EXCURSIONS IN WORLD MUSIC

Seventh Edition

Excursions in World Music is a comprehensive introductory textbook to world music, creating a panoramic experience for students by engaging the many cultures around the globe, and highlighting the sheer diversity to be experienced in the world of music. At the same time, the text illustrates the often profound ways through which a deeper exploration of these many different communities can reveal overlaps, shared horizons, and common concerns in spite of, and because of, this very diversity.

The new seventh edition introduces five brand new chapters, including chapters by three new contributors on the Middle East, South Asia, and Korea, as well as a new chapter on Latin America along with a new introduction written by Timothy Rommen. General updates have been made to other chapters, replacing visuals and updating charts/statistics. *Excursions in World Music* remains a favorite among ethnomusicologists who want students to explore the in-depth knowledge and scholarship that animates regional studies of world music.

A companion website with a new test bank and instructor's manual is available for instructors. Numerous resources are posted for students, including streamed audio listening, interactive quizzes, flashcards, and an interactive map with pinpoints of interest and activities. An ancillary package of a 3-CD set of audio tracks is available for separate purchase.

Bruno Nettl is Professor Emeritus of Musicology at the University of Illinois School of Music, and recipient of the Charles Homer Haskins Prize (by the American Council of Learned Societies) as a distinguished humanist.

Timothy Rommen is Professor of Music and Africana Studies at the University of Pennsylvania.

To the Memory of John Blacking (1928–1990)
In a world such as ours . . .
It is necessary to understand why
a madrigal by Gesualdo or a Bach Passion, a sitar melody from
India or a song from Africa, Berg's 'Wozzeck' or Britten's
'War Requiem,'
a Balinese gamelan or a Cantonese opera, or a symphony by
Mozart, Beethoven, or Mahler, may be profoundly necessary for
human survival . . .
How Musical Is Man? (1973)

EXCURSIONS IN WORLD MUSIC

Seventh Edition

*Bruno Nettl, Timothy Rommen,
Isabel K.F. Wong, Charles Capwell,
Thomas Turino, Philip V. Bohlman,
Byron Dueck, Richard Jankowsky,
Joshua D. Pilzer, and Jim Sykes*

Routledge
Taylor & Francis Group

NEW YORK AND LONDON

Seventh edition published 2017
by Routledge
711 Third Avenue, New York, NY 10017

and by Routledge
2 Park Square, Milton Park, Abingdon, Oxon, OX14 4RN

Routledge is an imprint of the Taylor & Francis Group, an informa business

© 2017 Taylor & Francis

The right of Timothy Rommen, Bruno Nettl, Isabel K. F. Wong, Charles Capwell, Thomas Turino, Philip V. Bohlman, Byron Dueck, Richard Jankowsky, Joshua D. Pilzer and Jim Sykes to be identified as authors of this work has been asserted by them in accordance with sections 77 and 78 of the Copyright, Designs and Patents Act 1988.

First edition published by Pearson, 2001
Sixth edition published by Pearson, 2012

Library of Congress Cataloging in Publication Data
Names: Rommen, Timothy, author.
Title: Excursions in world music / Timothy Rommen [and 9 others]
Description: Seventh edition. | New York : Routledge, 2016. | Includes bibliographical references and index.
Identifiers: LCCN 2016026536 (print) | LCCN 2016026883 (ebook) | ISBN 9781138666436 (hardback + cd pack) | ISBN 9781138666443 (pbk. + cd pack) | ISBN 9781138101463 (pbk.) | ISBN 9781315619378
Subjects: LCSH: World music—Analysis, appreciation.
Classification: LCC MT90 .E95 2016 (print) | LCC MT90 (ebook) | DDC 780.9—dc23
LC record available at https://lccn.loc.gov/2016026536

ISBN: 978-1-138-66643-6 (hb pk)
ISBN: 978-1-138-66644-3 (pb pk)
ISBN: 978-1-138-68856-8 (hb)
ISBN: 978-1-138-10146-3 (pb)
ISBN: 978-1-315-61937-8 (ebk pk)
ISBN: 978-1-138-68803-2 (audio CD set)

Typeset in Janson and Optima
by Florence Production Ltd, Stoodleigh, Devon, UK

Senior Editor: Constance Ditzel
Editorial Assistant: Peter Sheehy
Production Manager: Mhairi Bennett
Marketing Manager: Jessica Plummer
Copy Editor: Florence Production Ltd
Proofreader: Florence Production Ltd
Cover Design: Mat Willis

Printed and bound in the United States of America by Sheridan

CONTENTS

6 MUSICS OF EAST ASIA III: JAPAN

Isabel K.F. Wong

7 MUSIC OF INDONESIA

Charles Capwell

ABOUT THE AUTHORS

Bruno Nettl studied at Indiana University and has taught at the University of Illinois since 1964. He has done fieldwork in Iran (where he studied the Persian setar), among the Blackfoot people of Montana, and in South India. He is the author of *The Study of Ethnomusicology, Blackfoot Musical Thought: Comparative Perspectives, Heartland Excursions: Ethnomusicological Reflections on Schools of Music*, and *Nettl's Elephant: On the History of Ethnomusicology*.

Timothy Rommen studied at the University of Chicago and has, since 2002, taught at the University of Pennsylvania. Working primarily in the Caribbean, his research interests include folk and popular sacred music, popular music, ethics, diaspora, critical theory, and the intellectual history of ethnomusicology. He is the author of *"Funky Nassau:" Roots, Routes, and Representation in Bahamian Popular Music*, and *"Mek Some Noise": Gospel Music and the Ethics of Style in Trinidad*.

Charles Capwell studied at Harvard and taught at the University of Illinois. He has conducted field research among the Bauls of Bengal, India, and in Calcutta (where he also studied sarod), and he has studied Muslim popular music in Indonesia. He is the author of *Music of the Bauls of Bengal* and of numerous articles on aspects of South Asian musical culture.

Isabel K.F. Wong studied at Brown University and taught Chinese and other East Asian musics at the University of Illinois. She has done research on a large variety of music of her native China, including music drama, urban popular music, politics and music, and the history of musical scholarship in Chinese culture. More recently she has devoted herself also to the study of Chinese American musical culture.

Thomas Turino studied at the University of Texas and taught at the University of Illinois. He is the author of *Moving Away from Silence; Nationalists, Cosmopolitans; Popular Music in Zimbabwe* and *Music as Social Life: The Politics of Participation*. In 1992 and 1993 he lived in Zimbabwe, where he did research on village music and musical nationalism. He is an expert performer on the African mbira and founder of the Peruvian panpipe ensemble at Illinois.

Philip V. Bohlman studied at the University of Illinois and has, since 1987, been at the University of Chicago. He has done fieldwork in ethnic communities in Wisconsin, Chicago, and Pittsburgh, as well as Israel, Germany, and Austria. He is the author of *The Land Where Two Streams Flow*; *The Study of Folk Music in the Modern World*; *World Music: A Very Short Introduction*; *Jewish Music and Modernity*; and *Music, Nationalism, and the Making of the New Europe*. He is the artistic director of The New Budapest Orpheum Society, a Jewish cabaret ensemble at the University of Chicago.

Byron Dueck studied at the University of Chicago and is Lecturer in Music at the Open University in the United Kingdom. His research interests include North American Indigenous music and dance, popular music in Cameroon, and jazz performance in the United Kingdom. He is the author of *Musical Intimacies and Indigenous Imaginaries*, the coeditor with Martin Clayton and Laura Leante of *Experience and Meaning in Music Performance*, and the coeditor with Jason Toynbee of *Migrating Music*.

Richard Jankowsky studied at the University of Chicago and teaches at Tufts University. His research interests include music of the Middle East and North Africa, trance and healing, and Islam. He is the author of *Stambeli: Music, Trance, and Alterity in Tunisia*; and co-editor of *The Continuum Encyclopedia of Popular Musics of the World: Genres of the Middle East and Africa*.

Joshua D. Pilzer studied at the University of Chicago and teaches at the University of Toronto. His research interests include the relationships among music, survival, memory, traumatic experience, marginalization, socialization, gendered violence, public culture, mass media, social practice, and identity. He is the author of *Hearts of Pine: Songs in the Lives of Three Korean Survivors of the Japanese "Comfort Women."*

Jim Sykes studied at the University of Chicago and teaches at the University of Pennsylvania. His research interests include the relations among sound, personhood, modernity, aesthetics, and the politics of disaster in the Indian Ocean region. He is currently writing a book about music, Buddhism, and the politics of the past in post-war Sri Lanka.

FOREWORD

Bruno Nettl

THE WORLD OF MUSIC HAS CHANGED

Each of the peoples, ethnic groups, and nations of the world have their own music. We take this for granted, but we also take for granted, generally speaking, that just about all people in the world can listen to virtually any kind of music at will, on the Internet, on the radio, or with CDs. Some of this music may sound very attractive to us—whatever our own national or ethnic background— some of it may sound just terrible, some of it boring, some disturbing. But every kind of music sounds familiar, cozy, grand, ideal, heart-warming, or inspiring, to the people who make it. One major purpose of this book is to help readers and students understand what makes these musics different from each other, and how the different peoples of the world think about music. But we take it for granted that we can hear any of this music whenever we wish.

It's useful to remind ourselves that about 120 years ago, most people in the world, and surely most people in the United States, only got to hear music that belonged to their own culture. Someone in a small Midwestern town about 1910—if you are a student, it might have been your great-grandmother—might have heard some popular songs, sung hymns in church, and might possibly even have taken an excursion to the big city to hear a symphony concert. She very likely also heard some Sousa marches on the Fourth of July, heard some folksongs that her grandma had learned, and listened to some songs sung by a German or Polish choir at a festival. Your great-grandma's musical life—in some ways it is surely a rich musical environment—might be considered very restricted compared to our ability today to be musical omnivorous. If someone in that small town in 1910 had heard Japanese, African, or even Native American music, they might have said, "oh, that's so strange, I can't listen to it," or even asked "is this really music"? Today, members of all of the world's societies hear each other's music, and recognize that every society is musically different, that the world consists of a large number of musics. What has also happened is that people take elements they find attractive from strange musics and combine them, fuse them, with their own, inventing new, hybrid kinds of music in the process. Millions of people take part in discovering, interpreting, and re-creating the musics of the world.

The people who are most concerned with trying to figure out what makes musics different from each other (and why they are different), and to figure out how different peoples think about and use music are members of a profession called "ethnomusicology." Ethnomusicologists (and their predecessors, who called themselves comparative musicologists, or had no designation at all) began to work—at first in tiny numbers—in the late nineteenth century, when it became possible to travel to obscure places to hear music and to make recordings on wax cylinders. About 1900 there might have been about a dozen of them, and now there might be about 5000 in the world—still not a very large profession. In that time, they have tried to learn what the world's musical cultures were like, and to teach about what they found out in schools and colleges and through publications; they have tried not only to preserve the world's musical diversity by encouraging the world's peoples to maintain their old traditions, but also to figure out why and with what mechanisms musics change. The authors of the chapters in this book are ethnomusicologists, and while this is not a book actually about ethnomusicology, it may help the reader to understand a bit of how the minds of ethnomusicologists work—if I may put it that way.

ETHNOMUSICOLOGISTS CONTEMPLATE THE WORLD'S MUSIC(S)

How did our attitude toward listening to sounds from a distant land and saying, "can we even call that music?" or "this must be some kind of prehistoric sound" shift to thinking, instead, "well, this sounds strange to me, but it might not if I got to know it better" or, "sounds a bit weird, but then, our music probably sounds weird to those people, too?"

There are several ways of going at this question, but let me try just one. Ethnomusicologists have changed in their way of interpreting the world of music. The person who is sometimes thought to have blown the first trumpet, Alexander John Ellis, a British polymath, writing, in 1885, said in effect that all musics were equally natural and normal. After that, students of the world's musical cultures tended to adopt an "ours—not ours" attitude. They saw Western classical music as the purview of academics who called themselves historical musicologists, and everything else—the music of non-Western cultures and the folk music of all peoples—as the subject matter of ethnomusicology. Later on, the people who called themselves ethnomusicologists divided music into the categories of folk, classical, and popular musics—folk music as the music of oral transmission, classical music as the art of highly skilled professionals, and popular music as the music promulgated by mass media (recording, radio, TV) and often the result of cultural mixes. We still use these categories.

But also, in the early days before about 1955, ethnomusicologists looked at the world of music as one vast continent, variegated, to be sure, but something one could learn to understand with a single set of methods and approaches, and by finding ways of comparing musics with each other. Later they began to look at the world of music as a group of distinct musics—more like islands, as it were—each of which could be best comprehended by using a distinct approach derived from the way the people who created that music viewed it.

That included intensive fieldwork, and perhaps also learning to be part of that musical culture by performing the music. We still maintain this view, but we have also added a further one: We think of the world of music as distinct units relating to each other in many ways, like islands connected by bridges, realizing that in addition to studying the world's musics as individual systems, and perhaps getting insight from comparisons, we are enormously interested in how the world's musics interrelate. And so, studying what I've labeled as "bridges" between these islands has become one of our major tasks. And indeed, a very large proportion of the music that the peoples of the world perform and listen to today is based on many different kinds of fusion, combination, and interaction.

HOW WE GOT TO THIS BOOK

This is a book that tries to inform the reader about the music of the world's cultures, presenting each of the world's principal cultural areas such as East Asia or sub-Saharan Africa by looking in some detail at the music of one of its cultures or societies. It has changed through its seven editions that have appeared every few years, trying to reflect advances in the approaches of ethnomusicologists as well as changes in the world of music, and the authors are proud now to join the distinguished program at Routledge, which has made many significant contributions to ethnomusicology and world music. But it is still, in essence, the book that first appeared under the title "Excursions in World Music" in 1992. Let me give a personal account of its genesis, beginning with its prehistory.

Ever since Alexander Ellis made his point about the diversity and equality of the world's musics in 1885, various scholars have tried to provide overviews of this realm—well, more accurately, of the world's musics outside those of Western civilization. Before 1950, the authors of these accounts were largely German or Austrian—I'll just mention some of their names, because they are major figures in the early history of this field: Carl Stumpf, Robert Lachmann, Curt Sachs, Marius Schneider. They tended to think that the diversity of the world's musics represented stages through which all musics were passing, some more quickly than others.

But none of them wrote books that were directed to students or to laypersons; that came to be an American specialty. By now, as I write, there are a number of books that try in various ways to survey the world's musics. Today, too, virtually every music department at an American university or college offers at least a survey of the music of the world's cultures, and there is a widespread need for textbooks. But when I began teaching, in the 1950s, there was no textbook or set of readings that I could recommend to my students. In the six decades since then, various approaches to teaching have been developed, and these books surveying world music constitute a kind of genre. But in the development of this genre, the previous publisher of the book at hand, Prentice Hall (and publishing houses related to it) played a major role. Let me tell you a bit of the role of Prentice Hall in this history.

In 1961, I received a call from H. Wiley Hitchcock, a distinguished music historian specializing in American music then teaching at the University of Michigan, telling me that he had undertaken to edit a series of textbooks to be titled *The Prentice Hall History of Music Series*, which was to consist of nine volumes—six about the major periods of European classical music, one about the classical music of the United States, and two about, well, everything else. Mr. Hitchcock asked me to write one of these volumes, and told me that William P. Malm, a professor at Michigan and an authority on Japanese music, would write the other. What, you might exclaim, seven volumes on Western classical music, and only two for everything else? Indeed. But I know that Mr. Hitchcock had a hard time persuading the publisher that even two volumes for "everything else" were justified. Anyway, what was being requested was material that might satisfy the need of courses people were actually teaching or planning to teach.

Two volumes for music of the non-Western cultures, and for all folk music? But how were we to divide this world of music into two halves? Well, Mr. Hitchcock said, it's up to you guys to decide, you can duke it out. Well, Professor Malm and I did just that, and while we've never been quite sure that we did a good job—it has been a half century since that time—we have a drink in honor of our peaceful division of the world's musics. The books in that series did appear between 1964 and 1966, Mr. Malm's volume, titled *Music Cultures of the Pacific, the Near East, and Asia*, and mine, *Folk and Traditional Music of the Western Continents* ("Western" included the Americas, Europe, and Africa.) These short books were revised a few times and continued to be published and to be used as texts rather widely for some thirty years. Indeed, they were published in Spanish, Korean, and Japanese translations.

Well, there were many things about my volume, at least, that one might criticize, but one fundamental weakness—and this applies to William Malm's volume too—was that while each of us had done field research as ethnomusicologists, most of what we wrote we knew only from books and records. Another was our inability to integrate Western music with the rest of the world, and a third one was the absence of popular music.

To address this last issue, Prentice Hall in 1975 brought out a text titled *Contemporary Music and Music Cultures*, by Charles Hamm, Ronald Byrnside, and Bruno Nettl. Never widely used, because it did not fit a sufficient number of courses, its nine chapters included essays on music and society in twentieth-century USA, jazz improvisation, current developments in the music culture of Native Americans and in Iran, and the fusion of musics in American popular music.

Through the 1970s and 1980s I kept in close touch with editors at Prentice Hall, who recognized that courses on world music were becoming an academic standard, and one of them said to me in about 1985, "when you write a text on world music you owe it to us." Indeed, I had all along felt very much at home in the publishing world of Prentice Hall. But I didn't think I should try to write a book about world music by myself; those early days when one person could survey the music world seemed long past. Parenthetically I had better point out that today there are still authors willing to try this, but most of their books don't pretend to be comprehensive but provide spot-checks largely from the authors' own research experiences.

Now, to the book at hand: The moment came in 1987, when ethnomusicology at the University of Illinois, at which I had been teaching for years, had developed sufficiently to employ four of us. And further, our sister-campus, the University of Illinois at Chicago, had also appointed an ethnomusicologist, Philip Bohlman, to its faculty. When I thought about the interests of these colleagues, a light went on in my head: We really, in our research experience, did do a pretty good job of covering the world. And so, in the late fall of 1987, the five of us—Charles Capwell and his wife Isabel Wong, Thomas Turino, Philip Bohlman, and myself—sat for three or four hours in the Capwells' kitchen, brainstorming an idea for a text that we could present to Prentice Hall.

Our plan was to provide a book of ten essays plus an introduction, each of them based on an area of the author's expertise, providing some introduction to the area in the broad sense, but with a focus on the nation or culture with which the author had worked. Thus, Tom Turino would write about Latin America, with emphasis on Peru; and on Africa, with emphasis on Zimbabwe. I would write about Native Americans, concentrating on the peoples of the Northern Plains; and on the Middle East, with emphasis on Iran. Philip Bohlman, writing about Europe, would find ways to integrate Western classical music. Prentice Hall approved, and we stuck to that plan as much as we could. We decided that each author should write essays appropriate to his or her personal style of writing and research, but we also agreed that all chapters should have things in common. For one thing, of course, the length. More important: We thought that the best way to introduce students to a music would be to present, right off the bat, one aspect of the culture in detail. Usually it might be a musical event—performance or ceremony, but it could also be an instrument or a particular musician. This would provide the basis for expansion into the musical culture as a whole, and into the larger musical area. Thus: my description of a Blackfoot powwow would expand into the ideas about music and the musical style of Blackfoot culture and then further into the things that Native American musics had in common, and the ways in which they exhibited significant diversity, and also how they had interacted with the musical cultures of white and Black Americans.

One other thing we agreed on: Each chapter would talk about the music itself, its sound and style, instruments; but also about the role of music in culture, the ideas about music and the musical events that characterized each society we discussed. All of this we presented to our editor at Prentice Hall, with a plan for recorded musical examples and black-and-white photographs.

Well, with quite a lot of support and encouragement from the publisher, we completed a manuscript, and the first edition appeared in late 1991, with editions following in 1997, 2001, 2004, 2008, and 2012. In the fifth edition, Timothy Rommen was added to the roster of authors, in 2012, Byron Dueck, and in the current one—which also finds *Excursions in World Music* looking to the future with a new publishing home at Routledge—Richard Jankowsky, Joshua D. Pilzer, and Jim Sykes join the conversation. Over the years, we have added devices to help students and teachers—definitions and verbal illustrations in the text, teacher's manuals, more color photos, and more sound examples with better Listening Guides. But the basic structure and the principles with which we began have, in essence, remained.

A NEW KIND OF ETHNOMUSICOLOGY

We, the original authors, are happy to have some of our work replaced by younger scholars who are more up on recent technologies and current events in world music. We can't deny it: The world of music has changed a lot even in the twenty-five years since we began working on this book, and the world of ethnomusicology too has changed. Ethnomusicologists look at the world of music somewhat differently than back in the long-ago era of the twentieth century. Some of these changes in both music and ethnomusicology are reflected in the most recent editions of *Excursions in World Music*.

How have we, the kinds of people who write books like this one, changed our attitudes? Let me give a couple of examples: They—well really "we"—have stopped looking for "authentic" music. Decades ago, listening to Native American music, we would ask ourselves whether this was really like the music the singer's grandfather had sung; whether it was truly the music accepted by the entire nation or tribe; whether it showed influences of the music of white people; whether, in other words, it was or wasn't "authentic." We don't worry about that any more but have not entirely abandoned that concept. Second—and I've mentioned this already—we are more interested in music that exhibits fusion, music that combines elements from various cultures, and that we once scorned. Along with that, we are much more interested in the study of popular music, music disseminated by the mass media, and in the role of technology such as the Internet in the culture of music.

And finally, we have begun to take a greater interest in discovering how music can help people. We continue to try to discover what the musics of the various peoples of the world are like, as sound and also as bodies of idea and concept. Maybe even more, we are interested in how music is used to express identity, to communicate inside the society, and with the outside world, and with the supernatural, and what different societies believe music can do. Ethnomusicologists in fairly large numbers have begun to use this knowledge to do people some good—helping to develop equitable systems of music education, to aid in conflict resolution and in the problems occasioned by forced migrations, to understand the potential of music in healing, and even to do our part to fight the effects poverty and help to save the environment.

Learning something about the world's musics can lead to great aesthetic and intellectual experiences, to an understanding of art and of society. It can also show us that music can be a powerful force for good of all kinds.

PREFACE

Excursions in World Music, Seventh Edition is designed to draw you into a series of musical encounters that open onto the widest possible range of social, political, ethnic, religious, racial, historical, and economic concerns facing communities throughout the world today. But this book is also designed to achieve this broad scope while remaining very accessible to you. Without requiring a working knowledge of music theory or harmony, the chapters in this book invites you to consider many pressing questions: How does music function? What does it mean to (or accomplish for) the communities who produce it? How is it mediated and circulated and why do these flows of sound, bodies, and capital matter? How does music illuminate or complicate race, ethnicity, gender, and sexuality? What are the spiritual implications of performance? How do dance and theater participate in these musical contexts? In what ways do history and geography contribute to the conditions of possibility for musical creativity? What, moreover, can we learn about ourselves in the process of learning about the many musics of the world?

FEATURES

Your excursions will take you into the middle of Bira ceremonies in Zimbabwe; immerse you in a Japanese Kabuki theater production; allow you to get a working understanding of Javanese Gamelan performance; and challenge you to think with and listen to popular musicians hailing from Trinidad to Korea and from India to Colombia and that's just a start. *Excursions in World Music* is:

- Organized along an area studies model, in which individual chapters work to represent the multiple musical cultures of a given region.
- Comprised of a set of essays—by nine different scholars describing, with conviction and a sense of devotion, cultures in which they have had substantial field experience and done personal research, providing information and in-depth syntheses of the musical cultures of the world.
- Dedicated to illustrating what Bruno Nettl has, in his Foreword, called the "bridges" that exist between these various regions and nation-states.
- Written for students with no formal musical training, and challenging them to engage with the musics of the world and become motivated listeners.

- A complete course with book and dedicated web site that hosts instructor and student resources.

NEW TO THE SEVENTH EDITION

The most significant new component of the seventh edition is the inclusion of five new chapters, which incorporate new musical developments in these regions, integrate new approaches within ethnomusicology, and open new ways of considering these musical communities in global perspective. Four replace existing chapters from the sixth edition, and one is entirely new to the seventh edition. These include:

- A new Introduction, written by Timothy Rommen, replacing the previous chapter by Bruno Nettl.
- South Asian music, written by Jim Sykes, replacing the previous chapter by Charles Capwell.
- Music of the Middle East and North Africa, contributed by Richard Jankowsky, replacing the previous chapter by Bruno Nettl.
- Music of Latin America, written by Timothy Rommen, replacing the previous chapter by Thomas Turino.
- Music of Korea, contributed by Joshua D. Pilzer and adding a new chapter with a much-needed additional perspective to the East Asian content of the sixth edition (China and Japan).

Further, the authors of *Excursions in World Music* continue in this edition their commitment to the approach, structure, and content with which they have always conceived this work. The seventh edition:

- Responds to many of the significant changes that the world of music continues to experience (and this especially with regard to popular musics)— Chapter 2, for instance, considers the importance of Coke Studio for the production of South Asian popular musics.
- Interprets the rapidly changing conditions, repertories, and styles of world music since the beginning of the twenty-first century, focusing on traditional, art, and popular musics throughout the world. Chapter 3, for instance, explores the music and politics of the Arab Spring.
- Explores the world as a collection of places in which globalization, the explosion of new technologies, media flows, and the often dramatically shifting landscapes of a postcolonial and neonationalist world dominate the musical scene. Chapter 10 for instance, presents champeta (Colombia) and nortec (Mexico) as examples of how music is shaped by all of these factors. Enhances the instructional resources for educators with a test bank, PowerPoint slides, and a thoroughly updated instructor's manual written by Greg Robinson.

HOW TO USE THIS BOOK

Each chapter has several features that will enable you to get the most out of your experience with *Excursions in World Music*. Each chapter includes:

- An Opening Vignette that introduces the musical ideas and social contexts you'll be studying for the rest of the chapter.
- A Running Glossary that helps you keep track of key words and concepts, and familiarizes you with vocabulary you might not have encountered before.
- A series of Listening Guides that help you listen closely to examples of the musical genres and instruments under discussion throughout the chapter. These Listening Guides offer you the chance to follow along and come to a deeper understanding about the structure and technical aspects of the musical examples. Where appropriate, they also offer translations of the lyrics.
- Icons in margins alerting you to supplemental materials on the companion website. These icons come in three varieties:

 LISTEN: These are placed above the Listening Guide and direct you to the website for streamed listening within an interactive Listening Guide that is posted online, for most tracks. Other musical examples are linked to YouTube or Spotify, where you will need to establish a (no charge) account to listen to certain tracks. See www.spotify.com.

 REVIEW: These are placed at the end of each chapter and alert you to the set of resources available for studying. These include flashcards for key terms and ideas, interactive quizzes for your practice, and an instrument chart sorted by country or continent.

 EXPLORE: These are placed at various points in the margins, illuminating topics for which we have sought out additional information on the internet.

- A bibliography and discography compiled in order to provide you with additional reading and listening possibilities.
- An audio CD-set with a compilation of the tracks assigned for listening and demonstrated in the Listening Guides is available (and encouraged) for separate purchase.

 Note that tracks available on the CD-set will be marked with a CD-icon within the Listening Guide. The audio compilation is more complete than the hosted streamed tracks on the website, since some copyright holders would not permit their tracks to be licensed. While many copyright holders are contributors to the book, or fellow scholars who graciously permit use free of charge, several tracks are from publishing houses with firm conditions. You will have access to all audio examples if you access both the website and the CD-set.

COMPANION WEBSITE: www.routledge.com/cw/nettl

The website for *Excursions in World Music* hosts two separate sites for Instructors and Students. Entrance is password protected, and instructions are given when you open the home page.

Instructors will find an Instructor's Manual, Test Bank, a general essay on "Music Fundamentals" that presents some of the most common ways of talking about music and understanding concepts such as melody, harmony, and rhythm, and also available for students, and links to further resources for each chapter.

Students will have access to Learning Objectives for each chapter, Interactive quizzes, an Instrument Guide, aligned by country/continent, to the "Music Fundamentals" essay, and to "Explore" topics.

Both Instructors and Students have access to an audio compilation of tracks within an interactive Listening Guide, keyed to the textbook. These are organized by chapter. In addition to the streamed tracks, there are several which could not be streamed (as noted above, for copyright reasons), but are available on the CD-set and/or through YouTube or Spotify. URLs are on the website, but you must set up a (no-charge) Spotify account, www.spotify.com in order to access them.

FOR STUDENTS

You will find resources available both within each chapter and on the thoroughly redesigned companion website for the book. Within each chapter, you will be able to focus your learning with the help of integrated sidebar definitions of key terms; additional and, in many cases, updated photos; detailed Listening Guides; a word bank of key words and concepts, distilling the most salient ideas from each chapter; and updated bibliographies and discographies designed to point students toward further reading and listening. Callouts for additional material, housed on the companion website, are also common throughout each chapter. You can turn to the companion website for a range of additional resources including: videos and photos of instruments, ensembles, and genres discussed in various chapters; study guides and sample quizzes; flashcards; and audio Listening Guides keyed to those found in each chapter.

You should think of the audio examples, in particular, as a major component of your learning, paying close attention to the Listening Guides and working to understand the performances as growing out of and deeply connected to the issues and ideas each chapter's author is presenting in the text. Ideally, you'll find that the companion website gives you a wide range of material to take your inquiries further and ground your understanding in additional examples more deeply. Make sure you make use of both the book and the companion website in your studies, and you'll find that you'll gain a great deal more from your experience *Excursions in World Music* was written with a belief that knowledge of world music not only opens many doors to a better understanding of today's most pressing social, political, and cultural problems, but also engenders respect for those who make and experience music everywhere.

FOR INSTRUCTORS

You will find the seventh edition of *Excursions in World Music* more explicitly dedicated to providing teaching resources and pedagogical support than ever before. The photos and videos available to students are also made available to you in a secure portion of the companion website, where you can also find: a completely redesigned instructional guide; a generous set of sample test questions; a general essay on elements of music that you may use to supplement your lectures or simply assign to your students; PowerPoint slides to supplement your lectures; and links to further resources for each chapter. The goal is to provide a ready set of tools that can be deployed in the classroom, both during lectures and for testing purposes and I believe that you will find the textbook more user-friendly and easier to teach from than ever before.

The authors of *Excursions in World Music* know that there is never enough time to cover every chapter in a given semester or quarter. As such, we have designed the chapters to work as discreet units. Feel free to teach them out of order, and to select those chapters that help you craft the narrative and set of issues you are most interested in conveying to your students. The companion website is envisioned as a repository of resources to help you manage the course, and I hope you'll make use of the PowerPoint slides, and the use guide in particular. You should feel free to modify the power point slides as you see fit, using them as templates for creating your own path through the material. They are, however, designed to provide you with the basics of what you'll need for each chapter. The user guide, too, is designed to offer you some starting points for lecture notes and to offer support for the concepts and issues that emerge in the course of each chapter. We hope that you'll also find the test bank and the essay on the elements of music helpful in managing the range of students and skill levels that you may encounter in the course of teaching this material.

ACKNOWLEDGMENTS

Many thanks to Greg Robinson for revising a new instructor's manual for the seventh edition, and Kendra Millis for composing the index. Thanks are also extended to Ben DuPriest and Hannah Judd for their assistance in preparing the manuscript for production and compiling the online content. I and my fellow authors also wish to express our gratitude for the numerous helpful suggestions provided by our students, and all loyal users of the book alike. Specifically, we thank reviewers for the seventh edition: Hubert Beckwith of George Mason University—Fairfax, Jennifer Canfield of Huntingdon College, Robert Catalano of University of LaVerne, Christian Hauser of Concordia University-Chicago, Peter Marsh of California State University-East Bay, Christina Placilla of Winston-Salem State University, John Robison of University of South Florida, Margaret Sarkissian of Smith College, Scott Shannon of Washington State University, Robert Templeman of Xavier University, Wilbert Watkins of Benedictine University, and several anonymous readers.

We are also grateful to Routledge editorial assistants Laura Briskman and Peter Sheehy, and Senior Editor Constance Ditzel, as well as the production team who copyedited, set up the design, and worked with our proof pages, especially production manager Mhairi Bennett and Florence Production. The result is a true example of teamwork and dedicated collaboration.

Timothy Rommen
June, 2016

INTRODUCTION

Studying Musics of the World's Cultures

Timothy Rommen

> For some people, when you say "Timbuktu" it is like the end of
> the world, but that is not true.
> I am from Timbuktu, and I can tell you we are right at the heart
> of the world.
>
> Ali Farka Touré, liner notes, *Talking Timbuktu*

A CONCERT AT THE MANN CENTER

It's a beautiful summer evening and my daughter, Natalia, and I have just managed to find our seats at the Mann Center for the Performing Arts in Philadelphia, PA. The Center is presenting a double billing that has brought people out *en masse*. It's still an hour before show time, and already the amphitheater is full. The lawn behind the covered seating area, moreover, is almost completely covered in blankets and lawn chairs as patrons mill about, making preparations for the evening's entertainment. Natalia and I have been looking forward to this evening, because we're going to hear the South African vocal group, Ladysmith Black Mambazo, open a show that also features the famous gospel group, the Blind Boys of Alabama. Both of these Grammy Award-winning ensembles are iconic in their own way, the former for showcasing a South African style of singing called *isicathamiya* and the latter for sustaining upwards of seven decades of innovation within the African American gospel tradition in the United States (the group was founded in 1939). Both of these groups have achieved notoriety within their respective national contexts and have also garnered tremendous international fame. Ladysmith Black Mambazo tours extensively and visits the United States regularly. The Blind Boys of Alabama are also veterans of heavy international touring schedules.

Ladysmith Black Mambazo take the stage around 8 pm and perform their trademark show, complete with stories from Joseph Shabalala, the group's leader and principal arranger, humorous and playful interactions between members of the ensemble, choreographed dancing, heavy on Zulu aesthetics, and, of course, complete control over their subtle and virtuosic vocal production. Most of the songs are sung in languages like Zulu and Sotho, and only a few are performed in English. The Blind Boys of Alabama, for their part, take everyone to "church." Dressed in matching, bright blue suits and gathering emotional momentum as the set wears on, they call boisterously to the audience for participation (and receive it), tell jokes, and generally put on a great show, singing in their trademark, close harmony while treating us to a series of gospel standards. The concert, as it turns out, is amazing, and both groups live up to their considerable reputations, leaving the audience buzzing about the night's musical experiences.

As Natalia and I walk to the parking lot, I am struck by how well this concert highlights many of the issues with which ethnomusicologists (and this book) are concerned. For instance, the concert offers a glimpse at the ambiguity inherent in the terminology we use to discuss the music of groups like Ladysmith Black Mambazo. The music industry, based largely in the North Atlantic, tends to market groups like Ladysmith Black Mambazo as "World Music," whereas

Ladysmith Black Mambazo.
Source: Steve Mack/Getty

Blind Boys of Alabama.
Source: Przemek Tokar/
Shutterstock.com

the Blind Boys of Alabama are categorized as "gospel" musicians. Ironically, the expansive-sounding label—World Music—achieves a rather delimiting effect. It inscribes difference, otherness, and, at times, exoticism onto musical practices that do not squarely fit into North Atlantic modes of traditional, popular, or art music. The many musics of the world are, thus, homogenized into a category that serves as a catch-all for the performances of artists who, unlike, say, the Blind Boys of Alabama, do not sing primarily in English and do not, generally, hail from a North Atlantic nation-state.

And yet, both of these groups are clearly "world musicians" in the broadest and best sense of the word—in the sense that opens the world to new sounds, new encounters, and new possibilities. The authors of this book explore the world's music in this broad, open-ended way. They consider each of the many musics of the world as offering meaningful and vital experiences both on the local and translocal levels. In this book, the authors explore how music functions in communities throughout the world; how musical practice intersects with politics and economics; how it is bound up in questions of ethnicity, class, race, and identity; how religion, aesthetics, and ideology affect the production and consumption of music; and how dance and art are intertwined with it, to name but a few of the book's major themes.

Setting its flaws and ambiguities aside for a moment, however, the music industry markets "World Music" with recourse to difference precisely because it is a quantifiable (if often over-determined and essentialized) performative and sonic reality. Indeed, the musics of the world are endlessly diverse. This evening's musical performances offer a good case in point, for the styles of these two groups are quite different from each other. Ladysmith Black Mambazo sing relatively softly, though there are many members in the group, while the Blind Boys of Alabama are few in number but are very loud in terms of their vocal production. Ladysmith's music is called *isicathamiya*, a Zulu-derived word that means something like "walk softly," and which conveys in the name of the genre itself the necessity for the low volume required of the early performers and innovators of this style. These performers, active in the early decades of the twentieth century, were employed as migrant laborers at South African mines and thus lived in the mine barracks. Their after-hours singing and dancing needed to be quiet enough so that the camp security would not notice and come shut them down. The gospel music sung by the Blind Boys, by contrast, is rooted in the notion of proclamation and is, thus, intended to be heard both far and wide.

Ladysmith works with small units of musical material that they gradually transform over the course of performances often lasting more than ten minutes, a compositional technique sometimes referred to as *cellular construction* and a hallmark of many sub-Saharan African musical traditions (see Chapter 8). The Blind Boys work mostly within a shorter, verse-chorus structure that easily opens up to an improvisatory vamp toward the end of the song—a vamp that can extend these three- or four-minute compositions to well over ten minutes as well. Ladysmith is an *a capella* group, which means that they sing unaccompanied by instruments, once again because the genre developed within a context where playing instruments would have, in many cases, been impractical. The Blind Boys, though, travel with a small gospel band (organ/piano, guitar, bass, drums). One group sings primarily in African languages; the other sings exclusively in English.

These divergent approaches to musical structure, aesthetics, language, dance, and style suggest an important way of thinking about musical difference: Difference, like sameness, is best understood as a matter of perspective. Sameness is constructed out of identifying difference and, as such, is bound up in who you are, the experiences you've been in a position to accumulate, and the traditions from which you are selecting in the process of assembling your own sense of the world. As we all know, throughout history, difference has been mobilized to tragically destructive purpose—genocide, slavery, the holocaust, exile, religious fundamentalisms, and exoticisms of one stripe or another have all been justified through such mobilizations of difference. And yet, difference can also become truly productive if it is mobilized in service of mutual exchange and open encounter. It is in this sense that ethnomusicology is engaged with the musics of the world.

Importantly, acknowledging the ways that the musics of the world differ from each other can (and often does) lead to new insights and to rich and meaningful musical encounters that illustrate sameness, solidarity, and shared horizons. Difference can, in other words, enable us to see (and hear) ourselves in the other and the other in ourselves. This is especially the case if we approach these musical encounters open to the possibility that our own perspective is subject to reinterpretation and to change in the face of new experiences. Returning to this evening's concert, these two ensembles share several significant themes in common. First, both groups have overcome devastating social inequality tied to race and class. Ladysmith Black Mambazo was formed during the height of the Apartheid regime in South Africa, while the Blind Boys of Alabama have lived and performed through Jim Crow laws and the Civil Rights Movement in the United States. In this sense, both groups have been affected by the prior and unequal movements of money, goods, and people that characterized the colonial period. Ladysmith's ancestors were witness to the colonial subjugation of the Zulu and the successive injustices that culminated in Apartheid. The ancestral heritage of the Blind Boys is rooted in West Africa, the slave trade, and the southern plantation economy. Both groups have chosen to perform music of deep spiritual significance, raising their voices in defense of social justice and contributing in significant ways to the ongoing process of articulating a way forward after Apartheid and in building on the as yet unfulfilled promise of the Civil Rights Movement, respectively.

Both groups have also benefitted from the long-term exchange of musical practices. This exchange has seen African practices inform musical lives throughout the African diaspora, including the musical practices of African Americans and Afro-Caribbean communities. As such, a whole host of musical ideas—often called African retentions, and including instruments, drumming styles, ensemble structures, dance styles, and rhythmic cells—have been incorporated into and adapted to the musical contexts of traditional, sacred, and popular musics throughout the African diaspora. This exchange has also witnessed the return of new genres and practices from the diaspora to Africa. For instance, *isicathamiya* is, itself, informed by the sounds of the vaudeville and ragtime groups such as the Virginia Jubilee Singers and Orpheus McAdoo who toured South Africa during the 1890s.

A closer exploration of these two groups, then, reveals a deep solidarity, born of shared social and political histories (though experienced in different contexts) and worked out in shared musical horizons through the multiple crossings and re-crossings of what has been called the Black Atlantic. Both groups, moreover, have remained committed to the musical traditions they grew into locally while collaborating with a wide range of other musical artists (including Peter Gabriel, the English Chamber Orchestra, Lucky Dube, Paul Simon, Bonnie Raitt, and Ben Harper to name but a few), thereby modeling the possibility of pursuing shared musical horizons and solidarity—of seeing the other in one's self and one's self in the other.

The historical, economic, political, and social horizons of Ladysmith Black Mambazo and the Blind Boys of Alabama are thus different in detail and local context, but very similar in terms of the way that music is being mobilized to address local issues and struggles. When viewed from this perspective, the concrete musical differences so obvious in their back-to-back performances are no longer central to an analysis of the musical power of these two groups. What emerges instead is an appreciation for the shared human concerns and histories that these two ensembles have consistently confronted throughout their careers, an appreciation that is deepened by the powerful illustration these two ensembles offer of the multiple musical paths that artists forge in addressing these concerns.

The title of this book, *Excursions in World Music*, then, is chosen in order to question and explore the overarching category "World Music." The book engages the many musics of the world, offering excursions that highlight the concrete differences and sheer diversity to be experienced in the world of music. At the same time, however, the text illustrates the often profound ways through which a deeper exploration of these diverse communities of practice can reveal overlaps, shared horizons, and common concerns in spite of and, at times, because of this very diversity.

PRESENTING THE WORLD OF MUSIC

As the preceding vignette has illustrated, an ears-wide-open approach to sameness and difference—a recognition that concepts like home and away, self and other, are constructed and constantly shifting based on one's perspective—is crucially important as we embark on journeys that explore the musics of the world. With this in mind, let's briefly explore how such an approach informs our answers to the following basic, yet foundational question: "What is music?" This question seems harmless enough at first but as soon as an explanation or definition of the term is offered, things become a bit more complicated. *Webster's New World Dictionary*, for example, offers the following entry for music: "Music 1. the art of combining tones to form expressive compositions. 2. such compositions. 3. any rhythmic sequence of pleasing sounds." Now, this definition introduces an array of additional concepts that, when we begin to unpack them, make an answer to our question more difficult to come by, for in defining "music" *Webster's New World Dictionary* invokes the concepts of composition, of time, and of aesthetics, each of which presents us with a set of serious complications on the road to a workable definition. In an earlier edition of this textbook, Bruno Nettl, one of the pioneers of ethnomusicology, suggests a more general understanding of music when he writes that music is "a group of sounds" (2011). You'll notice that Nettl avoids mentioning how these sounds are grouped, what they sound like, or even whether or not they are in sequence, for he understands the multiple ways that music is conceptualized around the world and has learned to be careful when dealing with words and or ideas that can delimit the horizons of possibility inherent in musical life. In fact, he points out that "to be properly understood, music should be studied as a group of sounds, as behavior that leads to these sounds, and as a group of ideas or concepts that govern the sound and the behavior" (2011).

Composition

In order to understand more fully why Nettl chooses such a broad definition over a more specific and bounded definition such as the one offered by *Webster's New World Dictionary*, let's take a closer look at the three concepts that Webster's definition raised. The first of these concepts is composition itself. Composition

Calypso singer.
Source: Wolfgang Kaehler/ Getty

is one of the most ubiquitous of all musical ideas, but by ubiquitous, I do not mean to suggest that everyone conceptualizes composition in the same way. For example, a composition in the Western art music tradition is inextricably tied to written notation—to a score—whereas a Trinidadian calypso can be famous and well-known as a composition but is almost never written down. So, we need to free the idea of notation from the concept of composition. While a composition can, and in many contexts does, exist as a text within a written tradition, it may also exist as a different kind of "text" within an oral tradition. In fact, oral traditions are much more prevalent throughout the musics of the world than are notated ones.

It is important for us to recognize from the outset, then, that the concept of composition suggests a combination of musical elements that somehow forms a logical whole—a unit of some sort—and this without regard to how that unit is preserved and transmitted. The emphasis here is on a unit of "some sort," for the authors of this book make a point of illustrating that the methods for generating musical elements as well as the combinations themselves are infinitely varied. For example, the concepts of scale and/or mode are articulated in most musical contexts, but the variety with which scales are built and modes function is virtually endless. The highly developed maqam system, used in one variant or another throughout North Africa and the Middle East, is predicated on the performer being able to hear and appropriately reproduce microtonal content that shifts in quality and quantity from maqam to maqam, of which there are dozens (hundreds according to some ways of categorizing them). More importantly, the maqam within which a performance is played determines which paths can be pursued in terms of modulations (i.e., some modulations

Oud player.
Source: ALI YUSSEF/Getty

[transitions from one maqam to another] are simply not possible from a given maqam, while others are common and conventional).

The tonal content of a Javanese gamelan, by contrast, is derived from just two scales or tuning-systems, one made up of five pitches (*slendro*), the other comprised of seven pitches (*pelog*). In addition, neither of these tuning systems is consistent from gamelan to gamelan, because the instruments of each gamelan are commonly tuned to each other without being tethered to a common reference pitch (like the A440 of Western art music). The compositional horizons of possibility in these two examples are thus shaped in very different ways, and this not least because the musical materials in play for compositional purposes grow out of radically divergent approaches to mode/tuning-system.

We also find that musical building blocks and techniques commonplace in one community of practice or musical context are almost unheard of in others. Take, for example, the practice of throat singing (sometimes called overtone or diphonic singing) in Tuva and Mongolia. Throat singing is predicated on singing a fundamental pitch as a drone and manipulating the tongue, lips, velum, larynx, and jaw in order to isolate and then amplify individual overtones already present in the fundamental pitch being produced, such that two pitches (and sometimes more) are simultaneously sounded by the performer. Entire melodies are then constructed from the overtone content that the performer isolates, and it is in this fashion and from these musical materials that songs are formed (composed). While throat singing is commonplace in Tuva and Mongolia, this technique for generating vocal music is quite rare outside of Central Asia (though the Xhosa in South Africa, and the Inuit also practice forms of throat singing).

Of course, the types of musical combinations at which communities arrive have a great deal to do with the functions assigned to music in a given society.

Gamelan performer.
Source: Education Images/
Getty

Before addressing the second concept introduced by Webster's definition—time—let's briefly explore the various functions that music fulfills and how these very functions can drastically impact the shape of music. Because music is so deeply implicated in human experience, we find that it enhances religious practices (trance, transcendence, ritual, meditation, etc.), politics (propaganda, nationalism, minority rights, human rights, etc.), social functions (such as weddings, funerals, life cycle events, and community festivals), and other arenas of human interaction such as work (threshing songs, boat launching songs, and sea shanties) and play (ring plays and chants at sporting events). What we find as students of world music is that it becomes increasingly difficult to know what functions music is fulfilling and what the basis of its role in society is without knowing about the society itself in some deeper way. In fact, if we only think about music from our own perspective, we might even make serious mistakes in our assessments of various "musics."

A case in point is found in the realm of Qur'anic recitation. This religious exercise, which sounds convincingly musical to many North Atlantic ears, in part because it is modeled on the conventions of Arabic Art music, is, in fact, not considered music at all in Islamic contexts. It is, instead, understood as a form of heightened speech fit for religious use. This is an extremely important point of distinction within Islamic thought—a distinction that develops out of an approach that confines "music" to the secular realm of human experience and, as such, makes it less suited for use as a sonic vehicle for the sacred (the Qur'anic text).

What the authors of this book stress—and what I'm sure will become very apparent over the course of the chapters that follow—is that ethnomusicology is, in fact, about people and that we, as students of world music, are therefore ultimately concerned about what is important to people as reflected in the ways that they use and configure their various musics. As such, ethnography (fieldwork) is a crucial methodological element in pursuing the study of the musics of the world, for it allows us to engage with people about the musics that they love, use, and produce, both within and outside of their communities. And it is in this context that the merits of Nettl's choice to omit specific discussion of musical elements such as "composition" and "time" from his definition begin to shine. These musical specifics are, according to Nettl, best explored through encounter rather than delineated at the outset, and the flexibility inherent in this approach is central to ethnomusicology as a discipline and to the excursions that follow. In other words, we come to understand what music is not only through attending to sound itself, but also by studying it ethnographically as "behavior that leads to these sounds, and as a group of ideas or concepts that govern the sound and the behavior" (2011).

Time

It is surely clear from the preceding pages that this book's authors are committed to encouraging a relativistic approach to studying music. In other words, we are going to take Nettl's lead and examine each musical context on its own merits and attempt to understand it on its own terms. This intellectual stance is extremely important in every facet of our study, and the concept of "time," introduced to us in Webster's definition, provides us with an apt illustration. North Atlantic conceptions of time have consistently stressed linearity, the teleological idea that things progress from a beginning to an end. It should come as no surprise that this understanding of time is reflected in the way that music is put together.

If we explore, for instance, the way that the great majority of canonical, Western art music is structured (think of composers like Brahms, Beethoven, and Mozart), we find a few clues to the way that linearity informs compositions in this tradition. Small units like motives (from as short as a few notes to slightly larger structures) are combined to create phrases that, when combined with other phrases, themselves form periods. Periods, in turn, combine with each other to form sections that, when combined with other sections form entire movements and pieces. There is, in other words, a progression from beginning to end based upon the very way that pieces are constructed. The average rock song is no different in this regard. If you've ever played in a band or memorized your favorite tune, you'll no doubt recognize the following structure: Intro, Verse 1, Chorus, Verse 2, Chorus, Bridge, Solo, Verse 3, Chorus, Chorus, Outro. The musical materials here can be schematically represented as follows: A, A1, B, A2, B, C, A solo, A3, B, B, A. So, there are basically three ingredients with regard to melody and chord progression in this (admittedly formulaic) rock song. "A" covers the intro, outro, solo, and all the verses; "B" stands for the chorus; and "C" is the bridge. Each of these ingredients is connected to the next through time in performance (or recording) in order to create a linear progression from beginning to end.

South and Southeast Asian conceptions of time, however, are often cyclical as opposed to linear in nature. Although they, too, unfold through time and are, in this sense, progressing linearly through the performance, the musical emphasis is placed on returning to points that have already been visited—to cycling through instead of moving through musical material. For example, the system of talas in Hindustani music (a bit like time signatures in Western traditions, but much more complicated in its implications for performance) is predicated on returning to the beginning, and musicians (especially drummers) go through incredibly complex calculations in order to ensure that their improvisations arrive back at the place where they started. Within jhaptal (just one of the many talas available to musicians), for instance, each cycle consists of ten beats (2+3+2+3) and the goal is to move as elegantly and virtuosically as possible through the cycle, completing beat 10 (and approaching beat 1 of the next cycle) anew each time throughout the performance. Arrival is, as such, by necessity also a new departure. Drummers in particular have developed this cyclic approach to time into an art, and aspiring tabla players apprentice themselves for many years in order to learn from masters how to perform effectively and with sufficient improvisational creativity.

Sitar player.
Source: Jack Vartoogian/ Getty Images

At an even more fundamental level, however, the very concept of music within Hindustani thought offers a much broader view of time as it pertains to performance. For instance, each raga (part melodic possibility, part scale/mode) comes complete with an artistic rendering that describes in color and image the mood of the rag (called a dhyana), a short poetic vignette of the main characteristics of the dhyana, and a prescription for the time of day in which the particular rag should be performed. There is, in short, a much more cosmological, temporal framework in place in North Indian thought about music than we tend to find in Western art music. And, just as days, weeks, and seasons are cyclical, so too the approach to performing a rag in a particular tal is conditioned by a cyclical conception of time.

If we think of the ways that time is configured when it is combined with and subsumed into religious practices, then additional possibilities emerge. Within Aboriginal Australian ritual life, for instance, there are, in fact, two distinct modes of interacting with time. On the one hand stands the clock time of everyday life—a type of time with which we are all familiar. On the other hand stands the spiritual realm, which can be accessed through what is commonly called dream time. It is during excursions into this ritual time, into this time-out-of-time, that musicians are given songs, artists are inspired to paint, and clock time becomes meaningfully filled. Trances associated with music, too, function in conjunction with but also outside of clock time, affording both individuals and communities the opportunity to experience time anew. In each of these contexts, time is experienced and conceptualized in specific and localized fashion. Depending on the context, then, referring to music as consisting of a "sequence" of sounds, as Webster's definition does, can describe local conceptions of time in ways that are by turns apropos, misleading, or flat out inaccurate. So we see, once again, the reasoning behind the thoughtful omission of these specific references to musical elements in Nettl's short definition.

Aesthetics/Culture

Now that I've briefly explored the ideas of composition and time, I turn to introduce the last of the concepts that Webster's dictionary invoked in defining music—aesthetics. Unlike the first two concepts, which are concerned with the sound and structure of music, aesthetics is ultimately bound up in the tastes and values of a particular community or society and extends right down to individuals' preferences and conceptions of beauty. As such, it trades on the dynamic I've already raised regarding sameness and difference. For the purposes of this book, the way that aesthetics is deployed—and this by critics and practitioners alike—offers a window onto the larger concept of culture. "Culture" is one of the least defined but most used (and perhaps misused) words of all time and it has, for good reason, been subjected to increased scrutiny within academic circles since the 1980s. Think, for example, of how the concept of culture has been mobilized to justify hesitant action or inaction in the face of human rights abuses (like genocide) or, conversely, to advocate for imposing political and economic encroachment by one group on another (colonialism, neocolonialism, even war). Think of the ways that culture has, in conjunction with difference, been used to "naturalize" hierarchies of power (narratives of savage–civilized, third world–first world, for instance), and this even as it continues to thrive in everyday parlance (think of comments you've likely heard, such as "it's really multicultural" or "that's her culture," etc.). The concept of culture, then, is not benign, and can be turned to destructive ends in spite of its rather ubiquitous presence in our everyday discourse.

The authors of this book are keen to create an intellectual atmosphere within which a healthy skepticism about the idea of culture as it is generally (and uncritically) deployed—that is, as referring to a group of people, or a region of the world, wherein most people share the same values and like the same things—can be questioned without abandoning the concept out of hand. This monolithic approach to culture was popular in anthropology during the 1950s, when scholars attempted to describe the world by splitting it up into what were then called "culture areas." But, in a world that is increasingly globalized in terms of communications, technology, and travel, in a world where we are all, to some degree, travelers, the idea of a "culture area," or even of a culture in the singular, becomes suspect. So, in order to get at any working definition of culture, it is important for us to view culture not as a monolithic set of values and practices that a particular society claims as its own, but as something far more complex, fluid, and negotiated. To that end, I would like to steer our understanding of culture in a direction that will be more fruitful and that is able more accurately to portray the everyday workings of social interactions.

In order to illustrate this, let's take a closer look at the idea of aesthetics. Clearly, none of us are going to be able to agree on what is beautiful or on what sounds good all of the time. Just think for a moment about the arts and entertainment section of any major online magazine, dedicated blog, or newspaper and you will find critics who vehemently disagree with each other over films, plays, and music that are all considered a part of "our culture." Performers, too, struggle with aesthetics, disagreeing with each other about how best to play, say, bluegrass, tango, or salsa. The aesthetic, along with the authentic, then, is always negotiated in practice and subject to change, for the fact of the matter is that each "culture" also incorporates many subcultures within its broad umbrella, some of which are entirely opposed to the normative values and structures promoted by the society (or community of practice) in which they happen to be living. Multiply this complexity within individual communities out across the globe and it becomes clear why an approach to culture that privileges sameness (patterns of homogeneity) is no longer considered a viable analytical tool for studying the musics of the world.

It is more productive to approach culture by focusing on the multiple registers within which cultures are in motion (changing and fluid, that is). There are many arenas within which we can observe and analyze this motion, including ethnicity, technology, finance, media, and ideas/ideology, to name a few. Because there are multiple arenas of action and flow, there are also different rates and directions of cultural change occurring at any given time across these arenas. So, for instance, technology might rapidly be moving from an industrialized nation to a developing one, but a simultaneous movement of media (fueled by that very technological change) might be streaming back to that industrialized nation (among others), contributing to changes in perceptions of that developing nation and inspiring new cultural practices in both locations.

What I like very much about exploring culture through recourse to several arenas of action (what Arjun Appadurai has called scapes [as in techno-scape and media-scape]) is that this approach goes a long way toward explaining the movements we see all around us, not only within but also between cultures. And if we remember that these arenas are activated by human interactions, if we make the people who are animating these contact zones from day to day central to our efforts at understanding a given cultural context, then we will come to appreciate the degree to which the musics of the world are consistently at play in these arenas, affected by and also affecting the ever-shifting terrain we think of as culture.

The popular forms of World Music often provide excellent examples of this kind of dynamic change, for we can witness how technology, money, media, religion, and ideology variously shape the efforts of artists and even the formation and dissemination of new styles such as hiplife (Ghana), zouk (French Antilles), dangdut (Indonesia), and K-pop (Korea), to name but four. The authors of this book are thus committed to viewing culture as a concept that should immediately suggest many levels of complexity and movement, and this both within and between individual cultural contexts.

Although I have only begun to unpack the concepts of composition, time, and aesthetics (along with culture), I now return to the definitional task at hand. At this point, it should be clear why Bruno Nettl suggests that music constitutes "a group of sounds." This definition affords the greatest amount of flexibility for addressing the variety and multiplicity of musics and musical approaches on offer throughout the world. Unlike Webster's definition, Nettl chooses to allow encounter with a given musical context to flesh out the structural, temporal, and cultural details. And yet, I think we can make this definition a bit more specific without sacrificing its flexibility. I suggest that we add an observation by Martin Stokes to Nettl's words. Stokes (1997) defines music as follows: "music is what any social group consider it to be." When combined with the more element-oriented words of Nettl, this definition is about as close as we are likely to get to a working definition of music—"Music, being a group of sounds, is what any social group consider it to be." This definition successfully sets up the study of the world's musics—of ethnomusicology, that is—as an intellectual enterprise that requires: flexibility; a recognition that sameness and difference are a matter of perspective; an understanding that musical approaches to composition and musical materials, to formal structures and to time itself, as well as to aesthetics are all negotiated in and through practice; and a commitment to people (to ethnography), for we need to engage with "social groups" in order to better understand what sounds and practices they recognize as constituting music.

A MODEL FOR STUDYING MUSICAL CULTURES

The preceding pages have introduced some of the complexities attendant to the study of World Music and they have also offered an introduction to the way that ethnomusicologists go about thinking musically with people. The definition we have arrived at is, itself, subject to critique, of course, but it has the benefit of further articulating the intellectual approach we will be pursuing throughout this book. It also maps well onto a three-part model for the study of music articulated by one of the pioneers of ethnomusicology, Alan Merriam. Merriam posited that music should be analyzed in three arenas of action: sound, behavior, and conception.

Sound

Musical instruments, tuning systems, rhythmic ideas, ensembles, genres, styles, vocal timbre, language use, and a whole host of music-specific "nuts-and-bolts" elements fit into Merriam's category of "sound." One of the tasks that ethnomusicologists have set for themselves throughout the last century or so has been to categorize and come to a better understanding of all of the elements that contribute to sound. So, for example, Alexander John Ellis classified as many scales as he could during the late nineteenth century and also worked extensively on measuring pitch (suggesting the cents system still in use today). In the same spirit and at roughly the same time, Erich M. von Hornbostel and Curt Sachs developed four categories of instruments as a means of clarifying their sonic principles and also in order to distinguish them more carefully from one another. These included: areophones, chordophones, idiophones, and membranophones, to which another classification—electrophones—was later added.

Classification of Musical Instruments

- Aerophones (wind instruments)
  — Flute-like
  — Trumpet-like
  — Reeds
- Chordophones (string instruments)
  — Zithers
  — Lutes
- Idiophones ("self"-vibrators)
  — Rattles/shakers
  — Gongs
  — Xylophone

- Membranophones (membrane instruments or drums)

- Electrophones (electronic instruments)
  — Synthesizer
  — Computers

These classifications are still apropos and useful, but in an era of increasingly digital circulations of sound, and in a moment when phones, tablets, and computers are becoming ubiquitous platforms for both production and consumption of sound, new tools are necessary. So, although ethnography remains firmly at the core of how ethnomusicologists approach their research, ethnomusicologists are also incorporating ideas from disciplines such as new media studies and sound studies (among others) in order to explore and explain "sound" in the contemporary moment.

Behavior

Merriam's category of "behavior" focuses attention on how people interact with music and with each other (how people engage with music at concerts, for example); the contexts within which it is performed (is the event occurring at a church, in a concert hall, or on an urban street-corner?); and the kinds of conventions that govern interactions among musicians and within audiences (who leads, who gets to sing, who dances, gender issues, class issues, etc.?). It should be clear that behavior often results in direct consequences for the way that music sounds. For instance, social conventions and gender roles often impact directly on who sings, who is able to perform on instruments, or who dances. Often it is in the controversy generated by non-normative performance and in the sounds that such performances generate that a great deal can be learned about "behavior." Merriam's categories are, as such, crosscutting and overlapping. It may also be obvious to you that ethnomusicologists regularly draw on ideas and literatures across a wide range of disciplines in order to find vocabulary and achieve analytical sharpness in the process of thinking about "behavior." So, for example, if an ethnomusicologist is working on women practitioners of sacred music in an Afro-Caribbean context, it is likely that she will, in addition to her ethnographic work and musical expertise, at the very least, also incorporate ideas from religious studies, gender studies, transnational studies, and post-colonial studies.

Conceptions about Music

The category that Merriam calls "conceptions about music" incorporates more abstract ideas relating to music that, nevertheless, often dramatically affect the sound and attendant behavior of musical life in a given context. Time, composition, aesthetics, philosophy, ideology, theology, nationalism, ethnic identity, and ownership, to name but a few common sources of these conceptions, are thus intimately involved in the formation of "behavior" and "sound." In this connection, recall our earlier exploration of the complexities attendant to cyclic time and the incorporation of these principles into Hindustani musical performance. With regard to ownership, in particular, one important area of ethnomusicological inquiry involves work on intellectual property rights and questions surrounding appropriation. Here, too, ethnomusicologists find themselves pursuing their projects in interdisciplinary fashion, requiring tools from legal studies, globalization, economics, and, depending on the communal context at hand, also indigenous studies.

SUMMARY

REVIEW CHAPTER RESOURCES

Merriam's model, thus, helps open our excursions into the musics of the world to the whole range of ideas, practices, and sonic experiences that comprise musical practices the world over. It also helps focus attention on the necessarily interdisciplinary nature of ethnomusicological thought. The authors of this book put this model into action in the chapters that follow, offering insights into all three of these categories and illustrating how they are interdependent and mutually entangled. Applied to specific case studies, this model affords us a means of encountering the musics of the world in a way that encourages us to decenter our own perspective in the process of centering the sounds, behaviors, and conceptions of others such that we can understand that "music, being a group of sounds, is what any social group consider it to be."

BIBLIOGRAPHY

The Field of Ethnomusicology Rolf Bader, Christiane Neuhaus, Ulrich Morgenstern, Eds., *Concepts, Experiments, and Fieldwork: Studies in Systematic Musicology and Ethnomusicology* (New York: Peter Lang, 2010). Gregory F. Barz and Timothy J. Cooley, *Shadows in the Field: New Perspectives for Fieldwork in Ethnomusicology* 2nd ed. (New York: Oxford University Press, 2008). John Blacking, *How Musical is Man?* (Seattle, WA: University of Washington Press, 1973). Benjamin Koen and Jacqueline Lloyd, Eds., *The Oxford Handbook of Medical Ethnomusicology* (New York: Oxford University Press). Ellen Koskoff and Suzanne Cusick, *A Feminist Ethnomusicology: Writings on Music and Gender* (Urbana, IL: University of Illinois Press, 2014). Alan P. Merriam, *The Anthropology of Music* (Evanston, IL: Northwestern University Press, 1964). Helen Myers, Ed., *Ethnomusicology: An Introduction* (New York: Norton, 1992). Bruno Nettl, *Nettl's Elephant* (Champaign, IL: University of Illinois, 2010). Bruno Nettl, *The Study of Ethnomusicology: Thirty-Three Discussions*, 3rd ed. (Urbana, IL: University of Illinois Press, 2015). Bruno Nettl and Philip Bohlman, Eds., *Comparative Musicology and Anthropology of Music: Essays in the History of Ethnomusicology* (Chicago, IL: University of Chicago Press, 1991). Svanibor Pettan and Jeff Todd Titon, Eds., *The Oxford Handbook of Applied Ethnomusicology* (New York: Oxford University Press, 2015). Jennifer Post, *Ethnomusicology: A Guide to Research* (New York: Routledge, 2004). Timothy Rice, *Ethnomusicology: A Very Short Introduction* (New York: Oxford University Press). Henry Stobart, *The New (Ethno) Musicologies* (Lanham, MD: Scarecrow Press, 2008). Ruth Stone, *Theory For Ethnomusicology* (New York: Routledge, 2007).

Surveys of World Music and Musical Cultures The Garland *Encyclopedia of World Music*, 10 vols (New York: Routledge, 1997–2001). Philip V. Bohlman, *World Music: A Very Short Introduction* (Oxford: Oxford University Press, 2002). Philip V. Bohlman and Goffredo Plastino, Eds., *Jazz Worlds/World Jazz* (Chicago, IL: University of Chicago Press, 2016). Patricia Shehan Campbell, *Lessons from the World: A Cross-Cultural Guide to Music Teaching and Learning* (New York: Schirmer Books, 1991). Peter Fletcher, *World Musics in Context* (Oxford: Oxford University Press, 2002). John E. Kaemmer, *Music in Human Life* (Austin, TX: University of Texas Press, 1993). Ellen Koskoff, Ed., *Women and Music in Cross-Cultural Perspective* (Urbana, IL: University of Illinois Press, 1989). Kip Lomell and Anne Ramussen, Eds., *Musics of Multicultural America* (New York: Schirmer Books, 1997). Fiona Magowan and Louise Wrazen, Eds., *Performing Gender, Place, and Emotion in Music: Global Perspectives* (Rochester, UK: University of Rochester Press, 2015). William P. Malm, *Music Cultures of the Pacific, the Near East, and Asia*, 3rd ed. (Englewood Cliffs, NJ: Prentice Hall, 1996). Elizabeth May, Ed., *Musics of Many Cultures* (Berkeley, CA: University of California Press, 1980). Terry Miller and Andrew Shahriari, *World Music: A Global Journey* (New York: Routledge, 2006). Bruno Nettl, *Folk and Traditional Music of the Western Continents*, 3rd ed. (Englewood Cliffs, NJ: Prentice Hall, 1990). Bruno Nettl with Melinda Russell, Ed., *In the Course of Performance: Studies in the World of Musical Improvisation* (Chicago, IL: University of Chicago Press, 1998). Jennifer Post, Ed., *Ethnomusicology: A Contemporary Reader* (New York: Routledge, 2006). David Reck, *Music of the Whole Earth* (New York: Scribner's, 1977). Kay Shelemay, *Soundscapes*, 2nd ed. (New York: Norton, 2007). Lawrence Sullivan, Ed., *Enchanting Powers: Music in the World's Religions* (Cambridge, MA: Harvard University Press, 1997). Jeff Titon et al., *Worlds of Music*, 4th ed. (New York: Schirmer Books, 2002). Thomas Turino, *Music as Social Life: The Politics of Participation* (Chicago, IL: University of Chicago Press, 2008).

Musical Change Gerard Behague, Ed., *Performance Practice: Ethnomusicological Perspectives* (Westport, CT: Greenwood, 1984). Stephen Blum et al., Eds., *Ethnomusicology and Modern Music History* (Urbana, IL: University of Illinois Press, 1991). Ola Johansson, Thomas L. Bell, Eds., *Sound, Society and the Geography of Popular Music* (Burlington, VT: Ashgate, 2009). Charles Keil and Steven Feld, *Music Grooves* (Chicago, IL: University of Chicago Press, 1994). Bruno Nettl, Ed., *Eight Urban Musical Cultures: Tradition and Change* (Urbana, IL: University of Illinois Press, 1978). Bruno Nettl, *The Western Impact on World Music* (New York: Schirmer Books, 1985).

Instruments The New Grove Dictionary of Musical Instruments (New York: Macmillan, 1984). Sibyl Marcuse, *Musical Instruments: A Comprehensive Dictionary* (Garden City, NY: Doubleday, 1964). Curt Sachs, *The History of Musical Instruments* (New York: Norton, 1940).

Determinants of Music John Blacking, *Music, Culture, and Experience* (Chicago, IL: University of Chicago Press, 1994). Martin Clayton, Richard Middleton, and Trevor Herbert, Eds., *The Cultural Study of Music* (New York: Routledge, 2003). Alan Lomax et al., *Folk Song Style and Culture* (Washington, DC: American Association for the Advancement of Science, 1968). Curt Sachs, *The Wellsprings of Music* (The Hague: Martinus Nijhoff, 1961).

Views of Western Music Kurt Blaukopf, *Musical Life in a Changing Society* (Portland, OR: Amadeus Press, 1992). Henry Kingsbury, *Music, Talent, and Performance: A Conservatory Cultural System* (Philadelphia, PA: Temple University Press, 1988). Bruno Nettl, *Heartland Excursions: Ethnomusicological Reflections on Schools of Music* (Urbana, IL: University of Illinois Press, 1995). Bruno Nettl, Gabriel Solis, Eds., *Musical Improvisation: Art, Education, and Society* (Champaign, IL: University of Illinois, 2009). Christopher Small, *Musicking* (Hanover, NH: Wesleyan University Press, 1998).

Periodicals These provide articles as well as book and recordings reviews. *Asian Music*; *Ethnomusicology: Journal of the Society for Ethnomusicology*; *Ethnomusicology Forum*; *Popular Music*; *Popular Music and Society*; *The World of Music*; *Yearbook for Traditional Music*.

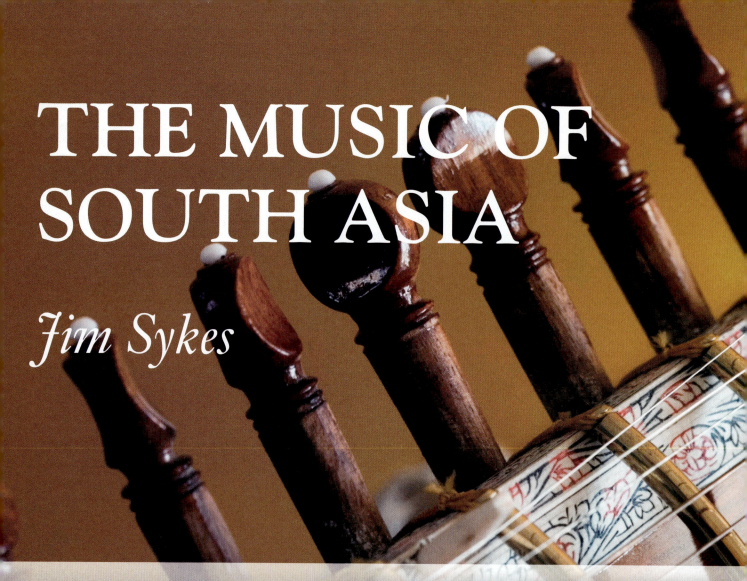

THE MUSIC OF SOUTH ASIA

Jim Sykes

INTRODUCING SOUTH ASIA

By the year 2050, India is expected to have a population of 1.6 billion, surpassing China as the world's most populous nation. India is already the world's largest democracy, and in the first two decades of the twenty-first century, India emerged as a global, economic powerhouse. Regardless of whether this era really turns out to be the "Asian century," India will undoubtedly have an essential role to play in shaping the world's dynamics for years to come, from geopolitics and information technology to debates on environmental regulations.

It is worth emphasizing, then, that if India seems to be just on the verge of achieving a global prominence worthy of a population of over a billion people, Indian culture is already globally ubiquitous. Bollywood films are screened on international flights around the world and watched daily in places like Nigeria, Indonesia, Peru, and Hong Kong. Classes on Bollywood dance can be found in

small towns and cities across the world—places like Florence, Kentucky and Florence, Italy (I found this out by googling "Bollywood class in Florence"). Yoga is so ubiquitous that some of its practitioners probably don't know it has Indian roots. Buddhism, a religion whose founder lived in what is now a border region between India and Nepal, long ago spread around the world but achieved much recognition in the West in the nineteenth and twentieth centuries. And while the Beatles inspired a generation of Westerners to turn to India in the 1960s through their use of the sitar (a North Indian lute instrument), musicians in recent decades have continued to reference Indian musical ideas, such as the sampling of Indian sounds in many hip-hop songs.

In the past few decades, Indian pop musicians have broken through the global mainstream, perhaps most notably AR Rahman with his music for the 2008 film

"South Asia" is the collective name for the countries of India, Afghanistan, Pakistan, Sri Lanka, Nepal, Bangladesh, Bhutan, and the Maldives. The category "South Asia" is a term used by scholars rather than the people of the region, and the countries included in South Asia has shifted over time. For instance, sometimes Tibet is considered a part of South Asia, though we do not include it here. *Source: Courtesy of the University of Texas Libraries, The University of Texas, Austin*

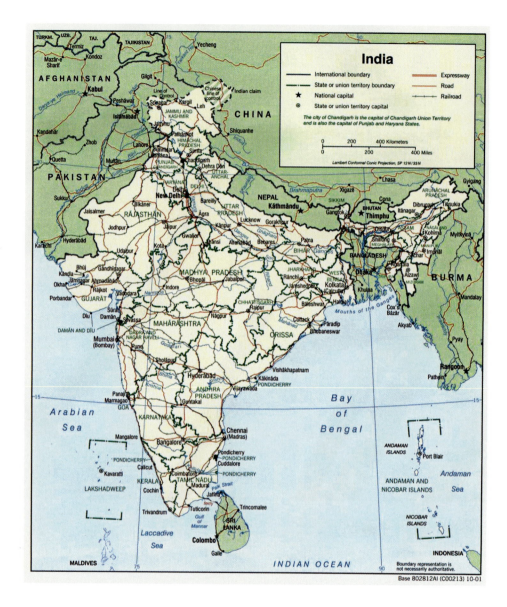

Slum Dog Millionaire. Before this breakthrough, however, the British Indian electronic music artist Panjabi MC, who performs a modernized version of a traditional folk music genre called bhangra, reached a global pop audience in the 1990s. Perhaps no South Asian musician has captured the attention of a global audience in recent years, though, like the rapper and visual artist Maya Arulpragasam (better known as MIA), who is not from India but Sri Lanka, a small island that lies off of India's southeastern coast.

Amidst this rampant circulation of South Asian cultures and sounds, the musicians who perform the region's "traditional" music genres are hardly standing still. The two Indian classical music systems—Hindustani music (from North India) and Carnatic music (from the South)—continue to develop in the digital age. Today, Indian classical musicians travel all over the world to perform and give clinics, after which they might log on to Skype and teach one of their students (who could live in India, New York, Copenhagen, or anywhere else around the globe). While the musical knowledge contained in North India's famous gharanas (regional traditions) used to be heavily guarded and revealed only through a long and arduous apprenticeship to a guru (esteemed teacher), today it is easy to gain at least a cursory musical knowledge of different regional styles by searching for and comparing videos online—a situation that does not please musical purists.

Hinduism is a vastly diverse religion whose followers constitute about 80 percent of the populations of India and Nepal, with significant numbers of followers in Sri Lanka and Bhutan. South Asian Hindu cultures are globally audible, as well, though here it is worth considering their *physical* presence and musics in the world's global cities. London, Johannesburg, and Kuala Lumpur (Malaysia) are all cities with significant Hindu populations, and Hindu temples in these cities routinely hold festivals and processions. The annual Thaipusam festival held at a cave complex (Batu Caves) just outside Kuala Lumpur now draws 1.5 million spectators and participants a year. At this and other Hindu temple festivals, an icon of the resident deity or deities of a temple may be taken out and wheeled around the neighborhood on a chariot accompanied by musicians, bringing Hindu religious sounds to ethnically mixed public spaces and diverse audiences.

Likewise, Islam is a vastly diverse religion whose followers constitute the majority of the populations of Afghanistan, Pakistan, and Bangladesh. The mystical form of Islam, called Sufism, emerged in the Middle East and found roots in South Asia many centuries ago. A network of saints' shrines developed across the region and expanded to other places where South Asian Muslims settled, such as Singapore and Malaysia in Southeast Asia. These shrines draw pilgrims back and forth between South and Southeast Asia, as devotees attend prominent events (like the commemoration of a Sufi saint's birth or death) held at different shrines (or dargahs). South Asian Sufi musics became globally known through the performances of Nusrat Fateh Ali Khan, a Pakistani singer of Qawwali (see below for more information), who achieved global fame via the world music circuit of the 1990s.

Finally, a discussion of South Asian religious musics should not skip over Buddhism, Jainism, and Sikhism, three major South Asian religions with a global reach. Buddhism is a majority religion in Sri Lanka and Bhutan, while significant Buddhist communities exist in Nepal and the regions of Ladakh and Sikkim in India. For many centuries, the growth of Hinduism in India facilitated a decline in the number of Buddhists in India, as Buddhism was spreading far and wide to places like Thailand and China. Sites associated with the Buddha's life in North India fell into disrepair, though a move was made to revive them in the nineteenth century and promote them as pilgrimage sites for Buddhists. Though Buddhism is today a small, minority religion in India, one can find Buddhist shrines and pilgrims in many places, particularly Bodh Gaya (where the Buddha found Enlightenment) and Sarnath (where he taught his first disciples). In turn,

South Asian Buddhists have moved throughout the world, opening temples and bringing Buddhist chant and lay devotional musics to diverse regions where Buddhists settled, from small Midwestern towns in the United States to Australia and beyond. While Buddhism is not globally famous for music, farther below in this chapter we will consider one example of a lay Buddhist musical tradition from Sri Lanka, a country with a majority Buddhist population. Jainism is a religion from Western India that dates back to the time of the Buddha, which still thrives; and Sikhism (which we return to below) is associated with India's Sikh community who trace their heritage to the Punjab region now split between India and Pakistan.

Given the astounding circulation of Indian musical traditions, one could be forgiven for thinking "South Asian music" is synonymous with "Indian music." But as we have already glimpsed above, this would be a mistake. The impact of India's musical reputation on other South Asian musicians was brought home for me by a story recounted by the anthropologist Anne Sheeran in her dissertation, where she researched Sri Lankan music in the mid-1990s. A tiny island nation, Sri Lanka is roughly the same size as the U.S. state of West Virginia, but is home to about twenty million people (roughly the same number as Australia). Sheeran found the Sri Lankan people to be welcoming, but when she mentioned she was there to study music they looked bewildered: Didn't she know that India is so nearby, and so much more famous for music? As one local put it, "Music in Sri Lanka? Haven't you come a bit too far south?" South Asian musics are not equivalent to Indian musics, but as Sheeran's experience shows, musicians from other South Asian nations now have to grapple with India's global musical prominence. Afghanistan, Pakistan, Bangladesh, Nepal, Bhutan, Sri Lanka, and the Maldives each has its own musical traditions that are worthy of recognition.

It is important to stress at the outset that the borders of today's South Asian nations are modern constructions. What is now known as India was throughout history a number of regional kingdoms, whose populations spoke different languages and had their own cultural traditions. A number of regional identities are still evident today in India, such as the Tamils (an ethnic group comprising 61 million people who live in the southeastern Indian state of Tamil Nadu, and who speak the Tamil language); the Bengalis (a population whose global total is estimated to be about 300 million, whose homeland is split between the Indian state of West Bengal and the country of Bangladesh, and who speak Bengali); and the Malayalis (who live in the southwestern state of Kerala, number about 33 million, and speak the Malayalam language). Amidst such regional identities are smaller populations, such as the scattered indigenous peoples that the Indian government calls "Scheduled Tribes," who tend to live in rural areas (such as the Nilgiri Hills in Tamil Nadu) but who make up a significant portion of the population of India's northeastern territories.

Medieval Muslim travelers from Central Asia were apparently the first to use the term "Hindu" as a geographical designation—it originally referred to "the people who live beyond the Indus River". Something more closely resembling today's national borders arose through the efforts of the Mughal

Empire (1526–1857), a dynasty of Central Asian Muslim migrants and their descendants, whose power spread throughout much of the Subcontinent. The growth of a Muslim influence on the cultures of North India began a few centuries before the Mughals took power, and we will see below that it would forever change North Indian musical cultures, marking a contrast with South Indian musics that lasts to this day.

From the early seventeenth century, European traders began coming to South Asia, including the Portuguese, Dutch, British, and French. By the late nineteenth century, the British had gained control of the old Mughal provinces while forging treatises with some nominally independent regional kings, essentially ruling over the entire Indian Subcontinent, as well as Ceylon (the British name for Sri Lanka) and the territories that make up present-day Burma, Malaysia, and Singapore. Not long after World War II, in 1947, India finally achieved independence, but the achievement was bittersweet, as the growing divisions between the region's Hindu majority and large Muslim minority resulted in a cataclysmic event called Partition—the largest mass migration in recorded history—during which a huge chunk of northwestern India was split off and became Pakistan, and Hindu and Muslim populations traded sides (India still has a sizeable Muslim minority, however). Meanwhile, another region with a large Muslim population, Bengal, had by 1947 already been long divided between Hindu and Muslim populations, but with Partition the Muslim-majority part of Bengal became East Pakistan (in 1971, it would split off and become the independent country of Bangladesh). Finally, there was much movement between Sri Lanka and South India over the centuries, and a sizeable Tamil population has long been resident in Sri Lanka's north and east; but the British ruled Ceylon as a separate province, and in 1948 the entire island became an independent country (later renamed Sri Lanka). Other countries in the region have had similar border changes, including Afghanistan, Nepal, and Bhutan.

So where does this leave us for our discussion of South Asian musics? For simplicity's sake, in what follows I adopt a "national" lens, by describing musical genres and histories of various South Asian nations; but I wish the reader to keep in mind that, as Anne Sheeran's story above shows, the historical construction of South Asian borders is perhaps most important as a factor that has shaped how South Asians understand their own music histories today, rather than something that can be taken to mark natural divisions between people.

In sum, to know South Asian musics is to know the historical construction, similarities, and differences between musics in places like India and Pakistan, Bangladesh and Nepal; between the wide range of "folk" and "sacred" genres in places like Rajasthan (a state in northwestern India) and Kerala (a state in southwestern India); between the famous classical dance traditions of the North (such as Kathak) and those of the South (such as Bharata Natyam); between the music performed by India's small Christian minority (say, in the South or northeast) and the hip-hop and rock music performed in cities like Mumbai, Bangalore, and Delhi. These days, knowing Indian musics requires knowing about Coke Studio (a television show created by MTV India, and sponsored by Coca-Cola), in which pop musicians may record music live on television with

EXPLORE

Kathak Dance

folk performers; it requires knowing about the schedule of the annual music "conferences" (a word that in India means a music "festival"); it requires knowing regional differences between, say, the Hindu musics of Tamils in the South and the Hindu musics of Gujaratis in the West. In other words, knowing South Asian musics requires knowledge of a range of pop, classical, folk, and sacred music traditions; it requires being able to place some of these within specific regions, while drawing commonalities between them; and it requires realizing that terms like "Hindu" and "Muslim" denote populations with a lot of regional musical variation.

Are you confused yet? The rest of this chapter attempts to unpack this overwhelming buzz of musical, cultural, and demographic diversity. I will try to simplify the discussion to leave you with a basic knowledge of key musical genres, terms, musicians, and instruments that collectively make up some of the more well-known South Asian musical traditions. If India is global and Indian music is just about everywhere, not many people around the world can distinguish different kinds of Indian music, nor the musical differences between South Asian countries. It is a goal of this chapter to help reverse this trend. As Anne Sheeran's experience shows, many non-Indian South Asians are aware of the musical powerhouse that is India, and yet, as I hope to make clear, other South Asian countries have their own music that deserves recognition. By cutting through this overwhelming musical variety, I strive to recognize the musical importance of India, while including other South Asian nations in the narrative.

HINDUSTANI MUSIC: THE GROWTH OF A TRADITION

VEDAS
The holy scriptures of Hinduism, traditionally recited by Brahmins and passed down by them orally.

According to Indian lore, the country once had a uniform musical tradition that dates back to the time of the **Vedas**, the ancient Hindu texts whose earliest sections were completed sometime around 1200 BC (though people refer to the Vedas as Hindu "scripture," they were initially passed down orally for many centuries, and only written down much later). One book of the Vedas, the Sama-Veda, contains hymns that were sung to a collection of melodies, called the Samagama. The Rig-Veda is a collection of poems that tells the stories of Hindu deities. In the Vedas one finds the earliest articulation of India's "caste system" (varna), through which people were divided into different categories based on profession (each with their own subcategories and regional differences), including the Brahmans (ritual specialists), Kshatriya (warriors), Vaishyas (merchants, landowners), and Shudras (servants and subordinates). The Brahmans received an extensive education in memorizing and reciting the Vedic hymns. The sound of the recitation was crucially important for Vedic recitation to work, more than the meaning of the text recited. The proper pronunciation was necessary for the gods to accept the offerings made by the Brahmins in ritual contexts (this connection between recited words and supernatural power can still be found in many South Asian religions today).

At the bottom of the list of varnas, or technically outside of it, were peoples who became known in English as "untouchables": they were formally outside the caste system, considered impure because they were forced to engage in impure activities, such as playing drums at funerals or cleaning latrines. Scholars still debate the historical emergence of the caste system and its relative strength or weakness in Indian society today, and later on I will consider its continuing musical importance.

Sometime before the fifth century CE, a treatise called the *Natyasastra* was written that would have an enormous impact on the Indian arts. As with the Vedas, the Natyasastra was written in Sanskrit (an ancient and sacred language of Indian origin that spread throughout South and Southeast Asia). According to legend, it was written by a person named Bharata, though scholars believe it may have been compiled by several individuals. The text provides detailed discussions on music, dance, and drama, showing an affinity for complex systems of categorization—a tendency that one still finds in Indian music traditions. Over thirty-six chapters, the Natyasastra describes three types of acting and ten types of theater. It is perhaps most famous for its theorization of *rasa*, a term usually translated as "moods" or "emotions," though it is perhaps best to think of it as the particular "flavor" produced through artistic expression. Over the centuries, rasa became integral to understandings of Indian music.

The twelfth century was a watershed period when the musical system of North India is said to have broken off from the South, due to the musical influence of Muslim migrants mentioned above. Two systems of Indian music emerged that remain separated to this day: *Hindustani* and *Carnatic* music. The conquering Mughals were descendants of the Mongol Empire who lived in the Central Asian Turkestan region, but they spoke Persian—a language from Iran, which had widespread cultural currency during this period. The classical music tradition of the north, Hindustani music, became heavily influenced by this Persian cultural tradition, and one can still find similarities between Hindustani, Persian, and other musical traditions of the Middle East (such as in Turkey, Iraq, and Egypt).

Hindustani music developed as an orally transmitted tradition whose musical knowledge was owned and guarded mainly by Muslim families of professional musicians. By the nineteenth century these musical lineages, called *gharanas*, were well defined and associated with certain places across the north of the Subcontinent. A rigorous system for learning Hindustani music developed. It involved years of training through apprenticeship to an *ustad* (a Muslim musical master) or a *pandit* (a Hindu musical master). In this day of easy access to information over the Internet, it may surprise readers to learn how difficult it was to obtain the most esteemed musical knowledge. As a student apprentice (*shishya*), one might labor for a few years simply doing household chores for one's teacher (*guru*)—the goal at this point would be just to hang about and try to soak up musical knowledge. It could take a few years before one would be allowed to learn anything substantial on one's instrument, and the more guarded musical secrets could take the better part of a decade or more.

NATYASASTRA
An early Indian treatise on the performing arts attributed to Bharata and concerned with music, dance, and theater and drama.

RASA
The affect or emotional state associated with a raga or other artistic expression.

HINDUSTANI
In music, referring to North Indian musical style.

CARNATIC
In music, referring to South Indian musical style.

GHARANA
A school of professional musicians who originally traced their heritage to a family tradition but which now includes non-biological descendants as well.

SHISHYA
Pupil of a Hindu master.

GURU
A Hindu teacher.

Many of the best musicians during the Mughal and British periods were associated with the courts of regionally based kings. This continued for much of the British period, even though these courts eventually lost their political power. One famous example is the court of Lucknow, a city southeast of Delhi, which before and during the rule of Wajid Ali Shah (ruled 1847–1856) was well known for its musicians and dancers. The British exiled the king to a suburb of Calcutta (in Bengal), where he brought many of his musicians and dancers in what now seems like a golden age for the Hindustani arts—an achievement that occurred during a time of immense political loss and social turmoil.

There are many legendary stories about the lengths students would go to in order to obtain proper training and musical secrets from gurus. One of the most famous stories is about Baba Allaudin Khan (c. 1862–1972), one of the twentieth century's most revered virtuosos on the sarod, a fretless plucked lute. As a boy, Khan was fascinated by music, but his parents tried to turn him away from the profession. At the age of ten, he ran away and joined a musical theater group. Lured to Calcutta, the biggest city in Bengal, he learned singing and instrumental music as a young man from two well-known gurus. But his musical curiosity was not satiated. Khan's dream was to go to the court of Rampur, a city east of Delhi, to learn from the esteemed sarod player Wazir Khan, who was a court musician and descendent of the famous Mian Tansen (c. 1493–1586), one of the most revered Hindustani musicians of all time. According to legend, every day Allaudin Khan went to the gates of the Nawab (an honorific title granted by the Mughal emperor to semi-autonomous Muslim rulers), to ask to learn music from Wazir Khan. Every day he was turned away. Allaudin Khan was married by this point, and he had given up his family in the hopes of studying with Wazir Khan.

Ali Akbar Khan. *Source:* Jack Vartoogian/Getty Images

According to legend, one day Khan wrote a suicide note and tied a cyanide capsule around his neck; when the gates opened and the Nawab left his estate, Khan flung himself on the Nawab and said that he was determined to study with Wazir Khan, or die. When the Nawab learned that Khan had left his family to study music, he remarked that he must be very serious indeed. The Nawab invited him inside, whereupon Khan dazzled him with a virtuosic display of his performance ability on several musical instruments—but this is not the end of the story. For a few years after this, Khan was allowed only to do chores and simply watch Wazir Khan. It was only after this point, after another bout of desperation, that Khan finally managed to gain a proper audience with Wazir Khan, after which he became his favorite disciple, and the rest is history. Allaudin Khan's son, Ali Akbar Khan, would go on to become one of India's most famous musicians in the twentieth century, eventually setting up a music school for the Indian arts (the Ali Akbar College of Music) which still exists in California today. Another student, the sitar player Ravi Shankar (1920–2012), would achieve global fame in the latter twentieth century on account of his association with the Beatles and concert tours.

EXPLORE

Ravi Shankar

One can imagine what kinds of musical complexity are involved in a tradition that requires such devotion, dedication, and—in myth if not in reality—such suffering for one's art. Indeed, Hindustani musicians are famous for virtuosity, a skill they achieve through hours of laborious practice—though whether such feats are real or exaggerated is open for debate. In his study of the Hindustani gharana tradition, ethnomusicologist Daniel Neuman (1990) describes Hindustani musicians' practice routines as a common topic of conversation, something that musicians brag about to others, in order to display their prowess. One well-known trick, associated with the tabla (a set of bowl-shaped drums) player Ustad Ahmed Jan Thirakwa, was to grow his hair long and tie it by a rope to the ceiling, so that when he fell asleep his head would jerk and he would wake up, so that he could keep practicing.

HINDUSTANI MUSIC: THEORY AND PERFORMANCE

EXPLORE

Hindustani Music

RAGA

A scale and its associated musical characteristics such as the number of pitches it contains, its manner of ascending and descending, its predominant pitch, and so forth.

TALA

Meter.

ALAP

Raga improvisation in free rhythm.

JOR

The section of Hindustani instrumental performance that follows alap and introduces a pulse.

JHALA

The concluding section of instrumental improvisation following jor in Hindustani music during which the performer makes lively and fast rhythmic patterns on the drone strings of an instrument.

TIHAI

A formulaic cadential pattern, normally repeated three times with calculated rests between each statement so that the performance ends on sam.

TAAN

A rapid and florid kind of improvised melodic passage in Hindustani music.

The standard melodic framework for Hindustani music is called *raga*, and the rhythmic framework is called *tala*. Each raag (the singular) is not only a scale (a precise ordering of tones in a row) but also a system of rules about how to play that scale. For instance, a raag might have a slightly different scale going up and down, and it might necessitate emphasizing one note in the scale over others. The musicologist Harold Powers came up with a way to define the word "mode" that can help us here (raga is a good example of a "modal system"). To paraphrase Powers, he said that if we think of a continuum with a basic "scale" at one end and a full-fledged "tune" at the other, "mode" falls in between. A particular raag might have some melodic turns of phrase that frequently appear when it is performed—i.e., it is more than just a scale—but these phrases do not coalesce into a specific melody that defines the raag. It is best to think of each raag as a modal framework (a scale plus a set of rules that state how to perform that scale) in which performers improvise.

Hindustani raags are classified according to many extra-musical criteria, according to their rasa (mood, emotion, flavor). Traditionally this includes a specific time of day or season when the raag should be performed; some were accorded supernatural power, such as one raag that is supposed to start fires, and another that drives away evil spirits. Rag Malhar, for instance, is thought to bring down buckets of rain. While raags continue to hold such metaphysical connotations today, it is common nowadays to perform Hindustani music on a concert stage and merely tell the audience (if they are not already familiar) what the raag's name is and what its extra musical associations are (especially the time of day at which it is supposed to be performed). Raags might also connote stories about Hindu gods and goddesses, as well as colors, flowers, and animals. Medieval Indian painters even devised a style of painting that represents each raag visually, and they often strung together such paintings in a series, called ragamala, or "garland of raga."

The opening of a Hindustani classical music performance begins with a section called *alap*—an unmetered, free-flowing introduction without percussion —in which the soloist explores the musical makeup of the raag. I like to think of the alap as akin to the carving of a statue: unlike a pop song, where a riff or melody may be presented right away, in an alap the characteristics of the raag are revealed gradually. It takes much experience with Hindustani music to understand the rasa of each raag. In an alap, the instrumentalist or vocalist typically begins at the low or middle of the scale and starts off slow, eventually going up higher and then descending in fast runs, while picking up speed.

After the alap section, the percussion usually kicks in, which in Hindustani music is typically played on the tabla (two bowl-shaped drums, played with the fingers while sitting down). At this point the soloist, along with the percussionist, improvises not only in a raag but also in a system of "beat cycles" called tala. Each *taal* (the singular) includes a set amount of beats that are *additive* in nature.

For instance, Jhaptal has ten beats and is counted 2 + 3 + 2 + 3, while Rupak Tal has seven beats and is divided 3 + 2 + 2. Most taals are easier than this, however; for instance, the most widely played taal is probably "Tintal," which has sixteen beats split into four divisions of four each (it sounds a lot like the Western meter called "4/4"). Just as each raag includes rules about what to do

TRACKS 2.1 and 2.2 **Performed by Allyn Miner (sitar) and Aqeel Bhatti (tabla)**

I**T CANNOT BE** stressed enough that each raag is much more than a musical scale: each raag contains rules that state *how* its scale should be played going up and going down, as well as details on *when* it should be played, and its association with gods, colors, and objects. Here is how *The Raga Guide* (pg. 164) describes Rag Yaman:

> Since Mughal times, Kalyan (today usually referred to as Yaman) is described by Meshakarna (1570) as a "lord in white garments and pearl necklace on a splendid lion-throne, under a royal umbrella, fanned with a whisk, chewing betel." Later authors also describe him as a brave, noble-minded hero . . .

From here, *The Raga Guide* describes the performance aspects of Rag Yaman, for which you will need to know something about the Indian solfege system. You may already be familiar with Western solfege (do-re-mi-fa-sol-la-ti-do), which applies certain words to represent notes in a scale. The Indian solfege system is "Sa-Re-Ga-Ma-Pa-Dha-Ni-Sa." *The Raga Guide* says,

> In today's Yaman, both Sa and Pa are frequently omitted in ascent . . . The ascent may begin on low Ni or low Dha [that is, notes below the lower Sa]. Ga and Ni are the sonant-consonant pair, while Pa and Sa are frequently sustained and function as final notes. When natural Ma is occasionally added in a concluding figure leading to Sa, the raga is known as Yaman kalyan. In other respects, today's Yaman kalyan is so similar to Yaman that many musicians do not recognise it as an independent raga. Time: early night, 9–12.

This Listening Guide includes two recordings (2.1 and 2.2). The first is by the sitarist Allyn Miner, who plays a short alap in Rag Yaman. Note that her performance here is shortened and only intended to demonstrate the different sections of an alap: in an actual recital, the alap would go on much longer, perhaps an hour or more. Miner's performance begins with an unmetered alap, followed by **jor** (which introduces a pulse to the music) and the up-tempo **jhala** (the concluding section, which includes fast rhythmic strums on the drone strings of the instrument). Listen to how she concludes with a short **tihai**, a cadential pattern that is played three times.

The second recording in this Listening Guide is a performance of Rag Yaman by Miner with a tabla player, Aqeel Bhatti. After a short alap, the tabla enters (at 00:57). What they are playing here is a gat, in middle speed Tintal, a common 16-beat cycle. A gat is an instrumental composition that is always set to a taal and played with the tabla. It usually consists of three composed lines, called sthai, manjha, and antara. Miner plays these, and then some variations, called **taan**. A longer performance would have more and longer taans.

BOL
Rhythmic syllable in Hindustani music.

and not to do while performing in it, each taal has its own rules as well. Most importantly, each taal contains "claps" and "waves" that denote which beats are stressed (those are the claps) and which are not stressed (those are the waves). In Tintal, for instance, the claps land on beats 1, 5, and 13 (that's every four beats, skipping over beat 9, which is not stressed—that is the wave). An audience will commonly clap or tap their leg on beats 1, 5, and 13, and wave (usually marked by simply turning one's hand upside down while tapping one's leg) on beat 9 (the term for the "wave" is khali, which means "empty"). The khali is important for tabla players: in Tintal, for instance, drummers will often leave out the lower-pitched tabla drum between beats 9 and 12, creating an audible emptiness due to the lack of a bass sound; the drummer then returns with the low drum from beats 13 through 16, creating heightened tension (perhaps adding

---

LISTENING GUIDE

DEMONSTRATION OF TALA

 **LISTEN**

TRACKS 2.3 and 2.4 **Performed by Aqeel Bhatti (tabla)**

THROUGHOUT SOUTH ASIA, drum strokes are given specific names—that is, hitting a drum in a certain place (such as hitting the edge of a drum and letting it ring, or hitting the middle of a drum and dampening it by pushing one's fingers into the drum head) is given a specific name. For example, when playing tabla, striking near the edge of the drum with the index finger is called 'ta', while arching the wrist and hitting the middle and ring fingers in the area between the middle and edge of the drum is called 'ghe'. In a Hindustani music performance, these drum strokes are placed in a system of 'beat cycles' called tala. Try clapping (and waving) these examples of taals so that you can gain a better understanding of how they sound and feel. Keep in mind that the **bolded** words are the 'claps' (stressed beats), and the *italicized* words are the 'waves' (unstressed beats).

(1) Tintal—16 beats (4 + 4 + 4 + 4): **dhaa** dhin dhin dhaa / **dhaa** dhin dhin dhaa / *dhaa* tin tin taa / **taa** dhin dhin dhaa
(2) Ektal—12 beats (2 + 2 + 2 + 2 + 2 + 2): **dhin** dhin / *dhaage* tirikiTa / **tu** naa / *kat* tin / **dhaage** tirikiTa / **dhi** naa
(3) Jhaptal—10 beats (2 + 3 + 2 + 3): **dhi** naa / **dhi** dhi naa / *ti* naa / **dhi** dhi naa
(4) Rupak Tal—7 beats (3 + 2 + 2): *ti* ti naa / **dhi** naa / **dhi** naa
(5) Dadra Tal—6 beats (3 + 3): **dhaa** ge naa / *dhaa* ti naa
(6) Keherwa Tal—8 beats (4 + 4): **dhaa** gi naa ti / *naa* ka dhi naa

Tabla drummers have taken the art of naming drum strokes to a complex level. Tabla **bols** (syllables) can be arranged in elaborate compositions and improvisations. In this listening example, hear how the tabla player This Listening Guide includes two recordings (2.3 and 2.4). In the first, Aqeel Bhatti demonstrates three taals: Tintal, Jhaptal, and Rupak Tal. He follows these with a peshkar (meaning "to commence"), a kind of tabla composition with variations that is played at the start of a tabla solo. Peshkars introduce the different sounds of the tabla gradually, building in complexity. In the second recording, Bhatti plays more advanced tabla compositions at a fast tempo.

MEDIUM AND FAST GATS IN RAGA YAMAN

 **LISTEN**

TRACK 2.5 Performed by Sudhir Phadke (sitar) and Anand Badamikar (tabla)

THIS PERFORMANCE in Rag Yaman illustrates several of the musical structures already introduced. Performed by Sudhir Phadke (sitar) and Anand Badamikar (tabla), it includes an example of a short alap, followed by a **gat-tora** section. The gat-tora section alternates a pre-composed melody (called a gat) with improvised sections (tora). An important component of gat-tora is the **mukhra**—the initial phrase of the gat (melody). The mukhra is used as a way of ending the improvisatory sections and returning to the gat. Another structural feature that you will hear in the gat-tora section is called a tihai. The tihai is a pre-composed phrase that, as noted earlier, is repeated three times to add emphasis to an arrival or to signal a shift to a new section. Following the gat-tora, you will hear a transition to a fast (drut) jhala. A jhala can be performed after a gat-tora, in which case it is accompanied by tabla, unlike the jhala that occurs in the sequence of alap, jor, jhala, each of which is customarily unaccompanied.

The pitches included in the raag performed here—*Rag Yaman*—are C-d-e-F♯-g-a-b (where C indicates the first note in the raag and does not necessarily match what you might be used to hearing as the pitch "C" in concert tuning). The raag is performed in Tintal (4+4+4+4).

MUKHRA

1	2	3	4	5	6	7	8	9	10	11	**12**	**13**	**14**	**15**	**16**
	clap				clap					wave				clap	

TIME	SECTION	MUSICAL EVENT
0:00–0:08	**Alap:** Listen for how the performer systematically explores the individual pitches of the raag.	The sitar player strums across the open strings of the instrument as an opening gesture. Listen for the sound of both the melody and the drone strings.
0:09–0:23		The performer begins the alap by moving slowly up the raag, exploring the first few notes.
0:24–0:45		This process continues until the performer eventually reaches the highest note.
0:46–1:10		A zigzag motion back down the raga eventually reaches the original opening pitch.
1:12–1:14		A second open-string strum ends the alap section.
1:15–1:38	**Gat-Tora in Medium Tempo:** Listen for the alternating sections of melody (gat) and improvisation (tora) in this section.	The sitarist plays vilambit (slow) gat, beginning on beat twelve, and repeats the melody twice, concluding with the mukhra (b-a-b-e-d-e-e) ending on **sam** (beat one). If you're having trouble hearing the mukhra, the tabla joins after the very first statement of the mukhra, playing a single stroke at [1:18] before joining in earnest.

continued

TIME	SECTION	MUSICAL EVENT
1:39–1:44		The sitarist continues without pause into improvisation (tora) for the rest of the tala cycle until mukhra is picked up at beat 12 again, ending on the next sam.
1:45–2:11		Further improvisation in higher range until full gat returns.
2:12–2:22		Restatement of gat.
2:23–2:26		Tora.
2:27–3:44		Mukhra, followed by tora, etc. . . .
3:45–3:54		At the close of the gat-tora section, the sitarist performs a tihai leading to sam and a change to fast (drut) gat.
3:55–4:50	**Brisk Jhala in Fast Tempo:** Listen for the increasingly virtuosic melodic and rhythmic explorations on the sitar and tabla.	The sitarist begins to play increasingly elaborate melodic explorations, alternating melody and drone.
4:50–5:55		The transition to jhala is complete and the sitarist signals this with rapid strokes on the drone strings, inserted between melody tones (a hallmark of jhala); the tempo (laya) also increases to about 240 beats per minute at this point.
5:55–6:15		Sitar and tabla join in rhythmic improvisation that takes the raga to a dramatic conclusion.

GAT-TORA
The section of Hindustani instrumental performance, accompanied by table, in which a short composed melody, the gat, is alternated with improvisational passages, tora.

MUKHRA
Initial phrase of a khyal or gat used as a cadence for improvisational passages in Hindustani music.

SAM
The first beat in a tala.

some complicated fills along the way) that resolves on beat 1, after which the cycle then repeats. The first beat of each cycle is called the *sam*, an important concept in Hindustani music: as the music gets more and more complicated, performers will often make eye contact before the sam, and smile when they reach it—for it means that they have made it through a difficult section of music without messing up!

After a virtuosic moment of improvisation, as well as at the very end of a performance, performers typically play a tihai, a cadence that is usually repeated three times. Once you learn to listen for tihais you will find them hard to miss; usually, they involve a fast, virtuosic run that is played three times, and then that whole pattern of three is repeated three times. In other words, a tihai is a pattern of three that contains within it other patterns of three.

Have you ever *seen* a sitar up close? A plucked lute instrument, it has around eighteen to twenty strings, including six or seven that lie above the frets, with the rest being smaller strings that lie *beneath* the frets and which are not usually played by hand. These smaller strings are "sympathetic strings" that resonate when particular pitches on the main strings are played. In other words, playing one note on the sitar will automatically resonate the sympathetic string tuned to that pitch. Many Indian instruments have sympathetic strings, but they are perhaps most famously associated with the sitar, giving it the bright, chiming sound for which it is well known.

I already mentioned the sarod (another lute instrument) above, which is originally from Afghanistan (where it is called the rubab) but found its way into Hindustani classical music; though it, too, has sympathetic strings, unlike the sitar it is a fretless instrument, and to my ears it has a less smooth (though no less beautiful) sound to it, somewhat like plucking an acoustic guitar with a coin. Other famous Hindustani instruments include the sarangi, a bowed instrument that used to play an accompanying role but which is now commonly used as a lead instrument; the bansuri or flute; and the santoor, a hammered dulcimer associated with the folk music of the Kashmir region (its ancestor is a Persian dulcimer called the santur)—the santoor has a mellow, reverberating sound and in the twentieth century it also found its way as a lead instrument. The tanpura is an interesting case: it is an instrument with four simple strings that only provides a droning sound, which forms the backdrop for a performance. The tanpura is traditionally played by a shishya, who sits on stage and provides the drone while watching the guru.

Finally, no discussion of Hindustani musical instruments is complete without mentioning the harmonium, a hand-pumped organ similar to an accordion and also of European descent. The harmonium has always been controversial in India, for some Indian music purists feel that it cannot

Various Hindustani musical instruments, including harmonium, bansuri, sitar, swarmandal harp, and tabla.
Source: © Dinodia Photos / Alamy Stock Photo

adequately capture the nuances of the instrumental or vocal music, which traditionally included much vibrato (a kind of trill, or shaking of a note subtly into another). Traditionally, Hindustani and Carnatic musics incorporate microtones (notes that cannot be found on the keys of a piano), called shrutis; the harmonium, with keys spaced apart identically to a Western keyboard, is accused by some to have changed Hindustani performance by forcing musicians to approximate Western scales (the harmonium can be found in the South but it is less prominent, and not typically used in a Carnatic recital).

CARNATIC CLASSICAL MUSICS: THE GROWTH OF THE SOUTHERN TRADITION

EXPLORE

Carnatic Music

Because the Beatles went to North India, they popularized Hindustani music in the West. To this day, South Indian Carnatic music remains less well known in the West, but this is not because of a lack of quality or historic importance. Carnatic music has its own stylistic and formal, as well as favored instruments. While I focus more on Hindustani music in this chapter, in this section I want to provide some of the basics of Carnatic music, after which I will expand the discussion to include Hindu ritual drumming and classical dance.

Carnatic (sometimes spelled Karnatak) music stems mainly from the music of Hindu wandering minstrels in South India in the late eighteenth and early nineteenth centuries. To be clear, there is a long tradition of music and dance (which have always been closely related) in South India for centuries before this, such as during the golden age of the medieval Tamil Chola Dynasty (circa 9th–13th centuries), where there was an elaborate system of music and dance that grew up in Hindu temples. But it was only later that what is now known as Carnatic music developed.

The grandfather of Carnatic music is considered to be Purandara Dasa (1484–1564). He was born in what is today the southwestern Indian state of Karnataka. Purandara Dasa gave away his possessions at the age of thirty to join an itinerant Hindu sect called the Haridasa. He is famous for, among other things, developing a system for teaching Carnatic music that continues to be used today. What we now call Carnatic music, though, was not fully developed until a group of three composers, now called "**The Trinity**," emerged onto the scene: Tyagaraja (1767–1847), Muthuswami Dikshitar (1775–1835), and Syama Sastri (1762–1827). These composers lived at roughly the same time as Beethoven (1770–1827), and the idea of a canon of "great composers" may have arisen through colonial influence—the British were ruling South India during this period. The Trinity's compositions have a unique style that came to define Carnatic music. They also developed a number of structural forms that continue to be used in Carnatic music today. Each composer is known for certain compositions: Tyagaraja is so famous that he is treated as a saint in his hometown of Thiruvaiyaru, and a music festival is held in his honor every year

THE TRINITY
Three foundational com posers of Carnatic music: Tyagaraja (1767–1847), Muthuswami Dikshitar (1775–1835), and Syama Sastri (1762–1827).

in Cleveland, Ohio, where musicians from all over the world come to sing Tyagaraja's music.

Though Carnatic music is associated with the Tamil people who live mainly in the modern state of Tamil Nadu, most of the classical Carnatic compositions are not sung in the Tamil language—Purandara Dasa sang in the Kannada language (of his native Karnataka region), Syama Sastri and Tyagaraja sang mainly in Telugu (a language associated with the state of Andhra Pradesh, just north of Tamil Nadu), and Dikshitar sang almost entirely in Sanskrit. Most composers that followed them did not sing in Tamil, a situation that meant that by the early twentieth century, Carnatic music was performed mainly by Tamils but not sung in Tamil. This would lead to the growth of a "Tamil Music Movement" in the twentieth century, through which more Tamil music was unearthed and composed.

Upon first listen, one could be forgiven for thinking that Carnatic and Hindustani musics are one and the same genre. In fact, they are quite different, though they share some vocabulary (for instance, the melodic system in the south is called ragam and the rhythmic system is called talam). Perhaps the most important difference is that, while the Hindustani tradition is famous as an instrumental, improvised tradition, Carnatic music is based primarily on a set of compositions whose composers (such as Tyagaraja) are known. But here is where confusion sets in. Hindustani music *does* have its own vocal genres (which I have not discussed here, for simplicity's sake), and it does have its own prominent vocalists who sing various types of poetic compositions, some of which date back centuries. Meanwhile, Carnatic music *does* have many kinds of improvisation, and improvisation occurs during the performance of compositions. The distinction between improvisation and composition (as mapped respectively onto Hindustani and Carnatic traditions) is thus problematic, though it may be useful as a general framework for beginners to comprehend South Asian musics.

Two musical forms in Carnatic music are the most revered. The first type of composition is the *kriti*, which is typically the main type of composition performed at a Carnatic recital. The structure of a kriti includes three sections: pallavi (refrain), anupallavi (second verse), and charanam (final, long verse). As one might expect from a refrain, the pallavi appears at the end of the anupallavi and charanam. Meanwhile, the charanam will often borrow elements from the anupallavi. A performance of a kriti may be preceded by an improvised exploration of the ragam in free meter, called alapanam (this is the Carnatic version of what in Hindustani music is called alap). The kriti traditionally ends with the composer's signature, or mudra, a set of words (which may include the composer's name and/or favorite deity) that identifies the piece as being composed by a specific composer.

After the kriti is completed, the performer might play *ragam-tanam-pallavi*, an improvisational sequence that itself can be performed as a separate component of a Carnatic concert, and which is the second important structure of Carnatic music. The ragam is the alapanam (unmetered introduction), the thanam is the improvisation on "nonsemantic syllables" like "nam," "na," "thaa," and "thom,"

KRITI
The major song type of Carnatic music, divided into three parts: pallavi, anupallavi, and caranam.

RAGAM-TANAM-PALLAVI
A form of Carnatic music that favors improvisation.

KRITI BY TYAGARAJA, "BANTURITI"

LISTEN

TRACK 2.6 **Vocal: Seetha Rajan; mridangam: N. Venkataraman; violin: Jayashankar Balan**

LET'S CONSIDER this brief but complete performance of the kriti "Banturiti." Composed by Tyagaraja, this kriti illustrates many of the musical ideas discussed in the section on the Carnatic recital. After the briefest of alapanams in a ragam called Hamsanadam (scale C-E-F♯-G-B), the singer begins the kriti, which is in the most common talam, called Adi. This eight beat talam is indicated by a clap on samam (the first beat) and two other claps on beats 5 and 7; the three beats following samam are indicated by tapping the fingers of the right hand, starting with the little finger, on the palm of the left and "waving" the right hand, that is, turning it palm upward on the palm of the left hand, for beats 6 and 8. These claps and taps are not audible in the recording, but serve as a customary way to orient oneself in relation to the music.

1	2	3	4	5	6	7	8
Clap	Tap	Tap	Tap	Clap	Wave	Clap	Wave

The eduppu or opening phrase of this song falls midway between beats 2 and 3—that is, after a clap and a tap of the little finger—and the performer must return to this point accurately whenever finishing a passage of niraval or kalpanaswaram, improvisation. Alternatively the performer may choose to conclude at samam.

In this performance, the singer is accompanied by violin and mridangam (double-headed, barrel-shaped drum); note that these instruments are briefly heard alone after the conclusion of the pallavi and anupallavi. When these instruments are next heard alone, about midway through the charanam, the singer is alternating niraval improvisation with the violinist; then the performance quickly proceeds to kalpanaswaram as she improvises by singing the note names—sa, ri, ga, ma, pa, dha, ni—before coming to a conclusion by returning to the pallavi theme.

TIME	SECTION	MUSICAL EVENT
0:00–0:03	**Alapanam:** Listen for the way that the performer systematically, though quite rapidly, explores the individual pitches of the ragam, revealing its shape in the process.	Brief drone introduction by the violin.
0:03–0:31		The vocalist begins the alapanam, rapidly introducing the full shape of the ragam.
0:31–0:42		The vocalist and violinist exchange improvised melodic fragments as they complete the alapanam.
0:43–0:49	**Kriti: Pallavi:** Listen for the clear articulation of the eduppu.	Pallavi theme is introduced. The theme includes the melodic fragment called the eduppu that initiates the pallavi theme. The eduppu falls on beat 2.5 and is followed by the whole melodic phrase. (If you're having

continued

TIME	SECTION	MUSICAL EVENT
		trouble hearing the eduppu, listen for the return of the first word "Banturiti," for example, at approximately [00:49–00:50], and approximately every 5 seconds thereafter through the pallavi.)
0:49–0:55		The pallavi theme is repeated.
0:56–1:35		Repetitions of the pallavi theme with variations (called sangati).
1:35–1:40	**Kriti: Anupallavi:** Listen for the introduction of the new melodic/rhythmic theme and for the return of the pallavi theme as a refrain.	The first half of the anupallavi phrase is introduced.
1:40–1:55		The full first phrase is introduced and repeated.
1:55–2:14		The second phrase of the anupallavi theme is introduced, followed by a repeat of the first and second phrases.
2:14–2:30		The pallavi theme returns as a refrain (listen for the eduppu beginning with "Banturiti").
2:30–2:53	**Kriti: Charanam:** Listen for the introduction of new charanam text, but sung to the established pallavi and anupallavi melodies. Listen also for the niraval and kalpanaswaram improvisation so prominent throughout this section of the performance.	Introduction of the charanam text, but performed by using the melodic materials of the pallavi theme.
2:54–3:24		Repeat of theme from the first phrase of the anupallavi, also with charanam text. This is followed by niraval improvisation on this theme.
3:24–4:02		The vocalist and the violinist are alternating their improvisations during this portion of the performance.
4:03–4:21		The niraval section of improvisation is concluded by the vocalist.
4:22–5:15		Introduction of kalpanaswaram improvisation. The voice and violin again alternate throughout this section.
5:15–5:55		Vocalist returns to anupallavi theme and then concludes with an ornamented pallavi refrain.

and the pallavi can be the first section of a kriti or new music composed by the soloist. There are many kinds of improvisation in Carnatic music that are woven into these formal structures, and it will take a student much time to learn how and when to use them. Some examples include niraval (improvising on a line from a kriti, thereby bringing out the essence of the ragam), kalpanaswaram (improvising on solfege syllables), and trikala (doubling, tripling, and quadrupling the duration of the notes of the pallavi). After such demanding music, a Carnatic

A veena being built.
Source: © Dinodia Photos / Alamy Stock Photo

MRIDANGAM

Double-headed, barrel-shaped drum of Carnatic music.

Saraswati and Veena.
Source: Heritage Images/Getty Images

recital will often conclude with lighter compositions that are less virtuosic, such as padams and javalis—genres that are historically associated with dance.

Carnatic music has its own musical instruments associated with it. The veena is about four feet in length, with a thin neck and two large gourds holding up each end. While the Hindustani sitar is held at a sharp angle (almost as one holds a guitar, but much more upright), the veena is often held horizontally along the ground, or at just a very slight angle. While the sitar has moveable frets, the veena's frets are built into the instrument. The veena is sometimes called the Saraswati Veena, as it is the instrument associated with Saraswati, the Hindu goddess of knowledge and the arts. You may wish to search online for performances of the veena, sitar, and sarod, and see if you can hear the differences between them.

Three percussion instruments stand out in the South: the *mridangam*, a thin, barrel-shaped drum played with the hands, which is usually the main drum used in a Carnatic classical music performance; the ghatam, which is a clay pot played with one's fingers and also used widely in Carnatic music (sometimes a performance might include a mridangam and a ghatam); and the thavil, a fatter, barrel-shaped drum played with one stick and one hand, which is associated with the auspicious music played in Hindu temples

Carnatic women's ensemble.
Source: The India Today
Group/Getty Images

(the thavil is usually found along with the nadaswaram, a very long and loud reed instrument that is used in Hindu temples and at temple festivals).

It is important to stress the importance of the violin to Carnatic music, a European instrument that has long been indigenized and which is played in South India with a unique style. While in the North the sarangi is the main bowed instrument, in the south this honor goes to the violin, which may be played as a lead instrument or as an important accompanying instrument during vocal performances. When the singer improvises, the violinist plays just behind the singer, mimicking the vocal melody and providing a mellifluous backdrop for the singing.

HINDU MUSIC AND DANCE: TEMPLES, GENDER, AND CASTE

Throughout India, dance maintains a vitality, vibrancy, and cultural relevance perhaps unparalleled in the West. Music and dance should be understood as deeply integrated in South Asian thought and practice: though we are focusing on music in this chapter, it is important to realize that historically, South Asian musics often developed in contexts where dance was prevalent. In medieval South India, a practice grew up whereby women were married to gods in formal wedding ceremonies, after which it was their job to dance and sing for the deity in a Hindu temple. These women, called *devadasis*, had become controversial by the late nineteenth century. During that era of conservative Victorian mores, India's British colonists looked down upon devadasis, defining them as "dancing girls," and assuming they were prostitutes. Due to the efforts of Hindu social reformers, some of whom came from devadasi families, being

DEVADASI
A Carnatic dancing girl whose art was dedicated to temple deities.

Bharata Natyam dancers.
Source: MANJUNATH
KIRAN/Getty Images

a devadasi was eventually outlawed in India, though today some devadasi communities do still exist. Scholars continue to debate whether such women are or were always prostitutes, but the current scholarly consensus is that the devadasis were treated unfairly. Rather than being in a destitute position, some devadasis enjoyed a kind of freedom not possible for some Hindu women of the day. They were allowed to have romantic partners outside the temple and many had children, but they did not face the stigma that attached to widows, for their husbands (the gods) never die.

In the early- to mid-twentieth century, an enormous transformation occurred in devadasis' dance, which was then called sadir. Some upper caste Brahman women lamented that the most developed and highly esteemed dance tradition of South India was performed by women of such "low" standing. A move was made to take sadir from the devadasis and transform it into a "respectable" dance that would be suitable for Brahman women to perform. This was portrayed as a project of redemption, reclamation, and progress, a saving of the dance from a community of prostitutes so that it could be remade as the dance of the nation. The woman most responsible for this was Rukmini Devi (1904–1986), an upper-caste choreographer and dancer. She initially faced skepticism and hostility from some upper-caste South Indians on account of her promoting what was then considered a degraded art form. She eventually succeeded, though the result was that the devadasis no longer had control of their tradition. The new version of the dance was called ***Bharata Natyam*** ("Indian Dance"), and Rukmini Devi emerged as one of its most well-known practitioners.

In hindsight, we can see that both sadir and Bharata Natyam should be valued, and they differ from one another in many ways. A famous dancer in

BHARATA NATYAM
Major dance style of South India.

the old style was Tanjore Balasaraswati (1918–1984, often called "Bala" for short), a woman from a devadasi family who persisted and achieved much acclaim despite the changes to her dance form. Bala's style is emblematic of the traditional sadir, as it is much slower with more hand gestures and facial expressions (abhinaya). (One of India's premier filmmakers, Satyajit Ray, made a 1976 documentary about Bala—simply called *Bala*—that can be found online and is well worth watching.) Bharata Natyam tends to be faster and involves much elaborate footwork; unlike the dance of the devadasis, Bharata Natyam dancers do not sing (both versions involve musicians sitting off to the side of the stage, with the dancer's guru usually playing the role of singer). Bharata Natyam is now a global phenomenon, learned by many (especially South) Indian women.

As mentioned above, according to the Hindu caste system there are some individuals who are considered so low, so impure, that they are technically outside the system. To put it simply, if the caste system stipulates that some groups are pure, then some must be impure—otherwise there would be no such hierarchy. Such outcastes, who are often called "untouchables," were and in some cases still are a downtrodden group in India. Historically, their job was to perform services for the middle and upper castes that those castes did not want to perform themselves. One of the untouchable communities, the paraiyars (from whom we derive our English word "pariah"), performed drumming in a number of different contexts (including some auspicious occasions), but they are most associated with performing work that has to do with death. This includes drumming at funerals, and scavenging dead cattle for drum skins. The paraiyars traditionally lived in their own villages or on the outskirts of villages, were not allowed to wear shoes, and could not enter Hindu temples. In the early to mid-twentieth century, a reformer named B.R. Ambedkar promoted the rights of the untouchable groups; he helped usher in a change in their name, as they are now called Dalits (a Sanskrit-derived word meaning "crushed" or "broken")—a politically correct term that acknowledges the historically downtrodden situation of untouchable groups but which avoids the stigma associated with their original names.

The paraiyars (that is, Dalits) play a frame drum called the parai. Ethnomusicologist Zoe Sherinian has documented a revival and resignification of the parai drum currently underway in South India: some Dalit groups have embraced the drum as a way to make money by playing at staged events—a transformation of their ritual music into "culture" and a form of entertainment. Anti-caste and Dalit activists have begun to embrace the drum (originally a source of the paraiyars' stigma) as a way to generate communal pride.

BOLLYWOOD

EXPLORE

Bollywood

Chances are you have heard of Bollywood, the Indian film industry based in Mumbai (India's most populous city, which used to be called Bombay). You may not know that Bollywood emerged out of a lively and already globally influential

Indian musical theater scene in the nineteenth century. A small community of Persian descent, called the Parsis, has long lived in the Indian city of Mumbai, and in the last decades of the nineteenth century they set out on steamships to travel around the Indian Ocean, performing a hodgepodge of music, theater, dance, and drama, now referred to as "the Parsi Theatre". The style found its way to Sri Lanka, where it was adopted and turned into a local style called nurthi, and to Malaysia and Singapore, where it gave birth to a musical theater form called bangsawan. These theater forms were a syncretic mix of Indian and sometimes Middle Eastern plots, and bangsawan in particular used a diverse set of actors including Indians, Arabs, Javanese, Malays, Ceylonese, Eurasians, and Chinese.

The first Bollywood film productions grew directly out of the aesthetics of the Parsi Theatre and a few other comparable theater genres of the day. Film song (*filmigit*) emerged as an essential component of Bollywood films. At first, much of this music was played in a "light classical" style that used the tabla, sitar, harmonium, and flute, but over time Bollywood musics developed sounds that owed much to the global popular musics of any period (such as 1970s disco, or Michael Jackson in the 1980s), while retaining a unique Indian feel that, in turn, would influence the globe. Most Bollywood films are not about music *per se* but include song and dance sequences; occasionally, however, films use music and dance to conjure up specific communities and time periods. The 1960 film *Mughal-e-Azam* (*The Emperor of the Mughals*), for instance, includes scenes of dancers and musicians at the court of the Mughal Emperor Akbar. Many films include renditions of folk or wedding songs; one example (chosen at random, for there are many) is the 2011 film *Jugni*, which includes modern versions of Punjabi folk songs. Indian films do not have to include only classical, folk, or religious traditions: the 2011 film *Rock Star*, as its name implies, is about a debaucherous Indian rock star who seemingly has it all, except for love. It is worth stressing that there are many regional cinemas throughout South Asia besides Bollywood. A good musical example is the 1968 Tamil film *Thillana Mohanambal*, which is in the Tamil language and tells the story of a nadaswaram player who falls in love with a Bharata Natyam dancer.

As the Indian film industry was being established, a system emerged whereby films often passed through the same recording studios. Many songs were recorded by the same artists, even though they were lip synced by someone else onscreen. The singers who sing Bollywood songs but do not appear in the films themselves are called playback singers. One of the world's most famous playback singers is Lata Mangeshkar (born 1929), who has recorded music for over a thousand Hindi films and sung in over thirty languages (mainly in Hindi and Marathi, the latter being the main language in western India). Lata has always had a sibling rivalry with her younger sister, Asha Bhosle (born 1933), who also has recorded music for over a thousand films, supposedly for a total of over 12,000 songs. She was certified by the *Guinness Book of World Records* as the most recorded vocalist in history. If you have spent any time listening to old Bollywood songs, you may remember a high-pitched, nasal-sounding female

FILMIGIT
Popular songs composed for Indian films.

voice—if so, it is probably one of these two singers you are imagining. The British rock band Cornershop had a #1 hit on the UK chart in 1998 with their song "Brimful of Asha," a tribute to Asha Bhosle.

IMPORTANT GENRES AND REGIONAL STYLES: QAWWALI

Film songs are not the only popular music in South Asia—far from it. One genre that straddles our standard genre distinctions between folk, classical, sacred and popular is *Qawwali*. The genre is a Sufi Muslim music that is spread throughout North India and Pakistan and contains many vernacular styles (and thus can also be considered a kind of folk music). It is also a national music, for it is now considered the national music of Pakistan, and yet it is also a popular music, as many Qawwali songs have become enormous hits—sometimes by appearing in Bollywood films!

As mentioned above, *Sufism* is the mystical dimension of Islam. As with Islam itself, Sufism emerged in the Middle East toward the end of the first millennium CE. It spread rapidly in many directions, and Sufi orders (tariqa) were established in places like Turkey, Central Asia, and North India (the famous Sufi poet Rumi was born of Persian parents in present-day Afghanistan, and his tomb is in the city of Konya, in present-day Turkey). A Sufi pir is a guide who instructs disciples how to follow the Sufi path; a key Sufi practice is dhikr (or zikr), a word that means "remembrance" and which often involves the chanting of the words for God, but it can also be taken as a generic name for Sufi devotional practices. One kind of dhikr is sama (or sema), a word that means "listening" and which refers to Sufi rituals involving music, dance, recitation and poetry.

Qawwali is a kind of sama that is traditionally held at Sufi saints' shrines in North India and Pakistan. The genre has an important connection with Hindustani classical music that must be emphasized. Qawwali as we know it today it is said to have developed through the efforts of a legendary thirteenth-century poet and musician, Amir Khusrao, who is widely considered one of the founders not only of Qawwali but of Hindustani music in general. Khusrao resided in the city of Delhi and was a member of the Chisthi order (a Sufi tariqa with roots in Afghanistan); legend has it that he invented the tabla by taking the pakhawaj (a barrel-shaped drum) and splitting it in two (though this story is probably more of a legend than historical truth, it demonstrates Khusrao's importance to Hindustani tradition). Khusrao was a disciple of the Sufi master Nizamuddin Auliya, and today you can visit the tombs of each, which are situated next to each other at the Nizamuddin Auliya shrine in Delhi. Amir Khusrao is famous for his poetry (composed in Persian), which still forms the content of many of the Qawwali songs sung today. The main poetic form he used is called ghazal, and it consists of rhyming couplets and a refrain. The ghazal is essential to a Qawwali performance; its themes often revolve around unrequited love. In one memorable poem, "Nami Danam Che Manzil" (which is still performed as a Qawwali song today), Khusrao exclaims,

QAWWALI
A genre of Sufi Muslim music popular throughout North India and Pakistan, which uses harmonium and tabla, and involves the singing of Persian poetry (particularly the poetic form called ghazal).

SUFISM
Form of Islamic worship involving communal ritual ceremonies featuring participatory practices such as singing, chanting, music, and dance.

EXPLORE
Qawwali Music

EXPLORE
Ghazal

I wonder what was the place where I was last night,
All around me were half-slaughtered victims of love
tossing about in agony.
There was a nymph-like beloved with cypress-like form
and tulip-like face,
Ruthlessly playing havoc with the hearts of the lovers.
God himself was the master of ceremonies in that heavenly court,
oh Khusrao, where (the face of) the Prophet too was shedding light
like a candle.

Often in ghazals, the love that is spoken of is not for a lover but for God. Qawwali singers take great care in repeating the lines of ghazals, for repeating them in different ways can bring out radically different meanings.

Nowadays, the standard instrumentation for Qawwali includes one or two harmoniums, a chorus of singers who sing and clap, and a lead vocalist (often one of the harmonium players acts as a secondary vocalist, trading off with the main singer). A Qawwali group is called a "Qawwali party," and sometimes they are family bands. The most famous Qawwali singer, Nusrat Fateh Ali Khan (1948–1997), was born in Faisalabad, Pakistan (his family had migrated there from a city in West Punjab, India, during Partition). Nusrat's father was a Qawwal (a singer of Qawwali), and from a young age he sang in his family's Qawwali party. After his father passed away in 1971, Nusrat became the head of the Qawwali party and the group began appearing steadily on radio and national television. During the world music craze of the 1980s, Nusrat appeared at the WOMAD festival in London (this is an organization founded by the British singer Peter Gabriel), and he eventually signed to Gabriel's Real World Records. Nusrat became an enormous star, gracing the world's largest stages; he even

Abida Parveen.
Source: Mail Today/Getty Images

QAWWALI*

 **LISTEN**

TRACK 2.7 **"Nât Sharîf," The Sabri Brothers**

THIS SONG is a *na'at*, a type of poem that praises the Prophet Muhammad. It is sung here in Urdu, the national language of Pakistan (which is mutually intelligible with Hindi—the most widely spoken language in North India—but written in the Persian script with many Persian loanwords). The form of a *na'at* is similar to that of a ghazal in that it alternates between sections called sthayi (an initial phrase that is returned to throughout as a refrain) and antara (verse), usually in the following order: (1) sthayi, sthayi (2) antara, sthayi (3) antara, sthayi. The sthayi tune thus appears in the *first* line of the *first* couplet, after which it appears in the *second* line of each remaining couplet. The antara sections are where improvisation usually takes place; they are often sung solo, while the refrain (sthayi) is typically sung by a chorus of singers (in this example, though, the antara is sometimes also sung by a chorus, interspersed with solo improvisation; there is also some solo improvisation on the sthayi at the very beginning of the track, which may have occurred in light of a positive response from the audience).

This particular *na'at* is by the famous Sufi poet Amir Khusrao (1253–1325). The track fades in with the song already in progress. What we hear first is a solo improvisation on the sthayi, followed by a group singing of the sthayi (0:55). The lyrics to the sthayi are, "Woh hai kya magar, woh hai kya nahin, yeh muhibb habib ki baat hai" ("But what is that? What isn't it? This beloved is the [desired] object of the lover"). This is followed by the *fourth* verse of Khusrao's poem, including (1) an antara sung by a chorus, followed by solo improvisation, and then a return to a shtayi. (2) Then we hear a fifth verse with an antara ("Tujhe"/"Dare") and sthayi ("Jo nashin"/ "Yeh bare naseeb") that is then repeated ("Tujhe"; "Jo nashin"), (3) followed by a new antara (or this may be just improvisation, it is hard to tell), ending with the sthayi.

TIME	MUSICAL EVENT
0–0:55:	improvisation on the sthayi, "Woh hai kya magar, woh hai kya nahin, yeh muhibb habib ki baat hai" ("But what is that? What isn't it? This beloved is the [desired] object of the lover").
0:55–1:10:	Clear rendition of the refrain (sthayi)
1:10–2:07:	Section of improvisation, where singers take turns improvising on text and the chorus repeating it. (antara)
2:07–2:30:	refrain. (sthayi)
2:30–3:45:	another section of back and forth vocal improvisations on text. (antara)
3:45–4:14:	refrain. (sthayi)
4:14–4:48:	another section of back and forth vocal improvisations on text. (antara)
4:48–5:08:	refrain. (sthayi)
5:08–5:30:	another section of back and forth vocal improvisations on text. (antara)
5:30–end:	refrain (5:38: the tempo drastically slows down). (sthayi)

* Thanks to Katherine Butler Schofield for help preparing this Listening Guide.

had moments of pop crossover, such as the two duets he sang with Pearl Jam's vocalist Eddie Vedder on the soundtrack to the 1996 Hollywood film *Dead Man Walking*.

While most Qawwals are male, a special mention must be made of Abida Parveen, a highly regarded female Pakistani Qawwali singer, who has been active since the early 1970s. Parveen sings ghazals and kafi (another kind of Sufi poetry), and she has become a pop icon in her own right, singing fusion music and collaborating with pop musicians at Coke Studio, as well as appearing as a judge on *Sur Kshetra*, a singing talent show (like *American Idol*) that stages singing contests between Indian and Pakistani singers.

IMPORTANT GENRES AND REGIONAL STYLES: AFGHANISTAN

EXPLORE

Afghanistan

Given the political turmoil that has torn Afghanistan apart in the past few decades, readers may be surprised to learn that this country had a vibrant pop music scene in the years before it was devastated by violence. Ahmad Zahir (1946–1979) was the son of a doctor and health minister (who was Prime Minister of Afghanistan, 1971–1972). Zahir is referred to as "the Afghan Elvis" because of his sideburns and Elvis-like swagger. He began playing in pop bands in high school (groups which included instruments like the piano, guitar, and congas) and then graduated into singing Persian poetry. He wound up recording over thirty albums that show an incredible range of sounds and lyrical themes, including social commentary and criticism of the government of his day. The music is hard to categorize—his voice typically has a lot of reverb placed on it, his tone and style (and lyrics) are often romantic, and the instrumentation may include the tabla and harmonium—though some of his songs used a drum set and they often have a rock and roll vibe. Zahir died at age 33 in mysterious circumstances, in a car crash that is widely seen as having not been an accident. This was just after the communist takeover of Afghanistan, which Zahir did not support (this would be one of many changes in governance that Afghanistan would experience over the following decades). Zahir's music is still widely remembered by Afghans all over the world, and it now conjures a golden age for music in pre-war Afghanistan.

While Herat is a city with a clear Tajik majority, Kabul is more ethnically mixed (with a majority Tajik population and large numbers of Hazaras and Pashtuns); by contrast, the city of Kandahar is a Pashtun-majority city (in sheer numbers, the Pashtuns are the ethnic majority of Afghanistan). Located in the west of the country, Herat looks more toward Iran for musical inspiration, while Kabul is located in the northeast and traditionally turned more toward India for musical inspiration.

In the 1860s, the Amir Sher Ali Khan of Kabul invited a number of Hindustani musicians from hereditary Muslim families in North India to move to the city to serve as his court musicians. While this is usually considered as the first wave of Hindustani musicians brought to Afghanistan to serve as court

A mural of Ahmad Zahir.
Source: AFP/Getty Images

musicians, ethnomusicologist John Baily (2011: 15) has argued this was in fact the second major wave, the earlier one coming during the rule of Dost Mohammed (1833–1863). The musicians brought by Amir Sher Ali Khan, it seems, were musicians who supplied music for female dancers. Whatever the case, by the early twentieth century, these Hindustani musicians were maintaining ties with Hindustani ustads through intermarriage and discipleship, and performing art music rather than dance music. A tradition called Klasik grew up, which is essentially the Afghan version of Hindustani classical music.

The term "Klasik" is obviously derived from the English term "classic" and the term probably spread from India; Baily (1980:76) notes that the term in its narrowest usage was applied to vocal music, but he also met Afghans who also used the term to mean "difficult." The phrase "naghmeh-ye-klasik" (classical instrumental piece) refers to the performance of instrumental music, typically on a rubab (a plucked lute, of which the sarod is a descendant), with tabla accompaniment. While the approaches and terminologies of Klasik and Hindustani musics are largely shared, there are some differences in performance style. Klasik is usually heard as having a rhythmic style all its own that distinguishes it from Hindustani music—call it a groove, an attitude, a way of strumming, plucking, and phrasing. In his book on the music of Herat, Baily documents the naghmeh-ye-klasik as having two sections, the first an instrumental solo in free rhythm, the second a fixed composition in tintal (sixteen-beat cycle).

The musical situation in Afghanistan would change drastically with the coming of the Taliban (a Pashto word meaning "students"). After the Communist takeover of Afghanistan in 1979, a long war was fought (a proxy war between the United States and Soviet Union) that devastated the country. (As is well known, the group that fought against the communists, which received funding from the CIA, were called the mujahideen, and included a young Osama bin Laden.) The Taliban trace their origins to this group of mujahideen, though they emerged in full in the Pasthun-majority city of Kandahar in the mid-1990s, eventually taking over the country in the years before the U.S. government's response to the September 11, 2001 attacks.

The Taliban are infamous for their ban on music, which they believe to be so sensual as to lead people into improper behavior. For justification they turned to the sayings of the Prophet Mohammed (called hadiths), one of which states, "Those who listen to music and songs in this world, will on the Day of Judgment have molten lead poured into their ears." (It should be stressed that many Muslims disagree with the Taliban's readings of the Qur'an and hadiths on music.) Upon gaining control in Kabul in 1996, the Taliban issued an infamous decree stating that those with cassette tapes would be imprisoned. Musical instruments and cassettes (along with television sets) were hung in mock executions or publicly burned, people were publicly flogged and even had limbs amputated.

Here we would do well to consider once again the work of ethnomusic-ologist John Baily, who has also written about the Taliban's ban on music. Baily rightly points out that the Taliban are not the only people to have taken an extreme stance on music—though they are unquestionably extreme in their attitude. Baily notes, for instance, that he comes from a Christian Quaker back-ground, and this group at one point in English history also had an extremely negative stance toward music. (I have already mentioned above that Theravada Buddhism looks down upon certain kinds of music, deeming it unacceptable for monks.) Baily emphasizes that the Taliban didn't ban all music, since they allowed the frame drum (daireh) which is often played by women and was sanctioned by the Prophet Mohammed. They also developed their own "musical" genre, a kind of chanting that they forced some singers to sing at the radio station, with lyrics praising the Taliban, which was not considered music because it didn't contain instruments. In Afghanistan, Baily emphasizes, "music" has historically meant "instrumental music," so vocal chants are in a different category. For Baily, what the Taliban initiated was a competition between kinds of "music," though undoubtedly the Taliban took an extreme position that had a terrible impact on the country's musicians—though many of these had already been persecuted during the period when the mujahideen had control of the country (who were also generally against music).

Though the Taliban were driven out of Kabul during the 2001 invasion, they remain an active presence in the country, particularly in the Pashtun-majority provinces in the south. The hereditary professional musicians who used to live in the musicians' quarter of Kabul have by now been living for a long time in Peshawar, a Pashtun-majority city over the border in Pakistan, while more affluent and educated amateur musicians have moved to various sites known for Afghan migrant populations, such as Fremont, California. In 2011, a rock music festival was held in Kabul, the first such performance in over thirty years.

The event was held within the walls of the Bagh-e Babur (Gardens of Babur), a park that houses the tomb of the first Mughal Emperor, Babur, who had captured Kabul in 1504 and died in 1530. The festival returned in the years after its debut, growing in size to become categorized as an "alternative arts festival," with bands from mainly Central Asian and European countries.

IMPORTANT GENRES AND REGIONAL STYLES: THE BAULS OF BENGAL

It would be hard to find a community more different from the Taliban than the *Bauls*, a community of itinerant musicians in West Bengal (India) and Bangladesh who preach tolerance and oneness through music and dance, drawing on religious traditions in a syncretic fashion. "Baul" is derived from the Sanskrit word *vatula*, meaning "mad," "possessed," "lashed by the air," or "crazy." The Bauls are not insane, for their madness is their passion for God. Rather than argue that one religious stance is more pure than another, the Bauls' general attitude is that we each contain divine power inside us, and we should enjoy the world's pleasures without becoming attached to them. They tend to wander and perform music for sustenance. Culturally speaking, the Bauls draw on aspects from Sufism and Vaishnavism (the worship of the Hindu god Vishnu), both of which are found in Bengal and Bangladesh, though technically speaking they do not belong to either of these traditions. Their philosophy centers on Sadhana, a spiritual practice aimed at transcending the ego through spiritual practices intended for certain aims, a philosophy that can be found in different versions in Hinduism, Buddhism, and other South Asian religions (such as Jainism and Sikhism).

The Bauls are perhaps most famous for their music. Baul Sangeet (Baul music) involves singing and dancing, usually with an ektara ("one-string")— a skinny neck with one string, attached to a small drum at its base. The Bauls use this instrument because it is so simple and easy to make. They often wear jangles on their feet to keep rhythm when they dance. While Baul songs are learned orally and often improvised, Lalon Fakir (1774–1890) is a famous Baul whose songs are still known today.

BAULS
A community of itinerant musicians in West Bengal and Bangladesh who preach tolerance and oneness through music and dance.

Parvathy Baul, a well known Baul singer.
Source: Jordi Vidal/Getty Images

BAUL SONG

 **LISTEN**

TRACK 2.8 **Performed by Purna Chandra Das Baul**

IN THIS EXAMPLE, we hear all of the musical elements characteristic of the Bauls. The song begins with strumming on the *dotara*, a lute instrument that may have two, four, or five strings and is common throughout West Bengal, Bangladesh, and elsewhere in northeastern India. The singing then enters forcefully, on a high note that descends quickly and gets quieter, creating dramatic tension. The lyrics are then introduced on low pitches, after which the percussion kicks in. The percussion instruments typically used in Baul performance include a bowl-shaped drum called a *duggi* (sometimes the lower-pitched of the two tabla drums, the *baya*, is used), as well as a pair of handheld cymbals (*manjira*). Occasionally performers use *khartal* (wooden clappers with hard discs or plates that make a clapping sound when struck together). The *duggi* is typically held by a Baul singer along with the *ektara*, the one-string lute instrument that is a defining feature of Baul music, and which is often as much of a visual prop as it is a musical instrument.

This song has a clear verse/refrain structure, with occasional interludes of loud *dotara* strumming. Listen for the polyrhythmic nature of of this song; you can count it in a two- or a three-beat cycle, simultaneously. It is perhaps easiest to hear the duple (two-beat) meter in the cymbals, and the triple in the underlying drum and *dotara* rhythms. A few times in the song, the cymbal player further emphasizes the "duple" meter by providing a feel that resembles the Western meter 4/4 (listen at 1:24–1:29, 1:33–1:51; 2:42–2:47). Listen, too, for moments when the percussion and *dotara* suddenly fall silent, allowing the vocals to take center stage, thus creating dramatic tension and a quieting that is resolved when the percussion and dotara reenter again in dramatic fashion. The final moments of the song extend the refrain, until the piece dies down and comes to a quiet end.

TIME	MUSICAL EVENT
0:00–0:08:	the *dotara* strums loudly, while the *duggi* (drum) hits accents. Also heard in the background is the *ektara* (one-stringed instrument).
0:08–0:24:	a dramatic entrance of the vocals on a high pitch that descends in tone and volume, setting up dramatic tension by ending in a slight pause.
0:24–1:01:	The lyrics begin, followed by the ensemble joining to play and sing together. The *manjira* (handheld cymbals) enter at 0:30.
1:01–1:11:	short vocal refrain
1:11–1:23:	return of the introduction but with the whole ensemble; fast strumming on the *dotara*.
1:23–1:31:	a return of the first vocal entrance—a high pitch that descends—though this time with a slight variation and with the whole ensemble playing.
1:32–2:05:	second verse.
2:05–2:26:	second refrain (extended).
2:26–2:38:	return of the introduction.

continued

2:39–2:46:	return of the high vocal part.
2:46–3:13:	third verse.
3:13–3:22:	refrain (shorter version).
3:22–3:33:	fourth verse.
3:33–3:41:	refrain (shorter version)/
3:41–3:50:	*dotara* strumming.
3:50–4:18:	fifth verse.
4:18–4:33:	verse continues but the percussion stops and the music gets quieter.
4:33–5:05:	final refrain at a slower tempo (doubly extended version).

As with most Bauls, Fakir famously rejected belief in class, caste, and other such divisions between people. His poems were an inspiration to Rabindranath Tagore (1861–1941), a towering Bengali intellectual figure and one of the fathers of the Indian independence movement. A playwright, novelist, and musician with a famously long beard, Tagore was the first (and to date, only) Indian to win the Nobel Prize for Literature, in 1913. His lyrics echoed many of the themes found in Fakir's music, and today his music is recognized as a national treasure in India and is also considered the national music of Bangladesh. Tagore's songs (known as Rabindra Sangeet, or Rabindra songs) are compiled into a book (called Gitabitan, "garden of songs"), which contains six sections on diverse themes like love, God, and celebrations.

Tagore's biggest influence on South Asian music, however, probably comes from his founding of a school, Santiniketan, which would go on to be named Visva-Bharati University and become a leading institution for higher learning in India. Many musicians came to Santiniketan in the mid-twentieth century, from places outside Bengal (such as Sri Lanka). The musical philosophy taught at Santiniketan invested in music as the cultural heritage and lifeblood of the people, such that the musicians who came there often went back to their home region and searched for and documented the folk songs of their region. They also learned many skills in Hindustani music that they in turn brought back home. Perhaps the most important case of this is in Sri Lanka, where many of the island's best mid-century musicians studied at Santiniketan and incorporated Hindustani influences into their music.

IMPORTANT GENRES AND REGIONAL STYLES: SRI LANKA

In contrast to India, the musics of Sri Lanka are among the least known in the entire world. Ethnomusicologists have tended to pass the island by entirely, presumably because it is so much smaller than neighboring India. Yet Sri

Lankan musics display a number of important themes in the history of South Asian musics that *are* present in India, but which are too easily forgotten about when discussing Indian musics: namely Buddhism, Portuguese colonialism, and the impact of Portuguese and African musics. It should be stressed that Sri Lanka is radically diverse, containing numerous populations, including a significant Tamil population whose traditional homeland is in the north and east; here we are concerned with the musics of the island's ethnic majority, the Sinhalas (roughly 74 percent of the population), the vast majority of whom are Theravada Buddhist (Theravada means "Way of the Elders," and it is considered the oldest form of Buddhism, found in Sri Lanka and throughout mainland Southeast Asia in Burma, Thailand, Cambodia, and Laos).

Perhaps one reason Sri Lanka has been ignored in ethnomusicology is that the view persists that Buddhism is an unmusical religion. It is hard to pinpoint exactly where this view comes from, but it probably arises from a tendency to associate "Buddhist music" with "what monks do": Buddhist monks take a set of precepts, one of which says they should refrain from engaging in music, dance, and similar forms of entertainment. Music is believed to be too sensual and can lead one astray from the path toward Enlightenment. Such a situation, though, should not lead one into thinking that Theravada Buddhism looks down on all music and dance (this would be equivalent to defining "Christian music" as "what pastors do"). In fact, there are many traditions of lay Buddhist devotional music, and music that turns one's mind toward the Triple Gem (the Buddha, his teachings of Dhamma, and the community of monks or Sangha) is deemed acceptable according to Buddhist orthodoxy.

The interpretation of the most famous Sinhala Buddhist traditional music genre has been clouded by this notion of a separation between Buddhism and music. In Sri Lanka there is a caste of Sinhala Buddhist ritualists, dancers, and drummers called the berava (a word that means "drummer"), who give offerings of music, dance, food, incense, sung poetry, and other offerings to the Buddha and deities in all-night rituals. The rituals, which are held mainly in the south of the island, are split into three categories: deva tovils are offerings to deities for the purpose of avoiding various calamities, such as drought and chicken pox; these rituals are held primarily for two deities, the goddess Pattini and the god Devol Deviyo. Sinhala Buddhist deities are placed in a rank according to their karma (as are people); the gods are boddhisattvas, or "Buddhas-to-Be." Deities may be benign or malevolent, depending on their mood and whether they have received the proper offerings; for instance, while Pattini is cherished as a beneficent deity, she is traditionally considered the cause of chicken pox, so one ceremony is held for her for this (and other) purposes.

The second set of rituals are yak tovils, which heal people when they are affected by illnesses brought on by the malignant glance (disti) of a demon (yakkha) or demons (yakku). In these rituals, the demons are tricked by the offerings of music and dance: they are treated as if they are gods, a process that draws their glance to the ritual space, whereupon they appear as masked dancers who joke with the ritual specialists and dance to the music; during the appropriate time, a ritualist will recite mantras (magic spells found throughout

Dance students at a village school in southern Sri Lanka, after they performed excerpts of ritual dances (women are not allowed to perform in the ritual context, so this was a staged event). *Source:* Photo by the author

South Asia, uttered in a variety of languages) to eliminate their malignant glance on the patient. Finally, a third category of Sinhala ritual is bali, a single ritual consisting of offerings to the deities of the nine planets. While some people have questioned whether berava rituals are "Buddhist," they are performed by a group of Sinhala Buddhists (the berava) who conceive of the music, deities, and ritual through Buddhist aesthetics, mythology, and concepts.

Sri Lanka's coasts were conquered by the Portuguese (1505–1658) and Dutch (1656–1796); the British (1796–1948) took control of the whole island in 1815. During the Portuguese period, a number of people fled inland, and a kingdom in the interior, the Kandyan Kingdom (1469–1815) gained in power. The island's most renowned Buddhist temple, the Temple of the Tooth (dalada maligawa), contains the Buddha's tooth relic, which is historically associated with Sinhala Buddhist kingship in Sri Lanka. To this day, the Buddha's tooth is placed on the back of an elephant each year during the Asala Perahera, a grand procession around the city of Kandy, accompanied by hundreds of dancers and drummers.

The national music and dance genre of Sri Lanka, called Kandyan Dance, is derived from excerpts of a berava "up country" (Kandyan) ritual, called the Kohomba Kankariya, and the vannams, a set of dances depicting Buddhist themes and imagery that were composed during the heyday of the Kandyan Kings. It is now widely agreed that the prevalence of Kandyan music and dance in the years after the island's independence was achieved in part because Kandy was the last region to be colonized by the British, and at the time, Kandyan traditions seemed "more authentic" and "more Buddhist" than those elsewhere on the island. In fact, the "low country" (southern coastal region) has its own highly revered berava traditions, namely the deva and yak tovils, and is especially known for its colorful masks that depict demons in yak tovils.

The Kandyan drum is the gäta bera, a barrel-shaped drum played with the hands that resembles the South Indian mridangam, but its two ends are not of equal size. One side of the drum uses monkey skin, giving it a "squeaky," high-pitched sound ("like a monkey," musicians say). The low country drum, called yak bera, is also barrel-shaped and played with the hands, but the drum has a straight shape and its skins are made from the inner lining of a cow's stomach, producing an enormously low, booming tone ("like a cow," musicians say). Similar to Indian traditions, students learn music and dance through apprentice-ship, in this case with a berava gurunanse (esteemed teacher). Not only are the yak bera and gäta bera heavy, but in ritual performances, players stand upright with the drums and play vigorously, sometimes almost continuously, from 7 or 8 pm to 8 or 9 am in the morning!

The Portuguese brought African slaves with them (they hailed mainly from East Africa, probably Mozambique). The mixture of Portuguese and African musics generated a popular Sri Lankan music genre called baila, which continues to be popular throughout the island. In the late 2000s, a group of Sri Lankans of African descent, called the Kaffirs, were "discovered" in a small village about four hours north of the capital, Colombo (the word "Kaffirs" is generally considered derogatory around the world, but Sri Lankans of African descent use this word to refer to themselves, and it does not carry the same negative connotations it has elsewhere). The Kaffirs, of course, had been living there for several hundred years; but somehow the media recently picked up on them and their music. The members of the village still know the old songs and dances, sung in a Portuguese creole, and they don Portuguese-style dress and sing and dance, accompanied by percussion made of coconut shells.

This music is called Baila Kaffirinha (the Kaffirs' baila), and though it is clearly influenced by Portuguese colonial musics, it is known to have influenced Portuguese musicians in turn. The Portuguese version of baila relies heavily on the violin. In the 1940s, a singer named Wally Bastiansz (who was a policeman by trade) started composing songs in the baila style, which became pop hits. To our ears today, the melodies and lyrics sound light and playful; for instance, one song, "Nurse Nona," is an ode to a hospital nurse. But the baila did not stop there: it continued growing and accruing influences from around the world, such as calypso and disco. One kind of baila is called "non-stop" because record companies made cassettes (from the 1980s through the early 2000s), where the songs literally go non-stop, with no pauses between songs (these were often played on busses at top volume). While the baila has been somewhat supplanted in Sri Lanka by rock, hip-hop, and other global pop sounds, it remains a distinctly Sri Lankan genre with Portuguese and African roots) that can be traced back four hundred years.

COKE TELEVISION: ROCK, HIP-HOP, AND THE NEW FOLK MUSIC

EXPLORE

Coke Studio

In 2007, a show named *Coke Studio* (sponsored by the Coca-Cola Company) launched in Brazil, where performances held on a concert stage are broadcast for the viewing public; a year later, the company started *Coke Studio (Pakistan)*, which has a quite different format, as the performances are filmed in private in a recording studio. The show has been a surprise success, and is now widely credited as one of the most influential forums for South Asian musical invention in the past decade. What makes the show unique is its focus on live perform-ances, musical collaborations, and its dedication to providing a wide repre-sentation of religious and ethnic communities from various regions across Pakistan, as well as a mix of genres, from rock and hip-hop to Qawwali and beyond. The show makes good use of social media, providing free videos and MP3s of each performance online.

The Pakistani show became popular in India, and in 2011, an Indian version of the show was launched. *Coke Studio (India)* continues the same format, forging unique collaborations between musicians. To take one example, at some point producers came across a YouTube clip of a 75-year-old singer, Sawan Khan, who is from a rural area of Rajasthan, a state in northwestern India; they sent someone out to Rajasthan to search for the singer, who was eventually found and flown to Mumbai, where he performed an impromptu duet in a recording studio with a rock singer, Clinton Cerejo. Apparently the Rajasthani singer Khan expressed doubts he could sing before the performance, since he had never been in an air-conditioned room before. In 2012, *Coke Studio Bel 3arabi* premiered (the Middle Eastern version of the program) and *Coke Studio Africa* has recently emerged in Tanzania, Nigeria, Kenya, Uganda, and Mozambique.

THE SOUTH ASIAN DIASPORA

This chapter would not be complete without pointing toward the immensely large South Asian diaspora, who are influenced by South Asian musics and whose influence is felt in turn. As the East Indian community in the Caribbean is mentioned in the Caribbean chapter of this book, I will conclude this chapter by speaking of the musics of two important South Asian diaspora communities, Tamils and Punjabis.

In the nineteenth century, the British Empire moved many Indian laborers to plantations in their various colonies. Many of these laborers were from South Indian untouchable groups (see above), who certainly hoped for better opportunities outside India. Sadly, this was not always the case. The British set up tea and rubber plantations, in places like the interior of Ceylon (Sri Lanka), the island of Mauritius (in the western Indian Ocean), and colonial Malaya (now Malaysia and Singapore). The conditions were often squalid, and many laborers died. The system usually involved an English-speaking, comparatively elite

Indian or Ceylonese Tamil (called a kangani), who would round up the laborer (who was usually also Tamil) in South India, accompany them to the plantation, and act as a go-between on the plantation between the laborers and the British who owned the estate. These Indian Tamil workers often lived in housing estates called labor lines, which were sometimes decrepit.

Happily, this system has now fallen apart. While Indians remain a sometimes-stigmatized minority in Malaysia and Singapore (roughly 8 and 9 percent of the populations, respectively), they now have many more rights than they used to; in Mauritius, the Indians now form the majority population (the music performed in Mauritius, called Séga, is a hybrid African-Indian music and dance genre that is worth looking into, though outside the bounds of this chapter). An interesting outcome of these (mainly Tamil) diasporic populations is that they are in touch with Tamil culture from Tamil Nadu, mainly through Tamil films and Hindu religious developments. A kind of feedback loop has emerged, where cultural developments are transmitted between Tamil Nadu and the Tamil diaspora, in multiple directions rather than from one to the other.

One of the most exciting developments to come from this relationship is the emergence of a new kind of Hindu devotional drumming in Malaysia and Singapore, which in turn achieved popularity in Tamil Nadu and found its way into South Indian films. The genre is called urumi melam, a kind of drum ensemble performed at Hindu festivals in Malaysia and Singapore. Because many of the first migrants to Southeast Asia were from untouchable groups, they did not want to keep the tradition of playing the stigmatized drum; over the generations, a gap emerged in that much of the drumming at Hindu festivals involved playing on "found" percussion instruments like bottles and trashcan lids, or on non-Indian instruments like timbales. The urumi melams filled this gap by taking traditional Indian percussion instruments and playing them in an excited, fast, and brash way.

The style first developed in the town of Ipoh, Malaysia, in the late 1980s, after which it spread like wildfire throughout Malaysia and Singapore. The groups use a drum traditionally associated with Dalits, called the urumi, which is played with one stick and one hand, and which generates a unique sound due to the pushing and rubbing of the stick against the drum; the ensemble also uses the thavil (the drum used in South Indian Hindu temples) and a few other percussion instruments. The music tends to be extremely fast, with singers using a portable loudspeaker—this is necessary because the musicians walk with their drums in Hindu processions. The groups are typically composed of Tamil Hindu young men. A main place they perform is Thaipusam, the largest Hindu festival in Southeast Asia (the festival has Indian roots, but it is arguably more important today in Southeast Asia than in India). At Thaipusam, devotees perform acts of penance to the god Murugan, showing their devotion to the deity in return for a favor that has been granted. Some devotees undergo extreme acts of penance, such as piercing their tongues or backs, walking on spikes, and walking for miles with huge contraptions encasing them with metal rods piercing their chests. These contraptions are called kavadis (a word that means "burden"); the urumi groups accompany kavadi-bearers. The kavadi symbolizes the devotee's burden that he or she wishes to eliminate through penance for the god Murugan. Urumi melams are now ubiquitous at Hindu festivals on Thaipusam and other Hindu festivals throughout Malaysia and Singapore.

Perhaps the most widely heard example of an urumi melam is the track "Bird Flu," a song by the British-born, Sri Lankan Tamil rapper Maya Arulpragasam (better known as MIA). Born in West London, Maya and her family moved to Jaffna in northern Sri Lanka when she was just six months old. Sri Lanka had many political problems at this time, and the island's Tamil population was (and remains) highly disenfranchised. A rebel movement sprung up to fight for an independent homeland, which her father played a part in. The family moved back to London, where Maya gained fluency in English and pursued an interest in the visual arts.

No one could have expected MIA would blow up as much as she did. After achieving underground success, she signed to Interscope, and through her inclusion on the *Slumdog Millionaire* soundtrack, she became a global success and performed at the 2009 Grammys. In retrospect, one of the interesting and frustrating aspects of MIA is her engagement with Sri Lankan politics. When Sri Lanka's civil war was careening toward its end in 2009—a tragic moment when perhaps 40,000 innocent Tamil civilians were used as human shields by the rebel group the LTTE, and slaughtered by the Sri Lankan government— she was the only Tamil with enough of a public profile to speak out about the atrocity. She appeared on talk shows pleading the world's governments to intervene. Yet paradoxically, though she has tried to educate the public about the political situation in Sri Lanka, MIA has also produced some music videos that trade in a crass and obfuscating exoticism. For instance, her video for the

Urumi melam.
Source: CHEN WS/ Shutterstock.com

EXPLORE

Bhangra

REVIEW CHAPTER RESOURCES

KEY TERMS

Alap
Bauls of Bengal
Bhangra
Bharata Natyam
Carnatic
Devadasis
Filmigit
Gharana
Guru
Hindustani
Klasik
Kriti
Natyasastra
Qawwali
Raga
Ragam-tanam-pallavi
Rasa
Shishya
Sufism
Tala
The Berava
The Trinity
Urumi Melam
Vedas

song "Bad Girls" depicts women in burqas (an enveloping outer garment, including a head scarf), prominent mainly in the Middle East and only used in Sri Lanka by a segment of the Muslim population. The women in the video are shown racing cars and holding guns in a dusty, unspecified country. Through such imagery, the video regurgitates some traditionally Orientalist images of Middle Eastern women (in a song by a South Asian singer), along with the stereotypical imagery of Islamic terrorists. Even if MIA thought she was appropriating these images in order to resignify them, the effect is an undifferentiated mishmash. Nevertheless, MIA's story is a significant one, for perhaps no musician of South Asian descent has achieved such renown since Ravi Shankar.

Last but not least I turn backwards, to a genre that achieved much success in the diaspora in the 1980s—Bhangra—and its surprising persistence to the present day. Bhangra is descended from Punjabi folk music (the Punjab is an area split between northwest India and Pakistan) and is associated with the Sikh population that follows the monotheistic religion called Sikhism, which developed in the fifteenth century. In the 1980s, Punjabi DJs in the UK began spinning an electronic version of bhangra, a genre identifiable by its fast, fun, and unique beat (usually played on a large drum called a dhol). The genre took off to become the first globally recognizable Indian diasporic popular music. By the 1990s, the British Punjabi musician and DJ Panjabi MC was fusing bhangra and hip-hop. Since then, the story of bhangra took an interesting turn. Over the past two decades, the music has found a home on college campuses in the United States. Many Punjabi and Indian associations at U.S. schools have formed bhangra dance troupes, where students form elaborate dance routines—sometimes in elaborate costumes, to much cheering from the crowd—to bhangra music. Sometimes the performers in such troupes are not even Indian, such is the lure of the music and dance.

SUMMARY

No one knows how the story of South Asian music will grow in the next few decades. Undoubtedly, new musicians and genres will emerge, in accordance with the development of new media. The material presented in this chapter is a "tihai" of sorts, a cadence to the musical innovation and changes that characterized three domains of South Asian musics in the twentieth and early twenty-first centuries—classical, popular, and folk/religious traditions. What I have provided is a partial story that did not even consider certain countries that deserve broader musical recognition, namely Nepal, Bhutan, and the Maldives (the latter are a nation of islands off the southwest coast of India). I did not consider many regional Indian traditions, such as the widely known music of Rajasthan, nor did I consider certain Indian diasporic populations of growing global importance, such as the large community of Indians living in Dubai. Nevertheless, I hope this chapter can serve as a starting point for further exploration of South Asian musics, for which I urge you to consider the following bibliography.

BIBLIOGRAPHY

Hindustani/North Indian Musics

Andrew Alter, *Dancing with Devtas: Drums, Power, and Possession in the Music of Garhwal, North India* (Farnham, UK: Ashgate, 2008). Janaki Bakhle, *Two Men and Music: Nationalism and the Making of an Indian Classical Tradition* (New York: Oxford University Press, 2005). Joep Bor, Françoise "Nalini" Delvoye, Jane Harvey, and Emmie te Nijenhuis, Eds. *Hindustani Music: Thirteenth to Twentieth Centuries* (New Delhi: Manohar Publishers & Distributors, 2010). Katherine Butler Schofield, "Reviving the golden age again: 'classicization', Hindustani music, and the Mughals," *Ethnomusicology* 54/3 (2010), pp. 484–517. Martin Clayton, *Time in Indian Music: Rhythm, Meter, and Form in North Indian Rag Performance* (Oxford: Oxford University Press, 2000). James Kippen, *The Tabla of Lucknow* (Cambridge: Cambridge University Press, 1988). James Kippen, *Gurudev's Drumming Legacy: Music, Theory and Nationalism in the Mrdang Aur Tabla Vadanpaddhati of Gurudev Patwardhan* (Farnham, UK: Ashgate, 2006). Peter Manuel, *Cassette Culture: Popular Music and Culture in North India* (Chicago, IL: University of Chicago Press, 1993). Allyn Miner, *Sitar and Sarod in the 18th and 19th Centuries* (Wilhelmshaven, Germany: F. Noetzel, 1993). Anna Morcom, *Illicit Worlds of Indian Dance: Cultures of Exclusion* (London: Hurst, 2013). Daniel Neuman, *The Life of Music in North India: The Organization of an Artistic Tradition* (Chicago, IL: University of Chicago Press, 1990). Regula Qureshi, *Sufi Music of India and Pakistan: Sound, Context and Meaning in Qawwali* (New York: Oxford University Press, 2006). Stephen Slawek, *Sitar Techniques in Nibaddh Forms* (Delhi: Motilal Banarsidas, 1987). Bonnie C. Wade, *Khyal: Creativity within North Indian Classical Music Tradition* (Cambridge: Cambridge University Press, 1984). Margaret Walker, *India's Kathak Dance in Historical Perspective* (Farnham, UK: Ashgate, 2014). Richard Widdess and R. Sanyal, *Dhrupad: Tradition and Performance in Indian Music* (Ashgate, 2004). Richard Wolf, *The Voice in the Drum: Music, Language, and Emotion in Islamicate South Asia* (Champaign, IL: University of Illinois Press, 2014).

Carnatic/South Indian Musics
Matthew Harp Allen, "Rewriting the Script for South Indian Dance," *The Drama Review*, 41/3: 63–100. David Nelson, *Solkattu Manual: An Introduction to the Language of Rhythm in South India* (Middletown, CT: Wesleyan University Press, 2008). Ludwig Pesch, *The Oxford Illustrated Companion to South Indian Classical Music* (New Delhi: Oxford University Press, 2009). Indira Peterson and Davesh Soneji, Eds. *Performing Pasts: Reinventing the Arts in Modern South India* (New Delhi: Oxford University Press, 2008). Zoe Sherinian, *Tamil Folk Music as Dalit Liberation Theology* (Bloomington, IN: Indiana University Press, 2013). Davesh Soneji, *Unfinished Gestures: Devadasis, Memory, and Modernity in South India* (Chicago, IL: University of Chicago Press, 2012). Lakshmi Subramaniam, *From the Tanjore Court to the Madras Music Academy: A Social History of Music in South India* (New York: Oxford University Press, 2011). T. Viswanathan and Matthew Harp Allen, Eds., *Music in South India: Experiencing Music, Expressing Culture* (New York: Oxford UP, 2003). Amanda Weidman, *Singing the Classical, Voicing the Modern: The Postcolonial Politics of Music in South India* (Durham,

NC: Duke University Press, 2010). Richard Wolf, *The Black Cow's Footprint: Time, Space, and Music in the Lives of the Kotas of South India* (Delhi: Permanent Black, 2005).

Afghanistan, Bangladesh, Sri Lanka, Nepal
John Baily, *Music of Afghanistan: Professional Musicians in the City of Herat* (Cambridge: Cambridge University Press, 1988). John Baily, *Songs from Kabul: The Spiritual Music of Ustad Amir Mohammed* (Farnham, UK: Ashgate, 2011). John Baily, *War, Exile, and the Music of Afghanistan: an Ethnographer's Tale* (Farnham, UK: Ashgate, 2015). Debashish Banerji, *Rabindranath Tagore in the 21st Century: Theoretical Renewals* (New York: Springer, 2014). Charles Capwell, *Sailing the Sea of Love: The Music of the Bauls of Bengal* (Chicago, IL: University of Chicago, 2010 [1986]). Veronica Doubleday, "The Frame Drum in the Middle East: Women, Musical Instruments and Power," *Ethnomusicology*, Vol. 43, No. 1 (1999), 101–134. Garrett Field, "Music for Inner Domains: Sinhala Song and the Arya and Hela Schools of Cultural Nationalism in Sri Lanka," *The Journal of Asian Studies*, 73(4): 1043–1058. Anna Stirr, "'May I Elope': Song Words, Social Status, and Honor among Female Nepali *Dohori* Singers," *Ethnomusicology*, Vol. 54, No. 2 (2010), 257–280. Jim Sykes, "The Musical Gift: Sound, Sovereignty and Multicultural History in Sri Lanka," Ph.D. Dissertation, University of Chicago, IL, 2011. Jim Sykes, "Culture as Freedom: Musical 'Liberation' in Batticaloa, Sri Lanka," *Ethnomusicology*, Vol. 57 No. 3 (2013), 485–517. Richard Widdess, *Dāphā: Sacred Singing in a South Asian City. Music, performance and meaning in Bhaktapur, Nepal* (Farnham, UK: Ashgate, 2013).

Bollywood, Popular Musics, Diaspora
Falu Bakrania, *Bhangra and Asian Underground: South Asian Music and the Politics of Belonging in Britain* (Durham, NC: Duke University Press, 2006). Jayson Beaster-Jones, *Bollywood Sounds: The Cosmopolitan Mediations of Hindi Film Song* (New York: Oxford University Press, 2014). Gregory Booth, *Behind the Curtain: Making Music in Mumbai's Film Studios* (New York: Oxford University Press). Gregory Booth and Bradley Shope, Eds. *More than Bollywood: Studies in Indian Popular Music* (New York: Oxford University Press, 2013). Anjali Gera Roy, *Bhangra Moves* (Farnham, UK: Ashgate, 2010).

General Surveys
Allison Arnold, Ed., *South Asia, The Garland Encyclopedia of World Music*, Vol. 5 (New York: Garland Publishing, 2000). Gerry Farrell, *Indian Music and the West* (Oxford: Oxford University Press, 1997). Nalini Ghuman, *Resonances of the Raj: India in the English Musical Imagination, 1897–1947* (New York: Oxford University Press, 2014). Jaime Jones, "Music, History, and the Sacred in South Asia," in Philip V. Bohlman, Ed., *Cambridge History of World Music* (Cambridge: Cambridge University Press, 2013). Virinder S. Kalra, *Sacred and Secular Musics: A Postcolonial Approach* (London: Bloomsbury, 2015). Lewis Rowell, *Music and Musical Thought in Early India* (Chicago, IL: University of Chicago Press, 1992. Richard Wolf, *Theorizing the Local: Music, Practice, and Experience in South Asia and Beyond* (New York: Oxford University Press, 2009).

DISCOGRAPHY

Anthologies *A Musical Anthology of the Orient*, vols. 6, 7, 18 (Bärenreiter 30L 2006, 2007, 2018). *Classical Indian Music* (Odeon MOAE 147–9). *Anthology of Indian Classical Music: A Tribute to Alain Daniélou* (Auvldis/Unesco, D8270).

North India *Parween Sultana* (khyal) (Gramophone Co. of India ECSD 2785). *Ram Chatur Mallick* (dhrupad and dhamar). *Musiques de l'Asie Traditionelle*, vol. 9 (Inde du Nord). *Ravi Shankar* (sitar) (Gramophone Co. of India EASD 1307). *Ananda Shankar and His Music* (modern instrumental pop) (Gramophone Co. of India ESCD 2528). *Begum Akhtar Sings Ghalib* (ghazal) (Gramophone Co. of India ECSD 2399). *Film Hits from Hit Films*, vol. 2 (Gramophone Co. of India ECLP 5470). Joep Bor, ed., *The Raga Guide: A Survey of 74 Hindustani Ragas* (Nimbus Records, NI 5536/9).

South India *Kaccheri* (vocal) (Nonesuch H-72040). *Vidwan* (vocal) (Nonesuch H-72023). *Dhyanam/Meditation* (vocal) (Nonesuch H-72018). *Musik für Vina* (Telarc MC8); *S. Balachander: Veena Maestro of South India* (Odeon MOCE 1026). *Pallavi* (flute) (Nonesuch H-72052).

Afghanistan, Bangladesh, Sri Lanka, Nepal Ahmad Zahir, *Hip 70s Afghan Beats* (Guerssen Records, 2011). *Music of Afghanistan* (Folkways Records, 2012). Homayun Sakhi, *The Art of the Afghan Rubab* (Smithsonian Folkways, 2006). *Tablas and Drum Machines: Afghan Music in California*. DVD, 58 minutes, directed by John Baily.

Afghanistan Music Unit, Goldsmiths, University of London, 2005. *Scenes of Afghan Music. London, Kabul, Hamburg, Dublin.* DVD, 97 minutes, directed by John Baily. Afghanistan Music Unit, Goldsmiths, University of London, 2007. *Breaking the Silence: Music in Afghanistan.* Documentary film, 60 minutes, directed by Simon Broughton, BBC, 2002. Purna Das Baul, *Bauls of Bengal* (Crammed Discs, 1998). Bauls of Bengal, *Mystic Songs from India* (ARC, 2005). Bauls of Bengal, *Bauls of Bengal* (Essential Media Group, 2008). Various Artists, *Baila Ceilao Cafrinha! Sri Lanka The Journey of Sounds* (Tradisom). Sri Lankan Berava rituals (see YouTube, search for: low country dance, yak bera, kandyan dance, gata bera). Piyasara and Chandrakanthi Shilpadhipathi, *18 Vannams—Sri Lanka Traditional Dance Recital Music* (SAA Tunes, 2015). Sri Lanka Traditional, *Sri Lanka—Ceylan* (Air mail music, 2006). Sri Lankan Baila (see YouTube, search for: Wally Bastin, Desmond De Silva, MS Fernando, Gypsies). Kaffirs of Sirambiadi, *Kaffir Strella* (independently released). Urumi Melam (see YouTube, search for: Urumi Melam Masana Kali). Tirusuli Aiyanar Urumi Melam, *Ayyapa Samy Urumi Melam* (kmi).

Popular Music Various Artists, *Coke Studio Sessions* (see www.amazon.com). MIA, *Kala* (Interscope, 2007). MIA, *Matangi* (Interscope, 2013). Panjabi MC, *Beware* (Sequence, 2003). Various Artists, *The Rough Guide to Bhangra* (World Music Network, 2010). Various Artists, *Bhangra: Original Punjabi Pop* (ARC, 2003).

MUSIC OF THE MIDDLE EAST AND NORTH AFRICA

Richard Jankowsky

INTRODUCTION: A *SUFI* PERFORMANCE

Every May, Sufis from all around northern Tunisia gather at the shrine of Sidi 'Ali Hattab to kick off their fourteen-week summer ritual season of music and dance ceremonies. The shrine, built in honor of the thirteenth-century holy man Sidi 'Ali Hattab, is one of the most important sites of pilgrimage and sacred music and dance performance in northern Tunisia. During these three spring days, many different Tunisian Sufi traditions—each with its own distinctive musical and ritual practices—converge to perform in the shrine's vast courtyard in front of hundreds of visitors. While some of these visitors are Sufis, most are not. Instead, they are Tunisians from all walks of life who have come to the pilgrimage to socialize, partake in the food and spectacle, and to hear the music that, for many listeners, maintains a venerable Tunisian musical tradition that not only constitutes the historical source

of other Tunisian musics, but also demonstrates the power that music has to act on individuals, most dramatically evidenced in the act of trance.

Inside the courtyard, I am seated on the ground alongside a circle of about twelve Sufi singers from the 'Īsāwiyya (the Sufi order named after its founder, Sīdī Ben 'Īsā) as they perform the "entrance liturgy," the opening song of the musical part of their ritual called *ḥaḍra*. They begin by singing in unison:

> God's magnificence never sleeps
> He is unique and eternal in his kingdom
> O God, keep deprivation and misery far from us.

ḤAḌRA
The musical ritual ceremony of Sufis in North Africa.

This praise of God and supplication for protection is then repeated by a line of dancers, dressed in white robes, holding hands, and stepping forward and bending at the waist in time with the music. The call and response between the circle of singers and the line of dancers continues:

> God's magnificence never sleeps
> The light filled my heart
> O Master Ben ʿĪsā
> O sultan of the "intoxication"
> The sweetness filled my heart.

These words, which are emphatically repeated at the beginning of every ceremony, not only praise God and his saint Sīdī Ben ʿĪsā, but also emphasize the capacity for ritual to keep away misery and create joy in the form of sweetness and light filling one's heart, especially through the symbolic intoxication of music and trance. This "intoxication" is a focal point of the ceremony and a specialty of the ʿĪsāwiyya.

After the entrance liturgy, the singers and dancers transition to the second ritual section, called *mjarred*, which involves songs accompanied by handclapping in a five-beat rhythm (another specialty of the ʿĪsāwiyya): clap-rest-clap-rest-rest. The dancers, all in one line, step forward on the first clap and backwards on the second one, singing "hūwa" ("He," referring to God), in response to the circle of singers.

As the mjarred section continues, some of the Sufis pick up a number of percussion instruments, including several handheld frame drums (*bnādir*; sing. *bendīr*), a tambourine (*ṭār*), and a small pair of kettledrums (*naqqarāt*), and distribute them to the singers. The leader of the dancers dances over to the singers, stretches his arms outward, and brings his hands together in a dramatic clap that coincides with the thunderous first beat of the drums. This introduction of drums, which play the eight-beat rhythmic cycle called *bṭāyḥī*, marks the beginning of the trance or "intoxication" section of the ceremony.

As the singing and dancing gradually increase in tempo, one dancer breaks free from the line of dancers. He takes a position closer to the singers and continues to dance, but in a more forceful fashion than those of the line, gradually removing his robe and t-shirt. He is given two stalks of burning hay, which he holds in his hands as he enters into a trance dance, passing the flames underneath his bare, outstretched arms and across his chest, eliciting no apparent damage or pain. After several minutes of dancing with the flames, he drops the stalks on the ground and puts out the flames by slapping them with his bare hands. He resumes dancing for a few minutes before raising his hands in the air and trembling, a sign recognized by one of the Sufi leaders who holds the dancer, places a hand on his forehead, and recites Qur'anic verses into his ear to end the trance state. As the songs progress, other dancers occasionally leave the line in order to enter into trance. Some dance with fire or roll bareback over cactus stalks while others even eat shards of glass. Such profound states of trance are the domain of the few who are able and compelled to enter

Line of Tunisian Sufis dancing and drumming.
Source: Richard Jankowsky

them; trancers are understood as possessing a special ability to communicate with the divine and are held in particular esteem in Islamic societies. These dramatic acts of trance, all supervised closely by the elder Sufi sheikhs, draw gasps and celebratory ululations from members of the ever-growing audience, which forms an enormous circle that envelops the Sufis. The crowd only moves back during the final trance of the ceremony, which involves a dancer in chains who breaks those chains and escapes into the crowd, eliciting quick retreats by audience members. This dance is performed to the song called "Khammara Ya Khammār" (Fill My Cup with Wine, O Cupbearer), which, like some classical Sufi poetry, explicitly likens the sacred experience to intoxication. The dancer eventually returns to the performance area to be carried away by his fellow Sufis, and the ceremony ends with the recitation of the fātiḥa, the opening verse of the **Qur'an**.

After the ceremony, I spoke with several participants in order to get a better sense of the meaning of the ritual performance. I soon realized that there was no singular meaning, but rather a multiplicity of meanings and experiences. For example, when I discussed the ceremony with the singers, they spoke at length about the musical rules that dictate the progression of the ceremony. The ritual is structured, in part, in accordance with a strict succession of particular rhythms and percussive techniques. The ceremony begins with no percussion at all, then progresses to a section in which the rhythm is provided by hand claps in the mjarred 5-beat rhythm, then the drums enter with the *bṭayḥī* rhythm, which then gives way to the *barwal* rhythm; the ceremony ends with the *khammarī* rhythm. Every song is also in a particular *ṭabʿ*, or melodic mode, which implies not only a discrete, named set of pitches but also conventions of performance that shape how those pitches are used and organized in practice. Once the *bṭayḥī* rhythm begins, the lead singer must choose songs that remain in the same melodic mode of the previous songs; if not, the change indicates that the

QUR'AN
The holy book of Islam, considered the word of God.

subsequent songs must be in the new melodic mode, and the group is prohibited from returning to the previous melodic mode. Table 3.1 shows the progression just described.

TABLE 3.1 ʿĪsāwiyya ritual – musical progression

Ritual stage	Percussion	Rhythmic mode
Entrance liturgy	None	None
Mjarred	Handclaps	Mjarred (5 beats)
Intoxication (takhmīr)	Drums	Bṭāyḥī (8 beats)
	Drums	Barwal (4 beats)
	Drums	Khammārī (8 beats)

The musicians' concern with the details of musical performance reflects not only the artistic rigor of Sufi musical traditions in Tunisia, but also the specific role of ʿĪsāwiyya Sufis in preserving and developing the highly esteemed Arab-Andalusian musical tradition that would later become the basis for Tunisia's officially designated national music, called *ma'lūf*. In the eighth century AD, Andalusia (i.e., the Iberian Peninsula consisting of most of present-day Spain and Portugal) became part of the Islamic Empire and experienced an age in which music and the arts flourished. During the Christian Reconquista of Andalusia, which ended in 1492, Jews and Muslims were expelled from the region, many of them landing in North Africa. This influx of Andalusians influenced the secular and religious musical landscape of Tunisia, giving rise to what came to be called the Arab Andalusian musical tradition of North Africa. Before the emergence of music schools in the twentieth century, Sufi orders were considered veritable conservatories of this tradition. Indeed, many of Tunisia's most esteemed popular singers and musicians of the twentieth century were active in ʿĪsāwiyya Sufism. Moreover, some ʿĪsāwiyya orders, especially in Tunisian areas where many Andalusians settled, also featured small ***takht*** ensembles comprised of an *ʿūd* (fretless lute), *nāy* (endblown flute), *kamanja* (fiddle), and *ṭār* (tambourine) that would perform at weddings and after Sufi rituals to "cool down" the atmosphere.

Whereas the musicians were often preoccupied with the musical details of performing, several dancers told me they focused on the meanings of the sung words and the potential for the music to carry them to another level of consciousness. Many dancers find profound spiritual comfort in the words, some of which were written as early as the thirteenth century. Thus, while many of the lyrics praise God, the Prophet, and Muslim saints, they also keep history alive in the present by referencing people, places, and events from the past. Indeed, several ʿĪsāwiyya dancers told me they were proud to be following in their ancestors' footsteps. They described their trance state actions as evoking the legend of Sīdī Ben ʿĪsā and his followers running out of food in the desert

TAKHT
Small traditional ensemble in the Arab world, typically including the ʿūd, nāy, kamanja, and riqq.

'ISĀWIYYA MEDLEY

 LISTEN

TRACK 3.1 **Recorded by the author in Tunis, Tunisia at the shrine of Sīdī Belḥassen, June 27, 2014**

THIS TRACK is a compilation of excerpts of Sufi ritual songs from the 'Īsāwiyya Sufi order in Tunisia. The excerpts, which are presented in their prescribed ritual order, are meant to give the listener a sense of the rhythm-based ritual progression through the ceremony, beginning with no percussion, moving on to handclaps, and ending with multiple drums.

TIME	SECTION	MUSICAL EVENT
0:00–1:46	Entrance Liturgy section. Song selection: "'Aẓẓam 'Aẓẓam" (Magnificence, Magnificence).	The melodic mode of this first section is called rast dhil (scale: C D E♭ F G A B♭ C). There is no rhythmic mode, but there is a strong sense of pulse.
		Listen for the vocalists singing together in unison, the long duration of the sung syllables at this slow tempo, and the occasional shouts of encouragement to praise the Prophet Muhammed.

The lyrics to this section of the song are:

'aẓẓam 'aẓẓam b-illāh lē yanām	God's magnificence never sleeps
wāḥid fī maliki	He is unique and eternal in his kingdom
zād niyāra, niyāra	He increased the light in me
yā mawlā ben 'īsā el-ḥabīb	O Master Ben 'Īsā, the beloved
yā sulṭān el-khammāra, el-khammāra	O sultan of the "intoxication"

TIME	SECTION	MUSICAL EVENT
1:46–3:10	Mjarred section; song selection: "El-Kās Ydūr" (The Cup Turns).	After the entrance liturgy, the singers begin the mjarred section, which is distinguished by the 5-beat clapping rhythm of the same name: **Clap-Rest-Clap-Rest-Rest**.
		The melodic mode of this section is called hsīn sabé (scale: D E♭ F G A B♭ C D). Listen for antiphonal singing as two groups of singers take turns singing their lines. Additionally, you'll notice the line of dancers repeating the word "*hūwa*" ("He," referring to God) in the background.

The lyrics to this section include:

el-kās ydūr, el-kās ydūr	The cup turns, the cup turns
el-khamra l-ahl el-ḥaqīqa	The wine of the people of truth
yā khammār, w-yā 'ammār	O cupbearer
isqīnā khamra sharīqa	Pour us the wine of illumination
yā sattār, yā jabbār	O Veiler, O Almighty
ij'alnā min ahl al-ḥaqīqa	Make us the people of truth

TIME	SECTION	MUSICAL EVENT
3:10–3:43	End of Mjarred section. Song selection: "Anā Bdayt Bismillah"	At the end of the mjarred section the musicians sing a song that begins *anā bdayt bismillah al-ḥay el-'aẓīm* (I Began in the Name

continued

TIME	SECTION	MUSICAL EVENT
	(I Began in the Name of God).	of God the Living and Magnificent). The melodic mode is aṣbaʿīn (scale: D Eḫ F♯ G A Bḫ C D). Listen for increased intensification as the musicians speed up the tempo and transition, without stopping, to the trance section of the ritual at 3:43.
3:43–end	Takhmīr (trance; lit. "intoxication") section. Song selection: "Nibtada Bismillah ʿAlim bi-Kul el-Makān."	The first sounding of the drums announces the beginning of the takhmīr, or trance section, of the ceremony. This is the ritually appropriate time for individuals to move out of the line of dancers and trance dance near the singers. They rhythmic mode is an eight-beat pattern called bṭāyḥī: **dūm-dūm-dūm-tek-ess-dūm-tek-ess**. The melodic mode returns to ḥsīn sabé. The singers begin the song by singing *nibtada bismillah ʿalim bi-kul el-makān* (We begin in the name of God, knower of all places). Listen for unison singing, repetition of the sung melody, and the interplay between the frame drums and the tambourine.

Takht ensemble, Palais Jamai Hotel, Fez, Morocco. *Source:* © robertharding / Alamy Stock Photo (Alamy B5AKTO)

as they made their pilgrimage to Mecca in the sixteenth century. According to the legend, through divine intervention mediated by Sīdī Ben ʿĪsā, he and his followers were able to sustain themselves by eating whatever they found in the desert—including cactus, scorpions, and pieces of glass and metal—with no ill effects. Other dancers viewed trance as a test of their endurance and tolerance for suffering or as a form of physical and mental therapy, while others still understood it as a physical and spiritual need that they could not explain.

This performance, then, alludes to several themes that will be addressed in this chapter. Most obvious of these is music and affect, that is, the way music creates emotions and altered states of consciousness for listeners. However, the Sufi performance also illustrates other chapter themes, including music and religious expression, histories of displacement and migration, and the organization of musical performances through modality and progressive sequencing.

OVERVIEW OF THE REGION

This chapter on the music of the Middle East and North Africa stands apart from others in this textbook that define their subject matter by country, continent, or sea. Instead, the Middle East is a region defined by its relative proximity to those defining it (namely, Europe and the United States). The phrase "Middle East" is a remnant of a geopolitical system of classification in which Western powers, for the purposes of handling international affairs, conceptualized Asia, the Indian subcontinent, and parts of North Africa as the Far East, the Middle East, and the Near East, although consensus on which countries should be included in each designation was rarely achieved and changed over time. While "Far East" and "Near East" have fallen out of

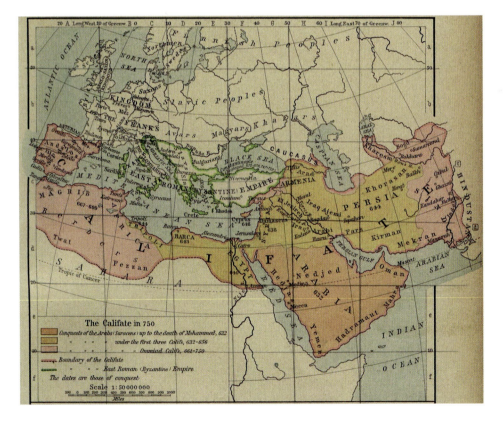

Map of the Islamic Empire. *Source:* Courtesy of the University of Texas Libraries, The University of Texas, Austin

Modern political map of North Africa and the Middle East. *Source:* MapMaster/CC/Wikimedia Commons

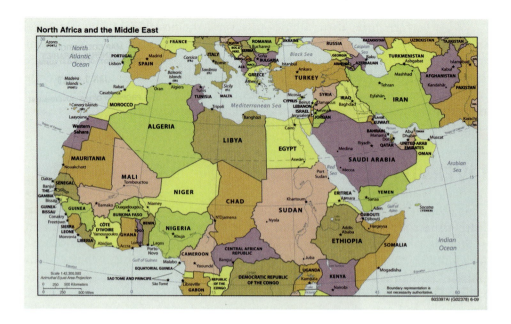

common usage, "Middle East" remains in use both inside and outside the region, although definitions still vary. Most include the west Asian countries, both Arab (Iraq, Jordan, Lebanon, Syria, and the Palestinian Territories) and non-Arab (Iran, Israel, and Turkey), as well as the countries of the Arabian Peninsula (Bahrain, Kuwait, Oman, Qatar, Saudi Arabia, Yemen, and the United Arab Emirates). The countries of North Africa (particularly Morocco, Algeria, Tunisia, Libya, and Egypt) are commonly grouped together with the Middle East, owing to certain commonalities in language, religion, and culture developed during their shared experience as part of the Islamic and Ottoman Empires.

The ambiguity that emerges from defining the borders of the Middle East and North Africa has historical precedent in the expansion and contraction of a succession of empires that dominated the region. From about the third century to the mid-seventh century CE, the region was roughly divided into two empires: the Byzantine in the west and the Persian in the east. By the end of the eighth century, major parts of these polities had been replaced by a rapidly expanding Islamic Empire that would eventually rule most of the Arab world as well as Turkey and Persia (modern-day Iran), stretching as far east as India and as far west as al-Andalus (modern-day Spain and Portugal) in Europe.

Throughout the extensive and multicultural Islamic Empire, there were no clear-cut boundaries between music cultures, and musicians travelled freely throughout the empire to learn neighboring styles and often borrowed from each other. Indeed, the important tenth-century treatise called *The Book of Songs* (*kitāb al-aghānī*) describes the travels of the innovative musician Ibn Muḥruz, who traveled to Medina (a city in modern-day Saudi Arabia), Persia (modern-day Iran), and Syria to learn the musics of those places, combining those influences to compose Arabic songs in a new style (Sawa 2002). By the middle of the thirteenth century, the empire, facing military attacks on numerous fronts, had fractured into various local polities, giving rise to the Persian Empire in the east and a succession of Arab and Berber dynasties in west. By 1574, the Ottoman Empire, based in modern-day Turkey, expanded to include most of the Arabic-speaking world as well as the Balkans and part of Hungary. While the Christian Church survived the Ottoman Empire in Europe, by this time Islam had become the dominant religion of the rest of the region and Arabic, the sacred language of Islam, gave the region a shared language of religious and literary expression, existing alongside local Arabic vernaculars as well as Turkish and Persian in their respective lands.

By the late nineteenth century, the Ottoman Empire had relinquished control of most Arab provinces to European powers, with France and the United Kingdom controlling most of the Middle East and North Africa, and Italy and Spain laying claim to some parts of North Africa. Anti-colonial movements in the twentieth century pushed the European empire out of the Middle East as most countries in the region achieved independence in the 1950s and 1960s. The establishment of Israel in 1948 had a profound political and geocultural impact on the region as it attracted hundreds of thousands of Jews living in Arab countries and largely dominated a succession of military conflicts with its neighbors. While the statehood of Palestine remains unsettled, much of the Palestinian population is spread throughout Israel, the Palestinian Territories, Lebanon, Syria, and Jordan.

The expansion and contraction of empires through history have helped shape the region's music culture, creating, as Philip V. Bohlman (n.d.) notes, a "top-down" unity of some fundamental musical principles that sometimes reinforces, yet often competes with, a "bottom-up" musical diversity. This diversity takes many forms. Numerous languages are spoken in the Middle East, including Arabic (both literary Arabic and the myriad local dialects), Armenian, the many varieties of Berber, as well as Hebrew, Kurdish, Persian, and Turkish, not to mention colonial languages (English, French, Italian) and liturgical languages (e.g., Aramaic and Syriac of Eastern Christian traditions). While Islam is the most widespread religion, it is important to keep in mind not only that there are multiple styles of Islam (including Sunni and Shi'a traditions, as well as more localized approaches such as Ibadhism), but also other traditions with centuries of history in the region, such as Judaism, Christianity, and Zoroastrianism. The geocultural distinction between rural areas and cosmopolitan urban centers provides yet another layer of diversity within the region.

As a region that touches three continents, the Middle East and North Africa also has been a historical site of exchange and intersection between Europe, Asia, and Africa. Major paths of exchange into and from the region include the trade ways of the Mediterranean Sea in the west, trans-Saharan trade routes to the south, and the Indian Ocean and Silk Road to the east. These routes have brought, for example, sub-Saharan instruments such as the *gumbrī* into Arab countries, and the Middle Eastern tambourine, shawm, and lute into Europe (in fact, the name of the latter derives from the Arabic name of the instrument, al-ʿūd). The musical landscape of the modern Middle East thus features layers of histories of intercultural contact. Today, in festivals and the media, on recordings, and in the digital circuits of exchange, localized village music may share a stage with classical art repertoires, and musicians on their way to perform a traditional healing ritual may listen to Arab hip-hop. The goal of this chapter, then, is twofold: to draw attention to this rich diversity of music cultures while identifying some common themes shared throughout the region.

THEMES IN MIDDLE EASTERN AND NORTH AFRICAN MUSIC

In this chapter, we will use four main themes to examine the musical traditions of Middle East and North Africa, including (1) modal organization (including musical sequencing, improvisation) and the significance of the voice; (2) music and affect, including various states of trance; (3) the dynamic relationship between music and religion; and (4) the musical experiences and contributions of migrants and minorities in the region. Along the way, additional themes will emerge, including philosophies and theories of music, the social meanings of particular musical instruments, the social status of musicians, and the relationship between music and politics.

MODAL ORGANIZATION

EXPLORE

Maqām

MELODIC MODES
Named musical scales that have conventions for how the pitches are used in performance and may be associated with particular moods or extramusical associations.

Much of the music in the Middle East and North Africa is conceptualized according to melodic and rhythmic frameworks that musicologists refer to as "modes." *Melodic modes*—called *maqām* (in the eastern Arab world) or *ṭabʿ* (in North Africa) in Arabic, *makam* in Turkish, and *dastgah* in Persian—are (1) discrete, named sets of pitches that (2) have rules or conventions for how those pitches are used and (3) have individual characters that may be related to specific moods, emotions, or extramusical associations. (To simplify matters, from now on I will use the term "maqām" unless discussing a particular tradition.) The thirteenth-century theorist Ṣafī al-Dīn Urmāwī organized the melodic modes according to whether they inspired strength, courage, pleasure, or sadness. However, while extramusical associations played a role in describing modes in medieval Middle Eastern music theory, today there are but faint traces of past associations for some modes. Modes named after specific places, such as Hijaz (a region in Saudi Arabia) or Nahawand (a village in Turkey), are unlikely to evoke those geocultural referents for musicians and listeners. However, many musicians and listeners continue to associate some maqāms with emotions; many listeners find rāst to evoke pride and soundness, while *ṣabā* may imply sadness or lamentation. Certain performance genres are also associated with particular modes, but not in a restrictive way: *bayyātī* and *ṣabā* are common in folk music, and bayyātī may also evoke religiosity because traditionally the cantillation of the Qur'an begins and ends in this mode. *Nahāwand* and *kūrd* are common modes for love songs. The most explicit extramusical associations have been preserved by religious communities, such as the Turkish Jewish liturgy

TABLE 3.2 Eastern Arab modes and their effects (Marcus 1989)

Rast:	dignity and gravity; religious songs
Nahāwand:	delicate and tender, suitable for sad or sentimental songs
Nawā Athar:	enchantment, sweetness, coquetry
Bayyātī:	folk songs, Qur'anic recitation, Coptic church weddings
Kūrd:	extreme longing, delicate and sweet
Ḥijāz:	simplicity and prettiness; enchantment of the "east"; religious songs
Ṣabā:	delicate and tender; sorrow
Sīka:	unsettled (it begins on a half-flat); many folk melodies
'Ajam 'Ushayran:	strength and sincere seriousness

BOX 3.1 MUSICAL MODES IN PRACTICE

IN THE MIDDLE EAST and North Africa, there are more pitches available to musicians than there are in most Western musics. For example, while in most Western musics the only available note between D and E is E♭, in the maqām there are two additional notes, D-half-sharp (D♯) and E-half-flat (E♭). These notes are not available on the piano; they would fall in-between adjacent piano keys, just as they would fall in-between adjacent frets on a conventional guitar. Yet they are easily playable on instruments with moveable frets, such as the Turkish *saz* or the Arab *buzuq*, as well as fretless instruments such as the 'ūd. Indeed, the 'ūd is considered the "king of instruments" in the Arab world, where analysis of its tunings and finger positions has been used a basis for Arab music theory and philosophy since medieval times.

Western system	D		E♭		E
Arab maqām	D	D♯	E♭	E♭	E

As in a Western scale, only one version of any note is allowed in a single maqām; thus E♭ and E would not be part of the same maqām. For instance, D E♭ F G A B♭ C D are the pitches of maqām kūrd, while just slightly raising the E♭ to E♭ produces maqām bayyātī: D E♭ F G A B♭ C D. Yet the difference between the two maqāms is not limited to their use of different tunings of the note E. Rather, it is also how the pitches are used that differentiate them, as each maqām has specific compositional and improvisational conventions that define them. For example, according to Scott Marcus (2002), maqām bayyātī has specific tunings for certain pitches (such as F and B♭, which are played slightly lower than their equal-tempered counterparts). Pieces in this maqām also tend to begin by emphasizing the middle of the scale (notes between F and B♭) and descend to the tonic D, as well as proceed through modulations to specific other maqāms in the higher register. These are not rules of composition per se, but are rather common conventions. These conventions are often featured in the taqsim—a solo improvisational piece in which performers can demonstrate their mastery of the maqām—and art compositions such as the samā'ī—an instrumental composition that often features a modulation to a new maqām in different sections.

| LISTENING GUIDE | TAQĀSĪM BAYYĀTĪ AND SAMAʿĪ BAYYĀTĪ AL-ARYAN |  LISTEN |

TRACK 3.2 **Ali Jihad Racy (ʿūd) and Souhail Kaspar (riqq)**

THIS IS A taqāsīm (taqsīm), a solo improvisation in free rhythm played on the ʿūd, followed by the first section of a samāʿī, a pre-composed instrumental piece accompanied by the riqq (eastern Arab tambourine). The improvisation and the samāʿī are in the maqām called bayyātī (scale: D E♭ F G A B♭ C D). Listen for the way Racy parses his improvisation into sections, creating momentary stops on his musical journey through the maqām. He also changes sonic density, with some sections featuring very sparse phrases while others have more rhythmic regularity and strumming. The song "SamāʿīBayyātī al-Aryan," which begins at 2:52, features the riqq playing the 10-beat samāʿī rhythm (D – – T – D D T– –). "Samāʿī" is the song form, "Bayyātī" is the maqām, and "al-Aryan" is the name of the composer. This is the most common form of naming compositions in Arab art music (form-maqām-composer).

TIME	SECTION	MUSICAL EVENTS
0:00–0:34	Taqāsīm (solo improvisation)	Begins in the middle of the scale, as is conventional in this maqām, descending to the resting note D (with lower octave duplication for emphasis) at 0:23.
0:34–1:05		Exploration of the upper notes of the scale (G A B♭ C), with hints of an alternative upper tetrachord (G A B C) AT 0:51.
1:05–1:37		Increase in rhythmic density with a repeated G, acting as drone, interspersed with stepwise motion down the scale.
1:37–2:05		More exploration of the upper region of the scale, emphasizing the base note D (1:36, 1:46) with leaps to the D an octave above (1:39; 1:59); explores the entire maqām scale from high D to low D.
2:05–2:52		Introduces B♮ in upper part of the scale until 2:20, then creates a succession of short, repeated phrases with rhythmic regularity; ends with the typical qafla (final phrase) for this maqām: F G F E♭ D.
2:52–end	Samāʿī	Samāʿī Bayyātī al-Aryan begins, featuring the riqq playing the 10-beat samāʿī rhythm: **dūm-ess-ess-tek-ess-dūm-dūm-tek-ess-ess**.
		Listen to how the percussionist is able to produce low sounds (dūm) and high sounds (tek), while filling the spaces in between by playing patterns on the cymbals of the instrument.
		Notice also how the melody aligns with the contour of the percussion part (many phrases, for example end on beat eight of the ten-beat rhythmic pattern).

that reserves the use of certain modes for certain times of day, holidays, and even texts (indeed, there is a different maqām associated with each of the Ten Commandments). Table 3.2 on p. 77 summarizes the terms introduced.

There is also a modal framework for rhythms, called *īqāʿ* in Arabic and *usul* in Turkish. An īqāʿ or usul is a discrete, named rhythmic cycle defined by the structural relationship between two drum strokes: low (sounded by hitting the drum near the center) and high (sounded by hitting the drum near the rim). Musicians learn these rhythms by memorizing these sequences of low and high sounds represented by the vocables "dūm" (rhymes with "room") and "tek" for the low and high pitches, respectively, and "ess" for rests or silences between the dūms and teks. For example, the 10-beat rhythm named samāʿī thaqīl is represented as:

dūm	ess	ess	tek	ess	dūm	dūm	tek	ess	ess
1	2	3	4	5	6	7	8	9	10

Rhythms can also be understood as modal because they (1) are named, finite and repeatable sets of sounds in time; (2) have conventions for how those sounds are played and varied; and (3) have extramusical associations that contribute to the "feel" of each rhythm. Samāʿī thaqīl, for example, is considered to be a stately, austere rhythm (heard toward the end of audio example 3.2), while maqsūm (featured on audio example 3.6) is considered lively and danceable. Others, such as *ṣaʿīdī*, are associated with particular geographic locations (in this case, the ṣaʿīd region of Egypt). While Middle Eastern music theorists have identified hundreds of **rhythmic modes** with up to 176 beats, in common practice most have anywhere from 2 to 16 beats, though some repertoires, such as that of the Turkish Mevlevi Sufis or Ottoman art music, regularly use cycles of up to 28 beats or more (audio example 3.3 has a 64-beat rhythmic mode). In the context of performance, these patterns are repeated throughout a piece until a modulation to another rhythmic cycle is called for. Percussionists rarely play only the dūm-tek rhythmic skeleton represented in their vocables. Rather, they embellish the rhythms with ornamentations, especially on the "ess" beats.

In Middle Eastern and North African art music traditions, entire performances are generally organized according to melodic mode. The eastern Arab *waṣla*, the North African *nūba*, the Yemeni *qawma* and *tawshīḥ*, and the Turkish *fasıl*, for instance, are all musical traditions featuring sequences of pieces unified by melodic mode (maqām) and diversified by rhythmic mode (*īqāʿ*). In other words, in these performances, most pieces are in the same (or a related) maqām, but different pieces will use different rhythms. These compound forms involve a mix of vocal and instrumental pieces, as well as precomposed and improvised sections (see Tables 3.3 and 3.4). They also often adhere to a logic of progression, such as moving from slower, more stately rhythms to faster dance tunes. The Iraqi *faṣl* is distinctive in that it adds a prescribed sequence of modulations and is based on a particular poetic text.

RHYTHMIC MODES
Named rhythmic patterns played in repeated cycles; they have conventions for how they are played and may be associated with particular moods or extramusical associations.

TABLE 3.3 Typical format of the Egyptian Waṣla (Racy 2003)

1.	ʿūd taqāsīm	Instrumental, improvised
2.	dūlāb or samāʿī	Instrumental, pre-composed
3.	nāy or violin taqāsīm	Instrumental, improvised
4.	muwashshaḥ	Vocal, pre-composed
5.	qānūn taqāsīm	Instrumental, improvised
6.	layālī and mawwāl	Vocal, improvised
7.	dawr	Vocal, mostly pre-composed

TABLE 3.4 Ottoman *fasıl* (Feldman 1996)

1.	instrumental taksim	Solo free-rhythm instrumental improvisation
2.	peşrev	Instrumental prelude
3.	vocal taksim (optional)	Solo free-rhythm vocal improvisation
4.	two beste	Vocal genre with long melody lines and numerous *usul*
5.	ağir semai	Vocal piece in the 10-beat *ağir semai* rhythm
6.	takim (small suite) of şarki	Suite of urban folk songs
7.	yürük semai	Vocal piece in the 6-beat *yürük semai* rhythm
8.	saz semai	Instrumental finale in the 10-beat *aksak semai* rhythm
9.	vocal taksim (optional)	Solo free-rhythm vocal improvisation

EXPLORE

Persian Classical Music

GŪSHE

Melodic phrases that constitute the main musical pieces of the Persian dastgah.

The Persian *dastgah*, while also based on the concept of modes, provides a rather different approach to modality. There are twelve dastgah modes, but in performance each one is not presented as a sequence of songs and interludes like the traditions mentioned above. Rather, a dastgah performance is based on an extensive collection of individual melodies called *gūshe*. Performers usually go through years of training memorizing these melodies but, crucially, must not play those melodies in performance. Rather, the **gūshe** melodies are used as musical themes that form the basis for vocal or instrumental improvisations. These improvisations can vary greatly; they can be as short as a few minutes or as long as an hour. However, there is a general formal contour for each performance: each gusheh typically has a prescribed progression, beginning with the *daramad* (opening), and progressing through the *owj* (climax) to the *forud* (closing). In such a system, there is no "composer" of a piece other than the performer who creates something new in each performance.

The Ottoman *fasıl* crystallized in the eighteenth century as a sequence of pieces juxtaposing vocal and instrumental selections, solo and ensemble textures, precomposed and improvised compositions, and different rhythmic cycles. The fasıl begins with an instrumental *taksim*, a solo, free-rhythm improvisation that introduces the makam of the fasıl. This is followed by the *peşrev*, an instrumental prelude played by the entire ensemble. After an optional vocal taksim, the group

LISTENING GUIDE

BUSELIK AŞIRAN PEŞREV

 **LISTEN**

TRACK 3.3 **Performed by the Dünya Ensemble**

THIS IS A 17th century instrumental prelude in makam Buselik Aşiran. The Turkish term for rhythmic mode is "usul"; the usul of this piece is called Havi, which has sixty-four fast beats. The original composer of this piece is unknown, but the melody was transcribed by Ali Ufki, the 17th century Polish captive of the Ottomans who converted to Islam and became a dragoman of the court. Instruments on this recording include: santur (hammered dulcimer), ud (fretless lute), ney (end-blown flute), rebab (spike fiddle), çeng (harp), nekkare (small kettledrums), and daire (frame drum with cymbals).

The Havi rhythmic mode is represented in the table below. You will hear the percussion begin on beat 57, playing the end of the cycle (marked in bold face) as a lead-in to the beginning of the Mülâzıme (refrain). Low-pitched sounds ("dūm") are indicated by the letter "D" and high-pitched sounds ("tak") are represented by "T." If you do not have a drum, you can play along on your thighs or a table by assigning the dūm sounds to one open hand and the tak sounds to your knuckles.

1	2	3	4	5	6	7	8	9	10	11	12	13	14	15	16	17	18	19	20	21	22	23	24
	T	T				T				T	T	T	T			T	T	T	T			T	
D				D				D				D						D					

25	26	27	28	29	30	31	32	33	34	35	36	37	38	39	40	41	42	43	44	45	46	47	48
				T	T	T	T			T	T			T			T			T		T	T
D		D						D				D	D			D		D	D				

49	50	51	52	53	54	55	56	**57**	**58**	**59**	**60**	**61**	**62**	**63**	**64**
	T	T			T	T			**T**			**T**		**T**	**T**
D				D				**D**		**D**	**D**				

TIME	SECTION	MUSICAL EVENTS
0:00–0:19	Serhâne (first verse)	Introduction with ud and çeng.
0:19–0:56	Mülâzıme (refrain)	Drums enter with an eight-beat lead-in. The sixty-four beat cycle begins at 0:20 with the entire ensemble entering on a shared low note (A).
0:56–1:31	Hâne-i Sani (second verse)	The rebab begins a new melody; at 1:15 the santur and çeng take over the melody.
1:31–1:50	Hâne-i Salis (third verse)	The nay flute is prominent here.
1:50–2:27	Mülâzıme	The Mülâzıme is repeated by the entire ensemble.

plays a series of *beste*, a vocal genre utilizing numerous rhythmic cycles and featuring long melodic lines, which forms the centerpiece of the fasıl. Next comes an *ağir semai*, a vocal piece in the 10-beat rhythm of the same name, followed by a small suite of urban folk song melodies called *şarki*. A 6-beat vocal *yürük semai* and an instrumental *saz semai* conclude the fasıl (with an optional vocal taksim).

It is not only art music that adheres to this kind of logic of progression. Many ritual traditions in the Middle East also feature prescribed sequences of pieces. Sufi liturgies, as well as traditional healing practices such as *zār*, *tambura*, and *stambeli*, often proceed in a descending hierarchical order that moves from praise for God and the Prophet Muhammad to songs for (or by) Muslim saints and other spiritual figures. As we saw in the introduction to this chapter, modal organizing principles may intersect with religious considerations.

Improvisation and the Voice

Improvisation is an important element in musics of the Middle East and North Africa, where it can take the form of a stand-alone piece composed on the spot or as an introduction to, or an interlude within, a pre-composed piece. The Arab **taqsīm**, Turkish taksim, and Persian avaz are all solo improvisational genres performed in a free, or non-pulsatile, rhythm. While the avaz may be vocal or instrumental, the taqsīm/taksim is instrumental. Musical improvisation in the region, as in other parts of the world, is not an exercise in absolute freedom in the sense that a performer may play anything that comes to mind. Rather, improvisation entails maintaining the balance of being faithful to the conventions of performing a particular mode and making an original musical statement within those conventions.

Vocal improvisation is especially prized. Arab music features two styles of non-metered vocal improvisation. *Layālī* refers to vocal improvisation on a single phrase, either "yā layl" (O night), "yā laylī" (O my night), "layālī" (nights), or sometimes "yā ʿayn" (O eye) or "yā ʿayni" (O my eye). Using these vocables, rather than a fixed text, enables singers to focus attention on the musical details of the improvisation, much like an instrumentalist performing a taqsīm. *Mawwāl*, in contrast, refers to vocal improvisation of a poetic text. This compels singers to match their musical decisions to the rhythm and form of the poetry. In Iran, singers performing a vocal dastgah also select poetry to improvise on. They also incorporate a distinctive vocal technique called *tahrīr*, which involves an emotive, quasi-yodeling oscillation in pitch.

The primacy of the voice and language is also evident in the prestige and ubiquity of sung poetry in the region. Sung poetic forms, such as the pre-Islamic Arabic **qaṣīda**, continue to enjoy great prestige in the Arab world, and the ability to spontaneously improvise creative poetic verses is highly valued. The musical expression of poetry takes many forms in the region. Epic singers create hours-long performances by reworking verses from an enormous corpus of memorized verses. Female poet-singers hired for wedding sing songs of passion, fertility,

TAQSĪM
Solo instrumental improvisation.

QAṢĪDA
An often improvised vocal piece based on classical Arabic poetic form of the same name.

LISTENING GUIDE

TWO FORMS OF VOCAL IMPROVISATION (ARAB LAYĀLĪ AND PERSIAN AVAZ)

 **LISTEN**

TRACK 3.4 Layālī and Mawwāl, performed by Ibrahim El-Haggar (voice) and Nussair (qānūn)

THIS EXCERPT is a layālī, a vocal form using the syllables "yā laylī" (O my night)and "ya 'aynī" (O my eye) as the vehicle for melodic improvisation. The two phrases evoke the beauty of the night and the eye as the beholder of beauty. The layālī is, in effect, the vocal equivalent of the instrumental taqsīm, allowing the vocalist to improvise a melody without worrying about conveying the meaning of a text (in this regard, this performance contrasts well with the song in Track 3.7, which is concerned with highlighting the meaning of the sung text). This vocal improvisation is in maqām bayyātī (scale: D E♭ F G A B♭ C). Listen to how the qānūn player follows the singer, sometimes anticipating him, and filling in the spaces in between vocal phrases with his own improvisations.

TIME	MUSICAL EVENT
3:48–4:10	The vocalist begins in the lower register of the scale, singing an improvised melody all on the phrase "yā laylī." The qānūn player follows quietly.
4:10–4:21	The *qānūn* plays a short improvisation in between vocal phrases.
4:21–4:57	The vocalist resumes singing and introduces the phrase "yā laylī" while continuing to improvise long, melismatic phrases.
4:57–5:13	The vocalist moves dramatically in stepwise motion up to the higher register of the scale of the *maqām* before descending back down.

TRACK 3.5 🔘 **Dastgah of Shour, performed by Khatereh Parvaneh.**

THIS EXCERPT is taken from a performance recorded by ethnomusicologist Ella Zonis Mahler and released in 1966 on Smithsonian/Folkways Recordings. It was thus recorded before the 1979 Revolution led many musicians and artists to leave the country. In this excerpt, vocalist Khatereh Parveneh sings the *dastgah* of *shour*, featuring the notes C D♮ E♭ F G A♭ B♭ C. For a text she selected verses of the *Masnavi*, the famous poem written by the thirteenth-century Sufi poet Jalal al-Din Rumi, who inspired the founding of the Mevlevi Sufi order in Turkey. The original recording provides a rough translation of the verse sung in this excerpt: *The cause of the lovers' illness is unique / to them, the religion and the cause is God.*

TIME	MUSICAL EVENT
0:00–0:33	The vocalist sings the first line of the couplet: *'ilati 'āshiq (x2) z-'ilat-ha jadāst.* At 0:17 you hear the first *taḥrīr* ornamentation. The santur can be heard following the singer and providing reference pitches in between phrases.
0:33–end	The vocalist sings the second line of the couplet: *'āshaqān ra (x2) madhhab u 'ilat khadāst.* Taḥrīr technique becomes more pronounced.

Egyptian epic singer with rebāb. *Source:* © David Taylor Photography / Alamy Stock Photo

and collective history. Public song duels bring battling poets to the stage to give and endure a barrage of insults and riddles. And ordinary men and women comment on social issues or express personal sentiments through short, clever, spontaneous verses of sung poetry.

Historically, the poetic traditions of the nomadic, desert-dwelling Bedouin served social functions beyond aesthetic enjoyment. They narrated history, conveyed news of recent events, and carried interpersonal messages. Bedouin poetry also exalts Bedouin cultural ideals such as generosity, honor, and heroism, while also encouraging the expression of individual sentiments of love and other emotions in socially acceptable ways. The *Sīrat Banī Hilāl*, a widely disseminated epic poem, features tales of heroism, romance, and intrigue within a broader narrative that recounts the migration of the Bedouin from the Arabian Peninsula, their conquests as they spread westward, and their final defeat in Tunisia. Professional singers of this epic poem accompany themselves on the *rebāb*, a two-stringed fiddle. In some areas, such as the Egyptian village where Dwight Reynolds performed his research, this instrument has negative connotations that denigrate its performers as "beggar-poets," a stereotype that the poets resist by portraying the rebāb as "the respected tool of the epic-poet profession" by associating it with the heroes and warriors exalted in the epic (Reynolds 1996: 208).

Sung poetry also provides women a forum for expressing their "veiled sentiments" (Abu-Lughod 1986) about love, marriage, family relationships, and society. Among Berber women in the rural Rif Mountain area of Morocco, composing and singing poetry is considered a virtue: "it is expected that each girl will be a poet just as it is expected that each woman will bake bread for her family" (Joseph 2003: 237). Groups of professional women poet-singers animate Berber weddings by singing *ʿaiṭa*, a tradition of sung poetry that recalls the deeds of heroes and extols the virtues of rural Berber society. It also takes license with traditional gender codes by sanctioning erotic images, the verbal abuse of unfit suitors, and social critique sometimes directed at government policy (ibid.). Sung poetry often serves as a strategic social device, enabling people to give voice to their feelings and concerns that might otherwise be considered unacceptable outside the formalized codes of musico-poetic performance.

MUSIC, HEALING, AND AFFECT

In the Middle East and North Africa, music is understood to have a powerful impact on its listeners. It is a defining feature of religious and secular traditions that produce at least three different kinds of altered states of consciousness, including: (1) a healing trance state that remedies psychological and physiological symptoms associated with affliction by spirits; (2) a religiously inspired trance state that brings listeners closer to the divine; and (3) a non-religious, heightened emotional state called ṭarab that is sometimes described as musical ecstasy.

Medieval Muslim philosophers and practitioners of musical healing encouraged the playing of certain maqāms to treat psychological and physical ailments. Al-Kindi, the ninth-century scholar known as the first Muslim philosopher, mapped onto the four strings of the ʿūd the four humors of the body (blood, phlegm, black bile, and yellow bile), four emotional attributes of accompanying poetry (bold, sad, soothing, cheerful), and the stages of human life (infancy, youth, middle age, old age), and prescribed certain combinations of strings (and their associated maqāms) be played to restore balance to a patient. While such approaches to music therapy are uncommon today (though there is renewed interest, especially in Turkey), there exist today numerous musical traditions in the region that are associated with healing, often through trance dancing. Such trances often take the form of spirit possession. Indigenous spirits known as jinn, which are mentioned in the Qur'an and therefore theologically sanctioned in Islam, may afflict humans and require certain rituals in order to be propitiated.

Music and Spirit Possession

In addition to indigenous jinn, other spirits were brought from sub-Saharan Africa to the Middle East and North Africa, where communities of displaced sub-Saharans developed musical traditions to treat people who were afflicted by the spirits. These traditions—such as the zār in Egypt, Iran, and the Arabian Peninsula, stambeli in Tunisia, diwan in Algeria, and the gnawa in Morocco—produce trance to alleviate the suffering caused by those spirits. In these traditions, the cure results from the patient temporarily giving up his or her body to the spirit so that the spirit may enjoy the sound of its song and the movements of its dance. This process is performed within the appropriate confines of a formal ritual ceremony. This is not a process of exorcism, but rather of bringing back into balance the relationship between the world of humans and a population of unseen beings that coexist within it.

Tunisian stambeli is one such tradition that was created by displaced sub-Saharans, many of whom were descendants of slaves forced northward across the Sahara Desert into North Africa. While subsequent generations of this sub-Saharan diaspora were born Muslim and spoke Arabic as a native tongue, they also developed a spirit possession music tradition that maintained some instruments, musical aesthetics, and linguistic influences from sub-Saharan Africa. The stambeli troupe is led by the gumbrī, the three-stringed lute that is said to "speak to the spirits." The gumbrī features three layers of sound: strings that are strummed, a drumhead that is struck with the fingers of the strumming hand, and a metallic plate nestled between the strings that ensures that every

Stambeli ensemble. *Source:* Provided courtesy of Richard Jankowsky

strum is accompanied by a subtle buzzing sound. The gumbri is flanked on either side by two to four musicians who sing and play metal clappers called *shqāshiq*. The lyrics they sing, some of which still feature words in Hausa, Kanuri, and other sub-Saharan languages, praise the tradition's sub-Saharan spirits and Muslim saints and invite them to join the ceremony to heal the dancer and bless the gathering.

Every spirit and saint in the stambeli tradition has his or her own song. The musicians perform a predetermined succession of songs, which means that every musical performance of stambeli is also a presentation of the spiritual beings of the tradition. While not every spirit or saint is conjured at every ceremony, each one does begin with songs for the Prophet Muḥammad and Bilāl, the first caller-to-prayer (**mu'adhdhin**) in Islam and one of the Prophet's companions. Bilāl was an African slave and one of the earliest converts to Islam; he is thus praised by many musical traditions developed by sub-Saharan communities in the Islamic world, who assert an African presence in Islam from its very origins.

MU'ADHDHIN
The person responsible for intoning the call to prayer five times per day in Islamic communities.

After these two songs, the musicians commence with the songs for the saints and spirits. Dancers, who often present with symptoms ranging from tremors and strange visions to partial deafness or paralysis, have gone through a process of diagnosis with a stambeli healer, who determines which of the dozens of stambeli spirits has afflicted her. Once the spirit has been identified, a ceremony is held to propitiate the spirit. Animal sacrifices (such as goat, lamb, chicken, or rooster, whose meat is then cooked for a communal meal) are made and the spirit's preferred incense is burned. Most important, the musicians play the spirit's preferred song while the patient dances and enters into a trance, opening herself up to possession by the spirit, who enjoys the rare opportunity to experience the world of humans by listening to music and dancing. The dance concludes once the spirit takes leave of the patient, who falls to the ground and often faints. This is a sign that the spirit has accepted the dancer's offering of her body and that the spirit will not harm the patient again for at least a year, when another ceremony will be held.

 LISTENING GUIDE   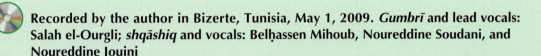 **"SĪDĪ MARZŪG"**    **LISTEN**

TRACK 3.6 🔘 **Recorded by the author in Bizerte, Tunisia, May 1, 2009. *Gumbrī* and lead vocals: Salah el-Ourgli; *shqāshiq* and vocals: Belḥassen Mihoub, Noureddine Soudani, and Noureddine Jouini**

"**SĪDĪ MARZŪG**" is a nūba (song) for the saint of the same name in the sṭambēlī tradition of Tunisia. This recording was made at a trance healing ceremony in northern Tunisia. Note the short three-stroke rhythm of the *shqāshiq* repeated incessantly throughout the song. Imagine yourself a trance dancer swaying forward and back to these rhythms for the entirety of the song. What might at first sound like an abrasive metallic clashing can become, over time and empathetic listening, more like a reliable rhythmic cushion supporting your physical and psychic movements, always ready to welcome you back in case you wander too far.

TIME	MUSICAL EVENT
0:00–0:36	brief instrumental introduction on the *gumbrī*, ending with the *shqāshiq* entering at a moderate tempo as soon as the *gumbrī* establishes a regular pulse. At 0:15 the *gumbrī* introduces the main melody of the *nūba*.
0:36–5:37	lead vocals begin, singing: *salēm 'alīh, salēm 'alīh, salēm 'alīh Sīdī Marzūg* (Greet him, greet him, greet Sidi Marzug). *Gumbrī* plays ostinato figure under the lead vocals.
At 0:42	the response singers enter, singing: *salēm ' alīh, salēm ' alīh, salēm 'alīh Bābā Marzūg yā m_l id-dīwān* (greet him, greet him, greet Father Marzug, master of the ceremony) as the *gumbrī* plays the main melody.

Call and response continues for the next several minutes. Notice the lead singer is free to alter the lyrics, often through substitution. Response singers also occasionally interject with shouts such as "Allah Allah"

At 3:55,	the lead singer raises the register of his singing, and adds emphatic plucks on the *gumbrī*
5:37–6:57	New, shorter repeated theme introduced
At 6:16,	the the main *gumbrī* melody returns, but at faster tempo and without vocals. Tempo continues to increase gradually until the end.

Music and Sufism

EXPLORE

Music and Sufism

While some Sufi orders are known for alleviating individual suffering from spirit affliction, most of them engage in communal devotional rituals called *ḥaḍra* that can carry listeners to a state of profound spiritual revelation or divine illumination. While Sufis are often called the "mystics" of Islam, it is important to note that they generally do not remove themselves from society or become ascetics. Indeed, Sufi orders (called *ṭuruq*, meaning "paths" or "ways"; sing. *ṭarīqa*) have been important social institutions throughout the Islamic world, providing social services such as education, dispute arbitration, and aid to the poor in addition to religious ceremonies. Most Sufi ṭarīqas perform some form of *dhikr* (Turkish: *zikr*; lit.: "remembrance"), a devotional practice that combines bodily movement and special breathing techniques with the communal chanting of the names or attributes of God. Some ṭarīqas, such as the Shādhuliyya of Egypt, only engage in chanting and unaccompanied singing, while others, for example the Sulāmiyya of Tunisia, add percussion. Some traditions, such as the Tunisian ʿĪsāwiyya, use wind instruments such as the *zukra*, while others, for example the Turkish Alevi, use stringed instruments like the *baǧlama*.

The most well-known Sufi tradition is that of the Mevlevi (the so-called Whirling Dervishes), which involves a highly choreographed spinning dance. Although the Mevlevi have become iconic of Sufism, they are in fact one of the most idiosyncratic forms of Sufism because they dance to the stately, gentle melodies and rhythms of an Ottoman classical music ensemble featuring *ney* (reed flute), *kanun* (plucked zither), *tanbur* (fretted lute), *kemençe* (upright, bowed lute), and *kudüm* (kettledrum). Mevlevi Sufism influenced the larger Ottoman music culture in numerous ways. Mevlevi lodges served as conservatories of music, transmitting the principles of Ottoman art music into the twentieth century and in some regions of the empire were the only social institutions teaching and performing art music repertoires. Their concerts, moreover, were designed to be both ritually effective for participants and aesthetically pleasing for an audience of non-members, including non-Muslims and women. Mevlevi lodges were constructed with a gallery designated for a nonparticipating audience and until the nineteenth century provided the only public art music concerts in Turkey (Feldman 1996).

Medieval Muslim philosophers and theologians debated the appropriateness of using music to achieve higher states of spiritual consciousness. The strongest proponents argued that music was the only known way to get close enough to God to have divine secrets revealed, while the strongest opponents argued that the devout should only be listening to the recitation of the Qur'an; these latter considered any other auditory practices to be *bidāʾ*, or religiously unlawful innovations, that drive the listener away from God. Between these two extremes was the influential argument of Sufis such as al-Ghazzali, who maintained that while *samāʿ* was indeed the most effective means of achieving divine inspiration, it needed to be performed at the right time and place and in the right company—that is, with other trained Sufis—to ensure that the exercise remained spiritual in nature.

Ottoman Mevlevi music ensemble. *Source:* Anadolu Agency/Getty Images

This debate is interesting to students of world music for two reasons. First, it was an argument about music focused explicitly on the act of listening to music, placing the listener at the center of the inquiry. In the world of Islam, listening is an active endeavor with ethical implications. Music is understood to have the power to bring listeners closer to the divine and toward right moral action, or away from the divine and toward questionable moral action. Second, all sides of the argument have in common the deep conviction that music has a profound power over its listeners and must be treated with great care. In this context, music has the capacity to affect the human soul, whether by tapping into a wide array of emotions or granting access to otherwise unattainable states of spiritual consciousness.

Ṭarab (Musical Enchantment)

Music's capacity to profoundly transform consciousness is not only relegated to ritual and religious traditions. Traditional Arab music is associated with the production of *ṭarab*, a heightened state of emotion that is often described as a kind of musical ecstasy brought about through deep listening. Tarab, which is mainly associated with urban musics of cities such as Cairo, Damascus, Aleppo, Jerusalem, and Beirut, is an elusive term with no exact equivalent in English. Under optimal tarab conditions, the listener may be emotionally transformed and may respond physically at musically appropriate moments with silence and stillness, verbal exclamations, hand-clapping, or even weeping. Ali Jihad Racy, the prominent musician and ethnomusicologist of Arab music, notes that the

ṬARAB
Heightened state of emotion or musical enchantment associated with listening to traditional Arab music.

Umm Kulthum.
Source: Howard Sochurek/
Getty Images

EXPLORE

Umm Kulthūm

maqām concept is central to ṭarab: musicians must not only firmly establish the pitches of the maqām, but must also internalize the characteristics of the mode to the point that they become "captivated" by the maqām and even "haunted" by its tonic pitch (Racy 1996). Through repetition, variation, improvisation, and creative engagement with song lyrics, musicians bring their listeners through a journey full of musical tension and release, suspense, climaxes, and un-expected detours.

A live performance by the legendary Egyptian singer Umm Kulthūm illustrates some of the conditions for cultivating ṭarab (see Track 3.8 for a detailed description). Umm Kulthūm was, hands-down, the most renowned and successful singer in the twentieth-century Arab world: to this day she is held up as a model of artistry and originality that embodies the ideals of Arab music performance. Although her songs were some of the most popular of her time, they were based on the modal principles and improvisatory conventions of classical Arab music, demon-strating that in the Middle East, the line between "art" and "popular" music can be a blurry one. It is difficult to con-vey the extent of her immense popularity, but photographs of the millions of Egyptians who flooded the streets of Cairo for her funeral in 1975 or the fact that her songs can still be heard regularly in taxis and cafes throughout the Middle East (and even on streets bearing her name) are suggestive. For forty years she gave Thursday evening concerts in Cairo that were broadcast throughout the Middle East; anecdotes from the period abound with stories of life coming to a virtual halt as communities across the region tuned into the live radio broadcasts.

One song that was performed at one of her monthly concerts and entertained millions of listeners at home and in cafés is "Ghannīlī Shwaya Shwaya" ("Sing to Me a Little"), composed by Zakariyya Aḥmed with lyrics by Bayram al-Tūnsī. The ensemble backing Umm Kulthūm includes orchestral instruments such as the cello, string bass, and numerous violins, as well as the traditional instrumental core of qānūn (plucked zither), ʿūd, nāy, *darbūka* (goblet-shaped drum), and riqq (tambourine). Typically, the entire orchestra, called a *firqa*, plays in unison for the introduction and some instrumental interludes, while only traditional takht instruments accompany the vocalist during the more improvisatory sections.

Spontaneity is an important element of the performance, and is necessary for cultivating the sense of anticipation and excitement that characterizes ṭarab. Listening example 6 illustrates how Umm Kulthūm circles back to particular lines, phrases, or even single words to repeat as she sets them to newly improvised vocal melodies. At the end of any given section of a song, her accompanying musicians often did not know whether she would move on to the next section, repeat the current line, or return to a previous line in this or a preceding section. There is thus often an audible sense of uncertainty in between sections as the musicians wait to see where the singer will take them. Rather than indicating professional unpreparedness, such musical moments of uncertainty are crucial to creating the ebbs and flows of tension and release, and show that the musicians must be highly prepared to go to or return to any part of the song at any time.

The lyrics of this song are about the power of music itself. Umm Kulthūm applies extensive techniques of repetition and variation when she arrives at the evocative line "music is the life of the soul" that begins the second stanza. It is at this point that the song modulates from maqām suznāk to maqām bayyātī. Bayyātī is a very common melodic mode that is especially prominent in religious music and the recitation of the Qur'an, adding another potential layer of aural associations to the sung text. Her virtuosic melodic variations on the words and phrases she chooses to repeat—especially *al-maghna* ("music"), *ḥayāt al-rūḥ* ("life of the soul"), and *wa-tdāwī* ("it heals")—are often met with approving exclamations and sighs of appreciation that are typical of ṭarab listening experiences.

LISTENING GUIDE | **"GHANNĪLĪ SHWAYA SHWAYA"** |  **LISTEN**

> **TRACK 3.7 Performed by Umm Kulthūm, Music: Zakariya Ahmed, Lyrics: Bayram al-Tunsi**
>
> **T**HIS RECORDING illustrates several aspects of how ṭarab in Arab music cultivates anticipation through spontaneity in live performance. The characteristics of ṭarab, or "musical enchantment," include performer-audience interaction, modulation, varying of textures, and repetition and variation. The lyrics to this song amplify the musical affect of the ṭarab experience by emphasizing the power of music. This example is the first eight minutes of a 22-minute live performance of the song by Umm Kulthūm from one of her famous Thursday night Cairo concerts. Umm Kulthūm's orchestra (firqa) features numerous violins, cellos, and other stringed instruments, in addition to the instruments of the takht ('ūd, qānūn, nay, and riqq). Notice how the entire firqa only plays together in between vocal sections; during the vocal sections only the traditional instruments of the takht support the singer. Notice also how the uncertainty of the musicians generates anticipation and excitement; they, too, are sometimes unsure of which musical choices Umm Kulthūm will make in her interpretation of the song.
>
> The song is in maqām suznāk (scale: C D E♭ F G A♭ B C), with a modulation (at 3:23) to maqām bayyātī on G (G A♭ B♭ C D E♭ F G). The selection begins with an īqā' called maqsūm [D T – T D – T –] played during the ensemble passages, with the sparser īqā' called waḥda [D - - T - - T -] played during the vocal sections.

continued

TIME	SECTION	MUSICAL EVENTS
0:00–0:18	Instrumental introduction	Entire firqa plays melody.
0:18–1:22	First verse	Umm Kulthūm sings the first line to the same melody as the instrumental introduction. The lyrics of the first line are: *ghannīlī shwaya shwaya, ghannīlī w-khudh 'aynaya* (sing to me a little and enchant me). She repeats this line a second time; between vocal sections the entire firqa repeats the melody.
1:22–1:50		The first verse continues with the lyrics:
		khalīnī aqūl alḥān titmāyil lahā as-sām'aīn
		wa-tarafrif lahā al-aghṣan an-nargis ma' al-yāsmīn
		wa-tsāfir ma'hā ar-rukbān ṭawin al-bawādī ṭayy
		Let me sing the melody that makes the listeners sway
		And the branches of the narcissus and jasmine trees flutter
		And travels with the Bedouin caravans crossing the desert
1:50–2:01		Qafla (octave descent) on last line of stanza:
		shwayya shwayya, shwayya shwayya ghannīlī ghannī, wa-khudh 'aynayya
		Just a little, just a little, sing to me, sing and enchant me
2:01–2:15		The firqa plays the main melody again as the crowd cheers.
2:15–2:54		Umm Kulthūm decides to return to line 2 of the first verse (*khalīnī . . .*), which she repeats twice before finishing the rest of the stanza.
2:54–3:23		The firqa repeats the main melody; slight hesitation due to uncertainty over where Umm Kulthūm will go next is audible at 3:09.
3:23–5:32	Second verse, line 1	Umm Kulthūm decides to continue on to the second verse, which begins with a dramatic decrease in tempo and a modulation to maqām bayyātī on G. The lyrics of this section emphasize the power of music, and Umm Kulthūm focuses on the first line, with its message that "music is the life of the soul, listening to it cures the ailing" (*al-maghnā ḥayat al-rūḥ, yasmahā al-'alīl tishfīh*). At 4:05 the musicians sing as a chorus responding to Umm Kulthūm, extending the repetition of this line of poetry and pleasing the crowd.
5:32–6:24	Second verse, line 2	Umm Kulthūm proceeds to the second line of the verse: *wa-tdāwī kabid magrūḥ* (it [music] heals the broken heart), alternating it with repetitions of line 1. The firqa quiets down and slows down to give her space to vary her repetitions through improvisation. At 6:01, notice how Umm Kulthum's repetitions and variations, particularly on the words tishfīh (it cures) and wa-tdāwī (and it heals), elicit responses of appreciation and encouragement from the audience.
6:24–8:00		A return to the beginning the second verse, followed by more repetition and variation on the words wa-tdāwī (and it heals), followed by completion of the entire verse before the return of the qafla closes the section.

MUSIC AND RELIGION

The diversity, widespread popularity, and historical depth of the musical traditions of the region that we have just encountered, along with the popular and ritual traditions we will read about below, all deny the common misconception that music is forbidden in Islam. The actions of some religious extremists, such as the ban on music and the burning of musical instruments by the Taliban regime in Afghanistan in the 1990s, should not be taken as representative of Muslim attitudes toward music. Indeed, only the Qur'an can indicate what is forbidden (*ḥaram*), and there is no mention of music in the Qur'an. There is a wide range of attitudes about the role of music in social and religious life, and most share the presumption that music has a power to lead individuals toward or away from the divine.

To fully appreciate the complexity of the matter, we should note that the Western concept of "music" does not translate cleanly onto many traditions in the Middle East, where there are roughly four categories of sonic expression: *mūsīqā*, *ghinā'*, *samā'*, and *qirā'*. The term *mūsīqā* (*mūsīqī* in Persian), borrowed from the Greek, historically has a much narrower meaning in the Middle East, where it refers mainly to secular and instrumental musical traditions, as well as the object of the scholarly study of art music. Ghinā' refers to vocal genres of music. Samā', discussed earlier in the context of Sufism, is framed in terms of the listener's responsibility to listen with moral acumen. *Qirā'* refers to recitation of the Qur'an, of which there are two kinds: *tartīl*, a plain, verbal chanting of the text mainly used in private devotion, and *tajwīd*, the highly ornamented, melodic recitation of the text that is based on the principles of maqām. The Qur'an, which is understood to be the word of God (transmitted with no modification to the Prophet Muhammad), is meant to be recited orally. In fact, the root of the word Qur'an means "recite," and even after it was first written down following the Prophet's death, an authoritative reciter accompanied each of the texts that were delivered to every village.

The tajwīd style of recitation requires that reciters be trained deeply in the maqām system, as well as in specific rules relating to pronunciation, syllable duration, and vocal timbre, among others, and is confined to the textual structure of the text. Due to the divine nature of the text, it is prohibited to "tone-paint" or repeatedly use particular musical phrases to express certain ideas or passages; rather, each recitation must be improvised anew. While recitation of the Qur'an is not considered "music" per se, it does share with music a basis in maqām, as well as a similar performer–audience interaction and commercial presence on recordings; moreover, talented reciters are considered artists and have dedicated "fans."

There are countless musical traditions associated with religious occasions, each with its own name, such as songs celebrating a pilgrimage to Mecca (*taḥlīl*), songs commemorating the Prophet's birthday (Arabic: *mawlid*; Turkish: *mevlut*), praise songs for God or his saints (Arabic *madīḥ*; Turkish *ilahi*), and the Shi'a community's praise for Husayn (Persian: *rowze*), to name just a few. Christian liturgies include those of Coptic Christians in Egypt, whose repertoire

QIRĀ'
Recitation of the Qur'an.

of chants is based on principles of Arab maqām, and Eastern Orthodox Christian traditions in Egypt, Israel, Jordan, Lebanon, and Syria, which are also modal, but based on the Byzantine *octoechos*, or "eight-mode," system.

Jewish communities throughout the Middle East developed their own musical traditions and contributed significantly to the musics of their non-Jewish neighbors. Pre-Biblical communities existed in Persia, Babylonia (Iraq), and Palestine; after the destruction of the Second Temple (Jerusalem, 70 CE, by the Romans), Jews dispersed from Jerusalem, forming sizable diasporic communities

LISTENING GUIDE — QUR'ANIC RECITATION —  LISTEN

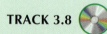 TRACK 3.8

THIS AUDIO EXAMPLE is a recitation of chapter 101 of the Qur'an, *Al-Qāri'a* (The Calamity), a verse about judgment day. According to Michael Sells (2007), who studied the ways that the auditory experience of recitation contributes to the production of religious meaning, this verse evokes imagery of the scales of justice that weigh human deeds and features an obscure term, *hāwiya*, which can mean either an abyss or a woman bereft of child. This term, as well as *al-qāri'a*, is presented as a mysterious concept because it is the object of the Qur'anic phrase "what can tell you of." The long pauses in between verses encourage listeners to ponder the meanings of the lines. This chapter capitalizes on poetic structures such as assonance at verse endings and a recurring long "ā" sound pattern. This style of reciting, called *tajwīd*, is based on the principles of maqām. Most of this recitation is in maqām sīka (scale: E♭ F G A B♭ C D E♭).

TIME	MUSICAL EVENT	
0:00–0:05	The reciter begins with the standard introduction to any recitation of the Qur'an by chanting "in the name of God, the Merciful and Compassionate" (*bismillah ar-raḥmān ar-raḥīm*)	
0:05–0:07	The calamity	*al-qāri'a*
0:07–0:13	What is the calamity	*ma l-qāri'a*
0:13–0:44	What can tell you of the calamity	*wa mā adrāka ma l- qāri'a*
0:44–0:57	A day humankind are like moths scattered	*yawma yakūnu n-nāsu ka l-farāshi l-mabthūth*
0:57–1:09	And mountains are like fluffs of wool	*wa takūnu l-jibālu ka l-'ihni l-manfūsh*
1:09–1:22	Whoever's scales weigh heavy	*fa ammā man thaqulat mawāzīnuh*
1:22–1:32	His is a life that is pleasing	*fa huwa fī 'īshatin rāḍiya*
1:32–1:42	Whoever's scales weigh light	*fa ammā man khaffat mawāzīnuh*
1:42–1:49	His mother is *hāwiya*	*fa ummuhu hāwiya*
1:49–1:57	What can tell you what she is	*wa mā adrāka mā hiya*
1:57–2:02	Raging fire	*nārun ḥāmiya*

across the Middle East and into Europe, Africa, and Asia. The Christian Reconquista of Spain, which ended in 1492 and expelled Jews and Muslims from the Iberian Peninsula, bolstered the preexisting Jewish communities of North Africa. Thus, Jews from North Africa and the Iberian Peninsula are called Sephardic (from the Hebrew for "Spain"), while Jews from the eastern Arabic-speaking world (especially Iraq, Syria, and Yemen) are generally referred to as Mizraḥi ("eastern").

Jewish cantors in the Ottoman Empire adopted Turkish and Arabic maqām practices in their liturgical services, which combined improvised and pre-composed pieces, both metric and non-metric, grouped according to mode. Paraliturgical songs called *baqqashot*, which are performed after midnight around the Mediterranean, are hallmarks of Moroccan and Syrian Jewish traditions. First developed in the sixteenth century, *baqqashot* are based on Kabbalic ideas about the esoteric value of midnight vigils and the power of music and song. These Saturday midnight vigils included prayers, sung *piyyutim* (sacred poems), and a qaṣīda (a classical Arabic genre of sung poetry—here based on a theme from the Torah). All of this singing was done a cappella, or without musical instruments. Some of the same repertoire, however, would also be performed, with instruments, at special concerts or family festivities. Many melodies for Hebrew-language piyyutim were borrowed directly from Moroccan Andalusian art music, while others were sung to melodies of popular Arab songs from the Middle East.

A synagogue in Tunisia.
Source: FETHI BELAID/Getty Images

LISTENING GUIDE

MOROCCAN JEWISH SONG

 **LISTEN**

TRACK 3.9 **Egyptian Melodies with Hebrew Texts: Aneh shav'ati yah u'shema**

THIS SONG was recorded by Paul Bowles in Meknes, Morocco in 1959. It is a Hebrew liturgical poem written by the Rabbi David Buzaglo, set to the melody of the Egyptian popular song 'Alayk ṣalāt allah wa-salāmuh (May you be blessed by God's prayer and salutation). The Egyptian song was composed by Farid al-Atrash and made famous by his sister Asmahan, who was an early musical "rival" of Umm Kulthūm's before Asmahan's early tragic death in 1944 at the age of 26. Because of its sacred nature, the Moroccan Jewish version of the song does not allow for musical instruments. Instead, the vocalists imitate the instruments, including the instrumental interjections (lāzima) in between phrases. The song is in maqām bayyātī (scale: D E♭ F G A B♭ C D).

TIME	MUSICAL EVENT
0:00–0:08	The piece begins with a textless mawwāl: a brief solo vocal improvisation on the syllable "doy."
0:08–0:47	First verse sung by soloist
0:47–1:23	First verse repeated by chorus
1:23–1:28	Soloist imitates instrumental interjection between sections
1:28–1:47	Second verse sung by soloist and fade out

Jewish musical activity was not limited to religious contexts. Jewish musicians and composers in prominent positions in the Ottoman court played key roles in the development of Ottoman art music. In their synagogues in North Africa, Jews are credited with preserving the ancient melodies of Arab-Andalusian music that they brought with them to North Africa after the Christian reconquista. In Morocco, prominent Jewish ensembles performed this Arab-Andalusian repertoire outside the synagogue in coffeehouses and private homes for Muslim and Jewish audiences. Jews were particularly important in developing the Iraqi maqām tradition, considered one of the oldest and most venerable art music traditions in the region, and Jews were among the most notable instrument makers and performers of the dastgah in nineteenth- and twentieth-century Iran.

POPULAR MUSICS, POLITICS, AND OTHERNESS

Major social transformations in the mid to late twentieth century, such as rapid urbanization, massive migration (especially rural–urban, but also of Mizrahi and Sephardic Jews to Israel beginning in 1948), post-colonial independence and nationalism, the emergence of consumer culture, and the spread of new technologies (especially the cassette) led to the creation of new genres of music that gave voice to the difficulties and contradictions of such rapid change.

During this time, nationalism led to the formalization and canonization of national musical traditions as part of larger projects that sought to (1) establish homogeneous national identities that transcended local class, ethnic, and religious ones; and (2) define the nation against its neighbors. Several new musical genres of the twentieth century, such as Turkish *arabesk*, Israeli *musica mizraḥit*, Algerian *raï*, and Berber rights music, challenged such constructions of homogenous national identities. While each of these popular music traditions emerged from, and spoke to, quite different local sociopolitical contexts and concerns, they all, to some extent, made musical and cultural connections across nation-state borders and to the nation-state's problematic "others," both internal and external. Since these genres relied on the recorded music market for their success, you can find many of the songs discussed in the remainder of this chapter on Internet sites such as YouTube.

EXPLORE

Popular Musics of the Middle East and Northern Africa

Arabesk

Both Turkish arabesk and Israeli musica mizraḥit emerged in the context of non-Arab nation-states whose cultural policies viewed Arab influences as a threat to establishing national identity. Turkish nationalist reforms of the 1930s operated under the assumption that in order for Turkey to become a successful modern nation-state, its citizens had to adopt European cultural and political ideals while embracing a rural Turkish heritage. This style of nationalism, championed by Turkey's first president Mustafa Kemal Atatürk (1881–1938), called for de-identification with the Ottoman past as well as the country's Arab neighbors. The Arabic script, which had previously been used to write Turkish, was replaced with a modified version of the Latin alphabet, and religious institutions such as the Mevlevi Sufi order were abolished. The makam system, as well as Ottoman art music—which was banned from state radio for years—were seen by nationalist reformers as unwelcome remnants of a pan-Islamic culture that they were trying to leave behind. Instead, the state invested deeply in institutions of European art music and in the documentation, study, and performance of Turkish folk music. In the wake of the growing popularity of Egyptian cinema, Egyptian films were only allowed in Turkey if the dialogue and songs were recreated in Turkish. By the time arabesk music emerged in the late 1960s, such reforms had been relaxed, but the legacy of the official devaluation of Arab or

"Eastern" culture ensured that arabesk—whose "Arabness" is announced in its very name—would be construed by some as an act of opposition to Turkish nationalism.

Arabesk was one of the most influential musical genres in Turkish popular culture from the 1960s to the 1990s. The most common instrumentation for arabesk includes the bağlama, a long-necked Turkish lute with moveable frets (and later, the amplified elektrosaz), a forceful percussion section featuring the darbūka, and a large string section that fills in between vocal sections, playing with a slow vibrato technique common in Arab popular music. The most definitive characteristic of arabesk, however, is the sobbing, emotional vocal style associated with Arab vocal improvisation, with lyrics based on themes of powerlessness in the grip of fate. Indeed, as Martin Stokes (1992) put it, arabesk implores its listeners to "light another cigarette, pour another drink, and curse the world and their fate."

Socially, arabesk is most associated with rural Kurdish regions of Turkey and the squatter towns on the periphery of western Turkish cities where many migrants from these regions settled during the urban expansion in the mid-twentieth century. In films, arabesk singers often played loosely autobiographical roles of poor urban migrants constantly defeated by unrequited love, betrayal, or corruption. A classic arabesk tune, Orhan Gencebay's "Batsın bu dünya" (1975), laments:

> A pity, a pity
> That fate should do such a thing, a pity
> Everything is darkness, where is the humanity?
> Shame on those who make a slave of the slave.
>
> Stokes 2010: 82

These lyrics were interpreted by listeners not only as cursing fate, but also as a cry against injustice, illustrated clearly in Gencebay's film of the same name in which his character, who faced constant humiliation and trauma at the hands of his debtors, finally decides to take revenge.

Musica Mizraḥit

A similar situation of musical border-crossing in the context of anxiety over "Arabness"—though in a vastly different sociopolitical context with different meanings—is evident in Israeli musica mizraḥit, a popular music style associated with working-class Israeli immigrants from Middle Eastern countries, especially Iraq, Yemen, and Morocco. When the state of Israel was established in 1948, Ashkenazi Jews dominated the political, economic, and cultural infrastructure of the state and had adopted a "melting pot" model of cultural assimilation to create a national unity out of the disparate diasporic groups that immigrated to the country. Ashkenazis largely identified with the art and popular musics of their Russian and European homelands, and encouraged the spread of Songs of the Land of Israel (*shirei erets Yisrael*), a genre of newly composed folk songs created during the formative years of statehood (1920–1960). While the musical influences of Songs of the Land of Israel have developed over the years—from the Eastern European ballads in its early years to more recent fusions with globally circulating musics, especially South American—its lyrical content, full of references to love of the land, indexes collective Israeliness.

Although half of the Israeli population was of Mizrahi or Sephardic origin by 1970, state media—which had a monopoly over radio and television broadcasts until 1990—would not air the Arab or Arab-influenced styles of music that these immigrants performed. The introduction of cassette technology, however, democratized the recording and dissemination of music, and would become crucial to the success of musika mizrahit. Musika mizrahit was mainly performed in nightclubs, social clubs, weddings, and parties. Many songs are covers of Greek, French, or Arab popular songs. Aesthetically, musiqa mizrahit combines Arab and Western pop/rock instrumentation. Cyclic Middle Eastern dance rhythms translated to the drum set were favored, as was a distinctive "shaking" vocal style and nasal timbre. Like their Arab counterparts, musica mizrahit songs often began with an introductory vocal improvisation (layālī or mawwāl). Haim Moshe's classic "Linda" begins with a high-pitched electric guitar (imitating the sound of the Greek bouzouki) performing an introductory improvisatory taqsīm, followed by a vocal layālī improvisation. The drum set plays a maqsūm dance rhythm. Moshe sings the song—a cover of an Arab song— in its original Arabic. Another good example is the hit "Ha-peraḥ Be-gani" written by Avihu Medina and sung by Zohar Argov, whose stardom was enshrined after his suicide in jail in 1987. The song begins with a layālī before jumping into a Yemeni dance rhythm played by the drum set. A Greek bouzouki is the main stringed instrument, along with the electric guitar.

Motti Regev and Edwin Seroussi (2004) suggest that musiqa mizrahit played such a central role in defining and mobilizing Mizrahi identity that it began to challenge other forms of music in the quest to represent the Israeli nation. In its trajectory from exclusion to inclusion in Israeli national culture, it gave voice to a new paradigm of national belonging, one that championed hybridity and border crossing, that now coexists alongside other models of Israeliness.

Algerian Raï

A succession of shifts in the social landscape also shaped the music of Algerian raï. Raï, which literally means "opinion" or "point of view," has a long history of giving voice to the concerns of those situated on the peripheries of society. Its origins are found in the women's urban songs of the early twentieth century in the Algerian port city of Oran (called Wahrane in Arabic). In the 1920s, as a port city with a continual influx of sailors, traders, and other transients, Oran had a bustling entertainment scene that included bars, hash dens, and cabarets where women singers and dancers represented and enhanced the pleasure associated with those venues. The songs featured risqué lyrics and social critique, and were performed to the accompaniment of the gaṣba (flute) and guellal (goblet-shaped drum), two Bedouin instruments brought to the city by immigrants from rural Algeria. Women were both singers and dancers who used their voices and bodies to crystallize desire in their male audiences. In a social context where there was a stigma attached to professional female entertainers, these singers, according to Marie Virolle, "had much to say, much to invent, and little to lose in this new genre." They adopted the title *shaykha*, the female variant of *shaykh*, a term used to bestow prestige on a profession, and adopted stage names to protect the honor of their families and assert their independence. Shaykha Remitti, considered the "mother of raï," has been described as an unwilling feminist, inspired to sing about her own troubled life as an orphan, migrant, and dancer. She became well known for her poetic technique that incorporates wordplays on an inventory of terms associated with red-light districts and bars (in fact, her stage name is adopted from the French command *remettez*, or "give me another [drink]"). Yet her songs also address the difficulties of migration and the solace of religion; these songs speak to the complexities of life in urban Algeria, with all its contradictions.

After Algeria won its independence from France in 1962, the government closed down many of the bars and cabarets where the shaykhas performed, and also limited the sale of alcohol and suppressed festivals associated with saints, another venue for the shaykhas. While women continued to sing their repertoire at weddings, men began to emerge as major voices in this genre, which became known as räi in the 1970s. They also experimented with new orchestrations, and instruments such as the trumpet and saxophone started to replace the gaṣba, and accordions and guitars, and eventually the synthesizer, became popular melodic instruments. The watershed moment in the development of räi—as in many popular musics around the world—was the introduction of cassette technology in the 1970s. This enabled musicians to record and distribute their music cheaply, while listeners could copy and exchange recordings. While the high rate of piracy meant that musicians rarely made money from their recordings, it also meant that their music was able to spread throughout the country, creating a national listenership for some artists.

While räi lyrics continued to draw on traditional texts and earlier räi songs in an intertextual manner, it was the theme of unrequited love that became particularly popular in the 1970s and 1980s, especially among the large population of young men faced with few prospects for employment or marital opportunities. Although räi is often compared to Western rock'n'roll, the authorship and production of räi songs differs in important ways from its Western counterparts. As Marc Schade-Poulsen (1997) shows, räi producers, who were usually the owners of recording studios, often hired songwriters whose lyrics were based on a common repertoire of textual references, but most importantly also a "key phrase" that would often become the title of the song. These lyrics would then be handed to the singer, who was expected to perform the song on the spot with no or minimal retakes. While some singers were able to vary the lyrics or inject their own (either intentionally or due to illegible writing), these lyrics do not represent the singer's ideas as directly as listeners

Khaled in Concert at La Cigale. *Source:* David Wolff-Patrick/Getty Images

of Western popular music might expect. This situation of indirect authorship challenges the marketing of raï music in the West, which often described räi as rebellious and as providing the voice of the youth, similar to punk rock or early rock 'n' roll in its challenges to social mores. As Ted Swedenburg (2001) has pointed out, räi may be most "resistant" in its new context of France, where it addresses issues of the pains of exile and anti-Arab racism experienced by North Africans living in France.

Music and the Berber Rights Movement

Berbers (or Amazigh, meaning "free people") are the indigenous inhabitants of North Africa. While many North Africans trace their roots to Berber communities, Arabic language and culture came to dominate the region with the westward spread of the Islamic empire that began in the late seventh century CE. While Berber communities were widely Islamicized, in some regions, such as the Atlas Mountains of Morocco and the Kabyle region of Algeria, they resisted adopting the language and culture of Arabs. Many Berbers, however, felt excluded and threatened as the newly independent countries legislated Arabic as official languages and suppressed public expressions of Berber identity. In the late twentieth century, a Berber rights movement developed that fought for recognition of Berber language and culture in Morocco and Algeria.

In these mostly remote areas, Berbers maintained communal musical traditions such as the Moroccan *aḥwash*, a festival music that relies on full participation of the village. In fact, a good aḥwash performance is seen as a symbol of healthy social relations in the village, while a bad performance is understood to represent discord. While the aḥwash is grounded in the village community, another tradition relies on individual musician-poets (*rways*) who travel among the villages and to the cities, playing the rebāb, accompanied by the *lotar* (four-stringed lute), and the *nāqūs* (bell). Traditionally, they would serve as reporters and moral guides, reporting on current events in songs that often had moral messages. One contemporary Moroccan *raysa* (the feminine singular of *rways*), Fatima Tabaamrant, is a popular singer with a strong media presence. She sees her role as carrying on the political commentary and social critique of the rways in her music, and bases her sound on the traditional music of the village. Tabaamrant is a rare example of a political singer who actually became a politician: she was elected to the Moroccan parliament, where she made headlines in 2012 by becoming the first member of parliament to ever pose an official question in a Berber language. This act drew attention to the secondary status of Berber in Morocco just after Berber rights activists finally succeeded in getting Berber to be recognized as an official language in Morocco in 2011.

In Algeria, Berber singer Lounès Matoub (1956–1998) became a martyr for the Berber rights cause after his assassination in 1998, and his songs continue to animate that movement. In his music, Matoub sang against the government, criticized religious piety and extremism, and fought for recognition of Berber language and history. He enraged both the government and the Islamists, the two forces that fought each other for control of the country during the Algerian Civil War (1991–2002). Government security forces shot and wounded Matoub in 1988 for supporting Berber rights demonstrations, while FIS (Islamic Salvation Front) militants abducted him in 1994 for being an "enemy of God." When he was assassinated in 1998, the GIA (Armed Islamic Group) took credit for the killing but to date no trial has been held and the exact circumstances of the event remain unclear (Aïtel 2014: 186–187).

The refrain to his song "An-nerrez wala n knu" (Better to Break than Bend) is a fixture at Berber rights demonstrations, signifying the deep commitment of activists:

> *An-nerrez wala n knu* (better to break than bend)
> *awal fi smaren rekku* (the word on which they spilled garbage)
> *s tirrugza a d-yeh* (will be restored with honor)
> *anta ttejra ur nesaa azar* (is there a tree without roots?)
>
> Aïtel 2014: 191

Matoub's final album, released posthumously, featured a provocative, irreverent version of the Algerian national anthem sung, defiantly, in Berber, with new lyrics accusing those in power of corruption, deceit, and destroying Berber identity. As a solution, the song calls for a separate Kabyle state.

> *I lasel ssamsen udem yeghma yejjunjer*
>   (They sullied the face of our ancestors, they soiled it)
>
> *Jeggren s ddin t-ttarabt tamurt n Lezzayer*
>   (They repainted Algeria's face with religion and Arabic)

D ughurru! D ughurru! D ughurru!
    (Fraud! Fraud! Fraud!)

. . .

Ddwa-s an cerreg tamurt an nebrez tura
    (The solution is to divide the country and we will improve it)

Amar assen ay atma at-tnaqel Lezzayer
    (So the day will come when Algeria stands up again).
(Aïtel 2014: 194)

Through the medium of music, singers such as Lounés Matoub and Fatima Tabaamrent championed Berber language, culture, and identity. The mass-mediated formats of records, cassettes, and compact discs enabled their activist messages to circulate throughout Berber society and across borders, subjecting them to multiple replayings, relistenings, and sharing. And they helped shape a Berber popular music culture that was contemporary and relevant, proving that Berber culture was not folklore relegated to the past but, rather, was alive and vibrant.

MUSIC AND THE ARAB SPRING

In November 2010, Tunisian rapper El-Général posted a homemade video of his new song, "Rayes Lebled" (Head of State) to his Facebook page. The song, which is in the form of an open letter to the president, presents a litany of injustices facing the Tunisian people, including systemic corruption, police violence, censorship, and continued widespread poverty. Some of the lines (presented here in English translation) accuse the president's circles of stealing public funds:

EXPLORE

Arab Spring

> They steal in broad daylight and take the land
> No need for me to name them, you know who they are
> A lot of money was pledged for projects and construction
> Schools, clinics, buildings, and improvements
> But the sons of bitches stuffed it into their potbellies
> They stole and looted clung to their seats of power
> I know that in their hearts the people have much to say, but
>   cannot
> If there were no injustices, I would have nothing to say
>
> *Chorus*:
> Mr. President, your people are dying
> Many are eating from the garbage
> You can see what's happening in the country
> Misery and homelessness are everywhere
> I speak in the name of those who are trampled underfoot.
(Gana 2012)

Such a direct and public criticism against the government was virtually unthinkable in the context of an authoritarian Tunisian regime and, as a result, quickly went viral. His song was spread via social media messaging that was also bringing together unprecedented numbers of Tunisians to the streets to protest against the regime. The protests had begun after the self-immolation of Mohamed Bouazizi, the fruit vendor from the impoverished town of Sidi Bouzid, who doused himself with gasoline and set himself on fire after being humiliated and harassed by the police as he tried to sell fruit from his cart. El Général's song captured the widespread frustration with systemic corruption and violence that Bouazizi was protesting and, when El Général was, inevitably, arrested later that month, protestors chanted the words to his songs.

Shortly after the protests in Tunisia forced Ben 'Ali to flee the country, mass demonstrations in Cairo's Tahrir Square presaged the overthrow of Egyptian President Hosni Mubarak. While El Général's "Rayes Lebled" was reportedly played, and sung, in Tahrir Square, it was singer-songwriter Ramy Essam's song "Irḥāl!" (Get Out!) that became a veritable anthem of the Egyptian Revolution. This song, written as the protests began and performed by Essam on guitar, has a chorus that was often repeated back by the crowds in Tahrir Square. In English translation, the chorus is:

> We are not leaving
> He will leave
> As one, we demand one thing:
> Leave, leave, leave!

Ramy Essam, a musician and writer of "Get Out," the song that has become popular among protestors in Tahir Square. *Source:* Michael Robinson Chavez/Getty Images

The Arab Spring protest movements quickly spread throughout the Middle East and North Africa, leading to major civil uprisings in Libya, Syria, Yemen, and Bahrain, as well as demonstrations in numerous other countries. In each case, local musicians captured the spirit of protest and helped mobilize demonstrators. While I have only mentioned two songs, it is important to recognize that a multitude of protest songs, in a number of different styles, played roles in the Arab Spring. Not all of these were rap or rock. In Egypt, the group Tanboura, which is reviving and disseminating the *simsimiyya* (5-stringed lyre) tradition of the Nile Delta, played to great acclaim, and important anti-Bashar Assad protest songs of Syria, such as "Yā Irḥāl Yā Bashar" (Leave, O Bashar), were composed in the style of *dabke*, the country's national communal dance music tradition. It is also crucial to recognize that it is not necessarily useful or accurate to consider rap and rock to be "foreign" musics in the region, any more than it is useful to consider the guitar (which has European and, indeed, Middle Eastern, roots) an import in the United States. Rock music has a longstanding presence in the region, while rap has been thoroughly indigenized, evoking and furthering a millennia-long heritage of sung poetry that speaks to power.

REVIEW CHAPTER RESOURCES

SUMMARY

Our excursions into the musics of the Middle East and North Africa have brought us from the energetic collective singing of trance rituals to the quiet contemplation of art music, and from the local specificity of village performances to the pervasive sounds of popular music spread through the mass media. We have examined songs sung in Arabic, Turkish, Persian, Hebrew, and Berber languages, and covered centuries of music history, from recreations of seventeenth-century court music to twenty-first century responses to socio political conditions. Throughout our journey, we have been attuned to the remarkable diversity of musics in the region, as well as four overarching themes that provide common threads linking many traditions.

Musically, we saw a widespread use of melodic and rhythmic modes, as well as many different kinds of traditions applying a sequential logic to the organization of performances. We encountered a diversity of musical instruments yet noticed the importance of improvisation and the primacy of the voice and sung poetry. The cultural expectation that music can provide different kinds of transcendent states of consciousness was our second theme. This ideal rests on the importance of musical sound to the religious experience in the Middle East and North Africa, which constituted our third theme. Finally, we saw how new musical genres across the region gave voice to populations in situations of social and political "otherness."

Like all excursions, ours had limited stops and therefore left many musics and themes unexplored. I encourage you to continue your journey by exploring other styles of music from the region (good starting points are the bibliography and discography at the end of this chapter) or coming up with your own themes that connect material from this chapter or other musical practices you encounter.

KEY TERMS

Arab music
Arab Spring music
Arabesk
Art music
Berber music
Berber rights music
Dastgah
Improvisation (taqsīm, layālī, mawwāl, avaz)
Israeli music
Melodic mode (maqām)
Musica mizraḥit
Otherness
Persian music
Popular music
Raï
Religion (Islam, Judaism)
Rhythmic mode (īqāʿ)
Spirit possession
Stambeli
Sufism
Sung poetry
Ṭarab
Trance
Turkish music

BIBLIOGRAPHY

General Philip Bohlman, "The Middle East" *Grove Music Online. Oxford Music Online.* (Oxford University Press, www.oxfordmusic online.com/subscriber/article/grove/music/19659). Virginia Danielson, Scott Marcus, and Dwight Reynolds (Eds.), *The Garland Encyclopedia of World Music Volume 6: The Middle East* (New York: Routledge, 2002). Richard Jankowsky (Ed.), *The Bloomsbury Encyclopedia of Popular Music of the World Volume 10: Genres of the Middle East and North Africa* (London: Bloomsbury, 2015). Jean Jenkins and Poul Rovsing Olsen, *Music and Musical Instruments in the World of Islam* (London: Horniman Museum, 1976). Kristina Nelson, *The Art of Reciting the Qur'an* (Austin, TX: University of Texas Press, 1985). Laudan Nooshin (Ed.), *Music and the Play of Power in the Middle East, North Africa, and Central Asia* (Farnham, UK and Brookfield, VT: Ashgate, 2009). Michael Sells, *Approaching the Qur'an: The Early Revelations* (2nd ed., Ashland, OR: White Cloud Press, 2007). Amnon Shiloah, The Dimension of Music in Islamic and Jewish Culture (Brookfield, VT: Variorum, 1993). Amnon Shiloah, *Music in the World of Islam: A Socio-Cultural Study* (Detroit, MI: Wayne State University Press, 1995). Owen Wright, *The Modal System of Arab and Persian Music A.D. 1250–1300* (London: Oxford University Press, 1978).

The Arab Middle East Lila Abu-Lughod, *Veiled Sentiments: Honor and Poetry in a Bedouin Society* (Berkeley, CA: University of California Press, 1986). Dalia Cohen and Ruth Katz, *Palestinian Arab Music: A Maqām Tradition in Practice* (Chicago, IL: University of Chicago Press, 2006). Virginia Danielson, *The Voice of Egypt: Umm Kulthūm, Arabic Song, and Egyptian Society in the Twentieth Century* (Chicago, IL: University of Chicago Press, 1997). Henry George Farmer, *History of Arabian Music to the XIIIth Century* (London: Luzac Press, 1996). Lois Ibsen al-Faruqi, *An Annotated Glossary of Arabic Musical Terms* (Westport, CT: Greenwood Press, 1981). Nouri Gana, "Rap and Revolt in the Arab World," (Social Text 30(4) 2012: 25–53). Moslih Kanaaneh, Stig-Magnus Thorsén, Heather Bursheh, and David A. McDonald (Eds.), *Palestinian Music and Song: Expression and Resistance Since 1900* (Bloomington and Indianapolis: Indiana University Press, 2013). Laura Lohman, *Umm Kulthūm: Artistic Agency and the Shaping of an Arab Legend, 1967–2007* (Middletown, CT: Wesleyan University Press, 2010). Scott Marcus, "Arab Music Theory in the Modern Period" (Ph.D. diss., University of California, Los Angeles, CA, 1989). Scott Marcus, *The Music of Egypt* (New York and London: Oxford University Press, 2007). Ali Jihad Racy, *Making Music in the Arab World: The Culture and Artistry of Tarab* (Cambridge: Cambridge University Press, 2003). Jonathan Shannon, *Among the Jasmine Trees: Music and Modernity in Contemporary Syria* (Middletown, CT: Wesleyan University Press, 2006). Habib Hassan Touma, *The Music of the Arabs* (Portland, OR: Amadeus Press, 1996). Lisa Urkevich, *Music and Traditions of the Arabian Peninsula: Saudi Arabia, Kuwait, Bahrain, and Qatar* (London and New York: Routledge, 2015). Earle H. Waugh, *The Munshidin of Egypt: Their World and Their Song* (Columbia, SC: University of South Carolina Press, 1989).

North Africa Fazia Aïtel, *We Are Imazighen: The Development of Algerian Berber Identity in Twentieth-Century Literature and Culture,* Chapter 4 (Gainesville, FL: University of Florida Press, 2014). Philip Ciantar, *The Ma'lūf in Contemporary Libya: An Arab Andalusian Musical Tradition* (Farnham, UK and Burlington, VT: Ashgate, 2012). Carl Davila, *The Andalusian Music of Morocco. Al-Āla: History, Society, and Text* (Wiesbaden: Reichert Verlag, 2013). Ruth Davis, *Ma'lūf: Reflections on the Arab Andalusian Music of Tunisia* (Lanham, MD: Scarecrow Press, 2004). Richard Jankowsky, *Stambeli: Music, Trance, and Alterity in Tunisia* (Chicago, IL: University of Chicago Press, 2010). Terri Brint Joseph, "Poetry as a Strategy of Power: The Case of Riffian Berber Women" *Music and Gender: Perspectives from the Mediterranean,* Tullia Magrini, Ed. (Chicago, IL: University of Chicago Press, 2003). Deborah Kapchan, *Traveling Spirit Masters: Moroccan Gnawa Trance and Music in the Global Marketplace* (Middletown, CT: Wesleyan University Press, 2007). Miriam Rovsing Olsen, *Chants et danses de l'Atlas (Maroc)* (Paris: Cité de la musique/Actes sud, 1997). Marc Schade-Poulsen, *Men and Popular Music in Algeria: The Social Significance of Raï* (Austin, TX: University of Texas Press, 1996). Philip Schuyler, "Rwais and Aḥwash: Opposing Tendencies in Moroccan Berber Music and Society," *The World of Music* (1979).

Iran Jean During, Zia Mirabdolbaghi, and Dariush Safvat, *The Art of Persian Music* (Washington, DC: Mage, 1991). Bruno Nettl et al., *The Radif of Persian Music: Studies in Structure and Cultural Context in the Classical Music of Iran* (Champaign, IL: Elephant & Cat, 1992). Laudan Nooshin, "Underground, Overground: Rock Music and Youth Discourses in Iran," *Iranian Studies* (2005). Laudan Nooshin, *Iranian Classical Music: The Discourses of Practice and Creativity* (Farnham, UK and Burlington, VT: Ashgate, 2015). Bronwen Robertson, *Reverberations of Dissent: Identity and Expression in Iran's Illegal Music Scene* (London: Continuum, 2012). Owen Wright, *Touraj Kiaras and Persian Classical Music: An Analytical Perspective* (Farnham, UK and Burlington, VT: Ashgate, 2009). Ameneh Youssefzadeh, "The Situation of Music in Iran since the Revolution: The Role of Official Organizations," *British Journal of Ethnomusicology* (2000).

Turkey Eliot Bates, *Music in Turkey: Experiencing Music, Expressing Culture* (New York: Oxford University Press, 2011). Koray Değirmenci, *Creating Global Music in Turkey* (Lanham, MD: Lexington Books, 2013). Walter Feldman, *Music of the Ottoman Court: Makam, Composition and the Early Ottoman Instrumental Repertoire* (Berlin: International Institute for Traditional Music, 1996). Karl Signell, *Makam: Modal Practice in Turkish Art Music* (Seattle, WA: Asian Music, 1977). Martin Stokes, *The Arabesk Debate: Music and Musicians in Modern Turkey* (Oxford: Oxford University Press, 1992). Martin Stokes, *The Republic of Love: Cultural Intimacy in Turkish Popular Music* (Chicago, IL: University of Chicago Press, 2010).

Israel Philip Bohlman, *"The Land Where Two Streams Flow": Music in the German-Jewish Community of Israel* (Urbana, IL: University of Illinois Press, 1989). Philip Bohlman and Mark Slobin, Eds., "Music in the Ethnic Communities of Israel," Special Issue of *Asian Music* (1986). Benjamin Brinner, *Playing Across a Divide: Israeli-Palestinian Musical Encounters* (New York: Oxford University Press, 2009). Amy Horowitz, *Mediterranean Israeli Music and the Politics of the Aesthetic*

(Detroit, MI: Wayne State University Press, 2010). Motti Regev and Edwin Seroussi, *Popular Music and National Culture in Israel* (Berkeley, CA: University of California Press, 2004). Assaf Shelleg, "Israeli Art Music: A Reintroduction," *Israel Studies* (2012). Eric Werner, *A Voice Still Heard: The Sacred Songs of the Ashkenazic Jews* (University Park, PA: Pennsylvania State University Press, 1976).

DISCOGRAPHY

Regional Compilations The Music of Islam (15-vol. set, Celestial Harmonies 13140–2—13155–2, 1998). *Middle East: Sung Poetry* (UNESCO D-8025, 1999).

Arab World Arabian Music: Maqam (UNESCO Collection, Philips 6586–0006, 1971). Egypt: Taqsim and Layali (Philips 6586 010, 1972). *Ensemble al-Kindi: The Aleppian Music Room* (Chant du Monde CML 5741108—CML 5741109, 1998). *Mystical Legacies: Ali Jihad Racy Performs Music of the Middle East* (Lyrichord LYRCD 7437). The Music of Arab Americans: A Retrospective Collection (Rounder 1122, 1997). The Rough Guide to the Arabic Revolution (World Music Network RGNET 1295, 2013).

North Africa Racines Maghreb: Terre d'envoûtement (Wagram 3056962, 2000). *Rough Guide to the Music of North Africa* (World Music Network RGNET 1011 CD, 1997). *Anthologie Al-Âla: Musique andaluci-marocaine* (Maison du cultures du monde, 12 vols., 1989–1999). *Tunisie: Anthologie du Malouf* (INEDIT/Maison des cultures du monde, 5 vols., 1992–1994). *Music of Islam and Sufism in Morocco* (Rounder Records CD 5145, 1999). *Morocco: Berber Music from the High-Atlas and the Anti-Atlas* (Harmonia Mundi MCD 20330, 1994). *Rai Rebels* (Earthworks CAROL 2407–2, 1988).

Iran Anthology of Persian Music, 1930–1990 (Mage CD 22–1, 1991). *Classical Music of Iran: Dastgah Systems* (Smithsonian/Folkways CD SF 40039, 1991). *Radif: The Integral Repertory of Persian Art Music* (5 vols, Al Sur ALCD 116–120, 1992). *Without You: Masters of Persian Music* (World Village 468011, 2002). *A Persian Heritage: Classical Music of Iran* (Nonesuch H-72060, 1974). *Iranian Underground* (Bar-Ax, 2010).

Turkey Music of Turkey: The Necdet Yaşar Ensemble (Music of the World CDT-128, 1992). *Folk Music of Turkey* (Topic TSCD908, 1994). *Gazel: Classical Sufi Music of the Ottoman Empire* (CMP Records CD 3012, 1991). *Archives de la musique turque* (Ocora C 560082, 1995). *A Story of the City: Contantinople, Istanbul* (European Capital of Culture Agency, 2010). *Music of the Whirling Dervishes: 800 Years of Mevlana Rumi* (ARC Records EUCD 2086, 2007).

Israel Rough Guide to the Music of Israel (World Music Network RGNET 1168CD, 2006). *Morasha: Traditional Jewish Musical Heritage* (Folkways FE 4203, 1978). *Israël: Traditions liturgiques des communautés juives* (Ocora 558.529, 1977). *Israel Unleashed: The Best Rock and Metal from the Holy Land* (JMG, 2007).

MUSICS OF EAST ASIA I: CHINA

Isabel K.F. Wong

INTRODUCTION

Today's China is the product of more than four thousand years of interaction with many other civilizations around the globe, receiving contributions from these civilizations and in turn enriching them. The population of the People's Republic of China (PRC), established in 1949, exceeds 1.3 billion and includes some 56 officially recognized ethnic groups, known as "nationalities" (*minzu*). Among these, the Han nationality is the largest and is, in fact, the world's largest ethnic group; it comprises more than 93 percent of the country's population. Other major nationalities include the Zhuang, Mongolian, Manchu, Tibetan, and a large group of nationalities who are followers of Islam: the Hui, Uyghur, Kazak, Tartar, Kirgiz, Tajik, and Uzbek, to name a few. Among the Muslim groups the Hui and Uyghur are the largest. The ancestors of the Hui were Arabian, Persian, Central Asian, and Mongolian Muslim merchants, militia, and officials, who first settled

CHAPTER

4

in northwest China from the seventh to the fourteenth centuries and later spread all over China. The Uyghur (meaning "united" or "allied") are one of the ancient Turkic people, who were originally nomads and around the sixth century settled as farmers in what is today's Xinjiang Uyghur Autonomous Region of the PRC, as well as in central Asian countries such as Kazakhstan, Kyrgyzstan, and Uzbekistan. The Uyghur already had high culture and written language in the fifth century. They first practiced Buddhism and served as important transmitters of this religion and concomitant Indic civilization to China prior to the tenth century CE; thereafter, however, they were converted to Islam.

Among the 55 minority nationalities, only the Hui and Manchu use the Han language (Chinese, or *putuaghua*, meaning the national tongue, and known in the West as Mandarin). The others speak their own languages: twenty-nine groups use languages in the Sino-Tibetan language family, and they live in central, south, and southwest China; ten groups use languages in the Altaic language family, and they live in northeast and northwest China; in addition, some other groups speak Indo-European languages. Often, the various minority groups speak each other's languages, as well as the Han language. Tajiks, Uzbeks, and Tartars speak Uyghur, a Turkic language, for instance.

BEIJING

Beijing, meaning "capital (*jing*) in the north (*bei*)," is a municipality that serves as the capital of the PRC and hence as its administrative, political, and cultural center. However, prior to the establishment of the PRC in 1949, Beijing had served as the capital city for three dynasties: the Yuan dynasty (1206–1368), established by the invading Mongols; the Ming dynasty (1368–1644), established by the Han, who replaced the Mongols; and the Qing dynasty (pronounced "ching"; 1644–1911), established by the invading Manchu, who destroyed the Ming forces. Yet, first-time visitors to Beijing today who expect to see an ancient city may be surprised to find a brash and modern metropolis crisscrossed by many freeways and flyovers and spiked with high-rises. Between the swaths of concrete and glass, however, visitors may still find some old temples, drum and bell towers, and remnants of traditional quadrangle courtyard housing complexes known as *si he yuan* (four buildings surrounding a courtyard) hidden in old alleyways known by the Mongolian term *hutong*. And certainly, modern visitors to Beijing will visit the grandest remnant of all, the imperial palace of the Ming and Qing dynasties known as the Forbidden City, because common people were forbidden to enter it unless summoned by the emperor. The Forbidden City, which occupies more than three square miles and consists of nearly a hundred grand pavilions with yellow tile roofs, is situated at the central axis of old Beijing. For today's modern dwellers of a much expanded Beijing, the Forbidden City is still regarded as the city's cardinal point.

Just to the north of the city, within a day's trip, visitors can visit the Great Wall (*chang cheng*) nearly 3,000 miles long and extending from east to west China. Begun in the Warring States period (435–221 BCE), the Great Wall was completed by the first king of the Qin dynasty (pronounced "chin"), who reigned during 221–209 BCE. In the subsequent Han dynasty (206 BCE–220 CE), the Great Wall was extended further west. Part of the Han dynasty wall still exists in Gansu province in the west. Most of the Great Wall north of Beijing, where most of today's tourists go, was reconstructed in the Ming period.

Despite its long presence as a capital city for various Chinese dynasties, Beijing is a latecomer in Chinese history. Earlier capitals—Chang'an (today's Xi'an, in Shanxi province) and Luoyang (in Henan province) for the Han and Tang dynasties (618–905 CE) and Kaifeng (in Henan province) for the northern Song dynasties (960–995 CE)—are all situated in north-central China west of Beijing. Prior to the thirteenth century, Beijing was but an insignificant trading center in the north for Mongols, Koreans, and local Chinese people. Its predominance began in the mid-thirteenth century with the formation of Mongol China (Yuan dynasty) under Genghis Khan (c. 1162–1227) and later his grandson Kublai Khan (1215–1294), who took control of the city in 1264 and established it as his capital. Marco Polo (fl. 1254–1324), the Venetian who had worked in Beijing under the Mongol government in the Yuan dynasty, reported that the city had many merchants from all over the world. According to him, a thousand merchants daily arrived in Beijing with camel or donkey carts laden with gemstones, spices, and incense. On their return, they carried with them precious cargos of silk, tea, and porcelain. This international commerce made Beijing very wealthy and cosmopolitan.

Beijing's wealth came from the city's position, beginning in the thirteenth century, as the terminus of the Silk Road, the name given to the ancient caravan trade routes by a German geographer in the 1870s. These routes were first developed by an emperor of the Han dynasty to bring China's capital, Chang'an, in the center of the country, into contact with Central Asian kingdoms (many of which were founded by the ancestors of the Uyghur people), and ultimately several great East-West trade routes joined the many Uyghur oasis cities along the northern and southern rims of the Taklamakan Desert, continuing on to the Middle East and ultimately reaching the Mediterranean.

More than just a series of trade routes, the Silk Road was also an ancient superhighway for cultural exchange. Manicheanism (an early form of Christianity originating in present-day Syria) and Buddhism (originating in India) came to China along the Silk Road. Through it, music and musical instruments and dance from India and the Middle East also came to China. For example, the popular plucked string instrument known as the *pipa* was imported to Tang China from Kucha in today's Xinjiang Autonomous Region of the PRC.

Though today the Silk Road frequently serves as a popular metaphor for East-West cultural exchange (for example, cellist YoYo Ma's Silk Road Project), it no longer functions as the main trade route connecting China with the rest of the world. Beijing, however, continues to be one of several important hubs for international travel and trade, where hundreds of international diplomats, tourists, and businesspeople arrive daily.

Beijing continues to be a cosmopolitan city in a contemporary way. For example, many Western-style nightclubs and bars are found around the city featuring the latest DJs flown in from the West and Japan to cater to an international clientele living in Beijing. Concerts of classical Western music and jazz are a regular feature in Beijing's cultural scene, and appearances on the Beijing concert stage by internationally renowned musicians such as YoYo Ma and Itzhak Perlman are by no means rare. Furthermore, the city boasts two fine music academies. One of them, the Central Conservatory of Music, regularly produces many international award-winning string and piano players and opera singers. For example, the pianist Lang Lang, internationally popular—and perhaps controversial—for his flamboyant virtuosity, is a product of the Central Conservatory of Music, from which he went on to continue his studies at the Curtis Institute of Music in Philadelphia. Less-glamorous career opportunities

Ensemble of Uyghur musicians performing in a restaurant in Uruthe capital city of Xinjiang Uyghur Autonomous Region of China. *Source:* Charles Capwell

for students of the Conservatory are offered by the many tourist hotels who desire to create an elegant atmosphere with background music for their guests.

In terms of demography, Beijing is a microcosm of China. Its inhabitants come from every one of the twenty-one provinces of China. People from virtually every of one of the fifty-six nationalities are also well represented. Today's visitors to Beijing can taste many different kinds of cuisine and snacks not only of the Han majority but of other minority nationalities as well. For example, several restaurants in Beijing serve typical Uyghur food, such as lamb kabob, flat bread called *nan*, and a delicious *pulao* rice dish mixed with lamb and carrot. A restaurant I enjoy going to in the northwestern part of the city frequently has performances by Uyghur musicians and dancers from Kasghar (or Kashe) of the Xinjiang Uyghur Autonomous Region.

Beijing also has a sizable Mongolian population, and more than 200 of the best musicians from the Inner Mongolian Autonomous Region currently reside in Beijing. Whenever I am in Beijing, I often join my friend, Professor Chogjin, in visiting a Mongolian nightclub, where we can listen to both traditional and popular music performed by these musicians while enjoying a bottle of strong Mongolian liquor with some tasty snacks.

Among the musical attractions of contemporary Beijing is **Peking Opera**. Indeed, a visit to a performance of Peking Opera has become a regular feature for organized group tours to Beijing, together with a dinner of the famous Peking duck. Big tour groups are likely to be taken to the Liyuan Theater (Pear Garden, or Liyuan, is a metaphor for theater). Built inside a modern tourist hotel situated south of the Forbidden City in an area called the Xuanwu district, which was the birthplace of Peking Opera, the Liyuan Theater has an audience

PEKING OPERA (JINGJU THEATER)
The main type of Chinese popular musical theater that first emerged in the Chinese capital Beijing (Peking) in the later eighteenth century.

capacity of 600 and a modern proscenium stage, but its seating arrangement is modeled after that of traditional Chinese theaters with square tea tables surrounded by several seats facing the stage. Tea and snacks such as peanuts and watermelon seeds are served, in keeping with long-established custom. The usual program for an international audience consists of several scenes with acrobatic displays and mock fighting, but very little singing, which is one of the most important elements of Peking Opera. But because the acrobatic displays are so spectacular in Peking Opera, they provide an attractive introduction to this many-faceted and sophisticated theater.

When a performance troupe from Beijing, led by China's foremost Peking Opera actor Mr. Mei Lanfang, toured San Francisco, Chicago, New York, and Washington, D.C., in the early twentieth century, reporters named the theatrical style Peking Opera. In China, however, this theater is known as **jingju**, that is, theater of the capital. First formulated in the capital city around the mid-eighteenth century, this theater drew its musical and dramatic elements from several older theaters that were current in Beijing at that time but were first developed in other parts of China. After several decades of performing in Beijing, the actors of these theaters from outside Beijing learned from one another, and after a period of such cross-fertilization, a new theater emerged, which is what we know as jingju today. At first, jingju was shunned by the Han educated class because of its popular origin and its lack of sophistication, but the common people in Beijing took to it right away because of the liveliness of its plots—which are presented in easy-to-understand vernacular language—and the exciting rhythmic drive provided by a battery of percussion that includes drums and clapper, gongs, and cymbals. Soon jingju also gained the favor of the Manchu imperial household, particularly its female members, and this patronage by rulers of the Qing dynasty gave much prestige to jingju and helped to overcome the disdain of the Han intellectual class. With the active participation of educated Han and Manchu men to remold jingju into a more sophisticated theater, it soon gained a dominant position not only in Beijing but also in other parts of China. For more than a hundred years, jingju dominated the national theater until the advent of the Cultural Revolution (1966–1976), a complicated, xenophobic, and ultimately ruinous period in modern Chinese history when a group of radicals—encouraged by the late chairman of the PRC, Mao Zedong—ravaged China with continuous and violently destructive political campaigns. This is not the place to discuss the Cultural Revolution; suffice it to say that jingju—together with many other traditional musical genres—was almost destroyed during this period because it was considered to be the cultural product of an old and discredited society. The musicians, actors, and producers connected with these old cultural products became objects of persecution, and many were killed or committed suicide. Although jingju was not completely destroyed by the Cultural Revolution, the end result of its having being silenced for ten years was that the generation who grew up during that period were never exposed to it and hence were totally ignorant of it. Without a knowledgeable audience today, jingju's chances of survival have been greatly weakened.

JINGJU
Chinese term for Peking Opera. It means "theater of the capital."

In 1978, a new, more rational leadership took control of the government, immediately eradicated most of the radical policies, and restored stability to Chinese society. To save China from the danger of bankruptcy brought about by the policies of the Cultural Revolution, the new leadership encouraged foreigners to invest in China by establishing business concerns and manufacturing enterprises. These policies, still in effect today some thirty-five years after the Cultural Revolution, have transformed China into the world's second-largest and fastest-growing economy. Culturally, this new leadership advocated a policy of diversity and encouraged a revival of many of the venerable traditions discarded by the radicals, including jingju. This open-door policy has ushered in not only foreign investments but foreign culture as well.

Pop songs, particularly those from the United States, Hong Kong (which became an integral part of China in 1997), and Taiwan, were among the first cultural products to arrive in China. The younger generation of Chinese who came of age after the Cultural Revolution (which makes up more than 35 percent of China's current population) are avid consumers of foreign pop culture. Since the early 1990s, however, homegrown Chinese pop songs have begun to take over a significant part of the pop song market. Today, if visitors to Beijing wander into its record stores, they are likely to find only pop song recordings.

So, imagine my surprise during a visit to Beijing in May, 2006, when I wandered into the New Dongan Mall—a huge complex that would not be out of place in St. Paul, Minnesota—and I heard the sound of drum, cymbals, and gongs that reminded me of the percussion music of jingju. I thought to myself: "Could it really be live music? No, it must be a recording." Nonetheless, I followed the source of the sound and found myself in a little teahouse that also sells souvenirs. Poking my head in, I saw a small stage at one end of the shop on which a man was standing and singing an aria of jingju, although he was in simple street dress and not the elaborate makeup and costume used for theatrical performance. On stage right there was an instrumental ensemble made up of bowed and plucked strings and percussion accompanying the singing. I immediately recognized that this was a traditional *qing chang* (singing without staging, costume, and makeup) performance, which usually includes the participation of talented jingju fans. I could not quite believe what I saw and heard in such an unlikely setting, but I hurriedly went inside, found a chair next to a tea table, and joined about twenty other people who were listening attentively.

Soon a woman came to serve me a cup of tea together with a big thermos of hot water for making more tea and a dish of peanuts and asked me to give her 10 yuan (Chinese currency, 10 yuan being equivalent to about US$1.50) as tea money and entrance fee. I settled down to survey my surroundings and noticed a red-colored wooden board on the back of the stage, with two gold-color Chinese characters "*fu*" and "*shou*" (meaning, respectively, happiness and longevity) engraved on it. A microphone was in the center of the stage, and a half dozen of instrumentalists sat on stage right. Suddenly I heard sounds of enthusiastic applause, as a dignified-looking middle-aged woman stepped onto the stage, followed by a man who carried with him a *jinghu* fiddle, the chief melodic instrument for jingju. As she stepped onto the center of the stage, she pushed away the microphone, walked to the back of the stage, and waited. The jinghu player who was originally among the instrumentalists stood up and deferentially gave his seat to the newly arrived player. I noticed that both the woman and the fiddle player assumed a confident air, and the audience hushed and waited with anticipation.

The fiddle player began an introduction to a jingju aria called *nan ban zi* from the famous jingju excerpt, *"Bawang Bie ji"* ("The King's Farewell to his Concubine"), the signature aria of the famous jingju actor Mei Lanfang, who was a consummate female impersonator for the *dan* role (principal female character). As the fiddle introduction came to a certain point, the woman singer walked toward the front of the stage in elegant, mincing steps typical of the dan role while raising one hand expressively and started to sing. The vocal melody was full of elaborate and subtle ornaments punctuated with irregular syncopated rhythm, but the fiddle matched the intricacy of the vocal line and the articulation of the singer faithfully; periodically the vocal part came to a rest, and the fiddle provided brief interludes until the vocal part resumed. I then noticed that the teahouse had become full—standing room only—and all listened with rapt attention. When the rendition finally came to a close, the audience broke into loud applause and called out *"Hao!,"* an equivalent of "Bravo!" in Chinese. Realizing that the performers must be well known, I leaned over to my neighbor and asked: "Who are the performers?"

"Don't you know?" he replied. "She is a famous professional jingju actress of the dan role, now in retirement, and the fiddle player has been her personal accompanist for years!"

"Who are the usual performers here, then?" I inquired.

"Anybody who loves jingju and can sing its arias or play instruments. Most are just amateurs who are fans of jingju, but occasionally professionals come too, like today. The gathering occurs daily here from 3:00 to 6:00 p.m., and the venue is provided by the city government, which also pays salaries for a group of instrumentalists and for two service persons to take care of the place and audience. This place was just opened six months ago, and I really hope it can be maintained."

The next singer to step onto the stage was a middle-aged man who told the instrumentalists what he wanted to sing, and then the fiddle began an introductory passage. Somewhat bashful and timid at first, he soon warmed up and starting to sing with gusto, if not with expertise. The audience laughed and encouraged him by clapping the rhythm with him; when he got stuck with an intricate rhythmic passage, someone from the audience sang the passage aloud to help him out.

The next person on stage was a fashionably dressed woman with dyed blond hair, wearing high heels. When she opened her mouth to sing, out came a powerful masculine low voice, and I realized that she was a practitioner of the principal old male role called *lao sheng* (old man), and she was good. So the audience rewarded her with "Hao!" In jingju, the gender of the performer is not necessarily the gender of the character he or she portrays.

I stayed for a couple of hours. The teahouse was noisy not only because of the percussion but also because people talked loudly with one another, as it was also a place to socialize. Most of the audience smoked, and cell phones rang incessantly. But I was thankful that I had the chance to experience a piece of old Beijing in New Dongan Mall.

MUSIC OF THE HAN NATIONALITY

Traditional music of the Han nationality includes many types of instrumental music (solo and ensemble), musical narratives, musical theaters, and folk songs of different regions. In the following sections I will discuss a few representative types: music for a seven-stringed zither called the *qin* (pronounced "chin"), one of China's most venerable instruments; music for a four-stringed lute called *pipa*, an instrument imported to China through the Silk Road; and finally, music of the jingju theater.

The Qin and its Music

EXPLORE

Qin

The qin is the most highly regarded of Chinese musical instruments because of its antiquity and its rich legacy of associations with scholars and poets. It is made from a hollowed board approximately four feet long and three inches deep with a convex curve to its top. The qin has seven strings of varying thickness stretched over the entire length of the board. Its body is painted with layers of dark lacquer, and although it has neither frets nor bridges, it does have thirteen studs or position markers called *hui*, which are made of mother-of-pearl or other semiprecious material and are embedded along the outer edge of the instrument to indicate finger positions for stopping the strings (i.e., pressing a string against the body of the instrument to shorten its length and thereby change its pitch). The open strings are usually tuned C–D–F–G–A–C–D. The flat, smooth underside of the instrument has two openings called "sound pools," and it is usually engraved with the name of the owner and the given name of the instrument, indicating that the qin is a highly personalized instrument.

Qin playing involves various ways of plucking the strings with the thumb, index, middle, and ring fingers of the right hand (the little finger, which is called *jinzhi*, or "forbidden finger," is not used) and stopping them with the four fingers of the left hand (the little finger is again not used). Using these techniques, a qin player can produce many different types of ornaments, including vibrato (slight rising and falling in pitch), portamenti (slides from one pitch to another), and harmonics (bell-like tones produced when a string vibrates in segments rather than as a single length).

WENZIPU (PROSE TABLATURE)
Archaic Chinese tablature for the qin written in prose.

Around the sixth century CE, detailed explanations were written describing the techniques required for producing each and every sound on the qin. This kind of notation, called tablature, is known as **wenzipu** (prose tablature). Later,

A Guqin performance in Qingyang Gong Taoist Temple. *Source:* China Photos/Stringer/Getty Images

in the Tang dynasty (618–906 CE), a new type of tablature was created that consisted of clusters of abbreviated symbols derived from Chinese characters; these specified the string number, the stopping positions, and the hand, finger, and direction of plucking. This tablature is called **jianzipu** (abbreviated characters tablature), and its evolved form is still in use today.

Throughout Chinese history, the qin has been associated with sages and scholars (male only), giving it a special place in Chinese life and culture. The earliest mention of the qin is found in the *Shujing* (Book of History, compiled c. sixth century BCE). Learning the qin was already a requirement for scholars and gentlemen before the third century BCE. At that time, however, the qin was employed primarily to accompany poetry recitation, as a member of the large orchestra for the court ceremonial music known as **yayue** (elegant music), or to form a duet with the *se* (a twenty-stringed plucked zither). A duo of qin and se symbolized a harmonious spousal relationship or friendship. After the Han dynasty (206 BCE–290 CE), as ceremonial music at court gradually declined, the qin emerged as both a solo instrument and the accompanying instrument for chamber vocal genres. During the end of the Han period and thereafter, the literati initiated the scholarly study of the qin and wrote compositions specifically for the solo qin, and thus its status and prestige were enhanced. In the subsequent periods of the Sui and Tang dynasties and the Five Dynasties (581–618, 618–907, 907–960), the playing of qin and qin scholarship were restricted to court circles only; outside the court, the qin was neglected.

Not until the Song dynasty (960–1027) was there a renaissance of qin music. An ideological system for the qin was developed by fusing Confucian philosophy with Daoist (Taoist) and Buddhist mystical symbolism. According to this ideology, the playing of the qin is an act of contemplation, self-purification, and self-regulation. Hence, it should be played in private, amid charming scenery, under pine trees and beside running creeks, in the privacy of one's garden, or in the cloister of one's own library with incense burning.

JIANZIPU (ABBREVIATED CHARACTERS TABLATURE)
Tablature for the Chinese seven-stringed zither, the qin; it is made up of clusters of abbreviated Chinese characters.

YAYUE
Literally meaning "elegant music," it was Chinese court music of imperial China.

The qin vogue among the scholars reached its height in the Ming dynasty (1368–1644), when numerous treatises and handbooks were printed. But in the early twentieth century, rapid social change brought about a sharp decline in interest in the instrument. The number of talented performers dropped to just a handful, and scholarship came to a virtual halt. After the establishment of the People's Republic in 1949, under government encouragement, research in qin music and its history was revived, particularly during the 1950s. In recent years, the qin has been brought into the new context of the modern concert stage, and with the appearance of a younger generation of qin virtuosi, interest in the qin has grown among members of the educated circle. Among the general populace, however, the qin, with its associations with past literary and philosophical traditions, is too exclusive and inaccessible and has therefore been largely neglected.

The earliest extant qin manuscript, dating from the Tang dynasty, contains the composition "*Youlan*" ("Orchids in a Secluded Valley"), which is written in prose tablature. The first printed qin handbook, the *Shenqi mipu* (*The Mysterious Secret Handbook*), compiled by Prince Zhu Quan of Ming, appeared in 1425 and was followed by numerous other woodblock handbooks, together comprising more than three thousand compositions notated in the abbreviated-character tablature. Only about eighty pieces, however, have survived in the oral performance tradition.

In qin handbooks, tempo is indicated by terms such as "Slow down," or "Speed up," but durational symbols are totally absent. These omissions indicate the importance placed on oral tradition and the realization and interpretation of the music by the performing artist. A process of reconstructing ancient pieces from qin tablature through the aid of oral tradition is called *dapu* (literally, "to obtain from the notation"). This process of reconstruction (i.e., realizing the qin tablature into actual sounds by a qin player) has become a venerable tradition. Qin meters vary among free meter, duple meter, and sometimes triple meter, often within the same piece.

Qin notation is very difficult to read, even for those who are literate and cultivate their skills, and this contributes to its exclusive nature. In the famous eighteenth-century novel *The Story of the Stone* (also known as *The Dream of the Red Chamber*) by Cao Xueqin (d. 1763), a passage conveys this well. This greatest of Chinese novels depicts in meticulous detail life in a wealthy and influential family, in particular the love and fate of the hero, Jia Baoyu, and his cousin, Lin Daiyu, two extremely talented, cultivated, and precocious teenagers. In Chapter 86, Baoyu seeks Daiyu out in her quarters and learns something about qin tablature and its philosophy, although his wry concluding comment seems to indicate he takes it all with a grain of salt:

Daiyu was sitting at her desk reading. Baoyu approached her, saying cheerfully, "I see that you left Grandmother's place early." Daiyu responded with a smile and said, "Well, you wouldn't speak to me, so why should I stay any longer?"

"There were so many people there, I didn't have a chance." As he replied he tried to see what she was reading, but he couldn't recognize a single word. Some looked like the character for "azalea," some looked like the character for "hazy." Another had the radical "big" on the left, the character for "nine" next to it, and a large hook underneath it with the character for "five" written inside. . . .

Baoyu was curious and puzzled. He said, "Sister, I am more and more impressed by you. You must be reading a secret Book of Heaven!"

Daiyu couldn't help laughing. "Here is an educated man! Don't tell me you have never seen a musical score!"

"Of course I have," he replied, "but I don't know any of those characters. Why don't you teach me to read some of it? . . . For example, what do you make of this character 'big' with that long hook and a character 'five' stuck in the middle?"

With a laugh Daiyu replied, "This character 'big' and the character 'nine' mean that you press on the ninth stud with your left thumb, and this big hook with the character 'five' inside means that you hook inward the fifth string with your right hand. This whole cluster is not a word; it stands for a musical note. There is really nothing to it. You have also many kinds of left-hand techniques such as the quick vibrato, broad vibrato, upward glide, downward glide, trill, quick glide, and so forth."

Baoyu was hopping with joy, saying, "Come on, dear sister, since you know so much about it, why don't we try it out?"

"It is said that the zither is synonymous with the word for self-restraint. The ancients intended it to be used for discipline, for tranquilizing one's emotions, and for suppressing excessive and frivolous desires. In playing the zither, you must select a quiet and secluded place. It could be in the top story of a building, in the forest among the rocks, at a mountain precipice, or at the edge of the water. The weather should be calm, with a light breeze or a clear moon. You have to burn some incense and meditate for a while. . . ."

"As to the performance itself, the fingering and the intonation have to be good enough . . . the position of your heart should be in a line with the fifth stud on the instrument. . . . Now you are ready, bodily, and spiritually."

Baoyu said, "Can't we just do it for fun? It's next to impossible if we have to go through all that rigmarole!" (Adapted from a translation by Rulan Chao Pian)

Practically all qin compositions have programmatic titles either derived from common poetic and mystical images or alluding to Chinese history or legends. The titles evoke a mood or atmosphere familiar to the Chinese.

A typical qin composition usually contains several sections:

1. *Sanqi* (introduction): Begins slowly in free rhythm. Its function is to introduce the principle notes of the mode used in the piece.

LISTENING GUIDE

"LIU SHUI" ("FLOWING WATER")

LISTEN

TRACK 4.1 Performed by Professor Wu Wenguang on the qin

"**L**IU SHUI" ("Flowing Water") is a famous composition for the qin. The performer is Professor Wu Wenguang of the China Conservatory of Music in Beijing, the foremost qin player in China today. Wu Wenguang studied the qin under his late father, the famous qin master Professor Wu Jinglue, and his performance is based on his father's 1960 interpretation of the tablature notated in a handbook dated 1876, entitled *Tian Wen Ge Qinpu (Tian Wen Ge Studio Qin Handbook)*. It is a rhapsodic piece of descriptive music portraying a waterfall cascading from a mountaintop, falling through various levels of rock, and then becoming a rapids, eventually running out to the sea.

The composition of "Flowing Water" is attributed to Boya, a great qin master who lived during the Spring and Autumn period (770–476 BCE). Boya's friend, Zhong Ziqi, was an attentive and imaginative listener to Boya's music. As the story goes, when Boya played the piece "Flowing Water" and conjured up the scene of a high mountain in his mind, Zhong Ziqi right away got the idea and said: "Ah! I am thinking of Mount Tai (China's tallest and most sacred mountain)." When Boya thought of flowing water as he played, Zhong Ziqi echoed his thought and said: "How excellent!—broadly flowing rivers and streams." When Zhong Ziqi died sometime later, Boya felt that nobody could match his understanding of the music he played, and so he broke his qin and never played again. Thus, the deeper meaning of this piece is as a symbol of deep friendship. From this story arose the phrase, "*zhu yin,*" literally meaning "a good friend who understands my music," and it is still popularly used today to signify profound friendship.

TIME	SECTION	MUSICAL EVENTS
0:00–0:49	**Sanqi (introduction):** Listen for the way that the portamento is used to glide or slide both small and great distances between pitches. Also notice the delicate quality of the harmonics produced by the qin.	The melody is performed with a lot of **portamento**. Some pitches are reinforced by the lower octave. This section of the piece is in free rhythm.
0:49–1:15		The melody is rendered with harmonics and in a more regular rhythm.
1:16–1:50	**Rudiao (exposition):** Continue to listen for the way that portamento informs the melody. Also notice the degree to which strums across all of the strings add a rich texture to the performance.	The melody is performed in a faster tempo and with wide, sweeping portamenti.
1:50–2:17		In this passage, the tempo is increased yet again.
2:17–3:31	**Ruman (becoming slower):** Notice the extremes of volume and the	Melody and portamenti are embedded in a strumming accompaniment produced by sweeping across all the strings.

continued

TIME	SECTION	MUSICAL EVENTS
	density of texture that the qin can produce.	This portion of the performance culminates at [3:11], after which the strummed portamenti dissipate in a decrescendo and diminuendo to [3:31].
3:32–3:43		A short passage of harmonics.
3:43–4:11		The performance then returns to the strumming style of [2:17–3:31] and again concludes with energetic strumming.
4:11–4:43	**Weisheng (tail sounds):** Notice the delicacy of the harmonics and their slow decay at the end of this performance.	This final section serves as a conclusion and features harmonics again.

2. *Rudiao* (entering the music, or exposition): The meter is established, and the principal motives of the piece are introduced, which are then varied by means of extension, reduction, and changes in timbre, tempo, and register. This part is usually the longest and musically the most substantial.

3. *Ruman* (becoming slower): The principal motives undergo further rhythmic variation, and modulation to other keys may occur. In some larger compositions, motivic materials occurring in the second part may be restated and reinterpreted here; this is called *fuqi* (restatement).

4. *Weisheng* (tail sounds): A short coda concludes the composition. The coda, always played in harmonics and in a slackening tempo, reiterates the important notes used in the composition.

The *Pipa* and its Music

The *pipa* is a four-stringed, fretted lute with a bent neck and a pear-shaped body. The prototype of this instrument, which had five strings, was imported to China from present-day Kucha (known in ancient China as Qiuci), which was one of the largest of the thirty-six ancient Uyghur kingdoms, and in 91 CE it was under the suzerainty of the Han. By the fourth century, the Kuchan Kingdom of Qiuci had become an important center for Buddhist learning imported from India, as well as the center for Central Asian trade and Indo-European culture, as trade routes running across the Taklamakan Desert intersected with the Silk Road at Kucha. Today Kucha is still a major town in the Xinjiang Autonomous Region in the PRC.

From numerous written accounts (in both Chinese and Uyghur) and the iconographic evidence found in the frescos of many Buddhist grottos along the Silk Road, we can surmise that the five-stringed pipa—which was held horizontally and played with a *plectrum*—originated in Qiuci (Kucha), from where it traveled east to Han China and west to Persia and Arabia. Because of this, it

EXPLORE
Pipa

PORTAMENTO
A slide or sweep between two pitches.

Wu Man on pipa performs at Symphony Space's Thalia Theater. *Source:* Hiroyuki Ito/Getty Images

was often called the Qiuci pipa. By the Sui and the Tang periods (respectively 581–618 and 618–905), when Han China entered one of its most cosmopolitan epochs, music and dance from Qiuci—featuring the pipa either as the principal solo instrument or as a member of an instrumental ensemble—formed an important repertory for refined entertainment at court and in homes of aristocrats and wealthy people. The pipa thus became extremely popular in Tang China, and many noted Qiuci musicians gained employment at court and in the homes of the wealthy. After the five-string Qiuci pipa was adapted in China, it underwent transformation and evolved into a four-stringed instrument, although it was still played with the plectrum. This form of Qiuci—inspired entertainment music, known in China as *yan yue* (banquet entertainment music), was imported to Japan around the Tang period. There it became part of the repertory of Japanese court music known as *gagaku* (elegant music), and the four-stringed pipa, played with a plectrum, also went to Japan at the same time and became known as *biwa*.

After the Tang period, the pipa became an instrument for courtesans who were well trained in music and dance, and because of this, the pipa has been associated with artistic entertainments, gaiety, and romance. In a famous long poem entitled "*Pipa Xing*" ("The Song for the Pipa"), the famous Tang dynasty poet Bo Ju-I (772–846) provided a vivid description of a pipa performance by a courtesan:

Pipa Xing (Song of the Pipa)

. . . The lowest string hummed like pouring rain;
The higher strings whispered as lover's pillow talk.
Humming and whispering intermingled
Like the sound of big and small pearls gradually falling into a jade
    plate.
Sometimes it sounded like liquid chirping of orioles hidden
    among flowers;
Sometimes it sounded like a brook sobbing sadly running through
    a sand bank.
A strong sweep across the strings sounded as though they had
    been broken
And the notes suddenly died down.
The music became a lament expressing the deepest sorrow;
The silence revealed more emotion than the actual sound.
Suddenly it sounded as if a silver vase had broken, and the water
    gushed forth,

Or as if armored horses and weapons were loudly clashing.
Then, before she laid down her plectrum, she ended the music
    with one stroke
Sweeping all four strings boldly and making a sound like the
    rending of silk. . . .

                                    (Translated by Isabel Wong)

Chinese written records show that in subsequent periods until the mid-Ming period (around the fifteenth century), the pipa was still played with a plectrum and held horizontally by the player. It was only since the late fifteenth century that the pipa has been held upright on the player's crossed knees and played with the fingers.

The modern pipa has twenty-three to twenty-five frets placed along the neck and the soundboard of the instrument; the four strings are usually tuned to A–d–e–a, and a complete chromatic scale can be produced. The pipa player employs a wide variety of playing techniques, the most distinctive of which are the following:

- Harmonics
- Tremolo, produced by rapidly and continuously plucking a string with all five fingers consecutively
- Portamento (sliding from note to note), produced by deflection of a string before or after it has been plucked
- Percussive pizzicato, produced when a string is plucked violently enough to cause it to snap against the body of the instrument
- Percussive strumming of all four strings

The music of the pipa, characterized by flexible tempi and frequent alternation between softer and louder passages, encompasses many moods ranging from the contemplative and the lyrical to the heroic and even to the comical. Chinese musicians divide the pipa repertory into two categories according to structure: the "big pieces" and the "small pieces."

"Big pieces" are usually quite long and are of three kinds:

1. Continuous (not divided into sections)
2. Divided into many sections that follow a theme and variation structure with themes derived from preexistent materials
3. Divided into many sections that alternate songlike with percussive material

"Small pieces" are usually quite short, each containing about sixty to one hundred beats or so. Most of these pieces are in sectional form.

Pieces in the traditional pipa repertory are also divided into the *wen* (lyrical) and the *wu* (martial) categories. Wen category pieces are expressive in nature and in a slow or moderate tempo, and they tend to employ various kinds of finger techniques to produce embellishments and microtonal ornaments. Wu category pieces tend to be percussive, loud, and in fast tempo—fast strumming techniques are often employed to produce a martial effect.

Sectional pipa pieces, be they "big" or "small," frequently employ a rondo-variation principle in which basic melodic material returns periodically, but in a more improvisational manner than is usual in the Western rondo or variation form.

Pipa pieces often have programmatic titles, and some of these contain clearly descriptive musical elements directly related to their titles; others, however, are more abstract and have only a poetic relationship to their titles.

Notation for the instrument, again a kind of tablature, combines symbols indicating pitches of the diatonic scale and an additional set of symbols indicating various finger techniques. There are approximately a dozen printed collections of music for the pipa, the earliest of which dates from the early nineteenth century. Prior to that time, music for pipa circulated in manuscripts, some of which still exist today. Notation has always been a secondary aid for the transmission of the repertory, as it exists primarily in oral tradition.

In traditional society, the pipa was usually performed in an intimate surrounding, either in a private banquet or in a teahouse. Nowadays, the pipa continues to be a popular instrument, with many young virtuosi being trained in conservatories, but performances usually take place in a modern concert hall.

Winds and Strings Ensemble in Shanghai

Shanghai, China's commercial capital, is situated south of Beijing at the mouth of the Yangzi River. Part of modern Shanghai was built by the British in the mid-nineteenth century. Today, Shanghai is starting to take on the chic of Paris, the sophistication of New York, and the futuristic vibes of Tokyo. It already boasts the world's fastest train (a magnetic levitation train that takes less than eight minutes to run the thirty kilometers from the Pudong international airport to the city), the longest underwater pedestrian tunnel (under the Huangpu river), and one of the world's tallest hotels—the 88-story Grand Hyatt. However, in some pockets of Shanghai, traditional modes of life are still common, and traditional kinds of music can still be heard there in appropriate surroundings.

One of these is the chamber ensemble of winds and strings called **Jiangnan sizhu**. Jiangnan, meaning "south of the river," which is the designation for the Yangzi Delta region in southeastern China, of which Shanghai is a part. *Si* literally means "silk," and it denotes stringed instruments because strings used to be made of silk (nowadays they are usually made of steel for greater volume). *Zhu* literally means "bamboo," a material from which some wind instruments are made.

Jiangnan sizhu was formerly a favorite pastime of the gentry and educated classes of the urban centers in the Jiangnan region. People gathered at the many private clubs to play and while away a pleasant afternoon or evening. As a rule, the performers of Jiangnan sizhu are amateurs who play for their own enjoyment. In Shanghai today there are still half a dozen or so Jiangnan sizhu

JIANGNAN SIZHU
Chinese chamber instrumental ensemble made up of strings ("silk") and winds ("bamboo") popular in the areas around Shanghai.

EXPLORE

Jiangnan Sizhu

clubs whose members are retired urban workers, some of whom belonged to the gentry class before 1949.

Jiangnan sizhu performances generally take place in neighborhood teahouses. The teahouse where I usually go to listen to Jiangnan sizhu is located in the Square of the Temple of the City God in the Old City of Shanghai, a picturesque area lined with many small shops selling all kinds of traditional wares and souvenirs. The old teahouse, always thronged with people, is an elegant structure built on an artificial lake teeming with goldfish, and it is approached via a zigzag footbridge. It is a hexagonal wooden building of two stories, lacquered with dark-brown paint and has intricate latticework windows open on all sides. It has double-tiered black tile roofs with elongated eaves swooping out in a complex pattern of upturned curves.

There is no entrance fee, but customers are required to pay a modest price for a pot of tea. The performance usually takes place in the afternoon when the players arrive one by one, place their instruments on a big table situated at one side of the teahouse, and then sit around it with the string players and the player of the drum and clapper in an inner circle and the rest in an outer one. The player of the drum and clapper (gu ban) serves as a conductor by beating time, and everybody plays from memory.

There is no formal announcement of the program, nor are there program notes, because the audience is familiar with the small, anonymous repertory, which consists of only about two dozen pieces that all have descriptive titles. The first piece for the afternoon—played by the novices—is always short and slow, and more complex pieces are played as the afternoon progresses. Each piece usually lasts ten minutes or more, and some may be played more than once. After one piece is finished, some players may get up from the table, and others sitting among the customers may come up to join the performers, the most skillful and respected players joining in around 4:30 P.M. to perform pieces that are fast and require greater expertise.

When the novices are not playing, they usually sit around the big table listening to and watching the more skilled players. There is no formal instruction, as learning is entirely by imitation, and when novices are considered ready to play, the more skilled players will give them criticism or suggestions.

Jiangnan sizhu pieces always begin slowly and gradually accelerate, ending in a fast tempo. Although the drum-and-clapper player is supposed to provide the beat for the music, the players typically are not overly concerned with rhythmic exactitude. In addition, all the instruments play together most of the time. The overall fuzzy timbral quality of this purely melodic music is attributable not only to the combination of plucked and bowed strings with winds but also to the fact that they play in a relatively high register and use several slightly different tunings.

When I first heard Jiangnan sizhu music, I could discern no break within a given piece. It seemed to me that, once started, it went on without break until the end. I later found out that every piece is divided into sections, but because the end of a section is always overlapped by the beginning of the next, a piece usually gives the impression of being seamless.

Another characteristic of Jiangnan sizhu is the extensive use of improvised embellishments on the basic melody. Every melodic instrument plays the same basic melody, but each player applies the improvised embellishments according to the conventions of his instrument, creating a complicated texture of **heterophony**, which—like the variations in tuning—adds to the fuzzy or thick quality of the melody. Because of this freedom in adding improvised embellishments, no two performances of one piece are exactly alike, and the more skilled the performers, the greater the differences may be.

One of the most important features of Jiangnan sizhu is the use of a technique of structural expansion known as "**fangman jiahua**" ("making slow and adding flowers"), in which the musical materials are expanded by slowing down the tempo of the original melody, and as the notes of the original melody become further apart temporally, other notes are inserted, or interpolated. The result is a new piece that may have sixteen or more notes corresponding to each note of the original melody.

As I mentioned before, the teahouses where Jiangnan sizhu is performed are always noisy, as the customers chat among themselves or come and go. The players are oblivious to the commotion, and in fact, when some of them are not playing, they also chat with their friends! Jiangnan sizhu, like much other traditional Chinese music of a popular nature, is considered a kind of background music to enhance the ambience of a pleasant social environment.

HETEROPHONY
Two or more performers play the same melody, but with small differences in timing or ornamentation.

FANGMAN JIAHUA
Literally "making slow and adding flowers." A technique through which the tempo is slowed to achieve temporal space between the notes of the melody. This space is then ornamented with additional notes.

LISTENING GUIDE

HUA SAN LIU ("EMBELLISHED THREE-SIX")

 **LISTEN**

TRACK 4.2 Featuring Lu Chunling (dizi); Zhou Hui (yangqin); and Ma Shenlong (pipa)

THE BEGINNING and conclusion of the first part of this piece are excerpted.

TIME	MUSICAL EVENT
0:00–0:28	Introduction: Performed here in free rhythm. The dizi stands out because of its distinctive timbre and greater ornamentation.
0:28–1:33	The melody is now performed in regular meter. Listen for the slight differences in ornamentation and tuning among the different instruments. This excerpt fades out at [1:31–1:33].
1:37–2:05	The second excerpt fades in as the performers are approaching the end of first section of the piece. They are playing at a faster tempo than they had adopted at the outset [0:28–1:33].
2:05–2:46	The dizi jumps to the upper register while the other two instruments continue to play the melody in the usual range. The performers execute a ritard (slowing) just before concluding the first section of the piece.

The Jingju Theater

At the beginning of this chapter I described a performance of the nonstaged variety of Jingju in a teahouse-gift shop in Beijing. Before the Cultural Revolution, staged performances of Jingju by professional actors used to take place daily, but nowadays, these performances do not take place often, except as tourist attractions, which nevertheless may help stimulate a revival of the art among native connoisseurs.

As theater, Jingju is a conglomeration of the dramatic presentation of plots using music, speech, stylized gestures and dance movements, acrobatics, mock combat scenes, and fanciful makeup and elaborate costumes. Personages of Jingju are divided into four main categories and their subcategories according to sex, age, social status, and character. Each role type is defined by the costume and makeup the actor wears and the prescribed physical movements of each. All the characters sing, but each employs distinct vocal techniques, timbres, and singing styles.

The four main categories of actors are sheng (male role, divided into old male, young male, and warrior subcategories); dan (female role, divided into old female, young refined female, young flirtatious female, and female warrior subcategories); *jing* (painted face, a rough or heroic male role whose face is painted with intricate colored patterns); and *chou* (a male comic role). The basic musical elements of jingju are arias, heightened speech, and instrumental music.

Instrumental music in jingju has many functions. The first and foremost is to accompany the singing and the physical movements and dance. To an audience familiar with the conventional musical code of jingju, it may also describe a dramatic situation and action, indicate the spatial dimension of the setting, convey the moods and psychological makeup of characters, and provide a soundscape or sound effects connected with a particular dramatic moment. With such musical clues, an educated jingju audience will be able to form a mental picture of the temporal and spatial aspects of the drama and respond to them with appropriate emotion and understanding.

The instrumental ensemble is made up of two components: the melodic, or **wenchang** (civic instrumentation) ensemble, and the percussion, or **wuchang** (military instrumentation) ensemble. In the musical communication of information, the percussion ensemble plays a more important function than the melodic group. The percussion ensemble also provides rhythmical punctuation for movements and singing, and it serves to combine all the discrete elements of a play, musical as well as gestural, into a complete whole.

The percussion ensemble is made up principally of five instruments: *danpigu* (a single-headed drum), *ban* (a paired wooden clapper; danpigu and ban are played by one person, who functions as the conductor), *daluo* (a big gong that produces a falling pitch), *xiaoluo* (a small gong that produces a rising pitch), and *naoba* (a small pair of cymbals). In addition, a few other percussion instruments are used for special effects: *datangu* (a big barrel drum), *xiaotangu* (a small barrel drum), several other gongs and cymbals of different sizes, a *muyu* (a "wooden-fish" slit drum), and a pair of small handbells.

EXPLORE

Peking Opera (Jingju)

WENCHANG

The instrumental ensemble in Peking Opera made up of melody instruments.

WUCHANG

The instrumental ensemble in Peking Opera made up of percussion.

Scene in a popular play based on the women generals of the Yang Family legends in Song Dynasty, at the Peking opera. *Source:* Zhang Peng/Getty Images

The music of the percussion ensemble includes some sixty conventional rhythmic patterns, each of which is identified by a proper name and a specific syllabic pattern. The five principal instruments are combined in different ways to indicate different kinds of dramatic situations, atmospheres, or moods. The three basic percussion combinations are as follows:

1. A trio made up of the big gong, the small gong, and the cymbal, with the big gong as the principal instrument. This combination is usually employed in scenes of pageantry featuring a big crowd of actors and also in dramatic scenes that require strong emphasis.
2. A duo made up of the cymbal, as the principal instrument, and the small gong. This combination usually accompanies tragic scenes.
3. A small gong solo. This is generally used in scenes of a tranquil or lyrical nature.

Besides these basic combinations, other additional combinations include a duo of the big and small barrel drums (used in acrobatic and fighting scenes), a duo of the small gong and the big cymbal (played in a specific way to indicate underwater and thunder sounds), and so forth. The sixty or so named conventional percussion patterns, each requiring different instrumental combinations and varying tempi, perform many functions. These include indicating entrances and exits of dramatic personages and their social status; emphasizing a word, phrase, or name of a person or place; accompanying fights and battles; and producing special sound effects.

A blind man plays an "erhu" instrument, busking in Beijing. *Source:* ED JONES/Getty Images

The melodic ensemble features mostly strings and winds, as well as a set of ten small, suspended pitched gongs called the *yunluo*. The strings are the *jinghu* (the leading melodic instrument, a two-stringed bamboo, spike fiddle with a very high and piercing pitch), the *erhu*, the *yue qin* (a four-stringed plucked lute with a round sound box), a *sanxian*, and a *ruan* (a large plucked lute with a round sound box). The winds are the *dizi* transverse flute, the *sheng* (mouth organ), and the big and small *suona* (conical double-reed oboes).

The primary functions of the melodic ensemble are to play introductions and interludes for arias, to double aria melodies, and to play incidental music for dance and miming movements, but the strings and the winds perform somewhat different functions. The strings, with the jinghu *as* their principal instrument, accompany the two main types of arias known as the *xipi* and the *erhuang*, which were derived from some folk predecessors of jingju. In addition, the strings play various incidental pieces—all of which have proper names—to accompany some miming movements such as sweeping, changing clothes, putting on makeup, drinking wine, and walking, as well as to accompany scenes of banqueting and general pageantry, celebration, and dance. Each individual piece of named incidental music has an association with specific dramatic situations and moods, and each requires different playing techniques on the various strings for the production of varying volumes and timbres.

The winds—the dizi and the sheng only, without the suona—sometimes in combination with the sanxian and the erhu, accompany arias in scenes derived from the repertory of the older classical theater called **Kunqu**, another predecessor of the jingju, which uses the dizi as its principal melodic instrument.

KUNQU
Classical Chinese musical drama.

Kunqu-derived scenes are usually lyrical in nature, and in these scenes the yunluo gong set is also used. The winds are also used to accompany arias derived from folk tunes that have been absorbed into the jingju repertory. Furthermore, the winds play specific named incidental pieces to accompany dances derived from kunqu.

Finally, the big and small suona (oboe) are always used in combination with the percussion ensemble exclusively to accompany arias sung by a chorus. Named incidental pieces specially associated with scenes involving military maneuvers, fighting, marching, hunting, or processions are also played by the suona-and-percussion ensemble.

Only nine basic players are in the jingju ensemble, but the performers, who are versatile, usually play more than one instrument. For example, in the percussion ensemble, the conductor, who plays both the single-headed drum and the clapper, also plays the big or small barrel drum. One person plays the various sizes of cymbals, and another plays the various sizes of gongs. In the melodic ensemble, the jinghu and erhu players also play the big cymbals when the music only involves the wind players, and sometimes they may have to play the suona and the dizi as well. The yue qin and sanxian players also play the suona, the dizi, the sheng, and even the yunluo or the barrel drums.

Vocal music in jingju comprises arias, recitative-like short phrases, and heightened speech, which is a type of stylized stage speech having steeply rising and falling contours that exaggerate the natural tonal contours of the Chinese language, in which the meaning of a word depends as much on its melodic contour and relative tessitura as on its particular arrangement of vowels and consonants. The arias express the lyrical sentiments of the character, whereas the recitative-like phrases and the heightened speech propel the narrative of the dramatic action. Heightened speech is used exclusively by important characters and characters of high social status, whereas everyday speech in the Peking dialect is used by the comics and characters of lower social status. In general, arias, recitatives, and speech are performed as solo numbers, but there are exceptions when these are performed by an ensemble.

In jingju, the aural and visual elements are of equal importance. The conventions require that an actor master highly stylized acting techniques as thoroughly as he or she does singing. Just as knowledgeable Chinese audiences would not excuse bad singing, neither would they excuse bad execution of movements on stage. For a jingju actor, the appearance demanded by his conventional role, his capacity for wearing the costume pertaining to it, and the scores of strictly defined movements and gestures are of vital importance. The actor is the focus of attention, the central point of that harmony of movement, which is the essence of a theatrical performance. The costumes are designed to assist and emphasize that movement, together with instrumental music, speech, and arias, all interdependent on one another.

Such a highly stylized and conventional theater requires an audience that possesses "the art of watching and listening" to appreciate it fully. Unfortunately, in recent decades, audiences have been rapidly shrinking. The conventions of jingju are deeply rooted in an old society based on Confucian moral precepts

Wind chamber and mouthpiece of a Chinese Sheng. *Source*: Philip Dowell/Dorling Kindersley Media Library

PEKING OPERA ARIAS

 **LISTEN**

TRACK 4.3 and 4.4 **Jingju: Narrative Aria, Vocal: Jiang Qiulian and Jingju: Dramatic Aria, Vocal: Qi Puqiang**

ALL JINGJU ARIAS derive from a group of some thirty preexistent skeletal tune-and-rhythm pattern types called *ban* (literally "beat," but best translated as "melody-rhythmic type"). By setting the same *ban* to a different text, a new aria is produced.

Most arias contain a two-phrase unit that sets a rhymed couplet. The constituent lines, which are of equal length, may have either seven or ten syllables grouped into three prosodic units, 2 + 3 + 2 for seven syllables and 3 + 5 + 2 for ten. The melody for each phrase, however, is always arranged in a five-bar structure, juxtaposed with the three-prosodic-units-per-line textual structure.

Defined in terms of their rhythm, tempo, and corresponding dramatic functions, these are the five main aria types:

1. The narrative aria in 4/4 meter and moderate tempo is usually used to provide narration in an unemotional manner (Track 4.3).

TIME	MUSICAL EVENT
0:00–0:02	Brief intro on clapper and drum (*bangu*).
0:02–0:18	Instrumental introduction: Strings (jinghu and yue qin) and *bangu*.
0:18–0:45	Voice enters—follows closely melodic line played by strings, with many sliding "leaps" between tones.
0:46–1:08	Instrumental interlude.
1:08–1:29	Voice returns (2nd verse).
1:29–1:48	Instrumental interlude.
1:48–2:07	Voice returns (3rd verse); fades out [1:57–2:07].

2. The lyrical aria in 4/4 meter and slow tempo is used at lyrical moments and is usually melismatic.
3. The animated aria in measured rhythm, and fast tempo is used to reveal a character's psychological state.
4. The dramatic aria in free rhythm, always accompanied by a steady beat from the clappers and the fiddle, is used to propel the dramatic action or to add tension to spoken dialogue (Track 4.4).

TIME	MUSICAL EVENT
0:00–0:27	Dramatic, nonmelodic introduction called "slow, long strokes" (*man chang chui*) indicating entrance of an important character; with cymbals (*naobo*) gongs (*xiao luo*), with high, rising tone; *da luo*, with low, falling tone); and drum (*bangu*) (builds in intensity to dramatic pause at [0:19]).
0:27–0:44	Strings (jinghu and yue qin) and *bangu* perform instrumental introduction.
0:45–1:11	Character (painted-face role) freely sings short melodic phrases with string and drum accompaniment; brief instrumental interludes "reply" to voice.

continued

TIME	MUSICAL EVENT
1:11–1:40	Gongs, drum, and cymbal—reminiscent of opening pattern, starting slowly and building in intensity; drum alone [1:35–1:39] announces transition to next section.
1:40–1:52	Melodic interlude by strings, clapper, and drum.
1:52–2:05	Voice returns for second verse; track fades [1:57–2:05].

5. The interjected aria, usually very short (only one phrase) and in free rhythm, is sung at a highly dramatic moment as a signal or a call.

These five melody–rhythm types are divided into more than ten categories, each of which has different melodic characteristics. The two most important ones are the xipi and the erhuang, which, respectively, derive from a northern and a southern regional theater. In addition, folk tunes of various regions and arias of kunqu have also been absorbed into jingju.

and political outlook, and these ideals have been thoroughly discredited by the contemporary socialist state. It is small wonder that young people who have grown up in this state find the art archaic and alien; they prefer programs on television and pop music. In recent years, the government has tried to remedy this situation by taking certain reform measures, which include the creation of libretti with modern themes, reorganizing troupes to streamline the companies, giving more financial incentives to able actors, and introducing electroacoustic instruments, but these measures appear to have met with little success.

General Characteristics of Music of the Han People

Although the Han people are relatively homogeneous in their cultural outlook and values, and all of them speak a number of related Sinitic languages that are known collectively as Chinese, the various dialects such as Putonghua (Mandarin), Wu, Xiang, Min, Hakka, and Yue (Cantonese) are mutually unintelligible when spoken. However, the use of a common written language and ideographic writing system enables all literate Chinese to communicate with each other. The existence of many regional styles of Chinese music reflects this diversity, too.

Musically, each major linguistic region possesses its own vocal styles and forms. The major types of vocal music of the Han, such as musical narratives and musical theatricals, have been profoundly influenced by the linguistic characteristics of each region. According to Chinese statistics, there are about 317 regional dramatic genres in China today. Instrumental music is also regional in character; for example, the Jiangnan *sizhu* is predominantly a genre of the Jiangnan region, whereas the Fujian province in the south has its own instrumental ensemble style called the Fujian *Nanqu*, and the Guangdong province in the deep south has its own Guangdong *Yinyue*. Some of the same instruments, however, are used in most major instrumental ensembles, such as the dizi and the yangqin (dulcimer).

Despite the regional differences, some common stylistic characteristics result from extensive borrowing of musical styles from region to region. When a particular regional style such as the famous jingju becomes widely adopted throughout the country, a national style is formed.

The Value and Functions of Music

For centuries, the Chinese have equated enjoyment of music with the natural human desire for aesthetic and sensual gratification such as the taste for food, the need for sex, and the satisfaction of seeing beautiful things. Music has traditionally been treated as one of the component phenomena that make up an environment for living. Thus, music has not only served as a means of expressing emotions such as joy and sadness or as a vehicle for spiritual or religious contemplation, but it has also always been integrated into events such as rituals, banquets, weddings, funerals, festivals, harvest celebrations, and so forth. In addition, music has always been conceived of as an integral part of other performing arts such as dance and drama. Furthermore, reference to some types of music has conventionally been used to evoke certain moods and atmospheres in literature, poetry, and painting. This complex and integral view of music and its functions had already become well established in the Zhou dynasty in the first millennium BCE.

Kong Fuzi, or Master Kong (551–479 BCE), known to the West as Confucius, founded the school of philosophy (popularly called Confucianism) that had the greatest impact on subsequent Chinese thought. Confucius maintained that music has positive and negative powers to stimulate related behavior and desire. Positive music, or *shi yin* (proper sound), features the attributes of harmoniousness, peacefulness, and appropriateness; it is an important educational tool capable of inspiring virtue and appropriate attitudes. In contrast, the music he described as negative, or *chi yue* (extravagant music), had the attributes of inappropriate loudness (like thunder and lightning) and wanton noisiness and stimulated excessive and licentious behavior.

Confucius lived during the end of the Zhou period in a time of constant warfare and chaos. He hoped to restore China to the peaceful feudalism of the early Zhou years, but felt that the only way the hierarchical system could be made to work properly was for each person to correctly perform his assigned role. "Let the ruler be a ruler and the subjects be subjects," he said, but he added that to rule properly, a king must be a virtuous person, setting an example of proper ethical conduct. To Confucius, social stratification was a fact of life to be sustained by morality, not force. He greatly stressed the possibility of remolding men's minds through education (in which music and dance were important parts of the curriculum) and taught that proper inner attitudes could be inculcated through the practice of rituals (which, to be effective, must have proper ritual music) as well as through the observance of rules of etiquette and decorum.

In the twentieth century Mao Zedong (1893–1976), chairman of the Communist Party from 1949 to 1976, like Confucius, viewed music and the arts as important educational tools. But Mao's practical application of this view was vastly different from that of the Confucianists. To Mao, music and the arts were important tools in the propagation of state ideology. Couched in the language of Marxism–Leninism as interpreted by Mao, the state ideology plays a key political role in the People's Republic; it defines, explains, and rationalizes the whole range of human activities and thinking in the society. Endowed with the sanctity of unchallenged truth, the state ideology constitutes the basis and substance of political values and is buttressed by the fullest extent of coercive power inherent in a sovereign political system. Few in China are able to ignore the all-pervasive influence of ideology. Propagation of ideology is a premier function of the Communist Party acting on behalf of the state, and music and the arts are important components of this propaganda machine.

Mao, like Confucius, differentiated proper and improper kinds of music. The proper or "correct" kinds are those that have been sanctioned by the state and that contain "correct" ideological messages. Improper kinds of music (or politically incorrect music) are those that have been construed by the state to contain "poisonous" influence, either from the discredited "feudal" society of the past or from the capitalistic, decadent West, and as such they must be censored or eliminated.

Authorship and the Creation Process

Before the twentieth century, the idea of an original composition identified with a particular person was foreign to the Chinese, and only a few traditional musical pieces had any attributed authorship. The sources for most traditional Chinese music were anonymous folk or popular materials transmitted orally or through written notation in manuscripts or printed music handbooks. In the traditional method of composition, these were rearranged in different ways, resulting in newly recomposed versions of the older models. The rearrangement process, however, is genre specific; that is to say, each genre has its own procedures and rules regarding rearrangements.

Some genres of music require a measure of improvisation during performance, such as adding improvised embellishments in Jiangnan sizhu. By adding improvised embellishments and varying the dynamics and tempi of the music according to established conventions during a performance and, most importantly, by extending or subtracting portions of the thematic materials in a spontaneous fashion, a performer is in fact acting as a composer as well.

With the introduction of Western ideas to China in the twentieth century came the Western musical repertory, compositional processes and techniques, and the idea of composership. Like their Western counterparts, modern Chinese composers regard themselves as individual creators of original music; the idea and emotion associated with a particular piece of music are regarded as the unique, individual expressions of the composer alone.

Amateur and Professional Musicians

Before 1949 the status of a musician was determined by his education and his occupation. Professional musicians, who relied on music for their livelihood and usually had little formal education, had rather low social status, particularly those who performed entertainment music catering to members of the unlettered class. Unlike the professional musician, the amateur, who did not rely on making music for a livelihood but was accomplished in music, well educated, and cultivated, was regarded as the ideal gentleman. In Chinese history, many distinguished amateur musicians such as players of the qin, who usually came from the leisured class, were given high acclaim as musicians and mentioned in historical documents. Records of professional musicians, on the other hand, were few and far between until the twentieth century.

After 1949, the Communist government hoped to create a classless society, and the stigma on professional musicians was removed. For nationalistic and propagandistic purposes, many forms of traditional entertainment music and folk music that had been frowned on by orthodox Confucians in the past were elevated as China's national heritage, as was the status of their practitioners. The government established many modern conservatories, whose curricula included Western art music as well as traditional Chinese music. Distinguished performers of traditional music, both amateur and professional, were hired as equals to teach in these conservatories.

NEW MUSICAL DIRECTIONS IN THE TWENTIETH CENTURY

In 1911, a Chinese revolution overthrew the Qing dynasty. In its place, a Republic was founded by Dr. Sun Yatsen (1866–1925), a revolutionary with liberal ideas who attempted to model the Republic of China (1912–1949) on the constitutional government of the United States. But China was not yet ready for such an experiment, and Sun's effort was largely a failure. However, the establishment of the Republic of China represented a clean break with old values and practices that had existed for millennia, and in this process traditional music was neglected, and a new type of music was born.

At the beginning of the twentieth century, reformers such as Kang Youwei (1858–1927) and Liang Qichao (1873–1929) advocated the establishment of a new type of school that included in its curriculum practical subjects such as arithmetic, geography, knowledge of the natural world, and classroom music. The reformers contended that traditional Chinese music (such as jingju, Jiangnan sizhu, and music for the qin and the pipa) was unsuitable for modern classroom music. Therefore, a new type of school song was adopted whose melodies, at first borrowed from school songs of the West and of Japan, were given didactic Chinese texts to inculcate a new sense of nationalism in young students. By the end of the first decade of the twentieth century, however, Chinese songwriters, many of whom had received some elementary music training in Japan, began themselves to write didactic school songs. The three most notable were Zeng Zhimin (1879–1929), Shen Xingong (1869–1947), and Li Shutong (1880–1942). The songs they wrote were simple and short, with a limited range and a square, march-like rhythm, and they were predominantly syllabic, reflecting the influence of early Japanese school songs. The song texts were simple and direct messages related to patriotism, self-discipline, military readiness, and civic spiritedness. In the decades that followed, the derivatives of these didactic songs became the main musical diet of the majority of Chinese students.

As the new China faced challenges from the West and from Japan in the early twentieth century, protest songs began to be written. In 1914, at the beginning of the First World War (1914–1917), Japan attempted to seize control of China. Immediately, the Chinese people expressed their outrage in protests, demonstrations, and strikes. Songs denouncing Japanese aggression and the weak Chinese government were part of the protest movement and circulated widely in schools, universities, and nationwide workers' strikes and demonstrations. The musical style of these protest songs resembled that of the school songs, but they were set apart by their texts. Whereas the texts of school songs usually expounded the general principles of good citizenship, discipline, patriotism, and nationalism, those of the protest songs focused on the current political issues and used terse, slogan-like language. These protest songs were the predecessors of the later political songs known as Revolutionary Songs, or "Songs for the Masses," which were developed by the Chinese communists.

During the First World War, Japan formed an alliance with Great Britain against Germany, with the ulterior motive of seizing Germany's colony in China, the Qingdao (Tsingtao) peninsula, as its own colony. China entered World War I in 1917 to declare war on Germany in the hope of recovering Qingdao, then claimed by Japan. But at the Versailles Peace Conference of 1919, the victorious Western powers confirmed Japan's seizure of Qingdao. This act engendered a strong reaction against Japan and the Western allies among the Chinese, who used protest songs to stimulate nationalist sentiment. Then on May 4, 1919, this ferment culminated in a mass student demonstration at the National Peking University. This was the first time that the modern educated class made its mark on Chinese politics, and a precedent was set. The political activities and the intellectual currents set in motion by these students developed into a broad national intellectual awakening known as the May Fourth Movement.

The May Fourth Movement affected the development of modern Chinese music profoundly. The hub of the Movement was Beida (National Peking University) under the administration of its remarkable and liberal chancellor, Cai Yuanpei (1867–1940), who fostered freedom of thought and education.

Cai was well versed in the tenets of both Confucianism and Western philosophy, and he wanted to synthesize the Chinese classical tradition and the libertarianism of the modern European West that characterized the May Fourth Movement. When he became chancellor, Cai endeavored to create opportunities for the students to receive an aesthetic education that included music and art, which he maintained were essential subjects in modern education.

Cai felt that the reform of traditional Chinese music was necessary to bring it up to date, by borrowing elements from Western music. In 1916, Cai established an extracurricular music study group at Beida, staffed by both Chinese and Western teachers, which offered students instruction in Chinese and Western vocal and instrumental music; the teachers were also charged with the responsibility of finding ways to modernize traditional Chinese music. This music group eventually was reorganized and expanded to become China's first academic music department. Under the leadership of the composer Xiao Youmei (1884–1940), who was trained in Japan and Germany, this department offered instruction in music theory, composition, and the academic study of music, in addition to instrumental and vocal instruction. Xiao pioneered the reform of Chinese music by incorporating Western elements, notably harmony. In this way, he put into musical practice for the first time the self-strengthening slogan of 1898, "Chinese culture as the essence, and Western learning for practical use."

Another development initiated at Beida that had significant implications for the future development of the field of Chinese musicology was the Folk-Song Campaign. Inspired by the Russian Narodniki Movement of the 1870s, it called for educated youth to go into the countryside to educate the peasants. Following this philosophy, a group of Beida students encountered folk song and folk art (which were considered unworthy of attention by most of the members of the elites of the old regime) and came to recognize their value. These efforts eventually produced the systematic collection and scholarly research of folk song, which laid the foundation for the future development of Chinese musicology.

The May Fourth Movement also affected the development of modern Chinese music by promoting the use of Chinese vernacular language as a written medium of communication in all fields, including scholarship, in place of the cumbersome literary Chinese that had been the language of literature and scholarship for millennia. Using the vernacular, the young writers introduced a new popular literature that emulated Western forms and spread it through numerous periodicals and newspapers. Inspired by this development, some songwriters began to set new vernacular poems to music. One pioneer was Zhao Yuanren (Y. R. Chao, 1892–1982), a naturalized American who was an internationally known linguist and a composer. Combining elements of traditional Chinese music with Western ones such as harmony, Chao wrote songs with vernacular poetic texts and piano accompaniment. He is now considered the creator of the modern Chinese art song.

One of the most enduring aspects of the May Fourth Movement was the change in the ideology of China's educated class, brought about by the attack on Confucian values. Using newspapers and journals such as *The New Youth*, modern scholars condemned as tyranny the subordination of subject to ruler, wife to husband, son to father, and individual to family, all of which were regarded as remnants of a feudal society. Because the traditional Chinese musical theaters, such as jingju, promoted these feudal values, the merit of such theaters became a subject for debate. Some writers advocated the total elimination of traditional theater, including jingju; others advocated reform by emulating the theater of the West. Though these debates lasted only a few years (mainly from 1917 to 1919) and failed to produce any immediate, tangible reform, they did create a general disdain for traditional music and theater among the modern educated class. Moreover, a lingering sentiment for reform of traditional theater never went away, and when Jiang Qing (1913–1991), wife of Mao Zedong, became the cultural dictator during the Cultural Revolution, she drastically reformed jingju by incorporating elements of Western orchestral and harmonic practice into the music, of ballet into the choreography, and of scenic design into the stagecraft, as well as by replacing the traditional stories with revolutionary plots; this reformed musical drama came to be known in the West as "Model Opera."

At the time of the May Fourth Movement, authoritarian parties were proving successful in Europe, most notably in Russia, where revolution had established the triumph of the Communist Party. The success of the Russian revolution and its Marxist–Leninist political philosophy inspired some of the leading writers and thinkers of the May Fourth Movement, who eventually founded The Chinese Communist Party (CCP) in 1921. It became the major opponent to the ruling Kuomintang (KMT, or Nationalist Party), and the two struggled for control of China for several decades.

By 1923 the impact of Marxism-Leninism on Chinese thought and on Chinese arts and music began to be felt as these came to be viewed as political tools for propaganda. The introduction of the "Internationale" to China in 1923, a song closely identified with the European labor movement of the 1890s and with the Bolshevik Revolution in Russia, came to be regarded as the signal of China's entrance into the world communist movement.

In the ensuing years, the increase of Japanese aggression in China stimulated many more protest songs against Japan, and Russian revolutionary songs began to be heard in leftist circles. The war of resistance against Japan from 1937 to 1945 during World War II stimulated a further outpouring of songs with patriotic themes; composers of all political persuasions joined forces to produce songs in support of the war. Through being used in war films, many of these songs became popular with general audiences, and after the establishment of the People's Republic in 1949, the production of thousands of "Songs for the Masses" became one of the important functions of the propaganda machine.

When I was a young student in the PRC in the early 1950s, the sole musical diet for my contemporaries and myself consisted of nothing but "Songs for the Masses." These songs, whose origins may be traced back to Western Protestant hymns and school songs, modern Japanese and Chinese school songs, Chinese folk songs, and Russian revolutionary songs, are short and simple, use the Western, diatonic scale, and have texts that are slogan-like ideological messages of communism and nationalism. We sang these songs in music classes and numerous political rallies and demonstrations, during the labor sessions in the countryside that every student had to participate in, and in our leisure time to amuse ourselves. One of the outstanding examples from the 1950s is "We Workers Have Strength." In the listening example the song is sung antiphonally between solo and chorus, but when sung in the classroom, the students sing the complete song in unison.

LISTENING GUIDE

"WE WORKERS HAVE STRENGTH"

 LISTEN

TRACK 4.5 A "Song for the Masses" composed by Ma Ke

TIME	MUSICAL EVENT
0:00–0:04	Western-style orchestral introduction.
0:04–0:08	Solo vocal line.
0:08–0:10	Choral response.
0:11–0:14	Solo vocal line.
0:15–0:17	Choral response.
0:17–0:25	Chorus sung by all.
0:25–0:36	Rapid back and forth between soloist and chorus.
0:37–0:40	All together.
0:41–0:47	More rapid interchanges between solo and chorus.
0:47–0:51	Final refrain all together.
0:51–0:58	(Track fades as two vocalists begin singing the next verse).

THE RISE OF POPULAR MUSIC

Modern Chinese popular songs, transmitted through recordings, radio, movies, and print, first appeared in Shanghai, China's most cosmopolitan and modern city in the first half of the twentieth century. A port city on the banks of the Huangpu River, an estuary of the Yangzi River, modern Shanghai was built by Europeans in the mid-nineteenth century on a piece of farmland adjacent to the old Chinese walled town. This piece of land had been ceded to the British after the Opium War (1839–1842), and on it the British built a Western-style city to serve as a toehold for commercial penetration to all parts of China.

But China also benefited, for from here Western ideas and culture, including music, as well as technology and modern business practice, were disseminated to all parts of the country. Soon after the establishment of modern Shanghai, people from other North Atlantic countries, such as Germany, France, Belgium, Russia, Italy, and the United States, as well as from Asian countries, such as India, Japan, Thailand, Vietnam, and the Philippines, all came to invest, live, and work, thus contributing to Shanghai's commercial and industrial development and to its cosmopolitan atmosphere.

From the beginning, however, Chinese contributions to Shanghai's development were significant, both in the form of capital investment and of manpower. Large numbers of Chinese workers migrated to Shanghai to seek work in Shanghai's factories, providing a labor pool that fueled the city's industrial development. Many could not find work, however, and the women among the unemployed frequently ended up as taxi-dance girls—women paid to dance with customers at cabarets for a short unit of time—or prostitutes. By the early decades of the twentieth century, Shanghai emerged not only as the financial, industrial, and cultural center of China and Asia, but also became Asia's entertainment mecca and a frontier for jazz in Asia. Shanghai also served as the major distributing center of Hollywood movies in Asia, and it was the home of China's domestic movie industry. Cinemas showing Hollywood or Chinese movies were everywhere. Shanghai became a hot tourist stop, and famous jazz musicians from the United States frequently made a stop in its cabarets, which inspired many aspiring jazz musicians from Japan and the Philippines to go to Shanghai for their first lessons in jazz. Already in the 1920s, the city was home to some twenty domestic radio stations, and the number grew rapidly. It was also home to some major Western-owned recording companies.

The bourgeoisie of Shanghai led a hedonistic life style, as vividly described in a 1930s Shanghai guidebook for tourists:

> Whoopee! What odds whether Shanghai is the Paris of the East or Paris the Shanghai of the Occident? Shanghai has its own distinctive night life, and what a life! Dog races and cabarets, hai-alai and cabarets, formal tea and dinner dances and cabarets, the sophisticated and cosmopolitan French Club and cabarets, the dignified and formal Country Club and cabarets, prize fights and cabarets, theaters and cabarets, movies and cabarets, and cabarets—everywhere, hundreds of 'em!
>
> —*All About Shanghai*, Hong Kong: Oxford University Press, 1983 (1934–1935), p. 73

LIUXING GEQU
Popular song produced in Shanghai since the late 1920s that is a hybrid of various Western and Chinese musical genres. Its lyrics are sung in the Chinese national tongue, the so-called Mandarin.

Shanghai popular song, known in Chinese as "**liuxing gequ**," is a quintessential product of this environment. This song form arose between the world wars, when Shanghai was at its peak. These songs have lyrics in modern vernacular Mandarin—the universal language of modern China—and melodies and rhythms of a cosmopolitan flavor with traces of Broadway and Hollywood hit tunes, jazz, Latin American rhythms such as tango and rumba, as well as of Chinese folk songs, urban ballads, and modern Chinese school songs.

The melodies of Shanghai popular songs were composed by Chinese, but the instrumentation and orchestration in some recordings was the product of a small number of White Russian musicians who had escaped to Shanghai from Russia during the Bolshevik Revolution and worked for recording companies in Shanghai. These composers, Western or Chinese, drew their sound materials from Shanghai's cosmopolitan soundscape and created a huge repertory of infinite variety catering to a diverse Chinese bourgeois audience with a multiplicity of tastes.

The lyrics of the Shanghai popular song were frequently written by noted popular fiction writers and newspapermen of the day. Drawing on their knowledge of and familiarity with the modern metropolis—both its opulent and seedy sides—these lyricists created a kaleidoscopic picture of modern city life and people, rich or poor, often with wit and verve.

Shanghai popular songs served many functions. They were repertory for nightclub singers in cabarets for dancing, accompanied in these settings by jazz musicians, many of whom were Filipinos. They were used as theme songs for Chinese song and dance movies, and through such exposure they were transmitted nationwide. At some radio stations, broadcast recordings of Shanghai popular songs made up the bulk of the programming; some radio programs also featured live performances by pop song stars singing audience-requested songs. And, as a source of individual enjoyment, these songs also were printed in the form of inexpensive, pocket-sized booklets that were distributed in neighborhood newsstands, drugstores, and bookstores.

Recordings of Shanghai popular songs were manufactured and marketed primarily by Western-owned recording companies in Shanghai—companies that employed both Chinese and European staff. The most important manufacturer of these songs was the Pathé Recording Company, which eventually monopolized the market.

Popular Music of Today

After the establishment of the PRC in 1949, Shanghai popular song was censored and denounced as "the dregs of imperialism, colonialism, and capitalism," but outside the PRC, fans of Shanghai popular songs continued to enjoy and circulate them. In the 1980s, the EMI Recording Company in Hong Kong reissued many of them on CDs to satisfy popular demand. Also in the 1980s, as China embarked on economic reform and ushered in a more tolerant attitude toward popular art, a small selection of Shanghai popular songs was allowed to be reissued by the government; the original jazzy accompaniments of many songs, however, were replaced by more insipid and square versions for synthesizer. Although technologically more modern, these new versions nevertheless demonstrated the government's continuing suspicion of the original sounds with their cosmopolitan qualities and association with a discredited era.

Coincidentally, as Shanghai struggled to reemerge as an international city, a Chinese film about colonial Shanghai, entitled *Night Shanghai*, was produced.

LISTENING GUIDE

"YE SHANGHAI" ("NIGHT SHANGHAI")

 **LISTEN**

TRACK 4.6 Performed by Zhou Xuan

ONE OF THE MOST representative Shanghai popular songs is entitled "Ye Shanghai" ("Night Shanghai"); it was the signature song of the most popular star, Zhou Xuan, and ever since its appearance, it has been considered the symbol of colonial Shanghai.

Ye Shanghai

Night Shanghai, Night Shanghai,
A city that never sleeps.
Neon-lights blazing, car horns blaring,
Singing and dancing in blissful oblivion.

Look at her, smiling and welcoming,
Who knows her sorrow and frustration?
Leading a life by night, paying for clothing, food and lodging,

Getting drunk, wasting youth recklessly.
Dawn arriving brings drowsiness, eyes heavy with sleep,
Everyone leaving for home,
The heart churning with the turning wheels,
Then pondering the former night life,
As if waking up from a dream,
Thinking of a new environment.

—trans. Isabel Wong

In "Night Shanghai," a brief instrumental introduction imitates the sounds of car horns and city traffic, after which comes the vocal part, whose diatonic melody is arranged in the **A–A–B–A** scheme followed by a great deal of North Atlantic popular song of the era. The jazz-like accompaniment is provided by a small band with prominent saxophone and piano parts in the rhythm of the foxtrot, one of the most popular dance steps of the time. In the lyrics, every index of modernity is there: automobiles, traffic, neon lights, and cabarets. A lifestyle that typifies Shanghai nightlife is encapsulated: alcohol intoxication, dancing, and the taxi-dance girl—the many nationalities of women selling sex for a living who personified colonial Shanghai.

In the last two lines the concept of a change to a new environment is introduced, and the song ends with the implication that the taxi-dance girl actually left the metropolis for a new environment—presumably the countryside—as if waking from a bad dream. These two lines touched on two recurrent themes in the cultural imagination of modern China—ambivalence toward colonial Shanghai as both a site of modernity and of corruption and destruction, and the other having to do with the city-country antithesis. The city is often presented in literature as a transient place of dislocation and loneliness,

continued

whereas the countryside represents enduring traditional values and a place of continuity. Shanghai popular song truly captures the spirit of its bygone era.

TIME	MUSICAL EVENT
0:00–0:10	Instrumental introduction starts with trumpet fanfare and ends with jazzy saxophone.
0:10–0:27	(A) First verse sung to regular 4/4 accompaniment, 8 measures.
0:28–0:44	(A) Second verse repeats tune with varied accompaniment, 8 measures.
0:45–1:09	(B) Contrasting bridge section, 12 measures.
1:10–1:28	(A) Return to opening melody.

The recording of Zhou Xuan's rendition of this song was used extensively as background music. Obviously, the symbolism of this song for Shanghai has not been forgotten as even a CBS news report attested in 1998. When President Bill Clinton visited Shanghai on June 29, 1998, the CBS report began by showing a nightclub scene with many couples dancing to a female vocalist's rendition of "Night Shanghai."

After 1949, new popular songs somewhat reminiscent of Shanghai popular songs were produced in Hong Kong and Taiwan and were sung by local singers. In the 1970s, however, their popularity in Hong Kong was eclipsed by the rise of Cantonese popular songs known in the West as "Canto Pop," which was inspired by White rock of the 1950s and uses synthesizers for accompaniment.

Meanwhile, in 1979, as China emerged from the ruinous Cultural Revolution, the government attempted to transform its centrally planned economy into one that borrowed some measures of a market economy, and it cautiously began to encourage private enterprises. To attract foreign investment, the government pursued an open-door foreign policy. Political pressure on the Chinese people, which used to be quite severe, became somewhat relaxed, and some influences from overseas were allowed to slip in. Beginning in the early 1980s, pop songs of Taiwan and Canto Pop from Hong Kong took mainland Chinese listeners by storm, particularly among the younger generation, and soon some mainland songwriters began to emulate the style of these imported models.

The transformation and expansion of the Chinese economy also stimulated the growth of China's fledgling popular song industry. Encouraged and controlled by the government until relatively recently, this industry began to recruit and produce its own composers, lyricists, and singers and to manufacture and market its own product. By 1984, Chinese popular music had definitely became commoditized, relying on the government mass media such as radio and television broadcasts and government-sponsored song and dance troupes for its dissemination and marketing, and its dominant concern was profit.

In the ensuing years, Chinese popular music proliferated, grew in strength and complexity, and began to compete for market share with the imports from

EXPLORE

Canto Pop/Mando Pop

Hong Kong and Taiwan. Drawing their musical inspirations directly from North American and European models such as jazz, blues, country, rock, and even Baroque music, new styles like *disike* (disco) and *jingge* (energy song) began to appear and gain widespread appeal.

In 1988, another new style called **xibeifeng** (northwestern wind) became extremely popular; its music is a combination of a disco beat and synthesized accompaniment with folk tunes of the Loess Plateau of northwest China, an impoverished region that had once been the cradle of the Communist revolution. Its lyrics are set deliberately in a simple, unsophisticated, and bucolic language addressing issues of feudalism and backwardness in rural northwest China. These songs were appealing to many urban dwellers, who were overwhelmed by rapid changes and inflation resulting from the economic reform and who yearned for the simpler lifestyle of a bygone time evoked in the folk-like music and simple lyrics of the "northwestern wind."

XIBEIFENG (NORTH-WESTERN WIND)
Popular Chinese song genre of the 1980s and 1990s. It combines a disco beat with Chinese folk music, and its lyrics are deliberately artless and simple.

LISTENING GUIDE

"HAVING NOTHING"

 **LISTEN**

TRACK 4.7 By Cui Jian

ONE OF CUI JIAN'S most popular songs is entitled "Having Nothing," which he delivers using a somewhat rough vocal quality. Its melody is forceful and direct and effectively projects a lyric expressing alienation and discontent.

By maintaining that he has nothing to his name, Cui Jian is rejecting the new materialism and loss of ideals that had swept China beginning in the late 1980s. The collective "you" points to corrupt officials who were unaware that calamity may happen, as "the ground is moving and water is overflowing." "Having Nothing" was a clarion call by idealistic youths, who were in despair in the midst of widespread corruption in the nation, and who were assuming a pose of nonconformity and detached individualism, protest, and rebellion, Cui Jian injected a whole new ethos into China's cultural consciousness, particularly among university students in the late 1980s, which concluded with the antigovernment demonstrations in Tiananmen Square in 1989.

TIME	MUSICAL EVENT
0:00–0:26	Introduction for synthesizer, guitars, bass, and drum set.
0:26–0:42	(A) First verse sung to folk-like melody over continuing accompaniment, 8 measures of 4/4.
0:42–0:58	(A) Second verse to same tune with slightly more active instrumental accompaniment, 8 measures of 4/4.
0:58–1:18	(B) Contrasting 4 measure melody with overdubbed vocal backing. This is repeated.
1:19–1 34	Return of A melody with the addition of a more active role for the drum set.
1:35–1:50	Variation of A melody, now with added flute (xiao) accompaniment.
1:51–2:07	Return of B melody and fade out [2:05–2:07].

Rock Music

Despite their diversity, these many new styles of popular songs, which the government has labeled **tongsu yinyue** (light popular music), have one thing in common: they are produced by a government-sponsored popular music industry, and the messages they impart are sanctioned by the government. In contrast, there is a small group of underground rock musicians who first appeared on the scene around the mid-1980s. Despite the government's disapproval and its efforts to marginalize rock music and musicians, Chinese rock nonetheless was able to not only survive but attract a significant number of devoted young followers from the urban educated circles. The most famous rock musician, Cui Jian, made his U.S. debut in New York in September 1995.

Chinese rock traces its ancestry directly to Anglo-American rock in terms of melodic styles, rhythms, performing behavior, instrumentation, and ideology. The rock musicians compose their own music and write lyrics that are intensely personal. Although a majority of the lyrics focus on individual expressions of strong inner emotion, others address contemporary cultural and political issues in a deliberately idiosyncratic and ambiguous language.

Rock musicians and their audience form a tight-knit social group. Concerts, never publicized and usually featuring many bands performing together, are named using the English word "parties." There are now about half a dozen bands in existence. Some label themselves as "zhong jinshu" (heavy metal), and others call themselves "benke" (punks).

MUSIC FOR AND BY MINORITIES

The relationship between Han and non-Han people in the PRC is complicated. Although in recent years the prevalent chauvinistic view of the Han, which tends to regard cultures of non-Han nationalities as somewhat inferior, has abated because of the increasing integration of non-Han nationalities into mainstream Han society. A sense of superiority among the Han, however, still lingers. In fact, through the centuries, Han culture has been much enriched by non-Han culture. This dialectic of power relationships between the Han and non-Han is well reflected in the musical domain.

For a long time the Chinese empire aimed merely to politically control the minorities in its territory and did not try to interfere with their culture and customs. By the time the modern Chinese Republic was established (1911–1949), however, the Republican government, influenced by Western concepts of the nation–state and nationalism, changed the policy toward the minorities to one of aggressive assimilation. The situation changed somewhat under the PRC, which recognized many more official national groups and proclaimed a commitment to protect their rights. But despite this new rhetoric and some real attempts at change, the PRC government neutralized its effectiveness by drawing on Marxist unilinear revolutionary theory, by which the Han were

TONGSU YINYUE (LIGHT POPULAR MUSIC)
Chinese popular music of the 1980s and 1990s.

EXPLORE

Chinese Rock

viewed as more advanced in terms of political, economic, technological, and cultural achievements. It thus produced a pseudotheoretical justification for the Han to control and to "help" the minorities.

In the musical domain, the discourse of this power relationship was reflected in the emergence, from the 1950s, of a huge body of revolutionary "Songs for the Masses" based on minority styles as a propaganda tool for legitimizing the PRC among the minority populations and fostering their loyalty to the regime. Distributed through the mass media to the entire nation, these songs were frequently performed by singers selected from the minorities and trained to sing with a vocal timbre that the Chinese call "*mei sheng*" (meaning "beautiful sound," a term translated from the North Atlantic term *bel canto*). This kind of North Atlantic-inspired singing style fostered by conservatories came to be regarded as a cultivated professional vocal style. Thus the PRC has created an official representation of what it regards as authentic minority music, which the majority of Chinese people have come to accept and enjoy as such. Mongolian style songs of this sort are particularly popular because of their haunting tunes, and a typical song lyric would usually mention the clear blue Mongolian sky with fluffy white clouds and galloping horses in the great grassland; the Mongolian people, living a happy life, proudly singing praise to the regime and the leadership of Chairman Mao Zedong and the Chinese Communist Party.

During the ten years of Cultural Revolution, music not sanctioned by the radicals who controlled the government was silenced, and this included the previously sanctioned official representation of minority music. Almost everyone suffered during the Cultural Revolution, but minorities suffered most, and this ultimately awakened their ethnic consciousness. When the turmoil ended and the leaders of the Cultural Revolution had been discredited, a new leadership adopted a more conciliatory and sensitive attitude toward minorities and in 1982 enacted more liberal laws to protect minority rights. This greatly encouraged minorities to reaffirm their ethnicity with more determination. Such a development was best reflected by the appearance, in the late 1980s and thereafter, of new cassettes and CDs of pop songs produced by minority singers, who now sang in their own regional vocal styles. This effort was also made possible by the availability of inexpensive means of reproduction and marketing, which has enabled minorities to produce their own music.

Music Performance in a Mongolian Nightclub

Earlier I mentioned that I sometimes visit a Mongolian nightclub in Beijing with my friend, Professor Chogjin, along with his journalist wife, Tana, and a few Han friends who are colleagues of Professor Chogjin at the Chinese Academy of the Social Sciences. The nightclub is situated in a spacious street in the Beijing diplomatic quarters. The inside of the nightclub is decorated like a Mongolian tent known as a yurt (a Turkic word taken into English from Russian; the Mongolian term is *ger*) with Mongolian carpets, furniture, and décor.

The waiters and waitresses are dressed in traditional Mongolian costume, a baggy shirt with high collar belted at the waist and loose trousers tucked inside high leather boots.

On one of our visits to the nightclub, while seated around a low table enjoying our food and drink, we chatted jovially in English and Putunghua. Like most educated people from the Inner Mongolia Autonomous Region (in the PRC), Chogjin and Tana are fluent in both Mongolian (belonging to the Altaic language group) and Putonghua of the Han people. A Mongolian colleague of Chogjin in the Academy named Professor Naqin came to join us and told us that we were in luck because Qifeng was singing that night. "Who is Qifeng?" I asked. Naqin pointed at a big poster on the wall, which was a close-up photo of a startlingly handsome young man with long hair, and said: "That's him, the most popular Mongolian pop singer today!"

As we waited for that night's special attraction, a group of young singers stepped onto the stage and began to sing Mongolian pop songs and folk songs to the accompaniment of instruments such as electric guitar and bass guitar, synthesizer, trap set, and several Mongolian instruments such as the *topshuur* (a two-stringed pluck lute), the *morin huur* (a two-stringed spike fiddle with horse-head decoration on the top of the neck), and the end-blown flute *tsuur*. Included in their presentation was a uniquely Mongolian singing style known as *höömii*, which produces a whistle-like melody by changing the shape of the oral cavity to reinforce selected overtones of a sung drone. Popularly known as throat singing in the North Atlantic, the effect of this music is ethereal, and we in the audience stopped talking and listened attentively. Gradually the place filled up, and soon there was standing room only. Most guests seemed to know one another and exchanged greetings in Mongolian. I said to Chogjin and Naqin: "Popular place, this." Chogjin nodded and smiled: "Yes, we come here to be Mongolians. We need to escape from you Han brothers and sisters every now and then." Chogjin continued: "We Mongolians are very hospitable and always welcome our guests with liquor and songs. Now to be a gracious guest you must drink up. *Gan bei* (bottoms up)!" Mongolian liquor, served in small shallow cups, is rather strong. It is either made of a combination of grains (barley, sorghum, wheat, and corn), which is clear, or of fermented mare's milk, which has a milky color. Jovially we toasted each other while eating noodles and boiled mutton.

Finally, a hush descended on the place as Qifeng entered dressed in a fashionably casual way with a loose shirt and a pair of faded jeans. He first looked around, nodded to a few people, and then came over to give Chogjin a hug and to share a toast. Only then did he walk toward the small stage. Curious about this respectful display, I asked Chogjin about it, and Naqin explained: "The local Mongolians respect him for his scholarly accomplishment and for his ability in gaining respect from the Han academic world!"

As Qifeng stepped onto the stage, the audience applauded. The synthesizer player already on stage started a soft introductory passage, and Naqin whispered to me: "He is going to sing his signature song entitled 'Blessing to My Dear Mother,' which made him a star." Included in the accompaniment were the guitars, the plucked lute (*topshuur*) the flute (*tsuur*), and the horse-head fiddle (*morin huur*). Qifeng's voice was natural, mellifluous, and expressive, quite unlike the nasal and tight-throated timbre used by most current Han pop singers. Although the melody was pleasingly sentimental and simple, Qifeng added lots of subtle ornaments that gave it a distinct Mongolian flavor. He sang two stanzas of the song, the first in the Han Chinese language (-*putonghua)*, and the second in the Mongolian language. A vocal interlude separated the two stanzas, which was sung in the Mongolian Long Song (-*urtyn duu*) style. A Long Song is a traditional Mongolian genre, which in 2006 was declared by UNESCO to be a Masterpiece of the Oral and Intangible Heritage of Humanity. In a traditional setting a Long Song is accompanied by the *morin huur*. But in Qifeng's rendition, the passage was accompanied by the whole ensemble, plus the trap set, giving it a contemporary popular urban twist.

In a Long Song the melody, sung with open throat and at full volume, progresses in wide skips and unfolds in a continuously linear and pulseless fashion; it is characterized by rich and frequent use of ornamentation and of falsetto. Individual pitches, phrases, and text syllables are indefinitely elongated, giving it a rhapsodic quality. It is a demanding vocal style, in which the musical qualities overshadow the text. A Long Song, sung by a skillful vocalist like Qifeng, can transport an audience to the wide-open spaces of the Mongolian steppes and serve as an important reminder of "home" for the urban Mongolians who came to this nightclub for just such an experience.

After hearing this song, I asked Chogjin why "mother" was used to represent Mongolia, when I had the impression that Mongol culture is rather male centered. Chogjin said: "Mother is a very important figure in Mongolian culture. She is the custodian of our legends, customs, genealogy, and history. Mongolian written script was invented very recently, and before that, our history was transmitted orally, and installed in our mothers' memory. The men were too busy engaging in warfare or animal husbandry. "Mother" is therefore an all-embracing metaphor for the land of the Mongols—not just modern Inner Mongolia, which is now an Autonomous Region in the PRC, or the modern Republic of Mongolia, previously known as Outer Mongolia, but the vast land of Genghis Khan's Mongols. The reference to the endless grassland, the soaring eagle, the nostalgia for a nomadic way of pastoral life, articulate a Mongolian consciousness, which to me is very real. The inclusion of the Long Song style is unprecedented. Partly because few Mongolian pop song singers can sing it, Qifeng learned it from a famous old Long Song singer. It is unprecedented also because Long Song is so unmistakably Mongolia—the yodeling style evokes a life out-of-doors in the grassland. To be frank with you, this very soft and mellow song is chock full of Mongolian nationalistic sentiments. It would not have been tolerated by our Han brothers even ten years ago! Naqin can tell you more about Qifeng because he is part of Qifeng's team. He writes some of the lyrics and is one of his producers."

At my urging, Naqin provided me with the following information: "Qifeng is the first Mongolian popular singer who has not received conservatory style vocal training in the so-called "mei sheng" (bel canto) style, whereas most of the popular Mongolian singers today sing in this academic style. He sings with his natural voice and utilizes indigenous Mongolian folk song vocal style. He is a skillful Long Song singer, having studied for a long time with the King of Long Song, Sularong (transliterated name). He could belt out an extended Long Song whenever he feels like it. In the late 1990s Qifeng first attracted national notice by making an appearance on the government-owned Central Radio Station in Beijing. When he appeared on the government radio and TV stations in 2004 and sang "Blessing to My Mother," it made him a household name, and his records sell in most popular recording stores in some major cities. Since then, he has decided to run his own business, becoming a private entrepreneur. He has gathered around him a group of good friends, both Han and Mongolian, who take care of publicity, arrange for public concerts and recording sessions, and write songs and lyrics for him. In 2004 and 2005 Qifeng sold 200,000 CD copies, which is considered a big figure in China's private enterprise pop music market today. Qifeng's audience comes not only from Beijing, but from other big coastal cities as well, particularly in the south, such as Guangzhou and Hong Kong. Members of his audiences include students and especially businessmen and taxi drivers; most of whom are Han. Of course we Mongols love his songs and are very proud of him, but the Mongol song market is too small. We need to attract the Han market, and therefore most of his songs are sung in Han Chinese, but he is fluent in both the Han and Mongolian languages."

I then asked: "Besides selling records, does Qifeng perform in public?" Naqin replied: "Oh yes, Qifeng constantly travels and gives concerts, usually on temporary outdoor stages, just like those of Western rock music concerts."

"Who decides what song to write, and how a song is produced?"

"Qifeng keeps close ties with his listeners, who write to him telling him what kind of songs they like most. Keeping their requests in mind, we write the lyrics first, and then a composer sets the lyrics to music."

The next day, I went to a record store in Beijing and asked for Qifeng's CDs, which are readily available. I asked the salesperson whether she liked Qifeng's music, and she replied affirmatively and enthusiastically: "Oh yes, we young people like his music very much. It is so different, and so Mongolian. His songs take us away from this congested and polluted city into the clear blue sky of the Mongolian grassland!" I asked: "Have you been to Mongolia?" She said: "Not yet, but I will, one day." I reflected that this is certainly a far cry from the attitude of the older generation. Twenty years ago when I told a friend I was going to the grassland of Mongolia, she said with shock and dismay, "What? You are going to that wilderness!" Now, through the medium of its haunting melodies and new modes of production, Mongolia has acquired new chic in the Chinese imagination.

In this chapter we have touched on only a fraction of China's enormously varied and valuable musical treasures, many of which have undergone traumatic periods of change, suppression, revival, and renewal in the twentieth century. When I think about the limited musical diet of my high school days in China and compare it to what is once again available today, I am excited by the musical vitality I encounter every time I go back. I feel proud when I see music by Chinese composers on programs of symphony orchestras in the United States or Europe, and pleased when I remember that that UNESCO has recognized the cultural importance and artistic worth of Mongolian Long Song and *Kunqu* opera. We can be assured that music in China will continue to play an important role in the social, political, and everyday world of the Chinese people, as it has been doing for several millennia.

REVIEW CHAPTER RESOURCES

SUMMARY

In our excursions through Chinese musical life we have been reminded that Chinese civilization dates back many centuries and includes many different ethnic groups, cultures, and languages under its umbrella. We have had occasion to encounter key instruments like the qin (zither) and pipa (lute). We've also explored traditional genres of music, including jingju (or Peking Opera), one of China's best-known theatrical/musical styles, featuring elaborate sets and costumes and a richly developed sung repertory. The contexts within which musical performances are held, moreover, led us to investigate traditional venues such as teahouses, where music is played by amateurs and professionals alike. We found that the audience at teahouses comes and goes as it pleases, often talking during a performance. The traditional music played in these venues is often highly improvised, with no announced program.

We also explored the political and philosophical context within which musicians and audiences have had to shape their relationship to performance. So, for instance, drawing on ideas developed within Confucianism, "good music" is understood as maintaining the proper social order and underlining the beliefs endorsed by the state; "bad music," however, leads to improper behavior or to criticism of the status quo. The rise of Communism and the successful 1949 revolution, introduced a new, didactic type of music, expressed well in the many "Songs for the Masses" and meant to instill the government's core message in the citizenry. This music drew on Soviet models. As Chinese society has opened up somewhat following the Cultural Revolution of the 1960s and early 1970s—and this especially in the 1990s and early 2000s—North Atlantic forms of both art music and popular song have become more accepted, though there remains an "underground" of unacceptable musical styles, many of which question the validity of the state's power. Finally, ethnic minorities within China have increasingly found a musical voice through which to assert their unique presence within China.

Though our excursions have been brief, I hope that these encounters with Chinese musical life will inspire you to continued exploration of China's long musical history and its many musical genres, instruments, and ensembles.

KEY TERMS

Dizi
Erhu
Jiangnan
Jiangnan
Jianzipu
Jinghu
Jingju
Kunqu
Liuxing gequ
Pipa
Qin
Ruan
Sanxian
Sheng
Sizhu
Sizhu
Suona
Tongsu yinyue
Wenchang
Wenzipu
Wuchang
Xibeifeng
Yanqin
Yayue
Yue qin
Yunluo

BIBLIOGRAPHY

Anne Birrell, *China's Bawdy: The Pop Songs of China, 4th-5th Century* (Cambridge: McGuiness, 2008); Szu-Wei Chen, "The Rise and Generic Features of Shanghai Popular Songs in the 1930s and 1940s" in *Popular Music* Vol. 24, No. 1 (Jan., 2005), pp. 107–125; Anthony Fung, "Western Style, Chinese Pop: Jay Chou's Rap and Hip-Hop in China," in *Asian Music* Vol. 39, No. 1, [Popular Music in Changing Asia] (Winter/Spring, 2008), pp. 69–80; Rachel A. Harris, *The Making of a Musical Canon in Chinese Central Asia* (Farnham, UK: Ashgate Publishing, 2008); Rachel A. Harris, Rowan Pease, and Shzr Ee Tan, Eds., *Gender in Chinese Music* (Rochester, UK: University of Rochester Press, 2013); Stephen Jones *Plucking the Winds: Lives of Village Musicians in Old and New China* (Leiden: Chime Foundation, 2004); Frank Kouwenhoven, "Meaning and Structure: The Case of Chinese Qin (zither) Music" in *British Journal of Ethnomusicology* Vol. 10, No. 1, Music and Meaning (2001), pp. 39–62; Frank Kouwenhoven, "Transcribing 'Time' in Chinese Non-measured Songs" in *The World of Music* Vol. 47, No. 2, Notation, Transcription, Visual Representation (2005), pp. 137–162; Frederick Lau, *Music in China: Experiencing Music, Expressing Culture* (Oxford: Oxford University Press, 2008); Francesca R. Sborgi Lawson, "Consilience Revisited: Musical and Scientific Approaches to Chinese Performance" in *Ethnomusicology* Vol. 56, No. 1 (Winter 2012), pp. 86–111; Mingyue Liang, *Music of the Billion: An Introduction to Chinese Musical Culture* (New York: Heinrichshofen, 1985); Ivan Mačak, "Questions Arising up from Thinking about Chinese Music," in *Studia Musicologica Academiae Scientiarum Hungaricae* 44, 1/2 (2003), pp. 263–267; Marc Moskowitz, *Cries of Joy, Songs of Sorrow: Chinese Pop Music and its Cultural Connotations* (Honolulu, HA: University of Hawaii Press, 2010); Yang Mu, "Music and Dance for Interment Rituals in a Chinese Village," in *Ethnomusicology* Vol. 56, No. 1 (Winter 2012), pp. 1–30; Lee Tong Soon, "Chinese Street Opera Performance and the Shaping of Cultural Aesthetics in Contemporary Singapore" in *Yearbook for Traditional Music*, Vol. 34 (2002), pp. 139–161; Tsan-Huang Tsai, "Is the Wind, the Banner, or the Mind Moving? The Concept of Body in Chinese Han Buddhist Ritual Performance and Its Musical Practices" in *The World of Music* Vol. 44, No. 2, 2002, pp. 73–92; J. Lawrence Witzleben, Ed. "China," in Robert C. Provine et. al. Eds., *The Garland Encyclopedia of World Music*, Vol. 7: East Asia (New York and London: Routledge, 2002); Isabelle K.F. Wong, "From Reaction to Synthesis: Chinese Musicology in the Twentieth Century," in Bruno Nettl and Phillip V. Bohlman, Eds., *Comparative Musicology and Anthropology of Music* (Chicago, IL: University of Chicago Press, 1991); Isabelle K.F. Wong "The Incantation of Shanghai: Singing a City into Existence," in Timothy J. Craig, Riachard King, Eds., *Global Goes Local: Popular Culture in Asia* (Vancouver: University of British Columbia Press, 2003); Su Zheng, *Claiming Diaspora: Music, Transnationalism, and Cultural Politics in Asian/Chinese America* (Oxford: Oxford University Press, 2010); Su Zheng, *Claiming Diaspora: Music, Transnationalism, and Cultural Politics in Asian/Chinese America* (Oxford: Oxford University Press, 2011).

DISCOGRAPHY

General *Anthology of the World's Music: The Music of China*, Vol. 1: Chinese Instruments, ed. and with notes by Fredric Lieberman (Anthology); *Chine Populaire, Musique Classique* (instrumental music) (Ocora); *Chinese Classical Music* (instrumental) (Lyrichord LL 72).

Jingju *The Chinese Opera* (Lyrichord LLST 7212 sides A & B); *The Peking Opera* (Seraphim SER 60201 sides A & B); *Ruse of the Empty City* (Folkways FW 8882 sides A & B); *Traditional Peking Opera* (Folkways FW 8883 sides A & B).

Kunqu Youyuan Jingmeng (A Dream in the Garden) (Art Tune Co. CO 228 & 229); *Kunqü Changduan Xuancui* [Selections of Well-known Kunqü Excerpts] (in six cassettes, Shanghai Audio Production). *Qin (Ch'in) Music* Ch'in Music of Ten Centuries (Museum Collection Berlin MC7 A & B); *Chinese Master Pieces for the Ch'in* (Lyrichord LLST 7342 A & B); *The Drunken Fisherman* (Lyrichord LL 72 B/3); "Youlan" ("Orchids in a Secluded Valley") (Art Tune Co. ATC 73 A/1); *Wumen Qin Music* (Compact disc, Hugo Production, HRP 712–2).

Pipa Music *Floating Petals . . . Wild Geese*, Lui Pui-yuen, pipa (Nonesuch Explorer Series, H-72085); *China, Music of the Pipa* (Complex Disc, Elektra Nonesuch 9 72085–2); *Ambush From All Sides* (Compact Disc, Bailey Record, BCD 90028, band 1); *Autumn Moon Over the Han Palace* (Compact Disc, Bailey Record, BCD 90029, bands 5 & 6); *Autumn Recollection* (Compact Disc, Bailey Record BCD 90030, bands 6 & 7).

Jiangnan Sizhu "Chunjiang huasyueye" ("The Moonlit Spring River") (Art Tune Co. ATC 16 A/1); *"Sanliu" ("Three Six")* (Art Tune Co. ATC 16 B/1); *"Huanlege" ("Song of Happiness")* (Art Tune Co. ATC 16 A/2); *Popular Jiangnan Music* (Hong Kong; under license from China Records Co., Peking).

Regional Ensemble Music Music of Amoy (Art Tune Co. AST 4002 A & B); *Shantung Music of Confucius' Homeland* (Lyrichord LLST 7112 A & B); *Chinese Masterpieces for the Erh-hu* (Lyrichord, LLST 7132 A & B). *"Songs for the Masses"* The East Is Red (China Records M 982); *Commune Members Are All Like Sunflowers* (China Records M 2265). *The Legendary Chinese Hits* Vol. 5 Chow Hsuan, EMI FH81005 2.

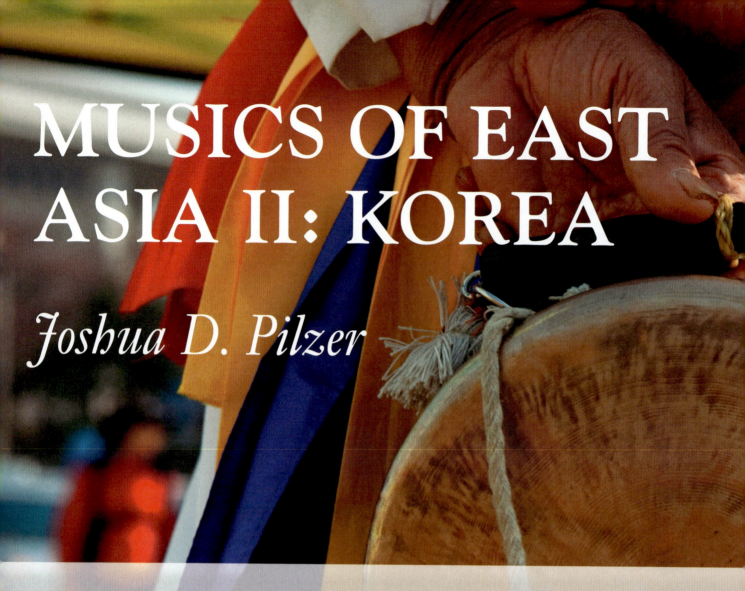

MUSICS OF EAST ASIA II: KOREA

Joshua D. Pilzer

WATCHING THE WORLD CUP IN SEOUL

On the evening of June 17, 2010, there are around 100,000 people in Seoul Plaza, outside Seoul City Hall. This is the center of the city, Korea's epicenter, a megalopolis of thirteen million inhabitants. Massive events of all sorts—protests, celebrations—have been held around here throughout modern Korean history.

We are here to watch South Korea play Argentina in the 2010 World Cup, on a giant Jumbotron. There is a stage set up to the side of the screen, and an MC. As the game starts the viewers begin to sing well-known soccer chants: "Oh, victorious Korea," "Daehan minguk" (the formal name of South Korea), and others. The chants are often initiated and led by the MC, but sometimes they begin somewhere in the crowd. At a particularly unfortunate moment for the team, the MC—looking to boost morale—leads the crowd in a rock version of Korea's

most famous song and unofficial national anthem, the "new folk song" (*sinminyo*) "Arirang."

When the game is over and lost, people cluster round to raise their spirits through music. The chants continue; a Western-style marching band comes to the fore, as well as a pop dance group, a club from a Seoul university; and when everything else is fizzling out a group of young Korean men come forward playing Brazilian *samba batucada*, an instance of Korea's assimilation of global soccer culture and of millenary South Korean multiculturalism.

Korean soccer culture and music are unsurprisingly deeply transnational, yet also profoundly preoccupied with defining and presenting "Koreanness" both to Koreans themselves and to an international audience. In this way Korean soccer

Seoul Plaza World Cup Soundscape. *Source:* Provided with permission of Joshua D. Pilzer

culture and its music are nicely representative of the quest for Korean national identity. The idea of national identity comes from abroad, and only makes sense in the context of a global system of nation-states. This *paradox of the transnational and the national* is a driving force in Korean musical culture. Prominent traditional percussionists claim to have created the national name chant ("Dae-han min-guk") in the spirit of traditional rhythmic patterns; but it is an appropriation of the UK Champions league's "We Are The Champions."

The World Cup event reveals another paradox of contemporary Korean life: the tension between *heterogeneity* and *homogenization*. On the one hand, modern Korea is a country characterized by contradiction. There are two Koreas, North and South. There is constant protest and controversy in South Korea, and growing class inequality. In both Koreas intense familialism and factionalism set people, regions, political parties, and businesses against one another in constantly shifting alliances. Yet both Koreas are also characterized by homogenizing social processes—national discourses of ethnic purity and homogeneity; normative genders, sexualities, and social roles; the cosmetic surgery boom in the South; mass culture and ideology in the North; and the standardizing force of the capitals Seoul and Pyeongyang and strong centralized governments. Korean culture in both places assumes—often unjustifiably—unity of purpose, and a unity in shared ethnicity and citizenship. The World Cup soundscape is a similar mass of contradictions, a vocal, musical, media display of unity and difference, order and chaos.

Most importantly, the World Cup festivities and their soundscape are a dream, a work of *imagining* the community that is the nation-state. It is an imaginative rendering of a certain kind of Korean present and future—

**LISTENING
GUIDE**

WORLD CUP

 **LISTEN**

TRACK 5.1 **World Cup Soundscape. Seoul City Hall World Cup Viewing, 2010.
Recording by Joshua D. Pilzer**

THE SOUNDSCAPE of the World Cup event is quite complex, including as it does a mixture of
live and recorded sounds, which often imitate one another. Some sounds emerge from the crowd,
whereas others originate on the stage or in the sound booth. The drums are in the crowd, not on the
stage; but there are drum samples played over the sound system as well. The overall effect is to composite
and blur the live and recorded, the staged and the spontaneous, the voices of the powerful and ordinary
people. As a metonym for the social, this soundscape is an attempt to make a coherent sound picture
of a heterogenous, complex social life. In so doing, it seamlessly integrates the national, the foreign,
and the transnational.

TIME	MUSICAL EVENT

Example 1

00:05	After a snare intro, the "We are the Champions" soccer chant is heard on the (live) bass drum.
00:07	The crowd answers responsorially with "Dae-han-min-guk," the formal name of South Korea.
00:28	After a *nanta* drumroll which completes the chant, we fade out and move to example two, a few minutes later.

Example 2

00:29	A recording of the familiar chant/rhythmic pattern in transnational sports, "Let's go!" which the crowd sings along to.
00:36	This figure is overlayed with a non-lexical (textless) chorus of "Arirang," a recorded track of an all-male chorus, dripping with testosterone. The crowd—composed almost equally of female and male participants—sings along, and the effect is to blur the lines between recorded and live voices. The song is presented in a four-beat rock version, not its original triple meter (see listening example 2, 1:17–2:01).
01:03	The recorded rock band kicks back in and the (texted) chorus of "Arirang" begins.
01:08	At the end of the first line of the chorus, the group and the recording answer themselves responsorially with "Dae-han-min-guk" (the formal name of South Korea).
01:45	We hear a plastic *vuvuzela,* the South African noisemaker, popular in global soccer cheering culture and Korean sports cheering in general.
01:47	A cheer to the tune of "When the Saints Go Marching in."

successful, dynamic, united if clamorous, at ease with its past and ready for a glorious future. This dream stands in stark opposition to the anxieties of modern South Korea—about economic instability, precarious international relations, the fragmentation of modern life, and the many patterns of social marginalization. Similar dreams of unity and flourishing are present in much of Korean and other musical cultures. If we sympathetically examine the dream and its music, look for its origins, peer into its shadows, and map its fault lines, then we will arrive at a sophisticated understanding of modern Korean life and its music, although one which is prone to its own kinds of dreaming.

HISTORY

Given the frenetic scene we have just witnessed, and the overwhelmingly urban image that Korea and most East Asian countries present internationally nowadays, it might be surprising to learn that at the close of the last Korean dynasty in the late nineteenth century, Seoul's population was less than 200,000. The urban population of the (then united) country accounted for less than 5 percent of the total of just over ten million people. Seoul is now a city of around thirteen million people, about a fifth of the inhabitants of South Korea. The urban population of South Korea is somewhere above 80 percent. The dynamic, urban, frenetic country is decidedly new.

People have lived in the Korean peninsula since prehistory, but the modern ethnicity known as "Korean" came together throughout the first millienium BCE and the first milllenium CE. The Korean language reflects the Northern wave of migration through the Korean peninsula to Japan, bearing trace resemblances to Mongolian and sharing a nearly identical grammatical structure with Japanese. The predominant religion on the Korean peninsula was shamanism until the middle of the first millennium CE, when it was supplanted (but not eradicated) by Buddhism, imported from Former Qin China (351–394). The Korean peninsula was essentially a collection of rival kingdoms until the Silla Dynasty unified most of the peninsula for the first time with Chinese assistance (668–935 CE). Its rule was supplanted by the Goryeo Dynasty (936–1392), which encompassed the Mongol invasion of the peninsula (1231–1259). In 1392 the Joseon Dynasty began, and its neo-Confucian government held power until Japanese colonialism in 1910.

There are a few points to bear in mind as we get to know Korean music that emerge from a consideration of Korean history pre-1910. First is the distinctness of topography, social life, culture, and music in each of Korea's many regions. All of these dynasties drew the bulk of their leadership from the Southeast; and from the Goryeo Dynasty onwards located their capitals in the central-western regions of Korea. The Southwest and Northeast, therefore, were relatively disempowered. Second is the influence of China. Since China helped the Silla Dynasty unify the peninsula in the seventh century CE, Korea long maintained formal relations of fealty to the Chinese Emperor—much longer than Japan, which has long had its own imperial tradition. Only in 1897 did the

Korean king declare himself an emperor, and that only for the few years before the Japanese colonization of Korea in 1910. This ideology of fealty, called *sadae*, "serving the great," meant on the one hand a long legacy of Chinese cultural influence, and on the other a relative lack of Chinese intervention in Korean government and society.

One of these impacts of Chinese culture has to do with the general and deeply hierarchical organization of Korean society: Korea, like China, was not feudal—based primarily on an aristocracy and a peasantry, with their corresponding court and folk musics. It was what is often called an "**agrarian bureaucracy**"—with a large bureaucratic class between the aristocracy and the various lower classes. By the Joseon Dynasty (1392–1910), Korean society was divided into an aristocracy (*yangban*), a bureaucratic middle class, a common class (*sangmin*), a lower class of "vulgar commoners" (*cheonmin*), and a class of untouchables (*baekjeong*). Many of these two lower classes were slaves, although slave status was not as hereditary and permanent as in other places in the world (such as the Americas). Each class had associated genres of music, and so hierarchy and genre in Korean traditional music are wickedly complex. This means that the terms "classical" and "folk music," so conventional in describing world musics, are wholly inadequate to the description of taxonomy in Korean music (they turn out to be inadequate almost everywhere, including in the West).

The third characteristic to bear in mind is the growing isolation which cut the Korean peninsula off from the rest of East Asia and the world in the late second millennium, prior to its "opening." The Joseon Dynasty grew suspicious of China after the onset of the Manchu-ruled Qing Dynasty in 1644. Joseon began to emulate the Chinese past and not its present, and the Korean peninsula became more and more isolated from its neighbors. Neo-Confucianism—a strict Confucian revival emphasizing hierarchy and filial piety—was in the ascendancy. This long period of relative seclusion accounts for much of the uniqueness of the Korean musical genres that we will encounter in this chapter; this radical difference among countries in East Asia is also why there is no "East Asian Musics" chapter in this textbook.

Fourth, Korea was characterized by religious syncretism, a multiplicity of interrelated religions. As dynasties gave way to others religions and philosophies—shamanism, Taoism, Buddhism, and Confucianism—layered on top of one another and intermingled, never really supplanting one another. This religious complexity left a profound stamp on Korean music and culture in the form of a deep heterodoxy. Finally, compared to other East Asian regions, the Korean peninsula was, for much of the first and second millennia until recently, characterized by relative political and social stability, and such stability made conditions ripe for certain kinds of cultural invention.

This relative stability meant that the radical upheavals of the twentieth century would cause great shock across the Korean peninsula. The mid-nineteenth century saw the major East Asian countries give way, one by one, to Western colonial pressure for international trade and exchange. China and Japan signed unequal treaties with Western powers in 1842 and 1854, respectively. After holding out for several decades longer against colonial pressure from

AGRARIAN BUREAUCRACY
A term used to describe the social structure of pre-20th century Korea and China, denoting a complex hierarchy of farming classes, administrative classes, elites, and various outcastes.

France, the United States, Russia, and Japan (who had jumped on the band-wagon of colonialism with remarkable speed), Korea gave into Japanese pressure and signed an unequal trade agreement in 1876. The Korean peninsula continued to be a warring ground of Russian, American, and Japanese colonial interests, however. Cultural importations of all sorts began, and military marching bands, Christian hymnody, Western popular musics, and Western music education and compositional technique came to Korea around this time. The last king, Gojeong, instigated a wide range of modernization projects. Despite this, the country was unable to rebuff the power of colonial interests, and Japan annexed Korea in 1910.

Modernization continued under Japanese colonialism in a profoundly colonial way, as Korean transportation systems developed, the country was radically industrialized, and the population was mobilized for the profit of the Japanese empire. Even more than the loss of national sovereignty, the often-forcible human displacements of the colonial era—for labor and war—would leave profound scars on Korean people and on Korean national consciousness. The mobilization of the population resulted in Korean diasporas in Japan, Soviet Central Asia, and Japanese colonial Manchuria, now Northeast China.

Japanese colonialism in Korea ended in 1945, with the end of the Asia-Pacific War (1931–1945), and Korea—despite having been a victim of the war—was divided into two protectorates, a Soviet-stewarded North and an American-occupied South. Both neocolonial powers laid the groundwork of respectively socialist and capitalist states; and the peninsula erupted in civil war—the Korean War—in 1950. The war never formally ended; hostilities ceased in 1953 with an armistice agreement. South Korea was governed, in the main, by authoritarian, aggressively development-oriented governments under the influence of American Cold War political pressure. The country developed an intensely export-dependent economy, which would go a long way toward explaining the state's preoccupation with identity and image. Long-standing movements for democratization, unification, and labor rights reached critical mass in the 1980s, and the authoritarians were forced out. The first free and direct presidential election in the country was held in 1987. The South Korean economy boomed throughout the 1990s, until the Asian Financial Crisis of 1997. An International Monetary Fund bailout the following year ushered in a new era of inter-national finance, neoliberal national flourishing, and runaway economic inequality. North Korea remains the South's poor, hermetic sibling, possessed of a relative political stability that puts the lie to the prevailing Western idea that the country is irrational and on the brink of collapse. The Cold War, which was over in most places in the early 1990s, continues in the Korean peninsula to this day. Both countries and their cultures are intensely militarized. In the South, the cultural influence of Japan was replaced by that of the United States. Large Korean diasporic communities sprang up in the United States and elsewhere throughout the English-speaking world. Among the elite and the poor, Christianity grew dramatically. All of this change has produced a rather profound anxiety in South Korea about the nature of Korean tradition and modernity; we shall see below the impact this has had on musical practice.

The turn of the third millennium saw the rise of a wave of interest in Korean culture in Japan, Taiwan, China, Southeast Asia, and beyond, dubbed the "Korean Wave," which heralded a new place for South Korea, anyway, in global public culture.

THE SOUTH KOREAN ROAD TO TRADITION AND NATIONAL CULTURE

Until the twentieth century, the Korean peninsula, like most other places in the world, was made up of people preoccupied with local concerns. Koreans more strongly identified as commoners, aristocrats, or other class- or vocationally-based identities rather than identifying as "Korean." The onset of Korean colonial and post-colonial modernity brought with it modern notions of citizenship, national systems of education, print media, radio, and other mediums that promoted national consciousness. In the post-colonial period, the Korean states, like many other post-colonial nations, took a pronounced interest in deciding how to represent themselves nationally and internationally.

This interest was fueled by the massive transformations and perceived cultural loss of Korean traditions in the twentieth century, and the South Korean nation-state in particular would prove anxious to define, preserve, and perpetuate its traditions, which had grown unfamiliar to most of its citizenry. As part of this, in South Korea various cultural institutions were established to codify and promote so-called national traditions. A courtly institution dedicated to the promotion and preservation of Korean imperial court music and dance was remade in mid-century as the Gungnip Gugagwon, literally the "National Institute for National Music." The name—and the current English name, the National Gugak Center—include the neologism for Korean traditional music, "national music" (*gugak*), born in the modern era and patterned after the Japanese *kokugaku*, which uses the same Chinese characters. At first, the Center was dedicated exclusively to the music and dance of the court and aristocracy, as befitting a state that stressed its connection to the culture of the elite as demonstration of its natural inheritance of the long political traditions of the Korean kings. In the late 1960s the Center began to include musics from other traditional classes; this initiative toward plurality emphasized the institute's connections to "the people," and argued for the coherence of Korea as a country historically. This involved the sleight-of-hand gesture of identifying "the people," the citizenry of the modern South Korean nation state, with "the folk," the commoners of traditional Korea. Such canonizing gestures also looked to folk culture as a means of claiming ownership of the profound connections to the land that agrarian commoners historically cultivate.

At around the same time, in the early 1960s, the South Korean state began a campaign to create a canon of traditional music, and preserve it against the perceived deleterious effects of the colonial era and rapid modernization in the post-colonial era. A "Cultural Properties" system—also modeled on the Japanese system—was put in place to recognize, support, and manage "national

GUGAK

"National music," a neologism generally used to describe music officially sanctioned as Korean traditional music.

traditions" and culture bearers. Designated masters of traditions, called "Human Cultural Treasures," and their apprentices receive small monthly stipends. The credibility and status bestowed by the designation makes tradition bearers preeminent in their fields, and gives them a tremendous advantage over other practitioners in terms of attracting students, concertgoers, and so on.

The Cultural Properties system and the National Center for traditional music have combined to codify what among the plethora of musics in Korea counts as tradition, and what does not. At the same time they have been instrumental in creating standardized formats for the presentation of Korean traditional music and dance for the Korean public and the international community. In this process of codifying tradition and its modes of presentation, the institutions of "national music" have designed a frozen musical image of "traditional Korea"—i.e., Korea before the tragedies of colonialism and modern war and the massive modern transformations of life. Korean traditions have been notated in Western staff notation, and reproduced by musicians as if they were masterworks of the European classical tradition. This cuts against the traditional flexibility and improvisation of Korean traditional music. These institutions and their subtle programs of national **canonization** and **Westernization** are central to the modern history of Korean traditional music.

Beyond the official spheres of national culture, however, we find Korean traditional music far more open to change, which most of it historically was. Common people continue to transform music to keep pace with the changeability of modern life, to make it suit themselves, and to put it to work in the course of life. We also find traditionalists and revivalists who are attempting to bring back improvisation and flexibility to traditional music.

CANONIZATION
The selection from a broad range of musical practices of a core of sanctioned pieces.

WESTERNIZATION
The variously voluntary and involuntary processes by which so-called non-Western cultures and societies adopt their versions of the qualities of "The West."

"ARIRANG" AND THE AGONIES OF KOREA'S MODERNIZATION

Perhaps no single piece of Korean music tells the story of Korea's fitful modernity more powerfully than its most well-known song, "Arirang," sometimes referred to as "New Arirang," and by other names, which I mentioned in connection with the World Cup event. "Arirang" is a song created in the early twentieth century but one that was inspired by a traditional song, one of many folk songs with the word "arirang" in the title. Such groups of songs with similar titles are common throughout Korea; they came into being as traveling entertainers and other migrants brought songs to different regions, where they remained behind and were transformed into regional versions. There are traditional "Arirang" from almost every region of the peninsula, and each follows the melodic characteristics of its region, which are quite distinct and function as a series of melodic "dialects" that distinguish regional musics.

The modern "Arirang" is modeled after "Jeongseon Arirang," a free-rhythm folk song (*minyo*) from the mountainous Central-Eastern Korean province of Gangwon-do. It, like many Korean folk songs, has a refrain and innumerable verses, which accrue to the song over time as different singers add their own verses. The song is a good example of the flexibility that is one of the most important characteristics of Korean traditional music. It can be modified to suit particular singers, and those singers will choose verses, tempo, and so on based on the occasion and audience. Much of Korean music was historically based in this sort of resolutely social improvisation, and was remarkably changeable in the interests of commenting on the present. "Jeongseon Arirang" is typically sung in a slow, flexible tempo, and can be somber in terms of content, in contrast with other members of the tune family, which can be quite up-tempo and humorous.

"Jeongseon Arirang" came to Seoul in the late nineteenth century, perhaps with migrant laborers, and the pathos of the song made it popular in Korea's uncertain, incipient modernity. A local version arose, which rewrote the melody to suit the scale and mode of Gyeonggi Province, the province surrounding Seoul. This version was adapted by filmmaker Na Un-gyu as the theme song of his 1926 film *Arirang*, one of Korea's earliest feature films. Audiences reportedly sang the song at the end of this silent film, which told the story of a Korean man who goes mad and kills a landlord and a Japanese police officer. The song became associated with the sorrows and psychoses of colonial life. It was quickly recorded by multiple singers, and became one of Korea's first true popular songs, in the sense that popular music is distributed by mass media.

The *sinminyo* (new folk song) genre to which "Arirang" belongs was inspired by a Japanese genre of the same name and basic composition. This genre was an attempt to find a middle ground between traditional musics and Western popular music. The Korean genre represented efforts to absorb venerated musical characteristics of the West—harmony, in particular—in the service of Korean popular music, and thus to help Korea make sense of "the West," via Japan; it also was an effort to find a place for Korean tradition in its burgeoning colonial modernity. The song was such a hit that it was recorded by Japanese singers in Japanese-language versions, and marketed to a Japanese public hungry for exotic representations of the colonies.

The new "Arirang" necessarily differs dramatically from its source tune. It was recorded from the beginning with Western band or orchestral accompaniment. Over time it was sung with progressively less of the melodic ornamentations of central Korea, and in a progressively Western style, with the same vibrato applied to each note. The intervals of the melody were nudged until they fit into a Western five-note (pentatonic) scale: in particular, the third scale degree of the provincial mode, just flat of a Western major third, became a regular Western major or minor third, depending on the version. It was based on relatively few verses, unlike the limitless verses of traditional songs, and thus a process of canonization and standardization was begun.

In recent years in the hallowed halls of national tradition and in the vague spaces of public culture and national consciousness, "Arirang" has undergone a process that we might call Koreanization or "traditionalization," which attempts to remove its patina of modernity through various means and make it sound more ancient and essentially Korean. In doing so, however—in demonstrating such anxiety about colonial modernity, the West, and national

SINMINYO
"New Folk Song," an early 20th-century genre that combined quasi-traditional Korean melodies with Western instrumentation and harmonies.

identity—it remains quintessentially modern. Above all, "Arirang," like the whole *shin minyo* (new folk song) genre and so many other kinds of music in the world in the era of the nation-state, has been nationalized—brought into service of the nation, demonstrating the nation's supposedly immutable essence that is untouched by the history of colonization and modernity.

LISTENING GUIDE

ARIRANG MEDLEY

 **LISTEN**

TRACK 5.2 **1:** "Jeongseon Arirang," performed by Cha Byeong-geol.
2: Yokota Ryoichi, "Ariran no uta."
3: "Arirang" performed by members of the National Gugak Center

THIS TRACK IS a medley of three pieces representative of the historical evolution of this "Arirang."

Example 1 is a version of "Jeongseon Arirang," the source song for the modern "Arirang." This tune has long been used as a kind of melodic material for singers to create verses, composite and borrow verses from other songs. It is a wonderful example of the flexibility long built in to Korean traditional music. The ornamentation, the flexibility, the solo singing—these are hallmarks of traditional Korean song. This version is sung by Cha Byeong-geol, an ethnic Korean living in Northeast China after being relocated there in the colonial period.

Chorus

Arirang, arirang, arariyo,   *Arirang, arirang, arariyo,*
Arirang gogae-reul neomeoganda   *Crossing over Arirang Pass.*

Verse

Musim-han gichaneun nal sireoda no-ko   *Oh indifferent train, you load me on . . .*
Hwangohyang sikiljul-ul wae molleuna?   *Why don't you know to take me home?*

This verse (0:26–0:50) is found also throughout the Korean peninsula. In a seeming paradox, this most traditional of "Arirangs" concerns the modern world. This is because it is traditional for Korean musicians to modify their material to suit the world around them, themselves, and their listeners.

Example 2 (1:17–2:01) is a Japanese version of the "New Arirang," which became popular in the early decades of the 20th century. This 1933 version by the Japanese tenor Yokota Ryo-ichi retains the words *arirang* and *goge* (mountain pass) from the Korean. The chorus says "I cross over *arirang goge*." Note the Western popular orchestral instruments and the harmonization of the verse—interestingly, the melody of the chorus is not harmonized, but presented monophonically. Also, note that it is up-tempo, despite lyrics about lovers parting; and it is firmly in Western waltz time, and meant

continued

to be danced to in a ballroom setting. In short, this is a rendering of a Korean folk song in the popular musical language of the time.

Example 3 (2:02 onwards), a performance from the 1990s of "Arirang" by musicians of the National Gugak Center, provides a remarkable contrast with the other two. "Arirang," is given an ultra-traditional setting, replete with Korean traditional instruments and melodic ornamentation. The traditional three-beat rhythmic pattern *semachi*, in 9/8, firmly replaces the 3/4 waltz time just as the traditional instruments replace the Western orchestra. The tempo is ratcheted down from the pop version, dropping from 137 beats per minute to just 79—the slowness denoting the calm of the past and grace. There is no reference made in the text to the modern world. What we get is the curse of a faithless lover, which has become absolutely canonical in the modern "Arirang," and which we heard in the World Cup recording:

Beloved who threw me away and left
May you only go three miles before your feet start to hurt.

SHAMANIST MUSIC: ROOTS, AND A RESOLUTELY MODERN TRADITIONAL MUSIC

The vagaries and ravages of colonial and post-colonial modernity produced an anxious discourse about culture and roots. One frequent refrain in this discourse is that the indigenous religion, *shamanism*, is the wellspring from which Korean culture sprang. Korean shamanism, as a form of *animism*, holds that matter is imbued with a complex pantheon of spirits. Houses have spirits, as do mountains, bodies of water, and so on. Spirits must be managed properly in the interest of prosperity.

Korean shamanism can be roughly divided into two kinds: ecstatic or spirit-descended traditions, traditional in central and northern regions of the peninsula, and hereditary ones, prevalent in the South and on the eastern seaboard. In the ecstatic tradition shamans are possessed by spirits in shaman rituals, whereas in hereditary traditions shamans act as intermediaries with the spirit world without experiencing spirit possession. In both branches of the religion the majority of shamans are female, although in ecstatic rituals they often wear traditional men's clothing, as they are often possessed by male spirits.

There are many reasons for shamanism's deep place in the national imaginary of Korean tradition and identity. First, shamanism is Korea's indigenous religion, and the oldest and most deeply ingrained in Korean culture. Different shamanisms exist all along the corridor that links Korea with Mongolia and Central Asia, and Korean shamanism demonstrates this cultural affinity. Second, many of the genres of traditional music that became most famous in the twentieth century have origins in or were inspired by shamanism and its practices. This could be evidence that this preoccupation with roots began a long time ago.

SHAMANISM

Typically a form of animism in which ritual specialists channel and manage complex pantheons of spirits and their place in the material world.

A third reason is that shamanism—especially the ecstatic variety—is a religion, which manages a complex and changing pantheon of natural, historical, ancestral, and other spirits, and is therefore always in touch with the present and its many crises, which it seeks to heal or mediate. It can respond to any crisis—from the Asian financial crisis of 1997, to the suicide of former President Roh Moo-hyun (No Mu-hyeon) in 2009, to the tragic sinking of the Sewol Ferry in 2014. Despite the efforts of some in modern Korean society, especially many of Korea's Protestant Christians, to stamp shamanism out, its concern with spirits resonates with the precarious nature of contemporary urban, capitalist South Korea and remains very useful in modern life. As economic life becomes more and more unpredictable, the last decades in South Korea have seen a revival of the shaman tradition. In particular they have witnessed a rise in the practice of ecstatic shamanism; and shamans who practice trance have become popular in the East and South, the traditional strongholds of the non-ecstatic, hereditary tradition. This is why I call shamanist music, despite its deep traditionality, "resolutely modern." It is thoroughly addressed to the present, and changes to accommodate it.

Ecstatic Shamanism: The Poetics of Crisis

In the ecstatic shamanism popular in the central and northwestern regions of the peninsula, one becomes a shaman as the result of contracting a "spirit sickness" (*shinbyeong*); shaman training is a process of learning how to manage this illness, a kind of breach in one's psychological makeup through which spirits can enter. The shaman then goes on to help others manage imbalances in the spirit world, which often manifest as illness or misfortune in the present. They are hired to contact spirits to make tribute to them and ask them for advice and blessings, and they preside over funerals. Throughout rituals, shamans are supported by instrumental accompanists, who also serve as vocal respondents and who may be shamans themselves, shamans in training, or professional male accompanists. They sing choruses, and also shout/sing a complex repertoire of vocal interjections, called *chuimsae*—this sort of vocal response by accompanists is present throughout most genres of Korean music beyond court and aristocratic genres. The art of *chuimsae* reveals that the accompanist is simultaneously a musician and a spectator, blurring the lines between performers and audience. Audience members also contribute these vocal interjections.

Ecstatic shaman rituals can last for several hours or for many days, depending on how much money is spent on the ritual, how many spirits need to be involved, and how long it takes to reach them and how long they stick around. Shamans dress in the clothes of the spirit they wish to attract. Rituals often have a basic macro-structure in which (1) the shaman or shamans purify the ritual space; (2) they make a "road" for spirits to travel to the ceremony and back along; (3) they explain the reasons for the ritual; (4) they invite, receive blessings and advice, entertain and send off spirits, in descending hierarchical order; and feed and ward off evil spirits. Music is present and essential throughout.

Human Cultural Asset Kim Geum-hwa performing a Hwanghae province-style gut (shaman ritual). *Source:* Provided by Dong-Won Kim

This macro-structure is by and large repeated at a smaller level in the individual sections (*geori*) of rituals, which are often but not always addressed to one particular spirit. First, they begin with a short performance by the instrumental accompanists. The hourglass drum *janggo* is requisite; other instrumentalists, whose numbers increase depending on how much money is available, play other drums and gongs, and perhaps (depending on the region) melodic instruments as well. Second, the shaman chants an invocation of the spirit, answered by a refrain from the other ritual participants (musician accompanists, other shamans, and lay people); there may be passages of unison or heterophonic singing as well. Third, she dances as the spirit descends and enters her body, to the accompaniment of the musicians. Fourth, when the spirit arrives there is a section in which people make gestures of reverence, the spirit demands various kinds of entertainment, and gives blessings and advice. Finally there is a chant to send off the spirit, capped with a short dance. The shaman performs feats associated with particular spirits: dancing on large straw cutting blades or drinking excessively without getting drunk in the case of warrior spirits, singing and dancing virtuosically in the case of entertainer spirits, and so on.

EXPLORE

Janggo

The musical accompaniment of ecstatic shaman rituals is based on traditional rhythmic patterns, *jangdan*, like most Korean traditional music. The core shamanist patterns, often in 12/8, with four beats each divided into three, are species of the most common rhythmic patterns in Korean traditional music, which is frequently organized around triple and compound meters. Each has a conventional tempo range, although the breadth of this range varies dramatically from genre to genre. *Jangdan* provide the rhythmic framework for the shaman's improvisations, and the rhythmic propulsion to allow possession and return to happen.

They also, through accelerations of rhythmic patterns, shifts between patterns, and sudden endings, create a sense of the flexibility of ritual time, and a sense of its transformation, a key aesthetic principle in Korean traditional folk music.

Much of Korean traditional music can be thought of as an art of transformation—of time, feeling, content, and so on—especially emotion, or spirit. This is one of the reasons why Korean music is so useful in everyday life—because it can be used to transform isolation into unity, and sorrow into exhilaration and joy. In ecstatic shamanism and in other genres, sequences of rhythmic patterns that create an overall arc of acceleration and emotional catharsis create this sense of transformation. The practice of changing and manipulating melodic modes in the course of performance is another means of creating this sense of transformation.

Managing spirits, coping with the fickleness of life, with accidents, with failures and illness—this is one key usage of ecstatic shamanism. But it is also a means of coping with general social tension, and provides many opportunities for the release of such tensions and the loosening of social rules. The best example, perhaps, is *mugam*, the dance in shaman's clothing. *Mugam* is performed

| **LISTENING GUIDE** | **HWANGHAE PROVINCE SHAMAN CEREMONY** |  **LISTEN** |

TRACK 5.3 Performed by Byeon Jaeseok

A YOUNG MALE SHAMAN, Byeon Jaeseok, practitioner of Hwanghae Province-style shaman ritual, performing the ritual section *sancheon geori*, a rite for mountain deities and other spirits.

TIME	MUSICAL EVENT
00:17	This is the dance and instrumental prelude. Players of *taepyeongso* (double reed conical oboes) and a *janggo* (hourglass drum) are visible in the foreground. The fast 12/8 rhythmic pattern accelerates throughout.
00:57	A section of invocation begins in a ten-beat rhythmic pattern, 2+3+2+3. Byeon sings to the accompaniment of the drum, cymbals, and *piri* (double reed oboe) and *daegeum* (transverse flute), and is answered by a chorus during the short refrains. At 3:08 he continues the invocation as a solo narrative, with only accompaniment by drums and cymbals in free rhythm.
03:56	The solo invocation changes to a non-lexical group refrain at 3:56, which is a brief transition device to a dance of invitation. At 4:47 he returns to invocation, praying for good fortune. At 5:38 the video cuts back to dance, and this is the dance of spirit descent and possession.
06:20	After several sub-sections of invocation and dance, a spirit begins to take hold, and Baek shakes visibly. His dance quickens and intensifies, and he begins to speak in the voice of a god. At 7:29 he continues the god-speak without drum accompaniment. Baek vocalizes in between the registers of song and speech. A colored flag divination dance follows; then the video cuts, skipping the dance of the spirit's return, to further sections of the rite, and we see Baek taking off the costume of a spirit and changing back into the basic attire of the shaman—a woman's dress, worn to attract male spirits.

by non-shamans, almost always older women. These women—often rather conventional elsewhere in life—put on shaman clothing, often the robes of a warrior spirit, and dance with knives, say outrageous things, yell and scream, and flail about. The dance points to the way that ecstatic shaman ceremonies, as places that exist between the present, past, and future, between the living and dead, are marked by a sense of being on the threshold, of being fluid spaces between relatively fixed modes of social being. This atmosphere allows for everyday people to set aside social strictures and express themselves; but it also allows shamans to work great acts of transformation in the fluid spaces in between relatively fixed realms of social life. Shamanist traditions and other ritual behavior the world over are marked by this threshold quality, which the eminent anthropologist Victor Turner called *liminality*.

Shamans themselves, of course, return again and again to this threshold in the course of everyday life, and some may be said to live in these threshold spaces. Shamanist culture has become a place in South Korean society where difference can remain and thrive. Many people of alternative sexualities find a home in shamanism, as do people with marked psychological gifts and differences (although shamans can be remarkably conventional as well). So the liminality principle that is so important to ritual has created a traditional social space for alternative identities; and these people officiate in the realm of the spirit.

Hereditary Traditions, Professional Music, and Spirit Management

The hereditary tradition has an independent history and has suffered a quite different fate. The Southwest of the Korean peninsula is, like the American South, a fertile agrarian region. As this part of the country was traditionally exploited by the centers of power for profit, it developed a rich and complex hierarchical social structure based on farm life, agrarian abundance, slavery, and a large agrarian bureaucratic class and aristocracy. Again like the American South, its peculiar combination of suffering and wealth marked its cultural productivity.

Like so many other things in this intensely hierarchical society, the spiritual needs of the wealthy were seen to by a professional hereditary class of specialists, in this case hereditary shamans. They belonged to the outcaste classes (as did the professional musicians who accompanied them, and professional musicians as a class), and combined great social power with low social status. The shaman ceremonies, which developed under the hereditary shamans, were not based on possession, but on the priestly work of mediating between the spirit world and the living through elaborately structured ceremonies.

Much of the rich legacy of Southwestern shamanism has been eclipsed by the turbulent transformations of twentieth-century Korea. But several rituals remain. Perhaps the preeminent surviving example of this is the cleansing funeral ritual (*ssikkim gut*) of Jindo Island in the far Southwest. The ritual begins in the early evening and lasts until morning, proceeding through myriad

LIMINALITY
The quality of being on the thresholds between states of being, characterized by loosening of social structure and the possibility of transformations such as healing an initiation.

SSIKKIM GUT
A ritual dedicated to assisting a recently deceased spirit in moving on to the next life.

formalized steps that facilitate the deceased's passage to the next world and help the living say goodbye. The shaman dresses in white, in contrast to the colorful costumes of ecstatic shamans. The many sections of the rite are elaborate and interlaced. After a number of beginning and cleansing sections, the rite properly begins. In the first section the body of the deceased is washed and purified for its passage. In the next, the shaman dances and unties knots in a long white cloth: these knots symbolize the resentments and attachments that bind the spirit to this world. Eventually this cloth is revealed as the road that the spirit travels from here to the afterlife. The ceremony culminates with the shaman and her assistants guiding a small, multicolored palanquin carrying the spirit along this road; the ceremony ends with a short closing section.

Throughout, the shaman chants and dances are accompanied by a varying ensemble of musicians, depending on how much money is available to hire accompanists. Instrumentalists divide into two groups: players of percussion instruments and of melodic instruments. The *janggo* hourglass drum, the most prevalent instrument in Korean traditional music, the barrel drum *buk*, and the large gong called *jing* make up the percussion instruments. *Ajaeng* (bowed zither), *piri* (double reed oboe), *haegeum* (bowed two-string spike fiddle), and *daegeum* (large, transverse bamboo flute) are the melodic instruments in current use. They play in a rich, polyphonic texture by which they interact with and support the shaman, and respond musically to one another. Most instrumentalists are also singers, and they switch, at need, between playing and singing. Melodic accompanists are generally professional male musicians, the descendents of the class of hereditary professional musicians and entertainers known as **gwangdae**. These men were also of the "vulgar commoner" class, and often related to shaman families by marriage or otherwise; they fulfilled a great number of ritual and entertainment roles throughout traditional Korean life, to the extent that there are *gwangdae-shin*, entertainer spirits, among the shamanist pantheon.

The structured Jindo funeral rite, although much more predictable than those of the ecstatic tradition, does not have a predictable script or scripted music. Rather the regular structural elements provide spaces of time for improvisation. The basic rhythmic patterns provide the rhythmic framework; and the instrumentalists ebb and flow in response to the improvisations of the shaman, who varies her routine to suit the particular occasion. Thus the musical texture continues to reflect the changeability and complexity of the spirit world and its interaction with our own. This forum for improvisation is one reason why Southwest shamanism inspired so many other traditional genres (see below).

The whole process of Korean modernity, in some sense, if it has created favorable conditions for ecstatic shamanism, has done the reverse for the hereditary tradition by radically undermining and questioning the legitimacy and viability of social class in traditional Korean life. In the mid-nineteenth century the slave registers were burned, and over the course of the late nineteenth and early twentieth centuries, many people worked assiduously to improve their social standing and shake off the stigmas of low class status. This included many descendants of shaman and shamanist musicians. Throughout

GWANGDAE
Professional male entertainers omnipresent in the musical landscape of 19th-century Korea.

the twentieth century the number of hereditary shamans practicing throughout the Southwest has steadily decreased, and they have often been replaced by ecstatic shamans. Ecstatic shamans have their own kind of intensely practical, spirit-focused musical and improvisational abilities, which contrast with the more aestheticized chanting and music of the hereditary traditions; and so the tradition is slowly changing into something more akin to its Northern cousins.

Due to the somewhat marginal and suspect status of shamanism in Korean life throughout the twentieth century, the government was slow to seek to the preservation of shaman traditions through the "Intangible Cultural Properties" system. But in the 1980s it began to designate shaman ceremonies as Cultural Properties; the Jindo ritual was one of the first to be awarded this status. In the Cultural Properties system, one or several individuals or groups are chosen to be culture bearers. Because of the social status conferred by the system, this small sample rises to the top in terms of ability to impact the tradition and disseminate their version of it.

Another axis of change in Southwestern shamanism is the transformation of the ritual into a stage performance—urged to a degree by the Cultural Properties system, which wants its beneficiaries to present their art to the nation. Performers of the Jindo rite, in making the transition to the stage, have created abbreviated versions; some have even added more performers, transforming the shaman's solo dancing into a choreographed group performance. Improvisation becomes difficult if not impossible if a group of dancers is expected to move in consort.

Yang Yong-eun and others performing a staged version of Jindo ssikkim gut (Jindo Island funeral ritual). *Source:* Provided by Pak Jeong-gyu

SHAMANISM'S DERIVATIVE GENRES: FROM RITUAL TO CLASSICAL

Sinawi and the Fate of Group Improvisation

SINAWI
A genre of simultaneous improvisation modeled after the music of shamanist ritual, particularly of Southwestern Korea.

GISAENG
A class of female professionals, many of whom were professional entertainers who were foundational in the history of Korean traditional music.

Shamanism, particularly the hereditary tradition of the Southwest, has inspired many genres of music, dance, and other performing arts. In the late nineteenth–early twentieth centuries, this music inspired an independent genre of polyphonic, improvisational chamber music called *sinawi*. This genre came about when two very fundamental groups of professional musicians—the *gisaeng* (female) and *gwangdae* (male)— members of the lowly *cheonmin* class, and often related to shaman families, began to play shamanist music in chamber settings for rural bureaucrats, aristocrats, and literati. The literati and bureaucratic classes in Seoul regarded the Southwest with a mixture of contempt and romanticism, much as American northerners have long thought about that country's South, and how the "Global North" generally thinks about the "Global South." So Southwestern genres and their musicians became popular throughout the country; members of shaman musician families had positions even in the Korean court. They performed for the Confucian literati and aristocratic patrons in general, and in this way came to influence and be influenced by elite culture. The whole creation of *sinawi* as a chamber genre is an example of this—music that had once occupied only rural, ritual contexts was transformed into a genre of instrumental music divorced from ritual, available for leisurely contemplation by the elite—the principle context in which elites listened to and played music. In the early twentieth century, *sinawi* began to be presented on stages for public audiences.

One of these performances would include about five to ten musicians, all improvising simultaneously—a phenomenon unheard of elsewhere in East Asian instrumental music. Contemporary performances may last from about ten minutes to almost an hour. In general the performances are suites of rhythmic patterns of increasing tempo. The rhythmic patterns are drawn from the shamanist tradition, and range from the quite long and slow, such as the very slow twenty-four-beat pattern *jinyangjo*, to the brisk and short, such as the quick three-beat *semachi* rhythm. The rhythmic transformation reflects the genre's origins in funeral and ritual contexts, which begin with spirits in stasis and isolation, and carries them to a place of movement toward an ultimate unity with the spirit world. In the context of instrumental music, it is often described as a transformation from sorrow to joy, paralysis to motion. This mechanism of transformation in *sinawi* and Korean traditional music generally is one of the reasons why traditional music retains such expressive power in the midst of the struggles and tragedies of modern Korea. Yet while this structure recalls the shamanist tradition, it also bears the imprint of the solo improvised genre *sanjo*, which we will learn about below.

Sinawi provides an excellent example of many of the key characteristics of Korean traditional music across genres in addition to the key facet of transformation. As a genre of simultaneous improvisation, it is a rather pronounced example of the many opportunities, large and small, for improvisation in Korean musical culture, which contrasts with the relative fixity of other East Asian musical cultures, especially Japan. This improvisation is one of many techniques by which musicians have latitude to develop and express their personal styles, and to make music relevant to the present and the audience.

Also, the music demonstrates a key principle of the melodic organization of Korean traditional music: it is based in what virtuoso Jin Hi Kim calls "**living tones**"—pitches that rise and fall in pitch and transform timbrally and dynamically (in terms of volume) as well, thus making pitch and ornamentation (limitless different kinds of vibrato, sliding, timbral and dynamic shifting, etc.) inseparable. Perhaps the most striking feature of *sinawi* and Southwestern music is its use of dramatic, raspy and rough timbres. These timbres are part of a continuum of timbral contrast in Southwestern music; performers employ them in contrast with clear and bell-like timbres to dramatic expressive effect. This makes the genre an excellent example of what educator and master percussionist Kim Dong Won calls "**rough beauty**"—a kind of stylized naturalness and grittiness that pervades many genres of Korean music, traditional and modern.

The Korean national effort to preserve tradition has meant making *sinawi* an "Intangible Cultural Property" and making transcriptions in Western staff notation of *sinawi* performances. *Sinawi* is now generally played according to memorized scores, either transcriptions of historical performances or newly composed pieces, or composits of transcribed solo performances from the solo *sanjo* genre, which exercises a profound influence on *sinawi* (see below). Like many other improvisational musics in South Korea, much of the improvisation in *sinawi* has disappeared in the interest of canonizing tradition, sharing in the high social status of Western-style composed musics, and pursuing rather problematic notions of authenticity. The irony of this is that while the musical surface remains the same, the performing manner, the experience of making music, and the course of music history are entirely transformed. In recent decades, however, we see signs of a return to improvisational practice. This return has been encouraged by Korean traditional musicians' interactions with jazz music and musicians, who demonstrate that music can be changeable and yet still hold high status as elite and manifestly modern culture, and also still be perceived to be authentic.

LIVING TONES

Experimentalist Kim Jin-I's term for describing how pitches in Korean music are not fixed, but alive—moving up and down, under-going dynamic and timbral transformations.

ROUGH BEAUTY

Percussionist and improviser Kim Dong-Won's term for the stylized roughness—raspy timbres, irregular instrument construction, and so on—intentional gestures toward nature and materiality that pervade much of Korean traditional music.

Sanjo's Scattered Melodies

In the nineteenth century, a solo form of shamanist-inspired improvisation developed, called **sanjo**, "scattered melodies." The genre, performed by one melodic instrumentalist with accompaniment of the hourglass drum, follows the same basic structure of suites of rhythmic patterns of increasing tempo as *sinawi*, and seems to have provided the blueprint for the development of that genre. It is characterized by intensive melodic exploration, often moving between different regional melodic modes.

SANJO

Originally suites of improvisations for solo instrument with hourglass drum (janggo) accompaniment based on rhythmic patterns of generally accelerating tempo; now generally notated and played rote.

The *sanjo* form developed as traditional professional folk musicians experimented with solo playing, gathering experience and melodic material from multiple masters and collaborative experimentations. But as *sanjo* entered the twentieth century, schools began to form around particular master performers, who passed on their style to their juniors. This pedagogical structure based on schools of playing was imported to Korean traditional music pedagogy from Japan, where it is prevalent. In the post-colonial period, when the genre was canonized as national culture, this school mentality persisted. *Sanjo* was written down, in the same manner that *sinawi* was, and people attempt to preserve it unchanged. The master performer whose name is given to a particular school of playing has attained a status akin to that of a Western classical composer. As Korean traditional music began its revival in the 1980s, *gayageum* (twelve-string plucked zither) studios sprang up all over the country, patterned very much on the model of the piano studio. These are institutions where (mostly) young girls cultivate a love of music and pick up artistic abilities that increase their attractiveness on the marriage market. In the *gagyageum* studios and in schools of "national music" the country over, *sanjo* is taught as the ultimate accomplishment of a zither player, the ultimate demonstration that the student has grasped the essence of Korean aesthetics.

The shift from shaman ritual music to staged performance in *sinawi* and *sanjo* is reminiscent of the many other kinds of art music worldwide, including sacred music in the West, which have gradually become independent of sacred contexts. This is a process by which musical sound became gradually more abstract, more conceived of as independent of not only ritual but dance and gesture—in other words, these processes are key in the historical evolution of the whole modern idea of music as exclusively *sound-based*. They are also important aspects of the process by which culture has been transformed to allow for its "presentation"—the display of music, as opposed to the use of music in the process of ritual or the course of life. The two genres also bear the imprint of the rise of radio and sound recording as, increasingly, the primary means of experiencing music. The ritual and social origins of the art forms, however, remain imprinted in the transformative structure of performances.

Pansori and the Poetics of Suffering

PANSORI
Solo epic story-singing with barrel drum (buk) accompaniment.

Another genre that is routinely claimed to have originated in shaman culture is **pansori**, musical epic story-singing performed by a singer and an accompanist playing the *buk* (barrel drum). With the aid of nothing but a hand-held paper fan and the accompanist, the *pansori* singer, through a mixture of song (*sori*), narration (*aniri*), and dramatic gesture (*pallim*, including gestures with the paper fan), relates a long tale from Korean folklore. By the twentieth century the many tales of *pansori* had dwindled to five, all concerned with the crisis and restoration of one of the five key Confucian relationships of filial piety: the relations between king and subject, husband and wife, parent and child, siblings, and friends. The singer may tell the epic tale in its entirety, or in part. The reciting

AJAENG SANJO

LISTEN

TRACK 5.4 Performed By Pak Daeseong

THIS IS A SHORT VERSION This is a short version of *ajaeng* (bowed zither) *sanjo* by the well-known performer Pak Daeseong. The *ajaeng sanjo* exemplifies the 'living tones' and 'rough beauty' concepts perfectly, as scraping sounds of the bow are a vital part of the music, contrasted with clear tones, and the sustain of the bow prolongs the life of each tone. The ajaeng is often said to be the instrument most able to imitate the human voice. This video shows the highly refined nature of the *sanjo* genre, as a representative of the professional folk music genres, and highlights the inadequacy of the concept of 'folk music' for describing these musics. It also shows an example of the arc of emotional transformation which structures *sinawi* and *sanjo*.

Pak begins with a free-rhythmic introduction called *daseurum*, which foregoes regular meter and drum to focus on introducing the melodic mode, *gyemyeongjo*. This video demonstrates this South-western melodic mode at its most pathos-ridden, with its aching vibratos and slides which evoke weeping and sighing. At 00:45, a tremendous scrape across the strings announces the beginning of the massively slow and stately *jinyangjo* rhythmic pattern. His first cycle takes about one minute; you can count the pattern as four groups of six very slow beats, which each in their turn are divided into three. So count one-two-three, two-two-three, three-two three, and so on up to six, and then start over. Four times through the group of six sees you through the pattern, which generally (but not always) corresponds o a complete melodic passage. The *jinyangjo* pattern is often expressed as four measures of 18/8, or 24: 3/8; although there is much variation in practice, and measures are added and omitted by soloists. There is a relatively heavy downbeat on the first beat of each group of six, and a high accent on beat five, which you can use to orient yourself.

We can hear the rhythmic, melodic, and emotive transformation effected by *sanjo* here. At the beginning of the track we hear two cycles of the pattern; the smallest beats, the eighth notes, come at about 80 beats per minute, accelerating to about 90 beats per minute by the end of the second pattern at 04:18. The acceleration makes the feel of the pattern lighter and more optimistic, and the melodic mode, with its cry-like vibrato, sounds more vigorous, edging away from tears and ever so slightly towards laughter. This measured, gradual transformation within the one rhythmic pattern has taken about four minutes; in a full performance of *ajaeng sanjo* it can take fifteen.

At 04:18 Pak slows down abruptly and plays a short downward glissando. This ends on the downbeat of the new rhythmic pattern, *jungmori*, a moderate 12/4, four groups of three, with accents on the first and ninth beats. This pattern is much shorter, taking only ten seconds to play through once; yet compared with the end of the last pattern, it feels slow, for a number of reasons. What is happening here is a kind of terraced, step-like acceleration, in which one pattern starts off slowly, accelerates, and is replaced by another pattern which slows down a bit, but begins with a quicker feel than the first pattern began with. The next change is at 7:00, with another downward glissando introducing the rhythmic pattern *jungjungmori*; more follow later on, all abiding by this rule of terraced acceleration. We will see this arc of acceleration again in this chapter, as it is one of the core techniques of emotional transformation in Korean traditional music.

of an entire story generally takes around two to four hours, but it can take up to eight, an enormous strain on both singer and drummer. There are several regional styles of *pansori*, but the style is generally thought to originate in the Southwest, and the genre is characterized, like Southwestern shamanism and its other derivatives, by timbral contrast, raspiness, and the alternately plaintive and vigorous melodic modes common to the region. Many-hour solo performance is exhausting on any instrument, but particularly taxing on the voice, and singers undergo rigorous training regimens to prepare themselves. There are famous stories of singers trying to out-sing waterfalls, or rehearsing until they spat blood. The point is to develop the vocal scarring that gives a singer a raspy voice, to be contrasted with relatively smooth timbres.

Pansori is thought to have originated in the seventeenth century or so among wandering *gwangdae* (male professional musicians) who had strong links to shaman culture and were often shamans or shaman accompanists. The genre originated as performances by "vulgar commoner" musicians for ordinary commoners, but as it developed it became patronized by the wealthy middle classes, the literati, and even royalty. This solo form with drum accompaniment—an ensemble which shows up elsewhere in Korean traditional music—became the predominant form of musical storytelling/acting in the Korean peninsula, in contrast to the group music-theatrical traditions of Japan and China: Japanese *noh* drama and *kabuki*, and the many varieties of Chinese music theater, such as *jingju* (Beijing opera) and *yueju* (Cantonese opera). UNESCO has declared *pansori* a Masterpiece of the Oral and Intangible Heritage of Humanity.

Pansori suffered the same fate in Korean modernity as the hereditary shaman tradition, as singers were eager to escape their low social status. In the nineteenth century *gisaeng*, female professional entertainers, began to perform in the genre.

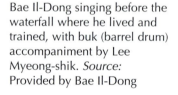

Bae Il-Dong singing before the waterfall where he lived and trained, with buk (barrel drum) accompaniment by Lee Myeong-shik. *Source:* Provided by Bae Il-Dong

The early twentieth century also saw the rise of *changgeuk*, an ensemble cast musical theater based on *pansori*, and the mid century saw the advent of *yeoseong gukgeuk*, its all-female counterpart, inspired also by Japanese *takarazuka* all-female theater. But as orthodox notions of tradition came to dominate Korean traditional performance in the latter half of the twentieth century, these genres would gradually wane, along with all the other genres that made public their efforts to mediate between Korean tradition and modernity.

In late-twentieth century Korea, *pansori* flourished as a kind of consolidating medium for expressing the sorrows of post-colonial modernity. The sorrowful "Western style" (*Seopyeongje*) of *pansori* rose in popularity, at the expense of the more vigorous Eastern style (*Dongpyeonje*). *Pansori* began to be described as the "sound of *han*," the emotional cluster concept often translated as "resentful sorrow," which many hold to be a core feature of what it means to be Korean. Like the blues, Portuguese/Brazilian *saudade*, and other emotional concepts held to be keys to identity, it is a complex concept, and there are almost as many definitions of *han* as there are Korean people. The idea of han as a national characteristic is a recent one, part of the modern search for national essences in the wake of colonialism, and in the midst of authoritarian capitalist development and national division.

It may seem surprising that *pansori* is called on to represent this emotion, as all of the surviving *pansori* epics end happily. But the characters travel through great hardship on the way to the happy endings, and this provides ample opportunity for the expression of *han*. This is especially true nowadays when excerpt performances are more common than complete ones, and one can focus on sorrow without reaching the happy ending. The 1993 film *Seopyeonje* ("Western style") provides an example of the recent canonization of *pansori* as the sound of *han*. The main character, a blind female *pansori* singer, ends the film with a recital of the penultimate scene in the *Song of Shimcheong*. In the song, the faithful daughter, who has literally sacrificed herself to restore her father's sight, is reunited with him and discovers that he is still blind. Soon he will open his eyes in his joy at her return, but the scene in the film ends before this happens and thus secures the unresolved, perpetual nature of *han*.

The late-twentieth-century history of *pansori*—with its canonization under the influence of the Intangible Cultural Heritage system and the **han** idea—has provoked waves of concern within the genre. Singers on the margins of the *pansori* world have responded to the codification of the genre by creating new stories about superheroes, political figures, and others. Others have responded by attempting to revive practices of improvisation and audience interaction, traditional pedagogy, and styles that have waned—in particular the vigorous styles of singing that fell out of favor as the softer and more melancholic rose to dominance. Bae Il-dong (see the listening inset) is one such singer. He has revived the defunct practice of training by waterfalls (see photo), and crossed the drawn lines of styles and schools in his training. Most importantly, he sings in a more than typically vigorous style for a younger singer (his 2014 North American tour was called "If Volcanoes Could Sing"). Some musicologists consider the rise of the softer and more melancholic Western style of *pansori* to have been

HAN
A complex emotional cluster often translated as "resentful sorrow." Thought by many to be essentially Korean, and by many others to be the product of modern, post-colonial efforts to create a "Korean" essence.

LISTENING GUIDE   **PANSORI**    **LISTEN**

TRACK 5.5   **Pansori from "Simcheong-ga." Performed by Bae Il-Dong (vocals) and Kim Dong-Won (buk)**

THIS IS AN EXCERPT from the *pansori* epic *The Story of Simcheong*, sung by Bae Il-dong, with *buk* (barrel drum) accompaniment by Kim Dong-Won. This is 'rough beauty' in one of its most extreme formulations. It also gives you some sense of the kind of stamina, power, and subtlety one needs to perform *pansori*. We hear throughout examples of onomatopoeia and mimetic speech, quotation, word painting, and all manner of musical devices for bringing the story to life. Importantly, Bae Il-dong holds to a basic outline of the story but varies it each time, based on his mood, the occasion, and the audience.

The story, in brief, describes how Simcheong, the only daughter of a blind man sold herself to sailors as a sacrifice to the god of the sea in exchange for rice, which she wanted in order to make an offering at a Buddhist temple in the hopes of restoring her father's eyesight. She throws herself into the ocean and drowns, but the god of the sea is moved by her filial piety, and sends her back to land and life. The emperor falls in love with her, and she becomes an empress. She invites all of the blind men in the area to the palace in an effort to find her father. When she finally finds him he is still sightless; but joy at being reunited with his daughter, whom he knew positively to have died, causes him to open his eyes.

This excerpt is from almost the very end, and describes the reunion of the father and daughter. Bae Il-dong opens singing to the slow 12/4 *jungmori* rhythmic pattern in the voice of the old man singing to an official at the palace. He describes how his daughter sold herself for 300 bags of rice, and how she died three years ago. He castigates himself for allowing her to do it, and begs the official for death.

At 1:13 a quicker 12/8 pattern, *jajinmori*, begins. The narrator describes Empress Sim's surprise at meeting her father. She runs to him without taking the time to put on shoes. He describes the sound using the onomatopoeia 'lulululululululu' (1:20). She reaches him at 1:24 and cries *"Aigo abeoji"*: "Oh my god, father!" Her father responds in tears: "Who is that calling me father?" He explains that his only daughter has died. The Empress mourns the fact that he is still sightless despite her sacrifice. He wonders if he too has died and gone to the palace in the sea, and is seeing his daughter there. He wonders also if he is dreaming. At 2:28 you can hear a long downward glissando and a florid passage on the word *sugung* (the sea palace), whose downward movement imitates a human body sinking in the ocean. The blind Mr. Sim expresses his desperate wish to see her; this desperation reaches a peak at 3:23, when he cries "Let's have a look at my daughter!" elongating the last words of the sentence as if using up his last remaining energy. At last, overcome by emotion, he blinks and opens his eyes (3:40). After a long section of *sori* (song), the narrator now slips into spoken-voiced narration (*aniri*) and Sim looks around, gazing on his daughter for the first time. This is the longest section in the sample thusfar of spoken narration, because the singer has stopped speaking as the various characters, who are voiced in song.

the result of the influx of the *gisaeng* (female professional entertainers) to the genre; and so the concern with reviving more vigorous styles is also a concern about "remasculinizing" the genre. Put most polemically, this is a concern about the so-called feminization of tradition during the colonial period. This anxiousness to make the genre more "manly" is just one of many instances of the attempt to masculinize Korean culture in the post-colonial, hypercapitalist era and its endless cold war.

Sinawi, *sanjo*, and *pansori* can be considered "folk art music"—music made by low-status but intensely professional performers with some connection to elite culture. The category of "folk art music" is just one of many in Korean music that casts doubt on the contemporary tendency to reduce all genres of traditional music to "folk" and "art" genres. But ironically it is precisely these genres that embody the twentieth-century transformation of Korean music from its fluidity and changeability to a scripted stasis, as they seek a kind of art music status. This might be thought of as a continuation of what we might call the "aristocraticization" of this music, the process by which low-commoner professional musicians have gestured toward elite musics in order to (variously) consolidate elite audiences and shore up social position. But revivals of improvisatory practice are underway as well, as we have seen and heard.

COURT MUSIC AND OTHER "ELEGANT MUSIC": MUSIC, THE STATE, AND SOCIAL ORDER

The elite musics to which so many other genres have aspired are many and varied. The category of *jeongak*, "proper music," embraces a wide number of genres from a broad range of traditional settings—everything from court ritual and entertainment music to the contemplative and pastoral musics of the literati and the bureaucratic middle class.

Two times a year, in the spring and fall, on the grounds of the Munmyo shrine in Seoul, a ceremony is performed in which highly formalized court dances are performed and sacrificial gifts are presented to the great Chinese Confucians. Between the dances, with measured stateliness, various offerings are set upon a shrine; the final gift is several cups of strong wine. These ceremonial events are accompanied by "proper music's" most elite genre, *a-ak* ("elegant music"). This is a two-piece repertoire based on melodies and instruments imported from China in the early second millennium CE. It is generally thought to be the most accurately preserved Chinese court music in the world. Chinese imperial court instruments were first donated by the Chinese emperor during the Song Dynasty in two envoys in 1114 and 1116; much of these collections were destroyed over the years, and other Chinese dynasties made supplemental gifts. The genre went through several rigorous processes of revival in the constant effort to make it more Chinese and more properly Confucian—by emulating historical documents, and squaring musical practice with contemporary interpretations of Confucianism. So despite its aura of eternal, unchanging stability, it has actually undergone profound transformations over the centuries, right up to the present.

The musical organization of *a-ak* may seem quite unusual. A number of percussive signals succeed one another as a kind of prelude; after this, the pieces consist of the orderly presentation of pitches in the original Yuan Chinese melodies, each of which bends up slightly at the end; this is followed by a coda similar to the prelude. The pitch-bending is thought to be a recent addition. The music is characterized by a remarkable lack of rhythmic precision—sounds in the prelude often seem to stumble one after the other, and the playing of the ordered pitches varies slightly in terms of time among the musicians. This is true for dance as well. This is because this music is about demonstrating ordered relations—of precedence and hierarchy among instruments and musicians, for example, or the relations between human beings, the earth, and heaven. It also has rhythmic flexibility because it is meant to accompany the ceremonial activities, which themselves vary in duration. This is a lovely example of a kind of music that is not about emotional expression, one of those things that people often assume is a universal feature of music. Nor is it about the intense transformations we have seen in many of the genres we have encountered thus far. It is about reflecting and attempting to create societal and natural harmony, about creating a sound image of a world in which things are in the proper hierarchical and geomantic (spatial) alignment, in which rule governs the passions and no dramatic change is required or desirable.

An elaborate performance of Korean ancient court music (with accompanying dance) known as Jongmyo jeryeak. *Source*: Wikimedia Commons

The next-most elite subsection of the *a-ak* genre, tellingly, is that for rituals to Korean royal ancestors at the Jongmyo shrine in Seoul. The fact that music for the deceased Korean royalty is less prestigious than music that honors the Chinese Confucians is evidence of the intensity with which the last Korean dynasty venerated China. This music is unusual in the landscape of Korean music because it combines instruments from the Chinese court ensembles with instruments that are considered indigenous (although the prototypes of many of them are originally from China), and makes use of the repertoire of Korean composition. Much of the usage of indigenous music and instruments in royal ceremonies was introduced in the era of King Sejong (1418–1450), a firm supporter of music, literature, scientific invention, and indigenous culture whose reign saw the reform of the calendar away from the Chinese model, the creation of the Korean alphabet, and much more. He in particular was instrumental in

EXPLORE

The Royal Ancestry Ritual and its Music

<table>
<tr><td>LISTENING GUIDE</td><td>ROYAL ANCESTRAL SHRINE MUSIC</td><td> LISTEN</td></tr>
</table>

TRACK 5.6   **"Chonpyehuimun": Royal Ancestral Shrine Music. Performed by members of the National Gugak Center**

THIS IS A SHORT EXCERPT from one of the main pieces of the music for the sacrifice to the royal ancestors.

At 00:00, various percussion instruments, mostly of Chinese origin, play a percussive prelude, as in the music for the Confucians. The percussive introduction starts and ends (00:11) with a single clap from the *bak* wooden clapper, played by the most senior performer.

At 00:12, the melodic instruments enter—including Chinese instruments, like the tuned bells (*pyeongjong*) and chimes (*pyeongyeong*), and also the melodic instruments indigenous to Korean court music. These include the *piri* (double reed oboe), *daegeum* (transverse flute), *haegeum* (two-stringed spike fiddle) and others. The piece is an orderly presentation of notes, each played a bit differently by the different musicians, making the melodic texture heterophonic. Note the contrast between the instruments of fixed pitch such as the bells and chimes and those that can bend—the aerophones all noticeably begin to vibrate pitches at the end, and the singer, in particular, demonstrates the most freedom to elaborate on the pitch being presented. The fact that even in this staid, courtly genre the instruments have some latitude to improvise in the idioms of particular instruments and personal styles, and in response to the situation of performance, shows the importance of improvisation in Korean traditional music. It is also evidence of the flexibility of this music, and a window through which the music could transform gradually over time.

The meter is slow and the melody is through-composed, structured around melodic phrases of varying lengths. If you have trouble counting time, that is because the measures from the beginning, are of six, four, five, five, seven, four, four, five, four . . . and so on. There is no regular repeating pattern. All of this corresponds with different aspects of Korean courtly numerology and geomancy: the number five is a particularly important one, as it corresponds to the five directions (north, south, east, west, and center).

changing the music for royal ancestral rites from Chinese ritual music to Korean royal banquet music, objecting to the use of Chinese music to honor the Korean royalty.

The remainder of the elite music repertoire can be divided into a few categories. First is music that accompanied other royal ceremonies and banquets, performed by the same professionals who accompanied Confucian and royal ancestral rites. This repertoire is generally divided between music of Chinese origin and music composed in Korea. Finally is the vast world of classical vocal and instrumental genres that the literati and middle classes practiced as amateurs for entertainment and as a kind of work of self-cultivation. *Pungnyu* ("wind and stream") was the instrumental music played in so-called *pungnyu-bang*, salons where the literati gathered to appreciate music, song, poetry, calligraphy, and art. The crowning jewel of the *pungryu* repetoire is the massive suite "Yeongsan hoesang," which is organized in order from slow to fast, another gradual acceleration across large forms in Korean music like those we have seen already. *Sijo*, *gasa*, and *gagok* are genres of sung poetry that were also appreciated and performed in the *pungnyu-bang*. They were composed in both Chinese and Korean. The song genres addressed all sorts of political, natural, and moral themes. Like related practices of poetry writing, songs were also an important part of the amorous back-and-forth with *gisaeng*, professional female entertainers, which went on in some salons. *Gagok* pieces are generally sung by a male or female soloist with instrumental accompaniment; there is one duet. Performances are given in the form of song cycles, which like "Yeongsan hoesang" are arranged from slow to fast.

In the South Korean present, these musics channel a Korea with an ancient civilizational tradition with close ties to China and a profound, contemplative sense of the relations between nature and humanity. The stately, slow elegance of the various elite genres projects a version of the Korean state before the turmoil of the colonial era, which undermined courtly and aristocratic traditions dramatically. It harkens back to a time before the hustle-and-bustle of the modern world set in. Judging from the not-quite 100 years of sound recording in the Korean peninsula, as modern Koreans have dreamed of an unruffled past this music has become even more ponderous and slow, as slowness is roundly associated with not just peace and the past but also with elite culture.

EXPLORE

Gagok

PERCUSSION TRADITIONS AND THE MODERN TRANSFORMATION OF TIME

Pungmul

So far, we have considered the music of the court, the literati, the middle classes, and the professional musician classes. What of the common people? In contemporary Korea the one tradition that is regularly called upon to represent the rural past and the common folk is the ubiquitous percussion and dance genre called ***pungmul*** (literally "wind objects"). The genre served four main purposes: first, it was performed as part of rural ceremonies to bless houses, crops, villages, and events. Second, it was used to accompany and encourage rural work, such as the planting of rice sprouts in paddies. Third, it was used in fundraising for village projects, temples and other institutions. Lastly, it was one of the principal forms of rural entertainment until the mid-twentieth century.

Like folksongs, there are numerous styles of percussion/dance band performance across the Korean peninsula, but they are unified by numerous facets. *Pungmul* processions—such as those that travel from place to place in a village bestowing blessings, scaring demons, and/or raising money—are led by a flag-bearer, who carries a tall rectangular flag with the name of the group on it, or more often a Sino-Korean inscription, which means "Farmers are the foundation of the Earth." In a typical procession the first musician is the player of the lead instrument *ggwaengwari* (small gong), a high-pitched and remarkably loud instrument that signals changes between rhythmic patterns and sets tempo, which gradually increases over the course of performance toward a climactic ending. Like many other genres in Korean music, *pungmul* is a means of transformation, and is characterized by the terraced acceleration we saw also in *sanjo*. The lead player may be followed by several other small gong players. The instrument is followed by the large gong *jing*. The *jing* typically marks metric divisions—playing only on the first beat of a rhythmic cycle, or only on accented beats. Next come a varying number of players of the lead drum, the ubiquitous hourglass-shaped *janggo*, with the hourglass tied around their waists. This drum plays a detailed version of each rhythmic pattern, articulating high and low accents with its high and low-tuned sides. It is followed by the barrel drum *buk*, a variant of the same drum used for *pansori* accompaniment. The *buk* plays a skeletal outline of the rhythmic pattern. The different instruments sometimes overlap and sometimes interlock, maintaining a complex balance of sameness and difference.

These four core instruments are typically followed in procession by dancer-acrobats who carry small drums called *sogo*. These drums are more important as ornaments for dance than they are as part of the sound of the music; but they highlight the inseparability of music and dance here—the visual effect of striking these drums is no less a part of the rhythmic life of music than is the rhythmic movements of the dancers. In processional performance, each rhythmic pattern has one or more designated walking or dance patterns that accompany it. In *madang-nori*, outdoor entertainments, performers move in complex, coordinated, patterned movements, twining together and apart.

In procession the *pungmul* group may be capped off by a troupe of actor-dancers, who portray various stereotypical figures such as Buddhist monks, aristocrats, scholars, hunters, and maidens. This group, known as *japsaek* (various colors), was one medium through which common people could parody the rich and the powerful. Buddhist monks—forbidden from sexual relations and alcohol—were portrayed drunk and chasing after young women. Aristocrats were shown exploiting commoners, or as oversexed wastrels with ruined complexions.

PUNGMUL
Farmers' percussion and dance bands ubiquitous throughout traditional Korea, and adopted by postcolonial protest movements.

 **EXPLORE**
Nongak

Yang Jin-Seong, playing ggwaengwari, and the Pilbong Nongak group at the full moon festival. *Source:* Provided by Yang Jin-Sung

In later years, this collection of characters would often change to admit stereotypical figures of Korean modernity—Korean and American generals, politicians, and so on.

The emptying of the countryside in the era of Korea's industrialization dramatically lessened percussion band culture, and in response several regional styles were been designated Intangible Cultural Properties. In the twentieth century many of the same effects of canonization we have seen elsewhere have been wrought upon percussion music—the diminution of improvisational practices, the centralization of authority in each tradition and the ossification of "schools," the evolution of pieces for presentation on stages, and so on. Also, in the late twentieth century, percussion and dance bands experienced a revival. In the 1960s a complex social movement for democratization, labor rights, and reunification began to grow, and reached its peak in the so-called *minjung* (mass) movement of the 1980s, which eventually toppled South Korean authoritarianism and substantially improved the fate of workers in South Korea. During the long social movement era, *pungmul* became a tool of protest. *Pungmul* came to represent, among the intellectuals and college students at the heart of the movement, a notion of the traditional Korean people that was powerful, durable, populist, and festive. In protest, drumming and dance encouraged protestors in their conflicts with riot police; it was a useful signaling medium, a way of communicating amidst the chaos of violent conflict. *Pungmul* performers who participated in movement events were jailed and even tortured along with other participants. In the subsequent decades of South Korean democratization, percussion and dance bands have continued to proliferate with continued interest in cities and colleges, including many abroad.

Samulnori

In the nineteenth century, bands of professional percussion and dance musicians roamed the countryside, playing at village entertainments, ceremonies, and so on. These troupes, the *namsadang*, emphasized technical virtuosity and spectacle, and included tight-rope walkers, plate spinners, puppet theater, and other entertainments. These travelling troupes, like the wandering *pansori* performers, were an important means by which news and also cultural exchange took place around the Korean peninsula until their effective demise in the twentieth century.

In the late 1970s, in the early days of the resurgence of progressive interest in Korean traditional folk culture, a group of musicians formed who were the sons of these professional itinerant performers. They called themselves *Samulnori* ("four things play") and developed a form of Korean percussion and dance music for stage performance. In the following decades this group became a national and international sensation. The timing of the emergence of samulnori—which went on to become a genre of the same name—followed the creation of a stage presentational form of Japanese *taiko* and the beginnings of its international export.

Samulnori, like the new *taiko* tradition, is made up of pieces that are pre-composed sequences of rhythmic patterns in a relatively fixed overall time.

SAMULNORI

A new genre of percussion music for stage performance derived from the farmers' band traditions and the traditions of namsadang travelling entertainers.

Samulnori founder Kim Deok-Soo (third from the left) and ensemble. *Source:* Provided by Lee Gyeong-pil

Compared with *pungmul*, which varies in content, tempo, length, and so on based on circumstance, *samulnori* is much more like a Western composition, varying only minimally based on the occasion of performance. We can sense here the global influence of Western notions of composition here—the idea of using traditional music as "materials" for new composition. This is a similar attitude taken by the proponents of so-called *changjak gugak*, newly composed traditional music. For this reason, among others, the debate rages as to whether or not *samulnori* is "traditional," whether it is authentically Korean, and so on. We might call it "traditionesque"—referencing tradition but not bound to it; or we could call the genre traditional, as it was created by the direct descendents of the *namsadang* tradition, which has long been known for its creativity. In any case, the genre provides a great opportunity to contemplate the meaning and the nature of tradition.

Another point of contention between the two genres lies in their different degrees of "swing" in the articulation of rhythmic patterns. Swing here refers to the sense of time being flexible—not made up of equivalent units, like seconds or eighth notes, but capable of being stretched and compressed, seeming to the uninitiated slightly early or (much more often) slightly late. Such practices are common the world over in percussion traditions; one such example is the practice, in musics of African American origin, of playing "in the pocket"— typically right behind the beat, if beats were measured as equal units. Farmers' bands famously include many such displacements; we find relatively more machine-like precision in *samulnori*. Some of this has to do with the speed at which performers play, which makes microrhythmic displacement difficult. But there may be other reasons as well.

The rhythmic life of music is one of its most pronouncedly social aspects. Gilbert Rouget, in his classic *Music and Trance*, called music an "architecture of time." Music helps to create and circulate the senses of time that hold sway in a culture. So in seeking an explanation for the differences in rhythmic feel and compositional/performance practice between *pungmul* and *samulnori*, we may look at the ways that music is transformed in its move from country to city, from agrarian to capitalist economies. Karl Marx famously found the abstract nature of money to be the key to capitalism—money places an abstract, rather than a concrete, value on human labor. In order for this economic transformation to take place, abstract values must correspond to equally abstract units of time. An instance of concrete time is the amount of time it takes to boil a pot of water, a length of time that may vary depending on all sorts of conditions. Abstract time is clock time, in which minutes and seconds are all identical to one another. In the emergence of the samulnori genre, with its compositions of relatively fixed durations and its performance manner that edges, virtuosically, toward abstract conceptions of time—in which one beat is absolutely identical in duration to others—we might suspect traces of the rise of this urban, capitalist time-sense. The rise of *samulnori* has even inspired some in the *pungmul* world to actually make their music swing even more, in a gesture—if our speculation is right—an authenticity which survives on the margins of capitalism and abstract time.

At the same time, *samulnori* is perhaps Korea's most popular **"traditionesque"** musical genre both domestically and abroad. The music is dramatic and transformative, starting slow and ending in blistering climaxes of speed. It represents Korean tradition and the Korean nation as this sort of powerful entity, possessed of tremendous energy. It is perhaps for this reason that *samulnori* was one of the iconic sounds and sights of "Dynamic Korea"—South Korea's first national slogan, launched in the first years of the twenty-first century. The drum and

TRADITIONESQUE
Describes cultural practices that reference tradition but maintain a flexible relationship to the past and its forms.

LISTENING GUIDE

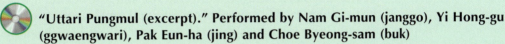

SAMULNORI

LISTEN

TRACK 5.7 "Uttari Pungmul (excerpt)." Performed by Nam Gi-mun (janggo), Yi Hong-gu (ggwaengwari), Pak Eun-ha (jing) and Choe Byeong-sam (buk)

"UTTARI PUNGMUL" is a blend of rhythmic patterns from Korea's Central-Western provinces, a piece by the four original members of the group Samulnori, which exemplifies their virtuosity and compositional practice and is one of the canonical pieces of the genre. The piece typically begins with an introduction, omitted from the textbook track.

The track begins with the *ggwaengwari* (small gong) playing one cycle of the *chilchae* (seven strokes) rhythmic pattern. The pattern is derived from farmer's band music, and is a long, lilting pattern used for parading. The name derives from the number of times in the pattern the *jing* (large gong) is struck in one repetition. The rest of the instruments enter, playing quietly, and the pattern is repeated.

It can be counted in the following manner:

3+2, 3+2, 3+3+3+2, 3+2, 2+3+3+2

The pattern, not being a simple repetition of one number, is what is typically called an additive meter. If we were to count it all up and express it as a Western time signature, we might call it 36/8. There are many such subtle and sophisticated rhythmic patterns throughout Korean music in general, but there are especially a lot among farmer's bands for parading. Watch out for the beginning of the last phrase, 2+3+3+2—that's where people often get lost, as the first 2 is unexpected after all the other phrases begin with three beats.

The pattern grows faster and faster, played in many variations, until at 3:30 it changes to another *jangdan*, the *yukchae* (six strokes) pattern, which slows down, but does not return to the starting tempo. Each of the sections, based on rhythmic patterns, does this—slowing down from the end of the last but maintaining an overall arc of increase of tempo. This terraced acceleration allows for the transformation that the music accomplishes to happen gradually rather than all of a sudden.

The next transition is rather remarkable—around 5:10 the *yukchae* pattern begins slowly to transform, seeming to melt into the next pattern, *madang samchae*. At around 5:25, with a signal from the small gong player, the fast 4/4 pattern *hwimori* takes over. At 6:16 the large gong player trades her instrument for a small gong, and the two small gongs play back and forth at one another in complex, interlocking rhythmic response. The terraced acceleration continues throughout; by the end, the lilting, irregular beat of the beginning has become a blistering 4/4, measuring 283 beats per minute.

dance traditions, whether onstage or in the village, are rather more congenial to contemporary South Korean capitalism than, for instance, the ponderous court music traditions. Samulnori is also, I believe, popular for the virtuosic way it stands between tradition and modernity—in terms of its blend of concrete and abstract time, its blend of Korean tradition and modern compositional practices influenced by the West, and its blend of ritual and staged performance. Finally, *samulnori* is popular because it seamlessly composites rhythmic materials from across the peninsula—something much easier to do than blending different regional melodic modes, for instance (which is done in *sanjo* and *pansori*, but these genres retain their origins in the Southwest). So the genre is a powerful tool of national unification in a time in which the Korean peninsula is fractured by political divisions, growing regionalism, and income disparity.

The story of *samulnori* internationally is similar. If someone from outside of Korea has ever heard Korean traditional music before, it will most likely have been *samulnori*. The complex melodic and timbral effects of Korean traditional musical genres such as *pansori*, *sanjo*, and others have been markedly difficult for people elsewhere in the world to digest—as they have been in Korea. But *samulnori* caught the attention of the Euro-American "world music" scene during its heyday of the 1980s and 1990s; its practitioners have undertaken collaborative projects with North American and European jazz musicians; and the genre has inspired community and university Korean drum-and-dance groups in Japan, the United States, Canada, the UK, Switzerland, and many other countries. In North America, Korean percussion—again like Japanese *taiko*—can be a forum for a dynamic and powerful solidarity that cuts against many disempowering racist stereotypes of Asian Americans.

MORE RECENT GENRES

The world of traditional music is only a very small part of the landscape of Korean music.

The influence of Western art music runs through the traditional music world, from the notions of composition that informed the museumization of *sanjo* and other genres and the compositional practices of *samulnori*, to educational reform along the lines of Western conservatories and piano studios, to the revision of traditional melody to suit the Western scale and harmony that we witnessed in the birth of "Arirang." This is only the case because Western art music has long flourished in the Korean peninsula. The story of the coming of and the development of Western art music in Korea is one key to understanding Korean modernity and music's place in it.

Western art music came to Korea in fits and starts at first, first with the late-nineteenth-century introduction of Western military bands to the peninsula, the concurrent rise of protestant missionary musical activism, and later the introduction of Western music pedagogy in school curricula. The first college music department, devoted exclusively to Western art music, was established in 1925; by the end of the twentieth century, the number of colleges offering specializations in Western art music had risen to more than ninety. Conservatories flourished as well, as did private studios. The number of Korean students studying Western art music performance and composition abroad is by now truly staggering; and the world stage is dotted with Korean singers and instrumentalists of Western art music, many of whom have achieved considerable fame. Western art music was at least until some years ago the third most popular genre of music in South Korea, after domestic and foreign popular music.

What explains the allure of this music, and its rapid proliferation? East Asian countries, who generally understand themselves to have joined the modern world later than "the West," emulated Western technological developments and economic systems throughout their incipient modernities; but they also emulated cultural forms as well. The development of Western art music in the Korean peninsula was a part of this modernizing mission; but at the same time it was, and continues to be, a dramatic romance by which individual Korean people fall in love with a fantasy of Europeanness and Westernness when encountering this music in churches, schools, concert halls, or recordings. While many attempt to explain the dramatic success of so many Koreans in the Western art music world as the result of some sort of cultural proclivity for music, it is more likely that this flourishing is due to the allure of the West in the context of Korea's modernity, and the urge to join that fantasy of a global, essentially Western modernity. As in many other places in the world, skill in or knowledge of Western art music proffers elite status and the social standing and security that goes with it. So one fascinating use of Western art music in contemporary South Korea is as a means for raising one's social standing; hence we find many middle-class households spending small fortunes on their children's Western music education.

Popular music, is another crucial key to understanding the texture of Korean modernity. The origins of Korean popular music, like those of Korean modernity in general, are bound up in the cultural productions and importations of Western and Japanese colonialism. They are also bound up in the history of technology in the Korean peninsula. One definition of popular music holds that it consists of music that is widely appreciated, created, and perpetuated in circuits of technologically mediated circulation. In other words, popular music is that in that sound recording, broadcast, and/or print media play a central role. It is a forum for mediating between the past and the present with its new and forward-looking technologies. Popular music is also a medium which brings large numbers of people into more intimate (if not more immediate) contact than before, and helps them to imagine themselves members of a national community. In Korea, sound recordings and playback technology began to circulate in the 1920s; the first recordings of what would become the colonial Korean pop music industry were made in the mid-1920s. Radio, controlled by the colonial state, came on in 1927. The fact that all of these technologies came from elsewhere meant that popular music provided not just a forum for mediating between past, present, and future, but also between Korea and the countries which, rightly or wrongly, were held to be more "technologically advanced" and more modern.

EXPLORE

Popular Music

Early Pop: Mediating Here and There, Now and Then

This effort at mediation is one crucial feature of early Korean pop music, which arises at the moment of so many encounters of Koreans with others and with each other. The late nineteenth and early twentieth centuries saw the emergence of two genres that exemplify these processes of mediation and translation. The first is the genre *sinminyo*, "new folk song," which we have encountered in Korea's most popular song and unofficial national anthem, "Arirang." New folk song attempted to find the space between Korea and the West, tradition and modernity in its combination of quasi-traditional melodies with Western instruments, harmonization, and song structures under the conditions of Japanese colonial modernity. The narrow, nasal voices of early-twentieth-century Japanese popular music became popular in the Korean peninsula and Korean new folk song. This Japanized Korean voice presented "traditionesque" melodies in the context of Western instruments and harmony.

CHANGGA

A turn of the 20th century genre with origins in Western folk songs and Christian hymns, modally similar to the music of central and south eastern Korea.

The second is *changga*, songs typically based on popular Western folk songs and Christian hymns. These songs are the legacy of Christian missionary work in Korea in the late nineteenth and early twentith centuries, and of the early-twentieth-century Japanese and Korean fascination with the United States and Britain. "Huimangga," "Song of Hope," was one of the most popular of the genre, and is a representative example of this dizzying colonial process—based on a Japanese popular song that was modeled after an American hymn, which in turn was drawn from an English folk tune. The song was first released in 1925 in a version by two *gisaeng* under the title "These Troubled Times."

The melodic material used for most *changga* was pentatonic and similar to the melodic modes of central and Southeastern Korea. This similarity is an effect of Christian missionary efforts in Korea, which used such music because of its melodic familiarity and appeal, and its clarity as a medium for text. In this respect the *changga* genre, like "new folk songs," was a means to create a music that mediated some part of the world to Korean people, and that explained Korean experience in the terms of that wider world. The first line of the "Song of Hope:" "In the face of these troubled times, where might hope lie?"

Trot: Post-colonial Soul

The next genre that arose in the late colonial era and held sway throughout much of the twentieth century is a genre based originally on the Japanese popular balladry called *enka*, a genre that itself was an attempt to find the space between Japan and Western popular music. The genre is now commonly called *teuroteu* (a Koreanization of the "trot" from "foxtrot"), emphasizing the transnational nature of the music, veiling its Japanese origins, and foregrounding the importance of rhythm and danceability. *Trot* was, in its origins, based on the Japanese *yonanuki* scale, a melodic mode that omits the fourth and seventh pitches of a

Korean survivor of the bombing of Hiroshima, Shim Jin-Tae, singing teuroteu on a tour bus: post-colonial soul. *Source*: Provided with permission of Joshua D. Pilzer

seven-note minor scale, a modern scale inspired by Japanese folk music. Trot imitated the common themes of the *enka* genre as well, focusing on heartbreak, urbanization, displacement, life abroad, and other aspects of modern life. But each of these themes was remodeled to suit Korean colonial modernity, reflecting the colonial exploitation and experiences of Korean people, and the genre became an important expressive resource for people victimized in the colonial period. All of this was generally veiled in metaphor and obscurity to avoid punishment or censorship by the colonial authorities.

In the post-colonial period the *trot* genre become Korea's most popular music. So tragically, the music most capable of expressing the sorrows and triumphs of modern Korean history was in its origins modern Japanese, translated to suit the terms of Korean colonial and post-colonial modernity. Songs ruminating on colonial experience, became canonical. In addition to content and language, the addition of Korean vocal signatures—timbres, kinds of vibrato, and other ornamentation—helped transform the genre into "Korean music." But at the same time, the genre still retained close connections to other popular musics—especially American and Japanese pop—throughout its post-colonial life. As a music industry, *trot* has continued to absorb domestic and international trends and styles in popular music all throughout its life as a genre, encountering and making sense of the wider world.

LISTENING GUIDE

TROT

 LISTEN

TRACK 5.8 **"A Person Like the Wind." Performed by Yi Yongsu**

POPULAR MUSIC circulates on recordings and through radio broadcast, and so the recorded medium seems like a hard, fixed object—THE song—which moves through society leaving a wake of influence behind it, and which molds people to it, resisting efforts by the rest of us to make it part of our lives on our terms. But in daily life around the world, "THE song" is susceptible to remarkable variation. Traditions of flexibility in Korean music have long made it possible for popular songs, even canonical ones, to change. The many occasions of group social singing in Korea allow for broad participation, challenging the boundaries between professionals and amateurs in the genre, and ensure a high average level of singing ability throughout both Koreas—we might call this Korea's "participatory culture." **Noraebang**, "song room," Korea's assimilation of Japanese *karaoke* technology and culture, is one such example of this, as are the innumerable "song parties" where older generations of Koreans sing by way of self-introduction or for mutual entertainment.

Many such parties take place on tour buses. The following track, a version of male *trot* singer Kim Gukhwan's 1998 "A Person Like the Wind," was recorded on a 2002 bus tour of Jeju Island, Korea's premier vacation spot.

0:00: The song begins with rhythmic mnemonic vocalization supporting the singer, and clapping. These rhythmic vocalizations provide an easy means by which listeners participate in performance. The singer participates in her own accompaniment by singing some of these prior to her first line of text, at 0:05.

0:21–24: Note the breaks in the singer's voice, a kind of ornamentation that references crying—common to sentimental balladry the world over, and important techniques of connecting music with everyday vocalization.

0:39: Other women in the audience begin to sing along to this well-known line—"Love, this thing called love—you can't trust it, you can't trust it, you can't trust it."

0:49: The singer modifies the text of this last line from "A person like the wind" to "That idiotic man," an example of textual versioning in the *trot* genre, common across the landscape of amateur folk song as well.

The bus tour was typical in many respects—particularly for the presence of the microphone, and the "song party"—the system by which the Japanese military coerced tens of thousands of girls and women into sexual labor for its troops during the Asia-Pacific War (1931–45)— who were mostly in their seventies and eighties at the time, and activists and volunteers who accompanied them. The singer is Yi Yongsu, a well-known survivor and activist from Daegu in Southeastern Korea. Because of the advanced age of the singers, many of whom are not used to singing with recorded background music, the built-in *karaoke* machine, which provides musical accompaniment and a screen with lyrics, was not employed. So the accompaniment had to be provided by those listening; and tempo, text and other parameters were not guided by the machine. As such, this is a wonderful example of the traditional principles of flexibility at work in Korean music—ironically here in a medium that is thought to be partly responsible for the near-death of Korean traditional music.

After Trot: Neocolonial Influences and the Dawn of Contemporary Korean Pop

When the Korean peninsula was divided in 1945, the South was ruled by a US military government for four years; the US military presence in South Korea has remained until this day (by contrast, the Soviet military left North Korea soon after the division). Simply put, after 1945, South Korea fell under the neocolonial cultural influence of the United States. American military radio, Armed Forces Network Korea, provided one main avenue for cultural importation, as did the availability of sound recordings and contact between Americans and Koreans in the neighborhoods surrounding the central US military base in Seoul. The Korean blues, rock and roll, rock, and other popular music scenes had their origins in this area.

The protest movements of the 1980s—much of which was hostile to the American military presence and the US in general—centered around a genre of music called *tong gita* (acoustic guitar), inspired by the American folk movement of the 1960s. At the same time, also in the manner of the folk movement, *tong gita* also was often radically opposed to war and American imperialism. This music, along with the protest song genre (*undong gayo*, ironically deeply influenced by military music stretching back to the Japanese period), was instrumental in bringing about the end of South Korean authoritarianism in the late 1980s.

The K-pop and Korean rap, which began to emerge in the 1980s and which have now reached near-global saturation thanks to Psy and "Gangnam Style" and other cultural exports, both originate and find sustenance in a healthy connection with American popular music. Indeed, the genre is characterized by its ability to blend aspects of prior Korean popular genres—timbres, melodic styles, lyrical themes, and so on—with the wide range of stylistic features of myriad established and emergent genres of Western popular music. Often this blend involves the mixing of Korean and English languages. K-pop is often said to have begun when Seo Taiji and Boys (Seo Tae-ji gwa ai-deul), the now canonical boy band, made use of elements of rap in their 1992 debut.

In our era of globalization the lines of cultural influence have broadened considerably, and influences from across Asia, Europe, and elsewhere have begun to make themselves felt in Korean music with new intensity. The remarkable production values of Korean music video, pop dance, and K-pop music have begun to leave their traces in the wider world of popular music, as a consequence of the "Korean Wave," which began in the 1990s in film and television drama and encompassed K-pop starting in the early 2000s. Indeed, these production values—backed by a sophisticated and regimented system of training for singer/dancers, and the whole advanced technological apparatus of South Korean society—are one of the hallmarks of the genre. Throughout Asia and elsewhere, K-pop fans respond to the patina of modernity, its spoils and possibilities that the genre projects.

The study of Korean popular music requires one to pay attention to the ways that transnational musical movements are embedded within Korean

NORAEBANG
Korean karaoke, private rooms where people gather to sing songs to the accompaniment of a song machine.

popular music; at the same time, it is important not to forget that this music is a facet of people's everyday lives, and useful to them in different contexts in ways that are often but not always framed by this transnationality. Popular songs, as media artifacts, travel through and beyond lives, through media circuits, and in so doing bind people, nations, transnational communities, scenes, and identities together. And in this process, these artifacts accrue meaning, like layers of sediment.

To take one example of the uses and the meanings that accrue to popular song: In 2007, Insooni, perhaps Korea's premiere soul singer, recorded a version of the 1997 pop ballad "Geowi-ui kkum" (A Goose's Dream), a song about rising above obstacles. Insooni, the child of a South Korean mother and an African American father, is one of the most prominent multi-ethnic personalities in South Korea, where interethnic couples and their children are still largely stigmatized. Growing up with this discrimination, she says, she overcame her difficulties through singing, and "A Goose's Dream" resonates with her experience:

> Before that cold standing wall called fate
> I can face up to it
> Someday I'll be able to rise above that wall and fly high up into
>   the sky . . .

The song borrows freely from African American vocal styles, but also harkens back to older Korean genres—the folk genres of the 1980s in particular. In 2014 rock ballad singer Kim Jang-hoon released a rather unusual version of the song on Youtube (www.youtube.com/watch?v=q89hTYJ470s). It was a duet with a high school girl named Yi Bo-mi, one of the victims of the 2014 Sewol Ferry disaster, in which 297 people died, mostly high school students on a school trip to the southern Jeju Island. Yi Bo-mi was an aspiring singer, and had filmed herself singing the song; the rock star, discovering this recording after her death, recorded the duet. The Sewol disaster—brought about by overloading an aged ferry—was a signpost in South Korean history: it exposed the raw fact that narratives of national progress can and do veil corrupt and questionable practices of contemporary transnational and South Korean neoliberalism. These practices victimize the citizenry, and worse, its children—the very people whom national progress is supposed to benefit. In Yi Bo-mi's version, the song was an effort to demonstrate the quality of her voice, and took part in that process by which she pursued her dreams. In the duet, the dream stands as a vicious indictment of greed and corruption in contemporary South Korean society, and a remarkable contrast to the spectacular dream of the World Cup celebration and contemporary South Korea nationalist and neoliberal triumphalism. The layered meanings and uses of "A Goose's Dream" encompass the transnational history of the pop ballad, the politics of race in South Korea, and the glories and travesties of the South Korean present.

The present life of popular music in South Korea is radically diverse, segmented into small scenes, nostalgias, and visions of the future. The remarkable centralization of Korean popular culture—which perhaps mirrored the centralization of authority in the authoritarian South Korea of the 1960s–1990s—witnessed dramatic diversification in the 1990s and onward—punk, extreme metal, EDM; if it's a genre, you'll find it in Seoul and beyond. South Korea, with the dawn of its relative economic prosperity and its new membership in the "first world," has more and more become interested in the rest of the world—in politics beyond East Asia and the United States, in philanthropy and missionary work in other countries, and in the food culture, and music of places beyond Korea, and the vaguely defined, mostly white entity called "the West." The nascent multiculturalism movement in Korea, which began in the late 1990s, has left a small mark on music curricula in schools; curricula began to include non-Korean/non-Western instruments about a decade or so after it began to include Korean traditional instruments.

BEYOND "KOREAN MUSIC"

South Korea's multicultural trend is in part a decision by the public to pay attention to the rest of the world in terms of politics, travel, culture, music, and so on. But it also is the result of the transformation of life through the internationalization of the country through labor migration and international marriage. For a long time in the twentieth century, the Koreas put a tremendous amount of energy into the myth of national homogeneity, although the peninsula did host small Chinese communities. At the same time, for years in the post-colonial period, South Korea was a source country for labor migrants, who traveled to Europe, North America, and the Middle East—some as immigrants, many as circular migrants with labor contracts abroad. But since the 1990s, South Korean prosperity has generated a lack of cheap labor, and the country began to recruit foreign workers from abroad for industrial work, domestic labor, and other jobs. Workers come from China, Vietnam, the Phillipines, Pakistan, North Korea, and elsewhere throughout Asia; there also are a great many foreign workers from Russia, parts of West Africa, and the United States. Since the 1990s as well, the number of international marriages—mostly of South Korean men to foreign women, often from China and Southeast Asia—has skyrocketed, particularly in the countryside.

On August 21, 2015, a friend and I attended Friday prayers at the Seoul Central Mosque, in the Itaewon district of Seoul, a neighborhood that serves as a hub of community for many of these workers, spouses, and other migrants. The mosque slowly filled up with around a thousand people, mostly men, who were from the Middle East, South and Southeast Asia, Africa, and elsewhere; there even were a few Koreans. A little after one o'clock a *muezzin* chanter sang the *azan* call to prayer. Typically *azan* are called from the top of a minaret, which crowns a mosque; but here the call is sung inside the mosque, and the amplified sound is not audible in the wider neighborhood—evidence of the combination of censorship and self-censorship that characterized the expressive lives of most non-ethnic Koreans in South Korea. Yet prayers are chanted, and music is nonetheless made. The shops in the Itaewon neighborhood for different

Friday prayer at the Seoul Central Mosque, August 2015. *Source:* Provided with permission of David Novak

migrant communities all had their sections of DVDs and CDs. The Filipino market that takes place every Sunday near Seoul's Hyehwa Cathedral, where the resident Filipino/a community gathers to worship every week, is evidence that some communities feel progressively more comfortable demonstrating aspects of their difference, ethnicity, and heritage in public.

MUSIC IN NORTH KOREA

There are many difficulties facing someone who wishes to learn about music in North Korea. It is often impossible to visit the country at all for most foreigners; the state wields a heavy hand in controlling what is known about the country, and it is quite rare to have opportunities to speak with ordinary people in North Korea. However, despite all of this, quite a bit is known about its musical culture.

Three years after the Korean Peninsula was divided into two protectorates in 1945, the Democratic People's Republic of Korea was established in the North. It was led until 1994 by Great Leader Kim Il Sung (1912–1994), who had been an anti-colonial guerrilla fighter during the Japanese period and who cleansed the state of its colonial bureaucracy, unlike the South, where it remained largely intact. For this reason, the North Korean state enjoyed from the start a tremendous sense of legitimacy, and was able to command a considerable amount of energy from its populace. In the Korean War, the Allies carpet-bombed and basically destroyed the entire industrial infrastructure of the country. But the country bounced back quickly with help from China and the Soviet Union, and was able to take part in the general prosperity enjoyed by the socialist world in the early decades following WWII; and it held this over the head of the struggling South as proof of its righteousness.

Revolutionizing Music Culture

Throughout its history, the North Korean state has taken a heavy hand in the cultural transformation of the country, as it does in most things. Under the influence primarily of China and Maoist thought about traditional culture, and following the dictates of Kim Il Sung, North Korea went about a program of cultural transformation meant to overcome the remnants of pre-modern, class-based society, and to cleanse culture of the influence of Japanese colonialism and capitalism and replace them with a vigorous Korean patriotism.

In the music sphere and the sphere of the traditional arts, this happened in several ways. First, music was created by state composers and lyricists, and content was and remains rigorously controlled and censored to keep it in line with state doctrine. This doctrine is a changeable, complex blend of nationalism, socialist ideology, militarism, and neo-Confucian thought. Contemporarily North Koreans are basically limited to watching domestic television stations, and the state has set up an independent internet and made it practically impossible to access the World Wide Web. This limitation resonates with the state doctrine of *juche*, self-reliance.

Second, the program of cultural transformation involved an aggressive Westernization of musical culture under the influence of China, as Western music was thought to be more "scientific" and rational. Kim Il Sung actively opposed many aspects of Korean traditional musics, such as complex vibrato techniques, the predominance of soloists, and so on, as decadent remnants of feudalism or bourgeois ideology. These "barriers to progress" were removed by adopting aspects of Western musical culture that were deemed more modern, rational and "scientific." Ironically, while the state attempted to demonstrate its independence from the West, North Korean musical culture was revolutionized through the adoption of Western vocal production techniques (*bel canto*, for example), Western-style melodic ornamentation, and instruments. The Western treatment of pitch, for instance, was deemed more rational because it relied on stable pitches arranged in fixed, equidistant intervals, and because the relative lack of ornamentation when compared to Korean traditional music allowed, presumably, for the clearer presentation of text. Western harmony was thought more rational because it focused on combination rather than difference, order rather than the controlled chaos of many Korean traditional musics. So traditional instruments were transformed to make them timbrally more like Western instruments—less distinct from one another and capable of harmonic playing. The *haegeum*, a two-stringed spike fiddle, for instance, became four instruments of four sizes, capable of playing as a quartet.

The other important revolutionary transformation of North Korean music was what might be called the "massification" of musical culture. At the same

Dancers and mass card display at the Arirang Mass Games. *Source:* Gilad Rom/ CC/Wikimedia Commons

time as state musical culture—song and musicals especially—emphasizes the importance of mass obedience to authority and glorifies labor, the musical ensembles reflect this importance of the masses: enormous choirs, monophonic textures that emphasize sameness and unity, and giant orchestras, often of people playing the same instrument—huge accordion ensembles, and others.

Perhaps the most spectacular realization of the mass cultural ideal is the "Arirang Festival," which has been held off and on since 2002. It is held in the massive Rungrado First of May Stadium in Pyeongyang (the capital), which can seat 150,000 people, making it the largest stadium in the world by capacity for seating. The festival includes music, parades, acrobatics, and, most famously, mass games, including the mass mosaic displays by around 30,000 trained performers in the seated areas who use cards to collectively create slogans and pictures.

Most of the things described above are based on material available online, or on the reports of scholars who have visited North Korea. These visits and this online content are vigorously monitored by the North Korean state; and so the picture we get of North Korea through these resources is extremely one-sided. Yet visitors report seeing all sorts of other musical activities on the street and in private. Traditional musicians continue with their art, although it has no place in public, and no state support, so it is rapidly disappearing. North Koreans of older generations and middle-aged people gather in public parks to sit around and sing old *trot* songs, mixed with contemporary North Korean popular songs. Some of these songs have become popular in South Korea, especially during the "Sunshine Policy" of South Korean President Kim Daejung in the late 1990s and early 2000s.

REVIEW CHAPTER RESOURCES

SUMMARY

We have only begun to scratch the surface of Korea as a musical place and a musical culture. But we know enough, anyway, to say that Korean music is one of the forums where the two Korean states and the many people who live in or identify with Korea struggle with the meaning of tradition, the vagaries of "cultural preservation," the quest for identity, and the relation of Korea to the rest of the world. Can music be fixed in amber? Does not the fixing itself constitute change, and if so, what kind? Should music be allowed to remain dynamic and flexible, yet suffer the fate handed to it by colonialism, war, the economy, and so on? Korea and its musics are swept up in powerful processes of economic, social, political, and cultural change, and musical lives have changed dramatically in a very short time. Popular musical culture in both Koreas has almost no sounding relation to "tradition"; yet those who try to dismiss it are confronted with people like Yi Bo-mi, for whom popular music is profoundly meaningful and useful in the basic process of being a person, having a future, and relating to others. Both traditional and popular musics are profoundly imprinted with the transformation of time in modern Korea, with the wounds of colonialism, war, authoritarianism, and rapid development, and with the dreams of the complex Korean present. All of the genres we have considered are to differing degrees the outcome of processes of transnational influence and cultural circulation. Most of all, they have all, in different ways, endeavored to be relevant to Korea's frantic present and to the ongoing projects of Korean identity.

KEY TERMS

Canonization
Colonialism and music
Improvisation and its
    social significance
Music and ideology,
    music and social order
Music and religion
Music and revolution
Musical and social time
Music as transformation
Participatory culture
Ritual and liminality
Suffering in music
Tradition and modernity
Transnationalism and
    nationalism in music

BIBLIOGRAPHY

General Bruce Cumings, *Korea's Place in the Sun: A Modern History* (New York: W.W. Norton, 2005). Nicholas Harkness, *Songs of Seoul: An Ethnography of Voice and Voicing in Christian South Korea* (Berkeley, CA: University of California Press, 2013). Nathan Hesselink, *Contemporary Directions: Korean Folk Music Engaging the Twentieth Century and Beyond* (Berkeley, CA: University of California Berkeley Center for Korean Studies, 2001). Keith Howard, *Korean Musical Instruments* (New York: Oxford University Press, 1995). Keith Howard, *Korean Music: A Listening Guide* (Seoul: National Center for Korean Traditional Performing Arts, 1999). Keith Howard, *Perspectives on Korean Music vol. 1: Preserving Korean Music: Intangible Cultural Properties as Icons of Identity* and *vol. 2: Creating Korean Music: Tradition, Innovation and the Discourse of Identity* (Aldershot, UK: Ashgate, 2006. Kyung Hyun Kim and Youngmin Choe, Eds., *The Korean Popular Culture Reader* (Durham, NC: Duke University Press, 2014). Byong Won Lee, *Style and Esthetics in Korean Traditional Music* (Seoul: National Center for Korean Traditional Performing Arts, 1997). Byong Won Lee and Yong-Shik Lee, Eds., *Music of Korea* (Seoul: National Center for Korean Traditional Performing Arts, 2007). Robert Provine, Yoshihiko Tokumaru, and J. Lawrence Witzleben, Eds., *The Garland Encyclopedia of World Music, vol. 7: East Asia: China, Japan and Korea* (New York: Routledge, 2002). Andre Schmid, *Korea Between Empires: 1895–1919* (New York: Columbia University Press, 2002). Gi-Wook Shin and Michael Robinson, Eds., *Colonial Modernity in Korea* (Cambridge, MA: Harvard University Asia Center, 1999). Bang-Song Song, Ed., *Source Readings in Korean Music* (Seoul: Korean National Commission for UNESCO, 1980). Judy Van Zile, *Perspectives on Korean Dance* (Middletown, CT: Wesleyan University Press, 2001).

Monographs and Articles Margaret Walker Dilling: *Stories inside Stories: Music in the Making of the Korean Olympic Ceremonies* (Berkeley, CA: University of California Berkeley Center for Korean Studies, 2007). Nathan Hesselink, *P'ungmul: South Korean Drumming and Dance* (Chicago, IL: University of Chicago Press, 2006). Nathan Hesselink, *SamulNori: Contemporary Korean Drumming and the Rebirth of Itinerant Performance Culture* (Chicago, IL: University of Chicago Press, 2012). Keith Howard, *Bands, Songs, and Shamanistic Rituals: Folk Music in Korean Society* (Seoul: Royal Asiatic Society Branch, 1990). Keith Howard, Ed., *Korean Pop Music: Riding the Wave* (Folkestone, Kent: Global Oriental, 2006). Keith Howard and Laurel Kendall, *Shamans, Nostalgia, and the IMF: South Korean Popular Religion in Motion* (Honolulu: University of Hawaii Press, 2009). Eun-Young Jung, "The Place of Sentimental Song in Contemporary Korean

Musical Life," *Korean Studies* 35/1 (2011). Andrew Killick, "Ch'angguk Opera and the Category of the Traditionesque," *Korean Studies* 25/1 (2001). Andrew Killick, *In Search of Korean Traditional Opera: Discourses of Ch'angguk* (Honolulu, HA: University of Hawaii Press, 2010). Yasue Kuwahara, editor, *The Korean Wave: Korean Popular Culture in Global Context* (New York: Palgrave Macmillan, 2014). Yong-Shik Lee, *Shaman Ritual Music in Korea* (Seoul, Jinmoodang, 2004). Yong-Shik Lee, Ed., *Pansori* (Seoul: National Center for Korean Traditional Performing Arts, 2008). Yong-Shik Lee, Ed., *Sanjo* (Seoul: National Center for Korean Traditional Performing Arts, 2009). John Lie, *K-Pop: Popular Music, Cultural Amnesia, and Economic Innovation in South Korea* (Oakland, CA: University of California Press, 2015). Roald Maliangkay, "Their Masters' Voice: Korean Traditional Music SPs (Standard Play Records) under Japanese Colonial Rule," *The World of Music* 49/3, 2007. Simon Mills, *Healing Rhythms: The World of South Korea's East Coast Hereditary Shamans* (Aldershot, UK: Ashgate, 2007). Mikyung Park, "Korean Shaman Rituals Revisited: The Case of Chindo *Ssikkim Kut* (Cleansing Rituals)," *Ethnomusicology* 47/3, 2003. Marshall Pihl, *The Korean Singer of Tales* (Cambridge, MA: Council on East Asian Studies, Harvard University, 1994). Joshua D. Pilzer, *Hearts of Pine: Songs in the Lives of Three Korean Survivors of the Japanese "Comfort Women"* (New York: Oxford University Press, 2012). Haekyung Um, *Korean Music Drama: P'ansori and the Making of Tradition in Modernity* (Farnham, UK: Ashgate Publishing Company, 2013). Heather Willoughby, "The Sound of Han: P'ansori, Timbre, and a Korean Ethos," *Yearbook for Traditional Music* 32 (2000).

DISCOGRAPHY

Korea: Shamanistic Ceremonies of Chindo (JVC VIGC-5214). *Kim Suk Chul Ensemble: Shamanistic Ceremonies of the Eastern Seaboard* (JVC VICG-5261–2). *Sinawi Music of Korea* (Seven Seas KICC 5163). Chi Soungja, Song Gumnyon: *Korea—Music of the Kayagum* (JVC VICG-5018). *Scattered Melodies: Korean Kayagum Sanjo from 78RPM Records* (Sublime Frequencies SF077). *Korea: The Folkloric Instrumental Traditions (I)—Sinawi and Sanjo* (JVC VICG-5020–2). *Korea: The Folkloric Instrumental Traditions (II)—Sinawi, Sanjo, and Taepungnyu* (JVC VICG-5021). *Kim So-Hee : P'ansori, Korea's Epic Vocal Art & Instrumental Music* (Elektra Nonesuch 972049–2). *Korean Court Music* (Lyrichord LYRCD 7206). *Corée: Musique Instrumentale de la Tradition Classique* (Ocora C558701). *Aak: Ancient Music of the Korean Royal Court* (Global Village iTunes release). *Samulnori: The Legendary Recording by Original Members in 1983* (Nonesuch 7559–72093–2). *Shin Joong Hyun—Beautiful Rivers and Mountains: The Psychedelic Rock Sound of South Korea's Shin Joong Hyun 1958–1974* (Light In The Attic LITA 065). *Radio Pyongyang: Commie Funk and Agit Pop from the Hermit Kingdom* (Sublime Frequencies SF023). Kim Young Dong, Song Kwang Temple Monastery: *The Buddhist Meditation Music of Korea* (Seoul Records SRCD3013). *Folk Songs I* (JVC VICG-5022–2). *Folk Songs II: Namdo Songs of Cholla Province* (JVC VICG-5023–2). *Korean Traditional Music* (Global Village iTunes release).

MUSICS OF EAST ASIA III: JAPAN

Isabel K.F. Wong

HOGAKU PERFORMANCE IN TOKYO

Tokyo, Japan's capital, is a crowded, bustling modern city of around 13 million people, nearly 10 percent of the country's population. Although a formidable city at first glance, Tokyo is more like a conglomeration of small towns and neighborhoods clustered together, each with its own shops and narrow, winding streets.

Tokyo is both new and old, Eastern and Western. The variety of Japanese, Asian, and Western musical performances that take place in Tokyo during the concert season (spring to fall) is a reflection of this fact. Any day during the concert season, the visitor is likely to find performances of Western art music or popular music, as well as performances of **hogaku**, Japan's traditional music. Some hogaku performances may take place in the concert halls clustered around the Tokyo Railroad Station, others in the recital halls inside great department stores in the

Ginza area, Tokyo's chic shopping district, and still others in the National Theater, situated across the street from the grounds of the Imperial Palace.

During one of my recent visits, I attended two musical performances at the National Theater, which was opened in 1966 for the promotion and development of traditional Japanese performing arts. It actually comprises two theaters: a large one seating nearly 1,800 people, which is used principally for the performance of **kabuki** musical drama, and a small one seating about 630, which is used to stage a variety of concerts of hogaku music and dance, as well as performances of puppet musical plays known as **bunraku**. Two restaurants are also attached to the National Theater: a larger one on the second floor that serves a set menu for dinner, and a smaller one at the front of the theater grounds that serves snack food.

A MIXED CONCERT

HOGAKU
Native Japanese music.

KABUKI
The main form of Japanese popular musical theater.

BUNRAKU
The main form of puppet theater in Japan.

One of the hogaku concerts I attended at the National Theater was a gala event commemorating the sixtieth birthday of a respected master. It took place in the small theater and started at 6:30 p.m., but most of the audience arrived before curtain time to have dinner at the restaurants. The concert was sold-out, and I was lucky to have obtained a standing-room ticket—the least expensive kind—at 4,000 yen (equivalent to about $40 U.S. in 1995). The audience was greeted by ushers at the door of the theater and handed program notes (in Japanese) about the four items to be performed; this included song texts and instrumentation and was followed by many advertisements. The inside of the theater included a proscenium stage and rows of seats. Both the program and the theatre's physical space, then, were similar to what someone attending a concert by the Berlin Philharmonic or the Chicago Symphony Orchestra might expect to encounter. The members of the audience were primarily well-dressed Japanese men and women wearing Western-style clothing, but some older women wore the Japanese kimono.

The relatively long concert, lasting more than three hours, began with three pieces for a chamber ensemble consisting of six musicians. The final piece of the program, which came after an intermission of about twenty minutes, called for a chorus and orchestra, each consisting of a dozen or so performers, as well as dancers. All the performers wore traditional attire and knelt on the floor of the stage with low music stands placed before them.

As each piece began, the performers picked up their instruments from the floor in front of them in a deliberate and uniform fashion. The attentiveness of the audience complemented the erect posture and strict decorum of the performers. At the end of each piece the performers replaced their instruments on the stage floor in the same way that they had taken them up, and only then did the audience applaud. The performers acknowledged the applause by bowing formally and then remained stationary until the curtain had descended completely.

Yuki Yamada playing the Japanese Koto with the Kifu Mitsuhashi Ensemble at the Japan Society, New York City, 2003. *Source:* Jack Vartoogian/Front Row Photos

The first piece in the program was an ensemble played by three *kotos* (long, thirteen-stringed zithers) and three *shamisens* (a three-stringed, long-necked, fretless lute, whose sound box is covered with cat or dog skin front and back and whose strings are plucked with a large plectrum). The musicians, who included both men and women, sang as they played. I noticed that the first and last sections were sung with instrumental accompaniment, whereas the middle section, which was the longest, was entirely instrumental. I also noticed that although the music was primarily **pentatonic**, it occasionally used auxiliary pitches. The voice, the kotos, and the shamisens seemed to share a basic melody, but each performed the melody in a somewhat different fashion, rhythmically as well as melodically, resulting in a texture that may be described as **heterophonic**. The second piece was a jiuta (a major koto genre). Broadly speaking, the term denotes a type of vocal piece having a lyrical text that is accompanied principally by the shamisen and sometimes by a koto as well. This performance included both shamisen and koto accompaniment, and the former was supplied by the vocalist herself. Like the previous piece, this too had three sections, of which the middle was a purely instrumental interlude.

The third piece was a trio for solo voice and two shamisens that was derived from a narrative genre called **shinnai-bushi**. The vocalist, who did not play any instrument, sang with a penetrating voice. The type of shamisen used in this piece had a thicker neck than those used in the previous pieces. While one shamisen played the basic melody, the other played a lighter and higher part, heterophonically elaborating the melody. In contrast to the others, this piece was divided into six sections.

During the intermission, people who had not had dinner before the concert—I among them—went to the theater restaurants to have a quick bite. The food was delicious and was served in beautifully decorated lacquered bowls and plates, but when the bell rang indicating that the curtain was about to go up, I hurriedly finished my dinner and returned to the auditorium.

The final piece, featuring some two dozen musicians, made me realize how much of a foreigner I was to Japanese music. Despite the magnificent costumes of the dancers, I had difficulty concentrating on the performance, because I found it disconcerting to have a variety of musical genres and instrumentations mixed in a single modern composition. Yet most of the audience appreciated the piece greatly and even seemed to prefer this composition to the others. The different types of instruments used included a number commonly associated with solo or narrative genres, such as the koto and shamisen, various types of *fue* (horizontal flute), the *shakuhachi* (end-blown, notched flute), and the *nohkan*, the horizontal flute of the Noh theater. Among the other instruments used, some

Taiso Yoshitoshi, "Enjoying Herself," 1888. Woodblock print. A music teacher of the Kaei era (1848–1854) smiles as she plays her shamisen. *Source:* Asian Art & Archaeology, Inc./Corbis

PENTATONIC
Having five pitches.

HETEROPHONY
Two or more performers play the same melody, but with small differences in timing or ornamentation.

SHINNAI-BUSHI
A musical narrative form accompanied by the shamisen, found in Shinnai Tsuruga.

GAGAKU
Japanese court orchestral music.

were borrowed from the **gagaku** court music ensemble, such as the *ryuteki* (a horizontal flute), the *hichiriki*, a double-reed oboe, which has a distinct and penetrating sound, and the *sho*, a mouth organ something like a harmonica. There was also a small percussion ensemble, comprising a small pair of cymbals, a small drum, a wooden clapper, and a small gong. This modern attempt to combine various kinds of traditional music and dance in a single new composition encompassed: fragments of a *jiuta* (played by a trio made up of shamisen, koto, and shakuhachi) an exerpt from the *nagauta* repertory of the *kabuki* theater, a bit of Buddhist chant called shomyo, a shamisen duet, and finally, materials deriving from folk song and dance. At the end of what seemed to this perplexed foreigner to be a tediously long and incongruous composition, the audience surprised me by rising and giving the performers a standing ovation. As soon as the curtain fell, however, the audience disappeared quickly, and clearly no encore was expected.

A KABUKI APPRECIATION CLASS

The second performance I attended at the National Theater was an appreciation class for the *kabuki* theater, which was extremely interesting and educational.

Kabuki, Japan's main popular theater, is regularly performed in several venues in Tokyo; among these, the most famous and best known is the *Kabukiza* (*za* means "seat," but today it has come to mean "theater"), which is situated in the Ginza and contains, aside from the theater, six restaurants. The Kabukiza has about eight or nine kabuki productions a year, each of which runs about twenty-five days. Usually two different programs are performed daily; matinees run from about 11:00 a.m. to 4:00 p.m., and evening performances run from 4:30 p.m. to 9:00 p.m.

The Kabukiza was built in 1887 and has been reconstructed many times since then. It is an impressive theater with more than 2,000 seats, a wide orchestra, and two balconies. The stage, almost ninety-three feet wide, is equipped with revolving platforms and trap lifts. In addition, there is a long runway, the *hanamichi*, connecting the stage with the rear of the theater, which is also part of the stage. In the lobby, various recordings of, and books in Japanese and English, about kabuki are sold along with various souvenirs. Foreigners who do not understand Japanese or are novices to the theater can rent earphones and listen to a simultaneous translation of the libretto.

Kabuki performances are also held several times a year at the larger hall of the National Theater, which also runs a "*Kabuki* appreciation class" for young people every summer. There are two such classes daily at 11:00 a.m. and 2:30 p.m., and I bought a ticket for the morning one.

When it was time for the class to start, all the lights in the theater were turned off except those on the bare proscenium stage, and a man in a kimono appeared on the stage.

"Hello everyone, my name is Iwai Hanshiro, and I am a kabuki actor. I am going to tell you something about the kabuki theater today so that you can

Togashi, a character in the kabuki theatre in a piece called *Kanjincho*. Written in the 19th century, it takes place in 12th century Japan. *Source:* FRANCE © Colette Masson/Roger-Viollet/The Image Works

appreciate it better. It is a pity that too many Japanese people nowadays cannot appreciate kabuki because they do not understand it. The purpose of this appreciation class is to tell you some of the fun and secrets of the kabuki theater, so you will come to the theater again and again."

"Let me first tell you a bit of the history of kabuki. The first performance was done in 1596 entirely by women. The government immediately banned female performance of kabuki, so the stage was taken over by a troupe of boys, but since 1652, kabuki has been performed by adult males, as it still is today, and female roles are impersonated by male actors. In the eighteenth century, when Japan was ruled by a succession of military strongmen known as shoguns and entered a long period of peace, kabuki developed into a definite cultural form for urban dwellers (*chonin*). You must remember that kabuki is predominantly a dance theater with musical accompaniment; it makes use of extensive and elaborate scenery, costumes, and properties, which I will show you later."

"Kabuki has borrowed a lot from other types of theater, such as the classical *noh* theater and the puppet theater bunraku. It has also absorbed folk dance and popular dance. How many of you have been to the noh theater?" Only a few hands were raised.

"Let me demonstrate some kabuki gestures that were derived from bunraku and noh."

At this point our lecturer made a vigorous gesture with his arms and legs, which was masculine, abrupt, and angular. "This gesture is an adaptation of puppet movement of the bunraku theater, known as *aragoto*, meaning 'rough business.'"

He then walked in stately, gliding steps, moving without any perceptible upper-body motion. "This gentle and refined movement came from the noh theater."

"Dance is very important in kabuki theater. A kabuki actor is primarily a dancer, and dance is an essential movement toward a climactic static posture." He now struck and held a dramatic pose, and then turned to us and said, "Now, this is the time for you to applaud me. We kabuki actors like to know that you appreciate what we do!" The young audience, encouraged by the lecturer, giggled and applauded enthusiastically. At that moment, a middle-aged woman sitting next to me shouted, "Bravo!" in Japanese, which was acknowledged by our lecturer with a deep bow in her direction. The young audience turned to look at her with puzzled expressions on their faces, whereupon our lecturer said, "This is a very appropriate and common way to give praise to actors. You may try it yourselves!" "Bravo! Bravo!" shouted the audience, greatly energized. Our lecturer bowed graciously to them.

"It is now time to show you something about the kabuki stage. It is equipped with several trap lifts, which are used to bring scenery or musicians from below the stage to the level of the stage floor, and vice versa." As he spoke, several men, who were holding musical instruments in their hands, suddenly rose up through the stage floor. The young audience, obviously loving this, burst into applause.

"There are more fun things to follow. The stage is also equipped with two revolving stages in the center, an outer one and an inner one, which are capable of being moved in opposite directions. These revolving stages are used to change the entire set at once and have been in use since the sixteenth century." As he spoke, a realistic set depicting a large rice field complete with stacks of grain, trees, and thatched huts suddenly revolved into the center of the stage. A few seconds later, this set disappeared from sight, and another one showing the inside of a house, with cooking utensils and straw mats on the floor, appeared in front of us.

Then our lecturer pointed in the direction of the raised runway connecting the stage to the rear of the auditorium, and asked: "How many of you know the name of this runway?" A few treble voices shouted, *Hanamichi!*" "Good!" our lecturer said. "You have been studying this in school, no doubt! The hanamichi is a unique feature of the kabuki theater. It serves as an additional acting space for the actors and as a more intimate acting area within the audience. There is a passageway built beneath the floor of the theater for actors to go from the dressing rooms behind the stage to the entrance of the hanamichi without being seen by the audience."

Suddenly, a man dressed in the costume of a peasant appeared on the hanamichi at the rear of the theater. He walked a few steps, paused, gently moving his head from side to side as if hesitating, and finally moved forward to the stage proper with an attitude of determination.

"Meet Hayano Kanpei, the hero of the play you are going to see after my lecture! Have you guessed that Kanpei is no peasant? He is really a ronin—that is, a samurai who has lost his master. He is disguised as a peasant to avenge his master's death. If you have been observant, you should have noticed that before he finally proceeded to the stage proper, he moved his head gently from side to side. A peasant does not move in such a refined fashion! The connoisseur would know from this gesture that his real social status is higher than that of a peasant." At this point, the actor who portrayed Kanpei gave the audience a bow and exited.

"Another important element of kabuki theater is music, and it is time to introduce the musicians! In general, there are two groups of musicians: those who appear on the stage, and those who do not. The onstage musician group is called the **degatari**, and the offstage group is called the **geza**." He gave a signal, and a pair of men were elevated from below to stage left. Both were kneeling, and one was holding a shamisen.

"This is the **chobo**, a pair of onstage musicians borrowed from the puppet theater. One is a narrator; the other one accompanies him on the shamisen. Even though they may sometimes participate musically in the events taking place on the stage, the chobo musicians are not actors."

"Let me give you an example. Suppose that I am a character in a play who is sobbing. The chobo narrator can take over the sobbing for me without a break, and the shamisen player in turn can imitate the sound of sobbing on his instrument, while all the time the sobbing is supposed to be that of the character onstage, and the accompanists do not participate in the action. The chobo musicians not only participate musically in the events on the stage, they also narrate and explain the plot to the audience; you could say that they are storytellers."

"Sometimes a character in a play may want to sing about his feelings, or another may want to perform a dance. Who will provide musical accompaniment? Another group of onstage musicians is called the **debayashi**, meaning 'coming-out orchestra.' These musicians are singers as well as instrumentalists, and their number varies according to the needs of the drama." He gave a signal, and from the rear of the stage a trap lift raised a two-tiered platform covered with red cloth on whose upper tier knelt six men holding shamisens; below them, on the level of the stage, six singers knelt behind low music stands.

"Let us hear their music!" the lecturer commanded, and the ensemble started to play. "This music is called *nagauta*, meaning 'Long Song,'" our lecturer said. "It is the heart of kabuki music. The music is produced by an ensemble consisting of singers, several shamisen, and sometimes a bamboo flute, plus a percussion ensemble borrowed from the noh theater that includes several drums and the flute called nohkan. Two or three of the singers are soloists; the rest of the singers sing the chorus part in unison."

"Now let us bring on the geza musicians." At this moment both the chobo and the debayashi musicians were lowered beneath the stage, and downstage left another group of instrumentalists and a large drum appeared.

"These are offstage musicians called the geza," we were told. "They normally sit in a room situated at stage right, where they can look out to the stage and the hanamichi through a bamboo curtain, and the audience cannot

DEGATARI
On-stage musicians in Kabuki theater. This group is divided functionally into two separate ensembles, called the chobo (storytellers) and debayashi (ensemble specializing in performing nagauta, or "long song").

GEZA
The off-stage music of the kabuki theater.

CHOBO
The Gidayu (musico-narrative) duo on the kabuki stage.

DEBAYASHI
The on-stage musicians of the kabuki theater.

LISTENING GUIDE

KABUKI NAGAUTA MUSIC FROM THE PLAY *DOJOJI*

 **LISTEN**

TRACK 6.1 **Performed by a Debayashi Ensemble**

THIS PERFORMANCE illustrates the sound of the debayashi ensemble in kabuki theater. Listen for the way that the vocalist, nohkan (bamboo flute), and shamisen take turns leading the performance.

TIME	SECTION	MUSICAL EVENTS
0:00–0:22	**Introduction**: Listen for the interaction between the shamisen players and the vocalist. They are performing similar melodic material but elaborating it in different ways.	The vocalist and shamisen perform together in this introductory section.
0:22–1:01	**Instrumental Section**: Notice here the sound of the nohkan (bamboo flute) and the drums, both of which join the shamisen. Also listen for the way the nohkan and shamisen take turns leading the ensemble.	The instrumental section gets under way, featuring a melody performed by the nohkan. It is accompanied now by shamisen and drum.
1:01–1:13		The nohkan drops out of the texture, making room for the shamisen to take the lead.
1:13–1:19		The nohkan returns momentarily.
1:19–1:22		The shamisen, once again, takes over the lead role.
1:22–1:41	**Vocal Section**: Listen for the expanded ensemble that accompanies the singer in this section.	The vocalist returns, accompanied here by a much more energetic ensemble including shamisen, nohkan, drum, and a small, bell-like gong.
1:41–2:05	**Instrumental Section**: By now you should be familiar with the sound of the ensemble, so listen now more closely to the way the parts fit together in this performance.	As during the first instrumental section, the nohkan takes the lead at first.
2:05–2:10		The shamisen takes over from the nohkan for a brief moment.
2:10–2:27		The nohkan re-enters as the principal melodic instrument.
2:27–2:40		The shamisen returns once more to lead the ensemble.
2:40–3:02	**Vocal Section**: The vocalist returns, accompanied by the full ensemble heard earlier.	Just as in the section heard at [1:22–1:41], the vocalist returns accompanied by shamisen, nohkan, drum, and bell.
3:02–3:15	**Instrumental Section/Return of Vocalist**: Listen for the short instrumental section here.	A short instrumental section, led by shamisen and then, beginning at [3:04] by nohkan.
3:15–3:35		The vocalist returns, and continues to perform even as the recording fades out beginning at [3:26].

see them. Their job is to provide sound effects for the dramatic action. The instruments are: the *o-daiko* (big drum), shamisen, nohkan, and gongs and bells. Let me show you the strokes of the o-daiko." As he was talking he picked up the two drumsticks and hit the drum with several types of strokes. "Some strokes indicate curtain calls; others create different atmospheres and moods; some strokes represent raindrops, the sound of wind, or thunder, and others represent the appearance of a ghost." When the demonstration was over, the geza musicians disappeared from the stage.

"I know you are very eager to see today's play, but I have yet one more important instrument to show you, and that is the *hyoshigi*." Immediately, a man appeared at the corner stage right, holding two rectangular woodblocks in his hand; he knelt and began playing the blocks in a series of accelerating beats.

"The player is called the *kyogenkata*; he is a stagehand, and the rhythmic pattern he just played announces the rise of the curtain." With this final demonstration, the actor concluded his introduction and called for the play to begin.

The play, about Kanji's revenge, employed all the devices, mechanisms, and musical groups we had just learned about, and using the simultaneous translation of the dramatic dialogue and explanation of the plot in English transmitted through the headphones I wore, I found that I could easily understand the plot and enjoy the drama.

Vocal and instrumental chamber music recitals and performances of kabuki can be heard and seen in Japan nowadays with some frequency, particularly in the four major cities: Tokyo, Kyoto, Osaka, and Nagoya. These types of hogaku music are essentially products of Japan's most recent "-ancient" period—that is, the time from the seventeenth to the nineteenth century known as the Tokugawa or Edo period, when Japan, ruled by the Tokugawa clan in the capital Edo (present-day Tokyo), experienced a period of uninterrupted peace. Cities such as Edo and Osaka grew into populous centers of trade and government, where a large and prosperous bourgeoisie developed, including tradesmen and artisans, who vigorously supported the developing arts and culture. It was under the patronage of this bourgeoisie that the kabuki theater and the many chamber vocal-instrumental genres involving the koto, shamisen, and other instruments came into being and flourished.

THEATER MUSIC

The culture of the bourgeoisie, essentially urban and popular, was characterized by a taste for romantic or comic novels, for salacious or witty lampoons, for brightly colored prints and paintings, and above all, for spectacular theatrical entertainment. The kabuki theater, with its lavish costumes and staging, its elaborate stage machinery, and its fondness for plots of romantic love, is representative of this culture.

EXPLORE

Japanese Theater Traditions

The Bunraku Puppet Theater

The other important popular theater of the Edo period, which can also be seen today, principally in Osaka and in Tokyo's National Theater, is the puppet theater called *bunraku*. Emerging at about the same time as kabuki and under the same circumstances and patronage—primarily that of the bourgeoisie or chonin of Osaka—bunraku both borrowed from and exerted influence on kabuki theater.

The bunraku puppet, made of wood, is moved by three puppeteers who manipulate its arms, fingers, legs, body, head, eyes, mouth, and even eyebrows. These movements are so realistic that the spectators can easily forget the actor is made of wood, even though the puppeteers are not hidden behind or above the stage. The two junior puppeteers are, however, completely shrouded in black and hooded, and only the senior puppeteer's face is visible.

The narration of the bunraku, both sung and spoken, is provided by a narrator-chanter, who is accompanied on shamisen. This is the same combination as the chobo ensemble we encountered in the kabuki demonstration. When a kabuki play is derived from the bunraku theater, the narrative and music accompanying the dramatic actions are provided by the chobo, in the same manner as in the bunraku theater.

GIDAYUBUSHI

A major Japanese musical narrative style accompanied by the Shamisen created by Takemoto Gidayu.

The narrative style used in bunraku is called **gidayubushi**, after its developer, Takemoto Gidayu (1651–1714) of Osaka. The vocal style of gidayubushi includes chants, heightened speech, and lyrical songs. The shamisen, whose music is made up of various arrangements of stereotyped patterns, plays preludes, interludes, and postludes to the singing. Bunraku rose to its artistic

Bunraku puppeteers operate a warrior puppet during the Kumagai Jinya scene from the play Ichinotani Futaba Gunki. *Source:* Jack Vartoogian/Front Row Photos

and popular height when Takemoto collaborated with the famous playwright Chikamatsu Monzaemon (1653–1725).

The Noh Theater

Edo-period musical theatricals are by no means the only kinds of traditional stage genres one can hear and see in Japan today. Among genres originating in other historical periods of Japan, the noh theater is particularly import- ant. Combining various folk dances, musical theatricals, and religious and courtly entertainment of medieval times, noh was transformed into a serious Buddhist art by the performer Kannami Kiyotsugu (1333–1384) and into a refined court art by his son, Zeami Motokiyo (1363–1444). Wearing a mask, brocade robes, and white socks, the chief actor moves and dances slowly on a bare stage with perfectly controlled and restrained movements. Accompanied by a male chorus and a small instrumental ensemble made up of a flute and three drums, he carries the spectator into the austere world of a medieval Japan deeply influenced by Zen Buddhism.

Noh was a product of the Muromachi period (1333–1615), which was marked by continuous military strife among the various clans of warriors (samurai). Exclusively an art of the ruling samurai class from the fifteenth to the nineteenth centuries, noh, with its performing style of elegant simplicity and restraint and its major themes of redemption of human suffering through the love of Buddha, is a direct antithesis of the flamboyant, colorful, and lavish theatrical entertainments of the Tokugawa bourgeoisie such as kabuki and bunraku.

In Zeami's day, a performance of noh consisted of at least five plays—a god play, a warrior play, a female-wig play, a possession play, and a demon play— interspersed with comic plays called *kyogen* for a change of pace. Today the usual program consists of two or three noh plays (each lasting about an hour) and one or two kyogen (lasting about thirty to forty minutes).

Supported mainly by intellectuals now, noh is performed in major cities in special indoor theaters that are owned and operated by five traditional schools of noh performance. In addition, noh plays are performed on various festival occasions throughout Japan on outdoor stages that are built in the compounds of Shinto or Buddhist temples.

The main element and action of a noh play is linked closely with its major actor, the *shite*. The supporting actor, or *waki*, provides a foil for the revelation of the shite's character and the explanation for his actions.

Noh plays are typically in two acts. Thematically, these acts can be organized into five major *dan* (sections or units). The first act comprises the first dan— an introduction—and the second, third and fourth dan—which together make up the exposition of the play—and ends with a dance called *kuse*, the high point of the play. This act provides a full exposition of the spirit of the *shite*. The second act consists of only the fifth dan; in this denouement the shite is transformed into a new character (usually a supernatural being), sings a couple

NOH
Japanese classical drama that originally developed in the early fourteenth century.

of songs, and performs another dance, called the *mai*, which reveals his new essence after his transformation.

Music for noh consists of songs (solo and choral) sung by the actors or chorus, recitative-like heightened speech for the actors, and instrumental music played by an instrumental quartet (a flute and three drums). The functions of the instrumental ensemble are to play introductory music and interludes, to set the scene or mood of individual units within the two acts, to accompany entrances and exits of actors, to accompany songs and dances, and to provide a rhythmic background for dialogue and action. The songs (*uta*), sung by either the actors or the chorus, are of two types—the **sageuta**, which are short, slow, and in low range, and the **ageuta**, which are longer and higher.

The instruments making up the instrumental quartet for noh are a flute called nohkan and three drums of different sizes. Unlike most bamboo flutes, which consist simply of a tube of dried bamboo, the nohkan is constructed from such a tube split lengthwise into strips that are then turned inside out, wrapped with cherry bark, and lacquered. It has seven finger holes and a mouth hole. Other elements of its construction and playing technique lend this flute a distinctive, piercing sound that helps it retain a strong individuality within the noh ensemble.

SAGEUTA

A type of song in lower vocal range used in Noh plays.

AGEUTA

A type of song in higher vocal range used in Noh plays.

(*left*) Sakiji Tanaka playing the Noh drum Taiko. *Source:* Shozo Sato/Isabel K.F. Wong

(*right*) Sakiji Tanaka playing the Noh drum Kotsuzumi. A kotsuzumi is an hourglass-shaped drum held at the shoulder and used in Noh theater. Other instruments include the nohkan (transverse flute), the okawa or otsuzumi (hourglass-shaped drum placed on the lap), and the taiko (barrel-shaped drum placed on a small floor stand and played with two sticks). *Source:* Shozo Sato/Isabel K.F. Wong

(left) Sakiji Tanaka playing the Noh drum otsuzumi. *Source:* Shozo Sato/Isabel K.F. Wong

(right) The Noh drum otsuzumi. The otsuzumi is one of four orchestral instruments (three drums and a flute) used to accompany the dances and songs of the traditional Japanese Noh drama. *Source:* Shozo Sato/Isabel K.F. Wong

The music of the nohkan is made up of various arrangements of a large number of stock patterns. Different pieces are produced by rearrangement of the sequential order of these patterns, and the use of certain sequences is determined by the dramatic conventions of the noh theater. The music for the nohkan serves as a marker for certain subunits of a dan, sets the tempo for the dances and accompanies them, adds a melodic layer to the drum patterns, sets the pitches for the chorus and accompanies it, and provides emphasis for certain lyrical passages of the songs.

The nohkan and the three drums used in noh are collectively called **hayashi** (a generic term for ensembles of flute and drums). The three drums are: the *ko-tsuzumi*, the *o-tsuzumi*, and the *taiko*. The first two are hourglass-shaped drums, whereas the taiko is a shallow barrel drum. Of the three, the smallest but most important is the ko-tsuzumi; although it derives from Chinese and Korean models, the manner of playing it in noh theater is entirely a Japanese development.

The three drums have wooden bodies with two skin heads that are stretched over iron rings and tied to the drum bodies with ropes. The special tone of the ko-tsuzumi is achieved by carving special patterns on the inside surface of the body and affixing bits of damp paper to the rear head, which is not struck.

HAYASHI
Generic name for ensembles of flute and drums.

The ropes holding the heads to the body may be squeezed to increase tension on the heads. The tension of the head of the o-tsuzumi is always at a maximum and thus cannot be altered by further tightening the ropes. In fact, before a performance, the drumhead is heated over a hibachi grill to increase the tension still further, and during a performance a newly heated drum may be substituted. All this tension creates a dry, hard sound that may be increased by the use of hard thimbles on the player's fingers.

The taiko is played with two thick sticks instead of the hands. The drum is placed on a special stand that grips the encircling ropes, lifting the drum off the floor for better resonance. The taiko is used sparingly, normally joining the other instruments for dance sections.

All three drums are capable of producing several basic sounds, and their varying combinations form stock patterns that are identified onomatopoeically.

An additional but integral part of noh drumming is the use of drum calls by the drummers. These **kakegoe**, as they are called, may have originated as practice devices, but they are now part of the overall sound of the music for noh and are certainly one of the distinctive elements that add to its strangely rarefied atmosphere.

Like the chobo ensemble of gidayubushi, the noh hayashi, has been adopted for some kabuki performances, where it always introduces a reference to classical, courtly culture.

The vocal part of noh, called **yokyoku**, is sung by both the actors and the onstage chorus. The melodic style of yokyoku is solemn and spare, betraying its origin in Buddhist chanting of medieval Japan. The articulation of every textual syllable is deliberate and prolonged, and their pronunciation is based on a stage convention different from everyday speech. Together with the actors' stately bodily movements and gliding steps, the music of yokyoku and hayashi contribute to the overall impression that noh theater is ethereal and other-worldly.

Yokyoku has two basic styles: the heightened speech called **kotoba** (words) and the aria called **fushi** (melody). Fushi is sung in two basic ways: the **yowagin** (soft) style, which is delivered softly and is used in lyrical scenes, and the **tsuyogin** (strong) style, which is delivered with strength and is used in masculine and warlike scenes.

The tonal system of the yokyoku is based on the interval of the minor seventh, coinciding with the same interval produced when the uniquely constructed nohkan is overblown. (Most flutes produce the octave when overblown.) Within this minor seventh, three notes making a conjunct pair of perfect fourths provide important tonal centers. If we designate the minor-seventh interval as being from A down to B, then the three tonal centers are A-E-B, in that order of importance. Around each of these tonal centers there is a cluster of notes forming a tonal system for melody.

The rhythmic structure of noh singing, like that for the hayashi, is based on an eight-beat framework, but in a flexible manner. The number of textual syllables in each poetic line to be sung within these beats varies, but a five-syllable line is most common.

KAKEGOE
Vocal drum calls used in noh theater.

YOKYOKU
Choral singing in noh.

KOTOBA
A heightened speech style used in the noh theater.

FUSHI
A term for melody in general.

YOWAGIN
Soft-style noh music.

TSUYOGIN
A strong-style noh music.

LISTENING GUIDE

EXCERPT FROM NOH PLAY *HAGOROMO*
("THE ROBE OF FEATHERS")

 **LISTEN**

TRACK 6.2 **Hayashi (instrumental ensemble) and chorus**

ONE OF THE most famous noh plays is *Hagoromo* ("The Robe of Feathers"). Belonging to the category of "female-wig plays," this one-act play in two scenes tells the story of a fisherman (portrayed by the waki) who stole the feather robe of an angel (portrayed by the shite) and thus prevented her return to heaven; however, he was so moved by her distress that he agreed to return it if she would dance for him. The second scene, consisting of a series of dances accompanied by choral chanting and the hayashi, is considered the high point of the play. The excerpt heard here basically alternates rather free-rhythm and ornamented vocal sections sung in the soft style with a more strident vocal and more regular rhythmic accompaniment.

TIME	SECTION	MUSICAL EVENT
0:00–0:25	**Waki sings with accompaniment**: Listen for the distinct contributions of the vocalist and the instruments. Notice the relatively free meter and the kakegoe (vocal calls) inserted by the drummers.	The vocalist opens this recording and is quickly joined by the drums, including the taiko, with its characteristic low, dull pitch. The drummers also intersperse kakegoe throughout this section. Notice how the drums are not functioning in this section to create a rhythmically stable backdrop for the vocalist, but rather to introduce their own "voices" into the texture of this free-metered section.
0:25–0:45	**Chorus enters**: Notice that the chorus and drummers settle into a steady rhythmic pulse by the middle of this section.	The chorus takes over the lead role in this section. The contrast between the soloist and the chorus helps delineate sections of the performance.
0:45–1:12	**Waki returns**: Listen here to the vocalist who, although he sings alone, is enveloped in kakegoe and occasional exclamations on the drums.	The waki returns and sings in free meter. He is supported here by intermittent kakegoe and strokes on the drums. Beginning around [1:01] the drummers begin to enter more deliberately into the texture and they also move the performance back toward a rhythmic pulse.
1:12–2:07	**Chorus returns**: Notice the increased activity of the drummers in this section.	The chorus enters and picks up on the regular pulse established at the end of the last section. The chorus continues to perform until the recording fades out, beginning at [1:58].

The individual musical elements of noh are conceived in a linear fashion, and the key to appreciating noh is to follow the various lines of the voices and the instruments. For example, the chorus and the nohkan may be involved in two completely separate melodic lines, while the drums may be playing a rhythmic pattern of a different length from either. As mentioned, the strong individuality of the components of noh is a characteristic feature, and relying on this, noh can create a complex art from few resources. The center of this art is the poetic text, and the musical elements revolve around it.

Noh plays are produced by a group of people: the poet supplies the text, and the actors, the chorus, and the hayashi compose their own parts according to the text. This creative process works for noh because the music is highly systematized.

THE RELIGIOUS TRADITIONS

Shintoism and Shinto Music

MIKAGURA
Japanese court religious (Shinto) music.

GAGAKU
Japanese court orchestral music.

SHOMYO
Japanese Buddhist chanting.

Among the ancient types of Japanese music that can still be heard today are court Shinto music, **mikagura**; court orchestral music, **gagaku**; and the Buddhist chant, **shomyo**. The latter two were originally Chinese inspired, whereas the first one is entirely indigenous.

The earliest Japanese religion shared many elements with the religions of other peoples of East Asia and only became designated Shinto ("the way of the gods") when confronted with Buddhism and Confucianism. Shinto is a loose agglomeration of local and regional cults with a diversity of gods and spirits, and it includes a variety of religious elements such as nature worship, animism, shamanism, ancestor worship, hero worship, fertility rites, phallicism, fortune-telling, and so on.

Constant change and adaptation is the norm of Shinto. It adopted and adapted gods and cults with ease, and there has seemed to be no clear conception of divinity and no real attempt to articulate a theology on a rational basis, nor is there an organized, hereditary priesthood.

Five elements or objects stand out in Shinto worship: the sun (or fire), water, mountains, trees, and stones. In ritual practice, Shinto ceremony consists essentially of attendance on a god and offerings to him or her, accompanied by invocations and prayers. Festivals represent special occasions for honoring the gods and establishing good rapport with them by offering food, drink, and music and dance. Shinto rituals generally take place during important occasions of life and of the agricultural year, such as birth, marriage (always celebrated at a Shinto shrine), the New Year, plowing, planting, and harvesting. Shinto has nothing to do with death, however.

Until the Edo period, musical creation was regarded as a gift from god and, like the beauty of nature, a miracle. Thus in the Shinto view, an appreciation

Ceremonial music, or "kagura" (entertainment of the gods). *Source:* John S Lander/Getty Images

of music sprang from admiration and awe at what is "natural," pure, and simple, rather than from a rational admiration of the artfully organized.

One type of ancient Shinto music, mikagura, can still be heard today in court Shinto ceremonies. It is performed by a male chorus and accompanied by the *wagon* (a six-stringed zither), the *kagura-bue* (a transverse bamboo flute with six holes), the hichiriki, and the *shakubyoshi* (a pair of wooden clappers). Fifteen songs are still preserved in the present-day repertory, and they are of two main types—the **torimono**, songs paying homage to the gods, and the **saibari**, songs meant to entertain the gods. Since the nineteenth century, mikagura songs have been performed by two choruses, each having its own repertory. The performance is initiated by the leader of each chorus, who sings the initial phrase of a song and accompanies himself on the clappers and is then followed by a unison chorus accompanied by the rest of the instruments. In Shinto ceremonies, dance is an integral part of the ceremony.

In folk Shinto rituals, the music used is called **satokagura**. There are two main types: The one used in shamanistic rituals paying homage to the gods involves a priestess who sings and dances and is accompanied by the *wagon*, the transverse flute, and the *suzu* (bell-tree). The other, used in Shinto festivals and called *matsuribayashi* (festival music), is performed by a hayashi consisting of the o-daiko, two taiko, a transverse flute, and a small gong, *kane*. This music is characterized by a lively syncopated drum rhythm, which accompanies a repeated melodic line played by the flute.

TORIMONO
Shinto songs in praise of the gods.

SAIBARI
Shinto songs meant to entertain the gods.

SATOKAGURA
Folk Shinto music.

Buddhism and Buddhist Music

Buddhism came to Japan in the sixth century CE from Korea and China. By this time it was already a thousand years old and a highly developed religion. The essential tenet of Buddhism concerns suffering and its elimination through the cessation of desire—the achievement of Nirvana. When it came to Japan, Buddhism gave the Japanese a means of dealing with death and suffering, something that Shintoism had not provided. It affected the Japanese deeply, but their innate delight in the simple joy of life also modified Buddhism by infusing it with an appreciation for life and nature.

During the Nara (553–794) and Heian (794–1185) periods, when Japan's capitals were in Nara and Kyoto, respectively, the great aristocratic clans adopted the Mahayana form of Buddhism. Great monastic systems were established and integrated into the court and its civil administrative system. The theology of Mahayana Buddhism asserted that salvation from suffering and death was open to all, and it attracted a huge following among the populace. The government decreed the building of many great monasteries and demanded religious services praying for peace and prosperity for the state. Scriptural verses called sutras were chanted in these ceremonies to secure good harvests and the welfare of the state.

The chanting of Buddhist sutras is called shomyo; it is performed by a male chorus in responsorial style, and the texts are in several languages. Those in Sanskrit are called *bonsan*; those in Chinese, *kansan*; and those in Japanese, *wasan*. The music consists of a series of stock patterns belonging to two different Chinese-derived scales, the *ryo* and the *ritsu*, each of which has five basic notes and two auxiliary notes. Shomyo chants may be **syllabic** or **melismatic**, and their rhythm may be more or less regular or free. A chant usually begins slowly and gets faster. During the Nara and Heian periods, the aesthetic aspect of Buddhism predominated, not only because of native Japanese sensitivity but also because the aristocrats admired beauty and elegance above all things. Aesthetic cultivation (the playing of music being one of the requirements), together with physical training and psychological discipline—all aspects of one personality— were involved in the attainment of Buddhahood, which was the goal of the Esoteric Buddhism practiced in the Nara and Heian periods. Consequently, ritual, art, and music were as important as scriptures and meditation. It was not just a matter of enlightening the mind but of affecting and transforming the whole world. This view of the world and of man gave great impetus to Buddhist art (including images of Buddha and mandala paintings) as well as Buddhist music.

The collapse of the Heian court and its civil administration in the eleventh century brought about profound changes in Buddhism. Religious institutions bound up with the fortune of the court nobility declined, while a highly aestheticized and sentimentalized religion, based on the refined enjoyment of beauty, could not meet the challenge of the difficult time ahead. With the constant warfare, famine, pestilence, and social disruption of the ensuing Kamakura (1185–1333), Muromachi, and Azuchi-Momoyama (1333–1615)

MELISMATIC-SYLLABIC
Performing a single syllable of text by singing multiple notes or pitches is called a melisma (melismatic). Syllabic singing, by contrast, matches one syllable to a single note or pitch.

periods, a new form of Buddhism arose, whose primary mission was to bring salvation immediately within reach. This Buddhism for the masses, called *Amida Buddhism*, had little to do with the arts and aesthetics.

Another form of Buddhism that arose during this difficult period was Zen Buddhism, whose roots were in China and India. Zen emphasizes personal enlightenment through self-understanding and self-reliance by means of meditation, using practices related to the yoga practice of ancient India. In Japan, Zen Buddhism was supported by the military class during the Azuchi-Momoyama period.

Aesthetically, Zen inspired many of the traditional arts of Japan, such as landscape painting, landscape gardening, swordsmanship, the tea ceremony, and noh drama. It was under the patronage of the Ashikaga shogun that Zen and its allied arts, including noh, evolved and developed.

A CONCERT AND A COURT TRADITION

Sokyoku

Popular koto-and-vocal music of the Edo period is known under the generic name of **sokyoku**. The koto is a long zither whose thirteen strings are stretched over movable bridges. The player places the instrument on a mat or low table and plucks the strings using plectra on the thumb and the first two fingers of the right hand. With the left hand, the player presses on the strings to the left of the bridges to create ornaments and new pitches by altering the tension of the strings.

There are two types of sokyoku. The first, **kumiuta**, is a koto-accompanied song cycle; the verses of each individual song, called uta, are derived from preexistent poems whose subjects are unrelated. Typically, an uta has duple meter and is in eight phrases, each divided into four measures. The second type, **danmono**, for koto alone, is in several sections (dan), each consisting of either 64 or 120 beats. The structure of danmono is akin to a loose rondo-variation form. The famous piece "Rokudan" (Six Sections) is a classic example of this form. A basic theme is presented and within each of the six dan the theme undergoes variation with interpolation of new material. "Rokudan" can be played by one koto as a solo piece or by two koto as a duet. Sometimes other instruments, such as the shamisen and the shakuhachi (an end-blown bamboo flute with four finger holes and one thumbhole, with a notch cut in the lip to facilitate sound production) may join in, as they do in the listening example "Rokudan No Shirabe".

Jiuta is an important hybrid form of koto music that combines the techniques of both kumiuta and danmono. It is sometimes called *tegotomono*, after the **tegoto**, the important instrumental interludes between vocal sections. Tegotomono usually contain three parts—a foresong (**maeuta**), an instrumental

SOKYOKU
Popular koto-and-vocal music of the Edo period in Japan.

KUMIUTA
A suite of songs accompanied either by the koto or the shamisen, or by both.

DANMONO
Sectional form.

JIUTA
A major koto genre that combines techniques of both kumiuta and danmoto. Sometimes called tegotomono.

TEGOTO
Instrumental interludes in koto music.

MAEUTA
The first song in a jiuta cycle.

ATOUTA
The last song in the jiuta
cycle.

SANKYOKU
Jiuta music played by a trio.

interlude (tegoto), and an after song (**atouta**). This basic structure may be extended (to include an introduction, for instance).

Today, jiuta is played by an ensemble called **sankyoku** (trio) consisting of koto, shamisen, and shakuhachi. The koto plays the main melody, while the shamisen and shakuhachi play an elaboration of the main melody, thereby producing a heterophonic texture.

LISTENING GUIDE

FIRST TWO DAN OF "ROKUDAN NO SHIRABE"

 **LISTEN**

TRACK 6.3 Performed by sankyoku trio of koto, shamisen, and shakuhachi by the Zumi-Kai Instrumental Group

THIS IS A RECORDING of the first and second sections, or dan, of "Rokudan No Shirabe," performed by a sankyoku trio of koto, shamisen, and shakuhachi. Each instrument realizes the melody in an idiosyncratic way, resulting in a richly heterophonic texture. The piece begins with a statement of the basic melody in a slow tempo. The performers, however, soon settle into a slightly faster tempo and proceed very gradually to increase the overall tempo of the performance. Listen for the distinctive "voices" of the three instruments. Listen also for the way that the second dan begins to elaborate and extend on the musical and melodic gestures of the first dan.

TIME	SECTION	MUSICAL EVENT
0:00–0:39	**First Dan**: Listen for the distinct contributions of the three instruments. Notice the relatively steady meter and the gradual increase in tempo. Listen also for the way the koto's sustained (ringing) tones carry through while the shamisen's comparatively rapid decay sets it apart from the koto.	The first few melodic gestures of the dan feature the koto and shamisen as lead instruments. The shakuhachi is playing along softly here. (If you're having trouble telling which string instrument is which, listen on a pair of headphones and notice that the koto is mixed more to the left ear and the shamisen more to the right.)
0:39–1:31		The shakuhachi enters more prominently during this part of the dan, mirroring the koto and shamisen.
1:31–2:04		The koto elegantly elaborates on the melody while the shamisen and flute play the basic melodic gestures. This continues until the first dan comes to a close at [2:02].
2:04–3:38	**Second Dan**: Notice that the tempo has increased slightly and that there is more elaboration of the basic melodic gestures in this dan.	The second dan features more frequent elaboration and ornamentation of the main melodic gestures. Notice that the tempo increases slightly here as well and that some new musical ideas are introduced along the way (not heard in the first dan, that is).
		The second dan comes to a close at [3:30] and the recording fades out as the third dan begins.

The koto tradition is perpetuated by various schools, the most important of which are the Ikuta School of Kyoto and the Yamada School of Tokyo, whereas the Meian and Kinko schools, also based, respectively, in Kyoto and Tokyo, represent the main traditions of shakuhachi performance. The latter have an interesting and colorful origin. They were founded in the Edo period by masterless samurai, who combined the profession of street musician with that of spy and informer and used their heavy bamboo flutes not just as musical instruments but also as clubs!

The music of the koto and the shamisen best represent the music of the Edo era. Although the shamisen belongs primarily to the world of the theater, with its colorful and exciting entertainments, the koto, by contrast, developed from a court tradition and gradually entered the home, played by members of the rising merchant class as an emblem of cultural accomplishment. In the modern era, the koto maintains a position in Japan similar to that of the parlor

LISTENING GUIDE | **"CHIDORI"** |  **LISTEN**

TRACK 6.4 Performed on two koto and shakuhachi, with voice, by the Zumi-Kai Instrumental Group

O NE OF THE MOST FAMOUS koto pieces is called "Chidori." In a full performance, it illustrates well the jiuta form (introduction—song—interlude—song). In this excerpt, we hear only the opening two sections—that is, the introduction and part of the first song (or maeuta). But this is enough to help us think through the alternating structure of the jiuta form (the movement between songs [which are sung] and instrumental sections). Although this particular recording features two koto and shakuhachi, it can also be performed as a solo piece, a koto duet, or a koto and shamisen ensemble.

TIME	SECTION	MUSICAL EVENTS
0:00–1:22	**Introduction**: This recording features two kotos and shakuhachi. Notice the stately tempo set in the introduction. Listen also for the timbre of the koto.	This opening section gives us a glimpse into what the tegoto (instrumental) section following the first song (maeuta) will sound like. Notice the way the kotos and shakuhachi combine to play the melody in heterophonic fashion.
1:22–1:54	**Maeuta (first song)**: Notice how the instruments support the vocalist in realizing the melody. Listen for the heterophonic way the ensemble works through the melodic phrases.	The vocalist enters and begins the maeuta (or first song).
1:54–2:03		The vocalist gathers for the next phrase while the instruments provide a brief interlude.
2:03–2:35		The vocalist re-enters and the ensemble continues the maeuta even as the recording fades out starting at [2:30].

piano in nineteenth-century America. It is a popular instrument for middle-class Japanese girls, who play it as a sign of good breeding.

Gagaku

Gagaku, meaning elegant or refined music, is the instrumental and choral music and dance that has been under the continual patronage of the imperial court for more than a thousand years. Influenced by the ancient music of China, Korea, and Sinicized Indian music, it has been carefully transmitted by generations of court guild musicians to the present day and is perhaps the oldest ensemble music in the world. Gagaku is also used to accompany dance; in this role it is called *bugaku*.

Gagaku was first adopted in the Nara period (553–749)—the first major historical period in Japan, during which the Japanese struggled to establish a national government modeled after that of China. Prior to the Nara period, Japan was ruled by various rustic clans, the most dominant of which were the Yamato, who originated on the southern island of Kyushu. Until the Nara period, Japanese history and mythology focused on the gradual northern extension of the imperial Yamato power and the justification for its dominance over other lesser clans of the land.

The construction of the city of Nara was begun in 708, and the court was moved there in 710. Fashioned as a miniature of the Chinese capital of Changan (present-day Xian), it captured perfectly the spirit of an age in East Asian history dominated by the pervasive influence of the great empire of the Chinese Tang dynasty. Nara was the first urban center in Japanese history. Its founding was accompanied by a great burst of economic, administrative, and cultural activities. One of the administrative measures taken was the establishment of a music bureau staffed by musicians from Korea and China. Musicians performed music and dance for court entertainments and rituals.

Nara's founding also ushered in the age of the court nobles, a period that lasted until the later twelfth century. Members of the imperial household, court ministers, and Buddhist priests contended for political power. The constant court intrigues suggest a fundamental instability in the ruling institutions. A century later, this instability was exploited by one court family, the Fujiwara, who were able to dominate the throne and subsequently the political affairs of the country for a long time.

The emperor Shomu and his consort, who was a Fujiwara, were fervent Buddhists, and their influence helped spread this foreign faith. In 737, Shomu ordered the construction of the Todaiji (Great East Temple) in Nara. Housed within the central building of the Todaiji is a huge bronze statue of the Buddha. The casting of the Great Buddha was an impressive technological feat for eighth-century Japan, and it also represented the first Japanese artistic representation of the human form.

At the "eye-opening" ceremony for the Great Buddha in 752, during which the statue was symbolically given life by having the pupils of its eyes painted

The Emperor and Empress attend the Gagaku, the Japanese Imperial Court Music Concert. *Source:* The Asahi Shimbun/Getty Images

in, all the great court dignitaries were in attendance. In addition, there were visitors from China, India, and other distant lands and some 10,000 Buddhist priests. It was without doubt one of the grandest occasions in all of early Japanese history. Hundreds of musicians and dancers performed, and many instruments dating from this occasion are still preserved in the imperial treasury of Nara, the Shosoin. Music thus became a part of important rituals pertaining to religious and court affairs.

All Nara court music was of foreign origin and was played primarily by foreign musicians in its original style. The subsequent Heian period (794–1185) showed signs that the Chinese influence was beginning to be assimilated and modified.

Heian (Kyoto), the newly constructed city to which the government moved in 794, remained the capital of Japan for more than a millennium (until the Meiji Restoration in 1868). At the end of the Heian period in 1185, a new military national government was established in Kamakura by the warrior family of Minamoto, bringing an end to the age of the court nobles and ushering in nearly seven centuries of dominance by the warrior class, until the restoration of the Meiji emperor in the late nineteenth century.

During the Heian period, great changes occurred in the governmental system, with the power of the emperor becoming eclipsed by that of the regent, who was controlled by the Fujiwara family. Buddhism continued to flourish in the Heian period, and it had become the principal intellectual system and one of the most important institutional systems in Japanese life. Heian nobles were preoccupied with etiquette and ritual, and they lived in a world governed by formal standards of beauty and the cultivation of poetry and music.

TOGAKU
Court music of Chinese and Indian origin in the gagaku repertory.

KOMAGAKU
Japanese court music of Korean origin.

Heian court music still employed a host of Chinese instruments and forms, but the musicians themselves were mostly Japanese. In the ninth century, a standard gagaku orchestra was created under order of the emperor, and a repertory of two main categories was standardized. The **togaku** repertory includes music of Chinese and Indian origin, whereas the **komagaku** includes music of Korean and Manchurian origin. Gagaku music was extremely popular in the Heian court. Not only was it a necessary component of all court ceremonies, but it was also practiced by the court nobles themselves. Amateur gagaku clubs flourished. The famous novel of the Heian period, *The Tale of Genji*, is full of descriptions of musical activities of the noblemen. Today about twenty gagaku musicians who are descendants of musicians of the professional guilds are maintained by the emperor, and amateur ensembles also exist outside the court.

The ensemble for gagaku consists of percussion, strings, and winds. The various instruments used in gagaku are described briefly under separate headings.

Percussion

1. The *da-daiko*, a huge drum struck by two thick sticks. It is only used in bugaku dance.
2. The *tsuri-daiko*, a suspended two-headed drum, only one side of which is struck with two sticks. It is a **colotomic** instrument—that is, it serves to mark off the larger phrase units.
3. The *shoko*, a small suspended gong played with two sticks. It is usually played on the first beat of every measure.
4. The *kakko*, a small drum whose two heads are struck with thin sticks. The kakko is the leader of the togaku ensemble. Its three basic rhythmic patterns are two types of rolls (a slow roll done with both sticks and a faster roll done on the left skin) and a single tap with the right stick. These patterns are played to regulate the tempo of the piece, and they are found mostly in free rhythmic sections; they are also used to mark off beats or phrases. The kakko is only used in togaku.
5. The *san-no-tsuzumi*, an hourglass-shaped drum with two heads, only one of which is struck. Korean in origin, it is played only in komagaku, by the leader of that ensemble.

Strings

1. The *wagon*, a six-stringed zither used in kagura.
2. The *gaku-so*, a thirteen-stringed zither, a predecessor of the koto. The strings are plucked by the bare fingers or with finger picks. The music for the gaku-so is made up of two basic patterns that are played to mark off sections.
3. The *biwa*, a pear-shaped lute with four strings and four frets played with a small plectrum. It is also used to mark off sections in a piece. The music

COLOTOMIC
Marking or delineating major phrases in a musical composition. Used to describe percussion instruments that have this function.

for the biwa consists primarily of arpeggios, which may end with short melodic fragments. The effect of biwa music in gagaku is primarily rhythmic. This instrument is similar to the old style of Chinese *pipa*.

Winds

1. The *hichiriki*, a short, double-reed bamboo oboe with nine holes, originating from China. Through use of the embouchure and fingering technique, tones smaller than a half-step can be produced. Its tone quality is penetrating and strong, and it is the center of the gagaku ensemble.
2. The *kagura-bue*, a six-holed bamboo flute that produces a basic pentatonic scale; other pitches may be produced by using special fingerings. The length of this flute varies, and thus also its actual pitch. It is used for Shinto ceremonies.
3. The *ryuteki*, a seven-holed bamboo flute of Chinese origin used for togaku music. It is the largest of the gagaku flutes.
4. The *koma-bue*, a six-holed flute of Korean origin used for komagaku music. It is the smallest of the gagaku flutes.
5. The *sho*, a mouth organ with seventeen reed pipes (two of which are silent) in a cup-shaped wind chest with a single mouthpiece. Its predecessor was the Chinese *sheng*. Chords are produced by blowing into the mouthpiece and closing holes in the pipes. Its primary function is harmonic. Typically, each chord is begun softly and gradually gets louder, whereupon the next chord is produced with the same dynamic swelling; this process is repeated continuously by inhaling and exhaling air.

The wind instruments are the heart of the gagaku ensemble; they play roles analogous to those of the strings in a Western symphony orchestra.

Different instrumentations are used for togaku and komagaku. The former uses three sho, three hichiriki, three ryuteki, two biwa, two gaku-so, one kakko, one shoko, and one taiko. Instrumentation for komagaku is similar in many respects but, nonetheless, distinctive. The *koma-bue* is used instead of the ryuteki, the san-no-tsuzumi instead of the kakko, and the strings are not used.

The musical style of gagaku is characterized by smoothness, serenity, and precise execution without virtuosic display. The melody, played on the hi-chiriki and the flutes, is supported by chords produced on the sho. An abstraction of this melody is played on the gaku-so in octaves and on the biwa in single notes. Although smaller sections of a piece are marked off by a biwa arpeggio, larger sections are delineated by tsuri-daiko and shoko strokes. Drum patterns played by the kakko or san-no-tsuzumi serve similar colotomic functions and also regulate the tempo of a piece. When a chorus joins in performing the melody of gagaku, it sings in a natural voice using very little ornamentation.

The melodies of gagaku use six modes theoretically based on the Chinese-derived ryo and ritsu scales. The rhythm is organized so that slow pieces have an eight-beat rhythm, moderately fast pieces have a four-beat rhythm, and fast pieces have a two-beat rhythm.

NETORI (PRELUDE) AND ETENRAKU IN HYOJO

 **LISTEN**

TRACK 6.5 **Performed by Nippon Gagaku Kai (Gagaku Society of Japan). Excerpt from a Gagaku Piece**

ETENRAKU IS THE MOST famous instumental piece in Gagaku and has no dance accompanying it. It was imported from Tang dynasty China, but over the centuries various tunings have been developed, so there are now three versions. The excerpts here introduce many of the instruments discussed in our text within a concrete musical example. This recording, performed in a pentatonic mode called hyojo, also gives a glimpse of the first two parts of the jo-ha-kyu scheme so central to the aesthetics of gagaku. Notice the continued accumulation of energy and volume during Etenraku, achieved, at least in part, by gradually adding more and more instruments into the texture.

TIME	SECTION	MUSICAL EVENTS
0:00–0:08	**Netori (prelude):** In this short opening prelude corresponding to the "jo" or introductory section of the jo-ha-kyu scheme, listen for the distinct "voices" of the six instruments that gradually enter.	The sho (mouth organ) opens the performance.
0:08–0:27		The hichiriki (bamboo oboe) enters, following the prescribed order of entries in netori.
0:27–0:36		The kakko (small drum) is added to the texture. And the ryuteki (bamboo flute) enters subtly in support of the hichiriki.
0:36–1:01		The ryuteki now takes a more prominent role and the hichiriki drops out.
1:01–1:30		The gaku-so (zither) and biwa (lute) enter and the ryuteki drops out. (If you're having trouble telling them apart, listen on headphones, where the gaku-so will be primarily on the left side and the biwa primarily on the right.)
1:30–1:36	**Etenraku:** This is the main portion of the performance, and you should continue to listen for the distinct instruments that continue to enter the ensemble. You might also want to think about this section as the "ha" (or development) section of the jo-ha-kyu aesthetic scheme.	The ryuteki returns and begins to introduce the Etenraku melody in a slow tempo, beginning the "ha" section of the composition.
1:36–2:17		The kakko returns and is joined by the shoko (small gong). At [1:41] these two percussion instruments are joined by the daiko (a larger drum). At [1:53] the kakko performs an extended roll.

continued

TIME	SECTION	MUSICAL EVENTS
2:17–2:37		The sho and hichiriki reenter at this point.
2:37–4:57		Gaku-so and biwa reenter, playing intermittently and completing the ensemble. This texture remains in place until the recording fades out beginning at [4:52].

Gagaku music, like most Japanese music that came after it, was conceived in an aesthetic scheme of introduction–exposition–denouement known as **jo-ha-kyu**, which has also influenced the aesthetic of noh. In gagaku, jo is the *netori*, a slow prelude that introduces the musical mode in which the piece is written. In a full-blown gagaku piece, the sho generally starts the netori, followed in turn by the hichiriki, the flute, and finally the kakko. The mood of the netori is generally subtle and serene and has a tentative feeling like a warm-up.

During the ha section, the rhythm becomes regular. Here the main body of the composition begins. The hichiriki and flute play the basic melody, the sho provides a harmonic background, and the percussion provides accompaniment; shortly, the strings also join in. Once the entire ensemble is playing together, there is no further change in the full ensemble sound.

Kyu is the rushing to the end. Here the tempo becomes fast. Toward the end, the pace slackens once again, and the instruments drop out one by one as the texture becomes thinner. Finally, only the biwa and the gaku-so are left. They play two or three slow notes, the biwa ending by plucking the dominant or the tonic of the mode, and the gaku-so completing the composition with one stroke on the tonic. Listening to the archaic sound of the gagaku, one may imagine going back into the rarefied time of the Heian court nobles and sharing with them, for a brief moment at least, their profound preoccupation with aesthetic self-cultivation.

JO-HA-KYU

A basic aesthetic concept in Japanese music. Jo denotes "introduction"; ha denotes "development"; kyu denotes the final section of a composition.

GENERAL TENDENCIES AND CHARACTERISTICS OF HOGAKU

Before closing, it may be helpful to provide some summary observations on the general tendencies and characteristics of traditional Japanese music, hogaku.

The rise and fall of a particular style of music through Japanese history has been closely linked with changes in political life, social conditions, and religious developments. For example, the gagaku of the Nara period was regarded as a symbol of the authority and power of the newly evolved imperial and national government, and no effort was spared to increase its grandeur.

The noh theater, with themes of redemption of human suffering through the love of Buddha, was exclusively an art of the ruling samurai during the long ages of military strife. It is, in particular, an expression of the samurai class's

EXPLORE

Japanese Traditional Music

KEY TERMS

Bunraku
Debayashi
Degatari
Fushi
Gagaku
Gidayubushi
Hayashi
Heterophony
Hogaku
Jiuta
Jo-ha-kyu
Kabuki
Koto
Mikagura
Noh
Nohkan
Shakuhachi
Shamisen
Shinnai-bushi
Sokyoku

preoccupation with Zen Buddhism, which emphasizes simplicity and personal enlightenment through self-understanding and self-reliance. Noh was also a political symbol of the samurai class. During the Edo period, it continued to be performed in the Edo castle, the political center of the Tokugawa military government. Finally, the popularity of the kabuki and the bunraku theaters was due entirely to the rise of the urban bourgeoisie and their patronage. As the bourgeois arts par excellence, they represent a fondness for popular entertainments and, in particular, lavish theatrical entertainments.

Japanese music is closely tied with ritual, literature, and dance, and these ties have remained unbroken through the ages. It was said that in ancient times, when the emperor or his courtiers asked for the pronouncement of an oracle, it was habitual to offer a musical performance first; therefore, the court has always kept musicians in its service.

In hogaku, vocal music predominates. Music serves primarily as a vehicle for words and literature. All Japanese instruments were developed to emulate the human voice. It is noteworthy that the first significant instrumental solos, the tegotomono, were created to serve as interludes to the verses of songs.

Among Japanese music genres, theatrical music is the most important. The course of Japanese music history is marked by a steady growth of theatrical music. This is due again to the Japanese love of storytelling and preoccupation with ritual.

Finally, we have noted the basic Japanese aesthetic concept of jo-ha-kyu (introduction–development–denouement) and the application of this concept in various kinds of music. We have also noted the propensity of the Japanese to use stock melodic patterns in creating new compositions. It remains to be noted that Japanese music is predominantly a chamber music in its conception; even the gagaku ensemble is essentially a chamber orchestra.

SUMMARY

REVIEW CHAPTER RESOURCES

Our excursion into the music of Japan has illustrated that Hogaku, or traditional Japanese music, comprises many different styles, from religious and dramatic music to court and popular genres. We learned that the earliest known Japanese musical style is gagaku, the traditional music of the court. Also fairly ancient are the religious Shinto music and the chanting of Buddhist monks, known as shomyo. The major Japanese theatrical styles we encountered are the kabuki drama; bunraku puppet theatre; and the earlier noh theater. We also learned that typical Japanese instruments include the shamisen (plucked lute), koto (plucked zither), shakuhachi (end-blown flute), and sho (mouth organ), along with various drums.

EXPLORE

Enka, Karaoke, and J-Pop

This chapter has only begun to explore the rich musical heritage of Japan and we have not had occasion to explore the popular music of Japan. That said, this chapter has opened a window onto the long and complex history of Japanese musical life and offers some guidance for those interested in exploring it further.

BIBLIOGRAPHY

Shawn Morgan Bender, *Taiko Boom: Japanese Drumming in Place and Motion* (Berkeley, CA: University of California Press, 2012); Gerald Groemer, "The Rise of 'Japanese Music'" in *The World of Music* Vol. 46, No. 2, Japanese Musical Traditions (2004), pp. 9–33; David Hughes, *Traditional Folk Song in Modern Japan: Sources, Sentiment and Society* (Folkestone, UK: Global Oriental, 2008); Jay Keister, "Okeikoba: Lesson Places as Sites for Negotiating Tradition in Japanese Music" in *Ethnomusicology* Vol. 52, No. 2 (Spring/Summer, 2008), pp. 239–269; Jay Keister, *Shaped by Japanese Music: Kikuoka Hiroaki and Nagauta Shamisen in Tokyo* (New York and London Routledge, 2004); Terence Lancashire, "World music or Japanese The Gagaku of Tôgi Hideki" in *Popular Music* Vol. 22, Issue 1 (January 2003), pp 21–39; William P. Malm, and Donald H Shively, *Studies in Kabuki: Its Acting, Music, and Historical Context* (Honolulu: University Press of Hawaii, 1978); Noriko Manabe, "New Technologies, Industrial Structure, and the Consumption of Music in Japan" in *Asian Music* Vol. 39, No. 1, [Popular Music in Changing Asia] (Winter Spring, 2008), pp. 81–107; Noriko Manabe "Globalization and Japanese Creativity: Adaptations of Japanese Language to Rap" in *Ethnomusicology* Vol. 50, No. 1 (Winter, 2006), pp. 1–36; David Novak, *Japanoise: Music at the Edge of Circulation* (Durham, NC: Duke University Press, 2013); Michael S. Peluse, "Not Your Grandfather's Music: Tsugaru Shamisen Blurs the Lines between 'Folk,' 'Traditional,' and 'Pop'" in *Asian Music* Vol. 36, No. 2 (Summer Autumn, 2005), pp. 57–80; E. Michael Richards and Kazuko Tanosaki, Eds., *Music of Japan today* (Newcastle, UK: Cambridge Scholars, 2008); Carolyn Stevens, *Japanese Popular Music: Culture, Authenticity, and Power* (London: Routledge, 2008); Toru Seyama, "The Re-contextualization of the Shakuhachi (Syakuhati) and its Music from Traditional/Classical into Modern/Popular" in *The World of Music* Vol. 52, No. 1/3, (2010), pp. 104–117; Alison Tokita and David Hughes, *The Ashgate Research Companion to Japanese Music* (Aldershot, UK: Ashgate, 2008); Bonnie C. Wade, *Music in Japan* (New York, Oxford: Oxford University Press, 2005); Bonnie C. Wade, *Composing Japanese Modernity* (Chicago, IL: The University of Chicago Press, 2013); Bonnie C. Wade, *Togotomono: Music for the Japanese Koto* (Westport: Greenwood, 1975); Christian Reiko Yano, *Tears of Longing: Nostalgia and the Nation in Japanese Popular Song* (Cambridge, MA: Harvard University Press, 2002).

DISCOGRAPHY

General   *Nihon No Ongaku*, 2 disks (Polydor MN-9041–9042) (notes in Japanese).

Instruments   *Traditional Music of Japan*, 3 disks, with notes in English and Japanese by Shigeo Kishibe (Nihon Victor, JL 52–54); *Japan: Semi-Classical and Folk Music*, with notes in English, French, and Italian by Shigeo Kishibe (Odeon 3 C064–17967); *Classical Music of Japan* (Elektra EKS 7285).

Shomyo   *Shomyo-Buddhist Ritual from Japan, Dai Hannya Ceremony-Shigon Sect* (UNESCO Collection Musical Sources, Philips); *The Way of Eiheiji, Zen-Buddhist Ceremony* (Folkways FR 8980) (everyday chanting of shomyo).

Shinto Music   *Edo No Kagura To Matsuri Gayashi* (Nihon Victor SJ 3004) (shinto festival and dance music).

Gagaku   *Gagaku Taikei* (Nihon Victor SJ 3002) (instrumental gagaku; another disc (SJ 3003) contains vocal gagaku); *Gagaku: Ancient Japanese Court Music* (Everest 3322); *Gagaku* (The King Record KC 1028).

Noh   *Noh*, 2 disks (Nihon Victor SJ 1005, 1006) (the most complete albums for noh; with history, music theory, libretti, photographs, and explanatory commentaries for each piece); *Hogoromo and Kantan* (Caedmon TC 2019) (contains two major noh dramas, sung and performed by players of the Komparu and Kanze School of Noh, Tokyo); *Japanese Noh Music* (Lyrichord LL 137).

Koto Music   *Sokyoko To Fiuta No Rekishi*, 4 disks (Nihon Victor SLR 510–513); *Japanese Koto Music, with Shamisen and Shakuhachi* (Lyrichord 131) (performed by masters of the Ikuta School).

MUSIC OF INDONESIA

Charles Capwell

JAVANESE MUSIC IN CHICAGO

A subtly glowing array of bronze ingots, pots, and gongs in intricately carved wooden cases painted indigo and red with flashes of gold leaf—this was the dazzling sight that greeted us, a small group of university students and faculty who had come to the Field Museum in Chicago for an afternoon's introduction to the performance of **gamelan** music. Gamelan—an Indonesian word meaning "musical ensemble"—can be variously constituted, but the one at the Field Museum is representative of those used at the princely courts on Java, the most heavily populated island in the nation of Indonesia. Nowadays, similar gamelan can be found in many universities and colleges in the United States and Europe. The Field Museum gamelan, however, has a special history: a couple of Dutchmen who owned coffee and tea plantations on Java brought the gamelan to Chicago, along with a

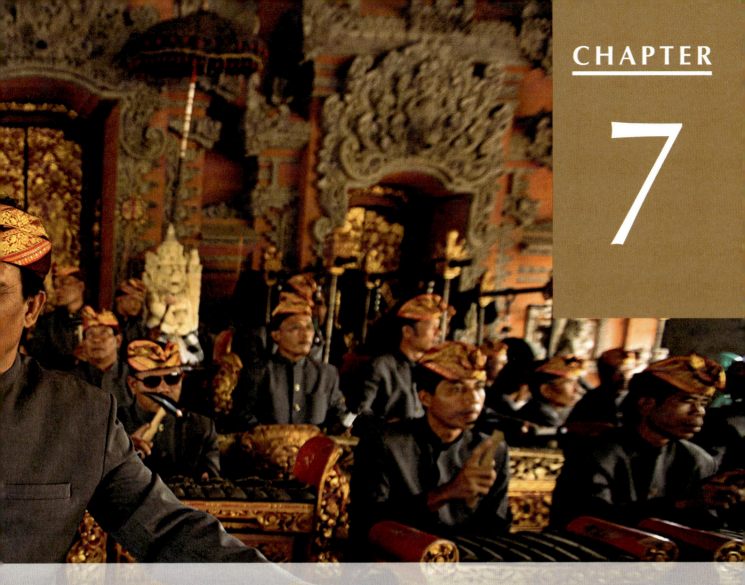

group of Javanese musicians and craftsmen, for the Columbian Exposition of 1893, a great world's fair. The same entrepreneurs had arranged similar contributions to an exposition in Amsterdam a decade earlier and to another in Paris in 1889. At the latter, the composer Claude Debussy was enchanted by the music he heard and later tried to capture what appealed to him in pieces of his own such as some in his *Préludes* and *Images* for piano.

Now that dozens of Indonesian gamelan of various types are to be found scattered around the United States in private and institutional collections, dozens of Americans have become competent performers and scholars of different types of Indonesian music. At the time of our visit to the Field Museum, Dr. Sue Carole DeVale, an ethnomusicologist with a special interest in the study of musical

GAMELAN
An ensemble of instruments such as those found in the central Javanese courts.

instruments (organology), took charge of our instruction. She had been fundamental in getting the museum to restore the gamelan, which had been more or less forgotten in storage for many decades, and had convinced them to make it available for use under her direction.

THE JAVANESE GAMELAN

Instruments in the Javanese Gamelan

METALLOPHONE
An instrument classification term for idiophonic instruments made of metal.

CHORDOPHONE
Scientific term for all types of string instruments, including violins, guitars, and pianos.

AEROPHONE
Scientific term for all types of wind instruments, including trumpets, flutes, and the organ.

MEMBRANOPHONES
Scientific term for all instruments using a stretched membrane for sound production, that is, all true drums.

Like most high-quality gamelan, this one consists largely of **metallophones**—in this case, instruments of gleaming bronze—but it also includes a **chordophone** (*rebab*, a two-stringed fiddle), a xylophone (*gambang*), an **aerophone** (*suling*, a notched vertical flute), and a couple of **membranophones** (*kendang*, drums).

Sitting among the metallophones, we became aware that the bronze had been fashioned in several different ways to make the various types of instruments. The *saron*s, for instance, had keys shaped like rounded ingots. These were pinned through the holes in their ends to the edges of a shallow trough made in a wooden case that served both to hold them in place and to increase their resonance. There were three different sets of sarons, each in a different octave. The highest, the *peking*, had a delicate but piercing tone; that of the middle range, *barung*, was mellower and longer-lasting; and the set in the lowest range, *demung*, had a powerful clang. The peking was sounded by striking the keys with a mallet of water-buffalo horn, but the others were played with heavier and less bright-sounding wooden mallets.

A similar three-octave range was found in the differently constructed *bonang*s, although there were only two of these. The lower-pitched bonang *barung* and the higher bonang *panerus* each spanned two octaves, with the higher octave of the lower instrument duplicating the lower octave of the higher one. The "keys" of the bonangs resembled overturned bowls with knobs protruding from the tops, which is where they were struck with a pair of baton-like mallets wrapped with string. Each instrument had two rows of bowls resting on strings that were stretched in wooden frames.

The *kenong* also had bowl-like individual components, but these were fewer and much larger than those of the bonangs, and each one was supported in its own case on a web of string. A single bowl, closer in size to one from the set of bonangs but flatter in contour, sat by itself and contrasted with all the other instruments because of its curiously dull-sounding "clunk"; this was the *ketuk*.

The most impressive bronze instruments, for both their size and their sound, were the hanging gongs. ("Gong," by the way, is a Malay—that is, Indonesian—word.) The largest, gong *ageng*, was nearly a meter in diameter, and its slightly smaller mate, gong *siyem*, hung by its side. A smaller gong, named kempul, was suspended on the end of the same rack that holds the two large gongs.

Musicians in the Gamelan troupe play traditional Balinese music to accompany dancers in a "Barong Dance show" in Ubud village. *Source:* saiko3p / Shutterstock.com

Like other names such as gong or ketuk, kempul is onomatopoetic and calls to mind the sound of the instrument it names.

In addition to these common instruments, the Field Museum gamelan also contained two others—the *jenglong*, similar to the kenong, which is found in gamelan from Sunda, the western part of Java, and the gambang *gangsa*, similar to the wooden gambang but with bronze keys like those of the saron instead of wooden ones. All in all, this original group of about twenty-four instruments was as impressive for its size as for its beauty; nevertheless, at the time of its use at the Columbian exposition, it lacked certain other instruments that have since been added.

Of the instruments that were lacking, perhaps the most important is the *gender* (pronounced with a hard "g" as in "good"). They come in two sizes (gender panerus and gender barung, like the bonang) and group thin, slab-like bronze keys in a slightly larger range than the saron. Much thinner than the ingots of the saron, the keys of the gender are struck with a pair of mallets with padded disks at their ends, and they produce a delicate, muffled ringing that makes up for their soft volume with longer-lasting resonance. The secret to the long-lasting sound is that each key has its own individually tuned amplifying resonator in the form of a tube. The key is suspended above this tube by strings, so that it is not damped by resting directly on the case (the saron keys rest on pads of rubber or rattan to lessen the damping). Another instrument similar in construction to the gender is the *slentem*, but it is struck with a single mallet and is similar in melodic function to the saron.

Originally, the kempul in the Columbian Exposition gamelan, as described, had been a single hanging gong, but additional gongs have been added to

Javanese gamelan instruments.
Source: Chris Stock/Lebrecht
Music & Arts

complete a full scale, as was also done for the kenong. Although the two-stringed fiddle, the rebab, was part of the original ensemble, the plucked string instrument *celempung*, a type of zither, was among the additions.

Tuning and Scales

Having familiarized ourselves a bit with the components of what at the start had seemed a bewildering array, we still had one further thing to learn before taking up our mallets to attempt our first piece: the instruments came in pairs. A complete Javanese gamelan is in fact two orchestras in one, for there are two different types of scales used in Javanese court music, one of five tones (pentatonic) and another of seven tones (heptatonic). Because the gaps (intervals) between pitches in one scale are different from those of the other, it is not possible to select five tones from the heptatonic scale to produce the pentatonic, and therefore there is a separate collection of instruments for each tuning system (**laras**). To play in laras *slendro* (pentatonic system), for example, the saron players faced front, and to play in laras *pelog* (heptatonic system) they had to make quarter-turn to the left. (You could get a general idea of the contrast between these by playing on the piano C-D-E-G-A as 1–2–3–5–6 of slendro and E-F-G-B♭-B-C-D as 1–2–3–4–5–6–7 of pelog.)

Although the Western scale, like that of the white piano keys, is heptatonic, too, we soon discovered that the seven pitches in pelog formed a different set of intervals from the regular half and whole tones on the piano. The difference was not so simple as merely being one between Javanese and Western scales, however, because each gamelan has its own unique slendro and pelog scales,

LARAS
Javanese tuning system; there are two primary types (1) slendro (with a five-note scale) and (2) pelog (with a seven-note scale).

unless it has been constructed purposely on the model of an existing gamelan. It is as though each symphony orchestra in the West used slightly different forms of major and minor scales, and as a result their performances of standard works like Beethoven's Ninth Symphony would all sound subtly distinct from one another.

Instrument Functions and Formal Principles

When we finally took up our mallets to play, we began with a **gendhing** (a piece of music for gamelan) in pelog called "Golden Rain." As the sarons attempted the first section of their melody, we sang along with them using numbers for the pitches and following our instructor: 6–5–3–2 we sang out as the sarons sounded the tones, all of equal duration. After repeating this phrase, we learned the next one, 3–3–2–3, and then returned to the original for the conclusion. On the last tone, the player of the gong ageng was given the signal to strike, and the awe-inspiring sound left little doubt that we had arrived at an important juncture. The role of the gong was just to furnish this most important punctuation at the end of every completed melody—a melody, in this case, with sixteen beats, with a single pitch on every beat. Two distinct musical functions were illustrated in this beginning: the sarons provided a "skeletal melody" (**balungan**) whose periodic punctuation (the **colotomic structure**) was provided by other instruments like the gong ageng.

The other colotomic instruments were the next to join in as the sarons grew more confident: the kenong sounded the appropriate pitch at the end of every group of four beats (**gatra**), and so every fourth kenong stroke sounded with the gong. In the same manner, the kempul sounded the pitch every fourth beat midway between strokes of the kenong, omitting the second beat, however, so as not to interfere with the continuing resonance of the gong. Finally, on every odd-numbered beat, the "clunk" of the ketuk was heard, so the beats in between kempul and kenong were marked, too.

The next instruments to join in were the bonangs, which added a third functional component to the music, that of elaboration of the balungan. Because their music was more elaborate, they required more dexterity and skill than the other instruments. Although we had been pleased at the ease with which we initially had picked things up, it became clear as we patiently waited for the bonang players to start mastering their parts that things were getting rapidly more complicated and demanding. Although the bonangs required more skill to play, the principle behind their basic method of melodic elaboration was easy enough to understand: As the kenong and kempul played every fourth beat, the bonang barung did the opposite and divided the beat in two, and the boning panerus divided it into four, doubling or quadrupling each pair of balungan pitches. The peking (highest-pitched saron) was also told to double the number of pitches to a beat by anticipating each balungan note. Thus, the first gatra (four-beat phrase of the balungan) came out like this:

GENDHING
A piece of Javanese music for gamelan.

BALUNGAN
Skeletal melody in Javanese music.

COLOTOMIC STRUCTURE
The marking of fixed beats within the metric structure of a musical piece by particular instruments; in gamelan music these include gong, kenong, kempul, and ketuk.

GATRA
A four-beat phrase in Javanese music.

bonang panerus	6	5	6	.	6	5	6	5	3	2	3	.	3	2	3	2
bonang barung		6		5		6		5		3		2		3		2
peking		6		6		5		5		3		3		2		2
Saron				6				5				3				2
kempul								5								
kenong																2
Gong																X

When we got the whole sixteen-beat phrase together, it sounded like a marvelous clock whose music was the actual time-keeping mechanism. Just as with a clock, the sounding of the gong signaled a conclusion that could also be the taking-off point for another cycle.

The drum player, our instructor, indicated whether or not we were to repeat this phrase. In regulating and supporting the pulse and rhythm of the music, the drummer fulfilled the fourth function in the ensemble so that the melody, its elaboration, and its punctuation were controlled from this instrument rather as the conductor in a Western orchestra controls the rest of the group. (In the eighteenth-century Western orchestra, in fact, the "conductor" was actually a performer, too—usually the first violin or the harpsichord player.)

When we had at last become comfortable with this first phrase, we went on to complete the piece with a second, similarly constructed phrase (7567 5672 2765 6765), which we now learned to call a **gongan**, that is, a phrase punctuated with a stroke of the big gong. As we have seen, each gongan was divided into four four-beat **kenongan** (punctuated with a kenong stroke), and each of these was further subdivided by a kempul stroke on the second beat and ketuk strokes on beats 1 and 3. Because this colotomic pattern is a fixed structure, it is common to a number of pieces differentiated from one another by, for example, their balungan, but similar in their colotomy. These make up a general category of small, simple pieces called **bubaran**.

The piece we had learned, as was mentioned, has the title "Udan Mas" ("Golden Rain") and is used to send people off at the end of a ceremony or concert. It served as our farewell too, as we had used up most of the afternoon and decided not to press our luck in attempting another piece.

The Variety of Styles and Forms

Although we came away feeling we had accomplished quite a bit in one afternoon, we had, of course, barely scratched the surface of this one type of Indonesian music. We hadn't even touched some of the instruments such as the genders, for example, because we played a "loud-style" piece in which gender, rebab, celempung, gambang, and suling do not participate. These difficult instruments are used for the elaboration of "soft-style" pieces, which may also include singing by a chorus of men (**gerongan**) and one or two female soloists (**pesindhen**).

GONGAN
A phrase concluded with a stroke on gong ageng or siyem.

KENONGAN
A colotomic phrase in Javanese music marked by a kenong stroke.

BUBARAN
A small-scale Javanese gendhing having sixteen beats.

GERONGAN
A male chorus that sings with Javanese gamelan.

PESINDHEN
Javanese female vocal soloist.

LISTENING GUIDE

BUBARAN "UDAN MAS" (GOLDEN RAIN)

LISTEN

TRACK 7.1 **Paku Alaman Court Gamelan in Jogyakarta**

THIS RECORDING ILLUSTRATES the main formal and rhythmic structures of a category of short gamelan pieces called bubaran. Bubaran are based on a sixteen-beat colotomy and "Golden Rain" incorporates two sixteen-beat phrases (gongan) punctuated at the end by the largest gong. Each gongan makes use of a balungan (skeletal melody) performed on saron and consisting of one pitch per beat. The following schematic representations of pitch contour and relative beats should assist you in picking out the two distinct melodies, and to see how they unfold within a sixteen-beat gongan structure.

Gongan 1:

Pitch (sarong)	*				*								*			
		*				*								*		
			*				*		*	*		*			*	
				*				*			*					*
Pitch number	6	5	3	2	6	5	3	2	3	3	2	3	6	5	3	2
Beat	1	2	3	4	5	6	7	8	9	10	11	12	13	14	15	16

Gongan 2:

Pitch (sarong)	*			*			*			*				*		
			*			*						*			*	
		*			*							*				*
								*	*							
Pitch number	7	5	6	7	5	6	7	2	2	7	6	5	6	7	6	5
Beat	1	2	3	4	5	6	7	8	9	10	11	12	13	14	15	16

TIME	SECTION	MUSICAL EVENT
0:00–0:07	**Introduction (Buka):** Notice the rounded tone and rapid decay (i.e., the notes fade out quickly without ringing out or sustaining their sound over time) of the	Introduction (buka) on bonang, joined by kendang and leading to first gong and first saron note at [0:07]. (The gong accents beat 16 in the colotomic cycle.

continued

TIME	SECTION	MUSICAL EVENT
	bonang. Also listen for the sound of the kendang, the drum that guides the performance and cues the performers.	You'll notice that the saron enters at the same time. It will be tempting to hear that as the first beat, but it's actually the last in the cycle, so count 16, 1, 2, 3, 4, etc. from the gong stroke.)
0:07–0:16	**First gongan**: Notice how much brighter and more sustained the sound of the saron is in comparison to the bonang. See if you can hear the melody clearly and follow along with the colotomic structure.	The first gongan, with balugan melody played on saron and marking one pitch per beat, is performed. Notice that the low gong is struck on the 16th beat. (If you're having trouble hearing it, listen for the most prominent instrument and follow along with the pitches indicated in the preceding schematic.)
0:17–0:26		The first gongan is repeated.
0:26–0:35	**Second gongan**: Listen for the new melodic content and for the way the colotomic structure remains stable. The gong is still articulating the 16th beat.	The second gongan is performed.
0:36–0:44		The second gongan is repeated.
0:45–1:03	**First gongan with repeat**: By now you should be familiar with the melody of the first gongan. This time see if you can hear some of the distinct rhythmic layers being performed by the gamelan. Notice, for instance, the rapid playing on the boning panerus (it generally plays four notes for every one note struck on the saron).	First gongan with repeat, beginning at [0:54].
1:03–1:20	**Second gongan with repeat**: Listen here for the way that the kendang drum interacts with the colotomic structure. Try to hear both the melody and the rhythmic and timbral complexities surrounding that melody.	Second gongan with repeat, beginning at [1:12]. Notice the gradual increase in tempo (accelerando) toward the end of the repeat.
1:20–1:34	**Repeat of both gongans**: Notice that the first gongan is played significantly faster, this time.	First gongan with repeat, continuing at the increased tempo achieved by the accelerando.
1:34–1:46		Second gongan is performed and a decelerando begins the process of slowing the tempo before the second gongan is repeated. The ongoing performance fades out during the repeat even as the decelerando continues.

We had naturally learned to play a short, simple type of piece, but among the types of other pieces for gamelan are some whose gongan, for example, have sixteen times as many beats as our sixteen-beat bubaran. And instead of playing just twice for each beat, the saron peking might play four times to fill in the great gap between one beat and another—so it might be as much as ten minutes between strokes of the gong ageng instead of the approximately ten seconds of our bubaran.

As an example of a small-scale, soft-style piece, we could consider *ketawang "puspawarna" laras slendro pathet manyura*. This is a work entitled "Kinds of Flowers" ("Puspawarna") that has a gongan of sixteen beats, like a bubaran, but it is divided into only two eight-beat kenongan, and therefore it falls into the class of **ketawang**. It employs the scale of the pentatonic tuning (laras slendro) in one of three particular ways or **pathet**, that is called "peacock" (manyura). (There are also three distinct pathet for laras pelog.)

"Puspawarna" is a popular piece played not only on the precious gamelan of princes but also on the modest two- or three-piece ensembles of itinerant street musicians. Despite its wide use for a variety of circumstances and audiences, however, it is not merely a piece intended for listening pleasure. It also has particular associations and prescribed uses, and even its title can tell us something about the political and cultural history of Java.

KETAWANG
A type of Javanese gendhing having thirty-two beats.

PATHET
A particular way of using a scale or laras in Javanese music.

THE CULTURAL AND HISTORICAL SIGNIFICANCE OF JAVANESE GAMELAN MUSIC

Ketawang "Puspawarna": A Piece for the Prince

Just as "Hail to the Chief" played by the Marine Band is often used to announce the arrival of the president at a function or ceremony, "Puspawarna" was played by the gamelan of the two subsidiary central-Javanese courts to announce the presence or the arrival of their respective princes. The main courts of the Sultan of Yogyakarta and of the Susuhunan of Surakarta (Solo) were established in the mid-eighteenth century when the Dutch succeeded in supporting their trade interests by asserting political control over much of the Indonesian archipelago. The central-Javanese kingdom of Mataram was divided at that time between two ruling families centered at Yogyakarta and Solo, with a secondary court, the Mangkunegaran, attached to Solo. Later, in the early nineteenth century, the Paku Alaman court was established as an adjunct to Yogyakarta, and the various princes had their own particular identifying pieces of music, with "Puspawarna" serving both of the subsidiary courts and symbolizing a family connection between them.

Because political power was largely in the hands of the colonial overlords, the wealth and energy of the courts was expended on the development of cultural

EXPLORE

Gamelan

KETAWANG "PUSPAWARNA"

 **LISTEN**

TRACK 7.2 **Paku Alaman Court Gamelan in Jogyakarta**

THIS **RECORDING ILLUSTRATES** the main characteristics of a soft-style piece. Included here are a solo female vocalist (pesindhen) and a male chorus (gerongan). The structure of ketawan pieces revolves around sixteen-beat gongan, and these are subdivided into two eight-beat kenongan. In addition to the introductory **buka**, this particular kenongan also incorporates two common structural components: an **ompak** ("bridge") which is repeated and precedes a contrasting **ngelik** section. A ngelik is usually longer than one gongan and, usually also where the gerongan (the male chorus) sings the main melody of the ketawan composition. Thus, the formal structure of the piece unfolds over the course of five gongan as follows: Gongan **A** (ompak); gongan **A** repeated (ompak); gongan **B, C,** and **A** (ngelik). This entire structure is then repeated.

TIME	SECTION	MUSICAL EVENTS
0:00–0:07	**Introduction (buka)**: The rebab (string instrument), joined by the kendang (drum), open this performance and lead up to the first gong.	Introduction (buka) on rebab, joined by kendang and leading to first gong at [0:07]. (The gong accents beat 16 in the colotomic cycle. It is tempting to hear that gong stroke as the first beat, but it's actually the last in the cycle, so count 16, 1, 2, 3, 4, etc. from the gong stroke.)
0:07–0:22	**Ompak section (Gongan A)**: Notice the entrance of the pesindhen (female vocalist) and also the dramatic slowing of tempo.	Gongan A is introduced at a brisk tempo but the tempo begins to slow almost immediately. At [0:18] the female vocalist (pesindhen) enters.
0:22–0:46		Gongan A is repeated with a continuing decelerando and reaches a settled tempo at the end of this gongan. Notice the continued presence of the female vocalist as well as the stylized male vocal cries that enter at colotomic points.
		During the repeat of Gongan A, you can find your bearings within the colotomic cycle by counting one beat for every four strokes on the drum, starting with 16 at the sound of the low gong at [0:22]. At beat eight, you will hear a particularly rich, sustained note in medium register (usually played just slightly after the beat), played on the kenong. This note cuts through the texture of the other instruments, and when you hear it once or twice, you'll be able to hear it every time. On beat sixteen, the lowest gong sounds out.
0:46–1:13	**Ngelik section (Gongan B, C, and A)**: Listen for the entrance of the gerongan (male chorus) and the melody that stretches across the three gongan (B, C, and A).	Gongan B is introduced and the gerongan enter between beats 5 and 6 of the colotomic cycle (the second syllable they sing is on beat six).

continued

TIME	SECTION	MUSICAL EVENTS
1:13–1:41		Gongan C is introduced and the gerongan enter here on beat 3. Notice the continuation of the melody. Notice also the continued presence of the pesindhen in the texture.
1:41–2:09		Gongan A returns, but as a vehicle to complete the gerongan melody. The chorus again enters at beat 3.
2:09–2:36	**Ompak section repeated**: By now you should be familiar with the overall structure of the piece. See if you can hear the contrasts between the Ompak and Ngelik sections. Also try to hear the gerongan melody as a whole statement across multiple gongan.	Gongan A.
2:36–3:04		Gongan A repeated.
3:04–3:32	**Ngelik section repeated.**	Gongan B.
3:32–3:59		Gongan C.
3:59–4:44		Gongan A.
		Notice the brief accelerando at [3:55] followed by a dramatic decelerando, initiated at beat 1 of the concluding gongan [3:59], but put to especially dramatic use after beat 8 [4:12], such that the last half of the gongan unfolds ever more slowly until the last gong stroke serves as a powerful concluding gesture.

matters such as music and dance as a means of both establishing and justifying their precedence and prestige. Mataram had been the last great native power in Java, a Muslim kingdom in a land where Islam had steadily been increasing its influence for several centuries. As the Sanskrit words in the title "Puspawarna" and in the name of pathet "Manyura" reveal, however, the culture of India and its Hindu and Buddhist religions had considerable influence on the elite and ruling classes in Java and other parts of the Indonesian region for a millennium or so before the establishment of Islam, which itself had been introduced in large part by traders from northwestern India. Although a segment of Indonesian society may follow a strict and conservative Islam that, among other things, condemns most musical and performing arts, the aristocracy of Java, while accepting the "new" belief, continues to prize the older spiritual and cultural concepts and also to accommodate indigenous practice and beliefs that antedate any of the imported ones.

BUKA
Introduction to a Javanese gendhing.

OMPAK
Refers to the opening, usually repeated gongan in ketawang pieces.

NGELIK
A section in ketawang pieces that contrasts with the surrounding material (ompak) and is usually longer than one gongan. It is also usually where the gerongan sings the melody of the ketawang composition.

Some Spiritual Aspects of Javanese Gamelan Music

We may discover something of the complex relationship between Islam and music in Java by citing some observations made about seventy years ago by the ethnomusicologist Jaap Kunst (1973, 266–67):

> The gamelan, found by the Islam on arrival in Java as an indispensable element of all Hindu ceremonials, has never become . . . an integral part of Mohammedan religious rite. Accordingly during the month of fasting, as well as on Fridays, all orchestras in the whole of the Javanese territory are expected to remain silent. (This rule is not strictly adhered to in the kraton [court]. All that is done there is to avoid beating the gong ageng, and to play the gong kemodong [a substitute gong] instead. The princes, for that matter, are regarded as above the adat [customary law]. When, for example, one of their memorial days falls in the fasting month, then the prohibition of gamelan-playing, it seems, is raised entirely. Then, however, a sum of money is paid into the mosque cashbox as a compensation of this breach of the religious adat.)
>
> *Music in Java: Its History, Its Theory, and Its Technique*, Jaap Kunst. © 1973 Martinus Niljhoff Publishers. With kind permission from Springer Science+Business Media B.V.

Princely privilege was partly related to the use of music in rites and ceremonies, and to do away with music altogether would have undermined it; yet acceptance of Islam required some recognition of its precepts. So a fine was paid to the mosque when a princely anniversary requiring musical performance to ensure its success violated the prohibition against playing the gamelan, or alternatively, the most imposing and important instrument in the ensemble was silenced, and a simpler substitute was used. In the latter case, the gong ageng no doubt stood as a metonymical symbol for the whole ensemble that could be considered silent, too, if it were absent.

The Power of the Gong

But another reason for silencing the gong might also be offered. In many cultures the blacksmith has held a special position, not simply because of his technological expertise but also because of his spiritual power (Eliade 1978, 238). Metallurgical skill was considered to require supernatural cooperation, and the smith, therefore, had to be possessed with special powers to accomplish his extraordinary task of converting earth and stone into metal. In Java, the smith in charge of forging a new gamelan used to prepare himself by fasting and other acts of purification, so that he could become fit for possession by the spirit of Panji, a culture hero who figures in many traditional Javanese stories. If the forging of the instruments was successful, they too would become the abode of a spirit, and the gong ageng, the most difficult instrument to make, would contain the greatest spiritual power.

Especially fine old gamelan—or their spirits—have even been ennobled. One at the Yogyakarta kraton, for example, that actually antedates the founding of the Sultanate in 1755 and that is used for special celebrations, such as those accompanying the birthday anniversary of Mohammed, is referred to as "Kangjeng Kyai Guntur Madu," or "Venerable Sir Torrent of Honey." For this reason, it remains proper etiquette when entering the gamelan to remove one's shoes and to avoid the rudeness of stepping over an instrument. Further, the spirit of the gamelan, embodied in the gong ageng, is paid homage with offerings of food, flowers, and incense. A rigidly orthodox Muslim might find such behavior to be verging on idolatry, so it is not surprising that even in the more flexible attitude found at the kraton, the gong ageng should be singled out for silencing on days of heightened religious significance within Islam.

A Christian, too, might object to venerating the spirit of the gong, but just as different attitudes prevail among the Muslims, Christians can also accommodate old patterns of behavior. Consider a story told to me by a dancer whose family had been performers connected with the Yogyakarta kraton and whose father had converted to Christianity. Once when he was rehearsing with a gamelan, he was disturbed by the gong's poor tone quality, even though it was supposed to be a very fine instrument. It was suggested that the spirit of the gong was disturbed and that an offering of incense and flowers should be made to it; when this was done, the dancer was pleased and surprised to notice that the gong began to sound resonantly and clearly again.

The spiritual power that is invested in old gamelan by tradition in turn invests power in their owners, for which reason they are important components of princely regalia (pusaka), over which battles have been fought in the past. The *gendhing* (musical work) played on these gamelan, too, may have such power that, for example, it was in the past forbidden to hum them casually. When transcribing them into notation—a practice initiated as a result of European influence in the nineteenth century—it used to be considered advisable to make an occasional mistake to prevent the power of the tune from being used inappropriately.

The Sacred Dance *Bedhaya*

The tunes accompanying the sacred dance bedhaya are considered especially powerful because of the reputed origin of the music and dance and their association with kingship, as illustrated in this paraphrase of a story from the *History of Gamelan* by Warsadiningrat:

> One night in the year 1643, Sultan Agung (the last great ruler of the kingdom preceding the establishment of Yogya and Solo) was meditating when he heard music that was so beautiful it gave him goosebumps. The next day

KRATON
Javanese royal court.

PUSAKA
Javanese royal heirloom.

BEDHAYA
Sacred court dance of Java.

he decided to form a dance troupe and called together musical experts to arrange the melodies for the accompaniment. Suddenly Kanjeng Sunan Kalijaga appeared; one of the nine saints legend credits with introducing Islam into Java, he was a noble Hindu by birth, who first became a notorious bandit and then converted to Islam after a lengthy period of continuous meditation in the manner of a Hindu holy man. Kalijaga congratulated the Sultan on his plans to create the gendhing bedhaya, for it was clearly a gift from He Who Is Great and Holy and meant to be a pusaka for the kings of Java that would bring blessings of peace, supremacy, and strength until the end of time.

Nine young girls from noble families were selected for their beauty and grace to dance the bedhaya. The bedhaya dance is important because (1) it contributes to an understanding of Javanese culture by providing a guide to meditation; (2) it explains certain strategies of war; and (3) it contributes to an understanding of music that portrays deep and noble emotions.

Just as the dance lessons were to begin, Kanjeng Ratu Kencana Sari, queen of all spirits, good and evil, suddenly arrived from her palace in the South Sea, in the dress and make-up of a bride. She appeared every day at dusk for three months to teach the dance, because she loved the noble and majestic melodies, and she still appears for this reason. Because of this, when the bedhaya is performed, complete offerings of many kinds are prepared and a great deal of incense is burned continuously throughout the performance, and all the performers—dancers, singers, and musicians—must be pure and clean.

(Becker 1987; Gertz 1973, 25–29)

As we see in this story, bedhaya is a remarkable example of the eclectic nature of Javanese elite culture and the way in which it is used to assert status. Music and dance that conjure an indigenous Javanese goddess from her home in the sea and receive the blessing of a legendary Muslim saint, whose conversion was accomplished through yogic meditation, constitute one of the special heirlooms that buttress the powers of the king.

The Shadow Play: *Wayang Kulit*

WAYANG KULIT
Indonesian shadow play accompanied with gamelan music.

The shadow-puppet theater, or **wayang kulit**, is another Indonesian performance medium using music that has achieved special prominence in Javanese culture and that may also be associated with extraordinary power. Whereas stories of Javanese and Islamic origins are performed in shadow plays, the stories derived from the Indian epics the *Mahabharata* and the *Ramayana* have the greater popularity and prestige, particularly the Mahabharata. Performed over the course of a whole night, the plays generally depict a battle whose turmoil is reflected in a disturbance of nature that, toward morning, is resolved when order is restored to human society and the world.

The Traditional Malaysian Shadow Puppet Show by Pak Daim in Kelantan, Malaysia. *Source:* dboystudio / Shutterstock.com

The stories of the wayang kulit revolve around Indic characters, but they have been Javanized by the introduction of a number of comic characters, who act as servants to the protagonists and incidentally serve as translators for the audience, because their masters speak a Sanskritized and poetic Javanese that is not commonly understood. This problem reflects the situation in contemporary Javanese, which has many styles of speech based on social class distinctions. (In Indonesia, whose motto is "Unity in Diversity," the Indonesian language—Bahasa Indonesia—has rapidly gained acceptance throughout the country as the lingua franca because it helps to overcome regional, ethnic, and class differences.) The chief of the clowns, Semar, is a fat, lazy, wily, lascivious, and obstreperously flatulent fellow, but he is also a mysteriously all-knowing sage who even takes precedence over the Hindu god Siva himself. Java may have been awed by exotic Indian culture, but it seems that autochthonous wisdom still earns the greater respect. Because Semar speaks colloquially, he has the advantage not only of entertaining the audience with his wit and shenanigans but also of giving good advice and wise counsel.

In fact, all the familiar characters in wayang communicate, at least by their actions, the various modes of human existence and manners of behavior. The shadow play has thus long been a medium for moral and ethical instruction and for discussion of contemporary events, and today it is often a medium for explaining government social programs as well.

All the different skills and knowledge needed to perform the shadow play come together in the **dalang**, the puppeteer, a man (rarely a woman) who commands a thorough knowledge of **karawitan** (musical repertory and practice). He is familiar with the many different stories of the plays and their appropriate-

EXPLORE
Wayang Kulit

DALANG
Master puppeteer of the Javanese shadow-puppet play.

KARAWITAN
Learned music in the Javanese tradition.

ness for particular occasions, speaks with a host of voices suited to everyone from the most refined gentleman to the crudest villain, and can skillfully move his puppets to convey an equal range of refinement and crudity. The dalang knows archaic languages and the full range of contemporary social dialects, is a repository of spiritual and cultural values, and is acquainted with the latest political events and social problems. No wonder he is often thought to be a kind of superman!

Seated between a light source and a thin screen, the dalang casts the shadows of flat leather puppets against the screen, all the while giving the appropriate signals to the gamelan for the pieces of music needed to accompany the scene, be it a moment of comic relief with Semar dancing, or a tremendous battle between the forces of good and evil. To set the mood for an upcoming scene, he sometimes sings, too.

Now that dalangs can learn their art in schools (just as gamelan musicians do), an abbreviation and standardization of the wayang stories and of the puppeteers' skills is occurring. This inevitably lessens the special aura of the wayang and of the dalang but helps to ensure them a continuing role in the cultural life of modern Indonesia.

MUSIC IN BALI

The arts of Indonesia, especially music and dance, have undergone many changes over the centuries as political and social circumstances have created different requirements and possibilities for performance. Among recent influences, the impact of tourism is certainly one of enormous significance, particularly for the arts of Bali, the small island just to the east of Java in the Indonesian archipelago. A jet airport that was opened there in 1969 has made Bali easily accessible to tourists from around the world, and they have been coming in ever-increasing numbers. Not that tourism is new to Bali: Some of its most famous visitors—painters, composers, anthropologists—arrived there in the decades prior to World War II and often stayed long enough to leave their indelible imprint on Balinese life.

Some Historical Events Influencing Balinese Culture

Before we discuss the impact of tourism on the music of Bali, we will first consider a couple of political events of singular importance in the history of Bali. Earlier, we mentioned the Islamic kingdom of Mataram in the discussion of ketawang "Puspawarna." This kingdom was the predecessor of the central Javanese courts founded in the eighteenth century through intervention of the Dutch, which still continue to exist in a ceremonial way in the present-day Republic of Indonesia. Mataram itself had earlier displaced the Hindu kingdom of Majapahit, whose refugees migrated to Bali in the fifteenth century. The elite Hindu-Buddhist-based culture of Majapahit introduced a new layer into the cultural fabric of Bali, and those who resisted its caste-based hierarchy and monarchical organization retreated to remoter areas of the island, where so-called Bali Aga or "old Bali" villages continue many of the pre-Indo-Javanese ways.

The other overwhelming event in Bali's history took place in 1908, when the kingdoms that had dominated the island for the previous several centuries were finally dissolved by the Dutch, who invaded the island and took over its administration. The effect of Dutch intervention on Bali was quite different from that on Java. In Java the newly established courts, provided with financial resources but given limited responsibilities of governance, evolved an elegant way of life that fostered the development of the arts as the most effective means of retaining exalted status. In Bali the courts were dissolved, and the descendants of nobles, who were often employed as agents of Dutch rule, rarely had the financial resources to maintain the elaborate musical establishments associated with courtly life.

Music in the Balinese Courts

Among the several different ensembles maintained by Balinese kings, with their different instruments, musicians, repertories, and functions, was the **gamelan gambuh**, a kind of opera derived from Majapahit models. Quite unlike the large gamelan of metallophones we encountered in Java, this one is smaller and consists of several extraordinarily long, vertical flutes (suling gambuh) and a rebab, with a few percussion instruments for punctuation and rhythmic control. The melodies of the flutes and fiddle are elaborately ornamented like those of the corresponding instruments in the Javanese gamelan, but rather than being part of a much denser and richer texture that competes with them, these flute melodies are the sole focus of attention. The flutes, whose tones have an ethereal quality, are played in such a manner that the melody is never interrupted when the player takes a breath. Using his cheeks as a kind of bellows, he inflates them before taking a breath so that he can continue to sound the flute with air from his cheeks while breathing in.

GAMELAN GAMBUH
An archaic type of Balinese court opera and its accompanying orchestra.

The long-winded melodies and unfamiliar orchestra, the stately progress of the action, and the archaic language of the actors and general lack of comic episodes have given gambuh the status of a venerated relic of the past, even though it has recently undergone something of a revival. Much more popular today is the **gamelan arja** theater, another type of operatic performance not associated with courtly ceremony. Although it is also accompanied by a small ensemble with flutes (of a shorter, more common type) and a few percussion instruments, it employs a greater variety of stories (including some on modern, topical subjects), female as well as male actors, and a lot of comedy.

GAMELAN ARJA
A type of Balinese opera.

Now rather rare, the "gamelan with the big gongs" (**gamelan gong gede**) is another ensemble that played an important role in the old courts. In its construction, it is more similar to the large instrumental gamelan of central Java than the gamelan gambuh. For instance, it incorporates colotomic instruments similar to those of the Javanese ensemble, such as gong, *kempur* (kempul), and

GAMELAN GONG GEDE
Older Balinese court music, used for court and temple rituals, similar in sound and style to the Javanese gamelan.

kempli (ketuk). The *gangsa*, instruments responsible for playing the core melody called *pokok* in Bali (balungan in Java), share similarities in construction and musical role with their Javanese counterparts, the saron and slentem. The *trompong*, an important lead instrument with structural similarities to the Javanese bonang, functions both to introduce pieces and elaborate the pokok. The gamelan gong gede was regularly played for public ceremonies and temple festivities and performed pieces with regular structures whose melodies, elaboration, colotomy, and rhythm were realized in ways broadly similar to those discussed earlier for Javanese gendhing. An important difference, however, is the fact that, like the majority of Balinese ensembles, the gamelan gong gede is a single orchestra with but one tuning system, pelog. Further, the version of pelog used is pentatonic—a selection of five pitches from the heptatonic pelog system scale. Like gambuh, this gamelan has a more popular and modern counterpart that we will discuss later.

A third court ensemble, **gamelan Semar pegulingan**, is a sizeable orchestra consisting largely of metallophones that was used to play purely instrumental arrangements of gambuh for the private enjoyment of the court. Because gambuh melodies use heptatonic scales, some gamelan Semar pegulingan used to have fully heptatonic instruments, but others played pentatonic versions of the melodies. Today this ensemble, with its peculiarly delicate sound, has been revived to play a variety of old-style, classically structured pieces as well as new compositions and arrangements.

A very modest ensemble, the **gender wayang**, has not suffered a loss of popularity or needed revival because of its association with the shadow play based on stories of the Mahabharata and Ramayana. This quartet of gender, similar in construction and playing technique to the gender of Java and tuned in laras slendro, is the sole accompaniment, other than the voice of the dalang, for the Mahabharata; some percussion and colotomic instruments are added to it for the stories of the Ramayana. The quartet consists, in fact, of two pairs of gender distinguished from one another by being in different octaves. Each instrument pair is also gendered, that is, a pair of instruments includes a male and female instrument. Within each pair, moreover, one instrument is distinguished from the other by being slightly "out of tune," that is, a particular key on one instrument is purposely made slightly higher or lower than its twin to create a sensation of acoustical beats that gives a shimmering quality to the pitch when the keys on both instruments are struck simultaneously. As the instruments of a pair are often played in unison, the result is a constantly throbbing resonance that almost seems to be breathing. Although particularly effective in the Balinese wayang quartet, this principle of purposeful "mistuning" is evident in other bronze ensembles as well and is especially noticeable when an octave is played.

The gender wayang continues to be a vitally important component of Bali's musical life, but the gamelan gambuh, Semar pegulingan, and gong gede have lesser roles as reminders of the past. With the passing of the courts, the patronage needed for the maintenance of the large numbers of instruments and for the support of the musicians, actors, and dancers disappeared. The common people of Bali, however, responded by filling the gap left by the absence of noble

GAMELAN SEMAR PEGULINGAN
Large, Balinese court orchestra that plays instrumental versions of gamelan gambuh melodies.

GENDER WAYANG
Four-piece ensemble of genders that typically accompanies the Balinese shadow play.

patrons, and this provided the impetus and stimulus for developing new types of performing arts. When Western intellectuals began to discover Bali between the World Wars, there was an efflorescence of the arts as they adjusted to the passing of old forms while accommodating new influences from the people and from contact with foreigners.

A Modern Form of Dance and Music: Kebyar

The most vibrant of the new styles was the result of the reshaping of the gamelan gong gede into the **gamelan gong kebyar** by dropping some instruments and modifying and borrowing others. The *trompong*, for example, was dropped because its function as the introducer of pieces and as elaborator of melodies became less important when gender-like instruments called *kantilan* started playing virtuosic interlocking patterns (**kotekan**) as the elaboration for kebyar. And the gangsa, the main melody instruments of the gamelan gong gede (responsible for the pokok, that is), yielded their role to other gender-like instruments with lower ranges than the kantilan.

Village gamelan clubs often bought older-style gamelan no longer maintained or needed by the courts and recast them into the new form, and the new music developed for these was a revolutionary departure from the sedate and majestic pieces of the repertory for the gamelan gambuh or gamelan gong gede. In the latter, predictably familiar formal structures, conventional instrumentation, stable rhythms, and relatively unvaried dynamics created a sense of classical elegance; but the music of kebyar was a revolutionary change—virtuosic, mercurial, flashy, and unpredictable.

In an old-style gendhing for the gamelan gong gede or Semar pegulingan, the introduction would normally be a somewhat tentative solo on the *trompong*, an instrument similar to the Javanese bonang. Kebyar music, on the other hand, immediately asserts its independence from older formal traditions by beginning with a loud, confident unison for the whole ensemble. Instead of the classical elegance and refinement of former times, it displays a willful exuberance, progressing in fits and starts with sudden dynamic contrasts, jerky syncopations, and breathtakingly rapid figuration. No wonder many older connoisseurs found kebyar a disturbing phenomenon when it first took Bali by storm around the time of World War I.

Originally a purely orchestral music ideally suited for musical competitions among different villages, kebyar was given a new twist when it began to accompany dance. About 1925, a young dancer named Maria made a particular impression with his version of a dance to go with this exciting music. Like the fixed structures of the classical gendhing, the various dances performed by trained court dancers or by people making

GAMELAN GONG KEBYAR
A modern type of Balinese music and the dance it accompanies, which is noted for its virtuosic and unpredictable playing style.

KOTEKAN
Often virtuosic and rapid interlocking rhythms important within gamelan kebyar performances and consisting of two parts (a lower part and a higher part) played on two separate instruments. Generally, multiple pairs of instruments are simultaneously involved in performing kotekan.

Balinese Kebyar dancer in performance. *Source:* Paul Kennedy/Lonely Planet/ Newscom

LISTENING GUIDE

GAMELAN GONG KEBYAR "KEBYAR TERUNA"

 **LISTEN**

TRACK 7.3 **Performed by Gamelan Gong Kebyar of Pliatan**

THIS RECORDING IS characteristic of Balinese gamelan gong kebyar performances. It incorporates many passages of kotekan, brilliant changes in tempo, dynamics, and texture that distinguish it from the older, more stately gamelan gong gede style, and produces the shimmering quality associated with the slightly different tunings achieved between the male and female counterparts of the various pairs of instruments in the gamelan.

TIME	SECTION	MUSICAL EVENTS
0:00–0:38	**Introduction**: Listen for the intense character of this introduction. Notice especially the sound of the ceng-ceng cymbals.	Introduction featuring almost the entire gamelan playing in unison. Typical of kebyar style, the introduction incorporates varied dynamics and tempi and irregular rhythms and syncopations.
0:38–0:42	**Passages featuring reyong and gangsa**: Take note of the different sounds produced by these two instruments.	Passage for reyong with kotekan (interlocking patterns). This passage introduces the reyong theme that will reappear in the next section.
0:42–0:48		Passage for gangsa with kotekan, introducing the patterns that will return in the calung-jegogan section.
0:48–1:24	**Section for reyong**: Listen for the way that the reyong plays kotekan within the structure provided by the gamelan. Notice also the dynamic shifts (changes in volume [loud-softer-loud]) in this section. Finally, notice that the kotekan being performed on the reyong are drawn from the patterns established during the reyong passage at [0:38–42].	The reyong is featured in this section. Notice that the lowest gong sounds consistently throughout this section. The kempli, which is struck but dampened with the other hand, and therefore sounds a bit dry and percussive, plays eight strokes per gong stroke. This underlying structure will help keep you oriented given the speed at which the kotekan moves.
1:24–2:00	**Section for calung/jegogan**: Notice the slower, lower-pitched melody emerge in the calung-jegogan. These instruments are in the same family group as the high-pitched gangsa, heard at [0:42–0:48]. Notice also that the kotekan played on the gangsa during that earlier passage reappear in this section.	The lower-pitched calung and jegogan are featured, but they are accompanied by kotekan in the higher-pitched gangsa. It is hard not to focus only on the dazzling figurations of the gangsa, but see if you can attend to the musical activity simultaneously unfolding in the other instruments. Again, you can orient yourself by listening for the 8/1 ratio of kempli to gong.
2:00–2:06	**Cadential pattern**: Listen for the way a syncopated, repeated figure brings the section to a close.	The cadential pattern, driven by the kendang (drums) and ceng-ceng (cymbals), is repeated once and then extended with a sustained stroke (not dampened, that is) on the reyong.

continued

TIME	SECTION	MUSICAL EVENTS
2:06–2:22	**Increased tempo and intensity**: Notice the dramatic and sudden increase in tempo here. Listen for the increasingly syncopated strokes on the reyong.	This section of increased tempo and intensity affords the most virtuosic drumming and ceng-ceng playing in the performance.
2:22–3:01	**Return of calung/jegogan section**: Listen for the return of the material used earlier at [0:48–1:24].	The material presented in the earlier calung-jegogan section returns here at a faster tempo and with more intensity. This section, because it is faster, provides for the most virtuosic kotekan passages. The performance continues as the recording fades out, beginning at [2:56].

offerings at the temple were based on traditional movements and gestures, and the stock characters of dramas like gambuh were confined to expressing the limited range of moods suited to them. But Maria's kebyar mirrored the fleeting moods and unpredictable contrasts of the music. The dancer performed in an unusual crouched position that was on the same level as the seated musicians with whom he sometimes interacted directly, seeming to tease and cajole. Alternately rising onto his knees and squatting, playing with a fan, flashing a bizarre series of glances that registered astonishment, pique, enticement, and fury in rapid succession, the dancer would interpret the music's every change. To top things off, he might conclude by joining his accompanists in a choreographically performed solo on the trompong (an instrument not much used in kebyar but symbolic of Balinese musical heritage), all the while continuing to bob up and down and back and forth on his knees, twirl his mallets like a drum major, and register a bewildering series of moods on his face. Although originally danced by boys or young men, today kebyar is also danced by young women dressed as men. This kind of cross-dressing in dance performance is nothing new, however.

The individual nature of kebyar gave a new importance to the role of the composer and choreographer, and for a while compositions were jealously guarded as the special property of a particular club. The concept of the "composition" in the view of the Balinese gamelan club, however, is quite different from how a piece, by Beethoven, for instance, is generally understood by orchestras in the North Atlantic. We can get an idea of how a Balinese composition is realized and treated from a memoir written by John Coast, an impresario who arranged the first world tour of the gamelan from Pliatan village in 1951. For this occasion, Coast wanted a special new piece, and he commissioned Maria to choreograph a new dance to go with it. Here is his account of how the gamelan learned the piece.

When we arrived about nine o'clock that night in the village we found the gamelan well into the first melody of the new dance [which they were learning by having each part demonstrated, as is customary, rather than from

GAMELAN GONG GEDE "TABUH EMPAT PENGAWAK"

 **LISTEN**

TRACK 7.4 Performed by Gamelan Gong Gede "Sekar Sandat" of Bangli

THIS RECORDING, excerpted from a typical old-style piece for gamelan gong gede, well illustrates the kind of music to which the new kebyar style presented such a startling contrast. The meandering trompong introduction is starkly different from the explosive beginning of "Kebyar Teruna" (Track 7.3), and the stately progression of the melody when the whole ensemble enters (at [2:00]) is rigidly organized with a regular tempo and equally regular ornamentation and orchestration.

TIME	SECTION	MUSICAL EVENTS
0:00–1:05	**Introduction**: Listen for the slow and deliberate way the trompong handles the introduction.	Introduction, featuring the trompong and performed in free meter.
1:05–1:23		The gong enters, marking both an end to the solo introduction and the beginning of a transition to metered, colotomic performance.
1:23–1:29	**Drums and remaining instruments enter**: Notice how the drums introduce a regular pulse and that, shortly thereafter, the entire ensemble joins the trompong. This is due, in part, to the fact that the tempo of the performance is now clear and the colotomic parts can be slotted into place.	The drums enter and immediately establish a regular beat.
1:29–2:00		The entire ensemble joins the trompong, regularly subdividing the beat in the colotomic fashion that should sound familiar to you by now.
2:00–2:29	**The main melody (pokok) enters**: Listen for the slow manner in which the pokok unfolds.	The pokok enters, performed on the gangsa at the rate of about one note every two seconds. The subdivided beat is emphasized by the ceng-ceng cymbals. The recording rapidly fades out at [2:28].

a score]; and it was Kebiar music, though new, Maria [*sic*] told us, having been composed originally by Pan Sukra for a club in Marga, near Tabanan, but it had never been used. And anyhow, these tunes were arranged for a girl dancer, while the original ones had been for a man.

It took about three weeks for the thirty minutes of music to be perfectly mastered by Pliatan, and at the end of that time Pan Sukra went home to his village. Then Anak Agung, Made Lebah, and Gusti Kompiang grinned freely. "Now it is our turn," they said.

"What do you mean?" we asked.

"Aggh! This is crude music. Now it is a matter of tabuh—style. You will see. It must be rearranged and polished by the club (Coast 1953, 109).

From *Dancers Out of Bali*, John Coast. GP Putnam & Sons, 1953. Used with kind permission of Laura Rosenberg at the John Coast Foundation for the Performing Arts in Bali.

As a comparison, we might think of the Boston Symphony Orchestra playing a composition originally composed for the New York Philharmonic and, when the composer had turned his back, rewriting it according to their own tastes! No doubt some instrumentalists in Boston would respond with that expressive "Aggh!" to a newly commissioned work, but it is highly unlikely they would have the temerity to suggest altering the piece once it was completed, even if the composer had once asked for their advice on how to arrange the parts for their particular instruments.

Even in matters of interpretation, the initiative is apt to come from the music director or conductor rather than of the rank-and-file instrumentalist. But in Pliatan, as in other Balinese gamelan, the repertory was shaped by the contributions of all the club members, although decisions may have been made by acknowledged leaders like Anak Agung, a nobleman, and Made Lebah, a commoner, both of whom were respected performers and teachers.

In his account of the creation of the dance to go with the new music, Coast (1953) again reveals the cooperative nature of the work.

And we saw the story of the dance unfold, as Maria had told us it would, creating itself bit by bit, with ideas thrown in from us all. We saw Raka as the little bumblebee sunning herself in a flower-filled garden, in moods of surprise, delight and fear; we saw the gaudy male bumblebee enter, and Sampih could pick up Maria's ideas with the speed with which a western ballet dancer follows an enchainement in class; we saw him spy the delectable little bee, zoom toward her, court her, frighten her by his advances till she fled from him. Then Sampih danced alone in baffled fury as the Kebiar music raged around him, and in the last rollicking melody he danced a Kebiar of sheer frustration around the whole gamelan, flirting desperately with its members. This was a development out of Maria's original Kebiar, and he called it now: Tumulilingan Mengisap Sari—the Bumblebee Sips Honey.

Luce was meanwhile busy with the costumes. . . . All our Pliatan family [*sic*] were engrossed in this dance, for it was a new thing and it was ours. (110).

To the creation of this new piece—which soon became a standard item in the repertory of the gamelan gong kebyar—even Coast and other members of the entrepreneur's retinue were able to make contributions as part of the "Pliatan family."

THE INFLUENCE OF FOREIGN ARTISTS AND TOURISTS

A Ramayana Performance: Kecak

KECAK
A type of dance drama accompanied by a large male chorus that chants rhythmically, usually performed for tourists.

Coast and his entourage were hardly the first outsiders to have an influence on Balinese arts. Two examples should suffice to illustrate this point. Walter Spies, a visual artist and musician who toured Indonesia (playing two-piano recitals) with the Canadian-American composer, Colin McPhee, in 1938, was involved in the development of **kecak**. This unusual performance medium is of particular interest because it has become a "must-see" item for tourists, who are often unaware that they are witnessing an art form specifically created to satisfy them. Because it is strange and disturbing in terms of Westerners' usual experience of performing arts, kecak has indeed satisfied millions of tourists as an experience of something powerfully exotic, without which the time and money spent in getting to new and distant places might seem poorly spent.

The kecak takes its name from the brusque, staccato monosyllables shouted by a large chorus of men in rapid and intricately interlocking rhythmic patterns. A few other men use their voices to imitate the sound of a small gamelan, and these two elements accompany a drastically shortened version of the Ramayana acted out by a few actor–dancers. The basic story is this: Sita, wife of King Rama, an incarnation of the god Vishnu, has been abducted by the demon Ravana, who carries her off to his palace in Sri Lanka, but Hanuman, general of the monkey army and devotee of Rama, pursues them and rescues Sita. Because the chorus of men intermittently takes on the role of Hanuman's monkey army and sounds like chattering monkeys, the performance is sometimes also called the "Monkey Chant."

The rhythmic shouting of the men is traditionally associated with rituals of divination, in which young girls are entranced so questions can be put to the spirits (*sanghyang*) that take possession of them. Although music and dance are frequently part of these rituals, dramatic stories from the Ramayana are not. Thinking that the kecak was an exciting and unusual kind of music, Spies suggested using it as the foundation for a concise presentation of the Ramayana that would give tourists, who were already discovering Bali before World War II, a professionally arranged and attractive means of experiencing it.

A Trance Dance: *Barong*

BARONG
(1) A mythical lion-like creature in Balinese sacred dramas; (2) a trance dance ritual adopted for performances for tourists.

Like kecak, **barong** is another kind of trance ritual that has been adapted as a regular performance medium for tourists. It is a kind of dramatic presentation accompanied by the gamelan gong or kebyar that represents the struggle between Good (in the being of the barong, an awesome but benevolent lion) and Evil (impersonated by a horrendous and malevolent witch). At the high point of the story, the supporters of the barong attack the witch with their *krises* (wavy daggers) and are forced by the witch's magic to turn them instead upon their own bodies, but the magic of the barong protects them from injuring themselves. During performances at village temples, many participants may fall into trance during and after the battle. Indeed the spirits that are normally thought to reside in the masks of the barong and of the witch may possess the men who wear them as well.

In temple rituals for the Balinese themselves, the barong is certainly an event of supernatural import, but that does not prevent it from being an entertainment as well. One village, in fact, may visit another to perform its particular version of the barong and be appreciated for the style with which it performs as well as for the evident power of its barong and witch. There are, in fact, trance performances in Bali and elsewhere in Indonesia in which the trancers are said to be possessed by animals or even inanimate objects and that seem to have the presentation of a type of entertainment as their sole or main purpose. In such circumstances, the entertainment of tourists with a barong performance seems to fit in with the Balinese view of things, but such a performance cannot mean the same thing as one in which the primary object is to create a sense of well-being and security for the community, rather than, for economic gain, to satisfy the curiosity of outsiders. Although many of the tourists may regale their friends back home with stories of the "authentic" rituals they witnessed, the Balinese probably have a clearer idea of the distinction between the different types of "authenticity" involved in the performance of barong for themselves and for tourists.

Changes in the motivations and presentation of performances of kecak or barong may bother those whose original associations with the performance have strong meaning. However, this is surely an inevitable part of human experience, because no society is static, and all culture must evolve and change or cease to exist. Just as the Sun Dance and other festivities of the Plains Indians in North America developed into pan-Indian powwow celebrations, and like the Medicine Dance of the San people of Botswana, which has evolved into a performance for others as well as for the San themselves, barong, too, may be undergoing a shift from an organic and vital part of specific Balinese communities to a "cultural performance" meant to help shape the idea of "Baliness" for the modern Balinese and for the outside world. Musical performances like barong, after all, can help mediate not just the contact between the human and the otherworldly but also the contact between groups of human beings, and we may hope that this latter role is no less powerful a validation of an art form than the former.

FOUR KINDS OF POPULAR MUSIC IN JAVA

Gambus

Entertainment and monetary gain are often thought of as the only reasons for the existence of many types of popular music. But when we think, for example, of how some people enjoy hip hop and willingly pay for the pleasure of listening to it, whereas others dislike it but are vehemently devoted to reggae or heavy metal, it becomes clear that more powerful motivations must also be involved. Like barong, popular music can shape an identity—for an individual or a group—and present it to the world.

In Indonesia, one of the pop musics that succeeds in doing this as well as providing its consumers a good deal of enjoyment is **gambus**, a genre named for an Arabic instrument that signifies connection with the homeland of Islam. Nowadays the gambus may be present only by virtue of having lent its name to the genre, the instrument itself having been replaced by the *'ud*, which has wider currency in the music of the Middle East.

Not just the instruments of gambus—which may include, for example, *marawis* (sing. *mirwas*), small double-headed drums from Yemen—but the musical style itself reflects Middle Eastern origins, with its short, often sequentially repeated phrases and simple, catchy, and danceable rhythms. Even the vocal timbre is often more that of Middle Eastern than of Indonesian singers although so-called modern gambus (*gambus moderen*) may use Indonesian lyrics. The dress of the performers as depicted on the sleeves of cassettes and CDs may include such articles as the kaffiyeh and agal, the Arab headdress worn by men. Although the texts of gambus may have Islamic subject matter, the songs are much appreciated for their musical qualities—too much so in view of the more puritanical Muslims who feel that music is not conducive to leading a proper Islamic life, because it directs the listener to focus on the sensual instead of on the spiritual. Perhaps one could imagine a similar confrontation in the United States between supporters of Christian rock and their adversaries.

GAMBUS
A type of Islamic song having Arabic influence; the name of the plucked lute originally used to accompany this song.

LISTENING GUIDE   **GAMBUS "CARI HABURAN"**    **LISTEN**

TRACK 7.5 **Performed by Orkè's Gambus Al-Hidayah**

TIME	MUSICAL EVENTS
0:00–0:21	Improvised prelude on gambus ('ud) and violins. One violin plays sustained bass notes while the other elaborates the melody.
0:22–1:23	Free rhythm rendition of first verses.
1:24–1:50	Voice concludes, and instruments continue melody with cadential accompaniment of interlocking drums (mirwas [pl. marawis]) At this point, the violin responsible for the bass notes becomes more actively involved in elaborating the melody as well.
1:50–2:48	Previously heard verses sung in free rhythm, now sung in 4/4 meter.
2:48–3:09	The interlocking drum cadence continues in similar fashion until the recording fades out at [3:00–3:09].

Dangdut

Dangdut is another popular music that is an extraordinary mix of Western rock and Indian film song. Its Indonesian texts have usually dealt with homiletic advice about leading a better, more productive, and uprightly Islamic life, although secular love lyrics are becoming increasingly common now. Its infectious rhythms have earned it the onomatopoetic name dangdut, which represents its characteristic drum sounds and, for those who deride it, its suspiciously worldly appeal. Dangdut was transformed into a popular medium for broadcasting Islamic values to the public in the seventies under the influence of the superstar Rhoma Irama. He was originally called Oma, but he added the "R" and "h" from Raden Haji, a title given those Muslims who, as he did, perform the pilgrimage to Mecca. Dangdut became the dominant pop music in the '90s, and like the Indian songs from which it borrowed so much, it has been featured heavily in films.

DANGDUT
Popular Indonesian musical style that combines Western rock and Indian

Kroncong

Dangdut, a relatively recent phenomenon, has had a fairly swift rise in popularity in the manner of many kinds of commercial pop, but **kroncong**, another popular style, has a long history in Indonesia stretching back to the first contact with European colonialism. The Portuguese ports in the East—such as Goa in India, Macao in China, and Malacca in Malaysia—and the Portuguese areas of southern Africa and the Azores linked Europe of the sixteenth and seventeenth centuries to the spice-growing areas of Indonesia. Before the Dutch established colonial hegemony in the Indonesian archipelago, the Portuguese outposts on the islands served as centers for the shipment of spices to Europe. These communities of mixed ethnic and racial background nevertheless maintained aspects of Portuguese culture such as the Christian religion and some types of folk music. In Indonesia, this music came to be called kroncong. During the late nineteenth and early twentieth centuries it had a somewhat unsavory reputation associated with urban violence and glamorous toughs called *buaya kroncong* (kroncong crocodiles), who were like the Malay pirates of some Hollywood movies in the twenties and thirties.

KRONCONG
A type of popular Indonesian music originating from Portuguese-derived sources.

 **EXPLORE**
Kroncong

   The typical instruments accompanying kroncong are of European derivation: violin, cello, flute, and plucked strings of various types; one of the strings, similar to a ukulele, has given its name to the genre. These provided a simple, harmonically based accompaniment to vocal melodies sung with a mellifluous sweetness Americans might think characteristically Hawaiian. When kroncong began to attract the interest of a more polite section of middle-class Javanese society in the twenties and thirties, it underwent a kind of acculturation to central Javanese style, and although the instruments were the same, they took on functional qualities similar to those of gamelan music. The flute and violin became like the suling and rebab, providing free, heterophonic elaboration of the melody. The cello, while continuing to provide a foundation for the harmony,

LISTENING GUIDE

"CURAHAN HATI"

 **LISTEN**

TRACK 7.6 **Grup Tanjidor Kembang Ros, Sophia Welly, vocal**

THIS EXAMPLE OF DANGDUT is performed by a **tanjidor** group—a kind of ensemble from the more rural outskirts of Jakarta. Unlike the heavily commercialized, professional, rock ensemble sound popularized by Rhoma Irama, tanjidor ensembles are comprised of amateur musicians and blend European-derived band instruments with local instruments. This recording features saxophone, clarinet, trumpet, a fiddle of Chinese origin (called a tehyan), and several local percussion instruments. Importantly, tanjidor groups do not generally focus on dangdut as a major component of their repertory. It is a testament to the immense popularity of the commercialized dangdut songs of artists like Rhoma Irama and Elvy Sukaesih (among many others) that these songs are being incorporated into the repertories of regional ensembles like the tanjidor. A song with lyrics about the complications of love, "Curahan Hati" means "From the Heart."

TIME	SECTION	MUSICAL EVENTS
0:00–0:33	**Introduction**	The ensemble plays a melodic theme twice through in heterophonic fashion. This theme becomes the basis for interludes later in the performance.
0:34–0:58	**Verse 1:** Vocalist enters and sings the first verse.	Notice the A [0:34–0:46] B [0:47–0:58] structure of the melody and that it differs from the theme played by the instruments. You'll notice that the B melody functions almost like a tag refrain in subsequent verses.
0:58–1:13	**Instrumental interlude**	The ensemble returns to the opening melodic theme.
1:13–1:59	**Verse 2:** Vocalist introduces new melodic content.	Notice that the first melodic phrase, which is repeated after a short instrumental break, C [1:13–1:26 and 1:33–1:45], is comprised of new material. This is followed by a move back to a variation of B, heard most clearly in the last line of text.
2:00–2:28	**Interlude:** This time the vocalist performs the opening theme with instrumental accompaniment.	After the vocalist sings the opening theme through once, the instrumentalists play a variation on that theme, closing with the familiar melodic material [2:16–2:28].
2:29–3:14	**Verse 3:** Vocalist introduces new text but follows melodic pattern established in verse 2.	
3:15–3:52a	**Conclusion:** The vocalist sings the opening theme twice through as the song comes to a close.	As before the instrumentalists accompany the vocalist as she sings the opening melody [3:15–3:29]. During the repeat, however, the instrumentalists join the vocalist in performing the melody, adding a bit of energy as the piece concludes [3:29–3:52].

KRONCONG "MORISKO"

 **LISTEN**

TRACK 7.7   *Performed by Orkes Kroncong Mutiara, vocal:* **Suhaery Mufti**

TIME	MUSICAL EVENTS
0:00–0:12	Introduction in free rhythm on flute.
0:13–0:37	Plucked strings set up accompaniment patterns regularly subdividing beat in a manner reminiscent of gamelan practice over which flute continues its ornamental floating melody.
0:38–1:20	Voice takes over melody of song, and flute adds ornamental flourishes in manner of gamelan suling at ends of vocal phrases.
1:20–1:23	Fades out.

was played pizzicato in rhythms resembling kendang-like drum patterns; and the kroncong, with its regular offbeat plucking, had a resemblance to the ketuk.

Some kroncong during this period also took on the typical 4 × 8-bar structure of Tin Pan Alley ballads, with a repeated first phrase that also returned after an intervening and contrasting second phrase: **AABA**. They also acquired a jazzy feeling with the addition of "blue notes." What had been an indigenously evolved, traditional popular music, based on very old importations, had evolved into a more internationalized commercial music at the same time that it was becoming more "Javanized."

With a variety of styles appealing to different ethnic groups and social strata, kroncong became a music of broad appeal. Its popularity was consolidated during World War II when the Japanese banned foreign popular music, thereby helping it become a vehicle for the expression of national solidarity and nationalist sentiment. Although newer styles like the rock-oriented kroncong pop have developed more recently, the powerful nostalgia evoked by the music from the war and prewar period gives it a strong appeal for an older audience, even as the young continue to turn toward music like dangdut.

Jaipongan

The *jaipongan* style of pop music has the unique characteristic of being derived from a type of professional folk entertainment of Sunda (West Java) and does not betray the foreign derivations or influences of gambus, dangdut, or kroncong. The Sundanese **ketuk tilu** (three ketuk) is a small ensemble of musicians playing rebab, gong, three ketuk, and drums, who accompany a female dancer-singer (and sometimes prostitute) in a kind of audience-participation performance during which various men get up to dance with her. Many similar

TANJIDOR
Musical ensemble from the outskirts of Jakarta that blends European-dervied band instruments with local instruments.

KETUK TILU
A small, Sundanese ensemble consisting of rebab, gong, three ketuk, and drums. This ensemble accompanies a female dancer/singer.

LISTENING GUIDE

> ### JAIPONGAN, "DAUN PULUS KESER BOJONG"

 **LISTEN**

TRACK 7.8 Performed by Gugum Gumbira and his Jugala Group, singer Idjah Hadidjah

TIME	MUSICAL EVENTS
0:00–1:14	Extended introductory passage highlighting the virtuosic and flashy Sundanese drumming style in which the drums are struck with the hands and even manipulated with the feet. Melody on rebab, and regular clacking of cymbal-like kecrek. Periodic shouts from the performers add to the raucous and rowdy atmosphere typical of jaipongan performance.
1:14–1:45	The performers yell the name of their group JU–GA–LA alternating with the leader who sort of groans it in a gruff voice.
1:45–2:13	Introduction concludes with entrance of sarons playing phrase with an answer by drums, both then repeated.
2:13–3:00	Singer briefly introduces song unaccompanied and is joined by other performers starting at [2:20]. Her highly elaborate melody is heterophonically accompanied by the rebab and progresses with occasional, startling comments from the drum.
3:00–3:03	The recording fades out.

JAIPONGAN
Popular Indonesian music that is derived from the native folk entertainment of Sunda (West Java).

 **EXPLORE**

Jaipongan

types of dance entertainments exist or existed in Java and Bali as well as other parts of Indonesia, and troupes were often hired for private parties or for celebrations connected with occasions like weddings or circumcisions.

Like dangdut, the word **jaipongan** was made up from syllables representing drum sounds, and flashy Sundanese-style drumming is basic to this style. A saron is generally added to the instruments derived from ketuk tilu. This adds another characteristic equally as attractive as the drumming and as typically Sundanese, because the saron is in slendro while the singer and rebab usually perform in another tuning such as pelog, adding ornamental pitches as well. According to Philip Yampolsky (in his liner notes for *Tonggeret*, Nonesuch 79173–2), a young musician named Gugum Gumbira was responsible for introducing the amalgamation of various Sundanese musical components that started the jaipongan craze in 1974. Its popularity soon caused it to spread beyond his original troupe to other parts of Java outside Sunda, as well as to take on the nature of a popular dance fad for couples.

Although the social-dance fad has waned in recent years, Gugum Gumbira has concentrated on creating staged performances, and as Philip Yampolsky remarks: "Today, Jaipongan is accepted as a 'national' stage dance." It is even included in cultural performances by Indonesian students in the United States for national-day celebrations.

UNITY IN DIVERSITY

"Unity in Diversity," as we pointed out earlier, is the national motto of Indonesia, a nation created within the memory of many of its present-day citizens. Creating unity is a primary concern in any attempt to form a nation, and is equally important to sustaining one. But the chore is a remarkably daunting one in a country with the topography of Indonesia and a population ranging from the industrialized city dwellers of Java to recently contacted groups of former headhunters in Papua (the Indonesian part of New Guinea) and Kalimantan (the Indonesian part of Borneo). In the scholarly view of music, the unity of the area is often related to the use of bronze-casting technology and cyclical musical structures that also link Indonesia to the Southeast Asian mainland, southern China, northeastern India, and the Philippines. Valid and interesting as this system of relationships is, it does not accommodate many other types of musical phenomena in Indonesia such as, for example, the various pipe ensembles of people in Kalimantan, whose music might be reasonably discussed in comparison with that of similar ensembles among the Andean Aymara or South African Venda.

The necessity of national "unity," evidenced in music by the establishment of government conservatories with standardized curricula, will present a challenge to the more marginal components of Indonesian society and to their cultural forms. These components of Indonesia's "diversity" will likely be neglected—as they have been in this chapter—but their lack of importance for the national scene does not necessarily indicate the inevitability of their disappearance or impoverishment. Thanks to the inexpensive and widespread technology of recording, many types of regionally circumscribed musics find a locally supportive market that helps to perpetuate them and at the same time alter their uses and associations. Rather than propagating a narrow range of musical product, the cassette, CD, and VCD industry in Indonesia has in effect created the audio equivalent of the country's motto, a wide range of music in a uniform medium.

Recorded sound has demonstrated the variety of Indonesia's music today, but it has also preserved the sound of its past: The gamelan brought to the Columbian Exposition of 1893 was recorded not only on film but also on wax cylinders, the audio-recording medium of the day. Although these are not the first recordings of an ethnomusicological nature—some earlier ones were made of Native Americans—they are among the earliest, and they help to lend a special aura to the instruments now housed in the collection of the Field Museum. What would those musicians recorded in 1893 have thought, I wonder, if they had been able to hear the performance of bubaran "Udan Mas" that was described at the start of this essay?

KEY TERMS

Balugan
Barong
Buburan
Colotomic structure
Dangdut
Gambus
Gamelan
Gatra
Gendhing
Gerongan
Gongan
Jaipongan
Kecak
Kenongan
Ketuk tilu
Kotekan
Laras
Pathetbedhaya
Pesindhen
Rebab
Suling
Tanjidor
Wayang kulit

**REVIEW
CHAPTER
RESOURCES**

SUMMARY

Gamelan is an Indonesian term for musical ensemble. In central Java, these are usually instruments of bronze—gongs and keys—with the addition of drums, a flute, a fiddle, a xylophone, and a zither.

As we have heard, the kinds of ensembles that are referred to as gamelan are diverse, indeed. The occasions during which gamelan becomes important to the event at hand are similarly diverse. In fact, Gamelan music serves ritual and spiritual, governmental, dramatic, and social functions. The shadow-puppet play—Wayang Kulit—in particular, is one of the major theatrical forms that uses gamelan accompaniment. We have also encountered some specific and characteristic musical ideas within Indonesia. So, for instance, we learned that Indonesian music is generally based on repeated musical phrases of varying length. We also learned that Javanese music uses two scales—a five-note (slendro) and a seven-note (pelog) one. In Bali, pelog predominates, but the important gender wayang ensemble for accompanying the shadow play uses slendro.

Our encounter with the music of Indonesia has also pointed out some of the differences between Javanese and Balinese gamelan music. So, for instance, Balinese gamelan sound is distinguished from its Javanese relative by the use of paired, gendered instruments that are tuned slightly differently, creating a shimmering or pulsating effect. Additionally, a type of gamelan music, called kebyar, is distinguished from its Javanese and Balinese antecedents by the virtuosic performance of kotekan and by the sudden rhythmic and dynamic shifts that characterize the style. As we have seen, the emergence of performance styles such as kecak and barong in Bali point to the ways that music can change and take on new forms and meanings in response to factors such as tourism. Finally, many newer popular styles (such as gambus, dangdut, kroncong, and jaipongan) combine outside influences—ranging from Arabic pop, Western rock, and Indian film music—with traditional Javanese musical instruments and ideas.

BIBLIOGRAPHY

Java Bernard Arps, Ed., *Performance in Java and Bali: Studies of Narrative Theater* (London: School of Oriental and African Studies, 1993); Bart Barendregt and Wim van Zanten "Popular Music in Indonesia since 1998, in Particular Fusion, Indie and Islamic Music on Video Compact Discs and the Internet" in *Yearbook for Traditional Music* Vol. 34 (2002), pp. 67–113; Judith Becker, *Traditional Music in Modern Java: Gamelan in a Changing Society* (Honolulu, HA: University of Hawaii Press, 1980); Marc Benamou, "Comparing Musical Affect: Java and the West" in *The World of Music* Vol. 45, No. 3, Cross-Cultural Aesthetics (2003), pp. 57–76; Ben Brinner, "Cognitive and Interpersonal Simensions of Listening in Javanese Gamelan Performance" in *The World of Music* Vol. 52, No. 1/3 (2010), pp. 580–595; Mantle Hood, *The Nuclear Theme as a Determinant of Patet in Javanese Music* (New York, Da Capo, 1977); Felicia Hughes-Freeland, *Embodied Communities: Dance Traditions*

and Change in Java (New York: Berghahn Books, 2008); Margaret Kartomi, "Meaning, Style and Change in Gamalan and Wayang Kulit Banjar Since Their Transplantation from Hindu-Buddhist Java to South Kalimantan" in *The World of Music*, Vol. 52, No. 1/3 (2010), pp. 476–514; Martin Richter, "Grounded Cosmopolitans and the Bureaucratic Field: Musical Performance at Two Yogyakarta State Institutions" in *Sojourn: Journal of Social Issues in Southeast Asia* Vol. 21, No. 2, Dynamics of the Local (October 2006), pp. 178–203; Henry Spiller, *Erotic Triangles: Sudanese Dance and Masculinity in West Java* (Chicago, IL: University of Chicago Press, 2010); Henry Spiller, *Javaphilia: American Love Affairs with Javanese Music and Dance* (Honolulu, HA: University of Hawai'i Press, 2015); Sumarsam, *Javanese Gamelan and the West* (Rochester, UK: University of Rochester Press, 2013); Christina Sunardi, "Negotiating Authority and Articulating Gender: Performer Interaction in Malang, East

Java" in *Ethnomusicology* Vol. 55, No. 1 (Winter 2011), pp. 32–54; R. Anderson Sutton, *Traditions of Gamelan Music in Java: Musical Pluralism and Regional Identity* (New York: Cambridge University Press); Susan Pratt Walton, "Aesthetic and Spiritual Correlations in Javanese Gamelan Music" in *The Journal of Aesthetics and Art Criticism* Vol. 65, No. 1, Special Issue: Global Theories of the Arts and Aesthetics (Winter, 2007), pp. 31–41; Susan Pratt Walkton, *Mode in Javanese Music*, Monographs in International Studies Southeast Asia Series No. 79 (Athens, OH: Ohio University Center for International Studies,1987); Andrew Weintraub, *Dangdut Stories: A Social and Musical History of Indonesia's Most Popular Music* (Oxford: Oxford University Press, 2010); Andrew Weintraub, *Power Plays Wayang Golek Puppet Theater of West Java* (Athens, OH: Ohio University Press, 2004); Sarah Weiss, *Listening to an Earlier Java: Aesthetics, Gender, and the Music of Wayang in Central Java* (Leiden: KITLV, 2006); Sean Williams, *The Sound of the Ancestral Ship: Highland Music of West Java* (Oxford: Oxford University Press, 2001).

Bali Michal B. Bakan, *Music of Death and New Creation: Experiences in the World of Balinese Gamelan Beleganjur* (Chicago, IL: University of Chicago Press, 1999); I Made Brandem and Frederik deBoer, *Kaja and Keod: Balinese Dance in Transition* (Kuala Lumpur and New York: Oxford University Press, 1981); Sonja Lynn Downing, "Agency, Leadership, and Gender Negotiation in Balinese Girls' Gamelans" in *Ethnomusicology* Vol. 54, No. 1 (Winter, 2010), pp. 54–80; Brita Renée Heimarck, *Balinese Discourses on Music and Modernization: Village Voices and Urban Views* (New York: Routledge, 2003); Edward Herbst, Voices in Bali (Hanover, NH: University Press of New England, 1997); Andrew C. McGraw, "The Development of the 'Gamelan Semara Dana' and the Expansion of the Modal System in Bali, Indonesia" in *Asian Music* Vol. 31, No. 1 (Autumn, 1999/Winter, 2000), pp. 63–93; Colin McPhee, *The Balinese Wajang koelit and its Music* (New York: AMS Press, 1936); Colin McPhee, *Music in Bali: A Study in Form and Instrumental Organization in Balinese Orchestral Music* (New York: Da Capo, 1976); Henry Spiller, *Gamelan The Traditional Sounds of Indonesia* (New York: Routledge, 2008); Kendra Stepputat, "Nice 'n' Easy: The Balinese Gamelan Rindik: Its Music, Musicians, and Value as Tourist Art" in *Asian Music* Vol. 37, No. 2 (Summer Autumn, 2006), pp. 84–121; Michael Tenzer, *Gamelan Gong Kebyar: The Art of Twentieth-Century Balinese Music* (Chicago, IL: University of Chicago Press, 2000).

DISCOGRAPHY

Java *Java Palais Royal de Yogyakarta: Musiques de Concert* (Ocora 558 598); *Java Historic Gamelans*, Art Music from Southeast Asia IX-2 (Philips 6586 004); *Musiques et Traditions du Monde: Une Nuit de Wayang Kulit Légende de Wahju Tjakraningrat* (CBS 65440); *Java Court Gamelan from the Pura Paku Alaman Jogyakarta* (Nonesuch H-72044); *Java Court Gamelan Istana Mangkunegaran Surakarta* (Nonesuch H-72074); *Java Court Gamelan Kraton Yogyakarta* (Nonesuch H-72083); *Sunda: Musique et Chants Traditionnels* (Ocora 558 502); *Tonggeret* (Jaipongan) (Nonesuch 79173–2).

Bali *From Kuno to Kebyar: Balinese Gamelan Angklung* (Smithsonian Folkways SFW 50411); *Semar Pegulingan: Golden Gong of Bali* (Grevillea Records GRV 1020); *Gamelan of the God of Love: Gamelan Semar Pegulingan* (Nonesuch H-72046); *Bali: Musique et Théâtre* (gender wayang, gambuh) (Ocora OCR 60); *Golden Rain* (kebyar) (Nonesuch H-72028); *Bali: Le Gong Gede de Batur* (Ocora 585 510); *The Balinese Gamelan: Music from the Morning of the World* (Nonesuch 72015); *Gamelan Music of Bali* (Lyrichord LLST 7179).

General *Music of Indonesia*, series of twenty compact discs issued by Smithsonian Folkways.

MUSIC OF SUB-SAHARAN AFRICA

Thomas Turino

A SHONA MBIRA PERFORMANCE IN ZIMBABWE

Heading toward the roundhouse after dark, I heard the powerful sound of people playing *hosho* (large maraca-like shakers) from some distance down the path. As I entered the dimly lit kitchen hut where the ceremony was being held, I could make out people clapping, singing, talking, and drinking; one frail old woman was dancing by herself in the center of the room. Beneath all of this there was still another sound, soft yet deep and moving like the combination of water and bells. This was the *mbira*. Two men, leaning against the far wall, sat with their hands hidden inside large calabash gourds playing mbira. They were the foundation of the musical activity, and the singers, dancers, and hosho players created their rhythmic patterns and improvised vocal parts based on the many simultaneous melodies that the mbira played.

During a break in the music, I asked the mbira players to show me their instruments. Twenty-two slightly rusted metal keys were tightly fastened over a metal bridge on a wooden soundboard, with bottle caps attached to a metal plate on the board. A necklace of bottle caps was also strung around the gourd resonators, creating the buzzing sound a torn stereo speaker makes. The musicians explained that without the gourds, the mbiras were too soft to be heard in occasions for communal music making, such as the *bira* (ceremony) that we were attending, and without the buzzing of the bottle caps, they would not sound like mbira.

The mbira belongs to a general class of instruments known as **lamellaphones** (plucked tongues or keys mounted on a soundboard or soundbox). It is sometimes referred to as "thumb piano" and thought of as a toy in the United States.

Shona instruments (left to right): karimba, hosho rattle, 22-key mbira in calabash gourd, 22-key mbira, side view. *Source:* Thomas Turino

LAMELLAPHONE
A general class of musical instruments that have tuned metal or reed tongues set on a bridge mounted to a soundboard or box; it is played by striking the keys. The mbira is but one example of this instrument type. Other lamellaphones used in Zimbabwe include the karimba, njari, and matepe.

Yet the mbira that these men were playing is one of the most highly developed classical instruments of the Shona, a Bantu-speaking people of Zimbabwe in southeastern Africa. Although different types of lamellaphones are played all over Africa, this class of instruments has been most highly developed by the Shona and other groups in southern Africa. The Shona play a variety of lamellaphones associated with different regions of Zimbabwe, including the *karimba*, the *njari*, and the *matepe*, but presently, the twenty-two key mbira is the most popular type. Shona mbira players often specialize on one variety of instrument, each with its own distinct scale pattern and playing techniques; changing from a karimba to an mbira or njari is like switching from a guitar to a mandolin or a banjo.

The musicians sat down and began playing another piece. Listening more closely to the mbira players this time, I could hear distinct bass, middle, and high melodic parts coming from the two instruments. I watched their hands closely. They played the same patterns for a long time before changing perhaps only one or two pitches by striking different keys and then repeated the new variation many times. But even when they were playing the same patterns, I sometimes thought that I heard changes in the melodies.

During their next break the musicians explained that it was always like that. Even simple mbira pieces contained many inner melodic lines that resulted not from changes in the keys played but rather from the particular combination of right- and left-hand parts that were played. They explained that mbira music was an art of creative listening as well as playing, and that the mbira itself seemed continually to suggest new inner melodic lines to the musician even when his hands continued to play the same keys. They told me that this was one reason why mbira players can perform the same pattern for a long time without getting bored or feeling the need to create constant contrasts. It was almost as if the mbira itself magically created its own variations; one simply had to have patience and learn to hear what it had to offer. I enjoyed talking to these musicians and was learning something of the art of listening to Shona music, but it was time for them to return to playing for the ancestral spirits in the *bira* ceremony.

The Bira

The Shona believe that their ancestors continually interact with and affect the lives of the living. As in many places, Shona people emphasize maintaining good relationships with their parents, grandparents, and other elder relatives; for the Shona, however, such relationships do not cease when someone dies. Interactions with deceased relatives take place through spirit possession when an ancestor enters and speaks through the body of a living person—a spirit medium. Not everyone who dies comes back as a spirit. However, those who do return select one person to be their medium for life. (Family spirits are usually within the past three generations.) Once spirits make themselves known in this way, family members can call them back to speak with them at a family-sponsored ceremony known as the bira. Misfortunes such as illness or losing a job are sometimes interpreted as the result of offending a particular ancestor. People also commonly turn to their ancestors for advice during times of trouble. Even when there is no specific problem, some families periodically hold ceremonies to honor an ancestor or simply to keep in touch (just as we might

BIRA
A Shona religious ceremony involving spirit possession.

Shona mbira players Emmanuel Chidzere and David Mapfumo with singer and hosho player Pyo Murungweni, Murehwa District, Zimbabwe.
Source: Thomas Turino

feel the need to call our parents when living away from them). In the central and some northern parts of Zimbabwe, these ceremonies often involve mbira music and dance to call the ancestors; in other Zimbabwean regions drums are used instead of mbira.

As the *bira* begins people arrive gradually; those already present casually talk and joke together to the music of the mbira and hosho, which will play all night. Mbira players are musical specialists who are invited to perform at the ceremony. They supply the musical foundation, but as the evening progresses, family and community members join in by clapping different patterns and dancing in the center of the room. Men and women also may contribute to the performance by singing melodies that weave in and out of the mbira's bass part or by performing in a high-pitched yodeling style. (Instead of singing actual words, the singers use **vocables**, rhythmic syllables that have no semantic meaning.) Both well-known verses and improvised words are also sung to fit the occasion, and the poetry moves people as do the dance and the music at this participatory event. After one piece has ended, the two mbira players begin again, each with his specific part, and again the different participants add what they will, until the performance becomes a dense, rich fabric of sound, movement, and feeling. As the spirit medium shows subtle signs that the ancestor is coming, the rest of the participants often begin playing, dancing, and singing more intensely. This collective energy helps to bring on possession.

Good mbira playing and concentrated communal effort are essential for the success of the bira because music is one of the main attractions that call the spirit into the ceremony. As the intensity mounts and the energy within the room becomes right, the spirit enters the body of the medium. Spirits are particularly attracted by the music that they enjoyed while they were living. Thus,

VOCABLES
Nonsemantic syllables that are sung; "nonsense syllables."

Shona women of Mhembere singing and playing hosho, Murehwa District, Zimbabwe. *Source:* Thomas Turino

playing the right tunes is important for bringing on possession. Once possessed, the spirit medium is usually dressed by an attendant in a special robe. The medium who now has become the spirit may continue singing and dancing, or may become quiet and withdrawn. After the spirit has participated in the event for a brief time, the music comes to a halt. The host of the bira welcomes the spirit, now sitting in the center of the room, with a formal greeting. He also offers special beer, brewed by the family for seven days, and snuff. The participants then consult the ancestor about the problem or issues that occasioned the bira, and a discussion ensues between the spirit and the concerned participants. After the consultation, the music, singing, and dancing start up again and continue until morning, even if the spirit decides to leave the medium some time during the night.

THE MBIRA AND SOME GENERAL PRINCIPLES OF AFRICAN MUSIC

A closer look at Shona mbira performance reveals a series of features and aesthetic preferences that are common to many sub-Saharan musical traditions. These include the practice of **interlocking**—fitting your pitches and beats into the spaces of other parts or alternating the pitches or phrases of one part with those of another to create the whole. As we will see, this occurs at a variety of levels in mbira performance and in the other African traditions we will study. **Call-and-response**—the alternation of leader and chorus parts or of a vocal and instrumental part—illustrates the principle of interlock at the highest level of musical organization. Call-and-response is a common practice all over sub-Saharan Africa.

A second general feature of African music is the aesthetic preference for dense overlapping textures and buzzy timbres that contribute to a dense sound quality. Third, African music is often cyclical and open-ended in form involving one or more repeated melodies or rhythmic patterns (**ostinatos**) as the basic foundation of a performance. These repetitive, cyclical pieces are often performed for a long time with gradual variations added as a performance progresses. Community participation is valued in many African musical traditions. Repetition and long performances facilitate participation by giving nonspecialized participants a chance to get their bearings and to enter the performance.

African music is famous for its rhythmic complexity. At the most basic level, this involves the juxtaposition or simultaneous performance of duple and triple rhythmic patterns (patterns of two against patterns of three). The multiple layering of different rhythmic patterns creates a tension and, at times, an ambiguity such that a listener can hear and feel the same music in a variety of ways depending on which rhythmic part or pattern he or she is focusing on. Another typical African musical trait is that melodies often descend (start high and end with lower pitches). A final general characteristic is that African

INTERLOCKING
The practice of fitting one's pitches and beats into the spaces of other parts, or alternating the pitches or phrases of one part with those of others to create the whole; also called *hocket*.

CALL-AND-RESPONSE
The alternation or interlocking of leader and chorus musical parts or of a vocal and instrumental part.

OSTINATO
A repeated or cyclical melody or rhythmic pattern.

music, and musical ensembles, often involve "core" and "elaboration" parts. The "core" musical roles and parts are those that must be in place for a performance to go forward. Core parts are the foundation that make other contributions, variations, and improvisations possible. In mbira performance, core roles include the basic rhythmic flow maintained by the hosho and the basic melodic–harmonic ostinato played in the midrange and bass of the mbira. The "elaboration" parts, no less essential to an artful performance, include clapped patterns, vocal lines, high mbira melodies and bass variations, and dancing.

General Characteristics of African Music

- Interlocking melodies and rhythmic parts
- Preference for dense, overlapping textures and buzzy timbres
- Cyclical forms (based on melodic/rhythmic ostinatos)
- Flexible approaches to rhythms often combining or juxtaposing units of twos and threes
- Descending melodic shape
- Musical roles including "core" and "elaboration" parts

Interlocking

The longest, lowest keys on the mbira are found in the center; the metal keys become shorter and higher as they fan out to each side. On the left side of the instrument, a row of longer bass keys is set directly below the midrange keys, with the row of the highest keys on the right side of the instrument. The keys on the left side are played by the left thumb, and the right thumb and forefinger play the keys on the right side. Mbira pieces are constructed so that the left thumb interlocks with the right thumb and forefinger to play a single midrange melody. On many pieces, the left thumb also alternates between the midrange keys of the upper-left row and the bass keys of the lower-left row to produce an independent bass line that interlocks with the midrange melody. Finally, the right forefinger plays the smallest, highest keys (far right) to produce additional descending high melodic lines. These pitches again are alternated with the left-hand part in interlocking fashion. The bass, midrange, and high melodies create a variable contrapuntal texture, and a listener's perception of the piece can change substantially by shifting attention from one line to another or to the resultant melodic patterns that emerge from the relations between different parts.

The hand-clapping patterns, dance movements, and vocal melodies performed by participants at a bira and other occasions frequently do not simply reproduce the basic beat and, typically, are not performed in unison. Rather, each participant may add his or her own clapped patterns, sung parts, or dance movements, so that they fall in between or around central beats and pitches—in the spaces—of other people's parts, thereby providing another series of interlocking aspects. A basic musical value among the Shona, and in many African societies, is the ability to add one's own distinctive part to the ensemble while making it blend with the whole. Call-and-response singing, an obvious form of interlocking, is also common in Shona music-making.

Density

The final contrapuntal, multirhythmic character of a communal Shona performance results from the interlocking and dense overlapping of the participants' contributions. The Shona, like many African peoples, prefer dense, rich sounds. Bottle caps or shells attached to gourd resonators and mbira soundboards create a buzzing aura around the discrete pitches that contrast with the clear, "pure" instrumental timbres (tone qualities) preferred in the European classical tradition. The multiple layers produced in a communal performance also add to the density of sound, as does the very nature of the mbira, on which keys previously struck continue to ring through the following pitches sounded, with each key producing multiple overtones.

Cyclical Form and Variation

The typical form of classical mbira music is a melodic–harmonic cycle, or ostinato, of forty-eight quick beats. The particular ostinato of most classical mbira pieces is divided into four twelve-beat phrases in 12/8 meter. As an mbira performance progresses, small variations, including traditional formulas and improvised lines, are gradually added to, and over, the basic ostinato. Mbira players say that a skilled musician must have patience and not rush the variations. It is not considered good playing to use overly apparent or dramatic contrasts; rather, one variation must be built on the last and subtly lead to the next within the ostinato cycle. Usually, each variation will be repeated a number of times before further development is attempted.

Conceptions of Music

The very definition of what constitutes a musical "piece" in Shona society, and in many sub-Saharan societies, suggests another characteristically African feature. Although mbira pieces have titles, the composition is conceived as an aggregate of musical resources that may be put together in different ways, making each performance recognizable as "the piece" and yet unique. These resources include the harmonic, temporal, and melodic character of the basic ostinato; a series of stock variations and motifs associated with the piece; and certain sung melodies and lines of text. The length of a given performance, the number of variations used and the order in which they are performed, the speed and

MBIRA MUSIC: "NHEMAMUSASA"

LISTEN

TRACK 8.1   **Chris Mihlanga and Bernard Matatfi, mbiras, Tom Turino on hosho**

ALTHOUGH THE MBIRA can be played solo, a piece is not really considered complete unless two players are present to play their separate, complementary parts that interlock to create the whole. One part is called the *kushaura* ("to lead the piece," to play the basic piece), and the other is called kutsinhira. The *kutsinhira* consists of a second, accompanying part. On many pieces the kutsinhira part is almost exactly the same as the kushaura, but it is played a beat behind so that each pitch played by the first part is doubled by the second. This doubling effect produced by the two instruments can be heard on the high descending lines of *Nhemamusasa*, which means "cutting branches for a shelter." This happens for the first time around [0:40] in the recording. With the exception of the high melodies, however, Nhemamusasa involves a second type of kushaura-kutsinhira relationship in which a completely different accompanying part is composed to interlock with the kushaura part. Listen especially to the ways that you can orient your listening to attend to either duple or triple meter throughout this performance.

You can follow the basic ostinato melody in the kushaura by counting one beat per note. Twice through this pattern constitutes one 48-beat cycle. Remember that this is very schematic and that small variations to the melody occur consistently throughout the performance:

In this example, each of the melody notes played on the kushaura counts for two beats. This can be represented rhythmically as follows:

Phrase 1

Beat	1	2	3	4	5	6	7	8	9	10	11	12
Kushaura melody	x		x		x		x		x		x	

The high descending melody can be represented as follows. Listen for the "echo" effect of the kutsinhira doubling the kushaura:

continued

The hosho provides a particularly good way of beginning to hear the interplay between duple and triple meter. The following representation of phrases 1 and 2 of the basic ostinato can help you orient yourself. If you listen to the hosho and count it as 123 456, 123 456 (or 1 – – 2 – – 1 – – 2 – –), then the melody played on the kushaura unfolds in triple meter against the hosho (three melody notes for every two strong beats on the hosho, or 1 – 2 – 3 – 1 – 2 – 3). The numbering above the notation is intended only to help you count the duple and triple feel. The smaller numbers underneath the notation reference the actual eighth note count in 12/8 meter.

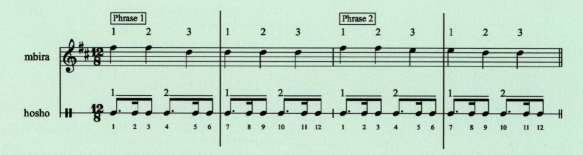

Again, this can be rhythmically represented as follows (just the first phrase). In order to help you hear the 3 against 2 rhythms, I highlight duple and then triple division of the twelve beat cycle in two successive tables:

Phrase 1 (triple meter)

Triple	1		2		3		1		2		3	
Beat	1	2	3	4	5	6	7	8	9	10	11	12
Kushaura	x		x		x		x		x		x	
Hosho	X	x	x	X	x	x	X	x	x	X	x	x

Phrase 1 (duple meter)

Duple	1			2			1			2		
Beat	1	2	3	4	5	6	7	8	9	10	11	12
Kushaura	x		x		x		x		x		x	
Hosho	X	x	x	X	x	x	X	x	x	X	x	x

continued

TIMING	SECTION	MUSICAL EVENTS
0:00–0:05		The recording fades in, playing the third phrase of the basic ostinato and completes the fourth phrase.
0:05–0:40	**Basic ostinato:** Try to hear the two mbiras and the hosho as distinct contributors to the overall texture. Notice the buzzing quality of the mbiras. Focus in on the melody being played on the kushaura.	Basic ostinato pattern begins. The 48-beat cycle consists of four 12-beat phrases. Try to follow along as the complete cycle is repeated four times.
		If you're having trouble hearing the phrases, you can use the timings below (for each phrase of the first cycle), to get your bearings:
		[0:05–0:07] Phrase 1
		[0:07–0:09] Phrase 2
		[0:9–0:011] Phrase 3
		[0:11–0:13] Phrase 4
		Different players "hear" the beginning of the cycle in different places. This aspect is not fixed, thus my designation of phrase numbers is somewhat arbitrary.
0:40–0:57	**High descending variation:** Notice the close imitation of the kushaura melody by the kutsinhira. Notice also how this high melodic variation provides contrast to the basic ostinato.	The high descending melody, also based on a 48-beat cycle, is introduced here and played twice. The timings for the first four phrases of the first cycle are given below:
		[0:40–0:42] Phrase 1
		[0:42–0:44] Phrase 2
		[0:44–0:46] Phrase 3
		[0:46–0:48] Phrase 4
0:57–1:15	**Basic ostinato returns:** Listen for the overall melody contained within the 48-beat cycle. Try to hear it as a total statement.	The basic ostinato returns and is repeated twice. To help you hear the overall melodic shape, listen this time for the whole cycle (instead of for the shorter phrases):
		[0:57–1:05] Cycle 1
		[1:06–1:15] Cycle 2
1:15–1:32	**High descending variation:** See if you can begin focusing on the hosho here. Try to hear the faster (123 456) rhythm, and notice how the melody played on the kushaura now takes on a triple feel (3 melody notes for every 2 accented notes played on the hosho).	Two cycles of the high melodic variation.
1:32–1:57	**Basic ostinato:** Continue to focus on the hosho. Try to hear the 3 against 2 texture. Also attend to the "inside and inner" voices (i.e., not melody and not bass, but	Three cycles of the basic ostinato, played with increased bass note accents. These bass notes should help you hear the 3 against 2 because they line up with the accents played on the hosho.

continued

TIMING	SECTION	MUSICAL EVENTS
	in-between) that animate this performance. The interlocking parts played on both mbiras can help you hear the duple and triple meters. Try to listen to these instead of the melody and you'll hear the piece differently.	
1:58–2:23	**High descending variation:** Now try to listen in duple again, that is, try to hear the melody independently of the hosho.	Three cycles of the high descending melody. Remember that one of the aesthetic principles at play here is being able to orient yourself as a listener and performer in either duple or triple meter.
2:23–2:48	**Basic ostinato:** Another exercise that will help you hear these ideas is to tap one hand to the accented hosho beats and your other hand to the melody notes played on the kushaura. Practice this and you'll be able to internalize the 3 against 2 rhythms at play in this example.	Three cycles of the basic ostinato.
2:48–3:04	**High descending variation:** Listen to the overall performance and work your focus between the various melodic and percussive parts.	Two cycles of the high descending melody.
3:05–3:28	**Basic ostinato**	Two full cycles of the basic ostinato are followed by a fade out during the third cycle.

character of development, and the improvisations on the basic patterns, however, make each performance distinct. This approach resembles that of jazz, blues, and some rock performers, indicating one way that people working in these styles may have been influenced by the African heritage.

In Shona villages, "the piece" and music itself are conceptualized as a process linked to specific people and particular moments or contexts, whereas for some musical traditions in the West, music has become a reproducible sound object that can be, and is, isolated and abstracted as a thing in itself. Recordings and written scores perhaps facilitate thinking about music as an object that can be purchased, consumed, collected, and copyrighted. It is significant that the Shona words for the two basic parts of a mbira piece—**kushaura** and **kutsinhira**—are not nouns, referring to things, but rather are verbs ("kushaura" means literally "to lead the piece"), underlining the notion of music as an interactive process.

KUSHAURA
"To lead the piece"; the first part, or lead part played by one Shona mbira player.

KUTSINHIRA
"To accompany"; the second accompanying part played by a second Shona mbira player.

AFRICA GENERAL AND AFRICA SPECIFIC

To this point, I have tried to link certain features of Shona mbira playing with more widespread African musical characteristics. Indeed there is a tendency among North Americans and Europeans to think of Africa as *one* place and African music as a single, identifiable phenomenon. The continent of Africa has over fifty countries, however, and linguists have identified at least 800 ethnolinguistic groups. In Nigeria alone, 386 different languages have been identified. The organization of sub-Saharan Africa into modern nation–states is primarily a colonial legacy based on the way the continent was divided by the European powers at the end of the nineteenth century. It has little to do with internal social divisions within these territories or with the linguistic groups that cross national borders. (Mande societies, for example, span parts of Senegal, Gambia, Mali, Burkina Faso, Côte d'Ivoire, Guinea, and Sierra Leone.) Because many musical traditions are linked to specific ethnolinguistic groups, it is often better to think about African music in these rather than in national terms.

In contrast to the stereotypic vision of small, so-called primitive tribes in Africa, various kinds of traditional political organization include (1) complex, hierarchical, centralized states with political authority vested in the hands of hereditary rulers; and (2) more decentralized, smaller-scale societies where political power was regulated by interactions between kinship groups such as clans or lineages. Centralized kingdoms with highly developed political organization have existed in Africa from early times. One example is the state of Zimbabwe (the modern country was named after this early empire), which was thriving by the twelfth century. On the other hand, small egalitarian bands of hunters and gatherers such as the BaMbuti Pygmies have lived for centuries in the central African rain forest. Hunter-gatherer groups such as the Pygmies and the San (Bushmen) are in a small minority, however. The majority of African societies depended on agriculture and animal husbandry for subsistence—stable agriculture being important for state formation. Just as political and economic systems differ widely between specific African societies, family and social structures are also diverse.

Sometimes there are important correlations between economic modes of production, social structure, and musical practices and style. Given the socio-economic diversity among African societies, we would expect musical diversity as well. Indeed, there are important differences in the styles, processes, and functions of music-making among different African societies, just as there are differences in conceptions about music, the role and status of musicians, and the types of repertory, instruments, and dances performed. As I suggested earlier, however, some basic similarities in musical style, practices, and aesthetics span the sub-Saharan region, even among such diverse groups as the Shona in southeastern Africa, the BaMbuti Pygmies in the central rain forest, and the Mande peoples in the northwestern savanna region. Taken at the most general level, these similarities allow us to speak of "African music" (much as the European harmonic system, among other general traits, allows us to identify mainstream "Western music"). Nonetheless, it is the facets that distinguish the different African musical cultures, rather than the similarities, that will probably appear as most significant to Africans themselves.

In the sections that follow, similarities with the major characteristics outlined for Shona mbira music will serve as a focus for the discussion of several specific African musical cultures. At the same time, differences among the musical cultures will be emphasized, and these differences will be considered in light of the distinct ways of life and worldviews that characterize different African societies.

MUSICAL VALUES, PRACTICES, AND SOCIAL STYLE

The Pygmies

The word *Pygmy* is an outsider generic term applied to social groups found in the equatorial forest area stretching from Gabon and Cameroon in the west to Uganda, Rwanda, and Burundi in the east. People in these groups self-identify by more specific terms such as BaMbuti, Bibiyak, and Baka. The Ituri Forest, bordering on Uganda to the east and Sudan to the north, remains a major stronghold for Pygmies, and about 40,000 live in this region. The majority of groups maintain a semiautonomous hunting-and-gathering existence. Centuries ago, the Pygmies found their central forest region invaded from the north by Bantu (a major linguistic category in sub-Saharan Africa) and Sudanic groups, who were cultivators and pastoralists. The Pygmy languages were abandoned for those of the neighboring groups, with whom they entered into types of patron-client relationships. The anthropologist Colin Turnbull, however, suggests that the BaMbuti Pygmies of the Ituri Forest lead a kind of double life, maintaining their own traditional ways (with the exception of language) when alone in the forest and taking part in Bantu ritual and musical life on their visits to the villages. Here we will concentrate on Pygmy life and music in their forest home.

The BaMbuti net-hunters maintain a nomadic existence, setting up camps for a month or so in different places in the forest as they continue their search of game. Net-hunting, like most aspects of Pygmy life, is a communal affair, with male family members stringing their nets together in a large semicircle and the women and children beating the brush to scare game into them. The catch is shared. Bands are composed of nuclear families, and although certain individuals are considered to have more expertise in some realms of activity than in others, there is little specialization of social and economic roles within age and gender categories. A formalized hierarchical system of leadership is not present. Because survival depends on cooperation rather than competition, the keystones of Pygmy society are egalitarianism, consensus, and unity. Because of their nomadic existence, the ownership of goods and property is minimal among most Pygmy groups.

EXPLORE

Pygmies of the Ituri Forest

All these aspects strongly influence their musical activities. The Pygmies have few musical instruments of their own. Pygmy instruments include whistles and end-blown flutes made from cane. They may be used to accompany singing or in duets for informal music-making. In flute duets, one instrumentalist plays a repeating ostinato pattern, while the other plays a part that interlocks and overlaps with the first, reminding us of the basic principles of Shona mbira performance. Rhythm sticks and rattles are found, as are several trumpet types such as the long, end-blown molimo trumpet. Some Pygmy bands also use a musical bow. A few other instruments, such as small lamellaphones and drums, may be borrowed from their Bantu neighbors.

Vocal music is at the core of Pygmy musical life. Some songs are sung by individuals informally such as lullabies and game songs; however, communal singing for collective ceremonies and occasions is considered much more important. Like most aspects of Pygmy life, musical performance is a non-specialized activity. As in net-hunting, where men and women fulfill different roles, musical participation may be differentiated by gender, depending on the context. For example, men are the primary singers for the **molimo** ceremony, through which the benign relationship with the sacred—and living—forest is maintained. Women are the primary singers for the **elima**, a puberty ceremony. On other occasions—for instance, before almost every hunt—men and women sing together.

Except for ritual occasions, when gender and sometimes age distinctions are made, musical performance involves anyone in the band who wants to sing. Song forms are varied but follow two basic principles that we have already encountered in the Shona mbira music and the Pygmy flute duets—the use of ostinato and interlock. A standard organizational feature found among the BaMbuti Pygmies and in many other African societies is the use of a leader and

MOLIMO
A Pygmy ceremony for the forest; a straight valveless trumpet used in the ceremony.

ELIMA
A Pygmy puberty ceremony for which women are the primary singers.

LISTENING GUIDE   ╭─────────────────────────────────────╮
                       │   **BAMBUTI VOCAL MUSIC:**   │    **LISTEN**
                       │   **"ELIMA GIRLS INITIATION MUSIC"** │
                       ╰─────────────────────────────────────╯

TRACK 8.2   **Recorded by C. Turnbull and F. Chapman**

THIS LISTENING SELECTION is divided into two excerpts ([0:00–1:48] and then [1:52–end]). In the first song, the "chorus" provides an eight-beat ostinato over which one—at first—and later several lead singers provide higher-pitched descending melodic variations (entering at approximately [0:06]). The leader-chorus relationship can be heard as an interlocking or call-and-response arrangement, but in illustrating the preference for density, the two parts continually overlap and are offset. The second song is performed in this same way. Note in both performances how individual singers provide slight variations on the chorus and lead parts adding to the density of the whole.

chorus in call-and-response format. The leader, or one group of people, sings a melodic phrase and is immediately answered by a second group singing another phrase so that the two interlock to create the entire melody. Pygmy vocal practice frequently uses the **hocket** technique (singers alternating short melodic fragments to create a melody), reproducing the same practice of interlocking parts. Yodeling is also frequently practiced by some Pygmy groups and is often considered a hallmark of their vocal style.

HOCKET
Interlocking pitches between two or more sound sources to create a single melody or part.

In its simplest form, the call-and-response phrases are simply repeated continually, creating a cyclical ostinato pattern like that described for Shona mbira music. People within an Mbuti chorus help to create a dense, layered sound by simultaneously singing a number of individual variations of the basic melodic parts. Among the Pygmies of the Central African Republic, ostinatos without call-and-response organization constitute a basic structure. On top of the basic ostinato, singers may add a second complementary ostinato, and others will perform variations on both melodies, thereby creating a dense, over-lapping contrapuntal texture (a texture consisting of different simultaneous melodic lines). The time span of the basic ostinato serves as the reference point for various clapped and percussion parts. Thus, one percussion part may be a six-beat pattern and another may last eight beats, dividing the overall time span of the song, say of twenty-four beats, into different-length cycles.

Certain individuals may begin or lead a song, just as different individuals are considered to have particular expertise in other realms of life. Once a performance is in motion, however, musical roles and leadership may shift, and different voices may move in and out of the background. Hence, Pygmy musical style and practice grows from, and reflects, the specific egalitarian nature of Pygmy social and economic life, just as certain features (e.g., ostinatos, density, and interlock) are consistent with African musical practice in other societies.

As in Shona societies, Pygmy musical performances often involve communication with the spiritual world. However, they have different ideas about the nature of the spiritual world and their own interaction with it. According to Colin Turnbull, the Pygmies recognize that they cannot see, truly comprehend, or give a single name to God. Because they view the forest as the benevolent provider of their lives and livelihood, however, they associate divinity with the forest, itself living and divine. They believe that the world and the forest are basically good, and if misfortunes—such as a bad hunting period, sickness, or death—come, it is because the forest is sleeping. Their response is to wake it by singing to it every night during a ceremony known as the molimo, which may last several months. The long, tubular, end-blown trumpet known as molimo is used to create the sounds of the forest and answer the men's singing, thereby realizing, through ritual, the relationship the Pygmies feel with their natural surroundings and the divine.

Unlike the Shona, who use elaborate and varied sung poetry in performances for the ancestors, communicating with the divine occurs among the Pygmies primarily through musical sound alone. Song texts are kept to a minimum, even to a single line such as "The forest is good." Because the Pygmy conception of the divine cannot be formulated with words, it may be that music, whose existence and meaning are likewise both concrete and diffuse, provides a more direct mode of relating to and representing God. Nonetheless, it is interesting that the Pygmies emphasize singing much more than instrumental music and yet grant so little attention to sung poetry and the power of the word. In this and other important respects, these people of the forest are very different from the Mande on the savanna in West Africa.

The Mande of West Africa

The Mande represent one of the most important ethnolinguistic groups in sub-Saharan Africa. A number of Mande subgroups, including the Mandinka of Senegal and Gambia, the Maninka of Guinea and Mali, the Bamana (or Bambara) of Mali, and the Dyula of Côte d'Ivoire, all claim a common descent from the thirteenth-century Mali empire. Connected historically to the Mali state, Mande societies are characterized by a social hierarchy as well as by occupational specialization. Although slavery once existed, the two main social categories in contemporary Mande societies are **sula** and **nyamalo**. Sula refers to "ordinary people," farmers, merchants, and people in urban occupations, and it includes the aristocracy as well. According to Roderic Knight, who has studied Mande music for many years, the term nyamalo designates those who rely on a specialized craft as a profession. In Mande societies these crafts include metalsmiths, wood and leather workers, and musicians, known by the term **jali**. The "material" that the musician works with is not the musical instrument (although they do typically make their own), but the *word*, whether spoken or sung.

In the traditional hierarchy, the craft specialists, as "service providers" to the king and the general population, occupied various slots below the general populace, but as the sole providers of goods and services needed for both agriculture and war, they were at the same time regarded with awe and respect. All the nyamalo, by virtue of their specialized knowledge, were regarded as having access to a special life force (the nyama) that gave them a certain power over others. The jali, with the power to manipulate words, had the greatest power. He or she (women being the prime singers) could praise when praise was due, or criticize if necessary, incorporating oblique commentary and poignant proverbs into their song texts if a public figure exhibited lackluster behavior.

At the present time the distinction between the sula and nyamalo social groups are not as strictly maintained as they once were. Yet the jali (pl., jalolu) still maintains many of his or her traditional roles as oral historian, musician, praise singer, genealogist, announcer for the aristocracy, and diplomat, and they still perform at important social events such as weddings, child-naming ceremonies, religious holidays, and affairs of state.

The Mande case clearly differs in some ways from conceptions about music and musicians within Pygmy society, where music-making is a nonprofessional, largely nonspecialized activity. In contrast, the jali is a hereditary specialist working as a professional musician and verbal artist, whose status position derives from hierarchical rather than egalitarian social relations.

SULA
Social category in Mande societies, referring to "ordinary people" in contrast to craft specialists.

NYAMALO
Craft specialists in Mande societies, a category including professional musicians.

JALI
The term for a hereditary professional musician in Mande society, who serves as an oral historian and singer/performer.

EXPLORE

Mande of West Africa

Another distinction between these two societies regards the power of the word and the importance of song texts. Although vocal music is important in both societies, jali performance often emphasizes verbal artistry and elaborate texts, whereas some of the most important Pygmy music such as singing for the molimo ceremony involves very little text. Nonetheless, certain features of Mande musical style are consistent with the general traits discussed for the Pygmies and the Shona.

The main instruments played by the Mande jali to accompany singing are the *balo* (a xylophone), the *kora* (a bridge harp), and the *kontingo* (a five-stringed plucked lute with a skin face like the banjo); male jalolu specialize on one instrument. The kora is unique to the Mande. It has twenty-one strings and a range just over three octaves. Cowhide is stretched over the gourd sound box, and strings come off the neck in two parallel rows perpendicular to the face of the sound box. The scale series alternates for the most part between the two rows and the two hands (right hand—do, left hand—re, right hand—mi, left hand—fa, etc.). The basic playing technique for the kora often involves plucking alternate notes by the right and left hands so that the melody results from the interlocking of these two parts, similar in principle to mbira playing and the principle of interlocking parts in general. Another similarity between the kora and the Shona mbira is the attachment of a metal plate with jangles to the bridge of the kora. This produces the buzzing timbral effect favored in so many sub-Saharan societies.

Mande music performed on the kora consists of several components. Each piece has a basic vocal melody known as **donkilo** and a second kind of improvised, declamatory singing style called **sataro**. Sataro sometimes receives major emphasis in jali performance, as does text improvisation and the insertion of proverbs and sayings appropriate to a given context. It was traditionally through the performance of formulaic praise and proverbs for a given occasion that the jali earned a living—praising a patron, telling a story, or recounting history. The use of songs to fulfill these social functions is widespread throughout West Africa and in other parts of the sub-Saharan region.

The jali accompanies his singing with the **kumbengo** part—a short ostinato, the most basic organizing feature of a performance—played on the kora. The kumbengo is played for long periods during which subtle variations may gradually be introduced, as in Shona mbira playing. Improvised instrumental interludes known as **birimintingo** are inserted between the long ostinato sections. The nature of the four components of a jali performance—kumbengo (K), birimintingo (B), donkilo (D), and sataro (S)—will become clearer by listening to "Ala l'a ke" and following along with the text.

Mande kora player, Kunye Saho, of the Gambia.
Source: Roderic Knight/Thomas Turino

DONKILO
The basic sung melody of Mande jali songs.

SATARO
A speechlike vocal style performed by Mande jalolu.

KUMBENGO
The basic instrumental ostinato, which serves as the foundation for Mande jali performance.

BIRIMINTINGO
An instrumental interlude or "break" during which a Mande jali departs from the basic ostinato.

LISTENING GUIDE

MANDE KORA MUSIC: "ALA L'A KE"

 **LISTEN**

TRACK 8.3 **Kunye Saho, kora, and voice. Recorded by Roderic Knight**

THE TEXT, designation of parts, and translation were kindly provided by Roderic Knight.

TIME	KORA	VOICE	
0:00	K		(Instrumental introduction.)
0:10			Kumbengo.
0:21	K	D	*A, Ala l'a ke, silan jon m'a ke* (Ah, God has done it, now it was not a man)
0:37	K	D	*Kuo bee kari bai.* (all things can be delayed.)
0:40	K	D	*Kunfai kuno te baila.* (but not the wishes of God.)
0:47	K	D	*Ala ye men ke te baila.* (What God has done can't be delayed.)
0:55	K	D	*Kori bali ku la manso le.* (The omnipotent king.)
0:58	K	D	*Kun fara kina ngana nin tabisi nani . . .* (head-splitting celebrity and . . .)
1:06	K	S	*N'ali be nganalu lala, nganalu man kanyan.* (If you are calling great people, they're not all equal.)
1:11	K	S	*Damansa Wulandin nin Damansa Wulamba* (Damansa Wulan the small, and Damansa Wulan the big)
1:13	K	S	*Moke Musa nin Moke Dantuma* (Moke Musa and Moke Dantuma)
			Tarokoto Bulai bangeta. (Tarokoto Bulai was born.)
1:16	B		*Birimintingo.* (Instrumental interlude, with vocable singing.)
1:44	K	D	*Ala ye men ke te baila* (What God has done can't be delayed)
			Dula be ngana juma fanan kilila (This song is calling the other celebrities too)
			Somani Tamba, a Bajo bane. (Somani Tamba, ah, only child.)
2:01	K	S	*N'ali be nganalu la la, nganalu man kanyan* (If you are calling great people, they're not all equal)
			E, nafa a barika. Sidi nuku makoto nin. (Eh, thanks for profit. Sidi the greedy one and buyer of gold, ah, king now.[?])

continued

TIME	KORA	VOICE	
2:17	K	D	*Dua le jabita, ban in fa dua le jabita.* (Prayers have been answered, mother's and father's prayers have been answered.)
			Lun min na nte lota julo da la *Wori jula nin sanu jala.* (On the day I stood at the trader's door traders of silver and gold.)
2:31	B		Instrumental interlude with singing in parallel.
3:44	K	D	*Suoluo, Samban Jime!* (The horses, Samban Jimeh!)
			Suoluo, Samban Jime! (The horses, Samban Jimeh!)

On this recording one can clearly hear the metal jangles buzzing and the relatively soft volume of the kora compared to the voice. As is apparent here, the birimintingo sections provide a greater degree of musical contrast, departing from the basic kumbengo ostinato. This type of instrumental interlude that alternates with the basic ostinato is distinctive from Shona mbira performance or a Pygmy song, where variations and improvisations are added to and over the basic cycle. Nonetheless, the conception of what constitutes a "piece," that is, a series of stock resources that are uniquely arranged and improvised on according to the needs of a given performer and occasion, is similar between the Mande and the Shona.

The Ewe of Ghana

North Americans often have the general impression that African music primarily consists of drumming. As we have seen, vocal music, strings, and other types of melodic instruments such as the mbira may have equally, or more, prominent positions in certain contexts. One of the most famous sub-Saharan regions for drumming, however, is the West African coast. Among the Anlo-Ewe of Togo and the southeastern coast of Ghana, dance drumming is the most important type of musical activity.

The Anlo-Ewe, who remain musically and socially distinct from other Ewe groups farther north and inland, work primarily as farmers and fishermen. Southern Eweland is divided into autonomous political districts, with the Anlo district having the largest population and cultural influence. This district, which traditionally functioned like an independent state, was ruled by a paramount chief, whose status was mainly ceremonial and sacred, although he had the important role of mediating disputes. The chief stands at the pinnacle of a political hierarchy over geographically organized territorial and town chiefs and finally over clan, lineage, and ward (village subdivision) leaders. The clans

Ewe Drum Ensemble: Gideon Foli Alorwoyie of Ghana. Lead drummer for the Yewe Cult, funeral music. *Source:* Art Davis/Thomas Turino

and lineages (tracing descent to a common male ancestor) and wards thus form an important basis of the social system. Age sets (groups of people of similar age who identify with each other on this basis) are another important feature of social organization. Social organization is often a key to understanding basic aspects of music-making, because the formation of ensembles, the definition of genres, and even the organization of musical events are frequently shaped by local conceptions of social hierarchy as well as according to the groups (e.g., gender, age, lineage) that people use to define their social identity.

Among the Anlo-Ewe, voluntary dance clubs, organized by individual villages, wards, or age groups, are the primary institutions through which the all-important dance-drumming traditions are performed. As villagers migrate to the cities, new dance clubs are often created on the basis of hometown identity, and these clubs may serve as the basis for social networks and support systems in the urban environment. According to David Locke, an ethno-musicologist and performer of Ewe music, the organization of some dance clubs traditionally reflected the political structure of the ward and lineage, although European influences have also by now been incorporated.

The dance-drumming clubs are generally led by a committee of men and women consisting of a chairperson, a secretary, and the leaders of different subgroups within the institution (i.e., dance leaders, and leaders of the drummers and the singers). Club organization may be seen as resembling the broader Ewe political hierarchy, which involves a paramount chief who presides over the leaders at the more specific levels of social organization (territorial, village, clan, etc.). Living in a hierarchical society ourselves, this might appear as a normal way to organize things, and yet we must remember that to the egalitarian Pygmies this might seem strange. Besides the officers already mentioned, another key figure in the club is the composer, who is responsible for creating the distinctive music and song texts that serve as identity emblems for his institution.

Unlike the Pygmy band, where some kind of music is likely to be performed almost daily, musical performance is less frequent among the Ewe. Occasions for club performance include the welcoming of government officials, the promotion of a political party, the formal presentation of a new club, or occasions for recreation. One of the primary functions of the clubs is to support its members during crises and especially on the death of a family member. Like the Shona, the Anlo-Ewe place great religious importance on the ancestors and the spirits of the dead, who are believed to intervene in the lives of the living. The Ewe thus place major emphasis on providing honorable funerals for the new spirits, and it is considered extremely prestigious to have a dance club perform at these events.

In terms of musical specialization and professionalism, we might think of the Ewe dance clubs as midway on a spectrum between the highly trained, specialized, and professional jali and the nonspecialist, nonprofessional Pygmy musician. For example, rehearsing is an important part of an Ewe club's activities, and learning to perform the dance and music is relatively rigorous, whereas among the Pygmies learning to sing, like learning to talk, is a normal part of socialization. Where the jali is a full-time musical professional, most members of the Ewe dance clubs can be thought of as semiprofessional at best. That is, except when fulfilling personal obligations to club members—such as performing for a funeral or for recreation—the organizations expect payment for their musical presentations, but the members usually only derive a small portion of their income in this way.

Ewe dondo drum player of Ghana, member of the Brekete Cult. *Source:* Art Davis/ Thomas Turino

LISTENING GUIDE

EWE DANCE DRUMMING: "GADZO," A THEATRICAL DANCE

 **LISTEN**

TRACK 8.4 **Two small drums, a mid-sized drum, bell, and several rattles. Recorded by S. K. Ladzekpo**

IN THE EWE GADZO DANCE, the singers begin the piece, and then the bells and shakers establish the basic time cycle before three drums enter with their interlocking parts to create a rich texture and rhythmic excitement. The hand clapping that remains consistently part of the texture offers a great way of switching perception between duple and triple meter. As the performance unfolds, identify and focus on the hand clapping to frame first two and then three claps of your own. This can be represented as follows:

Hand clapping	X					X					
Duple	x			x		x			x		
Triple	x		x		x		x		x		x	

TIME	SECTION	MUSICAL EVENTS
0:00–0:02	**Vocal introduction.**	The leader opens the performance with a speech-like call that is immediately answered by the chorus.
0:02–0:08		The leader then introduces the basic lead melodic part (**A**).
0:08–0:20	**Entry of bell, shakers, and hand clapping:** Notice how the bell, shaker, and hand clapping set the basic time cycle and groove for the performance. Listen for the hand clapping in particular, because you'll use this later to explore the 3 against 2 rhythms of the performance.	The leader and chorus then introduce the main call-and-response interchange melody (**B**). While they do this, the bell, shaker, and hand clapping are added to the texture. At [0:12] the lead drum begins to add sparse patterns to the texture.
0:20–0:27	**Lead vocal section (A):** Compare this repetition of the lead melody to the first instance [0:02–0:07] and notice how different it feels in terms of accents and structure now that it is accompanied by the percussion instruments.	The lead vocal section **A** returns, this time firmly embedded into the time cycle set by the percussion instruments.
0:27–0:49	**Entry of supporting drums:** Notice the return of the leader-chorus melody and the way the supporting drums intensify the rhythmic drive of the performance. Try to attend to the hand clapping in the background of the texture.	The leader-chorus call-and-response interchange returns **B**. The supporting drums enter at [0:28], playing interlocking patterns that strengthen the rhythmic drive. Once the entire drum ensemble is playing, the groove remains constant until the "coda."

continued

TIME	SECTION	MUSICAL EVENTS
0:49–0:56	**Lead vocal section (A):** Continue to listen for the hand clapping and prepare to tap along in duple and triple meter.	The lead vocal section (**A**) returns, this time carried along by the entire ensemble.
0:56–1:11	**Lead/chorus interchange (B):** Try to tap your hand along in duple time with the hand clapping (i.e., two times for every one hand clap on the recording).	The leader/chorus call-and-response interchange returns.
1:11–1:21	**Instrumental section:** Listen for the yodel-like vocalizations and shouted interjections by the singers. Keep trying to tap along in duple meter.	A short break in the **A–B** alternation creates an instrumental section.
1:21–2:47	**A–B alternation:** Listen to the overall flow of the leader-leader-chorus sections and attempt to tap along to the hand clapping in triple meter (i.e., three taps for each hand clap).	The **A** and **B** sections continue to alternate as follows: [1:21–1:27] A [1:27–1:48] B [1:48–1:54] A [1:54–2:15] B [2:15–2:21] A [2:21–2:47] B
2:47–2:58	**Coda:** Listen for the short instrumental break, followed by a vocal interjection by the leader, which is then repeated several times by all.	Notice the interjection by leader at [2:48] followed by the chorus as the recording fades out.

As Alfred and Kobla Ladzekpo have suggested, the drumming, dancing, singing, and hand clapping in an Ewe performance must be thought of as a unified whole. If any individual part is modified, the perception of the whole changes, because each part is heard as relative to and dependent on the others, as in a mbira performance. This characteristic, common to many African musical traditions, is a result of the practice of interlocking multiple parts.

The Anlo-Ewe perform a number of different dances. Depending on the specific dance tradition, each club uses various types of music. For example, clubs involved in the *takada* tradition have different genres for processions, more leisurely types of dancing, and the vigorous styles of dancing that are accompanied by the full drum ensemble. The specific instruments used also depend on the dance traditions performed by a given club, although certain instruments are widespread.

Typically, Ewe drum ensembles include a double-bell (*gankogui*), which often plays a repeated ostinato within a twelve-pulse cycle, serving as the organizational point of reference for the rest of the instrumental parts. A gourd shaker (*axatse*) performs a similar role. In addition, a series of four or more different-sized barrel-shaped drums (made of wooden staves and hoops, ranging from 55 cm to 124 cm in length) may be used for a variety of functions. The large drums (e.g., *atsimevu*, *gboba*) are used by lead drummers to create music from a repertory of established and improvised patterns. The middle-sized drums (*sogo* and *kidi*) serve the function of a chorus, playing a more limited variety of patterns in call-and-response fashion with the lead drummer, and they interlock their patterns with other percussion parts. In the takada tradition, the smallest drum (*kaganu*) plays a single repeated ostinato, which in combination with the bell and rattles creates the ground of the overall rhythmic organization that consists of the combination of the different parts.

Within these ensembles we thus find musical principles and aesthetic values that have already been discussed for other African societies: call-and-response, interlock, ostinato organization, improvised variation based on stock formulaic patterns, and density in the resulting sound of the entire ensemble. The drum ensemble accompanies both the dancing and the singing, and it is the songs themselves that are considered particularly important to Ewe participants for expressing the distinctive identity of the club. As elsewhere in Africa, the dance steps performed can be considered integral to the polyrhythmic fabric of the total performance.

EXPLORE

Polyrhythm

The Buganda Kingdom

Buganda is the name of the country that was formerly the most powerful independent kingdom in the Lake Victoria region in East Africa; *Baganda* is the term for its Bantu-speaking people. The kingdom was particularly well off economically thanks to favorable conditions for agriculture, particularly to the raising of bananas, the staple crop. Unlike many African kingdoms, the Ganda king, or kabaka, did not have "divine" or sacred status. His notably strong, centralized power was supported by a system in which the king directly appointed and could remove subordinate chiefs and by his ultimate control over many estates. (This contrasts with other African kingdoms, where middle-level chiefs could appoint their own subordinates, thereby creating an independent power base.) Although individual citizens belonged to clans and other social groups, primary allegiance was to the state and to the kabaka himself.

EXPLORE

Buganda Court Music

AKADINDA
Large twenty-two-key xylophone of the Ganda.

The kabaka's court was a major center for musical activity. The kabaka supported a number of different ensembles, and the musicians lived as retainers on land granted by the king. One important court ensemble consisted of at least five side-blown trumpets made of bottle-shaped gourds. The different gourd-trumpets each produced different pitches necessary to complete a melody and were thus played strictly in interlocking fashion. Like most of the Buganda instruments, the trumpets were associated with a specific clan. Another court ensemble, of less prestige than the trumpets, consisted of five or six end-notched flutes accompanied by four drums. An instrument specific to the court was the ***akadinda***, a large twenty-two-key xylophone in which the keys were freely set on two supporting logs running perpendicular to them. A single akadinda was played by six different musicians, three sitting on each side of the instrument. The most important royal ensemble of all was the *entenga*. This consisted primarily of twelve drums carefully graded in size and tuned to the local pentatonic (five-tone) scale, thus actually serving as melodic instruments. These were played by four musicians; they were accompanied by three other drums played by two drummers. The performance of the entenga was strictly limited to the royal enclosure.

The same principles of interlocking parts and ostinato organization that have been described for the Shona, Ewe, Pygmies, and Mande are also basic to entenga and akadinda performance. Each piece contains two distinct melodic rhythmic parts known as *okunaga* (meaning "to start") and *okwawula* ("to divide"), each of which is composed of two or more phrases. On the akadinda xylophone, the three players for one of the parts sit across the keys facing the three musicians who play the other. The pitches of the starter and divider parts literally alternate, thereby reproducing the basic hocket or interlocking technique between the players on opposite sides of the keys. The parts themselves involve ostinato patterns. A third part comprising only two pitches, called the *okukoonera* (or "binder"), emphasizes composite patterns formed by the interaction of the okunaga and okwawula. The okukoonera helps the players orient themselves within the dense ensemble texture.

The political importance of the royal drums is dramatically illustrated by the story of the Buganda kingdom. During the colonial period, African kingdoms were often left in place within the European colonies, because the native political systems could be used to rule African populations indirectly. Under an agreement with the British colonizers, the kabaka of Buganda was officially recognized in 1900 as the ruler of his semiautonomous state, with the provision that he obey the British governor of the Uganda Protectorate.

However, after independence, many new African states had to deal with the threat to state sovereignty that independent kingdoms within their boundaries might pose. Although such problems have been handled variously in different African countries, in Uganda violent means were used to suppress the powerful Ganda king. Only a few years after gaining independence in 1962, troops under Uganda's first leader, Apollo Milton Obote, stormed the kabaka's palace and sent him into exile in an effort to stamp out the independent kingdom.

It was no accident that the royal drums were among the things destroyed in the attack on the palace. Traditionally, the drums were such central emblems of the kabakaship that potential heirs to the throne were known as the "Princes of the Drum." In *Desecration of My Kingdom* (London: Constable, 1967), a book written in exile by the last kabaka, Mutesa II, he notes that

> Among the sad news of who is dead, who is in prison and what is destroyed comes the confirmation that the Royal Drums are burnt. I saw this work begun and feared that it must have been completed. These drums, of which there are more than fifty, are the heart of Buganda, some of them hundreds of years old, as old as the Kabakaship. To touch them was a terrible offense, to look after them a great honour. A Prince is not a Prince of the Blood

but a Prince of the Drum and his status is determined by which Drum. They all had separate names and significance and can never be replaced.

(p. 193)

With the destruction of the former political system and way of life in the name of nationalism came the demise of musical traditions that were central symbols of that kingdom. Although often less dramatic in nature, transformations of African musical life have taken place, and are still occurring, throughout the sub-Saharan region under the pressures of capitalism, nationalism, urbanization, and influences of cosmopolitanism.

A SAMPLING OF INSTRUMENTS

Judging from the few societies already touched on, we can see that African musical performance includes all the major instrument types (percussion instruments, skin-headed drums, winds, and strings), and the importance of given instruments may vary from one society to another. Vocal music, however, seems to be emphasized by a great majority of African societies, with the sung poetry often considered as important as the musical accompaniment—if not more so.

We have also seen that aspects of the social and economic organization influence the number and types of instruments used within a given society. For example, the Pygmies and the San of the Kalahari Desert have relatively few permanent instruments and a minimal material culture generally because of their nomadic way of life. In societies where the royal court was an important site for musical performance, the number, size, and complexity of instruments may be greater because of both available wealth and a more stable environment for performance. This was the case for the large Ganda drum-chime (*entenga*) and xylophone (akadinda) ensembles as well as for court traditions of other East and West African kingdoms.

The tremendous variety of African musical instruments, either played solo or combined in various types of ensembles, makes even a partial list difficult. It may be useful to highlight some of the most important instrument types as well as some that are less well known.

Percussion Instruments

Classified as percussion instruments, lamellaphones (known as *mbira*, *karimba*, *kisaanj*, *likembe*, and many other names, depending on the region) and xylophones are two of the most widespread and important instrument types in the sub-Saharan region. Although they have diffused to the Americas, lamellaphones like the mbira are instruments uniquely of African origin. Rattles, bells, cymbals, rhythm sticks, stamping tubes (hollow tubes with an open end made to sound when struck against the ground), and scrapers are also among the most common instruments found. For each of these general types, however, there are many different varieties, each with a specific local name. For example, there are rattles with the seeds inside the gourd (the *Shona hosho*) and those on which beads are sewn into a net stretched around the outside of the gourd (the Ewe *axatse* and the *sèkèrè* of the Yoruba of Nigeria). New materials such as soda bottles and cans are becoming increasingly important for the construction of percussion instruments.

Although percussion instruments such as bells, scrapers, and rattles primarily serve rhythmic functions, the aspects of pitch and timbre are important considerations in their construction and incorporation into a given ensemble. The parameters of pitch and timbre allow the given percussion instrument to contrast with and complement the other instruments used. For instance, the clear, high-pitched, metallic bell in Ewe ensembles contrasts in both pitch and tone quality with the drums, and the *hosho* both provides a timbral contrast and serves to augment the density in mbira performance.

Drums and "Drum Languages"

The variety of African drums and their social importance in many societies are striking. In Ghana, for example, the relative status of Akan chiefs of different communities and regions is indicated by the size of their *atumpan* drums. A subordinate chief cannot have drums larger than his superior's drums. Among the many Yoruba kingdoms of Nigeria, each court was said to have its own dance rhythms provided by a special set of royal drums. The very power of the drum music—and the styles played—were supposed to express the elevated nature of the aristocracy. Also among the Yoruba, some of the most important orisas (deities) have specific types of drums and repertories associated with them. Drumming is used to call the gods into their mediums during Yoruba spirit-possession ceremonies, much as was described for Shona ceremonies. Thus, in these societies, drums are tied to both political and spiritual sources of power.

African drums are usually carved from a single wooden log (e.g., the Ganda *entenga*, Yoruba *dundun* and *igbin*, and Akan *atumpan*, and the Shona *ngoma*) but may also be constructed with wooden staves and hoops, as described for the Ewe. Drums are also made from ceramics, gourds, and even tin cans and oil drums. Both double- and single-headed types are found in hourglass, conical, cylindrical, and bowl shapes, among others. Metal jangles, shells, or seeds are attached to drums among West African groups such as the Hausa, Dagbamba, Yoruba, and Akan peoples to create the same type of buzzing effect described for the kora and mbira.

The attention paid to the pitch of drums is notable in many African societies, and it may involve the combination of different-sized, fixed-pitch drums in ensemble. Some drums, like the Yoruba *dùndún* and the lunga of the Ghanaian Dagbamba, however, are used to produce multiple pitches. With these hourglass-shaped tension drums, the different pitches are produced by squeezing the lacing that connects the two drumheads under one arm while the other hand beats it with a curved stick. The importance of pitched drums goes beyond merely creating contrasts; as we have seen, it is sometimes extended to making tuned drums serve as melodic instruments (e.g., the entenga). More interesting still, pitched drums are used in many African societies to imitate speech.

Many languages in the Niger-Congo family, including the Bantu languages, are tonal; that is, the meaning of a word depends on the relative pitches applied to given syllables. Drums, lamellaphones, and even instruments such as the guitar are used by the Yoruba of Nigeria to articulate verbal formulas—for example, proverbs or praise names—by imitating the tonal patterns of the words. Longer messages can be played by drumming the tonal contour of different well-known stereotypic verbal formulas. Because many words may share the same number of syllables and tonal contours, the meaning of a given "word" (drummed tonal pattern) can be clarified by following it with a formula of its own (e.g., "cat" might become "cat walks quietly at night"), the tonal patterns of the whole phrase being easier to recognize. The social and "linguistic" contexts are crucial to interpretation. The Akan atumpan, a set of two large tuned drums, are used as speech surrogates, as are the Dagbamba lunga, drums of the Yoruba dùndún family, and wooden slit drums and paired skin-headed drums in the Congo region, among other examples.

Wind Instruments

In some societies, wind instruments, especially horns, are also used for signaling. Trumpets, made from metal or animal horns and often side blown, are particularly prevalent throughout the sub-Saharan region and are frequently played in interlocking fashion, as was described for the Ganda. Side-blown and vertical flutes

LISTENING GUIDE   GREETINGS AND PRAISES PERFORMED ON THE YORUBA DÙNDÚN DRUM    **LISTEN**

TRACK 8.5   **Recorded by Smithsonian Folkways Recordings**

THIS EXCERPT ILLUSTRATES how the dùndún is used as a "talking drum." The drummer first plays a pattern, and then another drummer recites the corresponding verbal phrase. Included are common greetings like "Good morning" as well as brief praises that would have been played in honor of a chief. The dùndún is an hourglass-shaped pressure drum. When the player squeezes and pulls the ropes that bind the heads on both ends of the drum, increased tension is created so that the pitch is raised; when the cords are relaxed, the tension lessens, and the pitch drops.

are widespread African wind instruments. It is perhaps less well known that panpipes are also found in different parts of Africa, including among the Venda of southern Africa, the Soga of Uganda, the Yombe of Zaire, the Shona, and in Mozambique. Ranging from a single tube closed at one end and blown like a bottle to instruments with multiple tubes and pitches, panpipes are usually played collectively in interlocking fashion, with the tones of the scale divided among the various instruments of the ensemble, so that each performer inserts the pitches that he or she has with those of others to create a complete melody.

Stringed Instruments

Although we usually think of the banjo as the most American of instruments, its prototype was brought by slaves during the colonial period. The banjo was modeled on West African lutes, which are known by various names, depending on the linguistic group and region (e.g., *tidinit* in Mauritania, *halam* among the Wolof in the Senegambia area, *kontingo* among the Mande). The sound box is made from a gourd or a carved wooden back with a stretched skin for the face. A neck is attached, and these instruments have between two and five strings, depending on the region.

A wide variety of harps exist in different African societies. The kora, which we have already discussed, combines features of the lute (with a sound box and neck) and the harp. Instruments of this type with both straight and curved necks are found all over the sub-Saharan region. Single- or multiple-string fiddles made with round sound boxes and skin faces are also important in West Africa (e.g., the *goge* of the Hausa people of Nigeria) as well as in central and eastern Africa.

The oldest and one of the most widespread stringed instruments of Africa is the musical bow. Like the bows used to shoot arrows, it consists of a single

---

LISTENING GUIDE   MUSICAL BOW PLAYED BY A NDAKA MAN    **LISTEN**

TRACK 8.6   🖸   **Recorded by Colin Turnbull**

WE HAVE ALREADY DISCUSSED the society and music of the BaMbuti pygmies. One of the most important scholars who studied and recorded their music and way of life was Colin Turnbull. He recorded this BaNdaka pygmy playing his musical bow, in this case made from a bent sapling, with a thin section of vine used for the string. The player holds one end with his toe against the ground, and the other against the edge of his mouth, which serves as a sound resonator. By flexing the bow, he shortens the string and raises the pitch. So pleased was he with his performance that he shouts "Budah!" in the middle of it, an expression of joy.

string attached to each end of a curved stick. Depending on the tradition, either a gourd attached to the stick or the mouth cavity of the player serves as a resonator. The string is either plucked or, alternatively, struck with another stick; it is sometimes stopped with a hard implement to raise the pitch. The playing technique results in a percussive and yet beautiful and delicate sound. One of the newest and most widespread stringed instruments is the guitar. Local acoustic guitar traditions exist all over Africa, and electric guitars have become central to the new urban styles.

POPULAR MUSIC IN THE TWENTIETH CENTURY

Over the course of the twentieth century, new popular music styles emerged in countries throughout the sub-Saharan region alongside the indigenous musical traditions that continued to be performed. African musicians combined European, North American, and Latin American musical instruments, scales, harmonies, rhythms, and genres with local musical instruments and styles to create their own distinctive forms of popular music. Local elements and musical sensibilities made each emerging style unique, whereas the cosmopolitan elements served as a kind of common denominator among them. During the first half of the twentieth century, European colonialism generated institutions and social attitudes that led to the emergence of new musical styles. Midcentury, African nationalism became a primary force for local musical creativity. By the 1980s, in the context of the "worldbeat" or "world music" phenomenon, African musicians were attracted by international markets and thus shaped their styles to cater to cosmopolitan audiences in Europe, North America, Japan, Australia, and elsewhere.

Through military conquest, various European powers colonized the sub-Saharan region to control resources and labor for production and ultimately to expand capitalist markets. Along with the use of force, colonial governments and missionaries also used legislation and education to teach Africans to accept European "civilization" as superior to their own ways of life and thus to accept their own subservient position. Through colonial education, a small African middle class began to emerge in the various colonies. Serving as clerks, teachers, foremen, and in other low-level administrative positions, this group understood European education as the means to upward social mobility within the colonial order. In the process, middle-class Africans internalized colonial values and aesthetics and became attracted to European and cosmopolitan music and dance styles.

European musical instruments and styles were first taught to Africans through two colonial institutions—military bands and schools. Particularly in the British colonies, Africans were trained in military band music, and these musicians often went on to form dance bands that played cosmopolitan styles such as European popular music and jazz; it was often these musicians who also created new local popular styles. In the process of Christian conversion, missionaries taught schoolchildren religious songs and hymns, which were sometimes translated into their own languages. Through singing in school and church, Africans learned how to read music, and they became accustomed to European diatonic melodies (i.e., melodies based on the standard do-re-mi scale) and harmonies with basic Western chords (I, IV, V). They also learned very different aesthetic values. For instance, instead of the dense overlapping sounds typical of indigenous performance, schoolchildren were taught to value clear, precise phrasing (e.g., everyone singing the same notes at exactly the same time) and precise vocal diction. These values influenced certain urban popular styles such as highlife in Ghana, and "concert" music in Zimbabwe that especially appealed to the African middle class.

In addition to schools and the military, commercial interests also played a key role in diffusing cosmopolitan instruments and styles in Africa. By the 1920s, a variety of relatively inexpensive instruments such as mass-produced guitars, harmonicas, concertinas, accordions, autoharps, and banjos became available in dry good stores in larger towns, cities, and mining centers. These instruments became popular among the emerging working class who, through wage labor, had some money to spend. Commercial recordings of European popular music, Latin American and Caribbean styles (especially Cuban son, and Trinidadian calypso), and U.S. popular music, including jazz, country and western, and popular groups such as the Mills Brothers, became available by the 1930s and 1940s, as rock 'n' roll, soul, and rap would become later.

By mid-century, local acoustic guitar styles had emerged in many parts of sub-Saharan Africa. Sometimes the guitar was simply adapted to styles formerly played on local indigenous instruments. For example, in Zimbabwe and South Africa, the guitar was used to play mbira and bow music or in West Africa to play music formerly performed on indigenous lutes (e.g., *halam*, or *kontingo*). In other cases, African musicians used the guitar to play foreign styles. Surprisingly, early American country and western performers such as Jimmie Rodgers and Tex Ritter were popular models for African guitarists in many regions. The acoustic guitar, usually accompanied by percussion instruments, was also used to play new styles that were fusions of foreign and local musical elements. Examples include West African "palmwine" guitar music and various acoustic guitar styles in the Congo region and in southern and eastern Africa. Common to African guitarists in many places, a two-finger (thumb and index) picking style was used to play independent bass and melody lines within simple chord progressions (e.g., I, IV, V; I, V; I, IV, I, V; I, IV, ii, V) in first position (on the first three frets of the guitar). By the 1960s, electric guitars had begun to replace acoustic instruments in popularity.

West Africa

In West Africa, dance-band **highlife** music originated on the Ghanaian coast, where the training of local African musicians in the brass-band idiom had begun

HIGHLIFE

A form of urban-popular dance-band music of Ghana; also played in Nigeria and elsewhere in West Africa.

<table>
<tr><td>

LISTENING GUIDE

</td><td>

I. K. DAIRO AND THE BLUE SPOTS, "SALOME"

</td><td>

LISTEN

</td></tr>
</table>

TRACK 8.7 Recorded in Lagos, 1962

AFTER AN ACCORDION INTRODUCTION, Dairo sings the text followed by a brief accordion solo (**A** section). The accordion then drops out for a new section (**B**). This section involves a percussion break in which the talking drum takes the lead playing verbal phrases that a unison vocal chorus repeats. At approximately [1:18], the talking drummer plays a short vocal phrase that is immediately repeated by the chorus in call-and-response, making the melodic (speech-song-like) quality of the talking drum particularly apparent. The **B** section ends with a bongo solo. A shortened accordion introduction and vocal material from the **A** section then comes back to conclude the piece, creating an overall **A B A'** structure. In addition to the combination of Yoruba and Cuban instruments, the piece incorporates the "clave" rhythmic pattern of the Cuban son (played by the "rhythm sticks," see chapter 10), which has influenced cosmopolitan music around the world. The text itself illustrates a combination of Yoruba and cosmopolitan elements—much of the text that Dairo sings falls squarely within the style of pop love songs. The texts drummed and sung in Section **B**, however, include Yoruba proverbs.

TIME

00:0	**Accordion introduction**
0:16	**Dairo singing:**

Sú sú sú bebi-o	(Shoo, shoo, shoo baby)
Bebi Salome mi-o	(My baby Salome)
Mo fé lo rí bebi-o Salome mi	(I want to go see my baby Salome)
Mámá Bekun mi	(Mother of Bekun)
Salome ó wùn mí-o	(Salome, she attracts me)
T' ó bá jé t' owó,	(If it is a matter of money)
màá tepá mó sé owó mi-o,	(I will work hard to make money)
Salome	
Salome ó dára l' óbìnrin iwa re l'ó wùn mi-o	(Salome, she is a fine woman, it is her character
Salome	that attracts me)
Eléyin'jú egé	
Eyín fún j'owó Salome,	(She has [egg] eyes that can trap)
Eyín m'énu gún-o	(Teeth whiter than cowries, Salome)
Oyínbó Salo, Salome	(Teeth that shape the mouth)
Salome, Salome, Salome, etc.	(Light-skinned Salo, Salome)

0:51	**Accordion solo**
1:10	**Percussionists' break**
1:18	**Dùndún talking drum:**

Emí ò ní sí níbè, émi ò ní sí níbe	(I will not be there, ×2)
Níbi wòb gbé sorí burúkú èmi ò ní sí níbè	(Where they have bad destiny, I will not be there)

continued

TIME		
1:26	**Vocal chorus:**	
	Emí ò ní sí níbè, émi ò ní sí níbe	(I will not be there, ×2)
	Níbi wòb gbé sorí burúkú èmi ò ní sí níbè	(Where they have bad destiny, I will not be there)
1:37	**Dùndún talking drum:**	
	Ire gbogbo kò ni s'èyìn mi, ní lé ayé ayé	(All the good luck will not happen when I am not present, in this life)
1:41	**Vocal chorus:**	
	Ire gbogbo kò ni s'èyìn mi, ní lé ayé ayé	(All the good luck will not happen when I am not present, in this life)
1:45	**Dùndún talking drum:**	
	Yes, ké, o béréfe	(Yes, you start to love)
1:47	**Vocal Chorus:**	
	Yes, ké, o béréfe	(Yes, you start to love)
1:48	**Dùndún talking drum:**	
	Yes, ké, o béréfe	(Yes, you start to joke)
1:50	**Vocal Chorus:**	
	Yes, ké, o béréfe	(Yes, you start to joke)
1:53	*O béréfe*	(You start to joke)
	O béréfe	(You start to joke)
	O béréfe	(You start to joke)
1:58	**Bongo solo**	
2:06	**Accordion reenters**	
2:10	**Dairo sings:**	
	Sú sú bebi Salo	
	Bebi Salome mi-o, bebi-o, bebi bebi-o, Salo, Salome-o	(Shoo, Shoo, baby, Salo) (Baby Salome, my baby, etc.)

as early as the eighteenth century and where port life had introduced the locals to many international musical styles. By the 1920s, big bands using brass instruments and playing European popular dance genres like the waltz and fox-trot began performing at upper-crust social affairs for the Westernized African elites and Europeans. During this period local Akan melodies and rhythms began to creep into the highlife repertory, thereby Africanizing what was more or less a Western musical style in terms of rhythm and orchestration.

It was not until after World War II, however, that the fusion of Western and African elements became more integral in big-band highlife. According to David Coplan, E.T. Mensah, the "King of Highlife," was the first to orchestrate both traditional themes and indigenous rhythms for dance band in conjunction

EXPLORE
Highlife

JÙJÚ

A form of Nigerian popular music associated with the Yoruba that combines electric instruments with indigenous drums and percussion.

EXPLORE

Jùjú

Nigerian musician King Sunny Ade and his band perform during the 31st Celebrate Brooklyn Summer Season's African Festival at the Prospect Park Bandshell. *Source:* Al Pereira/Getty Images

with the use of North and Latin American genres, such as swing and samba, and Caribbean genres like the Cuban son, and calypso (see chapter 11). By this time, the electric guitar had been incorporated, and Mensah's group used that instrument as well as trumpet, trombone, saxophone, string bass, and a Cuban-style percussion section. While these groups were playing for higher-class patrons, a parallel development of "guitar-band" highlife grew up among the lower classes in urban centers. This style fused the techniques and repertories of local Ghanaian instrumental traditions with those of the guitar and songs learned from sailors. The music of West Indian sailors, whose rhythms were originally based in African lamellaphone and string techniques, came full circle and began to influence West African highlife. "Palm-wine" music, played on acoustic guitar and accompanied by various percussion instruments, spread throughout British West Africa in informal settings. In Lagos, palm-wine and other syncretic urban working-class styles served as a basis for **jùjú** music among the Yoruba of Nigeria. During the 1930s performers such as Tunde King performed a small-ensemble style with guitar-banjo (banjo body with a six-string guitar neck) accompanied by a tambourine player and *sèkèrè* (rattle with beads on the outside of the gourd). Christopher Waterman suggests that after World War II, the use of amplification influenced jùjú's evolution to increasingly include both more cosmopolitan and indigenous African features simultaneously and to expand the size of the ensembles. With the use of amplified guitars and vocals, it became possible to introduce larger and more complex percussion sections using the Yoruba sèkèrè and the hourglass-shaped "talking drum," as well as other instruments often of Cuban derivation, such as bongos, congas, maracas, and *claves* ("rhythm sticks"). I.K. Dairo was a major juju star of the 1960s. At the height of their popularity, his group, The Blue Spots, included nine members and instrumentation typical of bands at that time: guitar, talking drum, bongos, congalike drums, claves, maracas, and agogo (double-bell); Dairo also occasionally performed on a single-row button accordion instead of guitar.

Now associated with the names Ebenezer Obey and King Sunny Ade, jùjú has become one of the internationally best-known "African-pop" styles. Ade has added the pedal steel guitar to the two or more electric guitars, bass, and large percussion section of his band. The highly polished "studio" sound of contemporary jùjú bands is also aided by the use of synthesizers. Jùjú groups combine the traditional functions of praise singing and social-dance drumming and perform both at urban bars and neotraditional Yoruba ceremonies (naming ceremonies, weddings, funerals).

Although Western harmonies are used, jùjú music is organized around a series of interlocking ostinato parts played by the guitars and drummers and leader–chorus call-and-response singing.

Congolese Guitar Music

Within sub-Saharan Africa, the urban-popular guitar music of the Congo region has had a more profound impact on musicians and audiences than any other single African style. Leading exponents of the style include Franco and his band O.K. Jazz, Docteur Nico, and Kanda Bongo Man, among others. Local likembe (lamellaphone) dance music (accompanied by struck bottles and a drum) and Afro-Cuban music, especially the Cuban son, served as the foundations of the Congolese style. By the mid-1950s, some musicians replaced the role of the likembe with acoustic guitar, and by the late 1950s Caribbean music became a primary model, with electric guitars as well as saxophones, trumpets, clarinets, and flutes sometimes being used. Different international "dance crazes" involving Afro-Cuban music were fueled throughout the Americas, Europe, Asia, and Africa by the recording and movie industries. The Afro-Cuban son, often referred to internationally as rumba, and the distinctive Cuban son clave pattern (heard in the I.K. Dairo example) took hold in the Congo region.

At first, Congolese "rumba" groups copied the Cuban recordings to the extent that some even imitated the original Spanish texts. As time went on, however, the Congolese bands began to develop their own distinctive sound as well as to incorporate new foreign influences such as riffs from North American soul music. Less rhythmically complex than jùjú, the Congolese style is organized around one or more guitar ostinatos, which serve to accompany the high, sweet singing style of performers like Franco. This style is now known internationally as soukous. A performance usually includes long improvised guitar solos as well as the sparse, orchestrated entrances of the horn section over a danceable rhythm in duple meter. Perhaps inspired by the Congolese "rumba" sound, the use of Cuban-style rhythms and rhythm sections can be heard in East and West Africa as well as in the modern music of Mali where, as in the music of the Super-Rail Band, such elements are fused with electric guitar ostinatos and solos that are clearly based on kora music.

South Africa

The urban-popular music of South Africa—a particularly early European settlement—differs in various ways from the styles created in other countries. The traditional music of the Nguni (Zulu-, Swazi-, Sotho-, Xhosa-speaking) peoples of the region is itself stylistically distinct from the music of other African areas. For example, in contrast to all the African musical styles that we have discussed so far, Nguni music is a predominantly choral-vocal style using slower tempos and lacking the polyrhythmic percussion accompaniments found in, say, West Africa. The music taught by Christian missionaries, also a choral tradition, had a particularly strong impact in South Africa, as did North American urban-popular music.

Various related syncretic choral styles were created using these sources in the context of the dismal living conditions of rural African migrant workers, who were forced by harsh circumstances to seek employment in the mines and cities. Within the workers' compounds, vocal-dance groups formed and participated in competitions, which became a primary social outlet. The competition song-dance genre known as isicathamiya blended the harmonies taught by missionaries with the slow Zulu choral style characterized by multiple overlapping ostinatos and an emphasis on the outer voices (low and high). The music of Ladysmith Black Mambazo and the earlier 1939 hit "Mbube" ("Lion," or "The Lion Sleeps Tonight") of Solomon Linda (popularized internationally by Pete Seeger) are examples that came from this line of development.

In addition to Christian vocal traditions, urban-Black South African music was also highly influenced by American popular styles, including that of minstrel shows, ragtime, jazz, and more recently soul, rock, and hip-hop artists. In the 1960s and 1970s, Zulu "jive" or mbaq'anga bands blended electric guitars, traps, and a particularly prominent electric bass line variably with accordions, violins, pennywhistles, and saxophones for a straight ahead, driving dance beat in 4/4 time. These bands also backed up vocal groups, such as the Mahotella Queens, with a male singer ("growler") and female singer–dancers. Black jazz, rock, and hip-hop groups continue to flourish in South African cities, and Capetown still celebrates carnivals with a performance tradition directly based on the American minstrel show of the nineteenth century.

EXPLORE

Ladysmith Black Mambazo

EXPLORE

Mbube

EXPLORE

Soukous and Mbaq'anga

Zimbabwe

Like elsewhere in Africa, Congolese rumba has been popular in Zimbabwe since the late 1950s, and South African styles such as mbaq'anga have also been influential among local musicians, as have North American rock and soul and Jamaican reggae. Two urban-popular guitar genres, however, stand out as unique to Zimbabwe. The most famous of these involves the performance of classical mbira and dance-drumming music by electric dance bands. The second genre, known as *jit* or jiti, is associated with dance drumming and songs performed in informal gatherings in Shona villages. Both mbira music and jit were played by solo itinerant acoustic guitarists by at least the late 1940s (at the time jit was called marabi, tsaba, and by other South African names). Similar to much Shona village music (but unlike mbira music), jit has a two-phrase ostinato, each phrase being twelve quick pulses with beats 1, 4, 7, and 10 receiving equal accents. These characteristics remain regardless of whether jit is performed by village drummers and singers, solo acoustic guitarists, or electric dance bands.

By the mid-1960s, young Zimbabwean rock bands began to add a few Shona village songs to their typical repertoires of Congolese rumba, South African mbaq'anga, and North American rock and soul. It was in the 1970s, however, during a period of heightened African nationalism and the violent war to end white rule, that urban audiences began responding to electric band renditions of Shona village music. Inspired by positive audience reactions, a number of Zimbabwean guitar bands increasingly began to play more local Shona music, including dance-drumming genres, mbira-based songs, and jit, in response to the social climate of the time. This original "neoindigenous" Zimbabwean guitar style continued to be refined throughout the 1980s by artists such as Thomas Mapfumo, an artist whose style has been called chimurenga music (a Shona word for "struggle").

Mapfumo's music is a wonderful example of the blending of indigenous African and cosmopolitan-popular musical elements. He began his professional career in the 1960s playing cover versions of English and American rock and soul music, as well as some Shona village songs. He recorded his first song based on classical mbira music in 1974. On this recording and throughout the 1970s, his bands played mbira, dance-drumming, and jit songs, as well as other genres, with electric guitars, bass, drums, and horns. In the mid-1980s, when he began to tour abroad, however, Mapfumo added an actual mbira player to pique the interest of cosmopolitan audiences; by the early 1990s he had three mbira players in the band.

Classical mbira pieces like "Nhemamusasa" are used as the basis for some of Mapfumo's pieces. Electric guitars might play the basic four-phrase kushaura ostinato as well as melodic lines that would be on the higher mbira keys; the electric bass plays the part of the lower mbira keys of the kushaura. In recent recordings, according to Mapfumo, the keyboard often plays the kutsinhira mbira part, and the mbiras divide these parts as they normally would. The drummer plays a rhythm on the highhat that sounds like the ho*sho* (gourd shakers) used to accompany the mbira, and Shona hand-clapping patterns and an actual hosho are also added. Mapfumo sings in Shona village style, including the high yodeling technique and low-pitched singing of vocables; he also sings traditional lyrics as well as texts of his own composition. Although Shona people who remain in the villages and who have migrated to the cities still play mbira and hosho, or drums, at spirit-possession ceremonies, Mapfumo's music, like that of urban-popular bands all over Africa, illustrates the creativity and adaptability of African musicians in the context of ever-changing social conditions.

Zimbabwean Chimurenga musician Thomas Mapfumo and his band, the Blacks Unlimited, perform at Carnegie Hall's Zankel Hall. *Source:* Jack Vartoogian/Getty Images

LISTENING GUIDE

"CHITIMA NDIKATURE" (EXCERPT)

 **LISTEN**

TRACK 8.8 Performed by Thomas Mapfumo and The Blacks Unlimited

THIS TRACK is an example of Mapfumo's mature style, which features one electrified mbira (bottle caps removed) with electric guitar, keyboards, bass, drums, hosho, and congas along with two female vocalists. This piece is based in the classical mbira repertory using a forty-eight-beat cycle (four twelve-beat phrases) and is related to the "Nymaropa tune family." Mapfumo performs with a softer, smoother vocal style here, as compared to his earlier recordings, but still uses indigenous Shona vocal techniques such as the singing of vocables with the lower lines of the mbira part. The allusive imagery of the sung poetry and its mosaic quality are also typical of indigenous Shona songs.

TIME	MUSICAL EVENTS	
0:00	Solo mbira plays the entire 48-beat mbira kushaura cycle.	
0:06	Trap drummer leads the rest of the band in beginning on the fourth phrase of the mbira cycle.	
0:10	Full band enters on the second phrase of the cycle, the electric guitar taking the lead.	
0:28	Mapfumo enters singing:	
	Ho yarira amai vemwana	(It has now started, my wife)
	Ho yarira mucherechere	(It has sounded now)
	Ho yarira ndisina kudya	(It has started before I've even eaten)
	Ho yarira mucherechere (stanza ×2)	(It has started now)
1:00	Guitar solo.	
1:07	*Iye zvandanga ndaona—Haa-a (×3)*	(What I had observed—vocables)
	Hona bhurukwa remwana rabvaruka	(The child's shorts are now torn)
	Hona mazuva angu asare mana	(I'm now left with four days)
	Hona vakomana mandiregerea—I yaa hoo	(You have let me down—vocables)
	Hona ndofa zvangu ndimire kani	(I am going to die without dignity
	—Iya hoo	—vocables)
2:02	*Hona musikana ndanga ndichikuda*	(Girl I loved you
	Iya hoo	—vocables)
	Hona ndakurarmbira mai varoyi	(I've changed my mind because your mother is a witch)
	Hona vanofamba nezizi mutswanda—Haa o	(She goes about with an owl in a basket)
	Hona vane mhungu inobika sadza—Haa o	(She has a mamba [snake] that cooks food)
2:34	*Hona nyamafingu ichiuhenekera—Haa o*	(While a viper holds a torch for it)
	Hona kwedu kure handingakusvike—Haa o	(I come from afar, I can't reach it)
	Hona ndotosvika mvura yanaya—Haa o	(I can only reach it after the rains)
	Hona chitima nditakurewo—Haa o	(Train carry me)
	Haa o, Haa o	

continued

TIME	MUSICAL EVENTS
3:06	Women singers enter with vocables:
	A ye iye ye (×2)
	Haa owoye o vakuru woye (×4)
4:01	Mapfumo enters singing:
	Ho chitima nditakurewo (×5) (Train carry me)

SUMMARY

Sub-Saharan Africa is a vast area with many different societies, each with their own distinctive music; however, we have identified some common general musical characteristics and approaches that pertain to many African societies. African music favors ostinatos (repeated rhythmic and melodic cycles), polyphony (multiple melodic parts performing at once), and interlocking parts. Musical performance, moreover, is often a communal participatory activity, and pieces often comprise a collection of melodic or rhythmic formulas that are subject to group variation and thus differ from one performance to another. In addition, we have discovered that many musical performances accompany religious or civic rituals.

Social structure and conditions influence music and performance. For example, the nomadic BaMbuti pygmies use fewer instruments and favor vocal performance. Those instruments that they do use tend to be smaller and lighter, fitting their traveling lifestyle. On the other hand, the Buganda kingdom, with a highly organized, centralized government, developed elaborate court music ensembles. The wide range of musical instruments used throughout sub-Saharan Africa include lamellaphones (for example, the mbira), strings (the kora and kontingo), xylophones, trumpets, flutes, musical bows, and drums.

During the twentieth century, cosmopolitan musical influences from the United States, Latin America, the Caribbean, and Europe, have been incorporated into the African musical scene and have been combined with local styles and practices for the creation of new, vital African musical styles. These styles include highlife, juju, soukous, and mbaq'anga, among many others. It should be clear that this chapter has only addressed a small fraction of the musical life of sub-Saharan Africa. That said, it provides a point of departure for further exploration.

REVIEW CHAPTER RESOURCES

KEY TERMS

Call-and-response
Chimurenga
Colonialism
Cosmopolitan
Cyclical parts
Dundun
Entenga
Ethnolinguistic groups
Highlife
Interlocking parts
Isicathamiya
Jali
Jùjú
Kora
Kushaura
Kutsinhira
Lamellaphone
Mbaq'anga
Mbira
Ostinato
Rhythmic complexity
Soukous
Spirit possession

BIBLIOGRAPHY

General Kofi Agawu, *Representing African Music: Postcolonial Notes, Queries, Positions* (New York: Routledge, 2003); Kofi Agawu, *The Invention of 'African Rhythm,'* Journal of American Musicological Society Vol. 48 No. 3, 1995, pp. 380–395; Robert Kaufman, "African Rhythm: A Reassessment," *Ethnomusicology* 24(3), 1980; J.H. Kwabena Nketia, *Them Music of Africa* (New York: W.W. Norton, 1974); Ruth M. Stone, *The Garland Handbook of African Music*, 2nd ed. (New York: Routledge, 2008); Stig-Magnus Thorsén, *Sounds of Change Social and Political Features of Music in Africa* (Stockholm: Sida, 2004).

Ewe and Ghana John Miller Chernoff, *African Rhythm and African Sensibility: Aestheticsand Social Action in African Musical Idioms* (Chicago, IL: University of Chicago Press, 1979); Jacqueline Cogdell DjeDje, *Fiddling in West Africa: Touching the Spirit if Fulbe, Hausa, and Dagbamba Cultures* (Bloomington, IN: Indiana University Press, 2008); George Dor, "Communal Creativity and Song Ownership in Anlo-Ewe Musical Practice: The Case of Havolu," in *Ethnomusicology* Vol. 48, No. 1 (2004); Steven F. Pond, "A Negotiated Tradition: Learning 'Traditional' Ewe Drumming" in *Black Music Research Journal* Vol. 34, No. 2 (Fall 2014).

Ganda Music Lois Ann Anderson, "Multiple Relationships in Xylophone and Tuned Drum Traditions in Buganda," *Selected Reports in Ethnomusicology* [Vol. 5] *Studies in African Music* (Los Angeles, CA: Program in Ethnomusicology, UCLA, 1984); Andrew Cooke and James Micklem, "Ennanga Hard Songs of Buganda: Temutewo Musasa's 'Gganga alula'" in *African Music* Vol. 7, No. 4 (1999), pp.47–65; Peter Cooke, "Ganda Xylophone Music: Another Approach," *African Music* Vol. 4, No. 4 (1970).

Mande Peoples Eric Charry, *Mande Music: Traditional and Modern Music of the Maninka and Mandinka of Western Africa* (Chicago, IL: University of Chicago Press, 2000); Graeme Counsel, *Mande Popular Music and Cultural Policies in West Africa: Griots and Government Policy Since Independence* (Saarbrücken: VDM Verlag, 2009); Banning Eyre, *In Griot Time* (Philadelphia, PA: Temple University Press, 2000);

Roderic Knight, "Music in Africa: The Manding [Mande] Contexts," in Gerhard Béhague, Ed., *Performacne Practice: Ethnomusicological Perspectives* (Westport, CT: Greenwood, 1984).

Pygmies Steven Feld "Pygmy POP. A Genealogy of Schizophonic Mimesis" in *Yearbook for Traditional Music* Vol. 28 (1996), pp. 1–35; Victor A. Grauer, "Concept, Style, and Structure in the Music of the African Pygmies and Bushmen: A Study in Cross-Cultural Analysis" in *Ethnomusicology* Vol. 53, No. 3 (Fall 2009), pp. 396–424; Colin Turnbull, *The Forest People: A Study of the Pygmies of the Cong* (New York: Simon & Schuster, 1962).

Shona of Zimbabwe Paul F. Berliner, *The Soul of Mbira* (Chicago, IL: University of Chicago Press, 1993); Thomas Turino, *Nationalists, Cosmopolitans, and Popular Music in Zinbabwe* (Chicago, IL: University of the Chicago Press, 2000); Claire Jones, "Shona Women Mbira Players: Gender, Tradition and Nation in Zimbabwe" in *Ethnomusicology Forum* Vol. 17, No. 1, 'Sounds of Power': Musical Instruments and Gender (Jun., 2008), pp. 125–149; Thomas Turino, "The Mbira, Worldbeat, and the International Imagination" in *The World of Music* Vol. 52, No. 1/3, The World of Music: Readings in Ethnomusicology (2010), pp. 171–192.

Studies in African Urban-Popular Music Eric Charry, Ed., *Hip Hop Africa: New African Music in a Globalizing World* (Bloomington, IN: Indiana University Press, 2012); John Collins, *African Pop Roots* (London: Foulsham, 1985); Veit Erlmann, *African Stars: Studies in South African Performance* (Chicago, IL: University of Chicago Press, 1991); Steven Feld, *Jazz Cosmopolitanism in Accra: Five Musical Years in Ghana* (Durham, NC: Duke University Press, 2012); Tsitsi Ella Jaji, *Africa in Stereo: Modernism, Music, and Pan-African Solidarity* (Oxford: Oxford University Press, 2014); Carol Muller, *Musical Echoes: South African Women Thinking in Jazz (Refiguring American Music)* (Durham, NC: Duke University Press, 2011); Christopher Waterman, *Jùjú: A Social History and Ethnogrpaby of an African Popular Music* (Chicago, IL: University of Chicago Press, 1990).

DISCOGRAPHY

Anthologies *Musical Instruments 1: Strings* Music of Africa Series No. 27 (GALP 1322); *Musical Instruments 2: Reeds (Mbira)*, Music of Africa Series No. 28 (GALP 1323); *Musical Instruments 3: Drums*, Music of Africa Series No. 29 (Kaleidophone KMA 3); *Musical Instruments 4: Flutes and Horns*, Music of Africa Series No. 30 (GALP 1325); *Musical Instruments 5: Xylophones*, Music of Africa Series No. 31 (GALP 1326); *Musical Instruments 6: Guitars 1*, Music of Africa Series No. 32 (GALP 1327).

Ewe and Ghana *Folk Music of Ghana* (Folkways FW 8859); *Drums of West Africa: Ritual Music of Ghana* (Lyrichord LLST 7307); *Ewe Music of Ghana* (Asch Mankind Series AHM 4222); *Songs of War from the Slave Coast: Abutia-Kloe Ewe* (Ethnic Folkways FE 4258).

Ghana *Uganda 1*, Music of Africa Series (Kaleidophone KMA 10).

Mande *Kora Manding: Mandinka Music of the Gambia* (Ethnodisc ER 12101); *Mandinka Kora par Jali Nyma Suso* (Ocora OCR 70); *Rhythms of the Manding Adama Drame (Jembe)* (UNESCO Collection, GREM DSM 042); *Malamini Jobarteh & Dembo Konte, Jaliya* (Rounder 5021); *Sounds of West Africa: The Kora & the Xylophone* (Lyrichord LLST 7308).

Pygmies *Music of the Rain Forest Pygmies* (Lyrichord LLST 7157); *Pygmies of the Ituri Forest* (Folkways FE 4457); *Music of the Ituri Forest* (Folkways FE 4483).

Shona *The Soul of Mbira: Traditions of the Shona People of Rhodesia* (Nonesuch H-72054); *Africa: Shona Mbira Music* (Nonesuch H-72077); *The African Mbira: Music of the Shona People of Rhodesia* (Nonesuch H-72043); *Rhodesia I*, Music of Africa Series (Kaleidophone KMA8); *Ephat Mujuru: Master of Mbira from Zimbabwe* (Lyrichord LLST 7398).

Urban-Popular Music *Ju Ju Roots: 1930s–1950s* (Rounder 5017); *King Sunny Ade and His African Beats; Juju Music* (Mango 9712); *Zulu Jive* (Earthworks ELP 2002); *Viva Zimbabwe* (Earthworks ELP 2001); *Voices of Africa: Highlife and Other Popular Music by Saka Acquaye and His African Ensemble from Ghana* (Nonesuch Explorer H-72026); *Black Star Liner: Reggae from Africa* (Heartbeat 41556); *Mbube Roots: Zulu Choral Music from South Africa, 1930s–1960s* (Rounder 5025); *Thomas Mapfumo and The Blacks Unlimited; Corruption* (Mango MLP 9848).

THE MUSICAL CULTURE OF EUROPE

Philip V. Bohlman

MUSIC IN THE LIFE OF MODERN VIENNA

Streets and Stages: A Musical Stroll

As we stroll through the streets of Vienna on a June evening, the sounds and symbols of music envelop us. Music is everywhere, and Vienna has derived ways to make its own musical persona obvious. Grandiose edifices, monuments, and statues attest to great musicians of the past and the extravagant performances of the present. The sounds of street musicians intermingle with insistent scales wafting from an open window in a music academy. Wall placards announce many upcoming concerts, and musicians with violin cases or armfuls of musical scores scurry into buildings on the way to rehearsals or concerts. Even restaurants and the foods they serve bear the names of composers and musicians. This is an image of Vienna as

the quintessentially musical city in a fundamentally musical nation in the heart of Europe, an image to which we are well accustomed. It is an image underscored by recordings and movies, history books and tourist literature, all conspiring to convince the world that Vienna is, above all, a musical city.

Continuing our stroll, we begin to see that the larger image of Vienna as a musical city is considerably more complex than its surface suggests. The map of Vienna in our hands tells a great deal about the interaction between the cultural core—symbolized by the city center (First District), which the Ringstrasse, with its governmental and cultural buildings, surrounds and the concentric ring streets that ripple outward toward the Alps in the west, the Czech and Slovak Republics in the north and east, and Hungary and Slovenia in the east and south. The major highways radiating from the center connect it with these other countries and cultures, which until little less than a century ago constituted an empire ruled by Austria. The Habsburg Monarchy is no longer a political reality, but Vienna still has the look and the sound of an imperial capital: We see many cars from the countries of Eastern Europe, and we hear street musicians singing in Hungarian or playing Slovak instruments. After the transition from communism to newly independent nation-states in the early 1990s, Austria's borders opened again, and musicians were among those who took advantage of the cosmopolitan musical life of its capital. As we listen to the many contrasting musics, it is apparent that Vienna attracts musical diversity and provides it with ample opportunities to express itself.

The annual Vienna Festival is in full swing during June, so it is hardly surprising that, as we head in the direction of the **Staatsoper**, many people are funneling into the front doors to see the nightly performance. Opera is an elegant affair, and many attend this evening's performance, dining before the 5:30 P.M. curtain and going to the nearby Mozart Café for drinks and desserts between acts. We check a kiosk to see what opera is on this evening, thinking it might be *Le Nozze di Figaro*. It is instead Richard Strauss's *Rosenkavalier*, although we see from the schedule of Vienna Festival events that *Figaro*, a Viennese favorite, will be staged later in the month.

Many symbols of Vienna's musical past lie within a few blocks of the State Opera. We walk a few blocks to the **Gesellschaft für Musikfreunde**, a large building with several halls for musical performances, a library, archives, and even

STAATSOPER
The National, or "State," Opera of Austria, serving the Habsburg court during the Austro-Hungarian Empire, until World War I.

GESELLSCHAFT FUR MUSIKFREUNDE
"Society for the Friends of Music"; institutional home to concert halls, archives, and artistic monuments that recognize the past history of Austrian music.

Staatsoper (State Opera House). *Source:* Lazar Mihai-Bogdan/Shutterstock

a showroom for the distinguished Austrian piano manufacturer Bösen-dorfer. We pass along Bösendorfer Street (the Austrians have a habit of giving musical names to just about everything) and enter the piano showroom. It is an imposing, even daunting, place, filled with pianos so highly polished that one hesitates to touch them and draped with huge posters of great Austrian pianists (and a few non-Austrians) staring or smiling down at us. Somehow, we get the impression of music that we should see and respect, even worship, but touching and playing seem out of the question just now.

We consider attending a concert in the Society for the Friends of Music—it hosts several evening concerts during the Vienna Festival—but everything is sold out, and, anyway, we are a little underdressed. Still, it is early summer, and our disappointment fades quickly as we resume our walk through Vienna. Many people are walking toward St. Stephen's Cathedral, the middle of Vienna's downtown. Kärntner Street, Vienna's main shopping thoroughfare, leads in that direction, and it is not long before we encounter numerous street musicians. They are of many types, and accordingly they are performing a remarkable variety of musical repertories. Flower vendors are selling an array of plants from the countryside and some imported from Italy and Spain, and they hawk their wares with a singsong style characterizing work songs. Several groups of street musicians have come to Vienna from Hungary, including a folk-dance troupe from a single village, whose performances are narrated by the local priest. The Hungarian musicians perform an amalgam of styles, mixing rural folk songs with contemporary popular hits. The young dancers even perform entire rituals, for example, a mock wedding. Everything, however, bears the stamp of the Hungarian language and an awareness of Hungarian instrumental styles.

We also encounter the rather raucous sounds of a young American singing chestnuts from the folk-music revival of the 1950s and 1960s, and with some embarrassment we throw a few coins into his guitar case. At the edge of the square surrounding St. Stephen's, we pause to listen to an Andean panpipe ensemble, performing songs of political protest in Spanish and attracting the largest crowd of all the street musicians. Whether or not anyone understands the lyrics, the Andean ensemble (no one seems to know whether they are Peruvian or Bolivian) obviously earns a considerable amount of money, probably enough to draw them back to this square through the rest of the summer. We conclude our excursion by entering St. Stephen's itself and are greeted by the magnificent sounds of an organ on which Bach is being played, the music of a North German Protestant in the cathedral of this largely Catholic Austrian city. The other visitors in St. Stephen's seem rather unsure whether the music accompanies a religious service, but they respond meditatively, remaining silent or only whispering nervously to their neighbors.

Just as nervously, we leave the cathedral and decide to spend the rest of the evening at a local wine garden, a so-called **Heuriger**, where we will enjoy the wine of the season and the urban music called **Schrammelmusik**, named after Johann and Josef Schrammel, two nineteenth-century musicians who made this style of "folk-like" (**volkstümlich**) urban music famous and contributed to

HEURIGER
Austrian wine garden, which is often a site for traditional music.

SCHRAMMELMUSIK
"Schrammel-music"; urban folk-like music of Vienna, named after a family of musicians.

VOLKSTUMLICH
"Folk-like" music of Central Europe, in which traditional folk and modern popular musics are often mixed.

SPANISH WORK SONG: "LA TRILLA"

 **LISTEN**

TRACK 9.1 **"La Trilla"**

THIS WORK SONG from the Andalusia region of Spain reveals many of the region's historical connections to the Muslim culture of North Africa, the Mediterranean, and the Iberian Peninsula. The song itself would traditionally accompany grain threshing, and it therefore reflects periods of repetitive movement and repose. The bells that begin the example and keep a steady sense of rhythm and meter are here more stylized because of the nature of recording in a studio, but originally they would have been attached to the animal assisting in the threshing.

The alternation between speaking voice and singing voice determines the structure of the song itself. The speaking voices communicate more directly to animals assisting in the work, whereas the singing voice employs melisma, the extensive performance of melody that creates the feeling of arabesque in this example. Witness, then, a shift between speech and song, hence the threshold between the use of voice in music and in communication that borders on music. Though used for a work song, the melody is very complex, showing a tendency to move between one mode, or collection of pitches, and another.

TIMING	SECTION	MUSICAL EVENT
0:00–0:06	**Intro**: The song is ushered in by the bells, accompanying the movement of work.	Traditionally these bells would have been attached to the animal assisting in the threshing.
0:06–0:13	**Communicative Speech**: The song gets under way with speaking. Speech will alternate with sung sections for the remainder of the song.	Speaking initiates the song as communication between the worker and the animal.
0:13–0:36	**Melismatic Singing**: This is the first section of the melody. The melody consists of several of these sections, and they are each bounded by communicative speech.	The first section of the melody is sung in melismatic style. Notice the subtle shifts in mode that signal deep historical connections to the Muslim culture of North Africa, the Mediterranean, and the Iberian Peninsula.
0:37–0:43	**Continued alteration between speaking voice and singing voice**: Notice the back-and-forth established between speech and song here, and remember that the whole song was historically accompanied by the physical work of threshing.	Communicative speech returns, punctuating the sections of song.
0:43–1:11		The second section of the song is performed in melismatic style.
1:12–1:24		Communicative speech returns, followed by a long break during which all we hear are the bells.
1:24–1:42		Return to melismatic singing (third section of song).
1:42–1:53		Speech returns to punctuate the section.
1:54–2:23		Return to melismatic singing (fourth section of song).

continued

TIMING	SECTION	MUSICAL EVENT
2:24–2:31		Speech returns to punctuate the section.
2:32–2:44		Return to melismatic singing (fifth section of song). Here we have evidence of the approaching conclusion because of the brevity of the section.
2:44–2:50		Communicative speech brings the song to its conclusion.

the compositions and performance practice of the tradition. By the end of the evening, we wonder whether there is any music that we did not encounter, and if so, whether we might have happened on it had we chosen a different route. Rumors fly about that there is good country-western music at a club called "Nashville." We hear, too, that some bands from the Celtic and **klezmer** revivals are playing in the city this evening. Just where are the limits of Vienna's musical life?

The Many Musics of Vienna

The musical life that we discover during an evening's stroll through Vienna sharply contrasts with many descriptions of this quintessentially Central European city. Music-history books, for example, contain labels for musical styles that are distinctively Viennese, such as "Viennese classicism," "-Viennese waltzes," and even the "Second Viennese School" of avant-garde composers in the early twentieth century. Could we also observe a similar "-Vienneseness" in our encounter with the vibrant musical life of the city on a summer evening? Surely there was no question that our expectation that Vienna would be a "very musical" city was fulfilled. It would hardly be an exaggeration to say that music—its presence as sound and idea—was everywhere. And yet it is not that easy to pin down what was especially "Viennese" about it or even any unequivocally Viennese trait connected to style, repertory, or performers. The street performers were often not even Austrian, and the multitude of musical sounds was more often mixed than identifiably of Viennese origin. Vienna's presence, nonetheless, was essential to our musical encounter. The city attracted these musicians, sanctioned their performances, and brought together the conflicting histories and cultural contexts in a unique way. What we heard during our stroll—indeed, what we would have heard on any stroll—*was* Viennese music.

Our firsthand encounter with Viennese music reveals that there are many possible ways of understanding just what it is. One view seems anchored in the existence of a historical canon, a series of repertories created by gifted composers who lived in Vienna because of the ideal conditions it provided for both the creation and performance of music. Music symbolizes something unbroken and

MELISMATIC
Performing a single syllable of text by singing multiple notes or pitches is called a melisma (melismatic). Syllabic singing, by contrast, matches one syllable to a single note or pitch.

KLEZMER MUSIC
Jewish instrumental musicians, active in social events and rites of passage in Eastern Europe prior to the Holocaust and revived in Europe and North America at the end of the twentieth century.

LISTENING GUIDE   "DAS WIENER FIAKERLIED" ("THE VIENNESE COACHMAN'S SONG")    **LISTEN**

TRACK 9.2 **Performed by Stewart Figa, baritone, and the New Budapest Orpheum Society, Philip Bohlman, Artistic Director. Composed by Gustav Pick**

"THE VIENNESE COACHMAN'S Song" (1884) was the biggest hit from turn-of-the-century Vienna. The song tells a rags-to-riches tale of a simple coachman who was able to offer rides to the most prominent citizens of the day. The journeys in the song, therefore, follow the city streets, and they also map the cultural history of a changing world, one in which the coach would eventually become obsolete as Europe modernized. The song, too, crosses a border between folk styles—it begins as a march from the country, and then the refrain is a waltz from the city. It uses urban dialects and the sounds of popular songs from the day, not unlike those that might have been flowing into and out of Strauss operettas and cabaret.

Stewart Figa sings in a style with the German inflected by Yiddish, signifying the growing immigration of Jews from rural Eastern Europe into modern Vienna (the composer, Gustav Pick, was an example of such immigration). Figa's performance career ranges from his profession as a Jewish synagogal cantor to work on the Yiddish stage, and with the revival cabaret ensemble, the New Budapest Orpheum Society.

TIME	MUSICAL EVENT
0:00	Introduction, cabaret-style band.
0:14	Verse one, in rural march style, evoking the horses who bear the coach.
1:19	The refrain begins, employing an urban waltz style.
1:50	Verse two begins.
2:53	Refrain of verse two.
3:25	Verse three begins, with the narrative bringing the coachman's life to a close.
4:26	Refrain of verse three.

Translation of "The Viennese Coachman's Song"

1. I drive two midnight horses.
    They pull my fancy coach.
    They're stronger than a Norse's,
    And far beyond reproach.
    It doesn't do to strike them.
    I never use a whip.
    I murmur, "Giddy-up, you two.
    Let's take another trip."
    In less than fifteen minutes,

    From Lamb Street to the club.
    We don't attempt a slow gallop.
    I push them faster, clop, clop, clop.
    They sound like shooting rifles.
    Then all at once I feel
    I'm not in charge of trifles.
    I'm a coachman, I mean real.
    Now, anyone can drive a hack,
    But Vienna calls for quite a knack.

continued

Refrain

I'm proud to be Viennese. Life suits me fine.
I serve as a coachman, the top of the line.
I fly through streets with speed like none other can.
I'm truly a Viennese man.

2. To be the perfect driver,
    You must be like a god,
    A silent, strong provider,
    You listen, think, and nod.
    I often take the rich men
    To visit "Number One."
    In fact, last night, Count Lamezan
    Stopped off to have some fun.
    I might pick up two lovers,

Improper true, I know.
If later someone asks me, "Who
Those lovers were?" What do I do?
I never stop to answer.
I glide on down the street.
It's safe for each romancer,
'Cause the horses are discreet.
If grandpa wants to have a fling,
That's fine with me, and I just sing.

Refrain

3. I'm turning sixty Monday.
    I've worked for forty years.
    But I would not trade one day
    For other bright careers.
    A coachman and his carriage
    Are mated well by fate.
    And when I die, hitch up my team,
    And mention heaven's gate.
    Just let my horses canter

As I go to my grave.
Direct them to the heart of town,
The smart, expensive part of town.
And though it's rather tiny,
I want the town to see,
My carriage black and shiny
Is the final ride for me.
Upon my gravestone, don't forget,
I would like this simple epithet.

Refrain

He was proud to be Viennese. Life suited him fine.
He served as a coachman, the top of the line.
He flew through streets with speed like none other can.
He was truly a Viennese man.

Taraful Marsa and Nea'
Vasile perform in Bucharest.
Source: Narcis Parfenti /
Shutterstock.com

persistent in the history of the city, and the language used to describe music's historical role—notably the stubborn word *classical*—tells us that the past has been important in the present.

Another view of Viennese music concentrates not on the central core but rather on the periphery, on Vienna's tendency to attract outsiders. Relatively few of the composers generally associated with Vienna were originally from the city or received their musical education there; Mozart, Haydn, Beethoven, Brahms, and Mahler were all outsiders, and their biographies demonstrate vividly that being accepted as an insider was no easy task. Clearly, the modern street musicians are not so different from the pantheon of Viennese composers in their relation to the city; the outsider status of the Hungarian folk singers or the Andean panpipe ensemble at once privileges and impedes, while making their presence almost unexceptional.

A third view of Viennese music challenges the historical nature of the first two and poses what we might call postmodern arguments. According to this view, Vienna forms a sort of cultural backdrop that permits unexpected—even jarring—juxtapositions. Accordingly, certain conditions foster Viennese musics at particular moments, but these are almost random. Such a view helps to explain why the old and the new, the classical and the avant-garde, opera and street music exist side by side. Vienna is no less important to the various juxtapositions, because it provides a cultural template that encourages them. Its concert halls, music academies, and streets all become the stages for a music that, whatever else it might be, is unassailably Viennese.

EUROPE AS A MUSIC CULTURE

Europe as a Whole

There is no more commonly held assumption about music's relation to cultural and geographical areas than that something called "European music" exists. Other categories are created to contrast with European music, for example, Middle Eastern music, whose position in a world culture is determined by Europe's geography, not its own. Throughout the world, students study European music; they call it by other names at times, perhaps "Western music" or "Euro-American music," but generally "European" became common parlance in the twentieth century.

Just what European music is, of course, is another question. Despite the lack of consensus, relatively few writers on music concern themselves with stating the limitations of European music or defining what it is. It might be easiest to suggest that it is the music of Europe or the music created in Europe. Would, then, the Andean panpipe ensemble we heard in Vienna be European music? And would the music of Islamic Spain in the Middle Ages be European music?

If we answer "no," we argue that Europe is more a shared culture than a unified geographic entity. If we answer "yes," we place greater importance on what happens within the geography, allowing even that the geography shapes the culture.

Europe is indeed unified in several ways. For example, it is a continent, largely though not completely bounded by water. Linguistically, most peoples of Europe are related, closely in several cases and more remotely in others. Those languages not related to the larger Indo-European family, such as Hungarian and Finnish, may demonstrate European interrelations of their own. The cultural history of the continent has a sort of unity, although sometimes that unity results only from barricading the continent from Asia and Africa. Religion unifies Europe. Europeans were historically largely Christian, certainly to a degree that distinguishes certain aspects of shared culture; to travel from Europe toward Asia, the Middle East, or North Africa brings one immediately into contact with peoples who are not primarily Christian. In Europe, the growing number of non-Christians today, particularly Muslims from the Middle East and South Asia, is seen by many as a fundamental transformation of European-ness itself. At the beginning of the twenty-first century, more nations are joining the European Union, thereby responding to calls for political and economic unity. All these cases for unity contain exceptions, but together they justify studying Europe as a whole.

Multicultural Europe

Despite the acceptance of Europe's cultural wholeness, individuals do not always—or even most of the time—identify with it. Instead, individuals identify more often with the culture of the town, region, or nation in which they live. Similarly, at the individual level, most identify more closely with a regional musical style than with an abstract European unity. It has been characteristic of music in Europe that patterns of regional and cultural identity have remained especially pronounced, even as mass culture encroaches in the twenty-first century. The geographic area surrounding Lake Constance in Central Europe, for example, belongs to a single cultural area in which a single dialect of German is spoken, and its musical styles and repertories are related by a long history. This small area nevertheless includes parts of four nations (Germany, Switzerland, Austria, and Liechtenstein). Even though the folk musics of Germany, Switzerland, and Austria are distinct at a national level, the Lake Constance region plays the decisive role in determining musical unity.

The musical areas of Europe also result from groups of people who share a way of life and a distinctive music, even when these have little to do with national and political boundaries. Jewish, **Saami**, and **Roma** (Gypsy) music cultures in Europe, for example, are circumscribed primarily by boundaries that arise within these communities. Roma communities exist throughout Europe, having adapted to many different socioeconomic settings. Roma musicians have traditionally adapted to the music in countries where they settled, often fulfilling specialized roles as performers in non-Roma society. This adaptability has not erased a distinctively Roma musical life. Bolstering that musical life have been the customs, languages, and social functions that are unique to the Roma community. It is not quite proper to speak of "Roma"—and surely not "Gypsy"—culture as a homogeneous whole. Instead, we must always keep in mind the distinctive linguistic and cultural communities that make up the whole.

If we were to generalize about the music of Roma and **Sinti** in Europe, we would need to take into consideration a process of negotiation between the community and the larger nation or cultural area of which it was a part. We would also need to incorporate the ways in which Roma and Sinti make distinctions among their own musics. The Saami in northern Europe have traditionally responded relatively little to the music cultures of Norway, Sweden, Finland, and Russia, whereas Jewish musicians have often been active participants in the musical life outside the community, so much so that certain differences of style and repertory have disappeared. The Roma musicians, for their part, often borrow from Jewish styles and repertory previously performed by Jewish musicians in northern Romania.

European Unity in Modern Europe

Many genres of European music reflect an underlying belief that unity of musical style is important. Hungarian and German folk-music scholars have created classification schemes that assert the historical presence and importance of these folk musics. European folk music in general falls into repertories that have national, linguistic, or cultural designations, suggesting that those who

SAAMI
Circumpolar peoples, living in northern Norway, Sweden, Finland, and Russia, whose musical practices in Europe mix indigenous and modern sounds.

ROMA
Transnational communities of people pejoratively referred to as Gypsies; active participants in Europe throughout history and across the continent.

SINTI
One of the largest communities of Roma, with a particularly strong presence in Central Europe.

"KHUSED" (CHASSIDIC DANCE)

 **LISTEN**

TRACK 9.3 **Performed by Gheorghe Covaci, Sr., and Gheorghe Covaci, Jr.**
Recorded by Rudolf Pietsch and Philip V. Bohlman, February 23, 1996,
Vadu Izei, Romania

TWO ROMA MUSICIANS, a father and son renowned throughout the Transylvanian Carpathian Mountains near the Ukranian border, perform a wedding dance from the Jewish repertory that had wide currency in Romania prior to the Holocaust. The dance itself is strophic, here with four verses, each increasing in tempo from its predecessor and revealing the generally ecstatic nature of the wedding celebrations of Chassidic Jews, observant communities following the spiritual traditions of the Baal Shem Tov, a rabbi from the eighteenth century.

The Covacis play a violin and a guitar, mixing Roma styles (e.g., playing the guitar upright in the lap) with Romanian styles. These musicians reveal the ways in which earlier Jewish repertories have come to serve other ethnic communities in Eastern Europe, and they particularly illustrate the centuries-long exchange between Roma and Jewish neighbors. The musicians play other repertories as well, for other ethnic and religious groups in the multicultural area of Transylvania.

TIME	SECTION	MUSICAL EVENTS
0:00–0:12	**Verse 1**: Listen to the three-part melody that makes up the verse (AABBCC).	The violin performs the first section of the melody. Notice that it consists of two short phrases that form a complete statement (AA') [0:00–0:06]. The guitar joins shortly after the opening gesture on the violin and the melody is repeated [0:06–0:12].
0:12–0:23		The second section of melody, again consisting of two short phrases, is introduced [0:12–0:18] and repeated [0:18–0:23].
0:23–0:34		The third section of the melody is introduced [0:23–0:28] and repeated [0:28–0:34].
0:34–0:44	**Verse 2**: Listen for the tempo increase that pushes up the intensity of the performance.	(A) section.
0:45–0:55		(B) section.
0:55–1:05		(C) section. Notice the rhythmically more complex strumming on the guitar during this section.
1:05–1:15	**Verse 3**: Now that you have heard the melody twice, listen for the increased tempo and intensity, and notice the nuanced strumming on the guitar in the (C) section.	(A) section.
1:16–1:26		(B) section.
1:26–1:36		(C) section. Notice, again, the rhythmically more complex strumming on the guitar during this section.

continued

TIME	SECTION	MUSICAL EVENTS
1:36–1:46	**Verse 4**: Listen for the increasingly ecstatic performance. In addition to the slightly increased tempo, the violinist plays more forcefully than in previous verses and the guitarist, for the first time, incorporates more complex rhythmic strumming into the (A) section of the melody, adding intensity to the performance.	(A) section. Notice the rhythmically more complex strumming on the guitar during this section.
1:46–1:56		(B) section.
1:56–2:08		(C) section. Notice the double stop (two notes bowed at once) on the violin to conclude the dance song.

describe these repertories feel that unity is fundamental to what folk music really is. Scholars in several countries have gone so far as to recognize patterns of unified history in their national folk musics. This is particularly evident in Hungarian and English folk music; but elsewhere, too, we encounter the belief that the music of the past is related to the music of the present.

Folk music can reveal and articulate history in both musical and cultural (or, better, political and nationalistic) ways. The classification of Hungarian folk song is based on claims about whether the progression of musical style has been relatively unbroken since the time Hungarian people lived in Asia (old style) or whether it has absorbed influences from surrounding European peoples (new style; see chart on page 316). Music Example 9–1, from Béla Bartók's collections of Hungarian folk song, demonstrates the characteristics of the old style in every way. Each characteristic is bracketed and numbered according to the chart on page 316 to help you identify the musical arguments that Bartók and other Hungarian scholars brought to their understanding of history.

PARLANDO RUBATO
Identified by Béla Bartók and characterized by a speech-like style that stresses the words while incorporating a great deal of give-and-take in the rhythmic structure. It is associated most closely with "old style" Hungarian folk song.

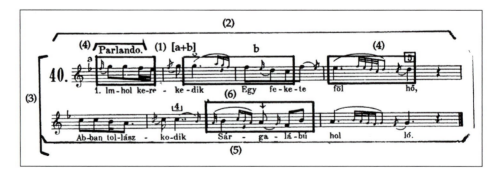

Music Example 9–1   "Imhol kerekedik"—Hungarian Folk Song in the Old Style. *Source:* Bartók, Béla. *Das ungarische Volkslied.* Berlin: de Gruyter, 1925, p. 11, Example No. 40.

One of the first things we notice when we compare the musical traits of the old and new styles is that there is much more flexibility in those traits recognized as "new." To fulfill the requisites for old style is difficult, but virtually any Hungarian song—folk, popular, or even religious—fits into the new style. If the two are compared even further, we realize that in certain ways they are not so different. The transposition by fifths is as much old as it is new style,

LISTENING GUIDE

"THE OWL WOMAN'S BALLAD"

 LISTEN

TRACK 9.4 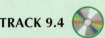 **Kati Szvorák, singer, and Ferenc Kiss, Jew's harp**

"THE OWL WOMAN'S BALLAD" is a clear example of the "old style" of Hungarian folk song. It has a four-line structure, (**ABAB**), in which the contour of the (**B**) lines are similar to those of the (**A**) lines, only at an interval of the fifth lower. The slow tempo and elaborate style are characteristic of what Béla Bartók called **parlando rubato**, a speech-like melody with much give-and-take in the rhythmic structure. The words are clearly important also because this is a ballad, in which a story is being told.

Kati Szvorák is one of Hungary's foremost singers of several styles of folk song. She has an immense command of traditional repertory, from which "The Owl Woman's Ballad" comes, but she also sings in the Hungarian "new folk" style, a hallmark of the ensemble, the Stonemasons, who often accompany her. She began her career singing with army folk ensembles, and then after the end of state socialism in Hungary, she branched into other styles, among them religious folk song from the countries surrounding Hungary.

TIME	SECTION	MUSICAL EVENTS
0:00–0:07	**Verse 1**: Listen to the four-line structure and for the melodic relationship between the (A) and (B) lines. Line (B) completes the melody initiated by line (A).	Line (A). Notice the melodic contour and see if you can hear it reappear in line (B).
0:07–0:15		Line (B), transposed down a fifth, as in the "old style."
0:15–0:22		Line (A).
0:22–0:28		Line (B) concludes the verse.
0:29–0:43	**Verse 2**: Listen to the melody and see if you can hear it as two statements of (ABAB).	Lines (A) and (B).
0:43–0:56		Lines (A) and (B) repeat.
0:56–1:10	**Verse 3**: Now that you have heard the melody twice, listen for the subtle accompaniment provided by the Jew's harp.	Lines (A) and (B). Song concludes without completing the four-line structure.

PENTATONICISM
Melodic structure based on scales with five pitches, often revealing an historically early stage of folk-music style.

excluding the fact that a falling melody should somehow be older. **Pentatonicism**, too, is not excluded from the new style, and one might argue that the ornamentation in the old style has a tendency to fill in the gaps in its characteristic five-note scale. Music Example 9–1, for example, is pentatonic when we consider only the main notes, but it has a seven-note scale when we add the ornaments, marked in Bartók's transcription with small noteheads.

The Hungarian construction of history from folk-song style has clear nationalistic implications, and these are important to understand as ideas about European music. Transposition by fifths was important to Bartók because it was quite rare in Western and Central European music, but more common in Central and East Asian traditions. A style of music that utilized transposition by fifths, therefore, proved that the integrity of the Hungarian people had been maintained to some measure, at least since they left Asia to settle in Europe. The close relation of the old style to speech (*parlando*) also reveals an attempt to link music to the uniqueness of Hungarian culture, because the Hungarian language is not a member of the Indo-European family. Clearly, identifying songs in the old style provided a strong argument for Hungarian nationalism. Recognizing that songs in the new style had been influenced from the outside—that their rhythms were regularized and loosened from their connection to language—made an equally strong nationalistic appeal. This interweaving of

COMPARISON OF OLD- AND NEW-STYLE HUNGARIAN FOLK SONG

OLD STYLE	NEW STYLE
1. A five-note, or pentatonic, scale, in which no half-steps were found.	Whereas pentatonic scales are occasionally found, more common are the so-called church modes or major mode.
2. Melodies or phrases that started high and ended lower.	Melodies are repetitive, and they form arches rather than descending contours.
3. A melody in two halves, in which the second half repeated the first, only at the interval of the fifth lower.	Four-line verses like the following (A^5 designates a phrase transposed a fifth higher); A A^5 A^5 A; A A^5 B A; A B B A.
4. A steady rhythmic style Bartók called parlando rubato (speech-like).	Rhythm is not "speech-like" but rather "dancelike," demonstrating what Bartók called tempo giusto.
5. Only Hungarian musical elements are heard.	Non-Hungarian musical elements have been incorporated.
6. No influence of popular song or other "outside" genres.	The influence of popular song, particularly Hungarian popular genres from the nineteenth century, is evident.

musical style, national history, and cultural ideology is such that we find it difficult to determine which characteristic of a song was determined for musical reasons, which for ideological for musical reasons, which for ideological reasons, and which for both.

LISTENING GUIDE	BÉLA BARTÓK: TWO DUOS	 LISTEN

TRACK 9.5   **Performed by Andrea F. Bohlman and Benjamin H. Bohlman. Recorded by Philip V. Bohlman**

Two Duos from the 44 Violin Duos, "Lullaby" and "Dance from Maramoros"

THESE TWO VIOLIN DUOS illustrate the contrastive styles of Hungarian folk music, the *parlando rubato* style of "Lullaby" and the **tempo giusto** style of "Dance from Maramoros." Parlando rubato is speech-like, and it follows the nuances of song and evokes in an instrumental piece the contours of language through embellishment. Clearly, a lullaby would be speech-like. A dance, in contrast, has a quick tempo that allows for rapid and coordinated movement on the dance floor. "Maramoros" is the Hungarian designation for Transylvania, which indicates that Bartók composed this dance to reflect characteristics of the region (the Roma musicians featured on Track 9.3 live in this region). In the "Lullaby" the two violins might represent a child and a parent at bedtime, one singing gently, the other declaiming forcefully that it might be time to go to sleep. In the "Dance from Maramoros" the variety of string sounds in Hungarian folk music is clear, from the percussive sound of the second violin to the plucking of the same instrument toward the end of the brief dance.

The two violinists, Andrea and Benjamin Bohlman, are young American musicians who specialize in the performance of chamber music for strings. Like the Roma musicians performing on Track 9.3 they are from the same family, in fact, that of the author of this chapter.

"Lullaby"

TIME	MUSICAL EVENTS
0:00	Solo voice, with gentle melody begins.
0:09	The other voice enters, showing firmness.
0:31	Dialogue, or conversation, begins between the two voices.
0:47	Gentleness increases in both voices.
0:53	The voices succumb to fatigue.

"Dance from Maramoros"

This dance is fast and through-composed, evoking the sound of a Hungarian string band.

TEMPO GIUSTO
Identified by Béla Bartók and characterized by a dance-like style that stresses strict adherence to meter. It is associated most closely with "new style" Hungarian folk song.

SPEECH ISLANDS
Sprachinseln, or the German-speaking cultural islands in Eastern Europe, given nationalist significance by Germany prior to World War II.

The concept of "music history," itself a particularly European notion, asserts that unity is somehow central to the formation of musical repertories. French music, then, is more than just music that utilizes the French language or music created or performed in France; rather, it is music that occupies a position within French music history, maintaining an essential style that is French. Whether the patterns of stylistic unity sought by European scholars are real or not is open to question. They have sometimes produced rather unfortunate historical distortions, for example, when some German musical scholars sought to equate pockets of German folk-music style (in French Alsace-Lorraine or in the so-called German speech islands of Eastern Europe) with colonialist expansion in the late nineteenth and early twentieth centuries. Nonetheless, the need to equate musical style with national and regional unity in Europe remains one of the most noticeable traits of the continent, even at the end of the twentieth century.

The "Europeanness" of music assumes many forms in modern Europe. However, motivations for retaining and expressing nationalistic or regional musical qualities have changed, as have the audiences who listen to popular and classical musics. A Polish popular singer must sing part of her repertory in English to ensure success in Warsaw, but that success allows her to sharpen the bite of the political message in her songs, both Polish and English. The mass media link the different linguistic regions of Europe in new ways, thereby empowering indigenous languages to claims of greater importance while permitting international languages to encroach at an increasing pace.

The Europeanness of music today is not unlike the attributes we observed during our stroll through Vienna. Seemingly unrelated traditions are juxtaposed in unpredictable ways. Elements of indigenous and foreign music commingle, and in some cases they demonstrate an affinity for each other. Revitalizing old folk music is not an uncommon way of highlighting contemporary political issues. The old and the new coexist. Just as Vienna shaped its conflicting musical parts into a unity that reflected the history and contemporaneity of Vienna, so too does the Europeanness of music today assert itself so that the changing complexion of Europe has a powerful musical presence. That European music so often combines such diverse parts is, as we shall see, fundamental to the basic ideas that Europeans hold about music.

IDEAS ABOUT MUSIC

The Concept of "European Music"

Music is many different things to Europeans. Still, we recognize that certain qualities make music "European" and enable us to discuss a European music culture. We commonly employ the term "European art music" to describe the classical music of the Western concert hall. "European folk music," too, provides a way of classifying shared musical activities.

Earlier in the history of ethnomusicology, music outside of Europe was defined by contrasting it with European music, calling it simply "non—European." Implicit in such terms was not the notion that all European music was the same, but rather that certain experiences, both historically and culturally, had produced musical activities and ways of thinking about music that were more similar to each other than to those elsewhere in the world. Hungarian and Norwegian folk musics, therefore, do not sound like each other, but both fulfill certain expectations of what folk music should be in rural European society and in the construction of national cultures, musical styles, and art musics.

Music in Peasant and Folk Societies

European ideas about music have a great deal to do with shared historical experiences and the ways these experiences have formed modern European societies. Early in European history, social relations were relatively undifferentiated and rural, and yet a common culture—consisting of language, folklore, and belief system—provided cohesion. Music played a role in expressing the common culture of a people because it was in a language shared by the people and was a part of their daily lives and rituals. Music was thought to be inseparable from the essence of a culture. As such, it could express the culture's past, share traits of a language, and articulate religious belief. In doing so, music differentiated one society from another on the basis of national, regional, and linguistic styles.

This type of music is, of course, what we call "folk music." Folk music is a particularly European concept. Johann Gottfried Herder, a German who grew up in the Baltic area of Eastern Europe, coined the term **Volkslied** in the late eighteenth century, and the collection and study of folk music spread throughout Europe by the end of the nineteenth century. The gap between a village folk song and a symphonic poem using it was massive, but it is significant for our consideration of European music that folklorists, composers, and many other intellectuals found it vital to bridge that gap. Folk music provided a means for understanding both the essence of, say, the Polish people and the ultimate expression of that essence in a national art music. Many twentieth-century European composers, such as Béla Bartók and Ralph Vaughan Williams, combined collecting and writing about folk music with composing in nationalistic styles.

VOLKSLIED
"Folk song"; the song of traditional European societies, included under a single umbrella term at the end of the eighteenth century.

Music in Urban Society

Most European concepts of folk music portray it as the product of rural life. A certain irony lurks behind the need to privilege the music of rural life, because European society has a long history of extensive urbanization. Markets, seaports, monasteries, courts, and fortifications all served as the kernels from which great European cities developed during the Middle Ages. European cities have often served as the gathering points for people from other places, that is, people singing in different languages and performing on different instruments. As we might expect, musical "trade" has been as common in the city as mercantile trade. During the Middle Ages, troubadours, **minnesingers**, and minstrels emerged as highly skilled musical specialists who traveled to urban centers, courts, and fairs, picking up new styles and repertories. Urbanization has also affected the manufacture of musical instruments and the mass production of music in all forms, ranging from printed broadsides in early modern Europe to recordings in the twenty-first century.

Cities may bring the musics of many different groups together, but by no means do they eliminate the distinctive qualities of these musics. This is particularly true of communities that were relatively independent of national folk music or European art music. Roma and Sinti musicians not only have a distinctive music culture, but they also perform as musical specialists in a variety of settings outside their own society, such as in the small courts of southeastern Europe prior to the twentieth century. Similarly, a wide variety of musical styles and repertories exist in European Jewish communities, while Jewish musicians are known for the specialist roles they play in non-Jewish society. Even the klezmer ensembles that performed widely for the rites of passage in the Jewish shtetls of Eastern Europe occasionally traveled to play at Christian celebrations.

MINNESINGER
Medieval singer, who often accompanied himself on the lute and was one of the first musical professionals.

Music Within the Nation, Music Outside the Nation

Music cultures such as those of the Saami and Jewish communities illustrate yet another characteristic of European music, namely the persistence of repertories that cross national borders. The boundaries of Saami music culture mirror the reindeer-herding routes in far northern Scandinavia and Russia. The Celtic folk-music traditions of Western Europe—traditions unified by the Gaelic languages and related stylistic traits, among them the harp and bagpipe—stretch from Brittany (western France) north through Wales and Ireland to Scotland. These traditions, moreover, have remained a vital part of the musical practices of Celtic communities living abroad—in places such as the United States, for instance. Modern political boundaries have failed to eliminate these traditions, and in fact their unity of musical style characteristic has ensured their cultivation during periods of revival.

The twentieth-century political state has become a significant force shaping modern ideas about music in Europe. Governments have been particularly supportive of music, providing financial support for folk as well as classical music and supporting festivals and broadcast media. When Bulgaria sought to create an international image of Bulgarian music in the 1980s, it toured its Bulgarian State Women's Chorus throughout the world. State choral ensembles from the Baltic countries of Lithuania, Latvia, and Estonia tour widely, promulgating an officially sanctioned national sound. It is hardly surprising that there is no single model for national music in Europe. A national music may have a style that

<table>
<tr><td>**LISTENING GUIDE**</td><td>**"BLACK IS"**</td><td> **LISTEN**</td></tr>
</table>

TRACK 9.6 **Performed by Anish (Ned Folkerth, Aileen Dillane, Kevin Moran, Aidan O'Toole, Brendan Bulger)**

IN THIS CONTEMPORARY version of "Black Is the Color of My True Love's Hair," folk music and popular music interact in complex ways. The text of the lyrical song is well known in Irish American traditions, and it has circulated through various folk and even country-music versions. In this performance, there is a healthy tension between the text and the instruments of a traditional Irish band, which improvise and vary in contrasting ways.

Anish is an Irish American band, with a shifting membership. It draws primarily on traditional repertories, but seeks new sounds and contexts in which to present them. The changing styles in the performance, therefore, reflect the changing landscapes of the Irish diaspora.

TIME	MUSICAL EVENTS
0:00	Introduction, with instruments entering to add new layers and dimensions.
0:35	First verse of "Black Is the Color of My True Love's Hair" begins, followed by multiple verses.
2:21	Instrumental interlude, with traditional and more contemporary improvisation.
2:57	Return of "Black Is the Color of My True Love's Hair."
4:16	Final vocal riffing on "Oh, I love the ground whereon she stands."

results from a unified history, or it may combine rather disparate styles from different parts of a country, symbolizing modern unity. Whatever the reasons for associating music with the state, politics have come to play a powerful role in twentieth-century ideas of European music.

Music and Religion

Religious concepts and experiences often provide keys for understanding music in European society. Both folk and scholarly classifications include categories that specify some forms of religious music, not infrequently relying on just two large categories, "sacred" and "secular" music. These broad classifications tend to mask a far more complex presence of religion in European ideas about music. If we consider the larger historical impact of Christianity on European culture, we see that systems of musical patronage often reflect the structure and hierarchy of the church. Indeed, much of the music studied as European art music was created for specific use in religious services. It was not uncommon for musical style to respond to the requirements of the church hierarchy, for example, the

Pilgrims arriving at the basilica of the Black Madonna of Czçestochowa, July 2005. *Source:* Philip B. Bohlman

COUNTER-REFORMATION
A period of Catholic revival (mid-16th to mid-17th centuries), energized in response to the Protestant Reformation.

POLYPHONIC
Generic term referring to all music in which one hears more than one pitch at a time, for example, songs accompanied by guitar, choral music, orchestral music, or two people singing a round together. Refers more specifically to music which incorporates two or more simultaneous melodic lines or parts.

call during the sixteenth-century **Counter-Reformation** for a **polyphonic** style that rendered text as audible as possible.

Folk music that accompanies ritual or that embodies spiritual themes is overwhelmingly religious in many communities. A harvest or wedding song, for example, may articulate a community's most fundamental sacred beliefs. Not only are Norwegian folk songs predominantly religious in thematic content, but many are actually variants of hymns that have entered oral tradition. Religious pilgrimages have generated new songs and formed new communities that give these songs special meaning and function. During the Cold War, religious music became a primary voice for resistance, especially in Eastern Europe. In the political transition in Eastern Europe, the music of pilgrimage has mobilized villages and nations alike as they sought new identities in shared religious experience; a recent example is the foot pilgrimage from Pope John Paul II's home village of Wadowice, whose participants sang on their way to the Black Madonna of Czçestochowa in the summer of 2005. Most recently, religious music has created venues for protesting violence against foreign workers and asylum seekers in Central Europe.

Concerts and Concert Stars

When most of us think about European music, we think also about how and where it takes place. In short, we equate European music with concerts. The concert is a specialized musical event, one in which the difference between performer and audience is very great, and the focal point of most activity is the singing or playing of music. At one level, the concert suspends the ritual of folk or sacred music by privileging the music itself, and social behavior dictates that one listen carefully to a particular musical text. At another level, concerts have generated their own rituals in European society, and audiences behave according to social requirements specific to the concert setting—dressing in a certain way, refraining from conversation, and listening attentively.

Concerts have become a form of musical ritual particularly suited to modern Europe. Some concerts may preserve one type of musical ritual, whereas others become the moment for radical innovation. The European concert empowers musicians to recontextualize music, to bring rural folk music to the streets of the city, or to relocate sacred music in a public auditorium. Though an idea shared by all Europeans, the concert has nevertheless remained one of the major sources of musical diversity in modern times.

Concerts inevitably shift a certain degree of attention to the performer as a result of splitting musical participation into the two groups of music makers and audience. The performer acquires importance because of the skill he or she possesses and the role the audience wants the performer to play. Virtuosity often becomes one of the markers of this role, and outstanding musicians become extremely important in European ideas about music. The virtuoso has taken many forms. We think first of the performer who plays the most difficult passages in a concerto cadenza faster than anyone else—the early-nineteenth-century Italian violinist Nicolò Paganini, for example. Some in the nineteenth century speculated—a few even seriously—that Paganini's virtuosity resulted from otherworldly influences, perhaps some sort of pact with the devil. Stories about the nineteenth-century piano virtuoso Franz Liszt chronicle his amorous skills, which were linked to his ability as a performer when he tossed broken piano strings to adoring women in the audience.

Although many stories about virtuosi are apocryphal, they reveal a great deal about European ideas about music. The virtuoso is somehow superhuman and can achieve things that no mortal is able to achieve. A sort of cult-figure worship develops around this superhuman quality. We find these ideas embedded elsewhere in European music, such as the association of certain instruments, particularly fiddles, or musical structures, especially the "devilish" interval of a tritone, with supernatural forces. The German philosopher Friedrich Nietzsche canonized these ideas in his writings about cultural superbeings, and music historians have applied them to virtuosi—composer, conductor, and performer alike. European music has been inseparable from the presence of individuals who stood out from the rest of society.

The Individual and Society, Creativity and Community

As a social counterpoint to the musicians who stand out as exceptional, more communal forms of music-making continue to thrive in European society. Musical ensembles in which the total musical product depends on a group's

"STEIRISCHER MIT GESTANZLN" ("DANCE FROM STYRIA, WITH STANZAS")

 **LISTEN**

TRACK 9.7 **Performed by Die Tanzgeiger ("The Dance Fiddlers")**

PERFORMED BY AUSTRIA'S premier folk-music ensemble, "The Dance Fiddlers," this dance moves across the cultural landscape of Austria and its changing history. The dance starts in Styria, the mountainous area with Graz as its provincial capital, and it eventually ends up in modern Vienna, the cosmopolitan world of the capital on the Danube. A "Steirischer," or "Styrian," is in this case a *Ländler,* a slow rural dance in triple meter, often used for social rituals and courting. Once the waltz begins about one-third of the way through the dance, the style changes. A "Gestanzln" is a style and genre with improvisatory verses, punctuated by instrumental interludes. There is much humor in the verses, actually a kind of jousting between the singers, each one trying to show that he is cleverer than his predecessor.

The traditional is relocated in the modern world in the style of performance championed by "The Dance Fiddlers." They collect many of the songs and dances they use as sources and then transform them to bridge the cultural worlds at the center of Europe.

TIME	SECTION	MUSICAL EVENTS
0:00–0:08		The ensemble sets the key and prepares for the Ländler.
0:29–1:00	**Ländler**: Listen to the melody and see if you can hear it in triple meter (1, 2, 3, 1, 2, 3).	The Ländler begins. It is a slow dance in triple meter. The form of the dance tune is (AABB).
1:00–1:16	**Waltz with Stanzas**: Now that you have heard the slow Ländler, listen for the increased tempo of the waltz and how the Gestanzln, or stanzas, are alternated with short interludes played by the ensemble.	Waltz begins. It is a fast dance in triple meter.
1:17–1:24		The first vocal stanza enters. Notice that it is sung as a trio (that is, three singers are harmonizing with each other).
1:25–1:32		Instrumental interlude.
1:32–1:40		Second vocal stanza enters, responding to the first.
1:40–1:47		Instrumental interlude.
1:47–1:55		Third vocal stanza.
1:55–2:02		Instrumental interlude.
2:03–2:10		Fourth vocal stanza.
2:10–2:17		Instrumental interlude.
2:17–2:25		Fifth vocal stanza, incorporating nonsense text of counting forward and backward.

continued

TIME	SECTION	MUSICAL EVENTS
2:25–2:33		Instrumental interlude.
2:33–2:40		Sixth vocal stanza, incorporating a joke about the nuclear disaster at Chernobyl.
2:41–3:07		Final instrumental section, transposed to a higher key for effect.

willingness to subsume individual identity into that of the ensemble reflect many ideals that Europeans associate with folk music. In the idealized folk society, all music theoretically belongs to the community, and because the means of producing music—family traditions, group interaction, community ritual—are shared, music becomes an aesthetic metaphor for communality. We recognize that this notion of communality is idealized, and yet we need not look far before discovering similar metaphors for other types of European music-making. The four voices of a **string quartet**, one of the most common ensembles, interact so that competition to make one voice dominate the others would undermine the performance. To symbolize this social equality, the chamber orchestra, the largest chamber ensemble in the classical tradition, often performs without a conductor. Not only does this avoid the symbol of power accruing to an individual, but it also assures the performers that their musical and social survival depends on functioning as a whole with interacting parts.

The folk-music or chamber ensemble may appear as idealized models for European society, but the complexity of European society, in which the parts do not always function as a whole, can also be symbolized by the musical ensemble. Folk-music ensembles—the **tamburitza** of southeastern Europe, for example—derive their structure in part from the soprano-alto-tenor-bass structure of choirs. European classical music ensembles became relatively fixed in this format in the late eighteenth century, and so we see that the tamburitza and the string quartet both symbolize a perception of gender roles in an otherwise egalitarian society.

German male choruses in the nineteenth century became a symbol for the power of nationalism embedded in and expressed by the *Volk*, the German people. Similarly, large choruses in socialist Eastern Europe during the second half of the twentieth century symbolized the achievement of the modern socialist state. Even though musical ensembles function in vastly different ways, their connection to the people as a collective society pervades European ideas about music. We witness a vivid portrayal of this in Mozart's opera, *Le Nozze di Figaro*, in which the peasant folk together constitute the choruses, who gather on the stage at the culmination of significant scenes to serve as the final arbitrators of the actions of peasant, specialized laborer, and noble alike. In the end, the chorus is what symbolizes the communal underpinnings of European society (see introduction for more information about this opera).

STRING QUARTET

The ensemble of European chamber music that idealizes the social and musical equality of the modern era—two violins, viola, and violoncello.

TAMBURITZA

String ensemble of southeastern Europe and in the diasporas of ethnic and national groups from the Balkans, with distribution of voices from low to high.

MUSICAL INSTRUMENTS

If we reflect back on our stroll through the streets of Vienna and take stock of the instruments we observed musicians playing, we might be struck both by the importance and variety of musical instruments. The pianos in the Bösendorfer showroom were displayed as if in a museum, untouchable and expensive symbols of an elite. No less untouchable was the organ in St. Stephen's, whose sounds filled every corner of the Gothic cathedral, yet failed to help us locate the organist tucked away in a loft somewhere. The instruments of the street musicians were equally symbolic of identity and social function. The distinctiveness of the Andean panpipe players comes most directly from their instruments; once considered a measure of music's universality, panpipes now serve as markers of a few musical cultures, especially those of the South American highlands (see Chapter 10).

Musical institutions in Vienna also bear witness to the importance of instruments. Museum collections juxtapose the so-called "period instruments" of early music with the experimental models of more recent times, and folk-music archives assemble folk instruments. The music academies are metaphors for the learning and specialization that musical instruments demand. Musical instruments are inescapable symbols of the unity and distinctiveness of European musical life. They may tell us that a musical style or repertory is European on one hand but Austrian, Hungarian, Sicilian, or Macedonian on the other. Instruments act as a vital material representation of musical life in Europe and as such embody its history and its great diversity.

Folk Instruments

Musical instruments have long served as some of the most commonly employed criteria for classifying music. Folk instruments were constructed within the society or community where the particular musical repertory was performed. Indeed, many thought that a folk instrument was one built by its player, therefore functioning ideally for the player's needs. An instrument imported from elsewhere, even a neighboring village, did not belong to the musical life of the community in quite the same way. In the idealized folk society of Europe, an instrument is somehow the extension of the individual musician and yet a marker of the community's musical identity. It is a specific product that we should be able to trace to its maker and the particular roles it plays in a given community.

Some folk performers do make their own instruments, but today the norm is that instruments come from elsewhere and are probably the product of an unknown maker or an industrial manufacturer. The willingness of European musicians to borrow an instrument from elsewhere is by no means a modern phenomenon. Instrument types and names reveal a long history of instruments traveling both within Europe itself and across its borders. European instruments such as the lute and the guitar came originally from Islamic North Africa, and the Ottoman presence in southeastern Europe induced a particularly rich

"TZARINA MILIČA AND DUKE VLADETA"

 **LISTEN**

TRACK 9.8 **Boro Roganovic, *Gusle* player. Recorded by Philip V. Bohlman**

THE MONTENEGRIN AMERICAN *guslar*—a player of the bowed spike fiddle, called the *gusle*—performs a traditional Balkan epic song from the *Kosovo Cycle*. The songs in this cycle move between oral and written traditions, and they describe, in a series of different accounts about historical events, the struggle between the Ottoman Empire and Christians for southeastern Europe.

The style of the song is typical of an epic song, with single lines of melody unfolding one after the other. The *guslar* performs this song more or less as he has his entire life, but he also introduces elements of improvisation, especially when accompanying himself. Boro Roganovic immigrated to the Chicago area in the late 1980s, and he performs primarily for cultural events in the large ethnic communities of Slavic language-speaking residents.

After a brief gusle solo, the singer begins at approximately [0:30] and then continues through a series of melodic variations until the song ends at approximately [6:28]. This is relatively short for this type of epic song, which can extend as long as necessary to tell a story.

exchange with Turkey. The **saz** has long been no less Balkan than Turkish. Instruments like the bagpipe and the violin exist in countless variations in folk-music cultures throughout Europe; local communities everywhere have adapted these instruments to their own music cultures, and individual musicians have personalized them. The Hardanger fiddle of Norway, a fairly recent adaptation of the violin, is indisputably Norwegian; a Swedish *hummel* is as likely to bear witness to the individual who performs it as is the *gusle*, or bowed lap fiddle, of a Montenegrin or Serbian epic singer. The ubiquity of such instrument types notwithstanding, they show that the tendency to use instruments to express individuality and community identity has not abated in modern Europe.

SAZ

Lutelike instrument used widely in Turkish art music and spread throughout the regions of southeastern Europe, into which the Ottoman Empire extended.

When Instruments Tell Stories

Europeans tend to anthropomorphize instruments and regard them as music makers with human qualities. We refer to the parts of an instrumental piece as its "voices," and it is fairly common to relate these directly to human vocal ranges. Europeans, like peoples throughout the world, ascribe human qualities to instruments (think of how many instruments have "necks," that part of the human body in which the vocal cords are located) and decorate instruments with human or animal figurations. Instruments become the musician's partner in music-making.

Musical instruments in Europe often assist in telling a story, which is one of the functions that makes them human-like. Among the earliest specialists who

"Klezmer House" in Kazimierz, the Former Jewish Quarter of Krakow, Poland. *Source:* Philip B. Bohlman

performed secular narrative song in Europe were those who sang by accompanying themselves on an instrument. The medieval *minnesinger*, for example, recounted tales of history and great heroes, encounters with lovers and with enemies, all the while relying on the narrative assistance of the lute. The importance of the lute to the German song tradition appears in a nineteenth-century interpretation in Richard Wagner's *Die Meistersinger von Nürnberg*, in which the mastersingers must prove themselves by playing the lute according to the rigorous rules imposed on the tradition.

Whereas Wagner's vision was particularly Romantic and German, the narrative epic traditions in southeastern Europe predate medieval Europe, evolving from the Homeric epic traditions of ancient Greece. The epic is a narrative genre in which the poet–singer performs tales from the life of a hero or heroine. The singer's instrument, the gusle, has become so closely identified with the genre that the singer's name, guslar (player of the gusle), is derived from the instrument itself.

The instruments of classical European music also demonstrate narrative functions, often in such ways that we recognize a close relation to rural society and folk beliefs. The twentieth-century composer Igor Stravinsky used the narrative potential of the orchestra to transform the pagan ritual of *Le Sacre du Printemps* (*The Rite of Spring*) and the Shrovetide folktale of *Petrushka* into classical ballets. The narrative power of the piano, too, marks the work of many composers; for example, Robert Schumann told the tale of attending a pre-Lenten party (again Shrovetide) in his *Carnaval*. Narrativity also distinguishes the symphonic tone poems of late nineteenth-century composers and the nationalistic works of composers seeking to use the orchestra to tell the stories most characteristic of their own history.

The stories told by musical instruments often acquire sweeping symbolic power. The revival of *klezmer music* has, for example, served as a powerful reminder of the destruction of European Jewry during the Holocaust, especially in countries such as Poland and Germany, where that destruction was extreme. Traditionally, klezmer ensembles comprised a group of instrumentalists—the Hebrew words *kleh* ("vessel") and *zemer* ("song") form the contraction, klezmer—who accompanied weddings, dances, and other events where strictly sacred music would be inappropriate. In the twenty-first century, klezmer ensembles play and record regularly in the cities that lost their Jewish populations, such as Kraków, where klezmer clubs even appear in the former Jewish quarter of Kazimierz.

EXPLORE

Klezmer

Musical Instruments in an Industrial Age

Although personal, communal, and human qualities continue to influence European concepts about musical instruments, modern European music would be inconceivable without technology. Technology's influence is evident in the development of new areas of musical life—for example, the dependence of rock-music instruments on mass-produced sound and dissemination. Perhaps less evident is the previous development of new instrument types during the rapid industrialization of European society from the end of the seventeenth century on, when instruments we now regard as standard—the piano, for instance—were invented and reinvented. The technology of musical instruments is also one of the primary musical exports from Europe, and we can recognize European influences on non-European musics by the adaptation of certain types of technology, such as the *harmonium* in North India and Pakistan. Moreover, technological developments have directly affected the reception of music, making it possible for larger audiences to hear a piano with a more powerful cast-iron frame or the amplified sounds of a folk-music ensemble using microphones.

No instrument symbolizes the impact of technology on European musical instruments as fully as the piano. Invented at the beginning of the eighteenth century in Italy, piano makers transformed the direct striking or plucking action of the clavichord and harpsichord into a more powerful action by employing a series of levers connected by joints. The piano's new design not only allowed a broader palette of sound colors but also made it possible for the piano to dominate the other instruments with which it was played. As the piano grew larger, so did its sound; as its machinery grew more complicated, the factories that manufactured it became more sophisticated and efficient. The technology to create pianos kept pace with the demand for an instrument that had its own solo repertory and a role in many other repertories. The piano both appeared on the stage of the largest concert hall and stood in the parlor of the bourgeois home.

A product of technology, the piano became the preferred instrument of the European "everyperson" by the mid-nineteenth century. It was an instrument that resulted from mass production and was capable of attracting mass audiences. Pianos followed Europeans as they settled elsewhere as both immigrants and colonizers. Yet the piano did not lend itself particularly well to other musics. Its technology was so highly developed that it could not be easily adapted to non-European scales. It stood apart in non-Western societies, effectively symbolizing the hegemony of European music in the colonial era.

Instruments and Musical Professionalism

Musical instruments often represent complexity, which is a musical quality highly valued in European society. Whereas both singers and instrumentalists generally practice and study to acquire their skills, playing an instrument is often regarded as less natural, less a product of pure gifts than singing. The distinction between vocal and instrumental forms of music is, in fact, universal, and in many societies, such as those of the Islamic world, instrumental music may be criticized or even prescribed because it is less human, that is, not directly tied to words. Restrictions on instrumental music are not unknown in Europe, where periodic attempts to keep instruments out of Christian religious music are among the hallmarks of conservative religious movements. When they ascended to power in 1649, forming the English Commonwealth, the Puritans inveighed against instruments in churches and ordered that organs be destroyed.

Instrumentalists therefore acquire the status of specialists and, very often, professionals. They stand out as exceptional in society because of the skills they command, and the best—that is, the most skillful—receive financial rewards for their labors. The exceptional role of instrumentalists does not always reflect public sanction; instrumentalists like the **becar** in southeastern Europe are sometimes regarded as ne'er-do-wells or troublemakers (and, not insignificantly, attractive lovers). The outsider status of the instrumentalist also empowers one to move with ease from community to community, or even to perform within several distinct societies. We have witnessed this already with Roma and Sinti musicians. Medieval minstrels, generally instrumental musicians, were also distinguished by relative mobility. In more modern times, the klezmer ensembles of European Jewish society have also been recognized as traveling performers. Increased mobility ensured the profitability of the instrumentalist's trade. We see again the European willingness to view music as a product, indeed one that a consuming society is willing to pay to hear.

BECAR

Instrumentalist and musical specialist in southeastern Europe, often distinguished by great mobility.

HISTORY AND SOCIAL STRUCTURE IN EUROPEAN MUSICAL LIFE

The Underlying Historicism of European Musical Thought

Throughout this chapter, we have seen that history is one of the primary forces unifying European concepts of music. Just as Europeans are aware of larger historical forces and moments—whether wars, religious transformations, or responses to other parts of the world—they also share a sense that a historical unity characterizes the musics of Europe. We witness such unity in phrases like "European art music" or "European folk music" (and conversely in phrases like "non-European music").

At least since the Renaissance, those who have written about music have largely concerned themselves with some musics of the past and the relation of these musics to a more recent time. It is hardly surprising that we commonly refer to scholars who write about European art music as music historians.

Individuals and Collectives in the History of Music

MENTALITÉ

A collective way of thinking, expressed in the cultural activities of a group or community.

History takes a number of distinctive forms in European concepts of the relation of music to a given community, society, or nation. Music may be a part of and serve as a voice for a people's **mentalité**. In contemporary usage, the mentalité of a people is that cultural profile existing apart from the actions of armies and political figures; instead, it forms from the everyday acts, aspirations, and belief systems of an entire society. The concept applies particularly well to an interpretation of musical life that emphasizes folk music as a body of expressive activities shared by an entire cultural group; in effect, folk music becomes the product of the group's mentalité.

We find a similar sense of collectivity in Johann Gottfried Herder's eighteenth-century model for the shared music of a people, *Volkslied*. Herder and nineteenth-century folk-music scholars steeped their concept of Volkslied in historical potential. The "-everyperson" in European society, therefore, continued to contribute to music history by sharing in a musical collective. Even attempts to reformulate the concepts of folk music into "people's music" (in Marxist thought) or "group song" (a formulation associated with the German scholar Ernst Klusen) retain the basic premise that it is a collective that shapes the formation, transmission, and history of music.

Few modern scholars accept the notion that a folk song or any other form of popular music came into existence simply because of the will and collective action of the community. Instead, an individual, usually a musician with some specialized role in the musical life of the community, creates a piece of music, "composes" it, and establishes its position in a particular music history. Folk songs might begin their history in oral tradition by first being printed on a broadside and sold on the street, largely to earn profit for the composer, printer, and hawker. The broadside ballad, which often appeals because it captures the news of the moment, is only possible if it embodies certain aspects of the community's mentalité and relies on the community's knowledge of common melodies, yet it is the individual who composes these relations in the ballad.

The broadside composer is often anonymous and represents one end of a continuum of individuals in music history. At the other end, we find the twentieth-century recording virtuoso, whose status as a cult figure would seem to stand outside of history (fans will regard the virtuoso's interpretations as superior to those fixed or limited by historical performance practice). The history of European music has gradually shifted more emphasis toward the individual. The notion of the individual musician standing out from his or her community was virtually unknown in the Middle Ages, but it began to form in the fourteenth century, when minstrels acquired names such as "Fiddler" or "Pfeiffer" (Piper) that help us to understand the relation between the musical specialist and the community. The designation of the individual as potentially exceptional, a musical genius, began only in the late Renaissance, but quickly became a primary impetus in European music history, and by the nineteenth century music historians were using "great composers" to mark the epochs of historical change (e.g., the "Age of Bach").

BROADSIDE BALLAD
A printed version of a folk song, usually combining a well-known melody with a topical text; printed on large sheets and sold inexpensively.

Modern Nations, Modern Histories, Modern Musics

Twice during the twentieth century, world wars radically redrew the map of Europe, creating new political entities while splitting and eliminating many old ones. The new face of Europe has had a profound effect on musical life in the continent. Just as new nations and cultural boundaries have developed, so too have new music histories emerged to interpret and, in some cases, to justify the widespread change. More than at any previous moment, the diversity of Europe's music at the beginning of the twenty-first century is a result of conscious historicism—the revitalization of a musical past in the present. On one hand, historicism interrupts the path of steady historical development by altering traditional social contexts. On the other, it collapses the differences between past and present, making it possible to combine musical styles and repertories in ways particularly appropriate to the political reality of modern Europe. Musical historicism recaptures the past in distinctly modern ways.

Just what can musical historicism capture from the past? In what ways do elements from the past effectively serve as the music of the present? There are no simple answers to these questions. Modern European musical cultures have employed historicism with quite different motivations. One of the most common motivations is nationalism. This reflexive impulse explains the urge to search for Czechness in the music of the Czech Republic. A nation of quite distinctive regional and minority cultures, the Czech Republic has nevertheless endeavored to establish the criteria that make music Czech, finding little consensus among composers or folk-music styles of the past. If Czechness in music is itself elusive, the motivation to discover a distinctive nationalism is not unique to the Czech Republic.

We find similar tendencies among the inhabitants of Southern Tyrol in Italy, who have carved out repertories of music that consist entirely of German-language songs and pre-Italian Latinate dialects, called **Ladino**, which also survive in the region today. Songbooks in the region simply do not contain songs in Italian, and the examples in German, Ladino, and English (the last usually from the American folk-song revival) reveal a clear pattern of choosing selectively from the past to build the repertory of the present. European institutions of classical music also arise because of the historicist impetus. The state or national academy of music, orchestra, or chorus has become normative throughout Europe. The new map of modern Europe has relied on the historical underpinnings of musical life to reformulate that life, to modernize it, and to link it to new historical conditions.

EUROPEAN MUSIC AT THE BEGINNING OF THE TWENTY-FIRST CENTURY

The Eurovision Song Contest

The spectacle of European nationalism is nowhere greater than during the annual **Eurovision Song Contest**, the largest popular-music competition in the world. The national entries, reaching forty by 2005, represent some aspect of the amalgam of cultures and the mixes of the local and the global that will appeal to the ultimate jury, European citizens themselves, who vote by cell phone through their national committees.

LADINO
The pre-Italian Latinate dialects of the southern Alps in Italy and Switzerland. Ladino is also the Romance vernacular language historically spoken by Sephardic Jews.

EUROVISION SONG CONTEST
The largest popular-song contest in the world, established in 1956 by the European Broadcasting Union and pitting national entries against each other in an annual spectacle judged by telephone voting from the entering nations.

The Eurovision Song Contest is a moment when Europe turns to popular song as a means of performing its national and global identities. On a Saturday evening each May when the Grand Prix ceremonies are broadcast by the member networks of the European Broadcasting Union, hundreds of millions of Europeans find themselves glued to their television sets to watch the national entries perform and to root for their favorite songs and national musical heroes. In many cities, crowds of fans flood the main public squares to watch the Eurovision on massive screens and to root not only for their national entries but also for the entries from nations regarded as cultural and political allies. Scandinavians vote heavily for other Scandinavians; the Balkan countries of Southeastern Europe back each other; even historical foes—the United Kingdom and Ireland, Greece and Turkey—trade votes; the former republics of the Soviet Union rarely give support to Russia.

In the world of popular music, the professional stakes for a good showing at the Eurovision are very high. The Eurovision played a signal role in launching the careers of the Swedish group Abba, the Canadian singer Céline Dion (performing and winning for Switzerland in 1988), the Israeli worldbeat star Ofra Haza, and the Celtic music phenomenon Riverdance, which was catapulted to prominence after its Eurovision intermission performance in 1993. Winning, or even doing well, in front of an international audience can mean lucrative recording contracts and a string of appearances for the European media who sponsor the Grand Prix.

All this sounds more like media hype and crass commercialism than a response to the Cold War, the reunification of Europe, and the countercurrents of old and new nationalisms. Once the different singers and groups start performing, the evidence for national identities becomes even more perplexing. European popular song at the Eurovision may not look particularly European, and it often does not sound European. In 2000 and 2001, African American styles were particularly prominent among the national entries, ranging from the blues to Motown to hip-hop. The entries from Southeastern Europe draw heavily on folk traditions, whereas former colonial nations, especially France, allow minority voices to emerge.

Ideology may be musically nationalist, for example, in countries with Muslim majorities, or internationalist. In 2006, Finland's heavy metal band, Lordi, won with the song, "Hard Rock Hallelujah," a throwback to a metal style of the 1980s, which on its surface had no more to do with Finland than Nokia telephones, Finland's internationally consumed gift to globalization. Lordi emerged, however, from a competitive field that included the Armenian singer André, whose entry, "Without Your Love," as the inaugural entry for Armenia, was politically innocent on its surface, but circulated in advance on a video that included overt references to a contested century of struggle with Turkey. Such mixes of the national and

EXPLORE

Eurovision Song Contest

Street musician at the 2005 Kyiv Eurovision Song Contest. *Source:* Philip B. Bohlman

Ukrainian Folk Chorus during the 2005 Kyiv Eurovision Song Contest, performing before the statue of the nineteenthcentury national poet, Taras Shevchenko.
Source: Philip B. Bohlman

EXPLORE
Celtic Pop

EXPLORE
Euro-Pop

the international have spread across the face of the Eurovision Song Contest for a half-century, from its earliest years after 1956, when popular song voiced a response to the Cold War, to 2006, when the national entries reached farther into the politics of the European Union and the cultural struggle between Christian Europe and Muslim North Africa and the Middle East.

Why should this surprise us, we might ask, for other international and hybrid popular styles also dominated previous periods during the half-century history of the Eurovision Song Contest. Celtic influences were most palpable in the 1990s, and before that Mediterranean song dominated, following on the era of rock 'n' roll and French chanson. Turkey and several nations from Southeastern Europe, wishing to draw attention to historical and musical connections to Islamic traditions, often combine Middle Eastern instrumental and vocal improvisatory styles.

Lest we think there is conformity, we find ourselves confronted by alternative styles as the gala performance moves from group to group. The entries from Southeastern Europe seem unwilling to buy into the prevailing musical fashions. The entries from Bosnia-Hercegovina, Croatia, Macedonia, and Romania have something else to say about the history of Europe during the dozen years of its reunification efforts. Regional and local politics find their way into national entries, such as Norway's 1980 entry, the Saami Mattis Hætta, who, together with Sverre Kjelsberg, performed the song, "Saamiid Ædnan," which was based on a Saami yoik and included extended passages of yoiking. In 1999, Germany's Sürpriz, herself Turkish-German, sang "Journey to Jerusalem," an acknowledgment of the cultural debt to and political difficulties of Germany's so-called guest workers from Turkey, who had historically been denied German citizenship. Eurovision entries that make political statements rarely win the contest or even place particularly high, but they are able to seize one of the most visible forums in the continent at a highly charged public moment. Eurovision songs produce controversy and create new possibilities for dialogue, and in so doing, they speak powerfully and globally for Europe today.

That song—popular and folk, local and global—engages directly with the New Europe, and its contradictions could not have been more evident in the 2005 Eurovision Song Contest in Kyiv, Ukraine. Following the winter of 2004–2005, when the Orange Revolution shook Ukraine, Eurovision echoed the struggle on the streets and gave voice to the movement to align the nation with Western Europe, particularly through eventual membership in the European Union. The Eurovision winner from 2004, Ruslana, lent her voice to the Orange Revolution, going on a hunger strike, while the 2005 Ukrainian entry, Greenjolly, openly called for revolution in its hip-hop entry, "Razom Nas Bahato, Nas Nye Podolaty" ("Together We Are Many, We Cannot Be Defeated"). The images from the 2005 Kyiv Eurovision reveal the extraordinary reach of national politics. Ukrainian popular musicians took to the streets of Kyiv, with folk accordionists providing counterpoint to workers' choruses at the feet of the nineteenth-century national poet, Taras Schevchenko. Other national entries took up the banner of the revolution, such as Norway's Wig Wam, calling for a "rock 'n' roll revolution." As the contest itself was broadcast on the final evening of the contest, 30,000 gathered in Independence Square, creating a sound mix of their own.

Depending on our musical preferences and political predilections, we can understand a Eurovision song as folk, popular, or classical, typically European or cosmopolitan, socially conservative, or liberal. As a juxtaposition of all these traits, it reflects a balance, and it is the nature of that balance that eventually establishes the relation of the Eurovision song as a musical symbol for Europe in the twenty-first century. That balance—struck and forged among the conditions of history, society, politics, geography, language, style, performance, musical instruments, and repertory—assumes myriad forms while charting the path of European music history. That balance, in fact, provides the dynamic tension that makes it possible to understand the music of Europe as a whole that achieves its identity only from its diverse, composite parts.

The Norwegian Entry, Wig Wam, at the 2005 Kyiv Eurovision Song Contest, waving the symbol of the Orange Revolution. *Source:* Philip B. Bohlman

SUMMARY

European music, as we have discovered, is a complex combination of different musical styles, created by many different peoples. It is used both to highlight individual experts (virtuosos, for example) and to affirm communal bonds (as is the case with folk ensembles). Music is mobilized by various European countries as a means of defining themselves and creating a unified culture, often resulting in articulations of musical nationalism. The story of Europe's music is, moreover, closely related to its history. European folk music, for instance, is often associated with a specified cultural group or regional area—determined, that is, by the long history of social and political interaction within Europe. The mobility of Roma and klezmer musicians is a stark reminder that musical interaction across national borders has a rich and deep history in Europe.

Urbanization, beginning in the Middle Ages, introduced a wider variety of musics and musical instruments to performers and audiences. As indus-trialization spread throughout Europe beginning in the eighteenth century, new instruments were invented—notably the piano—that revolutionized how music was performed. How people listened to music also shifted over time, and the formal concert developed in Europe as the primary way of hearing musical performance, with set rules for both the performers and the audience.

In the contemporary moment, the Eurovision Song Contest is an annual event that, since the middle of the twentieth century, has reflected the tensions

KEY TERMS

Becar
Broadside ballad
Eurovision
Gusle
Heuriger
Klezmer
Melismatic
Minnesinger
Parlando rubato
Pentatonicism
Polyphonic
Roma
Saami
Saz
Schrammelmusik
Speech islands
Tamburitza
Tempo giusto
Volkslied
Volkstümlich

Crowds gather to watch the 2005 Eurovision Song Contest in the host city Kyiv, Ukraine, May 21, 2005, Independence Square. *Source:* Philip B. Bohlman

The Wiener Stadthalle is prepared for the Eurovision Song Contest 2015.
Source: Muellek Josef / Shutterstock.com

REVIEW CHAPTER RESOURCES

between local and international musical styles and continues to underscore the diversity in European music today. The diversity represented in the Eurovision Song Contest also illustrates one of the central ideas of this chapter—the idea that the music of Europe achieves its identity only from its diverse, composite parts.

BIBLIOGRAPHY

Europe as a Whole Philip V. Bohlman, *Revival and Reconciliation: Sacred Music in the Making of European Modernity* (Lanham, MD: Scarecrow Press, 2013); Erik Levi, Florian Scheding, and Michael Beckerman, *Music and Displacement: Diasporas, Mobilities, and Dislocations in Europe and Beyond* (Lanham, MD: Scarecrow Press, 2010); Richard Middleton, *Voicing the Popular: On the Subjects of Popular Music* (New York: Routledge, 2006); Bruno Nettl, *Folk and Traditional Music of the Western Continents*, 3rd ed. (Englewood Cliffs, NJ: Prentice Hall, 1990); Timothy Rice, James Porter, and Chris Goertzen, Eds., *Europe: The Garland Encyclopedia of World Music*, vol. 8 (New York: Garland, 2000).

Cultural Life in Vienna and Austria Charlotte Ashby, Tag Gronberg, and Simon Shaw-Miller, *The Viennese Café and Fin-de-Siècle Culture* (New York: Berghahn Books, 2015); Walter Deutsch and Others, Eds., *Volksmusik in Österreich* (Vienna: Österreichischer Bundesverlag, 1984); Carl Schorske, *Fin-de-Siècle Viena* (New York: Alfred A. Knopf, 1980).

Folk Music Philip V. Bohlman, *The Study of Folk Music in the Modern World* (Bloomington, IN: Indiana University Press, 1988); Ralph Vaughan Williams, *National Music* (New York: Oxford University Press, 1954); Walter Wiora, *European Folk Song: Common Forms in Characteristic Modification* (Cologne: Arno Volk, 1966).

Eastern Europe Kati Agócs, "The Mechanics of Culture: New Music in Hungary since 1990" in *The Musical Times* Vol. 147, No. 1896 (Autumn, 2006), pp. 5–18; Béla Bartok, *Hungarian Folk Music*, trans. M.C. Calvacoressi (London: Oxford University Press, 1931); Béla Bartok and Albert B. Lord, *Serbo-Croatian Folk Songs* (New York: Columbia University Press, 1951); Philip V. Bohlamn and Nada Petković, Eds., *Balkan Epic Song, History, Modernity* (Lanham, MD: Scarecrow Press, 2011); Naila Ceribašić, "Social Canons Inherited from the Past: Women Players of Folk Music Instruments in Croatia" *Studia Musicologica Academiae Scientiarum Hungaricae* T. 44, Fasc. 1/2 (2003), pp. 147–157; Timothy J. Cooley, *Making Music in the Polish Tatras: Tourists, Ethnographers, and Mountain Musicians* (Bloomington, IN: Indiana University Press, 2005); Stephen Downes, *Music and Decadence in European Modernism, The Case of Central and Eastern Europe* (University Press, 2010); Sanja Radinović, Aranka Szücs, and Esther Helajzen, "Béla Bartók and the Development of the Formal Analysis of Serbian Vocal Folk Melodies" in *Studia Musicologica* Vol. 48, No. 1/2 (Mar., 2007), pp. 183–200; Daiva Šeškauskaitė, "Sutartin's and Balkan Diaphonic Songs" in *International Review of the Aesthetics and*

Sociology of Music Vol. 35, No 1 (June, 2004), pp. 71–92; Mark Slobin, Ed., *Returning Culture: Musical Changes in Central and Eastern Europe* (Durham, NC: Duke University Press, 1996); Jane C. Sugarman, *Engendering Song: Singing and Subjectivity at Prespa Albanian Weddings* (Chicago, IL: University of Chicago Press, 1996); Lajos Vargyas, *Hungarian Ballads and the European Ballad Tradition*, 2 vols. (Budapest: Akadémiai Kiadó, 1983).

Music of Central Europe Celia Applegate and Pamela Potter, Eds., Music and German National Identity (Chicago, IL: University of Chicago Press, 2002); Philip V. Bohlman, *Central European Folk Music: An Annotated Bibliography of Sources in German* (New York: Garland, 1996).

Music of Western and Northern Europe C.J. Bearman, "Percy Grainger, the Phonograph, and the Folk Song Society" in *Music & Letters* Vol. 84, No. 3 (Aug., 2003), pp. 434–45; Frances James Child, *The English and Scottish Popular Ballads*, 5 vols. (Boston, MA: Houghton Mifflin, 1882–1898); Mats Johansson, "The Gendered Fiddle: On the Relationship between Expressive Coding and Artistic Identity in Norwegian Folk Music" in *International Review of the Aesthetics and Sociology of Music* Vol. 44, No. 2 (December 2013), pp. 361–384; Cecil J. Sharp, *English Folk Song: Some Conclusions* (1st ed., 1907), 4th ed., rev. Maud Karpeles (Belmont, CA: Wadsworth, 1965); Leslie Shepard, *The Broadside Ballad: A Study in Origins and Meaning* (Hatboro, PA: Legacy, 1978).

Music of Ethnic Groups of Communities Stretching across Multiple Nations Samuel G. Armistead, Joseph H. Silverman, and Israel J. Katz, *Judeo-Spanish Ballads in Oral Tradition* (Berkley and Los Angeles, CA: University of California Press, 1968); Philip V. Bohlman and Otto Holzapfel, Eds., *The Folk Songs of Ashkenaz* (Middleton, WI: A-R Editions, 2001); Philip V. Bohlman, *Jewish Music and Modernity* (Oxford: Oxford University Press); Barbara Rose Lange, *Holy Brotherhood: Romani Music in a Hungarian Pentecostal Church* (New York: Oxford University Press, 2002; Anna G. Piotrowska, *Gypsy Music in European Culture: From the Late Eighteenth to the Early Twentieth Centuries*, trans. Guy R. Torr (Northeastern: 2013); Martin Stokes and Philip V. Bohlman, Eds., *Celtic Modern: Music at the Global Fringe* (Lanham, MD: Scarecrow Press, 2003).

Instruments Erich Stockmann and Ernst Emsheimer, Eds., *Studia instrumentorum musicae popularis* (Stockholm: Musikhistoriska Museet, 1969–present; currently 11 vols.).

Nationalism and Music Philip V. Bohlman, *Focus: Music, Nationalism, and the Making of the New Europe*, 2nd ed. (New York: Routledge, 2011); Sidney Finklestein, *Composer and Nation: The Folk Heritage in Music*, 2nd ed. (New York: International Publishers, 1989); Ivan Raykoff and Robert Deam Tobin, *A Song for Europe. Popular Music and Politics in the Eurovision Song Contest* (Aldershot, UK: Ashgate, 2007).

DISCOGRAPHY

Discographical Note Among the best surveys of national folk musics are those released on the Folkways label and rereleased on the Smithsonian label, with extensive critical notes geared toward students among others. A particularly good selection of Eastern European traditions is to be found on the Nonesuch Explorer label. The European recordings of the "Alan Lomax Collection" have been steadily appearing since the mid-1990s on the Rounder label, each of them with notes by well-known ethnomusicologists. The Rounder Lomax collections for Italy, Romania, Spain, and Yugoslavia are fairly extensive.

European academies of science and ethnological museums often produce recordings of extraordinarily high musical and educational quality, reproducing both modern field recordings and rereleasing historical collections from the first era of recorded sound. During the 1970s and 1980s, a period of widespread folk-music revival in Europe, and during the 1990s, when the European Union's political and economic influence spread, voluminous recordings of local, regional, and national folk-music traditions have appeared on CD.

The most comprehensive discographical guide to national and ethnic popular music is Simon Broughton, Mark Ellingham, and Richard Trillo, Eds., *World Music: The Rough Guide*, vol. 1: *Africa, Europe and the Middle East* (London: The Rough Guides, 1999). The *Rough Guides* also have published CDs of national and regional music in Europe, emphasizing ethnic and national styles of popular music.

Students will also wish to consider recordings of European art music and popular music, which are available in large numbers in libraries and record stores. When studying and listening to these recordings, however, the student may wish to make comparisons in new ways and to examine new issues that their mass production reveals—for example, just how are these genres marketed in different ways, or how do different nations produce the "same" music but in different ways?

Deutsche Volkslieder, 2 discs (DGG 004-157, 004-160); *Electric Muse: The Story of Folk into Rock*, 4 discs (Folk 1001); A.L. Lloyd and Ewan MacColl, *English and Scottish Popular Ballads* (Washington 715–723); *Folk Music of France* (Folkways P 414); *Folk Music of Hungary*, collected by Béla Bartók (Folkways 1000); *Folk Music of Portugal*, 2 discs (Folkways 4538); *Folk Music of Rumania*, collected by Béla Bartók (Folkways 419); *Islamic Ritual from Yugoslavia: Zikr of the Rafa'i Brotherhood* (UNESCO Collection, Philips 6586 015); *Le mystère des voix bulgares*, 3 vols. (Electra/Nonesuch 79165-2); *Liturgical Chant for Lent and Easter: Armenian Mekhitarist Community of Venice* (UNESCO Collection, Philips 6586 025); *Songs and Dances of Holland* (Folkways 3576); *Songs and Dances of Norway* (Folkways 4008); *Songs and Dances of Spain*, 5 discs, with notes by Alan Lomax (Westminster WF 12001-5); *World Collection of Recorded Music*, 6 discs, based on collections of Constantin Brailoiu (VDE 30-425-430); *Dancing on the Edge of a Volcano: Jewish Cabaret, Popular, and Political Songs, 1900–1945* (Cedille Records CDR 90000 065); *The Rough Guide Music of the Gypsies* (The Rough Guide RGNET 1051 CD); *Unblocked: Music of Eastern Europe*, 3-CD set (Ellipsis Arts CD 3570).

MUSIC IN LATIN AMERICA

Timothy Rommen

LOUIS TOWERS IN PHILADELPHIA

The announcement read: "Direct from Colombia! Champeta singer Louis Towers, with Palenke, brings danceable afro-Colombian rhythms to you." My colleagues in Latin American Studies and Africana Studies at the University of Pennsylvania had invited Towers to town and everyone was excited about the upcoming performance. The concert, took place at The Rotunda, a community arts space located in West Philadelphia on October 13, 2009. Well before the 7 pm start, the space had filled to capacity—in fact, the place was electric with anticipation. The audience for that night included Penn students and faculty, to be sure, but Philadelphia's Latino/a community was, by far, the largest constituency present at the show. Louis Towers and his band took the stage and simply owned the room, performing a generous set of *champeta* music that extended to well over two hours in length. Many in the audience danced, and a significant portion of the audience

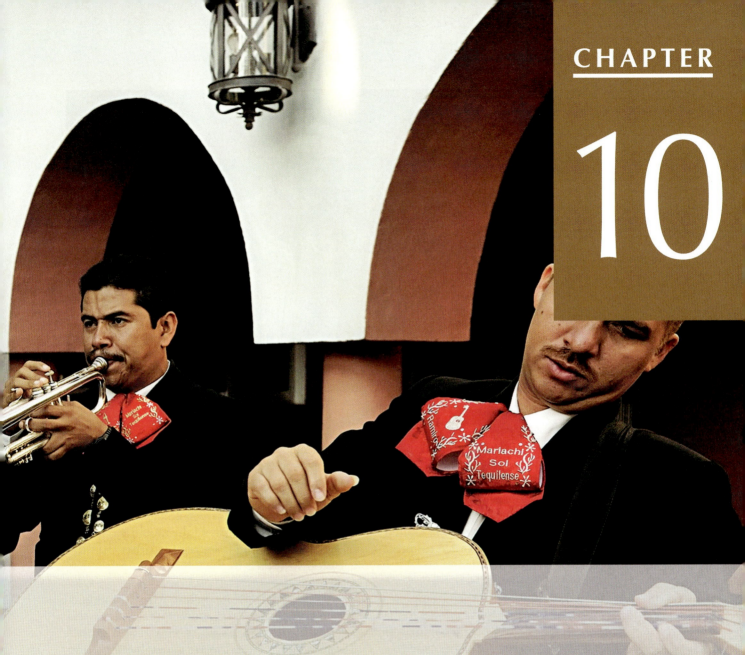

clearly knew most of the lyrics to his songs and performed their knowledge by singing along with the band. The highlight of the set was a powerful rendition of Towers' song, "Return to Your Roots / Mama Africa," in which he lyrically and sonically links his Afro-Colombian diasporic identity to the much longer history of his community's African heritage. In so doing, Towers is also making obvious connections with more pan-African sentiments articulated throughout the Americas. The lyrics, sung in both Spanish and a creole language called *Palenquero*, offer a vision of Mother Africa calling her children home.

The following morning, Towers and his band reluctantly packed their bags and headed back to Colombia. They had dearly wanted to spend some time in New York City, reconnecting with friends and family members living abroad and working to establish new professional relationships and networks in hopes of

Louis Towers.
Source: Provided with permission of Louis Towers

CHAMPETA
An Afro-Colombian popular music associated particularly with the címarron (maroon) village of Palenque de San Basilio and centered in the city of Cartagena.

PALENQUERO
A creole language, developed in Colombia, and mixing Spanish with Bant.

garnering future opportunities, but their visas were severely restricted due to the difficult post-9/11 political immigration climate in the United States. In fact, securing the visas at all (limited as they were) had been a rather protracted and unpredictable process in the months leading up to the show. The disappointment of missing out on the ancillary (and potentially career-enhancing) benefits of traveling to the United States highlights the precarity of the mobility required of (and afforded to) professional musicians hailing from regions other than the North Atlantic and I'll have occasion to return to this idea in the pages that follow.

In the contemporary moment, champeta is a popular Afro-Colombian dance music rooted in the Caribbean port city of Cartagena and the wider *costeño* region of the country. But the path to such success was a long one, and that history is instructive here. The beginnings of the genre are generally associated with large sound systems (called *picós*) that, beginning in the 1970s, would spin imported records (mostly of African and Caribbean genres) and provide entertainment for primarily black audiences in the poorer neighborhoods of Cartagena. Significantly the term champeta, the name of a local machete-like knife, was not initially associated with music at all. Instead, as urbanization drew more and more rural people to the city, middle- and upper-class inhabitants of Cartagena, as early as the 1920s, began derisively referring to the newcomers as *champetudos* in order to mark this growing community as lower class (economically insignificant), vulgar (culturally inferior), and black (other). In the 1970s, when the picós became popular, the term was repurposed by the economic elite in order to disparagingly class and racialize the community of listeners and dancers (Cunin 2003; Miranda 2007). By the early 1980s, however, having listened to a wide range of African and Caribbean genres at the picós, local Afro-Colombian musicians, many of whom hailed from a famous town called Palenque de San Basilio, began to integrate these sounds from abroad with local sounds creating a style that was initially called "Colombian therapy" or "creole therapy." Thanks to an internal revalorization of an externally imposed, negative term (champetudos), however, the community was soon calling the music champeta.

Champeta is conspicuously hybrid in its musical makeup. This is the case in large part because champeta grew out of a social and geographic context where the roots and routes of peoples, languages, and sounds all met, converged, and mingled. Nigerian, Congolese, and Caribbean sailors (among many others) exchanged their musical and cultural ideas with the local community at the picós, and these interactions became audible features of the style in the 1980s and 1990s. When listening to champeta today, it's easy to hear echoes of circum-Caribbean sounds, including styles as divergent as reggae, soca, *zouk*, *rumba*, dancehall, *son*, and calypso. It's also easy to make connections with African sounds such as *soukous*, *juju*, *mbaqanga*, and highlife. Local sounds, such as *cumbia*, of course, find their place in the mix as well.

EXPLORE

Son

But if we listen closely, champeta can also fill our ears with the sounds of history—with the sounds of slave resistance, of independent towns (like Palenque de San Basilio, the town whence many of the innovators of champeta came and where Louis Towers still lives), and of great struggles over language (Palenquero vs. Spanish), race (blackness in Colombia), and geography (rural vs. urban). Palenque de San Basilio, for instance, is the only surviving *címarron* (maroon) village among several founded in colonial-era Colombia. Against overwhelming odds, it survived from its birth in the seventeenth century, right up to the contemporary moment, developing its creole language (Palenquero), unique customs and music (especially burial rituals and the *lumbalú* music, which accompanies those rituals), and a rich diasporic imagination in the process. In the mid-twentieth century, as migration to urban centers began to draw more and more Palenque-born people to cities like nearby Cartagena, interactions, both musical and cultural, began to shape new practices and new sounds (including champeta).

Language, too, became part of this history, for Palenquero (a creole language mixing Spanish with Bantú), the primary language of the community at Palenque de San Basilio, found its way to the city and into champeta. To be sure, Palenquero is not winning its struggle against the national language (in fact, Palenquero is currently fighting to retain speakers against the twin pressures of urbanization and assimilation), but the spirit of resistance embedded in the language itself and in the community that developed it (San Basilio) remain powerfully symbolic. Champeta also highlights the social and cultural place of blackness within Colombia—a history that continues to be quite complicated (cf. Wade, 2000; Aldana 2012). But champeta gives artists like Louis Towers a voice in these negotiations, for many of these struggles are played out in the music itself, either as explicit political messages (singing in Palenquero) or as more subtle (but highly effective) claims to place, space, and identity.

<table>
<tr><td>LISTENING
GUIDE</td><td>RETURN TO YOUR ROOTS
"MAMA AFRICA"</td><td> LISTEN</td></tr>
</table>

TRACK 10.1 **Composed and performed by Luis Towers**

THIS SONG BY LUIS TOWERS is a good example of the popular music called champeta. The lyrics make a strong case for remembering Africa as a source of cultural production and heritage. They also illustrate the linguistic complexities at play in Columbia, moving between Spanish and Palenquero (a creole language developed from Spanish and Bantú sources) several times throughout the performance. The lyrics also offer a glimpse at the fraught racial dynamics at play within Colombia (and by extension, elsewhere in Latin America), highlighting stereotypical and racialized attitudes toward dancing bodies (verse 4). Like many genres of popular music, it is strophic in structure. The bridge, moreover, makes use of a formal device often deployed in champeta and called the *despeluque*. *Despeluque* means, roughly, losing one's composure or losing one's head, and is characterized by a very deliberate focus on the groove (often melody instruments drop out and percussion is foregrounded, as happens in this performance). Translation courtesy of Ann Farnsworth-Alvear.

TIME	SECTION	MUSICAL EVENT/LYRICS	
0:00–0:13	Introduction	Vocal callouts	
0:13–0:31	Verse 1	*Recordase en donde naciste—* *¡te acuerdas!* *Y la madre que te parió* *Eso que tu corazón dice— ay ómbe* *Lo que eres, tu propio yo*	Remember where you were born— You remember? And the mother who bore you Hear what your heart says—ay hombre (man!) What you really are, your own self
0:31–0:40	Instrumental interlude	Vocal callouts	
0:40–0:54	Verse 2	*Sientes muy dentro de tí* *Algo que te grita vuelve* *Esa es la propia raiz* *Que no se corte y que crece* *Dentro de tí*	You feel it way inside yourself, Something that calls to you: Come back That's it, that's the root It's not cut, it grows Inside of you
0:54–1:03	Instrumental interlude	Vocal callouts	
1:03–1:21	Chorus	*Mamá Africa te llama* *te llama Mamá Africa* *Mamá Africa te llama* *te llama Mamá Africa*	Mamá Africa is calling you She's calling you— Mamá Africa is calling you She's calling you—
1:21–1:30	Instrumental interlude	Vocal callouts	
1:30–1:58	Verse 3 with extension	*Si un día mientras caminas—* *te pones a bailar* *Al son de algo que no escucha—* *debes escuchar*	If one day when you're walking— you start to dance To a rhythm you don't hear— you should listen to it

continued

TIME	SECTION	MUSICAL EVENT/LYRICS	
		Piensa serio, no es excusa— *esa es la verdad*	Think, be serious, no excuse— it's the truth
		No se trata de una bruja— *esa es tu Mamá*	That's not a witch—she's your mother
		Que te llama vuelve—vuelve	She's calling you, come back—come back
		Que te grita . . . vuelve bis	She's shouting to you, come back bis.
1:58–2:24	Bridge/ Despulque	**Lyrics in Palenquero.** *Majaná,majaná* *onde jué ugtere ta majana*	
		[Rough translation from Palenquero: ¿Mi gente en donde estan? / Where are my people?]	
2:24–2:34	Instrumental interlude		
2:34–2:51	Verse 4	*Cuando un blanco baila sabroso—* *comentan*	When a White guy dances good— They'll talk
		"Esto no sé si sea verdad."	"Could it really be true?,"
		Que un negro lleva en el fondo . . . *ajá*	Since a Black guy has it deep down, ah—
		De su alma, dicen acá— *será mentira.*	In his soul, here they say that— "Maybe it's a lie."
2:52–3:01	Instrumental interlude		
3:01–3:19	Chorus	*Mamá Africa te llama*	Mamá Africa is calling you
		te llama Mamá Africa	She's calling you—
		Mamá Africa te llama	Mamá Africa is calling you
		te llama Mamá Africa	She's calling you—
3:19–4:13	Bridge/ Despulque	**Lyrics in Palenquero.**	

		Salino pa tiela ugtere	[Rough translation from Palenquero:	Come back to your land,
		Minino pa tiela mí	Regresen a su tierra, vengan a la mia.	Come to my land,
		Bukeno gende suto	Busquen a nuestra gente,	Find our people,
		Bukeno gende mí	busquen a la gente mia.	Find my people.

I open this chapter with a reflection on Louis Towers' music because the long history of champeta illustrates several of the recurring issues that we will encounter in our excursions in Latin America, including: (1) the reliance of the style on mobilities of various kinds; (2) the importance of race and ethnicity to the genre's meanings; (3) the crucial role that hybridity plays in shaping the genre's sound; and (4) the deep impact of urbanization on the style's development. Let me just briefly elaborate on these four themes. The concert at The Rotunda was brilliant, and left its audience buzzing. It was a unique moment of musical exchange and, accordingly, a significant event. That said, however, Towers' performance is also important precisely for its everyday ordinariness—for the mobilities it illustrates. In Philadelphia, any given week will find musicians and bands from Latin America and the Spanish-speaking Caribbean playing shows at local clubs, and these concerts draw the many Latin American expatriates living in the area (as well as other Philadelphia residents) to the venues. New York City, located just a short drive up Interstate 95, is embedded even more firmly within these fluid nodes and networks of mobility (of both musicians and their audiences).

Race and ethnicity, too, have shaped in powerful ways not just the music of Louis Towers, but the musics performed by and important to many Latin American communities. We will discover that Amerindian music, European-derived styles, and African aesthetics have all contributed to Latin America's rich musical traditions and that these are often at the heart of negotiations over space and place within the modern nation-states of the region. The notion of hybridity, moreover, so deeply rooted in Champeta's sound, also finds a ubiquitous, if widely variegated presence throughout the region. The notion of mixture embedded in the concept of *mestizaje*, for instance, is a powerful means of thinking through the many musical genres that have emerged in the course of colonial and post-colonial encounters between Amerindians and Europeans in the region. And, thinking about sacred sounds will lead us inevitably to explore the many beautiful ways that communities have made religious practice relevant and meaningful in their day-to-day experiences through recourse to *syncretism*. And finally, champeta isn't exceptional in terms of how urbanization has affected its sound and standing over the years. In fact, as we shall see, this is a recurring trope throughout the region, and one that has affected a great many of the musics we will be encountering in dramatic fashion. Our excursions in this chapter, then, will be directed toward thinking musically about these four themes and to illustrating, in as wide-ranging and representative a way as possible, the sheer variety of forms that they assume when communities wrestle them into meaningful sound.

LATIN AMERICA: DEFINITIONS AND SHARED HISTORIES

Before delving into our series of excursions, however, it is necessary to offer a few words about how this chapter will conceptualize the region as well as a few thoughts about the common themes that animate the long history of Latin America. For our purposes, Latin America comprises the Spanish- and Portuguese-speaking countries of North, Central, and South America. One way to organize and conceptualize the vast geography explored in this chapter is to think about the ways in which Latin America can be subdivided into smaller regions (see Box 10.1). These include North America (Mexico and the Latino/a community in the United States) and Central America (Guatemala, Belize, El Salvador, Honduras, Nicaragua, Costa Rica, and Panama). Within South

MESTIZO
A relative term referring to people and a social identity involving the blending of European and Amerindian beliefs and cultural practices. Although in the past used as a racial category, it now more accurately denotes the variable incorporation of Iberian (Spanish and Portuguese) and indigenous cultural heritages.

SYNCRETISM
A term, used within religious studies, to describe processes of mixture between religious traditions.

BOX 10.1: REGIONS WITHIN LATIN AMERICA

North America (Mexico and the Latino/a community in the United States)

Central America (Guatemala, Belize, El Salvador, Honduras, Nicaragua, Costa Rica, and Panama)

The Andean Region (Peru, Ecuador, Bolivia, Chile, and parts of Colombia, Venezuela, and Argentina)

Southern Cone (Argentina, Chile, Uruguay, Paraguay)

Portuguese-speaking Latin America (primarily Brazil)

Spanish-speaking Caribbean and circum-Caribbean (Cuba, Puerto Rico, the Dominican Republic, and Caribbean coastal regions of Central America, Colombia, and Venezuela).

America, several more regions are commonly recognized, including: The Andean Region (Peru, Ecuador, Bolivia, Chile, and parts of Colombia, Venezuela, and Argentina); the Southern Cone (Argentina, Chile, Uruguay, Paraguay); and Portuguese-speaking Latin America (primarily Brazil). Ordinarily, the Spanish-speaking Caribbean and circum-Caribbean (Cuba, Dominican Republic, Puerto Rico, and Caribbean coastal areas of Central America, Colombia, and Venezuela) are included as well, but since Chapter 11 covers the Caribbean, our excursions in this chapter will touch only briefly on the circum-Caribbean. Conspicuously absent here are the English-, French-, and Dutch-speaking nations of Guyana, French Guyana, and Suriname on the Caribbean coast of South America. But, for the purposes of this chapter, we will confine ourselves to exploring only the musical diversity of the Spanish- and Portuguese-speaking communities in Latin America.

Even after excluding the Caribbean, however, this chapter still aims to explore a tremendously diverse area, spread across two continents, and home to some 600 million people. How to begin to think about such a vast geography and such diverse communities? One place to start is to remind ourselves that there are some shared histories we can point to that, while experienced to different degrees and at varied moments, have contributed greatly to the shape of contemporary Latin American life. These include at least the histories of colonialism; the questions related to race and ethnicity that colonialism inevitably raised; and the powerful effects of urbanization on communities throughout the region. Let us briefly consider these interrelated histories.

COLONIALISM, RACE, AND URBANIZATION

What Christopher Columbus "discovered"—and what Europe quickly began calling the New World—wasn't at all new to a great many people who had lived there before he (and then many others) arrived in the region. Great civilizations had grown up centered in Mexico (Aztec), Central America (Maya), and Peru (Inca). Over many millennia, Amerindians had made the Americas their own, but within only a few decades, European colonial expansion devastated those communities unfortunate enough to have met these visitors. Exposure to European diseases (like smallpox), war, and forced servitude took a tremendous toll on these communities, reducing the population by 50–80 percent (even more in more in some regions). Within the next century, even the Inca, initially somewhat protected by geography itself, living as they did in the highlands of the Andes, fell into European hands. Only those Amerindians living in the most inaccessible locations (such as Amazonia) remained relatively untouched by the inexorable expansion of European colonial power in the region.

To one degree or another, this encounter between Europe and the Americas also raised questions about the value of human beings. Initially, Amerindians and, increasingly, African-born slaves were incorporated into a social order within that Europeans (*peninsulares* and *criollos*) held power and considered "others" inferior, and this both socially and culturally. This foundational struggle that indexed ethnicity and race in the service of power extended to inform attitudes toward mixture and cultural relevance, contributing a whole host of gradations in vocabulary designed to assign bodies a place within the social order. Terms like *castizo*, *mestizo*, *cholo*, *mulato*, *indio*, and *zambo* all delineated social rank within the caste system established in Latin America. Even after the Latin American Wars of Independence (fought during the first decades of the nineteenth century), these attitudes continued to inform the criollo elite, relegating mixed-race, Amerindian, and free black individuals to roughly the same positions they had occupied before. The fight for recognition and equality throughout Latin America continues in the contemporary moment and, as elsewhere in the world, it remains a pressing concern.

The twentieth century saw Latin America become the world's most urbanized region. In fact, the United Nations estimates that, by 2050, nine out of ten Latin American citizens will live in a city. This history of rural to urban migration has, as you can imagine, had major implications for populations throughout Latin America. It shouldn't come as a surprise that many of the region's poorest city dwellers are also racially marginalized, and that they live in the least desirable areas of these urban areas (the number of people living in urban slums throughout the region has recently risen above 110 million). The economic inequalities that emerge in the face of such rapid and pervasive urbanization, thus, parallel longstanding racial and ethnic fissures within Latin American societies. We will have occasion, in the pages that follow, to think about how music can highlight these processes by raising awareness and/or facilitating protest. But we'll also have a chance to explore the ways that music provides entertainment and fosters solidarities in spaces otherwise marked by these overarching issues.

THEMES IN LATIN AMERICAN MUSIC

Our excursions into the musics of Latin America will follow the themes outlined above, focusing on: (1) mobilities; (2) race and ethnicity; (3) hybridity; and (4) urbanization. Our case studies will cover both traditional styles and popular genres, and will visit as many musical communities as possible. Importantly, they will also illustrate quite consistently the ways that the themes suggested above blend and blur into each other as soon as we delve into specific musical histories and practices. Rather than thinking of these themes as separate from each other, then, it will be important to recognize the extent to which they can each participate in shaping any given case study. I use the themes, then, primarily to provide a general focus for our excursions, indicating points of connection between the themes along the way.

EXPLORE

Tango

Mobilities

Tango

Let us begin by thinking about the emergence of *tango* in Argentina, paying particular attention to the ways in which this genre has depended on mobilities of both sounds and people for its successful integration into the national and international scenes. The pre-history of tango is bound up in the ubiquitous narratives of urbanization in Latin America. Starting in the mid-nineteenth century, the image of the rural rancher, or *gaucho* (a kind of cowboy figure), was increasingly popularized in Argentina. The gaucho, associated in the public imagination with courage, individualism, machismo, and independence, became a figure easily mobilized to embody national values, traditions, and beliefs. This image was coupled with and subsumed into a massive labor migration to Buenos Aires, which was occurring at the same time, leading to a new social figure called the *compadrito*—as one commentator has succinctly put it, the compadrito was akin to a "gaucho unsaddled" (Gobello 1999). The men who adopted this persona tended to dress flashily and engage in petty crime, and also adopted and helped to develop a local dialect called *lunfardo*, which reinforced their social position (as lower class and ne'er-do-well) within Buenos Aires and the greater Río de la Plata region. The compadritos also developed a reputation for a machismo cultivated though skillful knife play, powerful song and dance, and success in romantic liaisons. They pursued this lifestyle in the tenements around Buenos Aires, called *conventillos*, which were growing rapidly at the time. Due to the overwhelming rate of labor migration to the city (primarily by men) the demographics of the conventillos eventually skewed to the point where men, far outnumbered women (5 to 1 by some estimates).

It was in this environment that, during the 1880s the tango emerged as a distinct social dance. Borrowing from earlier styles such as the *malambo* (a form of improvised male dance competition), *milonga* (a style of song that arrived to the city from the more rural areas of the Rio de la Plata region), the Cuban

TANGO

A form of popular dance music developed primarily in Buenos Aires and the greater Río de la Plata region.

GAUCHO

Residents of the South American pampas and particularly important to the national imaginations of Argentina, Uruguay, and Chile. A term roughly equivalent to the North American cowboy.

COMPADRITO

A stereo-typical character in the early history of tango. A male of modest means who makes do, both within and outside of the law, managing life with flair.

LUNFARDO

A particular approach to language (slang) that developed in the tenements of late nineteenth- and early twentieth-century Buenos Aires. Associated with early tango.

Carlos Gardel graffiti in Abastos Town in Buenos Aires. *Source:* Luis Davilla/Getty Images

TANGO-CANCIÓN
A form of tango music designed to be listened to instead of danced.

BANDONEON
A type of concertina commonly associated with tango music and particularly popular in Argentina and Uruguay.

habanera, and *candombe* (a practice with explicitly African roots, of which more a bit later), the music and dance became an integral part of the entertainment scene throughout the conventillos (and, just as an aside, here we have a great example of the kinds of mixtures and hybridizes that inform so many of the musical practices throughout Latin America). Because women were present in such small numbers in these communities, men often sharpened their dancing skills by dancing with each other, preparing themselves for the inevitable competition at brothels, where women had their pick of the best dancers or, alternatively, dancing with each other for the sheer pleasure of the experience (a homosocial and homoerotic narrative that has been downplayed in many of the historical accounts of tango).

Musically, tango developed into two distinct forms—one designed for accompanying dancing, the other for listening, called *tango-canción*. From the outset, tango lyrics focused on misery, lost love, pain, longing for better times, violence, and the effects of poverty. In short, the lyrics focused on what it was like to live in Buenos Aires at the time, and the foremost exponent of this style was Carlos Gardel, who became a legendary figure in the early tango scene.

The instrument most iconically associated with tango is the *bandoneon*, but it was really instruments such as guitars, flutes, and violins that initially provided the soundtrack to tango dance and song. In fact, it was common to use whatever instruments were on hand, and this often meant solo accompaniment (guitar, for instance). The bandoneon didn't make a permanent place for itself in tango until the first decade of the twentieth century, but once it did, it gradually became the principal sonic marker of the genre. Ensembles featuring two bandoneons, two violins, piano, and upright bass, became common, but bandleaders would,

 LISTENING GUIDE

TANGO: "EL CHOCLO"

TRACK 10.2 **Performed by René Marino Rivero**

THIS TANGO, WRITTEN by Argentine composer Ángel Gregorio Villoldo in 1905 and performed here by the Uruguayan musician René Marino Rivero is an excellent example of several features of tango. We can hear here four sections, which can be designated roughly as **ABA'A"**. In each of these sections, the rhythmic flexibility to slow down, stretch, or speed up the tempo is clear. We also hear the marcato style with the firm accented and on-beat chords played on the bandoneon. The regional character of the dance and music and the mobilities that underly its development and dissemination are highlighted here by the fact that an Uruguayan performer records this and includes it on an album entitled *Bandoneon Pure: Dances of Uruguay*. Each of the sections introduces new musical features and ideas into the performance, with the last two serving as variations on the first.

TIME	SECTION	MUSICAL EVENT/LYRICS
0:00–0:26	A	This section introduces the main melodic and harmonic themes of the piece, presented in a minor key. Notice the very slight stretching of the tempo around 0:10–0:12 that makes that melodic moment much more expressive. Listen also to the strong accent on the downbeat in the bass notes (a style of playing called marcato).
0:26–0:51	B	This section presents contrasting melodic and harmonic material.
0:51–1:23	A'	This section slows the tempo, presents a variation of section A in a major key and with the melody presented an octave higher than it was in the opening section. Listen also for the manipulation of tempo for expressive purposes.
1:23–1:58	A''	This section returns to the original octave and minor key introduced in the opening A section, but adds a great deal of additional ornamentation to the melodic line, making it the most virtuosic statement of the theme and a climactic ending to the piece. Notice again the dramatic stretching of the tempo in order to achieve artistic expression.

in subsequent decades, expand dramatically on the size of their ensembles. The composition of ensembles performing tango remains very flexible, even today. The dance (and it's musical soundtrack) developed into three substyles—tango, *milonga*, and *vals* (waltz). The tango (4/4) and milonga (2/4) are both duple-meter dances, while the vals (3/4) is a triple-meter dance. The tango is often characterized by strong accents at the quarter-note level, a technique called marcato. The milonga, for its part, is generally a bit faster and more energetic than the tango, offering a variant and contrast for both musicians and dancers (and the term also refers to the venues where tango is danced).

Due to the context within which tango was performed and danced, however, the upper class drew implicit links between poverty and indecency and, of course,

MILONGA

A style of song popular in the more rural areas of the Rio de la Plata region and influential during the early development of tango.

between wealth and decency. As such, tango wasn't initially widely accepted beyond the tenements and the working-class communities in which it was popular, although that did not prevent young members of the middle and upper class from frequenting the brothels and salons where tango was performed. And, in part because wealthy Argentines regularly traveled abroad for education and leisure, tango was eventually introduced to the dancing publics of Paris, where it was immediately seized on as the focus of a new dance craze. During the 1910s, tango rapidly became an internationally popular style, spreading to New York, London, and the rest of Europe. Several interesting developments are worth noting here. First, because of the popularity of tango dancing among communities who did not have direct access to the style's roots in the conventillos, tango developed a new, more generic choreography and was then incorporated into the ballroom dance complex. Second, the fact of tango's international popularity became the catalyst for a re-evaluation of the significance of tango within Argentine society. As the middle and upper classes began to realize that tango brought international approval, they quickly readjusted their own negative attitudes toward the music and dance (if not toward the communities in which it developed), incorporating it fully into the nation's narrative. It was in this moment that Osvaldo Pugliese and Anibal Troilo became two of the most famous bandleaders in the Argentine tango scene, even pushing tango into film.

The mobilities involved in creating such a reversal of fortune are important to keep in mind. Tango, itself a product of rural to urban migration and indebted to a particular combination of local and non-local musical influences for its sound, needed the international community to claim it as spectacular and worthwhile before the local Argentine elite took it seriously. Ironically, tango transcended both national boundaries and class boundaries in its rise to world prominence and to its place as a marker of Argentine identity. The 1930s–1950s were a period of tremendous growth for tango.

During the second half of the twentieth century, Astor Piazzolla, the innovative and controversial tango bandleader and composer, emerged into international stardom.

He lived between Paris, New York, and Buenos Aires, and connected tango deeply to jazz and Western Art Music. He tried many different configurations for his ensemble, but the most famous was his quintet, featuring bandoneon, electric guitar, violin, piano, and bass. He wrote material expressly intended for listening, not dancing, and sought to create virtuosic, avant-garde music. We can think of Piazzolla's reception in Argentina as parallel to the initial development and reception of tango in Buenos Aires. Both had to go away to come home, as it were. In the case of Piazzolla, it was only after his death that Argentina accepted his stylized and experimental music as a major contribution to tango. The formation of the National Academy of Tango in 1990 has helped this process a great deal.

Today, a new hybrid, fusing tango with electronic dance music and rock, is proving popular in Argentine clubs, and bands like Goapele Project and Bajofondo Tango Club are busy innovating new approaches to tango's sound and dance (and their videos are readily available on YouTube). Interestingly,

Astor Piazzolla and bandoneon. *Source:* Eugene Maynard/Getty Images

they are rethinking the originally myths about tango, exploring the homosocial and homoerotic possibilities embed in the long history of the genre and generally pushing questions of gender and sexuality to the foreground of their projects. These developments, too, are bound up in the ability of sounds and bodies to travel—in the mobilities of both musical style and individual artists and their audiences.

Salsa

Salsa counts among the most ubiquitous sounds traveling around Latin America. It has deep roots in the Spanish-speaking Caribbean, was developed in New York City, and then circulated throughout the region. Since the 1970s, it has expanded to inform and affect the popular music and dance repertories of the entire region. I include it here because of the particularly important ways that it illustrates mobilities, not just of people and musical practices, but also of the affinities and solidarities generated in and through its travels—solidarities that help shape the sounds and sensibilities of what many have called Latinidad.

During the 1930s and 1940s, New York City became an important fulcrum around which communities began to explore what it meant and sounded like to be Latino/a in the United States. People had moved to the city to find work, to seek education, and to join family. This growing community included Cuban master drummers, and Puerto Rican *plena* and *bomba* musicians (see Chapter 11). By the 1950s, famous bandleaders like Tito Puente, Tito Rodríguez, and Machito held court, playing mambos at the city's premier dance club—the Palladium. All of this musical activity was recorded, circulated, and

EXPLORE
Salsa

SALSA
A style of popular Latin dance music.

PLENA
A Puerto Rican folk song style associated with political and social protest and accompanied by frame drums and scrapers.

BOMBA
An Afro-Puerto Rican music and dance complex.

broadcast, moving around the region along with the people who came and went between Latin America, the Caribbean, and New York City. Many important intersections were being explored during these decades, including connections with jazz. For instance, a significant Cu-bob movement (bebop placed in dialogue with Cuban musical ideas) developed in the 1940s. By the 1960s a younger generation of Latino/a musicians in New York, tired of the sounds of the Latin Big Bands of the 1950s, was attempting to find their way into the mainstream US markets, creating a musical style that blended elements of R&B with latin percussion, using both Spanish and English in their lyrics, and generally working to create a party atmosphere (hand clapping, a live sound, etc.). This style came to be called *boogaloo*, but it was over almost as soon as it started (by 1968 it was effectively over). As the effects of the Cuban revolution, which occurred in 1959, began to be felt around the region, moreover, new artists and new ideas began to arrive in New York City, contributing their energy to the formation of what would eventually come to be called salsa. So, New York had already been a site for mixture, experimentation, and Latino/a sounds for decades before salsa emerged to prominence in the 1970s.

But musicians had also been doing their thing in places other than New York during this time. It is worth mentioning just two musicians here to illustrate how much the circuits of people and recordings during earlier decades impacted on the sounds of salsa. In Puerto Rico, Cortijo y su Combo created a formidable sound and mined the resources of local plena and bomba styles in order to create vibrant grooves that contributed in no small measure to the musical palette from which salsa musicians eventually began to choose. His band's popularity made a huge impression on many of the artists who would eventually rise to the top of the salsa scene. Similarly, a bit earlier, the Cuban bandleader, composer, and virtuoso tres player, Arsenio Rodriguez, created a richly percussive sound for his dance band. Playing *son* and doing so with an ensemble centered around a piano, *tres*, bass, two trumpets, and percussion (including congas), he influenced in very significant ways the formation of smaller, flexible ensembles for salsa. He also contributed one of the most recognizable rhythmic markers of salsa by codifying the conga part (still called the son conga today). The innovations of both of these musicians reached the bands and dancehalls of New York and, as boogaloo was fading, provided a way forward for the musicians seeking to play but uninterested in the big band sound of the 1950s.

By the 1970s, the larger Latin big bands had been replaced by more nimble and flexible ensembles and salsa had emerged as a viable genre. The style was initially dominated by a single record company—Fania Records—and the repertory was comprised of both new material and existing popular song from Cuba and Puerto Rico. Much has been made of the fact that many Cuban songs were recorded that circumvented the need to pay royalties because Cuba was being embargoed. But, because Fania was so dominant, a particular sound became a hallmark of their recordings, branding salsa in a way that became recognizable as a genre. Major stars became a part of the scene, too—artists like Celia Cruz, Willie Colón, Rubén Blades, and Héctor Lavoe wound up as household names.

BOOGALOO
A musical genre envisioned as a crossover between Latin and North American popular musics and actively pursued during the 1960s.

SON
A strophic song usually on romantic themes and in many regions characterized by sesquialtera rhythm.

And, because Fania promoted its sounds far and wide through record distribution, films, and touring, salsa began to find its way into communities around Latin America. Two of the most enthusiastic audiences for salsa were in Colombia and in Venezuela, where bands and dancing audiences sprang up almost overnight in response to the genre. So, in Venezuela, artists like Oscar D'Leon and bands like Dimension Latina entered the scene and began touring themselves. In Colombia, bands like Grupo Niche and Orquesta La Identidad achieved similar popularity. Both of these bands are based in Cali, which has come to be called the "World Capital of Salsa" in a move designed to replace New York City as the center of gravity for the genre. And, in some ways, this is a very accurate assessment of the state of salsa. By the time Fania Records began to falter and then fail in the 1980s, it had successfully seeded salsa in other places around Latin America, and Cali became one new center for the sound. Another way of thinking about it is that salsa became a thread that sonically tied the region together—a set of sonic practices in which the region could hear itself and with which it could identify.

The mobilities we can trace in and through salsa are, thus, really about: (1) the simultaneous movements of sound and people between several important nodes (New York City, Cuba, and Puerto Rico); (2) a secondary movement of sound and people to a wider range of locations, some of which (including Cali) then also became central nodes in a wider network; and (3) a development of solidarity in and around these very mobilities.

Race/Ethnicity

Race and ethnicity provide another perspective from which to explore the complexities of musical life in Latin America. The following excursions will very briefly consider several Amerindian, European, and African contributions to musical practice throughout the region. And, while the genres and styles we encounter here are understood as deeply ingrained in particular racial and ethnic pasts, they will, nevertheless, also provide us with a foundation from which to begin thinking about hybridity and mixture—a process ubiquitous throughout the region.

Highland Amerindian Musical Practices: The Aymara

The Aymara-speaking Amerindians living in the highlands of Bolivia and Peru and Northern Chile predate both the Inca Empire and the arrival of Europeans in the region. They have maintained a sense of solidarity across centuries, and in spite of the limitations imposed by the borders of modern nation states. They have, of course, also engaged with mestizos and with people of European heritage for much of that time. Many, for instance, travel from the highland region around Lake Titicaca to Lima in search of jobs, to join family, or to pursue their education. Conversely, many people and sounds also reach these highland communities even if they never leave home, contributing to new mixtures,

EXPLORE

Andean Music

Aymara pinkillu ensemble. *Source*: Thomas Turino

Aymara sikuri ensemble. *Source*: Thomas Turino

hybridities, and cultural formations in the process. As such, there is much in their musical lives that could fruitfully be discussed when we get to our considerations of hybridity and mestizaje in Latin America (and also in our previous considerations of mobility). That said, however, there are also aspects of their musical and aesthetic lives which have been maintained in spite of these histories of encounter, and it is these that I would like briefly to explore.

A preference for community over individuals characterizes Aymara social life. As Thomas Turino has put it in a previous incarnation of this chapter, "reciprocity, egalitarian relations, and community solidarity have come to constitute core values for ordering the Aymara social world" (2011: 297). And you might imagine that these values would surface in musical life as well. One area of performance where these social values become particularly evident is in the flute and drum ensembles so prevalent among the Aymara. I will focus here on an ensemble consisting of *siku* (cane panpipes) and large double-headed drums called *bombos* (also known as *wankara*), but several other types of flutes and drums (including a side-blown cane flute called the pitu, an end-notched vertical cane flute called the kena, vertical duct flutes such as the pinkillus and tarkas, and indigenous snare drums called cajas) also occupy a significant place within Aymara musical performance. A final note about these various flutes—only a single type of flute is used in any ensemble (so tarkas never play with kenas, for instance).

But let's now take a closer look at the siku ensemble. These ensembles are usually large, and they are formed in order to provide musical accompaniment for occasions ranging from harvest festivals and life-cycle events, to community projects and religious celebrations. The egalitarian values of the community emerge in the way the ensembles are structured, in the dynamics attendant to performances, and in the physical structure of the instruments themselves. The ensembles are comprised of any male who wishes to participate (regardless of musical knowledge or skill). Music is composed collectively during rehearsals, and a great deal of emphasis is placed on an aesthetic of unity. They play "as one"—in a manner that suggests a much smaller number of players than are actually performing, that is—a goal toward which the members of siku ensembles strive. The more the community can sound like a single entity, the more satisfying their performance becomes.

The process of creating a sound unified in this fashion involves some technique but is also reinforced by the physical makeup of the instruments themselves. In terms of technique, the music is performed in *hocketed* fashion, by which I mean that the melodies themselves can't generally be played by a single individual on a single instrument. Melodies (and the instruments) are structured such that two or more instruments (and players) are needed to realize the melody. But this isn't simply an aesthetic choice—the instruments themselves are designed such that the full range of notes is not available on a single instrument. This means that two instruments (like the two performers responsible for playing them) must combine their respective resources to perform the melody as one. Structural, aesthetic, and ideological reasons for privileging group over individual thus permeate musical life among the Aymara.

HOCKET

Interlocking pitches between two or more sound sources to create a single melody or part.

LISTENING GUIDE   PANPIPE MUSIC: "MANUELITA"    **LISTEN**

TRACK 10.3 **Sikuris Centro Social de Conima**
24 sikus (panpipes) of six different sizes; 2 bombos (drums)
Recorded by Thomas Turino in Lima, Peru, June 1986

LIKE THE VAST majority of music in Conima, this sikuri piece is in **AA BB CC** form. It is a slow piece in a genre simply referred to as *lento* (slow). The long-held chords at the beginning of the piece and at section endings are typical of all pieces in this genre. Note that this cadence formula is heard at the end of all sections except the second **B** and between the two **C** Sections. The accented strokes of the drumming pattern are designed to fit with the melody. Note the overlapping and blending of instruments to create a dense texture.

TIME	SECTION	MUSICAL EVENTS
0:00–0:03	**Introduction:** Listen to the long-held chord at the opening of this performance.	Long-held chord, a standard introduction for the lento genre.
		Try to remember the pitch of the highest panflute, because it is the highest note played throughout the performance and will help you identify the chord when it returns at the end of sections.
0:03–0:14	**"A" Section:** Listen for the breathy sound that the performers are producing on their flutes. Listen also for the syncopated melody (against the rather uniform beat provided by the drums).	The performers introduce Section **A**. Listen for the reappearance of the opening, long-held chord at the end of this section [0:12–0:14].
0:14–0:24		Section **A** is repeated. Listen again for the cadential (concluding) use of the introductory chord [0:23–0:24].

continued

TIME	SECTION	MUSICAL EVENTS
0:24–0:35	**"B" section:** Listen for the contrasting melody in this section.	The performers introduce Section **B**. Listen for the reappearance of the cadential chord you heard at the end of the **A** Sections [0:33–0:35].
0:35–0:44		Section **B** is repeated. This time, however, notice that the cadential chord is not used to transition to the next section.
0:44–0:52	**"C" section:** Notice that the melody is similar to that of Section **A**, but that the long-held chord that characterizes the opening gesture of the melody in the **A** Section is not part of the **C** Section.	The performers introduce Section **C**. Notice that the cadential chord is again left out in transitioning to the repeat of Section **C**.
0:52–1:01		Section **C** is repeated. Here, the cadential chord reappears in preparation for the return of the A Section [0:59–1:01].
1:01–2:00	**Repeat of AA BB CC:** Listen again for the overall form of the piece.	The performers repeat the entire song in the same fashion.
2:00–2:56	**Final repeat of AA BB CC:** Listen for the overall form of the piece, and see if you can begin to hear how the cadential chord helps mark the transitions from one section to the next.	The performers again repeat the entire song in the same fashion.
2:56–3:06		The song concludes with two long-held chords.

Lowland Amerindian Musical Practices: The Suyá

The Suyá, an Amerindian people living within Brazil's Amazon rainforest, is but one of many communities living within the vast Amazon region. The physical and logistical difficulties attendant to traveling deep into the Amazon rainforest have tended historically to contribute to more isolation for many of these communities (whether from colonial forces or, more recently, from national governments) than is the case with, say, the Aymara. That said, however, the Suyá have in recent decades established a working relationship with the Brazilian government. Among the Suyá, musical life has taken on a different shape than we see among the Aymara. Flute and drum ensembles are not the norm here—instead, vocal music, sometimes accompanied by rattles, takes center stage. The Suyá engage in a wide variety of vocal genres, and these range from speech-like and chanted oratory (political, historical, artistic) to different singing styles. Their social organization, moreover, is determined by gender and age cohorts, and different singing styles and genres are pursued by each such sub-group within the community.

For the Suyá as for the Aymara, joining together in collective participation is a major means of reinforcing social ties and the importance of community. But, unlike the Aymara, the Suyá also find room for songs that are individually owned (called *akía*) and, for music specific to particular age and gender cohorts. Songs are believed to be learned from animals, insects, fish, and plants, and Suyá festivals and song types are named for and often represent natural species (through costumes, dance, and style). Anthony Seeger has shown that some Suyá performances find a number of individuals singing their own different akía songs simultaneously within a musical context also including laughter, other vocal sounds, and shouts. This type of musical performance would likely feel quite disorienting to Aymara, who are committed to playing "as one." And yet, community and collective performance is deeply important in the Suyá context as well. What is different here is the role that individuals can play in contributing their distinct and unique voice to the communal effort. Whereas the Aymara are concerned with collectively sounding as close to an individual performance as possible, the Suyá are comfortable showcasing the many voices that make up the collective.

So, we can see in these brief contrasting examples a glimpse of the diverse approaches to music that exist among Amerindian peoples throughout the region. We will also see, a bit later on in this chapter, that some of the instruments and ideas about music prevalent among Amerindian communities have become embedded in the mestizo genres and hybrid sounds so ubiquitous throughout the region.

European Art Music

It should come as no surprise that European musical heritage is also strong throughout the region, and we can see this in many different areas of musical life, including within Latin American sacred, art, and folk musics. Within sacred music, in particular, Christian liturgical practices loom large, and the colonial period found many composers taking on the challenge of writing for the church or within the idioms favored by the church. Initially, this task was adopted by European-born composers like, for example, the Spanish-born Gutierre Fernandez Hidalgo (1553–1618), who served at the cathedral in Bogotá, and Juan Gutiérrez de Padilla (ca. 1590–1664), who served at the cathedral in Puebla, Mexico. And these composers introduced masses, psalm settings, Magnificats, motets, sacred *villancicos*, and other liturgical settings to the musical landscape. In efforts to convert local communities, liturgical texts were also often translated into local languages like Quechua and Nahuatl. Instrumental music and operas also found their way to the Americas and the techniques, instruments, and aesthetics attendant to all of these art music genres were passed on to new generations of local composers.

A vibrant art music tradition developed (and this especially since the nineteenth century) and composers of amazing creative scope have been working throughout the region ever since, including the Brazilians Antônio Carlos Gomes and Heitor Villa-lobos, the Argentine Alberto Ginastera, the Colombian Jaqueline Nora, the Venezuelan Paul Desenne, and the Mexican Hilda Paredes, to name only a very few. Efforts to connect to local folk music and dance have become a major theme within Latin American art music, and this has taken the

AKÍA

An individually owned and sung song of the Suyá Indians of Brazil.

VILLANCICOS

A form of polyphonic song, either secular or sacred, important to the development of Latin American art music from the late fifteenth to the eighteenth century.

form, for instance, of articulating a Yucatan Operatic tradition in Mexico (e.g. using local myth and folklore as the basis for librettos and musical material) and incorporating rhythmic ideas and melodic conventions from local folk practices into compositions. But the reverse trend is also important for our purposes here—the introduction of European instruments, musical ideas, and formal conventions into local popular and folk idioms has impacted regional musical life in profound ways as well. As we will see in the following section, string instruments of European provenance, in particular, have been adopted, rethought, redesigned, and then combined with flutes, local drums and percussion, to produce mestizo/hybrid ensembles. But European scales, formal structures (strophic music, for instance), and harmonic conventions also became integral to mestizo music throughout the region.

African-derived Musical Practices: marimba, candombe, candomblé

As with the Amerindian and European examples we've explored, musics connected to African aesthetics are also to be found throughout much of the region. This is the case not least because the slave trade brought so many Africans to Latin America. In fact, Brazil alone received four million slaves (1.5 million more than any other nation in the Americas). Even though Brazil is the prime example of the ways that the slave trade moved people from Africa to the Americas, African presence was and continues to be ubiquitous throughout the region. A few examples will illustrate this point.

Marimba

We might point, for example to the marimba—an instrument of African provenance and, for many in places like Ecuador, Colombia, and Costa Rica, a symbol of their heritage. The marimba and its repertory was also historically a major component of musical life in parts of Peru. Although the instrument takes different shapes and is accompanied by different instruments, depending on where you are, the African origins of the instrument are widely accepted. Chapter 8 introduces us to many of the ideas that animate sub-Saharan musical life. Let's explore these in relation to a community dance, prevalent along the Pacific coasts of Ecuador and Colombia, called the *currulao*. The currulao features the entire community and includes the marimba, single-headed conical drums in two different sizes (male and female), two double-headed drums (bombos), and bamboo shakers. The performance is a chance for the community to dance and features marimba playing that follows a basic ostinato pattern, varying it with improvisatory material. The drums and rattles interlock with each other, setting up a dense rhythmic backdrop against which the marimba sounds and to which the dancers move. Over the top of all of this, a singer and female chorus lock into a call-and-response pattern. All of these musical characteristics (collective participation; ostinato; interlocking rhythms; and call-and-response singing) point to the enduring presence of African musical aesthetics within Ecuador and Colombia.

CURRULAO

Afro-Colombian, Afro-Ecuadorian dance context in the Pacific Coast region in which marimba is featured.

LISTENING GUIDE

MARIMBA DANCE: "CURRULAO BAMBUCO"

TRACK 10.4   **Two-person marimba, drums, shakers, male and female voices**
Recorded by N.E. Whitten in Buenaventura

YOU CAN CLEARLY hear the African influences on this recording of "Currulao Bambuco." The instruments play interlocking duple and triple rhythms; the vocal parts are organized in leader-chorus, call-and-response patterns; melodies and rhythms are based on short, repetitive phrases (ostinatos); and the vocal style features yodeling and other vocal sounds. The primary ostinato on which this piece is grounded is supplied by the marimba, which with some variations continues throughout the performance. As the performance progresses, a female lead vocalist takes over from the male lead singer who is heard early on.

The following reductions are designed to help you key in on the simultaneous presence of duple and triple meters and to hear it with reference to several of the instruments performing on this recording. The marimba and one of the drums play rhythmic patterns that fall into duple meter, whereas the shakers and a separate drum perform patterns that are best heard in triple meter. See if you can follow along with one instrument at a time, first counting it in duple and then counting it in triple while listening to the song.

Aligned in duple meter (6/8):

Count	**1**			**2**			**1**			**2**		
Beat	**1**	2	3	**4**	5	6	**1**	2	3	**4**	5	6
Marimba, duple		x	x	**X**		x		x	x	**X**		x
Drum, duple		x	x	**X**	x	x		x	x	**X**	x	x
Shaker, triple	**X**	x	**X**	x	**X**	x	**X**	x	**X**	x	**X**	x
Drum, triple	**X**		**X**		**X**		**X**		**X**		**X**	

Aligned in triple meter (3/4 within 6/8):

Count	**1**		**2**		**3**		**1**		**2**		**3**	
Beat	**1**	2	**3**	4	**5**	6	**1**	2	**3**	4	**5**	6
Marimba, duple		x	x	**X**		x		x	x	**X**		x
Drum, duple		x	x	**X**	x	x		x	x	**X**	x	x
Shaker, triple	**X**	x	**X**	x	**X**	x	**X**	x	**X**	x	**X**	x
Drum, triple	**X**		**X**		**X**		**X**		**X**		**X**	

continued

As this song develops, listen for the marimba, which supplies the basic ostinato: two short six-beat phrases (in 6/8 meter). One of the drums reinforces this duple feel. Notice also that the shakers emphasize a triple pattern. One of the drums strongly reinforces this triple feel. Attempt to hear the performance as unfolding in triple meter and tap your foot or hand in duple meter. Now try hearing the performance in duple meter and tap your foot in triple meter. See if you get one foot or hand to mark time in duple meter while the other foot or hand marks triple meter.

TIME	MUSICAL EVENT
0:00–0:04	The ensemble is already in full swing when the recording fades in.
0:04–0:16	A male vocalist enters, singing a short phrase, and a female chorus responds [0:08–16]. The male leader uses a falsetto voice often throughout the performance.
0:16–0:21	The vocalists give way to the instrumentalists.
0:21–0:32	The male singer rejoins the ensemble, and the female chorus responds [0:28–032].
0:32–0:44	The vocalists give way to the instrumentalists again.
0:44–0:57	The male singer rejoins the ensemble again and the female chorus responds [0:48–0:57].
0:57–1:03	The vocalists give way to the instrumentalists yet again.
1:03–1:14	The vocalist rejoins the ensemble, and the male-call and female-response patterns become shorter.
1:14–1:29	The female chorus introduces a new melodic motif in yodeling style.
1:29–1:45	A female vocalist enters and sings a series of short calls, and the female chorus quickly responds with the new yodeling motif.
1:45–2:15	The yodeled motif is repeated numerous times by the female vocalists, who introduce some subtle individual variations.
2:15–2:37	The female vocalist reenters and sings a series of short calls, and the female chorus quickly responds with the new yodeling motif.
2:37–2:52	The female chorus continues to perform the yodeled motif.
2:52–3:09	The female singer adds a new, higher variation over the rest of the female chorus, and the track fades out even as the performance continues.

But, as with most musical matters, the on-the-ground situation is much more complex than it first appears, and this is the case not least because the marimba has also become central to the musical life of Amerindian communities and mestizo communities throughout Central America, Ecuador, and Colombia. Like all of our excursions, we can see here how musical style, musical instruments, and even aesthetics habitually transcend ethnic and racial boundaries, spreading across communities and into new spaces.

Candombe

CANDOMBE
An Afro-Uruguayan music and dance complex.

Another example of African presence within Latin America is the celebration of *candombe* in Montevideo, Uruguay. First called candombe in 1830, it developed as an expressly African practice within a European space (slaves never exceeded 26 percent of the population). Until the turn of the twentieth century, candombe was performed by and for Afro-Uruguayans in spaces set apart for

Unidentified Candombe drummers participate in the Montevideo annual Carnaval, in Montevideo, Uruguay. *Source:* Kobby Dagan / Shutterstock.com

themselves and called salas. During the early twentieth century, the practice was gradually incorporated into the nation's carnival celebrations and emerged from the salas, being staged instead in the streets of Montevideo. The practice has long been understood as African and includes masking traditions, parading, dancing, and drumming. The whole group of revelers, including the dancers, masqueraders, and drummers, is called a **comparsa**. But, for our purposes, let's focus on the drumming, in particular. Candombe drum ensembles, called **llamadas**, are the backbone of any comparsa and are organized around three different instruments, including the *piano*, the *repique*, and the *chico*. The piano is the biggest of the drums and holds down the basic rhythm. The chico is the smallest of the drums and the highest in pitch. This drum plays counter-rhythms and locks into the rhythms of the piano. The repique improvises over the texture laid down by the other two drums. All of the drums are played with a stick in one hand and the other hand free, and llamadas can be as small or large as a given comparsa requires. So here we see again the deeply African sensibility of interlocking rhythms, rhythmic density, and collective participation.

By 1920, candombe had become institutionalized within carnival. The drums (llamadas) now led the comparsas to and from street stages (through the crowd) and these drums became increasingly important markers of the nation, and this not only for the Afro-Uruguayan community but also for Uruguayan popular culture more generally—but this did not occur without struggle. The 1950s saw the beginning of an economic decline within Uruguay, a decline that culminated in the coup of 1973. Unfortunately, the new leadership prohibited the llamadas from performing in their traditional neighborhoods, destroyed a

COMPARSA
The name given to the entire group of candombe revelers, including dancers, masqueraders, and drummers.

LLAMADA
The name given to the drum ensembles features in Uruguayan candombe.

great deal of the cultural history of the country (including black shrines), and generally attempted to control the comparsas as much as possible by relocating them to a street of its own choosing. During these difficult years, however, a new counterculture began to emerge, one that was envisioned around the image of exile within the country's borders. As it turns out, candombe became a touchstone for a wide range of Uruguayans, such that it became broadly useful for artists, composers, carnival performers, popular musicians, etc. No longer confined to carnival, artists and musicians of various stripes shared stages, re-worked materials together, and generally created a very different sense of what candombe might mean in Uruguay. Democracy was restored in 1985 and candombe has been an important, if still contested, part of the national imaginary every since (see www.candombe.com for a nice collection of materials on this music). Importantly, candombe has, since 2009, been recognized as part of the Intangible Cultural Heritage of Humanity by UNESCO, a fact that grants it an international standing that greatly reinforces its value at home.

Candomblé

We can also find African provenance in the sacred practices of many communities. For instance, if we consider *candomblé* in Brazil, we can see deep connections to African religious sensibilities and cosmology as well as musical connections that tie the two together. In Brazil, African deities are called *orixas* (Yoruba orisa or orisha) and each orixa is characterized by particular colors, songs, anecdotes, objects, animals, plants, and atmospheric phenomena. Each candomblé devotee has a relationship to a guardian orixa—an orixa that she receives while in trance. Importantly, each orixa is also identified with one or more catholic saints. This was initially strategically important in order to camouflage African beliefs and to give the impression that Afro-Brazilians were "good Catholics" within a colonial context that would not tolerate any other religious sensibilities. Since that time, Catholic and African ideas, symbols, and practices have continued to mingle and merge, and candomblé is, as such, an excellent example of syncretic (or mixed) religious practice. In this respect, candomblé shares much with s*antería* in Cuba and *shango* in Trinidad. Importantly, candomblé is not a singular, unified practice. It might, in fact, be better to think of candomblé as a complex that encompasses many branches (nations). These branches are distinguished from one another by language, ethnic histories (Yoruba, Fon, Bantu, etc.), particular rites, region within Brazil, etc., but they are all, nevertheless, considered part of the candomblé complex. In Salvador, Bahia, the Ketu (Yoruba) branch is most prevalent.

The music for candomblé ceremonies is extremely important because it summons the gods—without music, worship couldn't happen. Three drums, called *atabaques* in some but not all traditions within candomblé, are used in ceremonies, including, in order from biggest to smallest, the *rum*, *rumpi*, and *lé*. Drums used for ritual purposes are baptized shortly after they are made, dressed (adorned with beads, shells, cloth), and fed (chicken blood, oil, honey, holy water). In candomblé, the lowest-pitched, biggest drum (rum) plays the intricate parts, leaving the two smaller drums to hold down the basic groove.

Procession before the Lavagem, the washing of the steps of the Itapua church. *Source:* Godong/Getty Images

Two other instruments are part of candomblé music: the *agogo*, a double bell struck with a metal stick; and the *ague*, a rattle that is basically a big gourd containing cowries, pebbles, or dry seeds. During candomblé ceremonies, there is a continuous exchange between drummers and dancers, and the master drummer (who plays the rum) is always in control, leading the proceedings through the appropriate songs. Add to this the solo male voice and the female chorus, and you have the sound of candomblé rituals. The singers basically accompany the drums, not the other way around. Many of the songs use a **pentatonic** scale, and all of them use call-and-response, often with a bit of overlap between leader and chorus.

PENTATONIC
Having five pitches.

As you might expect by now, the music of candomblé has had a major influence on carnaval in Brazil. From the 1880s on, carnaval became a battle-ground, and this especially after emancipation in 1888. The black population would come out into the streets of Salvador during carnival, celebrating in large groups and playing on candomblé instruments: atabaque drums, agogos, and gourd shakers. Serious controversy erupted as a result but, by the 1920s, a distinct movement called street candomblé or *afoxe* (fronted by priests who could tell the future) was codified. A period of less active Africanization of carnaval was followed in the 1970s by a real effort to re-Africanize the carnaval. Parading groups like Filhos de Gandhy, Ile Aiye, and Olodum emerged and re-centered the drums in important ways and extended the reach of candomblé beyond carnival to other festivals as well.

All of these excursions within the Amerindian, European, and African musical contributions to the region, however, must be carefully tempered by the reality that individuals of European descent were, almost always, in a position to impose their worldview and politics on those around them. Occasionally slaves were able to escape and form communities of resistance (like Palenque de San Basilio in Colombia, for example) and, as we've seen, some Amerindian communities remained isolated within the Amazon region, but these were exceptions that proved the rule. As such, the music of Latin America has been shaped by official and middle- and upper-class approbation and, more commonly, disapprobation, just as those communities that have chosen to remain mindful of their own heritage have often suffered politically, economically, and socially at the hands of others. In the midst of these challenges, and in part because of them, many adaptations, mixtures, and experiments have become a major hallmark of the region's musical life.

Mestizaje/Mixture/Hybridity

This insight brings us to our third organizing theme—mestizaje. The term points to a mixture between European and Amerindian provenance. This could (and very regularly did) take the form of inter-racial coupling, producing mestizo offspring. But freed from its biological meanings, the term has also been applied to make sense of the significant impacts that such extended encounter between Amerindian and European people and their cultural practices engendered throughout the region. Music is, it turns out, a particularly fruitful area within which to explore, and hear such mixtures. Let's briefly explore just two examples.

Mariachi

MARIACHI
Ensemble type originally from Jalisco, Mexico, consisting of two or more violins, vihuela, guitarrón, two trumpets, and various guitars.

RANCHERA
A Mexican song genre with rural and working-class associations.

EXPLORE
Mariachi

The modern *mariachi* ensemble developed in Jalisco (a state bordering the Pacific in central Mexico) during the mid-nineteenth century. The repertoire is quite diverse, including *rancheras*, waltzes, polkas, cumbias, corridos, huapangas, and son jalisciense, among other styles. The presence of waltzes (Europe), cumbias (Colombia), and polkas (which probably entered with German immigrants coming from the United States) should bring to mind just how much the repertory of mariachi ensembles has been shaped in and through the history of mobility in and around the region. One of the ways of understanding what mariachi is, then, is as a type of ensemble as opposed to a type of musical style or genre. That said, mariachi does have a particular sound and is easily identified. A modern ensemble usually includes two trumpets, three or more violins, guitar, vihuela (a five-stringed guitar-like instrument with a rapid decay), and guitarrón (which is kind of acoustic bass guitar). The ensemble can be quite large in cases where the mariachi is putting on showcases at, say, restaurants or festivals, but all you really need is one of each of the above instruments in order to produce a mariachi sound. Eight musicians are often considered an ideal number.

The ensemble evolved over time. There is evidence that the trumpet and violins replaced older, indigenous instruments like flautas (flutes) and that the

Mexican traditional mariachi musician Isabel Aguilar poses with her group. *Source:* ALFREDO ESTRELLA/Getty Images

guitarrón replaced the Jaliscan harp (another Native American instrument) by about 1900. There is, in fact, some tension between those who would wish to champion the European instruments that have replaced the indigenous ones as a sure sign of progress and modernity and those who acknowledge that these very same instruments are not being played in the manner of European instruments at all—that the mariachi ensemble still embodies Amerindian aesthetics, regardless of instrumentation. The mestizo character of the mariachi, then, is an important—a crucial, and much debated—feature of the ensemble's composition.

The nationalist ideal of the ranchera, which was promoted starting in the 1930s, is enshrined within mariachi repertory and was reproduced in song and in film throughout the twentieth century. A great example of this focus on the ranchera is the career of actor/singer Pedro Infante, who sang and performed his way through some sixty movies during his career. Using metaphors of women to reference both actual, physical relationships as well as relationships to nation, land, and region is very common in the repertoire. Beauty is, however, often connected to Iberian ideals at the direct expense of Indigenous or mestizo beauty. The repertoire thus wrestles with the specter of Spain in both its instrumentation and in its lyrics, and ethnicity and race remains a major area of negotiation within the mariachi complex. One more dimension worth thinking about here is a prominent rhythmic feature common across much of the mariachi repertory—the *compás*. This term refers to a rhythmic gesture, spread across two equal halves, that shifts the accent patterns to create syncopation. You can think of it as an approach to generating a triple over duple feel. The syncopation that results from the application of compás is called *sesquialtera* (see Listening Guide).

COMPÁS
Within Mexican traditional musics a rhythmic gesture, spread across two equal halves, that shifts the accent patterns to create syncopation.

SESQUIALTERA
The combination/juxtaposition of duple and triple rhythmic patterns, both simultaneously in different instrumental parts, or sequentially in the same part, hemiola.

MARIACHI: "LA MALAGUENA"

 **LISTEN**

TRACK 10.5 **Performed by Nati Cano's Mariachi Los Camperos**
Vocalist, vihuela, guitarrón, violins, trumpets

THIS RECORDING OFFERS a good example of the ensemble sound, singing style, and aesthetics of mariachi groups. In this performance, the singer is lamenting the fact that a beautiful woman "La Malaguena" is ignoring his advances—a fact that is leaving him lovelorn. The vocalist's consistent use of falsetto throughout the song helps to convey his pain and his longing for reciprocated interest. The performance is also a good example of a rhythmic feature called sesquialtera. Sesquialtera is created by the fact that both 3/4 (triple) and 2/4 (duple) rhythms are present at the same time. The easiest way to hear this is to listen for the (relatively consistent) eighth-note strumming pattern (also called a compás) established by the vihuela and then attempt to count it in both meters. The strumming pattern can be sketched as follows, with the "x" indicating the muted, percussion-like sound of the strings being struck but prevented from vibrating.

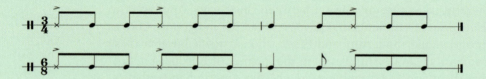

TIME	SECTION	MUSICAL EVENT/LYRICS
0:00–0:24	Introduction	During this introduction listen for the vihuela strumming pattern and notice also the other instruments involved: several violins as well as a lead violin, and the guitarrón (the bass instrument).
0:24–1:03	Verse 1	Listen for the singer's use of falsetto and for the first entrance of the trumpets at 0:35.
1:03–1:13	Transition to slower, more deliberate tempo	Listen for how clear the vihuela strumming pattern becomes as the tempo slows. See if you can follow along with the patterns above and hear it within the context of 3/4 and 6/8 meter.
1:13–1:47	Verse 2	The slower tempo and new melodic material in this section allow the singer to incorporate even more falsetto into his performance. Listen also for the way that the trumpets occasionally add their voices to the mix.
1:47–3:43	Chorus	Continue listening for the falsetto technique of the vocalist and consider the degree to which the vocalist, singing about his desire for the woman from Malaga, infuses his performance with a depth of emotion that you can hear.

Wayno (Huayno)

In Peru and throughout a good portion of the Andean region, *wayno* is ensconced as the most important mestizo genre. The ensemble (which accompanies a fast couples dance), along with the aesthetics animating the music, offers another great example of the extent to which hybridity and mixture permeate Latin American music. Several aspects of the wayno predate the colonial encounter, including some of the instruments employed, as well as some of the performing aesthetics (vocal quality, in particular). So, indigenous flutes, Andean harps, and bombas (see section on Aymara music) are all prominently present within wayno ensembles. Vocally, the timbre and quality is high-pitched and tense, reflecting Andean aesthetics. But the region's long history of contact with European musical ideas has found important markers of the genre incorporated from that stream as well. Guitars, mandolins, accordions, lutes, and violins, among other instruments, variously add their voices to the overall texture of the ensemble. This mestizo ensemble is simply called an orquesta típica. Wayno has also adopted the popular strophic form (two-, three-, or four-line texts over short, repeating melodic sections) from European models, resulting in strophes with *AABB* or *ABAB* melodic structures. The lyrics, usually centered on

EXPLORE

Wayno/Huayno

LISTENING GUIDE

WAYNO (HUAYNO): "QUISIERA OLVIDARTE"

 **LISTEN**

TRACK 10.6 **Performed by La Pastorita Huaracina (Maria Alvarado)**

THIS CLASSIC RECORDING was a hit record in Peru and is representative of the commercial wayno music that gained tremendous popularity in the 1950s and 1960s. Maria Alvarado, a long-time resident of Lima, is accompanied by a string band in the style of her native highland department of Ancash. The group comprises several guitars, mandolins, violins, and accordions. This is a strophic song in **AA BB′** form, with an animated closing section known as *fuga* (labeled Section **C**, melodic phrases **e** and **f**). Each section comprises two short phrases (**A = a, b; B = c, d; B′ = c, d′**) and each phrase features its own text line. The length of these phrases is also important to note. The **A** Section contains two asymmetrical phrases (4+6) whereas the **B** section includes two symmetrical phrases (4+4). Section **B′** is once again asymmetrical (4+6). The ensemble adds a three-beat extension to several of the phrases. The phrase structure of verse one can be sketched as follows:

Section:	**A**			**A**			**B**		**B′**		
Phrase:	**a**	**b**	Ext.	**a**	**b**	Ext.	**c**	**d**	**c**	**d′**	Ext.
Beats:	4	6	3	4	6	3	4	4	4	6	3

continued

Once the performance reaches the fuga, the length of phrases changes yet again. This time the predominant length is three beats. The fuga unfolds as follows:

Section:	C		C′	
Phrase:	e	f	e	f′
Beats:	3	3	3	4

Note the quick, high vocal ornaments (e.g., on the words "*he* podido" and "mald*i*to" so characteristic of highland women singers). Note also the humorous insults hurled at her lover in the final lines of the fuga.

TIME	SECTION	MUSICAL EVENTS		
0:00–0:08	**Instrumental introduction**	The performance is initiated by guitar.		
0:09–0:15		The ensemble joins the guitar in preparation for the first verse.		
0:16–0:23	**Verse 1**: Listen for the over-arching structure (**AA BB′**). Listen also for the way the **"b"** and **"d′"** phrases are extended by the ensemble.	A	**(a)** *Quisiera olvidarte* **(b)** *Pero no he podido*	(I would like to forget you). (but I can't)
0:24–0:31		A repeated.		
0:31–0:35		B	**(c)** *Este amor maldito* **(d)** *Rendida me tiene*	(This wicked love) (has conquered me)
0:36–0:43		B′ (lyrics repeated).		
0:44–1:11	**Instrumental interlude:** Listen for a repeat of the entire melody, including the extensions at the end of phrases **"b"** and **"d."**	AA BB′ Notice the words, clapping, and vocal sounds of animation included here. This is how it would be done to inspire dancers.		
1:12–1:20	**Verse 2**: This time, see if you can hear the way the **"b"** and **"d′"** phrases are extended by the ensemble.	A	**(a)** *Quisiera morirme* **(b)** *Para no olvidarte*	(I would like to die) (rather than forget you)
1:20–1:27		A repeated.		
1:27–1:32		B	**(c)** *Luego sepultarme* **(d)** *Dentro de tu pecho*	(then bury myself) (in your chest)
1:32–1:39		B′ (lyrics repeated).		
1:40–1:43	**Fuga section begins**: Listen for the shift to three-beat phrases and for the new melodic content.	C	**(e)** *Anda vete cholo* **(f)** *Ya no te quiero mas*	(Go away boy) (I don't love you anymore)
1:43–1:47		C′	**(e)** *Por más que te quiero* **(f)** *Te haces de rogar*	(For me to love you) (you will have to beg)

continued

TIME	SECTION	MUSICAL EVENTS	
1:47–1:51		**C** repeated.	
1:51–1:54		**C'** repeated.	
1:55–2:10	**Instrumental interlude**: Listen for a performance and repeat of the entire fuga melody.	**CC' CC'** (repeated). Notice the words, clapping, and vocal sounds of animation included here. This is how it would be done to inspire dancers.	
2:10–2:13	**Fuga section with new lyrics**	**C** **(e)** *Anda vete cholo* **(f)** *Ya no te quiero mas*	(Go away boy) (I don't love you anymore)
2:13–2:18		**C'** **(e)** *Por más que te quiero* **(f')** *Te haces de rogar*	(For me to love you) (you will have to beg)
2:18–2:21		**C** **(e)** *Anda vete sucio* **(f)** *Ya no te quiero mas*	(Go away dirtyboy) (I don't want you anymore)
2:21–2:33		**C'** **(e)** *Hasta que te bañes* **(f)** *Ya no te vuelvo querer*	(Until you take a bath) (I couldn't return to loving you)

humorous, romantic, or political topics, are rendered in Quechua or in Spanish, further underscoring the Amerindian and European contributions to the genre.

Rhythmically, wayno is distinguished by a pattern that varies between an eighth-and-two-sixteenth-note figure and an eighth note triplet within a two- or four-beat measure. An extra beat is often added at the end of phrases, creating a very distinctive and asymmetrical phrase structure (see listening example). Taken as a whole, the sound of the ensemble and the structure of the songs have absorbed influences from both Amerindian and European sources, making of wayno an expressly mestizo practice.

Vallenato

But mixture isn't confined to the binary of Amerindian and European cultural provenance. In fact, African instruments and aesthetics have consistently been incorporated into musical practices throughout Latin America, and I offer just one excursion here in order to move beyond specifically mestizo musics and toward a consideration of hybridity. *Vallenato* is a genre characterized by a history of mixture, in this case combining elements of African, Amerindian, and European contributions within its sound. For our purposes, let's call it a hybrid genre. The popular version of the genre gained world prominence during the early 1990s and, in 1996, it was even awarded its own Grammy category. But the genre has a much longer history. It's contemporary form started to develop in the 1940s within the Caribbean coastal region of Colombia (La Costa). According to the origin myth of the genre, carefully cultivated during the middle years of the twentieth century and tied to literary magical realism in complicated

VALLENATO
A traditional music of Colombia that has also found expression as popular music since the middle of the twentieth century.

 **EXPLORE**
Vallenato

but significant ways (see Ana Maria Ochoa), this style was originally played in rural areas. The ensembles of the mid-nineteenth century included European-derived instruments like the guitar, and instruments of Amerindian and African provenance such as the *gaita* (indigenous flute), *guacharaca* (a bamboo scraper), and *caja* (drum). The modern ensemble came into focus around the turn of the twentieth century, when the three-row button accordion was incorporated into the sound. The modern folk ensemble consists of the three-row button accordion, a *caja*, and the *guacharaca*. Primarily a dance genre, it was popularly played at parties, but also at parrandas, which were basically big festivals with lots of dancing and competitions. The repertory played by vallenato ensembles can be grouped into four main categories and two distinct metric groupings: The son and the paseo operate within a duple-meter framework. The son is generally slower and characterized by a "long/short/rest" bass pattern with heavy emphasis on the downbeat. The paseo, for its part, emerged in the middle of the twentieth century and features romantic, nostalgic, and/or regional lyrics. Within a triple-meter framework the merengue (not to be confused with a genre by the same name popular in the Dominican Republic) and the puya are common. The puya is, more often than not, a vehicle for displaying extreme virtuosity. Performers play very fast, incredibly complicated melodies and rhythmic patterns on their respective instruments during these showpieces.

A gradual move into urban centers since the middle of the twentieth century has created a popular version of vallenato, and these ensembles tend to include electric bass, one or two guitars (acoustic and electric), and drum kits, in addition to the traditional instruments of accordion, guacharaca, and caja. This popular form of the genre, though consistently maligned by traditionalists, has thrived, with the 1980s and 1990s witnessing the style's emergence into the international prominence. Carlos Vives is largely responsible for bringing the style to these new markets, fusing traditional vallenato with other genres such as rock, funk, and R&B to create a fusion that appeals to a wider base of fans. Vallenato, then, is a great example of a genre hybrid in its very creation and continuously exploring new mixtures and possibilities in its popular forms.

Urbanization

Vallenato offers a great example of hybridity, but it could just as easily have served as a case study within this chapter's final section on urbanization. After all, the popular version of the genre is characterized by a major move from rural to urban spaces and reflects these shifts in both sound and markets. In the pages that follow, I offer three case studies of urbanization, illustrating through them the immense changes that continue to play out within urban spaces throughout the region.

Forró

Forró emerged into the national imagination within Brazil in part because of rural to urban migration, and in part because the rather decentralized and vast Brazilian state was attempting to find its way toward a more centralized mode of engagement across the entire nation. A northeast to south migration from the mid-twentieth century saw a great many people moving from places like the *sertão* and the state of Bahia to the big cities of like Rio de Janeiro and São Paulo. In fact, Rio doubled in size between 1920 and 1950—in the space of just three decades, the city grew from approximately 1.2 million to 2.4 million, and many of these newcomers hailed from less developed and less urbanized areas around Brazil. As a consequence, Northeastern stereotypes grew up around these migrations. That said, Northeastern styles were already a part of the musical landscape in Rio. Artists and composers like Pixinguinha, Villa Lobos, João Pernambuco, and many others were playing Northeastern rhythms and singing about the region in their choros. Choro is a genre incorporating both composed and improvised material and was played in an ensemble that was quite fluid. Early on, the ensemble included flute, *cavaquinho* (like a ukulele and used as a strumming instrument), and guitar. This genre was pretty well established by the turn of the twentieth century. In the early years of the twentieth century, the ensemble was rounded out with mandolin, *violão* (tenor guitar), and *pandeiro* (tamourine/frame drum). These days, however, the violão is not much used. Many ensembles now use an additional, seven-string guitar for better bass lines. At any rate, these initial, nineteenth- and early-twentieth-century experiments with Northeastern lyrics and sounds met with some success.

In the 1930s, the Getúlio Vargas government, which was trying to centralize power, mounted a campaign against the political strength of the outlying regions. But, in the process of centralizing power, the Vargas government also needed to present a national face. In order to create this national narrative (Brazil: unified but diverse), the administration actively mobilized culture and folklore. Ironically, at the very moment that political power was being stripped from places like the Northeast, the roots of Brazilian culture were also being invented and then presented to the nation by drawing on and showcasing the Northeast's folklore and folk culture. This project was aggressively pursued through radio broadcasts featuring regional performances starting in the 1930s. It was within this political and cultural environment that several musicians were able to establish a new imaginary (mythical and thoroughly unnuanced) of the Northeast for the nation. On the one hand was the popular musician Dorival Caymmi, who traded on his Northeastern authenticity (he hailed from Bahia) in order to establish himself and his sound (a guitar-based samba feel). In the process of establishing his own career, however, he also helped solidify certain stereotypes in the Southeast about Northeastern culture. In his case, he traded on West African cultural heritage, erotic delights (the mulata), tropical languor, and general bliss in spite of poverty. He communicated these ideas through his lyrics, self-representation, and the iconic materials he chose for album covers and promotional materials (photos of him chilling out in a hammock by the beach, for instance). Caymmi offered a compromise that brought Northeast and Southeast together through samba.

On the other hand was Luiz Gonzaga, who came from the interior of the Northeast—from the sertão. He too, traded on his regional roots, reinforcing through his music stereotypes of the sertão, including hardship, rugged self-sufficiency, tendencies to banditry, and religious fanaticism. Gonzaga hit on a

EXPLORE

Samba

rhythm that was generically called baião and which made a big impression among his audiences in Rio. He sold his musical style, called forró, on radio shows, in concert, and on record. In the sertão, this music was traditionally played by ensembles for dances called *forrobodó* (great dances/parties) and, as we've seen elsewhere, these ensembles were quite flexible. The basic ensemble tended to include only an eight-bass accordion (called *oito baixos* or *sanfona*), a *zabumba* (two-headed drum played with a mallet in one hand [bass] and a thin stick in the other [treble]), and a triangle. Other instruments could include snare drums and flutes (small, six-hole, transverse instruments called *pífanos*). Gonzaga regularly recorded songs featuring the baião rhythm (also a designation for an accompanying dance) which, at its most basic, consists of a dotted eighth note followed by a sixteenth note and a quarter rest in 2/4 time. But there are, in fact, three main types of dances associated with forró: the xóte (the slowest of the three); the baião (medium tempo and with the characteristic rhythm very foregrounded); and the Arrasta-Pé (the fastest, with an almost polka-like feel).

The emergence of forró as a national genre within Brazil (along with the stereotypes it reinforced about the sertão) is directly related to the political need for centralization, to the economic need of so many laborers to relocate to urban centers, and to the ability of radio to create solidarities (i.e., listeners nostalgic for home) and imagined communities (Brazil as a unified nation). Urbanization puts new pressures on communities even as it opens up new opportunities and possibilities. In the case of forró, individual artists were able to capitalize on the tastes of a very large community of recently relocated workers from the Northeast and simultaneously tap into a new market of "local" listeners who were ready to hear regionally specific sounds.

Nortec

EXPLORE

Nortec

In contrast to forró, which thrived in a moment of intense rural to urban migration and national consolidation, let's explore the development of *nortec* in the Mexican border city of Tijuana during the late 1990s. Nortec can be read as a response to the failures of urbanization—as a creative rethinking of an urban environment historically plagued by poverty, transient labor, drugs, and tourism. Emerging toward the end of the 1990s, nortec rose to popularity and rather spectacular success by combining sounds from rural Mexico with techno and eletronica. This rather unorthodox combination of musical components worked in part because of the city's history, and in part because of the vision that accompanied the music. As Alejandro Madrid has pointed out, nortec as "sound" is only one part of a much larger artistic endeavor, involving art, architecture, and style.

Conceptually nortec is a new engagement with age-old questions of border relations, industrial architecture, cityscapes, and tradition. Nortec basically turns a generally negative set of stereotypes inside out, refiguring and reimagining them and offering an ironic but hopeful blend of symbols in the process. Musically, this takes the form of blending musical markers from norteño and the bandas sinaolenses with the most cutting-edge techniques of

Members of the band
Nortec Collective perform
during the Sabrosura Concert
Los Angeles. *Source:* JC
Olivera/Getty Images

live electronic dance music. But it is also a project that takes on the visual arts and architecture, along with style. So, guns and cowboy hats, old warehouses and abandoned buildings, mustaches and cowboy boots—all of these are reconfigured in a positive light as markers of identity within nortec. It is because of this careful balance between music, art, and architecture, all coalescing around this philosophical and audio-visual approach, that nortec achieved its success. The song "Odyssea" became a hit in the UK in 2000 and the song launched nortec into a wide range of transnational spaces.

Musically nortec is a dance genre, performed with both live and sampled sounds. The sounds and rhythms that characterize nortec are gathered from norteño music, from bandas sinaloenses, and from techno/electronica. Turning to the sounds of banda highlights the connections between Sinaloa and Tijuana (drug growing and drug trans-shipping). And the inclusion of norteño makes explicit the fact that nortec, like norteño is all about the experience of living in a border region, an experience shared by those living in Tijuana. A group of artists and producers, now known as the Nortec Collective, explored how to feature the accordion and **bajo sexto**, instrumental hallmarks of norteño bands, along with the tubas, trombones, *tarolas* (snare drums), and *tamboras* (bass drums) of the bandas sinaloenses, within a dance groove informed by techno and electronica. Blending samples with live instruments, they created a sound that juxtaposed rural and urban sounds, electronic and acoustic instruments, and live and sampled performances, thus highlighting the junctures and disjunctures of life in Tijuana. Actively turning negative stereotypes of the city and the border region into positive markers of space and place, nortec offers a counter narrative (if not a solution) to the challenges of urbanization.

BAJO SEXTO
A twelve-string guitar used in
Mexican norteño music.

CUMBIA
A Colombian traditional music combining Amer-indian, African, and European musical ideas and instruments. It has, since the middle of the twentieth century also become an internationally important popular music.

Cumbia

As a final example, let's take a closer look at **cumbia**. Many of the genres we considered in this chapter are obviously informed by several (perhaps even all) of our guiding themes, even though I chose to focus our conversations around a primary theme in each case. That said, cumbia affords a great opportunity to think about how these themes can combine in a single genre—an excursion that will also remind us just how complex all of the musical practices we've explored really are. The style, developed in and around the Caribbean coastal region of Colombia during the nineteenth and early twentieth centuries, has, in recent decades, become a transnational phenomenon. Mexico has become a premier site of production for the genre, and Peru and Chile have found it useful, modifying it to their aesthetic needs along the way. It continues to inform the popular music scene throughout the region and a brief history will offer some context for the genre's popularity.

Like tango, cumbia came into its own as a transnational genre once it reached a major urban area—a history that speaks to the importance of urbanization and various types of mobility. But cumbia's early history helps us understand the extent to which the genre is informed by our other two themes—race/ethnicity and hybridities. With these ideas in mind, let's briefly review some of the genre's history. Cumbia developed in the Caribbean lowlands of Colombia. The exact degree of African and Amerindian influence on early cumbia remains a matter of debate for scholars but, for our purposes, the important issue here is that the genre was, from very early on, an amalgam or mixture of African and Amerindian musical ideas. So, starting in the nineteenth century, during which time it was practiced as a courtship dance, the ensembles came to be characterized by drums, maraca (a gourd shaker), and *gaitas*. The drums come in three sizes with different, interlocking roles: the large *tambora* (which plays a long-short-short pattern on the wood of the drum, accented by a strokes on the drum head at regular intervals); the medium-sized *tambor alegre* (responsible for counter rhythms and improvisations); and the smaller *tambor llamador* (which plays consistently on the off-beats and gives a reference against which the other drums align themselves). All of this was organized within a duple-meter framework (most often 2/4). This percussion ensemble was augmented by indigenous flutes, called gaitas, which are long duct-flutes that are played in gendered pairs—the six-hole female (hembra) and two-hole male (macho). A great contemporary exponent of traditional cumbia is Totó La Momposina, whose recordings are readily available on YouTube and streaming services, and another important group is the ensemble called Los Gaiteros de San Jacinto.

As a working class and rural music, it was initially quite maligned by Colombian elites, but as urbanization began to affect the coastal region of Colombia, cumbia made its journey to the cities, taking on many new instruments and influences and eventually gaining recognition from both national and international audiences in the process. By the 1940s, cumbia had acquired a whole new, hybrid sound, though many of the rhythms that hold traditional cumbia together continued to characterize the genre. For a while the sound turned

EXPLORE

Gaita

LISTENING GUIDE

"FUEGO DE CUMBIA
(CUMBIA FIRE)"

LISTEN

TRACK 10.7 **Los Gaiteros de San Jacinto**

THIS RECORDING IS an excellent example of traditional cumbia music. The ensemble features two gaitas, three drums (more on these below), and maraca (a gourd shaker) plus vocals. The lyrics reflect on the racial complexities of the genre, making reference to Amerindian and African contributions to the cumbia and claiming it as a cultural heritage. The lead singer of the band, Rafael Pérez García, sings the following during the first verse:

Se encienden noches oscuras	Dark nights light up in fire
Como un jolgorio que encanta.	like a feast that enchants.
Los repiques de tambores,	The beating of the drums,
La raza negra levanta,	the black race rises up,
Y el indio pasivamente	and the Indian, passively
Con su melódica gaita,	with his melodic *gaita,*
Interrumpen el silencio	interrupt the silence
Cuando una fogata baila,	when a bonfire dances,
Y yo siento por mi venas	and I feel through my veins
Un fuego que no se apaga.	a fire that goes unquenched.
Es el fuego de mi cumbia;	It is the fire of my *cumbia;*
Es el fuego de mi raza:	It is the fire of my race:
Un fuego de sangre pura,	A fire of pure blood,
Que con lamentos se canta.	Sung in laments.

The three drums interlock with each other, each having a distinct role to play in the performance. The tambora (bass drum) is a double-headed drum played with two sticks. The performer plays a long-short-short pattern on the frame of the drum with the sticks and punctuates this pattern with strokes on the drum head at the end of each measure. The tambor llamador (calling drum) is the smallest (but not the highest-pitched) of the drums and plays a steady pattern on the off-beats so that the other performers can orient themselves around its sound. The tambor alegre (lively drum) is the most improvisatory of the drums, often interacting with the gaitas and the vocalist, and able to create a wide variety of tones and timbres depending on the techniques the performer applies to each stroke. Both the tambor llamador and the tambor alegre are played with hands not sticks. Added to this is the maraca, which plays a long-short-short pattern in support of the stick-work of the tambora. Over this rhythmic foundation, the gaitas coordinate repeating motives into a melodic groove.

TIME	SECTION	MUSICAL EVENT/LYRICS
0:00–0:07	Vocal Call	The vocalist sings the last two lines of the chorus to introduce the melodic contours of the piece and the lyrical themes that will be addressed.

continued

TIME	SECTION	MUSICAL EVENT/LYRICS
0:07–0:46	Instrumental Introduction	Led by the gaitas, the ensemble enters and establishes the melodic and rhythmic context. Listen here for the way one flute (the gaita hembra) plays a melody and the other plays the role of harmonic support and countermelody (the gaita macho). One is more active, the other a bit more restricted, allowing you to hear the fact that the gaita hembra has six holes and more possibilities as a result, whereas the gaita macho is more restricted because it only has two holes.
0:46–1:22	Verse 1	Listen for the way the vocals match the gaita hembra's melody. Also listen for the short instrumental interlude that sets up the chorus (1:17–1:22).
1:22–1:51	Chorus	Listen here for the alternation of lead vocalist, instrumental response, chorus repeat of the last two lines of text, and the instrumental response.
1:51–2:10	Instrumental interlude	Listen here for the drum that's playing most rapidly and improvising during the interlude. That is the sound of the tambor alegre.
2:10–2:45	Verse 2	Although the vocalist is now singing again, listen for the sticks and the maraca, noticing the long-short-short pattern that they are consistently playing. See if you can hear the lowest pitched drum regularly punctuating the long-short-short cycles. That is the voice of the tambora. Notice again the short instrumental interlude before the chorus (2:41–2:45).
2:45–3:14	Chorus	Listen here for the alternation of lead vocalist, instrumental response, chorus repeat of the last two lines of text, and the instrumental response. This time it should sound familiar and you should be able to anticipate the interactions between the ensemble and the vocalist/chorus.
3:14–3:51	Instrumental interlude	Notice that the gaita hembra takes center stage during this interlude, soloing and improvising around the established melody.
3:51–4:26	Verse 3	Listen here for utterly consistent stroke on the off-beat by the tambor llamada. Notice how it locks in with the maraca and the sticks, falling in the middle of the long-short-short cycle. And, again, be aware of the way the instruments provide the transition from verse to chorus (4:22–4:26).
4:26–5:26	Chorus	Listen now for the whole ensemble and how it fits together sonically. Notice that the chorus is extended here, with the chorus singing the last two lines of text two times, and the lead singer completing the song with an elongated, last repeat of those lines.

toward big band (that sound was everywhere during the 1940s and 1950s and radio was alive with these sounds). But ensembles with large brass sections were eventually trimmed down and electrified in the 1960s and 1970s. One of the most characteristic aspects of expressions within this more electric and urban cumbia is the bass-line, which often plays a half note followed by two quarter notes (long, short, short) thereby imitating the basic tambora part. Another marker is the highly accented cymbal/shaker/scraper work on 2 and 4 of each measure, which mirrors the role of the tambor llamador. By the 1960s, elements of salsa begin to find their way into cumbia, too. One of the most obvious of these is the piano part, which often plays an arpeggiated montuno pattern.

All of these changes to the traditional cumbia began to translate into new audiences, and the genre made a highly successful transition from traditional to popular music during these decades. As you can imagine, the rise of cumbia did not sit all that well with the elites, who found the dance too sensual and the music too lowbrow. But, radio made a huge difference and, by the 1960s, Discos Fuentes (the first Colombian record label) was disseminating the latest recordings at a rapid clip. This forced a change of attitude and cumbia has since become a major marker of the Colombian national imagination.

But some of the most interesting developments in cumbia since the mid-1960s have occurred outside of Colombia itself. This is the case not least because cumbia has achieved a level of mobility as great as or greater even than salsa, garnering vast fan bases in virtually every corner of Latin America. During the 1960s, cumbia made a journey to Mexico City, where it came to influence the recording industry in profound ways. Even as cumbia was conquering the popular music industry in Mexico City, it was expanding into Peru, Chile, and Argentina. In Peru, in particular, the genre was adopted and then merged with local Andean wayno to create a sub-style called chicha. And as cumbia continued to find new spaces within Latin America, it continued to inspire local versions. During the last few decades of the twentieth century, a whole range of sub-styles developed (including Argentine *cumbia villera*, Peruvian *tecnocumbia*, and Chilean "sound," to name just a few). So we see in cumbia a genre that requires us to think about it using all of the themes under discussion in this chapter in order to understand how it has developed and its significance around the region.

**REVIEW
CHAPTER
RESOURCES**

SUMMARY

This chapter has, of course, only explored the tiniest fraction of the diversity and richness of Latin American music. Even those genres I have managed to include in our excursions have only been introduced in rather schematic fashion. It is my hope, however, that the sounds and ideas you've encountered in this chapter will lead you to dig more deeply into the region's musical life—that you will be compelled to continue learning more about Latin American music. Although mobility, race/ethnicity, mixture/mestizaje/hybridity, and urbanization are particularly appropriate themes around which to organize our journeys through the region's musical landscapes, you'll no doubt find that they work quite well to think about musical communities in other regions of the world as well. I encourage you to take these themes and use them as a means for comparison across different musical contexts.

These themes also give you an opportunity to think about your own subject position. How does your own mobility inform your musical choices? What impact does your own race/ethnicity play in opening up sonic possibilities and how might this help you generate insights about yourself or the music you are listening to/making? What role (if any) does the concept of mestizaje or

KEY TERMS

Aymara
Candombe
Candomblé
Cumbia
Currulao
Ethnicity
Forró
Gaita
Hybridity
Mariachi
Mestizaje
Mobility
Nortec
Race
Salsa
Sesquialtera
Suyá
Tango
Urbanization
Vallenato

hybridity play in your own musical life? And, finally, how does your own geographic history (rural, urban) inform your musical horizons? In the process of answering these questions, you might find that you are drawn into new relationships to the sounds you encountered in this chapter and, for that matter, throughout this textbook.

BIBLIOGRAPHY

General Gerard Béhague, "Folk and Traditional Music of Latin America: General Prospect and Research Problems," *The World of Music* 25/2 (1982). Dale A. Olsen, "Folk Music of South America—a Musical Mosaic," in Elizabeth May, Ed., *Musics of Many Cultures: An Introduction* (Berkeley, CA: University of California Press, 1980). Dale A. Olsen and Daniel E. Sheehy, Eds., *The Garland Encyclopedia of World Music, vol. 2: South America, Mexico, Central America, and the Caribbean* (New York: Garland Publishing, 1998). Dale A. Olsen and Daniel Sheehy, Eds., *The Garland Handbook of Latin American Music* (New York: Routledge, 2008). John M. Schechter, Ed., *Music in Latin American Culture: Regional Traditions* (New York: Schirmer Books, 1999).

Highland Indigenous and Mestizo Music Max Peter Baumann, Ed., "Music of the Indios in Bolivia's Andean Highlands (survey)," *World of Music* 25/2 (1982). Robert Garfias, "The Marimba of Mexico and Central America," *Latin American Music Review* 4/2 (1983). Karl Gustav Izikowitz, *Musical and Other Sound Instruments of the South American Indians* (Göteborg, Sweden: Elanders Boktrycheri Aktiebolag, 1934). Zoila Mendoza, *Shaping Society Through Dance: Mestizo Ritual Performance in the Peruvian Andes* (Chicago, IL: University of Chicago Press, 2000). Manuel Peña, *The Texas-Mexican Conjunto: History of a Working-Class Music* (Austin, TX: University of Texas Press, 1985). Raul Romero, *Debating the Past: Music, Memory, and Identity in the Andes* (New York: Oxford University Press, 2001). John Schechter, *The Indispensable Harp: Historical Development, Modern Roles, Configurations, and Performance Practices in Ecuador and Latin America* (Kent, OH: Kent State Press, 1991). Helena Simonett, *Banda: Mexican Musical Life Across Borders* (Middletown, CT: Wesleyan University Press, 2001). Thomas Stanford, "The Mexican Son," *Yearbook of the IFMC* (1972). Robert Stevenson, *In Aztec and Inca Territory* (Berkeley, CA: University of California Press, 1968). David Stigberg, "Jarocho, Tropical, and 'Pop': Aspects of Musical Life in Veracruz, 1971–1972," in Bruno Nettl, Ed., *Eight Urban Musical Cultures* (Urbana, IL: University of Illinois Press, 1978). Henry Stobart, *Music and the Poetics of Production in the Bolivian Andes* (Aldershot, UK: Ashgate, 2006). Thomas Turino, *Moving Away from Silence: Music of the Peruvian Altiplano and the Experience of Urban Migration* (Chicago, IL: University of Chicago Press, 1993).

Amazonian Cultures Jonathan David Hill, *Made-from-Bone: Trickster Myths, Music, and History from the Amazon* (Urbana, IL: University of Illinois, 2009). Anthony Seeger, *Why Suyá Sing: A Musical Anthropology of an Amazonian People* (Cambridge: Cambridge University Press, 1987). Anthony Seeger, "What Can We Learn When They Sing? Vocal Genres of the Suyá Indians of Central Brazil," *Ethnomusicology* 23/3 (1979): 373–394.

African Traditions Gerard Béhague, "Patterns of Candomblé Music Performance: An Afro-Brazilian Religious Setting," in Gerard Béhague, Ed., *Performance Practice: Ethnomusicological Perspectives* (Westport, CT: Greenwood, 1984). Timothy Brennan, *Secular Devotion: Afro-Latin Music and Imperial Jazz* (New York: Verso, 2008). Harold Courlander, "Musical Instruments of Cuba," *Musical Quarterly* 28 (1942). Luis Heitor Correa de Azevedo, "Music and Musicians of African Origin in Brazil," *World of Music* 25/2 (1982). Larry Crook, "A Musical Analysis of the Cuban Rumba," *Latin American Music Review* 3/1 (1982). Alma Guillermoprieto, *Samba* (New York: Vintage Press, 1990). Katherine J. Hagedorn, *Divine Utterances: The Performance of Afro-Cuban Santeria* (Washington, DC: Smithsonian Institution Press, 2001). Peter Manuel, *Popular Musics of the Non-Western World* (New York: Oxford University Press, 1988). Peter Manuel, Ed., *Essays on Cuban Music: North American and Cuban Perspectives* (Lanham, MD: University Press of America, 1991). Chris McGowan and Ricardo Pessanha, *The Brazilian Sound: Samba, Bossa Nova, and the Popular Music of Brazil* (Philadelphia, PA: Temple University Press, 2009). Robin D. Moore, *Nationalizing Blackness: Afrocubanismo and Artistic Revolution in Havana, 1920–1940* (Pittsburgh, PA: University of Pittsburgh Press, 1997). Charles A. Perrone, *Masters of Contemporary Brazilian Song: MPB 1965–1985* (Austin, TX: University of Texas Press, 1989). Alison Raphael, "From Popular Culture to Microenterprise: The History of Brazilian Samba Schools," *Latin American Music Review* 11(1), 1990. Susan Thomas, *Cuban Zarzuela: Performing Race and Gender on Havana's Lyric Stage* (Urbana, IL: University of Illinois, 2009). Norman E. Whitten, Jr. and C. Aurelio Fuentes, *Black Frontiersmen: A South American Case* (New York: Schenkman, 1974).

DISCOGRAPHY

Highland Indigenous and Mestizo *Mountain Music of Peru*, vol. 2 (Smithsonian Folkways CD 40406). *Musik im Andenhochland/Bolivien* (Museum Collection Berlin [West] MC 14). *Huayno Music of Peru*, vol. 1 (Arhoolie CD 320). *The Inca Harp: Laments and Dances of the Tawantinsuyu, the Inca Empire* (Lyrichord LLST 7359). *Your Struggle Is Your Glory: Songs of Struggle, Huayno and Other Peruvian Music* (Arhoolie 3025). *Kingdom of the Sun: Peru's Inca Heritage* (Nonesuch H-72029). *Music of Peru* (Folkways FE 4415). *Mexico: Fiestas of Chiapas and Oaxaca* (Nonesuch H-72070). *Texas-Mexican Border Music [vol. 24]: The Texas-Mexican Conjunto* (Folklyric 9049). *Marimba Music of Tehuantepec* (University of Washington Press UWP 1002). *Music of the Tarascan Indians of Mexico: Music of Michoacán and Nearby Mestizo Country* (Asch Mankind Series AHM 4217). *Music of Mexico: Sones Jarochos* (Arhoolie 3008). *Music of Mexico [vol. 2]: Sones Huastecos* (Arhoolie 3009). *Amerindian Ceremonial Music from Chile* (Philips 6586026).

Amazonian Cultures *Why Suyá Sing* (cassette, Cambridge University Press). *Indian Music of the Upper Amazon* (Folkways FE 4458).

African American *La História de Son Cubano, Sexteto Boloña* (Folklyric 9053). *In Praise of Oxalá and Other Gods: Black Music of South America* (Nonesuch H-72036). *Afro-Hispanic Music from Western Colombia and Ecuador* (Folkways FE 4376). *Afro-Brazilian Religious Songs: Cantigas de Candomblé* (Lyrichord LLST 7315). *An Island Carnival: Music of the West Indies* (Nonesuch 72091). *The Sound of the Sun: The Westland Steel Band* (Nonesuch H-72016). *Meringues and Folk Ballads of Haiti* (Lyrichord LLST 7340). *Cult Music of Cuba* (Folklways FE 4410). *Music from Saramaka: A Dynamic Afro-American Tradition* (Folkways FE 4225).

REFERENCES

Aldana, Ligia. 2012. "Blackness, Music, and (National/Diasporal) Identity in the Colombian Caribbean." In *Let Spirit Speak!: Cultural Journeys through the African Diaspora*, ed. Vanessa Valdés. Albany, NY: State University of New York Press.

Cunin, Elisabeth. 2003. *Identidades a flor de piel. Lo negro en Cartagena*. Bogatá: Instituto Colombiano de Antropología e Historia, Universidad de los Andes, Instituto Francés de Estudios Andinos, Observatorio del Caribe Colombiano.

Escallón, Miranda. R. 2007. *La Polarización de la Champeta: Investigación que motivó el reconocimiento de esta cultura y de este género en el Salón Regional y Nacional de Colombia*. Roztro: Museo de Arte Moderno de Cartagena, vol, 1, no. 2.

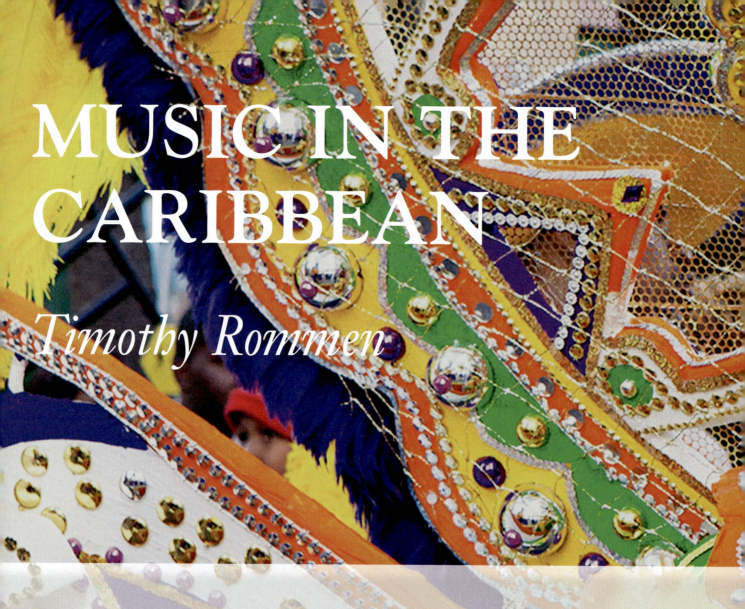

MUSIC IN THE CARIBBEAN

Timothy Rommen

CAT ISLAND, JUNE 2, 2006. NINTH ANNUAL RAKE 'N' SCRAPE FESTIVAL

It's pushing 8:00 P.M. on a Friday in June, and the crowd is packed into virtually every nook and cranny of the improvised fairground—a fairground erected next to the Arthur's Town airport especially for this event. The revelers have gradually assembled here over the past day or two, and although the crowd is predominantly Bahamian, a small handful of tourists and a group of folk music aficionados from Atlanta have joined the celebration. Cat Island is one of the many "Family Islands" in the Bahamas, and Arthur's Town is located on its northern end. For most of the year, Arthur's Town is a small village on a relatively small island (the entire population of Cat Island stands at about 1,600 people), but during the Rake 'n'

Scrape festival, which was first held in 1998, the island is bursting at the seams with people. As the festival weekend draws near, guest houses and private homes throughout the sixty-mile-long island are filled to overflowing with visitors. If you want to attend, then you'd better have made reservations a few months in advance.

The overwhelming majority of Bahamians live on New Providence and Grand Bahama (in the cities of Nassau and Freeport, respectively). The Family Islands have historically, and somewhat paradoxically, been touted as the greatest cultural repositories of the nation while, at the same time, receiving very little financial attention from the government. This state of affairs—which has led to increased migration out of the Family Islands in search of employment and educational opportunities—has been changing in recent years, though, and the Festival is a good example of current efforts to bring the Family Islands into the national limelight in tangible (and material and financial) ways.

The stage, set up at the far end of the fairgrounds, is flanked on either side by a giant tower of speakers, and several cabinets of subwoofers line the foot of the stage. The stage itself is arranged to accommodate both a full house band and a range of smaller ensembles. The perimeter of the fairgrounds, meanwhile, is completely overtaken by shacks (small temporary booths made of plywood) out of which Cat Islanders are serving food, straw work (for which Cat Island is famous), and other handmade souvenirs. I arrived here this afternoon from Nassau and am looking forward to hearing some of the very best rake 'n' scrape bands in the Bahamas perform. Ophie and the Websites are here, as are Bo Hog and the Rooters.

Rake 'n' scrape is a traditional music of the Bahamas, today usually played on accordion (most commonly on a two-row button accordion such as the Hohner that Ophie plays), saw (literally a carpenter's saw), and goatskin drum. Rake 'n' scrape ensembles traditionally accompanied **quadrille** dancing, and although quadrille is not as popular today as it was even twenty-five years ago, rake 'n' scrape artists have continued to play their tunes outside of that social context. Perhaps equally important, the rhythms and sounds of traditional rake 'n' scrape provide the foundation for a great deal of the popular music being performed in the Bahamas today. Musicians are increasingly exploring ways of incorporating rake 'n' scrape into the context of full dance bands, adding

RAKE 'N' SCRAPE
A traditional Bahamian music, usually played on accordion, saw, and goatskin drum.

QUADRILLE
A dance, originating in Europe and adapted to Caribbean contexts. It was historically performed by couples arranged in a square formation and following a series of set dance figures.

Ophie and the Websites, Saturday, June 3, 2006, in Arthur's Town, Bahamas.
Source: Timothy Rommen

saw, accordion, and goatskin drum to ensembles that already feature at least drum kit, bass, and electric guitar, and, sometimes, also keyboards and a horn line. In fact, one of the most exciting of these popular rake 'n' scrape singers is going to be performing tonight. His stage name is Ancient Man, and his songs, along with those of a few other rake 'n' scrape–influenced artists, including the Lassido Boys, Elon Moxey, and Ronnie Butler, are leading what might be considered a revival of sorts in Bahamian popular music—rake 'n' scrape style.

But this night isn't just about rake 'n' scrape; storytellers will precede the musical entertainment, and the audience has packed in to hear them. Storytelling was, not so long ago, a major pastime and an art form in its own right throughout the Bahamas (and the rest of the Caribbean, for that matter). Today, few can still tell the stories the way they used to be told, but there are active attempts to keep the oratory arts alive in the Bahamas, and the fact that it has been programmed into the festival is a good indication of that initiative.

The fairgrounds are cooling off nicely from the oppressive heat of the day, and the festival gets under way in earnest at about 9:30 P.M. After several rounds of storytelling by both children and adults, the sounds of rake 'n' scrape take over. First on stage are the Lassido Boys (a Cat Island band). They perform for nearly an hour, heating up the crowd before handing over the stage to Ophie and the Websites. In contrast to the Lassido Boys, who incorporate electric guitar, bass, and an additional percussionist into their rake 'n' scrape sound, Ophie and the Websites are a traditional ensemble consisting only of accordion, saw, and drum, and their set highlights many of the traditional tunes that Bahamians associate with rake 'n' scrape.

Ophie and the Websites's set is dominated by tunes that, not so very long ago, would have accompanied quadrille dancing. Although there isn't any organized quadrille dancing on stage this evening, something else is happening. Here and there around the fairgrounds, in small groups of two, three, and four dancers, the quadrille is being taught and danced. Mothers are teaching daughters, grandchildren are copying their elders. Rake 'n' scrape and quadrille dancing are, among other things, about being together—about enacting community—and tonight's festivities are providing a forum for doing just that.

As night turns to morning, Ancient Man takes the stage, singing his current hit single, entitled "I Ain't Asking for Much." He is wearing a scarf that bears the word "Kuumba." (Kuumba is the name of the sixth day of Kwanzaa and it means "creativity.") The scarf, moreover, is woven in Rastafari colors. By wearing this scarf, Ancient Man is simultaneously affirming his affinity for African American cultural symbols and his solidarity with his Caribbean neighbors. And this is not surprising, for he very deliberately foregrounds Bahamians' African heritage through his music, fashion, and spirituality. Earlier this afternoon I asked him why he chose to call himself Ancient Man, and his response was, "I didn't name myself. The spirits [specific to obeah, and pronounced "sperrets"] named me." Embracing and valuing African heritage is, for Ancient Man, an important key to thinking about identity in the Bahamas—a key that he embodies in his performances.

OBEAH
Bahamian folk belief and practice derived from African models and concerned with controlling and deploying powers in service of both good (i.e., healing) and evil (i.e., vengeance).

LISTENING GUIDE

RAKE 'N' SCRAPE: "TIMES TABLE"

 **LISTEN**

TRACK 11.1 🔘 **Ophie and the Websites**

THEIR RENDITION OF "Times Table" illustrates the principal musical characteristics of rake 'n' scrape. Listen especially to the rhythm played on the saw, which consists of a series of successive sixteenth notes, with an accent placed on the third sixteenth note of each beat (see Figure 10–1). This accent pattern emphasizes the "and" of each beat in a measure (one AND two AND, in 2/4 meter). If you listen carefully, you can also hear that the saw player is bending and releasing the saw to get different timbral effects. Notice, too, the way that the drummer interacts with the saw player. During the first phrase (four measures per phrase), the drummer generally executes a single low-pitched stroke on the "and" of the second beat of measures 2 and 4. The next phrase finds the drummer playing an extended fill that eventually culminates on the second beat of measure 8. This pattern is, of course, varied from time to time in the course of improvisation, but the variations are effective and interesting, thanks in large part to the fact that the general structure is firmly in place. Finally, notice the short melodic phrases, each four measures long, which are put together into a verse form (six phrases of four measures each, paired together to create a three-part structure [**ABA**]). The only exception to this pattern is at the very beginning of the performance, when the A section is played once as an introduction and then repeated as the first section of the **ABA** structure. The initial moments of the song can be represented as **A**(intro)–**ABA** (first verse).

Saw Pattern	x	x	X	x	x	x	X	x
Alternate Saw Pattern	x		X	x	x		X	x

Rake 'n' scrape rhythm (saw).

TIME	SECTION	MUSICAL EVENTS
0:00–0:07	**Introduction**: A section (two phrases of four measures each in 2/4).	Accordion begins and is immediately accompanied by strong foot stomping that marks the quarter note throughout the piece.
		Saw and goatskin drum enter in the third measure of the first phrase.
0:07–0:14	**First verse**: Listen for the ABA form of this strophic song.	A
0:14–0:22		B
0:22–0:29		A
0:29–0:36	**Second verse**: Continue listening for the ABA form.	A
0:36–0:43		B

continued

0:43–0:51		A
0:51–1:12	**Third verse**: Listen to the rhythms played on the goatskin drum.	The drummer marks the "and" of the second beat of the second and fourth measure in the first phrase of each section with a strong, single stroke.
		The drummer marks the third and fourth measures of the second phrase of each section with a fill that culminates "on" the second beat of the fourth measure of the second phrase.
1:12–1:34	**Fourth verse**: Continue listening to the goatskin drum.	The pattern sketched predominates throughout this performance with minor exceptions due to intensification or to improvisatory gestures.
1:34–1:55	**Fifth verse**: Focus on the saw.	The saw plays a consistent sixteenth note pattern that is accented on the "and" of each beat in a given measure (x x X x x x X x).
		The saw player subtly bends and releases the saw to create timbral effects that give the impression of changes in pitch (not unlike the effect created by a flanger).
1:55–2:10	**Sixth verse**: Listen for the intensification of melodic improvisation in the accordion in this last verse.	

Ancient Man performs a half-hour set backed up by the house band, and the band remains on stage to accompany the evening's remaining headliners, including Sparkles and Nita. The Lassido Boys come back on stage at about 1:45 A.M. and they play a short set to finish things off. The first night of the festival comes to an official close at about 2:30 A.M. The music continues, however, because many of the artists, along with a few hundred festival-goers, retire to a nearby nightclub, owned and operated by the Lassido Boys—a club called "Dis We Place." The festivities finally lose steam sometime around 4:30 in the morning, and I retire for a few hours of sleep.

For two nights (and well into the mornings) the audience at the festival is treated to both traditional rake 'n' scrape bands and to popular music heavily influenced by the rhythms and sounds of that musical tradition. On the third night, however, rake 'n' scrape takes a backseat to gospel music. All the performances this night are focused on sacred music traditions, from traditional anthems to songs influenced by African American gospel and R&B. Once again, traditional and popular forms share the stage, juxtaposed to highlight both distinctly Bahamian sounds (such as the anthems) and connections to broader musical and religious trends and sensibilities (like African American gospel music).

I should note here that Cat Island is, in Bahamian lore, a center not only of rake 'n' scrape, but also of obeah. Obeah is associated in the Bahamas with folk magic and (at times) with black magic. There are so many well-known tales

EXPLORE

Bahamian Music

Ancient Man in Concert at the Cat Island Rake-n-Scrape Festival, Friday, June 2, 2006. *Source:* Timothy Rommen

about obeah on Cat Island, that, in the weeks leading up to the festival, I have been regaled with stories and by turns solemn and joking warnings anytime I mentioned that I was going to be attending the rake 'n' scrape festival. The juxtaposition of Christianity with obeah—in this case by singing gospel music in what is considered by many to be quintessential obeah country—is a powerful reminder of the various negotiations that Bahamians (and inhabitants of the entire Caribbean region) have found necessary to make sense of their spiritual histories and futures. The gospel concert marks the end of the Festival, and along with a great many other visitors, I plan to make my way back to Nassau the following day.

The festival illustrates at multiple levels the simultaneous presence of unmistakably local characteristics and of elements drawn from (or present in) regional and transnational sources. For instance, the rake 'n' scrape rhythm, although performed in a particularly Bahamian instrumental configuration and claimed as a quintessentially Bahamian form of musical expression, is actually only one version on a theme that extends, in a great musical arc, from the Bahamas right down the Antilles. The rake 'n' scrape rhythm, altered a bit here and there, and played on different instruments, like shakers, washboards, squashes (a kind of guiro), and triangles, is called by other names depending on where you happen to be. So, in the Turks and Caicos Islands, it is called rip-saw; in the U.S. Virgin Islands, the rhythm is central to scratch bands; in the British Virgin Islands, it is known as fungi; and in Dominica, it is called jing ping. A festival highlighting the unique contributions of rake 'n' scrape, thus, points to the connections that exist between the Bahamas and the rest of the Caribbean (and vice versa).

Ancient Man's expressions of solidarity with Rastafarianism and Kwanzaa, moreover, illustrate his deliberate engagement with other locations in the Caribbean and with North America in the process of negotiating Bahamian identity. The sacred music performed at the festival underscores a similar set of relationships. The anthems, although sung in particular ways by Bahamians, nevertheless tie Bahamians to other Protestants throughout the Caribbean, whereas the North American gospel songs—and local artists like Tracy Tracy, who write and perform in that style—make explicit a strong connection between the Bahamas and the United States. More subtly still, because the festival takes place on Cat Island, the imagined heart of obeah in the Bahamas, the presence of syncretic religious belief here (and elsewhere throughout the Caribbean) remains an insistent companion to the proceedings. (*Syncretic* practices draw elements from two or more religious systems to create new ways of believing.)

SHARED HISTORIES, MUTUAL CHALLENGES

The Caribbean is marked by several shared and interrelated experiences that have contributed in significant ways to some of the common elements of the region's musical life. Yet, each of these experiences has been filtered through local circumstances, negotiated in particular contexts, entered into at different historical moments, and interpreted in diverse ways, evidence of which we can see in the great diversity of the region's cultural productions. So, for example, diaspora—the forced movement of ethnic groups from their homeland—plays a foundational role throughout the Caribbean. Everyone living in the region is, in one way or another, from somewhere else. The places that people called home before arriving in the region are varied indeed—West Africa, Europe, South Asia, East Asia, the Levant—and these people and their descendants have, over the course of several centuries and through a process often called creolization, become Caribbean nationals. The Caribbean also shares a colonial history. The region was born in the violence of the middle passage, slavery, indentured laborers, and imposed European laws, languages, religions, and economies. The consequences of the colonial encounter are in evidence in various ways in contemporary Caribbean life. For example, that encounter has left its mark in terms of political organization: the region includes nation–states (Cuba, Trinidad and Tobago, and the Dominican Republic); protectorates (Puerto Rico); overseas territories (British Virgin Islands); *departménts* (Martinique and Guadelupe); insular areas (U.S. Virgin Islands); and states within larger kingdoms (Aruba).

The shared colonial experience has also left a mark on the languages spoken throughout the region. The colonizers (Dutch, English, French, and Spanish) brought their own languages to the Caribbean, installing them as the "official" languages of government and business. The slaves that found themselves confronted by these languages, however, often developed new ways

DIASPORA

A term describing the movement of a group of people (generally sharing ethnic or national history) into forced exile. This exile in a place other than the group's ancestral homeland generally also precludes the possibility of return. The Jewish and African diasporas are two paradigmatic examples.

COLONIALISM

The administrative, economic, and political control of a territory (colony) by a colonial power (such as the British empire). This condition is maintained through exploiting unequal power relationships and by force, benefiting the colonial power and its center (the métropole) to a much greater degree than the colony itself in the process.

of communicating (French-based creole, various *patois*, and Papiamento) that combined their own native tongues with the European-imposed ones. These languages existed (and to varying degrees continue to exist) in a hierarchical relationship to each other wherein the official languages are considered proper (literate), whereas local forms are viewed as vulgar (oral). Language has, in fact become a ground on which musicians lyrically inscribe local identity, deploying local forms of language against the **métropole** (*zouk* [*creole*]), across class within a given nation–state (reggae and dancehall [I-ance and patwa]), and even to claim identity and express solidarity across national borders (punta rock [Garifuna]). I will return to these musics later. Religious life also reflects the colonial encounter. Although some have found a spiritual home within the Catholic and Protestant beliefs imposed on the region, many others have preferred to adapt their beliefs and cosmologies, giving rise to a great variety of sacred traditions that variously resist, combine with, or oppose Catholic and Protestant practices. The result is a wide range of religious practices, including *vodoun* (Haiti), *santería* (Cuba), obeah (Bahamas), shango and Spiritual Baptist (Trinidad), and myal, convince, and Rastafarianism (Jamaica), to name just a few. Many of these negotiations resulted in syncretic religious practices. That said, Hindu, Muslim, and Jewish religious practices have also found a home in the Caribbean.

The colonial encounter, moreover, almost immediately set in motion forces that devastated indigenous populations. This took various forms, but the principal mechanisms of the encounter included forced labor, often involving forcible removal of people from one location (such as from the Bahamas, where mineral resources were scant) and transfer to important centers of production (such as **Hispaniola**, where many Bahamian Lucayans eventually perished). Other forces contributed as well, including European diseases against which the inhabitants of the Caribbean had no immunity and warfare with Europeans and among themselves. The colonial encounter was so overwhelming that indigenous populations survive only in very small numbers and in but a few locations throughout the region today.

These shared histories are audible in the region's instruments and musical styles. As you might expect, African- and European-derived musical practices, aesthetics, and instruments predominate throughout the region. Many varieties of drums (batá, *gwo ka*, and bomba, to name just a few), various shakers and scrapers, bass instruments such as the *marímbula*, dances like rumba and bèlè, as well as rhythmic concepts such as timelines and clave are only the most tangible African-derived contributions to the region's musical life. More subtle, but equally significant, are several African-derived aesthetic and compositional concepts, including call-and-response structure, careful attention to the rhythmic complexity of music (syncopation, interlocking parts, 3+3+2 patterns), and what Peter Manuel has called *cellular construction* (taking a short repeating motive and treating it as an **ostinato** from which the form of a song emerges).

Stringed, wind, and brass instruments, pianos, and accordions are a few of the most prominent European-derived instruments. The European musical

MÉTROPOLE
From Metropolis, or "mother city." Also used for any colonizing "mother country."

HISPANIOLA
The name of the large Caribbean island shared by the modern nation-states of Haiti and the Dominican Republic.

OSTINATO
A repeated or cyclical melody or rhythmic pattern.

heritage has also contributed dance forms such as the waltz, mazurka, and quadrille and verse forms such as the copla and décima (a ten-line verse form). East Indians have contributed instruments and genres to the region's musical life—instruments such as the *dholak* (drum), *dhantal* (metal clapper), and harmonium—but these contributions remain comparatively localized (in places like Trinidad, Guyana, and Suriname). The *maraca*, a shaker usually made from gourds and dried seeds, is the principal Native American instrument thought to have survived the colonial encounter.

In a great many instances, these musical antecedents have been combined to create new, creole styles and musical traditions. Rake 'n' scrape is an excellent example of a Creolized musical style, because it is based on a combination of European and African instruments (accordion and goatskin drum) and on a successful combination of European and African conceptions of embodied rhythm (quadrille dancing and the rhythms played on the drum). In the end, rake 'n' scrape is a creole musical tradition, neither European nor African, but rather Caribbean—specifically, Bahamian. The Caribbean also shares a neighbor to the north, a neighbor that has grown ever more powerful both politically and culturally. The United States and, to a lesser degree, Canada exert a great deal of influence on the region, and that influence (at least in the cultural realm) is often exerted through the mass media. That said, however, the United States also has a long history of physically intervening in the region's political affairs, often deploying its military for strategic purposes in places like Cuba, Haiti, the Dominican Republic, Trinidad, and Grenada. This physical and media presence has profoundly affected the musical life of the region. Finally, the Caribbean shares, in a broad sense, a struggle to negotiate identity against the complex backdrop of diaspora, colonial histories, and influential neighbors, both leading up to and in the wake of independence.

COPLA

An Iberian-derived verse form with four octosyllabic lines per stanza.

DÉCIMA

An Iberian-derived, octosyllabic verse form with ten octosyllabic lines per stanza. The rhyming scheme is **ABBAACCDDC**.

THEMES IN CARIBBEAN MUSIC

Caribbean music has been shaped through the choices that various communities have made in responding to the presence of both European-colonial and African influences. As such, the range of musical styles and performing traditions is broad, indeed. Yet, several recurring themes illustrate some of the challenges that these shared experiences have engendered throughout the region. In this chapter, I'll introduce a number of musical case studies that explore the breadth of Caribbean performance traditions while simultaneously relating these musics to four interrelated and overlapping themes: (1) patterns of musical reception, (2) questions of identity, (3) class and cultural politics, and (4) tourism and travel.

Calypso in New York, Rumba in Paris: Patterns of Musical Reception in the Caribbean

I start this story in the Bahamas during the 1950s, when a performer by the name of George Symonette was riding high on the opportunities afforded by the early days of tourism in Nassau. The music that he played in those days—called goombay—included the rhythms of traditional rake 'n' scrape, played, in this case, on goatskin drum and maracas (instead of saw). But Symonette's goombay sound also included piano, guitar, upright bass, and clave. The songs he sang included original compositions, traditional tunes, and calypsos, all performed in goombay style. One of the calypsos in his repertory was especially popular; he called it "Love Alone." Symonette's performance of this song incorporates Trinidadian and Cuban influences without losing its distinctively Bahamian characteristics. The goatskin drum, for instance, incorporates a strong beat on the "and" of the second beat of each measure (2/4 meter)—a rhythmic marker of traditional rake 'n' scrape (see Track 11.1). The song itself, though, is a calypso (a Trinidadian genre), and the clave you hear is associated most closely with Cuban musics. Suffice it to say here that to accommodate the desires and tastes of tourists, goombay artists turned to a complex range of musical influences to create their sound, blending Bahamian, Cuban, Trinidadian, and even North American sounds into a genre unique to the Bahamas and yet audibly indebted to several other musical traditions throughout the Caribbean. But goombay's heyday in the 1950s and 1960s was made possible, in some respects at least, thanks to other musical successes, occurring in the years between the late 1920s and the early 1950s and involving at least the reception histories of calypso and commercial rumba.

Calypso

The Trinidadian Carnival Complex from Emancipation to "No, Doctor, No"

CARISO

Traditional French creole song. Early form of calypso, often employing insulting or satirical lyrics.

As early as the 1780s, the word **cariso** was used to describe a French Creole song and, in Trinidad, cariso seems to have been perfected by the (mostly female) chantwells during the first half of the nineteenth century. The chantwells, assisted by drums and alternating in call-and-response style with a chorus, were a central component of the practice called *kalenda* (stick—fighting). Kalenda bands (organized by neighborhood) would square off with each other, first through song and then, more often than not, through stick-fighting. Kalenda was a central component of early carnival celebrations in Trinidad, and after emancipation (1834), Afro-Creoles essentially took over the streets during carnival. Elite French Creole revelers, for their part, moved their carnival celebrations indoors and to private parties.

CANBOULAY

Processions that commemorated the harvesting of burnt cane fields before emancipation.

Official and elite unease over carnival revelry (which was considered violent and unruly) grew during the course of the next few decades, and in 1883 drumming was banned in an attempt to clean up carnival. This injunction came on the heels of a serious disturbance that occurred during the 1881 Carnival, known as the *Canboulay Riots*. **Canboulays** were processions during carnival that commemorated the harvesting of burnt cane fields during slavery, a process so labor intensive that it had often involved forced marches of slaves from neighboring plantations to more efficiently harvest the cane (once burned, sugar cane requires immediate harvesting or it spoils). These canboulay processions were quite popular and often incorporated kalenda. The government's attempt to ban the processions in 1881 resulted in open riots between Afro-Creole revelers and police, a turn of events that, not surprisingly, caused deep resentment within Trinidadian society toward the government's use of power. The open resistance of Afro-Creole revelers, of course, redoubled concerns among government officials over this potential threat to public order and led to an alternative strategy—the banning of drumming—in 1883. To make sure that the point got across, stick-fighting itself was banned in 1884.

An ingenious substitute for the drums and sticks, called *tamboo bamboo*, was introduced in the 1890s. **Tamboo bamboo bands** consist of three different instruments (each cut from bamboo): boom, foulé, and cutter. The boom serves as the bass instrument, is usually about five feet long, and is played by stamping it on the ground. The foulé, which is a higher-pitched instrument, consists of two pieces of bamboo, each about a foot long, and is played by striking these pieces end to end. The cutter, which is the highest-pitched instrument in the ensemble, is made from a thinner piece of bamboo (of varying length) and is struck with a stick. These three types of instruments combined to beat out rhythms that accompanied the chantwells and were a staple of carnival celebrations for many years (they were gradually rendered obsolete by the steel band).

One consequence of the ban on stick-fighting was that men became much more involved in singing carisos, thereby increasingly relegating women (formerly often participating as chantwells) to the sidelines. These cariso (*calypso*) singers gradually shifted their formerly physical competition to the lyrical content of their songs—lyrics in which boasting, double entendre, insults (picong), and powerful, satirical political and social commentary came to be central features. By the early years of the twentieth century, calypsonians began to perform in tents, leaving the streets to the tamboo bamboo, and in the 1920s they began charging admission to their shows. The 1930s saw contests between tents become a standard part of carnival, and in 1939, Growling Tiger was crowned the first calypso monarch of Trinidad (for his song, entitled "The Labor Situation in Trinidad").

During the 1890s—at roughly the same time that tamboo bamboo bands were getting up and running on the streets—string bands modeled on Venezuelan ensembles were coming to prominence in Trinidad. The string band usually consisted of guitars, violins, and *cuatros* (similar in sound and construction

A portrait of Calypso singer and musician Lord Kitchener. *Source:* Popperfoto/Getty Images

TAMBOO BAMBOO BAND
Bamboo percussion band used to accompany calypso songs during Carnival time in the late 19th–early 20th centuries.

CALYPSO: "NO, DOCTOR, NO"

 **LISTEN**

TRACK 11.2 **By The Mighty Sparrow (Slinger Francisco)**

THE MIGHTY SPARROW'S SONG, entitled "No, Doctor, No," illustrates many of the characteristics of calypso discussed so far. The ensemble includes a horn line, upright bass, guitar, and percussion and basically reflects the modern calypso sound (although this recording minimizes the drum kit and does not incorporate a keyboard—both of which are often featured prominently in calypso ensembles). Sparrow's lyrics engage with a political issue current in 1957 revolving around the (recently elected) government's failure to come through on campaign promises and the increasing cost of basic food and transportation. The verse-chorus structure, the call-and-response interplay during the chorus, the secondary importance of the music in relationship to the lyrics, and the aggressive tone of the lyrical content are all characteristic of calypso. Sparrow's self-identification with the lower class is significant as well in that it suggests the possibility of lower-class action of some sort should the political situation remain unchanged. The ability of calypsonians to mobilize public opinion continues to be a matter of concern even today, and the popularity of Sparrow's calypso, combined with the barely masked threats of lower-class action he incorporated into the lyrics, offers a case in point.

TIME	SECTION	MUSICAL OCCURRENCE/LYRICS
0:00–0:10	**Introduction of Sparrow**: Listen for tent atmosphere, announcer, and audience.	**Announcer**: The ever-popular King Sparrow and the situation in Trinidad.
0:11–0:30	**Introduction**: Music played here returns later as the chorus.	The instrumentalists introduce the chord progression and melody that forms the basis for the chorus.
		Notice that the ensemble includes an upright bass, guitar, percussion, and a horn line.
0:31–0:50	**Verse 1**: Listen for the repeating chord progression (ostinato) that drives the verse.	*Listen, listen carefully/I am a man does never be sorry (repeat)* *But I went and vote for some council men/They have me now in the pen* *After promising so much tender care/They forget me as they walk out of Woodford Square*
		Woodford Square is an important space for political debate in Port of Spain.
0:51–1:11	**Chorus**: Listen for the call-and-response interplay between Sparrow and the ensemble.	*Because they raise up on the taxi fare/No, doctor, no* *And they have the blasted milk so dear/No, doctor, no* *I want them to remember/We support them in September* *They better come good/Because I have a big piece of mango wood*
		The mango wood (club/stick) Sparrow sings about here is his way of promising retribution if the politicians fail to come through on their promises.

continued

TIME	SECTION	MUSICAL OCCURRENCE/LYRICS
		The doctor is none other than Dr. Eric Williams, the leader of the People's National Movement (PNM), who had recently been elected to power.
1:11–1:20	**Instrumental interlude**: Drawn from the last half of the chorus.	
1:21–1:41	**Verse 2**: Listen for the way that Sparrow plays with the rhythm beingset by the ensemble, speeding up and slowing down as he sings his lines against the ostinato.	*Well, people, plenty people sorry/Sorry they thrown down big belly* *Not me, I sticking my pressure/When I can't buy milk I use sugar and water* *Support local industries they done declare/They mean Vat 19 rum and Carib beer* *The way how they forcing we to drink Vat/It look as if they want to kill we in smart* "Big belly" references Albert Gomes (defeated by Eric Williams in 1956).
1:41–2:01	**Chorus**	
2:01–2:11	**Instrumental interlude**: Notice that the music is a vehicle for the lyrics and that the arrangement remains essentially unchanged throughout.	
2:11–2:30	**Verse 3**: Listen to the intensity in Sparrow's delivery in the last two lines of the verse.	*I only hope they understand/I am only a calypsonian* *What I say may be very small/But I know that poor people ain't pleased at all* *We are looking for a betterment/That is why we choose a new government* *But they raise on the food before we could talk/And they raise taxi fare so we bound to walk* Sparrow's suggestion that he is merely a calypsonian and that his words have a negligible impact is entirely satirical. Calypsonians were (and to some degree remain) very powerful within the Trinidadian social and political landscape.
2:31–3:02	**Chorus**: Listen for the change in lyrical content here.	*But still, I don't want them to catch cold sweat/No, doctor, no* *Because this mango wood talk is not a threat/No, doctor, no* *But still they must remember/We support them in September* *They better come good/I have no intention of throwing down my mango wood.* The withdrawal of the threat only to reinstate the possibility of violent action (he is not going to put down his stick) serves as a powerful warning to the government.

to the ukulele), but many groups also incorporated other instruments such as clarinet, trumpet, and even piano. String bands were the favored ensemble in elite circles and gradually came also to provide the musical backdrop for calypsonians, remaining a staple of calypso for decades.

Carnival festivities, then, split into two kinds of venues during the late nineteenth and early twentieth centuries, occupying both the street and more performance-oriented calypso tents. Both of these spaces, however, were the preserve of the lower class and of Afro-Creoles. Calypsonians were considered potentially dangerous by elites and government officials because they commanded large followings and could sway public opinion with their songs. The streets were also carefully monitored, setting up an atmosphere within which calypso and carnival were embraced by the lower class and kept at a distance by elites. The Afro-Creole middle class, moreover, working toward upward social mobility and thus concerned with aligning itself with the elite, also attempted to distance itself from carnival and calypso. C.L.R. James remembers this about calypsos: "Like many of the black middle class, to my mother a calypso was a matter for ne'er-do-wells and at best the common people. I was made to understand that the road to the calypso tent was the road to hell" (James, *Beyond a Boundary*, 1993 [1963], 16).

In the early 1940s, the United States built a military base in the northwest portion of Trinidad. The military presence in Trinidad provided many opportunities for calypsonians to write about current events and also contributed to a shift in the instrumental composition of the calypso ensemble. By the end of World War II, ensembles more reminiscent of jazz combos were taking hold, and a typical calypso ensemble today includes a horn line, drums, percussion, bass, guitar, and keyboard. A performance by the legendary calypsonian, the Mighty Sparrow, recorded in 1957 and entitled "No, Doctor, No," illustrates many of the characteristics outlined above.

"Edward VIII": Calypso in New York   In 1937, twenty years before the Mighty Sparrow wrote his politically charged calypso, several Trinidadian calypsonians traveled to New York to record the season's calypsos for the export market, a trend that had begun in the late 1920s. One of Lord Caresser's calypsos, entitled "Edward VIII," generated a huge amount of publicity that year and arguably contributed, at least in part, to the increased popularity and visibility of calypso in the United States during the 1940s and 1950s. It is a topical song that incisively relates a bit of current news and gossip (in this case humorously discussing the abdication of King Edward VIII to marry an American divorcée), and it revolves around a catchy refrain: "It was love, love alone, that caused King Edward to leave the throne."

Caresser's "Edward VIII" catapulted calypso into households throughout the United States and, significantly, helped initiate a sustained love affair with calypso outside Trinidad. Indeed, by the mid-1940s artists like the Andrews Sisters were covering calypsos like Lord Invader's "Rum and Coca Cola," which was a sardonic commentary on the U.S. military presence in Trinidad. In the 1950s, Harry

Belafonte ushered in the heyday of calypso's popularity in the North American market—and beyond. Everywhere that American tourists went—to the Bahamas, for example, where George Symonette covered Caresser's tune, calling it "Love Alone"—calypso followed. So, by the time that The Mighty Sparrow was singing "No, Doctor, No" in Trinidad, Harry Belafonte was making a career out of calypso in the United States, and George Symonette was covering calypsos to satisfy his audiences in Nassau's hotel clubs. In two short decades (1937–1957), calypso had become an internationally viable popular music.

Sweet Steel: The Steel Band in Trinidad and Abroad   While calypso was gaining popularity in the United States and finding expression in the nightclubs of Nassau, calypsonians were also winning fans in England, where performers like Kitchener, Lord Beginner, and the Mighty Terror were contracted for extended engagements. But calypso was not the only Trinidadian musical practice moving abroad in a big way during these years, for the 1950s also found the **steel band** making inroads in England and the United States. The steel band, which gradually replaced the tamboo bamboo ensemble during the 1940s, is composed of **idiophones**—called steel pans—made from oil drums that are "tuned" to play a range of pitches. The lower the pitch, the more area is needed on the surface of the drum, meaning that bass instruments have fewer notes on a given instrument than do melody instruments. Today several different sizes of instruments (or "pans") are used, and they have names like tenor, double second, cello, and bass (generally, the bigger the instrument [the more metal], the lower its register).

These instruments fill roles not unlike those found in a Western orchestra. The tenor pans generally play the melodies (like violins), the seconds handle harmonies and countermelodies (like violas), the cellos fill in harmonic materials (like cellos), and the bass pans, of which there are several different types, play the bass lines (like the double bass). Unlike orchestras designed to play Western art music—where the musicians rely on scores to learn and perform repertory— steel bands depend on arrangers. Arrangers fulfill multiple roles, adapting a given calypso or song to the steel band, assisting in the process of teaching the parts to the steel band, and once the arrangement has been learned, helping the steel band to polish the overall presentation for performance.

When playing in the Panorama Festival (a kind of massive battle of the bands, complete with big prizes and great notoriety, that parallels the Calypso Monarch competition), steel bands include as many as one hundred and twenty performers, of which several are responsible for running the "engine room," the battery of percussion (including a drum kit) that provides the rhythmic foundation for the band. But smaller ensembles are also common; the Trinidad All Steel Percussion Orchestra that toured London in 1951, for instance, included only eleven performers. It played to rave reviews and helped to bring steel pan into wider acceptance within Trinidad. Discussing this tour, Stephen Stuempfle (1995) noted: "Because British artistic taste was widely respected and often taken more seriously than local judgments, the critical acclaim that the

STEEL BAND
A band composed of oil drums that have been "tuned" to play a range of pitches.

IDIOPHONE
Scientific term for all instruments whose bodies vibrate as the principal method of sound-production, including rattles and many other percussion instruments.

Petrotrin Katzenjammers
Steel Orchestra performs
during National Panorama
Semi-Finals in the Queens
Park, Savannah as part of
Trinidad and Tobago Carnival.
Source: Sean Drakes/CON/
Getty Images

band received in the course of its tour brought greater legitimacy to steelband music at home" (Stuempfle, *The Steelband Movement*, 99). So, both calypso and steel pan went abroad in a big way between the 1930s and the 1950s, garnering enthusiastic responses from both European and North American audiences in the process.

At the very height of calypso's first international breakthrough in New York, however, the government in Trinidad was hard at work censoring calypsos, banning albums, and in general making life pretty miserable for calypsonians. Atilla the Hun wrote a calypso in response to this mistreatment of musicians, calling it "The Banning of Records"—and, yes, it was banned. One of the verses he sang included the following lyrics:

> *Imagine our records being banned/From entering in our native land!*
> *That they are obscene I must deny/But all things look yellow to the*
>   *jaundiced eye.*
> *I think that they have been ungenerous/To attempt to take our music*
>   *from us.*

It is not a coincidence that the first calypso monarch competition was held in 1939, some years after calypso had become an internationally viable and "hip" music. Calypso remained a threat to political figures and elites (and there are famous examples of confrontations between government officials and calypsonians over the contents of a given calypso), but came to be understood as an important genre, in part, through the recognition that calypsonians garnered abroad.

Rumba dancers in the Casa del Caribe in Santiago. *Source:* Günter Nindl/Getty Images

This heightened visibility and external approval generated the atmosphere within which steel bands and calypso, formerly quite maligned and considered the domain of ruffians and the lower class, became *the* symbols of Trinidad during the drive toward independence. It is no coincidence that the first Panorama competition occurred during the carnival following independence in 1963. This pattern of outside legitimation extends, in some form and to varying degrees, to many areas of cultural production in the region. The pattern of reception that I describe here is also intimately bound up in class conflicts and in questions of identity (can we really use steel band and calypso to represent the nation?), and dependent on travel (both of Trinidadian musicians and of the sounds of calypso [over airwaves, or relocated in Bahamian nightclubs]).

Rumba

Rumba developed as a secular African-derived drumming tradition in Cuba during the second half of the nineteenth century. The ensemble generally consists of a lead vocalist, a chorus, and at least three types of percussion instruments (clave, *palitos* [short sticks], and three conga drums [usually called *tumbadoras* in Cuba]). Several types of rumba developed, with three becoming widely popular: the *guaguancó*, the *yambú*, and the *columbia*. The most paradigmatic style for later Cuban dance band music was the guaguancó, and the characteristic rhythms of this style consist of the interlocking patterns created by the two-three clave, the palitos, the basic patterns of the congas, and the improvised play of the lead *quinto* conga.

RUMBA

Cuban dance form that developed at the end of the nineteenth century. The typical Rumba ensemble consists of a lead vocalist, a chorus, clave, palitos, and congas.

 **EXPLORE**

Rumba Guaguancó

LISTENING
GUIDE

RUMBA GUAGUANCÓ: "CONSUELATE COMO YO"

 **LISTEN**

TRACK 11.3   **Carlos Embale Ensemble: Clave, Palitos, Congas, Leader, and Chorus**

THIS RECORDING ILLUSTRATES the main formal and rhythmic structures of rumba guaguancó. The narrative section (canto) is followed by the montuno (beginning at [2:47]) and the clave, palitos, and congas all provide an interlocking, rhythmic foundation for the dancers. The quinto, or lead, conga, improvises over the top of the texture.

The song's lyrics are an encouragement to give up on love because it only leads to heartbreak.

> Console yourself like me, because I also had a love that I lost.
> And for this (reason) I say now that I won't love again.
> Because what good was love to you if that love betrayed you like it did me
> O my negra I love you but now I don't love anymore
> Hear me . . . Hear me well

> (trans. Jodi Elliott)

The clave, palitos, and congas play the following rhythms fairly consistently throughout the performance as shown here. Try to hear them individually. Although the clave in this performance follows a 3/2 pattern (that is a group of three strokes, followed by a group of 2 strokes) another very common clave pattern in rumba is the 2/3 pattern.

Clave:

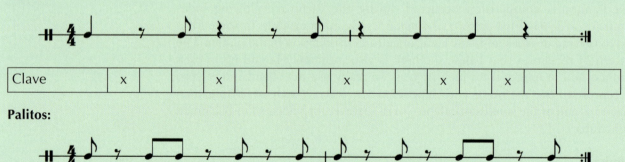

Palitos:

Conga:

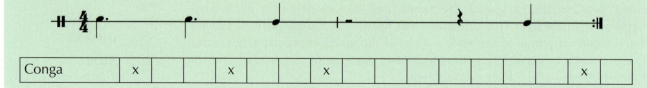

continued

The whole rhythmic texture looks like this:

Clave	X		X			X		X		X		
Palitos	X	X	X		X	X	X	X	X	X		X
Conga	X		X		X						X	

TIME	SECTION	MUSICAL EVENTS
0:00–0:06	**Canto**: Listen to the way this narrative section features the soloist/leader and his interactions with the chorus, who always sing the main melodic phrase with him. Listen also for the individual percussion instruments and see if you can hear their unique contributions to the overall rhythmic texture of the performance. Listen to this section multiple times. The first time, focus on the melodic and textual organization. Next, listen for the congas (the lowest-pitched of the percussions instruments). Then listen for and clap along with the clave (3 strokes, then 2 strokes). Finally see if you can hear and clap along with the palitos (the highest-pitched of the percussion instruments).	The clave, palitos, and congas open this performance, getting their interlocking rhythms set and preparing for the vocalists entry.
0:06–0:32		Lead vocalist improvises an introductory melody using vocables.
0:32–0:43		Chorus responds to the leader with the first phrase of the canto (and also the first phrase of the melody). *Consuelate como yo . . .*
0:43–0:59		The lead vocalist returns with another improvisatory flourish.
1:00–1:13		The chorus returns, repeating the melody and text. *Consuelate como yo . . .*
1:14–1:36		The chorus, now augmented by additional singers, repeats the first phrase of melody and text twice more.
1:36–2:00		The lead vocalist again improvises a text-less melody.
2:01–2:24		The smaller version of the chorus sings the second and third phrases of the melody, complete with new text, revealing the overall structure of the canto melody to be ABA.
2:25–2:46		The expanded chorus takes up the second and third phrases of the melody as well.
2:46–3:14	**Montuno**: Notice the slight increase in tempo and the new melody. Listen for	

continued

TIME	SECTION	MUSICAL EVENTS
	shorter intervals between the lead vocalist and chorus here and for the quinto solo.	Chorus and lead vocalist take turns singing short phrases.
3:14–3:33		The quinto, or lead conga, plays a solo. This is a good moment to see if you can hear the individual percussion instruments in addition to the solo.
3:34–4:00		The lead vocalist and chorus reenter, continuing their call-and-response interaction until the performance comes to an abrupt end.

Rumba consists of two main sections: *canto* (narrative text) and *montuno* (call-and-response with the chorus/percussion). Once the montuno starts, a male and female dance a ritualized enactment of male conquest. The male dancer uses surprise, stealth, and grace to get close enough to the female dancer to thrust his pelvis at her in a move called a *vacunao*. She in turn evades his moves, improvising her own playful dance steps in the process. As you might imagine, rumba caused a great deal of hand-wringing among the middle and upper classes, and it was banned or severely limited on several occasions throughout the late nineteenth century.

Bèlè and Bomba Rumba is not an isolated phenomenon within the Caribbean (though it certainly is uniquely Afro-Cuban). Indeed, rumba is one among a *series* of drumming traditions with accompanying dance that emerged throughout the Caribbean during the nineteenth century. It is important to think about these styles because of the significant, even foundational, role they have played in the development of popular musics throughout the region. Let's briefly explore just two of them: *bèlè* and *bomba*.

Bèlè drumming (also called belair) developed in rural Martinique and is played on a drum of the same name (a variant of this drumming tradition, played on a drum called a gwo ka also emerged in Guadeloupe). The drum is played by two performers: one straddles the drum, playing on the drumhead with both hands and a foot (which is used to dampen and undampen the drumhead to produce different pitches); the other performer uses a pair of sticks (called *tibwa*) to beat out characteristic and intricate cross-rhythms on the side of the drum. Bèlè is accompanied by call-and-response singing and by dancing. The dancers focus particular attention on close coordination between their steps and the improvisatory drum strokes (they have to pay attention to keep up with the drummer as opposed to dancing somewhat independently from the lead drummer as they do in rumba guaguancó).

This practice of West African origins was once prevalent throughout the Eastern Caribbean, but is today limited to folkloric exhibitions or to isolated revival movements (such a revivalist movement took place in rural Martinique in the 1980s). Although there are several different ways and styles of playing bèlè, one of the central rhythmic ideas of Martinician and Guadeloupean bèlè—the **cinquillo**—also provided serious inspiration first for *biguine* and then for *zouk* (two Antillean popular musics). In bèlè, the cinquillo is beat out by the tibwa, but it translates very well to shakers (called *chacha*) when the rhythms are applied to playing biguine. In zouk, as we shall see, the rhythm is often simplified to an almost-constant *3+3+2* motive and played with rim shots on the snare while shakers or hi-hats play the cinquillo rhythm. Another interesting aspect of the cinquillo is that it turns up over and over again throughout the region. As such it is not unlike the rake 'n' scrape rhythm—flexible and useful in a variety of musical contexts. For instance, the cinquillo, which came to be a central and defining feature of the light-classical Cuban salon music called *danzón*, is prevalent in popular genres like Haitian *meringue*, and even makes its way into other popular musics like calpso.

Bomba is a Puerto Rican tradition that emerged from the slave barracks, probably during the early decades of the eighteenth century. It is relatively rare to hear bomba today—it is preserved primarily in staged renditions and performed by folkloric groups. Nevertheless, there are places like Loiza, where young players are mounting a revival of the genre. The bomba was traditionally danced on special days—to mark the end of harvesting, for birthdays, christenings, and weddings. Bomba is a generic name that, like bélé, encompasses a wide range of rhythms and subtypes. The bomba ensemble generally includes dancers, a lead drum (*primo*), a second, lower pitched drum (*buleador*), sometimes a third drum (also called *buleador*), *cuá* (sticks), maracas, singer, and chorus (*coro*). The dance is essentially a challenge pitting the virtuosity of the dancers against the skill and speed of the lead drummer. Bomba dancing incorporates two levels of call-and-response: between the lead singer and the coro and between the lead drummer and the dancers.

Although bomba has declined in popularity over the course of the last century, the rhythmic ideas and aesthetic values embedded in the practice have found expression in Puerto Rican dance band music (notably in the repertories of performers such as Cortijo and Ismael Rivera during the 1960s). Bomba rhythms have also found their way into *salsa*, and bomba remains (along with *plena*) a firm part of Puerto Rican musical identity.

The Twentieth-Century Rumba   At the turn of the twentieth century, according to Robin Moore (*Nationalizing Blackness*, 1997), Cuban elites were looking for a musical identity for their newly independent nation. European-derived forms, including operettas (called *zarzuelas*), burlesques, and light classical salon and dance musics, all of which were common in Cuba at the time, were too European to offer a distinct national sound. There were, to be sure, Cuban elements that stood out. The habanera rhythm (from the *contradanza*) and the cinquillo (already discussed) were very popular both within Cuba and abroad. And yet, there was some concern that the musical genres within which these rhythms operated were, in the end, still too European to serve nationalist purposes. On the other hand, Afro-Cuban musics like rumba were

CINQUILLO
A rhythmic cell common throughout the Caribbean, containing five separate articulations and organized into a long-short-long-short-long pattern.

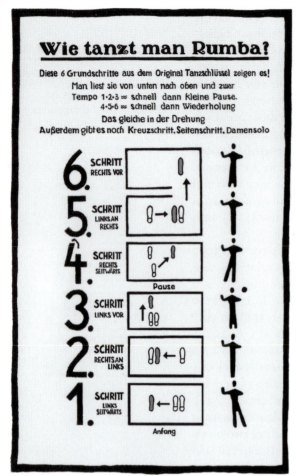

"Wie Tanzt Man Rumba?" Reproduction of a how-to guide for German-speaking rumba dancers, created by dance instructor Walter Carlos. Initially printed in the October 1931 edition of *Wintergarten* Magazine. Used by permission, Biblioteca Nacional Jose Marti with thanks to Robin Moore

considered too "primitive," too drum-oriented, and not modern enough for the new nation.

The central paradox was how to create a national culture (a project virtually inconceivable without incorporating Afro-Cuban expressions) and present it as civilized and modern (for which it seemed necessary to marginalize "blackness"). In short, how to find a way to "browning" Afro-Cuban music? Mirroring the state of affairs in Trinidad, members of the black middle class did not object to this project because they were attempting to distance themselves from their own cultural heritage to obtain a greater measure of acceptance within Cuban society. They resented the "blackness" of rumba as much as, if not more than, did the elite.

While elites were busy looking for their answers within Cuba, the World's Fair of 1889 in Paris had illustrated quite clearly the marketability of the primitive and of *negritude*. Composers like Debussy were fascinated by Indonesian gamelans, artists were thrilled by African masks, and a bit later, audiences went wild over Josephine Baker's revues. Jazz was beginning to make inroads in Europe and, by 1920, a tango craze hit all of Europe. People turned to *l'arte negre* for a variety of reasons, both aesthetic and philosophical, and the stage was set for a new dance craze to hit the streets. A few Cuban entertainers who had been performing rumba in a "cleaned-up," staged form in Havana found their way to Paris, where, in 1927, they performed with great success.

By the 1930s, this cleaned-up, commercial rumba was being danced all over Europe and in the United States— ironically solidifying precisely the "exotic" image from which Cuban elites were trying to distance themselves. While rumba swept through Paris and the world, the rumba of the urban lower class was still quite maligned in Cuba. When tourists became increasingly interested in rumba, however, things gradually changed. The top-tier clubs began hiring more Afro-Cuban musicians (in order to claim greater authenticity). Rumba found acceptance abroad and this led, at least in part, to its subsequent repositioning at home despite the fact that it was still symbolically tied to the legacy of slavery and to Africa.

A parallel development had, nevertheless, taken place within Cuba itself during these years. Elements of the traditional rumba had also become firmly entrenched in the formal structure and instrumentation of a new genre called *son*—the dance band tradition that gradually became the international face of Cuba. The clave and the two-part formal structure of *canto* (called *largo* in sones) and montuno, to name but two aspects of traditional rumba, became central to the sound of *son*, and *sones* rapidly became extremely popular in Cuba and abroad. So, rumba found its way into the world and into a more benign local genre (son), and the combination of these two processes made it possible for elites to embrace it—outside recognition, inside redefinition (Moore 1997).

The popularity of son was such that the sounds traveled throughout the region, contributing to the incorporation of elements like the clave into Trinidadian calypsos, Jamaican mento bands, and George Symonette's cover-tune, "Love Alone." By contrast to son, which has remained popular, rumba is today no longer widely popular in Cuba. However, several ensembles specialize in performing it, a fact that keeps rumba from becoming merely a folkloric music. This has also meant that rumba continues to serve as a source of musical inspiration for Cuban dance bands playing styles like son and, more recently, *timba*. This is another example in which questions and issues related to class, cultural politics, travel, tourism, and national identity all contribute to the ways that a musical practice is received and rethought. And, in similar fashion to calypso and steel pan, the sounds of rumba, and especially of son, had an effect beyond Cuba's borders as the music was "exported" through recordings, radio, and performing groups.

We, the People: Nation and Identity in the Caribbean

A second theme in Caribbean musics concerns how musical style reveals national or communal struggles with identity. The Bahamas offer a case in point. As the country moved to majority rule in 1967 and then achieved independence from Great Britain in 1973, a concomitant cultural negotiation was taking place. As in our example from Cuba, middle-class Bahamians felt that the island's cultural icons were too backward for mobilization in service of national identity. The long history of colonialism had ingrained a certain predilection for British culture, resulting in a parallel silencing of Bahamian culture. Significantly, musicians played an important role in bringing Bahamian customs, foods, clothing, language use, and musical traditions back into the public eye, both through their lyrics and by means of performance. In fact, **junkanoo**, a carnival-like festival celebrated on Boxing Day (December 26) and New Year's Day, gradually came to serve as an icon of Bahamian identity.

In the Bahamas, junkanoo developed during the nineteenth century and took the form of a nighttime festival during which slaves would get together to visit, celebrate, and socialize. After emancipation in 1838, however, it came to be associated in the minds of elites with loud revelry and violence (more imagined than real) and was generally disparaged. Junkanoo gradually became associated with a particular rhythm, performed on goatskin drums and accompanied by whistles, cowbells, and whatever other instruments people could get their hands on (bugles, bicycle horns, etc.). The characteristic rhythms of junkanoo developed over the course of some decades, but by the early twentieth century, they had codified to some degree into roles for the various drums and bells.

JUNKANOO
A Bahamian festival, celebrated on Boxing Day (December 26) and New Year's Day and including music, costume arts, and dance.

Dancer in traditional costume at Junkanoo Festival in Nassau. *Source:* Erkki & Hanna / Shutterstock.com

The festival was variously banned, threatened, and limited throughout the nineteenth and early twentieth centuries. Just as with carnival in Trinidad, elites felt threatened by junkanoo and passed injunctions, such as the Street Nuisance Act of 1899, that severely limited the festival (in this case by prohibiting junkanoo during the late nighttime hours when it was customarily celebrated). However, as tourists began to frequent the Bahamas more regularly in the years following World War II, they began to express real interest in junkanoo. Merchants along Bay Street in Nassau seized the opportunity and began to institutionalize the festival. During the 1950s there was a gradual recognition that this festival could generate tourist revenue. The drive toward independence began in earnest around the same time, and junkanoo thus began to factor as a marker of Bahamian identity.

By the time independence became a reality in 1973, junkanoo was a very different festival than it had been prior to World War II. It now took place in a centralized location with a set parade route (along Bay Street), had been recognized as an official competition (with rules, judges, and prizes), was broadly "Bahamian" and sponsored by the state (the Masquerade Committee had been absorbed into the Ministry of Tourism). Most importantly, junkanoo had become a positive source of identity for Bahamians (including elites). Junkanoo illustrates how a festival tradition gradually came to define for a nation–state an important aspect of its identity leading up to and in the wake of independence.

But the Caribbean also plays host to other political arrangements. The next two case studies consider what happens when identity is being negotiated in the context of a foreign *departmént* (that is, within the French Antilles, which are foreign *departménts* of France) and—more drastically still—when it is being negotiated by people who do not have any way of constituting themselves within the geographical boundaries of a nation–state (as is the case with the Garifuna).

Zouk

The French Antilles were not particularly active in the popular music scene during the early 1970s. *Biguine*, the local dance band music, had been a hugely successful genre earlier in the twentieth century and had, in fact, been one of the first Caribbean musics to attract early and sustained interest by recording companies (along with calypso). But biguine had gradually lost much of its popularity to other regional styles. George Decimus, a founding member of the band called Kassav', came to believe that this void—which was filled by nonlocal musics like merengue (Dominican Republic), cadence-lypso (-Dominica), and *konpa-direct* (Haiti)—was a result, ultimately, of a lack of confidence in Antillean identity. This belief led in 1979 to the birth of Kassav', a band explicitly committed to producing technically flawless, rhythmically complex, unquestionably Antillean music for world consumption.

The band implemented several strategies of representation, starting with its name. "Kassav'" is a local dessert that is made from manioc and needs to be carefully prepared, because if made improperly, it can result in a toxic cake. The band thus claimed local cuisine and folk knowledge as their own. Kassav' also decided that its lyrics would be sung in the local language, *creole*. Among Antilleans, creole had for the longest time been considered the language of the poor and uneducated, whereas French was considered proper and refined. The band featured the gwo ka (Guadeloupean bèlè drum) and foregrounded local rhythms to instill a sense of pride in Antillean sounds and instruments. The rhythms of the gwo ka were soon transferred to the drum kit, but nevertheless remain the basis for the music that came to be called zouk. Kassav' recorded in Paris to have access to the best equipment possible and was extremely sensitive to international sounds (especially to those of the World Beat craze of the late 1970s and early 1980s). In 1984 Kassav' released the song "*Zouk-la se sel medikaman nou ni*" ("Zouk is the only medicine we have"), and it was a huge success. Having gained traction on the international market, the band was forced to articulate their ideology more clearly to the public both at home and abroad. Among these ideas were: They wanted to create a music that would be picked up and understood by non-Caribbean ears, to write music that would defend the sounds of the Antilles and of the black diaspora on the international market, and to craft a current translation, with the available means, of the Caribbean musical sensibility, which enters into contact with all cultures. It is important to note also that the band boasted a broadly international membership. Originally a Guadeloupean band, the membership quickly expanded to include Martinician, Belgian, Cameroonian, French, and Algerian musicians. Finally, one of the remarkable aspects of Kassav's membership is the union of Guadeloupe and Martinique, a remarkable union because of the strong, long-standing mistrust and competition that has

ZOUK
Popular music style of the French Antilles, popularized in the 1980s by the band Kassav'.

 **EXPLORE**
Zouk

Jacob Desvarieux of the band Kassav' performs at the 'Setting The Stage 2015 And Beyond' concert at the United Nations in New York City. *Source:* Mike Coppola/Getty Images

divided these two *departménts*. So Antillean unity is a particularly salient message—a message that the band literally embodies.

As Jocelyne Guilbault (1993) noted, Kassav' foregrounds its hybrid nature and, in so doing, proposes a new vision of Antilleans as mixed and hybrid, culturally rich, and modern world citizens. There is also a peculiar logic to challenging the métropole with creole by so carefully appealing to the exoticism that drives the world music industry. In the end, Kassav' was able to turn both Paris and Fort-de-France in a big way—Fort-de-France, because creole thumbed its nose at Paris, and Paris because creole had found a space outside French national culture (the world music market) that could then be reabsorbed as French diversity by the urban elite.

Punta and Punta Rock

Garinagu is the name of the people of West African and Amerindian descent who settled along the Caribbean coast of Belize, Guatemala, Honduras, and Nicaragua during the nineteenth century. Garifuna is another, more common name for this people—a term that serves also to refer specifically to their language. The beginnings of the Garifuna trace to the island of St. Vincent, one of the few places in the Caribbean where Amerindians were able to successfully resist the colonial encounter well into the eighteenth century. On St. Vincent, the Amerindians met and intermarried with two shiploads of Africans, who had reached shore after their slave ships were wrecked in a storm on the way to Barbados around 1635. The Garifuna, known in St. Vincent as the Black Caribs, eventually found themselves at war with and technologically outmatched by the British, who had become increasingly interested in St. Vincent during the course of the eighteenth century. The Garifuna, led by a chief named Chatuye, were eventually defeated in 1796—a defeat that prompted a massive (and forced) Garifuna migration with eventual resting points in places like Guatemala and Nicaragua. This migration began with the exile in 1797 of some 2,000 Garifuna to Roatan Island off the coast of Honduras. The dispersal of the Garifuna from St. Vincent has led many to refer to themselves as the Garifuna Nation throughout the diaspora.

In 1802, Garifuna from Honduras began settling in Belize (then British Honduras), and on November 19, 1832, many of the exiles from Roatan Island joined the Garifuna who had already settled there, a day that, since 1977, has been recognized as Garifuna Settlement Day. There are six major Garifuna settlements in Belize today, but beginning in the middle of the twentieth century, large numbers of Garifuna have been migrating to the United States, where there are now sizable communities in New York, Los Angeles, and

Chicago. Oliver Greene has pointed out (2002) that in 1993 there were an estimated 225,000 Garifuna in Central America and about 90,000 in the United States. The difficulties of maintaining identity across several host nations and between multiple languages (Spanish, English, and Garifuna) has led many Garifuna to focus careful attention on preserving language, customs, music, and other traditions. This concern is illustrated in the creation of **punta rock**.

| **LISTENING GUIDE** | **PUNTA** |  **LISTEN** |

TRACK 11.4   **Performed by Henry, Bobsy, and Lena Núñez**

TIME	SECTION	MUSICAL ELEMENTS/LYRICS
0:00–0:20	Listen briefly for the three main elements: the vocals, the primero, and segunda drums.	This song is being performed by three children. The lyrics of the song are mostly in English: *When the teacher speaks I don't like it. Hey Dandi (Mountain Cow or Tapir) walking away.* *Hey, Tiligad's sister is walking away.*
0:20–0:40	The vocals: Listen for the English content in the lyrics.	The children are singing in a mixture of Garifuna and English. Recorded in 1982, at the very moment that the first punta rock artists were gaining popularity, this performance illustrates both the continuation of traditional forms of tutelage (these children learned how to drum and sing punta from their elders) and offers some sense of the felt need for a revitalization of Garifuna language (the children sing mostly in English).
0:40–1:00	The segunda pattern: Listen for the repeating ostinato in the segunda drum.	The rhythm that drives this song is played on the segunda. It consists of the following pattern: You can hear it in 2/4 or as a 6/8 pattern, but the actual feel is somewhere between these two:

2/4 feel

Segunda	x				x		x	x
Pulse	x				x			

6/8 feel

Segunda			x			x	x	x
Pulse			x			x		

TIME	SECTION	MUSICAL ELEMENTS/LYRICS
1:00–1:30	The primero: Listen for the improvisatory and virtuosic role of the primero.	The primero is free to improvise over the segunda pattern. In this sense, it fulfills a role not unlike the quinto drum in rumba ensembles.

PUNTA ROCK
Popular music style developed by the Garifuna, featuring call-and-response vocals and a rich percussion accompaniment derived from traditional punta music.

To understand the ideology and sound of punta rock, though, it is necessary to offer a brief introduction to its musical antecedent—punta. Punta is a song genre that symbolically reenacts the cock-and-hen mating dance and is usually composed by women. Punta is performed during festivals, at wakes, and at celebrations that follow *dugu* ceremonies (religious ceremonies during which a family appeals to the ancestors for help in solving a given problem). It is a secular, duple-meter genre, and the lyrics are often cast in the vein of other regional genres such as calypso, giving expression to strong currents of social commentary and political consciousness. It's a couples dance that features rapid movement of the hips and a totally motionless upper torso. Punta usually involves call-and-response singing, drums, rattles, and sometimes conch shell trumpets. The drums used in punta are called the *primero* and the *segunda*. As you might imagine, the primero improvises over a steady ostinato (repeating motive) laid down by the segunda.

"Punta" (recorded in 1982), illustrates both the extent to which children were still being taught Garifuna musical practices at that time and the increasing need for renewed attention to Garifuna language and identity. It reminds us that Garifuna were actively passing on traditions despite the rhetoric that accompanied the rise of punta rock while simultaneously offering a bit of perspective on the ideological position that artists took with respect to their project—not enough was being done to promote Garifuna lifeways. Accordingly, the late 1970s found a new musical approach gaining momentum among Garifuna. Indeed, punta was being consciously revitalized as popular music through a genre called punta rock. Punta rock is an adaptation of punta and to a lesser extent of *paranda* (a folk-song genre for voice and guitar) and is very popular in Belize and in places like Guatemala and Honduras (where only *cumbia* outstrips it in terms of popularity). The language of punta rock is Garifuna, a major marker of ethnicity and of identity for performers and fans alike. There are, to be sure, punta rock songs with English or Spanish lyrics, but Garifuna, along with the rhythms of punta, remain major markers of identity. Unlike punta, however, punta rock is composed and performed largely by men instead of women.

The shift from punta to punta rock was motivated in part by concern over the degree to which young Garifuna were identifying with the musical styles they were hearing primarily over the radio. Sounds from Bob Marley to James Brown were floating across the airwaves, and traditional punta simply couldn't compete. Initially (in the late 1970s) the traditional punta ensemble was merely augmented with a lead guitar and a turtle shell (to approximate a snare drum sound). Performers gradually added keyboards and drum machines (which replaced the segunda) in the 1980s, and the basic tempo of punta was increased, leading to a radio-friendly and ethnically marked popular music. One of the ways that the sound was adapted to more modern-sounding arrangements was to split the traditional punta rhythm (the segunda part) between kick drum and snare.

Garifuna continue to face significant challenges to their identity. They live in modern nation–states of which they form but a small minority. They share a common heritage, but are spread over several national borders, including the United States, making large gatherings for reunions or *dugu* ceremonies quite difficult to realize. Finally, they continue to eat, dance, sing, and speak in ways not recognized as mainstream within their respective nation–states, making it tempting for some to entertain the thought of blending in. These challenges, however, have been confronted with a focus on the shared history of the Garifuna—by a renewed interest, growing during the 1970s and 1980s, in preserving language, customs, and rites and by new artforms that include the creation and dissemination of punta rock. This is a story of identity quite different from zouk or junkanoo, but it offers another example of the challenges to identity that confront peoples living in the Caribbean region.

"All O' We Is One": Class and Cultural Politics in the Caribbean

Junkanoo also serves as an excellent introduction to the next theme in Caribbean music—class and cultural politics within the region. Junkanoo is touted as the great, national unifier by the Bahamas Ministry of Tourism and by participants alike. All Bahamians, whether day laborers or prime ministers, participate in the festival. For these two parades (Boxing Day and New Year's Day), at least, Bahamian society dissolves ethnic and class issues and celebrates together— so the argument goes. And yet, a closer examination reveals some very interesting trends within the structure of junkanoo groups themselves. Each junkanoo troupe is made up of a front line and a back line. The front line includes dancers (both choreographed and free dancers) and a range of set pieces designed to illustrate and explore the group's chosen theme. The back line consists of the instrumentalists: brass players, bellers (cow bell players), lead drummers, and bass drummers. Bellers and drummers also blow whistles along the parade route. The number of people who participate in these troupes is quite considerable. The largest groups, like the *Valley Boys*, *Saxons*, *Roots*, and *One Family*, for example, can bring as many as one thousand junkanooers to Bay Street for a given parade.

Vivian Nina Michelle Wood has pointed out that women generally gravitate toward the costume arts while men play instruments, and that drums are generally the domain of the grass roots while local whites play *mas* (i.e., masquerade). In other words, junkanoo groups tend to preserve an internal division of labor that traces some of the historical fissures within Bahamian cultural and social life. Metaphors of unity, then, only go so far toward explaining junkanoo. When subjected to a bit of analysis, it becomes clear that some of the struggles related to cultural politics within the Bahamas continue to rest uneasily at the very heart of this most powerful of national symbols. Junkanoo illustrates gender, ethnic, and economic fissures within Bahamian society and offers an introduction to a theme that plays out musically in powerful ways throughout the Caribbean.

Chutney and Chutney-Soca

An example of cultural politics as it relates to ethnicity can be found in Trinidad, where East Indians and Afro-Creoles continue to work out just what sounds and tastes should represent the nation. East Indians, the descendants of indentured laborers brought to the region from South Asia, are present in large numbers in Trinidad, Guyana, and Suriname. They arrived first in Guyana, where some 250,000 disembarked between 1838 and 1917. Suriname, getting a rather late start, imported some 37,000 East Indian laborers between 1873 and 1916. Trinidad followed Guyana's example more quickly and began importing indentured laborers in 1845. By 1917, some 144,000 East Indians had arrived in Port of Spain, and the resulting East Indian community has since grown to comprise approximately 41 percent of Trinidad's population.

Hindu and Muslim religious beliefs and practices were added to the growing number of religious systems in Trinidad, and the government's Population and Housing Census of 2000 suggests that approximately 30 percent of the population claims Hindu or Muslim faith. East Indians, of course, brought with them not only religious beliefs, but also ways of living, making music, and speaking, all of which added layers of complexity to Trinidadian society. Dr. Eric Williams, Trinidad's first prime minister, attempting to find a way of uniting Trinidadians toward the common goal of nation building in the early 1960s, tried to do away with this complexity by reconfiguring the way people thought about their place in Trinidadian society. In a now-famous address he suggested, "There can be no Mother India, for those whose ancestors came from India . . . there can be no Mother Africa, for those of African origin. . . . The only Mother we recognise is Mother Trinidad and Tobago, and Mother cannot discriminate between her children" (Williams, *Forged from the Love of Liberty*, 281).

And yet, Dr. Williams's attempt at using familial metaphors to unify a society splintered along ethnic fault lines foundered. One reason for this failure was that the cultural productions that the government chose to represent the way that Trinidad looked, sounded, and tasted, were, almost without fail, of Afro-Creole extraction. We have already seen that calypso, steel bands, and carnival came to hold a special place in terms of Trinidad's national identity. East Indian musical traditions, like Tan-singing, tassa drumming, and chutney, were not equally promoted. Although Dr. Williams's address posited Mother Trinidad as the only mother for all Trinidadians, the terms of *inclusion* into the ostensibly multicultural nation did not change appreciably for East Indians.

Added to this political dimension of interethnic relations in Trinidad has been the increasing economic success of East Indians. Afro-Creoles have found themselves increasingly economically outstripped by East Indians, whether in small business ventures or in terms of employment. By the mid-1980s, this growing East Indian economic power had translated into burgeoning political power. When, in the 1990s, East Indians succeeded in turning the political tables on Afro-Creoles, electing Basdeo Panday prime minister in 1995, there was a great deal of worry among Afro-Creoles that the cultural tables would be turned as well.

Musical style plays a major role in these cultural politics, each style carrying an extra measure of weight as an expression of a particular identity and subject position within the nation. Styles such as calypso and soca continue to be tied to the Afro-Creole community in Trinidad, whereas chutney and tan-singing are understood as "authentically" East Indian forms of expression. And although there were artists and fans who broke through these categories of musical ownership to explore mixtures or simply to sing or participate in a different style, these artists were the exception rather than the rule. It is predictable that these artists were often roundly criticized for these breaches of artistic (read cultural) propriety.

Even as recently as the 1990s, controversy raged over musical styles. A case in point is **chutney-soca**, which blends aspects of both *soca* and *chutney* to produce a hybrid drawing on both Afro-Creole and East Indian musical styles. As musicians began to sing chutney-soca in the tents during carnival and in the Soca Monarch competition, both Afro-Creole and East Indians raised concerns. Afro-Creoles were unsure how to judge chutney-soca in a competition designed to deal only with soca. East Indians were by turns aggravated at the fact that East Indian musicians and musical characteristics were even participating in carnival and upset at those Afro-Creole musicians who chose to perform "their" music—a musical blend that they had vigorously opposed in the first place. To satisfy both groups, a new category for competition, called the "Chutney-Soca Monarchy," was created in 1996. This move, although certainly making the job of judging the soca competition more clear-cut (a happy development for Afro-Creoles), continued to legitimize and further institutionalize the "separate but equal" policies for which East Indian leaders had been pushing (see Edmondson 1999; Manuel 2000). Musical ownership thus remains a major component of cultural politics in Trinidad.

Two other East Indian musics—Tan-singing (now on the verge of falling out of use) and chutney—further illustrate Caribbean cultural politics. *Tan-singing* is a light-classical tradition and features several different genres, the most important of which is Thumri. *Thumri* is, for many East Indians, a tangible link to South Asian musical practices, and although it is certainly indebted to South Asian models, it has developed as a uniquely East Indian musical practice. Thumri is a vocal genre accompanied by *dholak* (drum), *dhantal* (metal clapper), and harmonium, which doubles the vocal line in heterophonic style. And yet, this musical style is gradually passing from active performance into folklore. Most performers no longer can speak Hindi, and the tradition seems to be dying a slow death at the hands of chutney and Bollywood film music.

Chutney is a folk music of South Asian origin, usually sung by women for women at celebrations such as weddings. The lyrics are often humorously educational with regard to domestic and marital subjects. Traditional instrumentation for these songs is not unlike that for Tan-singing, employing a harmonium, dholak, and dhantal, although the performance style is no longer touched with the virtuosity of Tan-singing. This tradition continued through the 1960s, but starting in the 1970s, male East Indian singers like Sundar Popo began to explore chutney as a popular genre, performing it in public and even

CHUTNEY-SOCA
Popular music style of Trinidad that combines elements of two earlier styles, soca and chutney.

in carnival tents and adding other instruments to the ensemble, including keyboards, drum kits and drum machines, bass, and electric guitars. This move from the private to the public sphere—and from folk to popular status—caused a great deal of concern among East Indian leaders and was only exacerbated when women performers began to experiment with the style as well. And yet, chutney grew in popularity and, in the 1980s, helped to launch the hybrid I discussed earlier: chutney-soca. Both performance styles continue to be popular, and East Indian leaders seem to have resigned themselves to the fact that East Indian culture and social structures can no longer remain isolated from Trinidadian national culture. And yet, the separate but equal policies continue to be attractive, and Trinidadians continue to face serious challenges in the realm of cultural politics.

Merengue

MERENGUE
Popular dance music of the Dominican Republic.

EXPLORE
Merengue Típico

Merengue music of the Dominican Republic offers a very different example of class and cultural politics. During the mid-nineteenth century, merengue developed from the salon-type music popular throughout the region at the time (*danza* and *contradanza*). It was gradually picked up as a folk music, and this style came to be played far away from the dance halls and salons of Santo Domingo. It should come as no surprise that those in positions of power denounced this rural merengue as vulgar and primitive. The early merengue ensemble usually included *guira*, guitar/*quatro*, *marimba* (like the *marímbula*), and *tambora* (a double-headed drum), and by 1870, the button accordion took the place of the string instruments. Merengue was quite varied from region to region, but the style of the Cibao valley was most influential. By the 1920s merengue *típico* of Cibao had become somewhat standardized and could even include a saxophone playing melodies and countermelodies alongside the accordion. In contrast to many of the genres explored earlier, merengue focuses a great deal of its rhythmic intensity in emphasizing on-beats. So merengue is in 2/4 meter, and the "one, two, one, two" of each measure is pounded out by the kick drum and by the bass guitar (in contemporary ensembles), making this feel a prominent feature of the genre. The structure of these songs is similar to Cuban rumba/son in that there is a narrative section (called merengue) followed by a more syncopated call-and-response section (called *jaleo*). Early merengues also often included a short, march-like introduction, called a *paseo*, during which the dancers would make their way to the dance floor. This introductory section is rarely played in the contemporary moment. In the 1930s, nation, music, and ideology were linked by Rafael Trujillo, who rose to power in 1930 and remained in power until his assassination in 1961. Merengue was re-urbanized under Trujillo, who championed it as the national music (starting in 1936), using it not only to solidify his own dictatorial power, but also to posit a Dominican Republic distinctly different (in every possible respect) from Haiti. If Haiti was African, then the Dominican Republic was Iberian, and merengue from the cibao region appeared to support that claim. That merengue was already a thoroughly creole musical

MERENGUE TÍPICO:
"CONSANGRACIÓN DE CARIÑA"

 **LISTEN**

TRACK 11.5 **Accordion, saxophone, bass, guira, tambora, congas**

La India Canela

THIS RECORDING ILLUSTRATES the old three-part structure of merengue that used to be standard for merengue típico. It begins with a short, march-like paseo, which would have been used to give dancers enough time to escort each other to the dance floor. This is followed by the merengue section. At about [1:17], the performance moves into the third section, called *jaleo*. It is more improvisatory, more syncopated, and even moves between duple and triple meter toward the end. In the contemporary moment, most merengues will simply start with the merengue section, creating a two part merengue/jaleo structure not unlike the rumba/son structure explored earlier. The lyrics are an expression of true love:

You are so beautiful and so pretty that I love you.
I love all of you now and forever.
I dedicate to you my affection and help
and I'm thinking of loving only you eternally.
Yes! Before getting married, stop by here.
You belong to me and I will make you happy.
Before getting married, think it over.
Mami, you don't know how much I love you.
Listen beautiful negra, how do you know . . . how much I love you?
Nobody loves you like I love you!

(trans. Jodi Elliott)

TIME	SECTION	MUSICAL ELEMENTS
0:00–0:09	**Paseo**: This opening section presents only the accordion, bass, and guira. Notice the march-like quality, and think about how this short section provides just enough time to grab a dance partner and make your way to the dance floor.	The opening paseo melody is played by the accordion and accompanied by bass and guira.
0:9–0:18		The paseo is repeated.
0:19–0:32	**Merengue**: Notice the dramatic increase in tempo and the straight-forward 2/4 meter, emphasized by the bass, which plays on one and two consistently throughout this section. Listen also for the nimble counter-melodies and	The merengue gets underway, and the accordion and saxophone set the stage for verse one.

continued

TIME	SECTION	MUSICAL ELEMENTS
	harmonies played by the saxophone in response to the accordion.	
0:32–0:48		Verse one, delivered by two vocalists, is sung over an accompaniment accented by accordion and saxophone riffs at the end of phrases.
0:48–1:01		The accordion and saxophone take over and play an interlude.
1:01–1:17		The vocalists return and sing verse two.
1:17–1:36	**Jaleo**: This is the most syncopated, energetic section of the performance. Listen for the improvisatory explorations by all members of the ensemble and, in particular, for the sections, toward the end of the jaleo, during which the ensemble switches back and forth between 2/4 and 6/8 meter, creating sections during which 3 against 2 rhythms are prevalent.	The jaleo begins, and it is signaled by both a new melodic theme and by the shift in the bass guitar. Instead of playing on beats 1 and 2, the bass now intones notes on the off-beats of each measure (playing on the AND of 1 and the AND of 2). Notice that the end of this subsection ends in a repeated formula that signals the vocalists.
1:36–1:51		The vocalists take over, singing another verse.
1:51–2:10		The instrumentalists play another interlude, concluding with the repeated formula introduced earlier.
2:10–2:25		The vocalists take over again.
2:25–2:42		The instrumentalists return, this time playing in 6/8 time so that the rhythm shifts to 3 eighth notes per beat instead of 2 per beat as has been the case throughout the performance to this point. This 3 against 2 is heard most easily by listening to the bass guitar line. This shift to 3 against 2 heightens the intensity of the improvisations.
2:42–3:03		The instrumentalists return to the repeated formula that signals the return of the vocalists and also shift back to 2/4 meter in the process. Instead of bringing the vocalists back immediately, however, the accordion performs a solo over the repeating formula.
3:03–3:19		The vocalists return for a final verse.
3:19–3:44		The instrumentalists move again to a 3 against 2 feel in 6/8 meter. Listen for the bass guitar here, which improvises a bit within the harmonic framework.
3:44–3:52		The instrumentalists return to 2/4 meter and play a concluding figure to bring the performance to a close.

tradition, developed in and through negotiating both African and European influences, was expressly denied by Trujillo. This was to be a musical genre that countered Haitian musical styles, emphasized European aesthetic ideas, and would, so Tujillo hoped, unify the country with regard to class relations. He mandated that urban dance bands take up the merengue, and not a few merengues were composed in his honor. That lower-class, rural music was now being performed in elite ballroom settings was not a particularly satisfying turn of events for Dominican socialites, and yet Trujillo's mandates managed to firmly install merengue at the heart of Dominican national identity. The lower-class roots of merengue were resounded, in part through the use of swing bands, complete with trumpets and especially saxophones, that came to play a type of merengue called *orquesta* merengue. The piano accordion, moreover, became the instrument of choice in these orchestras because of the increased flexibility that it offers over the button accordion (which can play in only a few keys).

During the middle years of the twentieth century, both urban and rural styles of merengue existed side by side and were played on national radio, and although both remained tied to their class roots, both also served as markers of Dominican identity. The merengue típico of the Cibao has come to be called *perico ripiao* and remains the "roots" version of merengue. Following Trujillo's assassination in 1961, the orquesta merengue style gradually evolved into the popular, commercialized merengue (utilizing fairly typical electric dance band ensembles) that took the international scene by storm in the 1980s and 1990s and remains popular today.

Travel and Tourism: Reconfiguring Home and Away

As we have already seen, travel and tourism are important themes throughout the Caribbean—themes that play out in both centripetal (inward-moving) and centrifugal (outward-flowing) patterns. The musical styles that are created at "home" are affected by travel and tourism even as these creations, in going abroad, affect other places and musical practices. We will explore some of the other ways that travel and tourism can help us think about musical practices both within and outside the Caribbean by considering the several types of travel (both actual and imagined) with which the growing Caribbean diasporas in many locations throughout North America and Europe continue to negotiate their understandings of home and away, illustrating that Caribbean musics have participated in significant ways in globalized networks of music-making, and exploring several of the religious practices that have historically emerged in response to travel in the Caribbean. The emergence of major carnival festivities in New York (-Labor Day Carnival), London (Notting Hill Carnival), and Toronto (Caribana) reminds us to think about globalization as a double-edged and uneven process that globalizes the local while localizing the global. When we think about patterns of reception within the Caribbean, we also need to keep in mind that the movement outward from the Caribbean of these various musical styles and festival traditions does, in fact, affect in a tangible way the life of people in the métropoles even after it has returned "home." And this not least because many of these urbanites are Caribbean nationals who for educational or employment reasons have found themselves "abroad." The Labor Day Carnival works in large part because of the enthusiastic support of the Caribbean community in New York. Caribana represents not merely a chance to get together and play mas or to hear great artists, but also a means of recognizing publicly the twice-diasporized nature of life in a city like Toronto. That non-Caribbean participants gain exposure to and often appreciation for Caribbean Carnival arts and musical life is, of course, an important motivating factor and source of pride for those who are representing, say, Barbados at Notting Hill Carnival in London.

But travel and tourism also suggest the possibility of considering new relationships to the past and to "home" that are coming to characterize communities living abroad as well as those who have stayed behind. Nostalgia, for example, drives perceptions of home and away in significant ways. Take the lyrics of a Bahamian song entitled "Island Boy," and written by Eric Minns, which repeatedly assert: "Island Boy, you've got your mind on your job in New York but your heart's in the Caribbean." The new diasporas of the Caribbean configure themselves not only around family networks and everyday concerns related to employment and education, but also around memory and particular views of history that allow narratives of the past to be woven into a more nuanced sense of place in the present.

One strategy is to configure home as an idealized place that exists in the past (not just the good old days, but also that good old *place*). This process allows diasporic communities to view their "home" (say, Port of Spain) as simply a stopover on the road toward the "real home," but not really all that much better than their present physical location (say, London). This affords a new relationship to identity forged through recovering a way of being in the world (and of being in the present) that works toward that "good old place" (with all of the cultural and social implications that this idea entails), regardless of one's actual physical location. Importantly, this approach to home and away means that new traditions in new places not only become possible but desirable, and carnival celebrations in cities like London, New York, and Toronto are merely the most obvious examples of this trend.

Another example of this tendency is the musical effects that follow from the artistic interactions that occur between musicians from various locations throughout the Caribbean in places like New York. For instance, *salsa* is an example of how travel has influenced the music of the Caribbean and of Latin America. Salsa, which grew out of experiments by Latino musicians in New York during the 1960s, variously combined elements of Cuban and Puerto Rican musical styles (the principal, if not the only musical influences) to create a hybrid, flexible style that swept to popularity during the 1960s and 1970s. The presence of musicians from various locations throughout the Caribbean in New York and their musical interactions and negotiations led to a new genre that has since

Tarrus Riley performs during Reggae Sumfest in Montego Bay, Jamaica.
Source: Shelby Soblick/Getty Images

found a home (and legions of fans) in most urban centers of Spanish-speaking Latin America. Travel and tourism have led to new trends of music-making (salsa) and to new cultural practices (various carnivals) in those places outside the Caribbean where Caribbean nationals make their homes.

Caribbean musics have also had a global effect quite independent of Caribbean communities living abroad. Evidence of this can be seen in the immense global popularity of reggae, which took the world by storm during the 1970s and 80s, But reggae represents only one of the chapters of Jamaica's engagement with North American and globalized music markets. Jamaican popular dance music, in fact, has a long history of reciprocal exchanges with North American popular music. R & B heavily influenced the early history of ska in the 1950s and into the 1960s. While reggae was being sold to worldwide audiences by artists like Bob Marley, Peter Tosh, and Bunny Wailer (to name only three of the most iconic performers), *dub music* (versions of recorded reggae manipulated by engineers in ways that created new aesthetic visions of reggae) was beginning to influence the early explorations of hip hop in New York City. Dancehall, itself heavily influenced by hip hop, represents only the latest example within in a long history of these musical exchanges. Artists like Beenie Man, Sean Paul, Lady Saw, Buju Banton, Bounty Killer, and Elephant Man, to name just a few, are variously benefiting from collaborations with North American artists and finding it possible to release their own, very successful, records. It is important to recognize, then, that sound travels in different ways

EXPLORE

Jamaican Musics

and along different routes than do people, but that both of these patterns continue to create new and powerful musical practices that afford individuals, whether living within or without the Caribbean and irrespective of citizenship, new means of constructing their identities.

Some sacred musics offer another range of responses to questions of travel in the Caribbean. These musics are tied quite closely to diasporic narratives, growing from the need to address fundamental spiritual concerns in new contexts. Other sacred practices are clearly predicated on travel to the region by missionaries and, more recently, on the role of the mass media. All Caribbean sacred musics, however, give expression to the variety of ways that beliefs and cosmologies have been negotiated within the region. Catholic, Protestant, Hindu, Muslim, Jewish, and African religious contexts were all brought to the region during the colonial encounter. Of these religious systems, Catholicism and Protestantism were imposed on a great many people for whom these religions represented primarily another register of colonial control. One of the main results of these traveling (and imposed) religious practices has been religious syncretism, a strategy whereby elements from two or more religious traditions are combined into new practices. Stuart Hall (2001: 35) has remarked, "It is impossible, in my experience, to understand black culture and black civilization in the New World without understanding the cultural role of religion, through the distorted languages of the one book that anybody would teach them to read." His assertion rings true without regard to whether that one book was being taught by Baptists, Anglicans, or Catholics.

That said, African-derived drumming is a major component of the ceremonial music central to syncretic religious systems such as Cuban *santería*, Trinidadian *shango*, and Haitian *vodoun*, all of which have found ways of combining African deities and cosmologies with Catholic saints and doctrines. In santería the drums are called *batá*, and there are three main instruments in a batá ensemble: the *iyá* (largest drum), *itótele* (midsized drum), and *okónkolo* (smallest drum). The drums are considered sacred, and important rules and rituals circumscribe their construction, care, and use. Only initiated drummers may touch these drums, and the drums are imbued with a spiritual force, usually called *Añá*, upon their initiation. The drums are played without the improvisational elements present in genres such as rumba, bélé, and bomba. Instead, each drum plays more-or-less set rhythms that are associated with individual **orisha** and that also correspond, in part at least, to patterns and inflections particular to Yoruba language. These rhythms provide the foundation that the lead singer builds on in invoking the particular orishas toward which the batá drums are directed.

In Jamaica, a particularly rich range of responses to Protestant missionizing was deployed, including a practice called dual membership, whereby an individual could claim to be, say, Baptist, but would also participate in myal or convince rituals (both of which are local, African-derived religious practices). Rastafarianism, which developed in the 1930s, is significant in that it managed to link, albeit for a short time, its theological and social message to the

ORISHA
A spirit understood as one of the manifestations of God within Yoruba and Yoruba-derived religious practice.

soundtrack of reggae (thanks in large part to artists like Bob Marley). The message and the sound have been split from one another in recent years (especially with the rise of dancehall in the mid-late 1980s). Niyabinghi drumming, however, continues to be an important component of Rastafarian religious life. The *Niyabinghi* ensemble consists of three drums—*bass*, *funde*, and *askete* (which improvises over the solid rhythms performed on the other two drums)—an ensemble of instruments and an associated set of rhythmic ideas adapted from Jamaican Kumina rituals and from Burru drumming. Niyabinghi drumming is an excellent example of the ways that African-derived instruments and traditions can be "retuned" in the process of searching out and refashioning African roots.

During the middle decades of the twentieth century, Pentecostalist missionaries made significant inroads throughout the Caribbean (and in Latin America), as a result of which gospel music and contemporary Christian musical styles are now very prevalent in the region. Beginning in the 1970s, local genres have also been identified as potential evangelical tools, leading to new styles like *gospelypso* (calypso and gospel dancehall). These musical traditions often illustrate the complex ways in which church communities are utilizing regional and transnational styles both for their own local purposes and to participate in globalized forms of Christianity (see Rommen 2007).

Finally, there are also sacred musics that participate in religious networks separate from those that trace European and African religious travels. *Tassa drumming*, for example, accompanies the Hosay festival in Trinidad. *Hosay* is a Shia Muslim festival commemorating and celebrating the martyrdom of Husayn ibn Ali (the Prophet Muhammad's grandson). Ensembles include two primary kinds of drums—lead and second drums—and hand cymbals, but the number of players can vary greatly. Significantly, the Hosay festival has, in Trinidad, become a site of potential interethnic and interreligious participation. Hindu East Indians also contribute to the range of sacred musics circulating in the Caribbean. Two of the principal genres include **bhajans** and **chowtal**. A bhajan is a devotional song almost always incorporating a text dealing with a spiritual topic. In Trinidad, the bhajan is usually accompanied by a harmonium and sometimes by a violin, but because of the devotional nature of the material, virtuosity is consciously downplayed in bhajans.

One of the major Hindu festivals on the Trinidadian religious calendar is called phagwa, or holi. This festival is held in March and celebrates the victory of good over evil. Groups of East Indian men play and sing a style called chowtal during this festival, and there are often competitions during the phagwa season. Chowtal is usually accompanied by percussion (including hand cymbals, dholak, and dhantal).

The complex colonial encounter, coupled with the continued presence of missionaries, has created within the Caribbean a wide range of religious practices, each deployed to make sense of histories and futures, and each reflecting the need to make meaningful the present. Music has accompanied these travels and continues to offer audible and tangible support to people of faith throughout the region.

BHAJAN
Hindu devotional song.

CHOWTAL
A form of folk music associated with phagwa (holi) in Trinidad and having roots in Indian (Bhojpuri) folk music.

REVIEW CHAPTER RESOURCES

KEY TERMS

Bélé
Bomba
Calypso
Canboulay
Cariso
Chowtal
Chutney
Cinquillo
Copla
Décima
Diaspora
Junkanoo
Merengue
Obeah
Punta
Quadrille
Rake 'n' scrape
Rumba
Soca
Steel band
Tamboo bamboo
Zouk

SUMMARY

Cat Island, Monday June 5th: I am waiting at the Cat Island Airport, along with several dozen other late-departing festivalgoers, shooting the breeze and reliving some of the great moments of the weekend. We've heard storytelling, seen quadrille dancing, experienced traditional, popular, and sacred musics. In short, the festival provided a glimpse at many of the registers of musical life I have discussed in the preceding pages. In offering these short vignettes, I have juxtaposed each of these musics and themes to suggest ways they overlap, draw on each other, interact, and in general offer inspiration to each other. The unifying themes are powerful—rhythms like rake 'n' scrape and cinquillo, formal patterns like canto/montuno, ensemble aesthetics (like the predominance of three interlocking drum parts), and patterns of religious life, to name just a few possibilities, appear and reappear throughout the region. And yet, these common musical threads are highly individuated in terms of their local instantiations, accruing different meanings, diverse social functions, and new sounds, depending on where (and when) they happen to be performed. The cinquillo finds expression in rural, lower-class bélé drumming and in the elite spaces of Cuban danzón. The habanera rhythm finds itself equally at home in nineteenth-century Cuban contradanza and in today's reggaeton. Caribbean musics thus reflect the challenges of shared history while simultaneously reworking the present into sounds and shapes that offer new ways of making meaning and creating community. This holds true for nation–states and festivals like junkanoo, for the Garifuna Nation and genres such as punta rock, and for Arthur's Town, Cat Island, and that one rake 'n' scrape band: Ophie and the Websites.

BIBLIOGRAPHY

General Ray Allen and Lois Wilcken, Eds., *Island Sounds in the Global City: Caribbean Popular Music and Identity in New York* (New York: New York Folklore Society: Institute for Studies in American Music, Brooklyn College, 1998); Frances Aparicio and Cándida F. Jáquez, Eds., *Musical Migrations: Transnationalism and Cultural Identity in Latin/o America* (New York: Palgrave Macmillan, 2003); Kenneth Bilby, "The Caribbean as a Musical Region" in Sidney W. Mintz and Sally Price, Eds., *Caribbean Contours* (Baltimore, MD: Johns Hopkins University Press, 1985); Richard D.E. Burton, *Afro-Creole: Power, Opposition, and Play in the Caribbean* (Ithaca, NY: Cornell University Press, 1997); Belinda Edmondson, ed., *Caribbean Romances: The Politics of Regional Representation* (Charlottesville, VA: University Press of Virginia, 1999); Stuart Hall, "Negotiating Caribbean Identities" in Brian Meeks and Folke Lindahl, Eds., *New Caribbean Thought: A Reader* (Kingston, Jamaica: University of the West Indies Press, 2001); C.L.R. James, *Beyond a Boundary* (Durham, NC: Duke University Press, 1993 [1963]); Peter Manuel with Kenneth Bilby and Michael Largey, Eds., *Caribbean Currents: Caribbean Music from Rumba to Reggae*, 2nd ed. (Philadelphia, PA: Temple University Press, 2006); Peter Manuel, Ed., *Creolizing Contradance in the Caribbean* (Philadelphia, PA: Temple University Press, 2009); David Moskowitz, *Caribbean Popular Music: An Encyclopedia of Reggae, Mento, Ska, Rock Steady, and Dancehall* (Westport, CT: Greenwood, 2006); Dale A. Olsen and Daniel E. Sheehy, Eds., *The Garland Encyclopedia of World Music, vol. 2: South America, Mexico, Central America, and the Caribbean* (New York: Garland Publishing, 1998); Sandra Pouchet Paquet, Patricia J. Saunders, and Stephen Stuempfle. *Music, Memory, Resistance: Calypso and the Caribbean* (Kingston, Jamaica: Ian Randle, 2007); Susan Thomas, *Cuban Zarzuela: Performing Race and Gender on Havana's Lyric Stage* (Urbana, IL: University of Illinois Press, 2009); Eric Williams, *Forged from the Love of Liberty: Selected Speeches of Dr. Eric Williams*, Paul Sutton, Ed., (Port of Spain: Longman Caribbean, 1981); Kevin Yelvington, Ed., *Trinidad Ethnicity* (Knoxville, TN: University of Tennessee Press, 1993).

Monographs and Articles Frances Aparicio, *Listening to Salsa: Gender, Latin Popular Music, and Puerto Rican Cultures* (Hanover, NH: University Press of New England, 1998); Paul Austerlitz, *Merengue: Dominican Music and Dominican Identity* (Philadelphia, PA: Temple University Press, 1997); Gage Averill, *A Day for the Hunter, A Day for the Prey: Popular Music and Power in Haiti* (Chicago, IL: University of Chicago Press, 1997); Geoffrey Baker, *Buena Vista in the Club: Rap, Reggaetón, and Revolution in Havana* (Durham, NC: Duke University Press, 2011); Brenda Berrian, *Awakening Spaces: French Caribbean Popular Song, Music, and Culture* (Chicago, IL: University of Chicago Press, 2000); Curwen Best, *Culture @ the Cutting Edge: Tracking Caribbean Popular Music* (Kingston, Jamaica: University of the West Indies Press, 2004); Kenneth Bilby, *True-born Maroons* (Gainesville, FL: University of Florida Press, 2005); Rebecca M. Bodenheimer, *Geographies of Cubanidad: Place, Race, and Musical Performance in Contemporary Cuba* (Jackson, MS: University Press of Mississippi, 2015); Samuel Charters, *The Day is So Long and the Wages So Small: Music on a Summer Island* (New York: M. Boyars, 1999); Carolyn Cooper, *Sound Clash: Jamaican Dancehall Culture at Large* (New York: Palgrave Macmillan, 2004); Carolyn Cooper, *Global Reggae* (Kingston, Jamaica: University of West Indies Press, 2012); Carolyn Cooper, *Noises in the Blood Orality, Gender, and the "Vulgar" Body of Jamaican Popular Culture* (London: Macmillan Caribbean, 1993); John Cowley, *Carnival, Canboulay, and Calypso: Traditions in the Making* (New York: Cambridge University Press, 1996); Yvonne Daniel "An Ethnographic Comparison of Caribbean *Quadrilles*" in *Black Music Research Journal* Vol. 30, No. 2 (Fall 2010), pp. 215–240; Shannon Dudley, *Music from behind the Bridge: Steelband Spirit and Politics in Trinidad and Tobago* (New York: Oxford University Press, 2008); Shannon Dudley, *Carnival Music in Trinidad: Experiencing Music, Expressing Culture* (New York: Oxford University Press, 2004); Juan Flores, *From Bomba to Hip-Hop: Puerto Rican Culture and Latino Identity* (New York: Columbia University Press, 2000); Henry Frances, *Reclaiming African Religions in Trinidad: The Socio-Political Legitimization of the Orisha and Spiritual Baptist Faith* (Barbados: University of the West Indies Press, 2003); Oliver Greene, "Ethnicity, Modernity, and Retention in the Garifuna Punta" in *Black Music Research Journal* 22/2 (2002); Francio Guadeloupe, *Chanting down the New Jerusalem: Calypso, Christianity, and Capitalism in the Caribbean* (Berkeley, CA: University of California Press, 2009); Jocelyne Guilbault, *Zouk: World Music in the West Indies* (Chicago, IL: University of Chicago Press, 1993); Jocelyne Guilbault, *Governing Sound: The Cultural Politics of Trinidad's Carnival Musics* (Chicago, IL: University of Chicago Press 2007); Jocelyne Guilbault and Roy Cape, *Roy Cape: A Life on the Calypso and Soca Bandstand* (Durham, NC: Duke University Press, 2014); Katherine Hagedorn, *Divine Utterances: The Performance of Afro-Cuban Santeria* (Washington, DC: Smithsonian Institution Press, 2001); Dick Hebdige, *Cut 'n' Mix: Culture, Identity, and Caribbean Music* (New York: Routledge, 1987); Donald Hill, *Calypso Calaloo: Early Carnival Music in Trinidad* (Gainesville, FL: University Press of Florida, 1993); Nanette de Jong, "The Tambú of Curaçao: Historical Projections and the Ritual Map of Experi-ence" in *Black Music Research Journal* Vol. 30, No. 2 (Fall 2010), pp. 197–214; Michael Largey, *Vodou Nation: Haitian Art Music and Cultural Nationalism* (Chicago, IL: University of Chicago Press, 2006); Peter Manuel, *East Indian Music in the West Indies: Tan-Singing, Chutney, and the Making of Indo-Caribbean Culture* (Philadelphia, PA: Temple University Press, 2000); Elizabeth McAlister, "Listening for Geographies: Music as Sonic Compass Pointing Toward African and Christian Diasporic Horizons in the Caribbean" in *Black Music Research Journal* Vol. 32, No. 2 (Fall 2012), pp. 25–50; Elizabeth McAlister, *Rara! Vodou, Power, and Performance in Haiti and Its Diaspora* (Berkeley, CA: University of California Press, 2002); Rebecca Miller, *Carriacou String Band Serenade Performing Identity in the Eastern Caribbean* (Middletown: Wesleyan University Press, 2007); Robin Moore, *Nationalizing Blackness: Afrocubanismo and Artistic Revolution in Havana, 1920–1940* (Pittsburgh, PA: University of Pittsburgh Press, 1997); Robin Moore, *Music and Revolution: Cultural Change in Socialist Cuba* (Berkeley, CA: University of California Press, 2006); Viranjini Munasinghe, *Callaloo or Tossed Salad? East Indians and the Cultural Politics of Identity in Trinidad* (Ithaca, NY: Cornell University Press, 2001); Helen Myers, *Music of Hindu Trinidad: Songs from the India Diaspora* (Chicago, IL: University of Chicago Press, 1998); Sonjah Stanley Niaah, "A Common Space: Dancehall, Kwaito, and the Mapping of New World Music and Performance" in *The World of Music* Vol. 52, No. 1/3 (2010), pp. 515–530; Tejaswini Niranjana, *Mobilizing India: Women, Music, and Migration Between India and Trinidad* (Durham, NC: Duke University Press, 2006); Marc D. Perry, *Negro Soy Yo: Hip Hop and Raced Citizenship in Neoliberal Cuba* (Durham, NC: Duke University Press, 2015); Deborah Pacini Hernandez, *Bachata: A Social History of Dominican Popular Music* (Philadelphia, PA: Temple University Press, 1995); Raquel Z. Rivera, *Reggaeton* (Durham, NC: Duke University Press, 2009); Timothy Rommen, *Funky Nassau: Roots, Routes, and Representation in Bahamian Popular Music* (Berkeley, CA: University of California Press, 2011); Timothy Rommen, *"Make Some Noise:" Gospel Music and The Ethics of Style in Trinidad* (Berkeley, CA: University of California Press, 2007); Timothy Rommen and Daniel Neely, Eds., *Sun, Sea, and Sound: Music and Tourism in the Circum-Caribbean* (New York: Oxford University Press, 2014); Norman Stolzoff, *Wake the Town and Tell the People: Dancehall Culture in Jamaica* (Durham, NC: Duke University Press, 2000); Stephen Stuempfle, *The Steelband Movement: The Forging of a National Art in Trinidad and Tobago* (Philadelphia, PA: University of Pennsylvania Press, 1995); Ned Sublette, *Cuba and Its Music: From the First Drums to the Mambo* (Chicago, IL: Chicago Review Press, 2004); Michael Veal, *Dub: Soundscapes and Shattered Songs in Jamaican Reggae* (Middletown: Wesleyan University Press, 2007); Alexandra T. Vazquez, *Listening in Detail: Performances of Cuban Music* (Durham, NC: Duke University Press, 2013); Lise Waxer, Ed., *Situating Salsa: Global Markets and Local Meanings in Latin Popular Music* (New York: Routledge, 2002); Vivian Nina Michelle Woods, *Rushin' Hard and Runnin' Hot: Experiencing the Music of the Junkanoo Parade in Nassau, Bahamas* (Ph.D. diss. Indiana University, IN, 1995).

NATIVE AMERICAN MUSIC

Bruno Nettl

"NORTH AMERICAN INDIAN DAYS"

A Modern Ceremony

The scene is the town of Browning, Montana, in the middle of the Blackfeet Native American Reservation. To the west are the rugged mountains of Glacier National Park, and in all other directions one sees the yellowish look and the curved contours of the high plains in late afternoon. We are on the edge of the small town with its handful of stores, boarded-up businesses, and streets with potholes, and have gone to the center of a large circle of tents. Some are the kind you can buy at any camping store, but others are canvas versions of the grand tepees of the Plains tribes with their ceremonial painted decorations. We are entering a kind

of miniature stadium with entrances on four sides and an expanse of grass in the middle.

Some three hundred people are sitting on benches or folding chairs; about half of them seem to be Native Americans, the rest whites, many with cameras and cassette recorders. There is a podium on one side, and a master of ceremonies (MC) is speaking over a loudspeaker, asking dancers (who are not visible just yet) to prepare for the grand entry. Around the edge of the grassy center several bass drums are spaced, each representing a singing group of a half-dozen men that seems to be setting up amplification equipment. Eventually, eighteen singing groups take their places; a few of them include one or two women, but one of them is entirely made up of women. The MC proceeds to call the roll, naming and locating each group and giving it a number; each responds with a stroke on the drum. It turns out that the groups (also called drums) come from various locations on the reservation or from the Blackfoot reserves in neighboring Alberta. About half of them are from other tribes, from Eastern Montana, the Dakotas, Arizona, and Washington. Their names indicate locations or family names, and it becomes clear that the members of a "drum" are often members of an extended family.

Grand Entry

The MC, who happened to be the chief of the tribal council and a well-known politician in the Native American world of the 1970s, engaged in a bit of lighthearted banter and then called on one of the "drums" to sing the song for the "grand entry." Throughout the song, and, indeed, throughout most of the **powwow**, the members of the singing group sit in a circle, facing each other but essentially looking at their drums or the ground, bent forward, singing with great concentration, ignoring the audience and also the dancers when they finally enter the enclosure.

POWWOW
Tribal or intertribal gathering in twentieth-century Native American culture, a principal venue for performance of traditional and modernized music and dance.

Then, rather suddenly, we see dancers in flamboyant costumes entering from all four sides of the enclosure, each group in single file, moving to the right and steadily clockwise around the center of the circle, eventually making a wide stream of bodies, perhaps 150, moving rhythmically to the drumming. The men wear brightly colored cloth-and-feather outfits, each unique; the women wear long dresses decorated in various ways with beads and colored cloth, simpler and more modest than the men's costumes. Each dancer, however, has a costume in some sense of the word, while the singers wear blue jeans, T-shirts, and farmers' caps. From one entrance emerges a line of male dancers moving athletically, with large steps and jumps; on the opposite side, men with more restrained movements enter the enclosure. These two types of dancers are called fancy and traditional dancers, respectively. The women, though with much more restrained motions, divide themselves along the same lines in the other two entrances. All dancing is "solo." Couples do not dance, but while the men move singly and idiosyncratically, some of the women dance slowly, grouping themselves two or three abreast.

INTERTRIBAL
Songs or dances based on the Plains styles with which traditions of various other tribes are combined, developed for performances at modern powwows.

The song ends after seven or eight repetitions. The MC indicates that the next one will be sung by Drum no. 7 from Heart Butte (a small town thirty miles south of Browning) and that it will be (as most turn out to be) a type of song called **intertribal**. The singing and dancing begins again. It goes on like this for several hours, each drum or singing group taking its turn. The series of songs are frequently interrupted by related events such as a song and brief procession to mourn a recently deceased member of the community, different dances such as circle and owl dances (the latter danced by couples), dance

Powwow Festival: four Sioux male dancers with feather staffs dance in grand entry. *Source:* Tony Freeman/PhotoEdit

contests, and brief ceremonies. The style of the music is much the same throughout, and the singing groups from all locations sound similar and share a repertory. Members of the audience talk, walk in and out, speak with dancers and singers, take photos, and record the singing on cassettes. The scene is similar to that of a small-town sports event.

Ancillary Events

Although the main events of North American Indian Days take place in the dance enclosure, other activities with music are worthy of attention. In a small hut, a traditional gambling game, played by two teams facing each other and hiding a bullet or stick, is in progress. The team hiding the object sings constantly, songs with a limited melodic range consisting of the alternation of only two brief musical phrases, all the while beating rhythmically and rapidly on a plank. But the high, intense, pulsating singing of the dance songs is here replaced with a lower, more relaxed style. A couple of blocks away, a kind of barn dance is taking place in a parking lot, with a country-and-western band composed of members of the Blackfoot tribe singing old Nashville favorites. A half-mile further, south of the town, a small rodeo is in progress. It is billed as an "Indian rodeo"; its content is like that of other small-town rodeos in Montana, but the participants are all Native Americans. Before and between the events recorded music is played over a loudspeaker and attracts little attention; it is patriotic music, such as the national anthem, "America, the Beautiful," and also Sousa marches. The next morning there is a parade with

VOCABLE
Nonsemantic syllables that are sung; "nonsense syllables."

INCOMPLETE REPETITION
A song structure common in intertribal and Plains style and consisting of two sections. The first section includes a short melodic phrase, called a "push up" or "lead," followed by a repetition of that melody by another singer. This repetition is called the "second." The second section, called the "chorus" generally consists of two or more phrases and is, itself, repeated.

TERRACED MELODY
A melody structured so that it begins in a high register and "steps" or "cascades" down to a low concluding pitch.

BLACKFOOT WAR OR GRASS DANCE SONG

 **LISTEN**

TRACK 12.1 **Performed at North American Indian Days, Browning, Montana, 1966**
Sung by Heart Butte Singers (7 men)
Recorded by Bruno Nettl

THIS RECORDING ILLUSTRATES many features of the "plains" music area. The track fades in while the performance is in the middle of a stanza. We can clearly hear how the singers set up a steady rhythm by beating on the edge of their bass drum. When the first full stanza begins, the drum's leader sings an initial phrase in a falsetto voice—tense, harsh, loud, and ornamented [0:37–0:44]. This is often called the "push up" or "lead." The phrase is then repeated by a second singer. The whole group enters during this repetition, still singing softly. This portion of the strophe is called the "second." After this repetition, the whole group sings a stately melody, consisting of several short phrases and moving down the scale until it flattens out an octave below the beginning. The stanza comes to a close after this longer melodic section is repeated. This section is called the "chorus." The whole stanza is then repeated several times. Note that the first two stanzas are sung and drummed softly, and then tempo, intensity, and loudness increase rapidly (at about 1:30). The song has no words; only **vocables** or meaningless syllables are sung, but all of the singers perform these in unison. The overall form of the song can be represented as **AA BCDE BCDE**, with **BCDE** noticeably longer than **A**. In fact, **E** is a variation of **A**, an octave lower. This kind of song structure is called **incomplete repetition**. This type of melody, which begins high and gradually "steps" down to a low ending pitch, is often referred to as a "**terraced melody**."

TIME	SECTION	MUSICAL EVENTS
0:00–0:05	**Stanza 1:** The performance is already underway as the recording fades in. Listen for the clicks of the drumsticks on the side of the drum throughout this section. Listen also for the "hard beats" or "honor beats" toward the beginning of the second **B** Section.	The recording fades in as the repeat of Section **A** is under way (the "second").
0:05–0:22		Section **BCDE** (called the "chorus") is performed. Notice the clicking of the drumsticks on the side of the drum and the way the melody descends almost stepwise to its lowest notes at the end of the section. [0:05–0:08] **B** [0:09–0:12] **C** [0:12–0:16] **D** [0:17–0:21] **E**

continued

TIME	SECTION	MUSICAL EVENTS
0:22–0:37		Repeat of Section **BCDE**. Notice the incorporation of "hard" or "honor" beats at [0:27–0:29].
		[0:22–0:25] **B**
		[0:25–0:29] **C**
		[0:29–0:33] **D**
		[0:34–0:37] **E**
0:37–0:44	**Stanza 2:** Listen to the short **A** Sections, and notice the way that the melody is incorporated into the end of the "chorus" (phrase **E**), but sung an octave lower.	Section **A** begins the second stanza. This is sung by the lead singer. This is called the "push up" or "lead."
0:44–0:50		Section **A** is repeated, this time by a second singer. That singer is accompanied by the other performers (singing softly). This portion of the strophe is called the "second."
0:50–1:06		The "chorus" is sung by the whole group. Notice the melodic gesture toward the end of the section [0:57–1:01, phrase **E**] that mirrors Section **A** an octave lower.
1:07–1:23		The "chorus" is repeated, again incorporating "hard" or "honor" beats at [1:12–1:13].
1:24–1:30	**Stanza 3:** Listen for how the singer transitions the group from beating on the side of the drum to beating on the skin itself. Notice that the intensity increases markedly as all the performers begin to play on the skin of the drum.	"Push up" or "lead."
1:30–1:37		"Second," but this time the second singer begins to beat his drumstick on the skin at [1:33–1:37], signaling the whole drum to do the same. A crescendo (gradually increasing volume level) accompanies this shift and accomplishes a transition into the "chorus."
1:37–1:52		The crescendo carries into the "chorus." Notice that the intensity of the performance also increases at this juncture.
1:52–2:06		Chorus is repeated.
2:06–2:46	**Stanza 4:** Listen to the whole melody, and see if you can hear and feel it as a whole musical statement.	[2:06–2:11] "Push up."
		[2:11–2:16] "Second."
		[2:17–2:32] "Chorus."
		[2:32–2:46] "Chorus" repeated.
2:47–2:59	**Beginning of Stanza 5:** The recording fades out just as the repeat of Section **A** is begun.	[2:47–2:51] "Push up."
		[2:51–2:59] Fade out during the "second."

many dozens of floats representing businesses and institutions of the area—some are Native American, others white—this is a central event in North American Native American Days. Some of the floats have music, live or recorded, and for once one hears traditional Native American music—the modern intertribal songs—along with rock, jazz, and Christian hymns.

North American Indian Days is a spectacle that characterizes Native American culture in North America in several ways. First, it is a successor of the midsummer religious ceremonies that were held traditionally by many Native American societies. Furthermore, as an intertribal event, it symbolizes to both Native Americans and whites the broad Native American identity that is important to them. The fact that the same songs are known to singing groups from all over, that the same style (with some regional diversity) is used by many tribes, and that linguistic differences are submerged as the songs have no words (or occasionally English words) underscores that function of the powwow. The coexistence of several events, each with different music—gambling games from an ancient tradition, dancing from a modern Native American one, other events with Western music performed by Native Americans—symbolizes the present life of Native Americans as a separate population that nevertheless participates in the mainstream culture. The comparison of traditional and fancy dancers reflects the dual role of the event—traditional ceremony and modern entertainment. What is important for us to note is the way in which traditional Native American music is used to exhibit the old tradition but also to tie the various strands of the culture, old and modernized, to each other.

EXPLORE

History of Powwow

SOME OLDER CEREMONIAL TRADITIONS

The concept of "song" in most Native American cultures is a relatively short unit, rather like our nursery rhyme or hymn. Songs are ordinarily presented, however, in large groups and sequences as parts of elaborate ceremonies and rituals. Most religious ceremonies are elaborate affairs, lasting many hours or even several days. In many ceremonies, the songs to be performed and their order are specifically prescribed. In others they are not. In the **Peyote** ceremonies of Plains tribes, for instance, each singer must sing four songs at a time, but they may be any songs from the Peyote repertory, and only at four points in the ceremony must particular songs be sung.

Thus, the "Night Chant" (**Yeibechai**) of the Navajo, a curing ceremony, requires nine days and nights and includes hundreds of songs and their poetic texts. The **Hako**, a Pawnee ceremony of general religious significance, required several days and included about one hundred songs. The medicine-bundle ceremonies of the Northern Plains peoples might consist of several parts: narration of the myth explaining the origin of the bundle, opening the bundle and performing with each of the objects in it, a required activity (dancing, smoking, eating, praying), and the singing of one or several songs (usually by the celebrant, sometimes by him and others present) for each object.

PEYOTE MUSIC
Songs, in a characteristic style, accompanying a ceremony surrounding use of peyote, a drug derived from a cactus. The peyote religion is a major component of twentieth century Native American culture of the Plains and Southwest.

YEIBECHAI
A major curing ceremony, lasting nine days, of the Navajo; also known as "Night Chant."

HAKO
A complex ceremony of the Pawnee, carried out for the general welfare of the tribe and the world, requiring four days of singing, dancing, and ritual.

Native American drummers form a drum circle at the Cheyenne Arapaho powwow in Oklahama. *Source:* Allen Russell/Alamy

The Blackfoot Sun Dance, the largest and most central of the older tribal ceremonies of this culture, required four preparatory days followed by four days of dancing. The Peyote ceremony, which became a major religious ritual in many tribes of the United States in the course of the late nineteenth and twentieth centuries, consists of a night of singing. Each participant—there may be from ten to thirty sitting in a circle—sings four songs at a time, playing the rattle while his neighbor accompanies him on a special drum.

Secular events, too, are structured so that songs appear in large groups. The performance of a Stomp Dance, a social dance of southeastern origin performed by a line of dancers moving in snakelike fashion with responsorial singing, leader and group alternating, includes a dozen or so songs. The North American Native American Days powwow, described earlier, takes four days.

THE WORLD OF NATIVE AMERICAN CULTURES AND MUSIC

Native American Societies Past and Present

American Indian life today is highly variegated. Some tribal societies maintain their special identity; other groups of tribes were, through happenstance or force, obliged to share a reservation and have somehow fashioned a unified culture. Some activities and ceremonies, such as the powwow we have described, are of an essentially intertribal nature. Native Americans from various tribes find

CREEK STOMP DANCE SONG

 LISTEN

TRACK 12.2 **Song leader, John Mulley**

"**S**TOMP DANCE SONG" is really a series of songs to accompany a line dance, sung by the dancers. The dance leader is the song leader, and the form is responsorial, that is, the leader sings a short call or phrase, and the group responds by simply repeating what the leader has sung **(A)**, or something to complete his phrase **(B)**. This "call-and-response" is repeated a number of times until a high-pitched call ends the song and a new one begins. Ordinarily the first song consists of a call on one tone, the second expands the range, and others provide a slightly more complex melody. The singers accompany themselves with rattles. In form, melody, and rhythm the songs tend to become increasingly complex. The singers draw on a stock of traditional musical motifs whose content, variations, and order they improvise. This recording illustrates many characteristics of the "Eastern" music area.

TIME/SECTION		RHYTHM	FORM		MELODY
			Solo	*Group*	
0:07	Beginning call				
0:13	Song no. 1	Duple meter.	**A** (with variations)	**A**	Mostly on one tone.
0:30			**B**	**B**	Higher.
0:38			**C**	**C**	Triadic tune (like C–E–G).
0:47	Song no. 2	Triple meter (Beats: solo 1, 2; group, 3).	**D**	**E** (with many variations)	Higher. Note triadic melody throughout. Note the arc-shaped melodic contour, as the pitch gradually rises in the middle of the song and then descends.
1:07	Song no. 3	Five-beat meter (Beats: solo, 1, 2, 3; group, 4, 5).	**F**	**G**	Both F and G have more elaborate melodies than Song no. 2. Note the pentatonic bits of melody.
1:32	Song no. 4	Complex and varying meter. Sometimes solo has 8 beats, and group, 5.	**H**	**I** (much variation)	Melodic material more elaborate; scales are pentatonic, range over an octave.
1:46	**Rattle begins to be audible.**				
2:10	**End of excerpt.**				

themselves in large cities and join together to establish for themselves a common identity. In most respects, of course, they share the culture of their non–Native American compatriots, speaking English or Spanish. It is largely in music and dance that their Native American background is exhibited to themselves and to others.

Most of what is known about Native American music comes from the last hundred years, when recording techniques and ethnography were developed. Native Americans had, of course, already experienced much negative and positive contact with whites by this time, but in the early part of that period (late nineteenth and early twentieth centuries) one could still get a picture of what Native American music and musical culture may have been like before contact. It is clear, first of all, that each tribe had its own musical culture, repertory, musical style, uses of, and ideas about music. There were between one and two thousand tribal groups in North America, almost all speaking distinct languages. The average population of a tribe was around a thousand, but some were much larger, and others had only one hundred to two hundred persons. Each tribe, however, had a large number of songs and used them in many ceremonies, for curing, to accompany dances, and to draw boundaries between subdivisions of society such as age groups, clans, and genders.

Anthropologists have classified these cultures into six to eight groups called culture areas, each with characteristic types of housing, ways of acquiring and preparing food, clothing, religion, and economic and political structure. Thus, for example, the peoples of the North Pacific Coast fished, built wooden houses, had a rigid class structure including slaves, fashioned complex ceremonial sculpture such as totem poles and masks, and held special **potlatch** ceremonies to exhibit personal and family wealth and status. The Native American people of the Plains specialized in hunting buffalo as the prime source of food, housing, and clothes, first on foot with the help of dogs and later on horseback. They were nomadic, lived in tepees, and had a rather informal and egalitarian political structure. Their religion was based on guardian spirits that were acquired by men in dreams, and their ceremonial life included many kinds of acts that showed personal courage. The Pueblo Native Americans of the Southwest, on the other hand, lived in towns of cliff dwellings, grew corn and other plants, and had an extremely complex ceremonial life. In California, a great many very small tribes lived seminomadically, with complex ceremonial life, but subsistence based on hunting small animals, including insects, and gathering plants.

Unity and Diversity in Native American Music

Comparing the sound of North American Native American music with that of Africa or Japan shows that Native American music is relatively homogeneous. It is almost always **monophonic**, and with few exceptions it is vocal. Although there are a number of distinct singing styles, they have in common a tense sound and the use of pulsations on longer notes. Two or three types of forms

POTLATCH
A ceremony once common among the peoples of the North Pacific Coast, held to exhibit personal wealth and family status, and often commemorating important events in the life of the host (i.e., marriage, death, birth of a child, etc.). Potlatch ceremonies usually included a feast and the giving of gifts.

MONOPHONIC
Referring to music comprising a single melody; without chords or other melodic or harmonic parts.

predominate. There are strophic songs, rather like folk songs or hymns in that a stanza of several lines is repeated several or many times: some very short songs consist of one or a pair of lines repeated many times; and there are forms in which two contrasting sections of music, one usually higher than the other, alternate. Almost all the singing is accompanied by percussion, usually drums or rattles. Thus, the many Native American musical cultures have a good deal in common.

But if we were to go into great detail, analyzing hundreds of songs and making a statistical study of their characteristics for each tribe, we would discover that each group has a unique musical repertory and style. There are differences even between neighboring tribes. The picture is not totally confusing, however, as there are units, which we might call **music areas**, that coincide roughly, though not always precisely, with the culture areas. It is worth mentioning that they do not coincide well at all with language areas; that is, societies speaking related languages often do not share either cultural or musical characteristics.

MUSIC AREA
A group of Native American tribes who share similar musical styles, roughly corresponding to the cultural areas (but not by language).

Music Areas

The seven music areas are:

1. Plains
2. Eastern United States
3. Yuman (Southwestern United States and parts of Southern California)
4. Athabascan (Navajo/Apache; also Southwestern U.S.)
5. Pueblo (Papago; Southwestern United States)
6. Great Basin (Nevada/Utah)
7. Northwestern Coast (Oregon, Washington, and also some tribes in Alaska)

The Plains area coincides well with a culture area. It has the singing style most distant from standard Western singing, emphasizing high pitch, rhythmic pulsations on the long tones, tension, and harshness. Its characteristic form consists of stanzas internally arranged as follows: a short phrase is presented and repeated; there follows a descending line of three or four phrases ending with a low, flat cadence that is sometimes a version of the initial motif an octave lower; this long second section is repeated, so that the total may have the following scheme: **AA BCD BCD**. The Blackfoot song already discussed in connection with the great powwow (Track 12.1) is a typical Plains song.

The Eastern part of the continent has a greater variety of forms, which usually consist of several short phrases in different arrangements; a rounder and more relaxed vocal sound; some singing in which a leader and a group alternate brief bits of music, the so-called call-and-response pattern; and resulting from this, occasional bits of polyphony. The Creek Stomp Dance Song (Track 12.2) is typical of Eastern U.S. song.

A group of cultures representing the Yuman-speaking peoples of the southwestern United States and some cultures in southern and central California

LISTENING
GUIDE

WALAPAI FUNERAL SONG

LISTEN

TRACK 12.3 **Yuman style song**

THIS WALAPAI FUNERAL SONG illustrates two of the most prominent features of the Yuman music area. First, notice the relaxed vocal quality that the singers bring to the performance. Compare this, for instance, to the much more intense example of Plains style heard on Track 12.1. Second, the song structure incorporates a "rise." The overall structure combines two related melodic phrases (**A A′**) and repeats the pair four times before being interrupted by the "rise," which is higher in pitch and contrasting in character. After the rise is repeated, the performers return to singing **A A′**.

TIME	SECTION	MUSICAL EVENTS
0:00–0:03	**Fade in and A A′**: Listen for how the two short melodic phrases are paired together to create a repeating **A A′** structure.	The recording fades in as the performers complete Phrase **A′**.
0:04–0:08		Phrase **A**. Listen for the relaxed vocal quality of the performers.
0:08–0:12		Phrase **A′**.
0:13–0:17		Phrase **A**.
0:17–0:21		Phrase **A′**.
0:22–0:26	**Rise**: Listen for how the performers introduce a higher-register melody, the contours of which also contrast with the more static **A** and **A′** phrases.	The rise interrupts the lower-register melody, introducing a whole new range of higher pitches and a much more active melody line.
0:26–0:31		The rise is repeated.
0:32–1:17	**A A′ and Rise**: This time see if you can hear how these two, lower-pitched and more static melodic phrases work to set up the "rise." You'll hear four repetitions of the **A A′** pairing, followed by the rise. When the rise bursts onto the scene, listen for how much energy it injects into the song, not only because of the higher pitches and the more active melody but also because it takes a while to arrive.	[0:32–0:35] Phrase **A**. [0:35–0:40] Phrase **A′**. [0:40–0:45] Phrase **A**. [0:45–0:49] Phrase **A′**. [0:50–0:54] Phrase **A**. [0:54–0:58] Phrase **A′**. [0:59–1:03] Phrase **A**. [1:03–1:08] Phrase **A′**. [1:08–1:12] Rise. [1:13–1:17] Rise Repeated.
1:17–1:31	**Back to A A′ as a conclusion**: Listen for how a final statement of the **A A′** pairing brings the song to its conclusion.	[1:17–1:21] Phrase **A**. [1:22–1:31] Phrase **A′** and end of song.

GHOST DANCE
Native American (principally Plains) religious movement of protest against U.S. government excesses of the 1880s.

POLYPHONIC
Generic term referring to all music in which one hears more than one pitch at a time, for example, songs accompanied by guitar, choral music, orchestral music, or two people singing a round together. Refers more specifically to music that incorporates two or more simultaneous melodic lines or parts.

EXPLORE

Inuit Songs and Vocal Games

specialize in a form in which one section, a phrase or short group of phrases, is repeated several times but is interrupted occasionally by another, slightly higher and definitely contrastive section, called by some Yuman peoples and also by ethnomusicologists the "rise." Here also we have a relaxed kind of vocal style. The Walapai, a Yuman culture, are representative of this music area.

Also in the southwestern United States we have the Athabascan style of the Navajo and Apache peoples. Its typical traits are a large vocal range, a rather nasal-sounding voice, and even rhythms that can almost always be written by using only quarter- and eighth-notes.

The style of the Pueblo Native Americans shares features with those of both the Athabascan and the Plains peoples but has a low, harsh, pulsating vocal style and long, complex forms. Related to both Plains and Pueblo songs are those of the Papago people. The Great Basin style, found in Nevada and Utah as well as northern California, and also in the **Ghost Dance** songs of the Plains people, has songs with small vocal range and with a characteristic form in which each of a group of phrases is repeated once, for example, **AABBCC**. This style is illustrated in the Pawnee Ghost Dance recording (Track 12.5).

The Northwest Coast peoples and some of the Inuit share a typical singing style and complex rhythms, often pitting patterns in voice and drum against each other. The Northwest Coast is also the area richest in wind instruments and has a well-documented, if not prominent, **polyphonic** tradition.

IDEAS ABOUT MUSIC

What It Is and What It Does

For all their interest in music and their large repertories, Native American peoples did not develop longer, more complex forms with greater interactions. There are three main reasons why this didn't happen:

1. Oral tradition places some limitations on the complexity of materials to be remembered.
2. There is really quite a lot more complexity, at a microscopic level, than the listener may at first perceive.
3. Most important, the idea of technical complexity has never been a criterion of musical quality to Native American peoples. Rather, music is measured by such things as its ability to integrate society and to represent it to the outside, its ability to integrate ceremonial and social events, and its supernatural power. The rather athletic view of music taken in Western culture, where star performances by individual composers and performers and their ability to do difficult things is measured, is replaced in Native American cultures by quite different values.

Music has supernatural power. In Blackfoot culture, it is the songs that, as it were, hold the power. Thus, each act must have its appropriate song. In a ceremony in which a medicine man is trying to influence the weather, he will have a bundle of objects, which he opens and displays, but their supernatural power is not activated until the appropriate song is sung. In many Native American cultures, songs are thought to come into existence principally in dreams or visions.

Composition and Creativity

In the Plains, a man has visions in which powerful guardian spirits appear to him, and these are validated by the songs they sing to him. As many songs have no words, it is clearly not simply the texts but the act of singing—producing a kind of sound that has no other function in life—that embodies spiritual power. The strong association with religion, unusual even when we consider that religious music is a cultural universal, is characteristic of Native American music.

Beyond the composition of songs in visions by Plains people, the creation of songs is viewed differently in Native American traditions than in most European and Asian cultures. It may be that songs are thought to exist in the cosmos and need to be brought into human existence through dreams. In some tribes songs are extant in the supernatural world but need to be "unraveled" by humans in dreams to be realized. In an Inuit culture, there is a finite quantity of songs, and new ones can be made up only by combining elements of extant ones. In some tribes, making up songs is associated with emotional or mental disturbance. Except in modernized musical contexts, one rarely finds a situation in which humans are given credit for creating music. Specialists in making up songs are usually also experts in religious matters, and their technical competence or aesthetic creativity seems not to be an issue.

Music, a Reflection of Culture

In Native American cultures even more than others, the musical system is a kind of reflection of the rest of culture. A Blackfoot singer said, "The right way to do something is to sing the right song with it"; and indeed, in theory at least, the Blackfeet have particular songs for all activities. The more an activity is subdivided—as, for example, a ceremony—the more specific the association of songs with its various parts. For example, in the Beaver Ceremony, the ceremonialist has a bundle of 168 objects, mostly dressed skins of many birds and animals of the environment but also some handmade objects, rocks, and sticks. For each he must sing the appropriate song. Traditionally, the men of the tribe divided themselves into seven societies by age, and a man was initiated successively into them roughly every four years. Each society had its ceremonies and certain duties in social life and warfare, and each had its separate group of songs. There were special songs for warfare, riding, and walking. The most important social division, between men and women, was also reflected musically. Women had, so it seems, a separate and much smaller repertory, although they might join in singing certain men's songs; but more important, their singing style was different, with a smoother and more nasal tone than the men's, and with the pulsations being not rhythmic stresses but melodic ornaments. In many Native American cultures, the major divisions in society are paralleled in musical repertory and style.

MUSICAL INSTRUMENTS

Types of Instruments

In North America, the Native American music is prevailingly vocal. Almost all instruments are percussive, and their function is to provide rhythmic accompaniment to singing. Solo drumming is actually rare. But there is a great variety of drum and rattle types. Large drums with two heads or skins, small hand-drums with a single skin, kettledrums filled with water for tuning, and pieces of rawhide simply suspended from stakes are examples of drum types widely distributed. There are container rattles made of gourds, hide pieces sewn together, or a turtle shell; others fashioned of strings of deer hooves; and more. Although the musical function of these instruments is essentially the same, a culture may have many types, distinguished in the details of decoration with beads, feathers, animal skins, carving, and painting, each type associated with a particular ceremony. There are other idiophones as well such as notched stick scrapers, clappers, beaten planks, stamping tubes, and jingles. Small metal bells,

Plains Indian hand drum with drumstick covered with raw hide. *Source:* Wanda Nettl/Bruno Nettl

Northwest Coast Indian drum.
Source: Wanda Nettl/Bruno Nettl

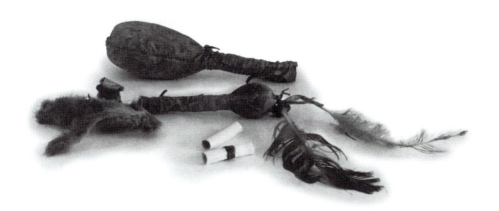

Blackfoot ceremonial objects: Two medicine bundle rattles, pair of gambling bones. *Source:* Wanda Nettl/Bruno Nettl

introduced centuries ago by Europeans, have become established and incorporated in some of the cultures.

The most widespread melody-producing instrument is the flute. Various kinds of flutes are found, including true end-blown flutes in which the player's pursed lips direct a ribbon-shaped column of air against an edge of the blowhole, as well as duct flutes rather like European recorders. In some tribes, the repertory of flute music consists simply of songs that may also be sung. Elsewhere, particularly in the southwestern United States, there is a separate repertory of flute music, although its style is not markedly different from that of the songs.

Among the instruments found in small numbers among a few tribes, we should mention the use of simple reeds and trumpets for recreational and ceremonial occasions on the North Pacific Coast. The musical bow, similar to or identical with a hunting bow, appears to have been used as an instrument in the southwestern United States and has been succeeded by the "Apache fiddle" or Navajo violin, a bowed instrument with one horsehair string and a cylindrical body about twelve inches in length, probably created as a combination of the bow and the Western violin.

EXPLORE

Native American Flutes

Instruments, Singing, and Words

Most important, however, the instruments of Native Americans are largely nonmelodic percussion instruments, and melody-producing instruments have special and restricted functions. In this respect Native Americans are similar to other cultures with small populations such as the tribes of Australian aboriginals, whose main instruments are percussion sticks of eucalyptus, struck against each other, and the *didgeridoo*, a long trumpet used mainly to play a single-tone drone. It is important to know, however, that the didgeridoo requires complex playing techniques such as circular breathing and changes in the shape of the mouth cavity for varying the tone color. In Polynesia, instruments are used mainly to accompany singing, and in Melanesia and Micronesia the principal instruments are panpipes.

If the relative dearth of melody-producing instruments is noteworthy in Native American cultures of North America, it is important to keep in mind that, in many of them, songs may not be primarily a vehicle for words. Although some Native American song texts, like those of the Navajo and Pueblo peoples, are often highly elaborate poems, in Plains people culture songs may have no words at all but only *vocables*. Where there are words, they are usually brief and occupy only a short portion of the melody. Here are the *complete* texts of two Blackfoot songs: "Sun says to sing" (song of the Sun Dance ceremony); and "It is spring; let others see you" (sung at the beginning of a medicine-bundle ceremony, before the bundle is opened). In a sense, we could conclude that songs without words substitute for the absent instrumental music.

ASPECTS OF THE HISTORY OF NATIVE AMERICAN MUSIC

Reconstructing Prehistory

There is little direct or written information about the history of Native American music, yet various kinds of circumstantial evidence permit reasonable guesses toward a rough reconstruction. Though there is still considerable debate about the early history of Native American presence in the Americas, most scholars agree that they originally arrived, probably in waves, from Asia at least 14,000 years ago and possibly much earlier. If there are musical styles and practices that Native Americans share with Asian cultures, they would have to be very ancient. The only musical material to which one can reasonably point is the existence, in many Indian cultures, of a stratum of short, simple songs consisting of one or two repeated lines and built on a scale of three or four tones, associated with children, games, and love charms. Among these, it is game songs, usually called gambling songs, that remain most widespread today.

This type of music, consisting of short tunes with few pitches repeated or varied many times, is found in many parts of the world and may possibly be a remnant of a highly archaic stratum of human music. Comparison of North and South American Native American music may also reveal some clues. There are musical styles shared by the two regions. For instance, peoples of the Gran Chaco, a region in the Rio de la Plata basin, South America, have forms and a singing style not too different from that of the North American Plains. Ideas about music—the reflection of cultural categories in modes of performance, music's central role in myths about the origin of culture, music as a way of com-municating within and with the supernatural world—often seem similar in the two regions. On the other hand, South American Native American music is, in most respects, very different from North American: there are more instances of major participation by women, and there is much more instrumental music. This suggests that the musical styles of North America developed independently and perhaps later. As cultures tend to hold on to their languages more

 **LISTEN**

TRACK 12.4    **Performed by Joe Washington and family**

ALTHOUGH THIS EXAMPLE is performed by the Lummi, who represent a Northwest Coast culture, this gambling song does not illustrate that music area's general song style or musical characteristics but belongs, rather, to the special style of game songs, which is distributed widely throughout the continent. This is a song that accompanies a game in which one team hides sticks, singing while the other team tries to locate them. Notice the subtle **A A'** form of the melody. The rough sketch of the contour of each melodic section that follows points out the main differences. The melody is also mirrored in parallel fourths (an interval). You can hear this by listening for a higher-pitched voice in the background, singing along with the main vocalist. Finally, notice that the song utilizes only four notes. You can see this in the representations shown here.

Compare the notation shown previously to this textual representation of the contour and follow along as you listen.

Section	A					
Highest pitch	long,	long,	short, short, short			
				short,	long	
					short,	long,
Lowest pitch						long (x2)
Section	**A'**					
Highest pitch	long					
		short, short,	short, short, short			
			short,		short, long,	short, short
Lowest pitch					long long, long,	

continued

TIME	SECTION	MUSICAL EVENTS
0:00–0:03	**A**: Listen for the melodic contour of the **A** Section. Notice also that the melody is being mirrored in parallel fourths by another vocalist (quite far in the background of the mix).	Steady drums provide a foundation for the song.
0:04–0:10		Section **A** is performed.
0:10–0:12		Notice that the vocals drop in volume once the lowest note is reached, thereby foregrounding the drums.
0:12–0:18	**A'**: Listen now for the ways that the **A'** section differs from section **A**. The second highest note becomes more important here than the highest note (which drives section **A**). The melody is also slightly more ornamented, with more neighboring notes incorporated into the contour. Finally, the section is slightly longer than Section **A**.	Section **A'** is performed, also ending on the lowest note.
0:18–0:21		The drums again take precedence as the vocalists end the phrase on the lowest note and prepare to transition to Section **A**.
0:22–0:39	**A and A'**: Listen to the whole melody again and see if you can hear and feel it as a whole musical statement.	[0:22–0:28] Section **A**. [0:28–0:30] Transition to **A'**; the drums are foregrounded here. [0:30–0:35] Section **A'**. [0:36–0:39] Transition to **A**; the drums are foregrounded here.
0:40–1:04	**A and A' and fadeout**: Listen to the whole melody again and this time see if you can hear and feel it as a whole musical statement without following along with the time markers. Can you hear the transition from section **A** to **A'**?	[0:40–0:46] Section **A**. [0:46–0:48] Transition to **A'**; the drums are foregrounded here. [0:48–0:53] Section **A'**. [0:53–0:57] Transition to **A**; the drums are foregrounded here. Fadeout begins. [0:57–1:04] Fadeout completed as Section **A** begins again.

tenaciously than to other things, and as language groupings do not often coincide with musical areas, the music of one society may have changed rapidly and frequently. If so, the picture of Native American music history must have been quite variegated, with tribes adopting new music as they changed important aspects of their culture.

It is assumed that large ceremonies and massed populations generally give rise to complex musical structures, and thus Aztec and Mayan societies had choral music and probably polyphonic structures. But this kind of correlation is not found in East Asia, and as few instruments were either extant or preserved in archeological sites, little can be known about the music of the classical Mexican cultures. Similarly, archeological sites in the United States and Canada give us little information about musical life.

Modern Music History

Since the Coming of White People Native American history is better documented, and aspects of it have been widely studied since the coming of white people. The tragic social and political history is accompanied by a great reduction in the content of musical culture. Clearly, as entire tribes were wiped out and virtually all Native American peoples were relocated, suffering cultural disintegration through devastating famines and epidemics, knowledge of ceremonies and rituals as well as social repertory decreased, and much was simply forgotten. As Native Americans were motivated to take up Western lifestyles and religion, they also began to participate in Western music and sometimes to adopt Western conceptions of music for their own musical culture. So in the Plains, for example, the notion that all songs have a supernatural origin has been replaced by the acceptance of human composition. And to the original emphasis on music as a carrier of supernatural power has been added the European concept of music as entertainment.

But the tragic history of the Native Americans also brought with it, as a happier kind of by-product, interesting new developments in music, as Native American people came to use music as a weapon to fight back against total absorption and to preserve their cultural identity.

The Ghost Dance The modern music history of Native Americans may be said to begin after the great tragedy of the massacre at Wounded Knee in 1890, which resulted in part because Sioux and Arapaho people had taken up the practice of the Ghost Dance religion. This messianic cult began in the Great Basin area (Utah and Nevada) and was taken up by the Plains tribes, who hoped that it would help them in combating and defeating the white people, bringing back the dead, and restoring the buffalo—in other words, bring back the good old days. As these Plains people learned the Ghost Dance ceremony, they learned its songs, which were composed in a simple style that also made them think of a simpler, better time. But these songs and their style also enriched Plains music. Typical Ghost Dance songs consist of a few short phrases, each of them repeated once: **AABBCC**. This style of music, taken up by many tribes—thus, an intertribal style—was superimposed on the older song traditions.

LISTENING GUIDE

PAWNEE GHOST DANCE SONG: "THE YELLOW STAR"

 **LISTEN**

TRACK 12.5 **Sung by Wicita Blain, c. 1919**
Recorded by Frances Densmore

FRANCES DENSMORE WAS among the first to record Native American performers. She did so on an early recording device—called a phonograph—that used wax cylinders to record the sounds. You'll notice that the sound quality on this selection is somewhat muffled and that you can hear a pulsing hissing or scratching in the background. That pulsing is caused by the way the needle amplifies the rotation of the wax cylinder during playback. This recording thus affords us a chance to hear both the machine and the performer, as it were. More importantly, because this recording is so early, we are afforded a chance to hear a Native American performer before the influence of twentieth-century mass media came to exert as great an impact as it would over the coming decades.

This recording is a Ghost Dance song in the style of Great Basin music, but it is sung by a Plains Pawnee singer. Its form is typical of Ghost Dance repertory, in that it consists of three short phrases, each of which is repeated before moving on to the next phrase; **AABBCC**. The phrases are, in fact, very short. Note, for example, that two repetitions of the **"A"** phrase take only about six seconds to perform.

TIME	SECTION	MUSICAL EVENTS
0:00–0:03	**Phrase A**: Listen for the distinct contour of this short phrase. Notice the repeat.	Phrase **A**.
0:04–0:06		Phrase **A** repeated.
0:06–0:09	**Phrase B**: Listen now for the ways that Phrase **B** is distinct from Phrase **A**, in both melodic contour and length (slightly longer).	Phrase **B**.
0:09–0:12		Phrase **B** repeated.
0:13–0:15	**Phrase C**: Listen for the unique character of Phrase **C**.	Phrase **C**.
0:15–0:17		Phrase **C** repeated.
0:18–0:31	**AABB**: Here, listen for the how phrase **A** and **B** complement each other. Phrase **A** includes the highest pitches in the whole song. Phrase **B** moves through a middle register to the lowest note in the song. Phrase **C** is not performed in this repetition.	[0:18–0:23] Phrase **A** and repeat. [0:23–0:31] Phrase **B** and repeat.
0:32–0:48	**AABBCC**: Having listened for the way that phrase **A** and **B** complement each other, now listen to how phrase **C** completes the structure. Phrase **A** includes the highest pitches in the whole song. Phrase **B** moves through a middle register to the lowest	[0:32–0:37] Phrase **A** and repeat. [0:37–0:43] Phrase **B** and repeat. [0:43–0:48] Phrase **C** and repeat.

continued

TIME	SECTION	MUSICAL EVENTS
	note in the song. Phrase **C** reinforces this low note and sets up a return to the higher register of phrase **A**.	
0:49–1:14	**AABBCC:** Listen here for the slight variations that are introduced especially in the **B** and **C** phrases.	[0:49–0:53] Phrase **A** and repeat. [0:54–1:01] Phrase **B** and repeat. [1:01–0:08] Phrase **C** and repeat followed by several seconds of silence at the end of the performance.

A tribe of Sioux Indians perform a Ghost Dance, a traditional dance thought to bring peace, prosperity, and a return of lost lands from The *London Illustrated News,* published in 1891. *Source:* MPI/Getty Images

Peyote Music   The songs of the Peyote religion (already mentioned in our discussion of ceremonies), like the Ghost Dance songs, are an intertribal overlay on the individual tribal and area styles. Although Ghost Dance songs are hardly ever sung any more, Peyote songs are a major element in the contemporary Native American music scene. Based on the hallucinogenic buttons of a cactus native to Mexico, the Peyote religion spread through much of the Native North American world between 1700 and 1940. Peyote religionists developed a distinct song repertory; you can easily recognize a Peyote song regardless of the singer's tribal identity. Their singing style is probably derived from that of the Navajo. The rhythmic structure uses elements of Apache rhythm—the "incomplete repetition" type of form and the descending melodic contour

<table>
<tr><td>LISTENING
GUIDE</td><td>KIOWA PEYOTE SONG:
"OPENING PRAYER SONG"</td><td> LISTEN</td></tr>
</table>

TRACK 12.6 **Performed by David Apekaun**

THIS EXAMPLE ILLUSTRATES the intertribal Peyote style and is sung by a Kiowa singer. This "Opening Prayer Song," using the syllables "he-ne-ne-ne-ha-yo-wi-tsi-na-yo," has a two-part structure in which a line is sung, repeated, and then replaced by another. A concluding line is then sung, followed by the closing formula "he-ne-yo-we." This pattern is then repeated with slightly different melody and a new line (**D**) and without the repeat of the **A** line, making the second part of the structure shorter than the first. The complete form of a verse can be sketched as **AABCX** (closing formula), **A'DCX** (closing formula). You'll notice that the last line and the closing formula remain constant in both parts of the verse structure.

It is best to listen by following the vocables or syllable sequences of this recording in order to hear the structure. I've indicated the syllables as they are sung. The syllables are also a guide to the rhythm. Shorter notes and syllables are combined with hyphens; longer notes and syllables stand on their own.

TIME	SECTION	MUSICAL EVENTS
0:00–0:03	**Introduction**: Listen for the opening gestures on the kettledrum (often called a water drum) followed by the entrance of the singer.	Drum enters. The recording fades in as the repeat of Section **A** is under way.
0:03–0:07		Introductory vocal: *he ne he ne he ne he ne ne.*
0:08–0:24	**Stanza 1**: Listen for the overall structure of the song by following along the vocables or syllable sequences.	[0:08–0:11] **First Section**: Line **A**. *ha (he) ne ne ha-yo-wi-tsi na yo* [0:12–0:15] Line **A** repeated. *ha he ne ne ha-yo-wi-tsi na yo.* [0:15–0:18] Line **B**. *ha na-yo-wi-tsi na hi-ya no ha wa.* [0:19–0:20] Line **C**. *ha hi-yo wa ne.* [0:20–0:24] Line **X** (closing formula). *ha-yo-wi-tsi na he ne yo we.*
0:24–0:34		**Second Section**: Line **A'**. Notice the same syllabic sequence as **A** in the first section, but a different melody here. *ha he ne ne ha-yo-wi-tsi na yo.* [0:27–029] Line **D**. Here both melody and syllable sequence are new, so a new letter is assigned (**D**). *he-ya-na-yo-wi-tsi na yo.* [0:29–0:31] Line **C**. *ha hi-yo wa ne.* [0:31–0:34] Line **X**. *ha-yo-wi-tsi na he ne yo we.*

continued

TIME	SECTION	MUSICAL EVENTS
0:35–0:50	**Stanza 2**: This time see if you can hear the closing formula at the end of the first and second sections of the stanza. This will help you get a feel for the shape of this song.	**First Section**: Listen for the closing formula [0:47–0:50]: *ha-yo-wi-tsi na he ne yo we.*
0:50–1:01		**Second Section**: Again, see if you can hear the closing formula [0:57–1:01]: *ha-yo-wi-tsi na he ne yo we.*
1:01–1:26	**Stanza 3**: Listen to the whole melody and see if you can hear and feel it as a whole musical statement.	[1:01–1:16] **First Section**. [1:16–1:26] **Second Section**.
1:27–1:57	**Stanza 4**: Now try once more to hear as many structural details as you can, including the closing formula at the end of the first and second section.	[1:27–1:41] **First Section**: Listen for the closing formula [1:38–1:41]: *ha-yo-wi-tsi na he ne yo we.* [1:41–1:57] **Second Section**: Again, see if you can hear the closing formula [1:48–1:52]: *ha-yo-wi-tsi na he ne yo we.* Notice that the drum speeds up during the closing formula, thereby emphasizing the conclusion of the song.

come from the musical practices of the Plains (and can be heard in Track 12.1), and the percussion accompaniment is a kettledrum filled with water that possibly originated in the southeastern United States.

You can identify a Peyote song by its words—or, rather, "meaningless" vocables or syllables sequences, as they are quite unique; examples are "heyowitsinayo," "heneyowitsine," and "heyowanene," and each song ends with an amen-like "heneyowe." The origin of these vocable patterns is not known, but conceivably they came from the Comanche language of the southern Plains. This is a religion that tries to tie Native American peoples together and takes a conciliatory position toward Christianity, and thus Christian texts in English are occasionally used. Here, too, we see forced culture change resulting in new musical style and the broadening of Native American musical culture.

Peyote songs must be sung at certain structural points in the nightlong ceremony, at the beginning, and at sunrise; most songs can be selected by the singers at their discretion, as long as they are Peyote songs. The Peyote religion has some Christian overtones; the name of Jesus appears occasionally among the vocables. Some religionists claim that "Indians know Jesus better than do white people," and the Peyote organization is known generally as a "church." Quite apart from Peyote music, there is also a body of Christian hymnody based on traditional Native American music, with hymnals that include traditional Anglo-American hymn tunes and monophonic songs in traditional style with Christian words.

EXPLORE

Native American Music and Christianity

The Powwow Culture   In the second half of the twentieth century, the most significant trend has been the development of the powwow culture. This is the most visible strategy for building an intertribal Native American culture and the consciousness of ethnic identity that goes with it, and it is joined by the establishment of a Native American popular music whose sound is clearly in the mainstream of American popular music styles, but that is still recognizably native. In a related development, Native American artists have made significant contributions to the world of concert music and dance.

This intertribal style, based on Plains music and forming a common song repertory for the powwow culture, was illustrated in our description of the Blackfoot North American Native American Days. However, powwows take place throughout the United States and Canada, in places of concentrated Native American population, where they celebrate ethnic identity and intertribal unity. Where there are few Indians, powwows are used to make nonnatives aware of Native American culture. Native Americans have used the powwow as a powerful wedge for making themselves—but also, it's important to note, others—aware that they are no longer the "vanishing American."

A celebration on the campus of the University of Illinois in Urbana dramatically illustrated the use of the powwow for education and empowerment. It was presented by a small number of Native Americans, largely visitors from out of town, with the main purpose of instructing local people in the structure, content, and functions of intertribal powwows. The visitors received pamphlets on "Powwow Etiquette" with instructions that included certain ritual actions: times to stand, to sit, to remove hats, to dance or not to dance, to take pictures and to refrain, but above all, to follow the directions of the master of ceremonies. All this was justified by reference to unspecified older sacred Indian traditions, but the main purpose of the rules was to create a situation in which a distinction between whites and natives was drawn—a distinction defined by the natives, but also intended in certain respects and at some moments, to be ignored or overcome. Music and dance were used to negotiate and symbolize, to establish times in which whites were to stay out of the native business, and other times in which they were to participate. As in the powwow at Browning, discussed at the beginning of this chapter, music and dance were used to cope with the nonnative "other" in a number of ways.

A part of the powwow repertory is the body of so-called forty-nine songs or forty-niner songs, which ordinarily have mildly romantic or amusing (and sometimes considered by powwow dancers as uproariously funny) words in English, such as "I don't care if you're married sixteen times, I will get you," or "When the Dance is over, sweetheart, I will take you home in my one-eyed Ford," or "My sweetheart, she got mad at me because I said hello to my old-timer, but it's just OK with me".

A Native American record industry marketing native music—primarily the intertribal powwow repertory—to Native Americans emerged in the 1950s (with the label North American Soundchief) and flourishes yet today. Clearly, many young Native Americans spend much of their music listening time with these CDs and tapes. The concept of music as mainly ritual and communication with

TWO MODERN POWWOW LOVE SONGS  **LISTEN**

TRACK 12.7   **Recorded by Willard Rhodes**

BOTH OF THESE SONGS alternate vocable verses with English language words. They are composed in a simple strophic format, **AABC** (first excerpt) and **AABB'** (second excerpt). The English language lyrics are introduced into this structure with a different melody, but they are worked into the overall form of the stanzas as follows: **DD'BC** and **CCBB'**, respectively.

TIME	SECTION	MUSICAL EVENTS
0:00–0:09	**SONG 1, Stanza 1**: Listen for the overall structure of this short verse—**AABC**.	[0:00–0:04] **A** [0:04–0:08] **A** repeated.
0:09–0:14		**B**
0:14–0:18		**C**
0:18–0:22	**Stanza 2**: Listen for the English language lyrics, sung to a new melody, but connected back into the structure of the stanza in the **B** and **C** phrases (sung, again in vocables).	[0:17–0:21] **D** (new melody). *When the dance is over, sweetheart.*
0:22–0:26		**D'** (**D** melody extended). *I will take you home in my one-eyed Ford.*
0:26–0:30		**B**
0:30–0:33		**C**
0:34–0:52	**Stanzas 3 and 4**: This time see if you can hear the way that these two, slightly different melodic shapes work together in alternation. The **A** phrase is sung with vocables and incorporates the highest pitches in the song. The **D** phrase contrasts with this because of its lower register and incorporates English language text. Both are unified by the **B** and **C** phrases.	Stanza 3: all vocables.
0:52–1:10		Stanza 4: English and vocables.
1:11–1:20	**SONG 2, Stanza 1**: Listen for the overall structure of this short verse—**AABB'**.	[1:11–1:15] **A** [1:16–1:20] **A** repeated.
1:20–1:26		**B**
1:26–1:33		**B'**
1:34–1:43	**Stanza 2**: Listen for the English language lyrics, sung to a new melody. There are more lyrics here than in the first song, but the performers still manage to get back to the structure of stanza 1 by the **B** and **B'** phrases.	**C** (new melody). *My sweetheart, hey-a-hey-a.*

continued

TIME	SECTION	MUSICAL EVENTS
1:37–1:43		C repeated and **B** (melody folds into **B** at the end of the line).
		She got mad at me because I said hello to my old-timer.
1:43–1:50		**B'**
		But it's just ok with me, oh wey-a-wey . . . hey.
1:51–2:12	**Stanzas 3 and 4**: This time see if you can hear how these two, slightly different melodic shapes work together in alternation. The **A** phrase is sung with vocables and incorporates the highest pitches in the song. The **C** phrase contrasts with this because of its lower register and incorporates English language text. Both are unified by the **B** and **B'** phrases.	Stanza 3: all vocables.
2:13–2:34		Stanza 4: English and vocables.

the supernatural has given way to one of music as entertainment and an expression of ethnic identity. There are now virtually countless singing groups, or "drums," some known only on their own reservation, others traveling widely, following the powwow circuit, entering contests that provide substantial monetary prizes.

Women in Native American Music   It is widely stated, and perhaps even true, that women's role in Native American musical activity before about 1900 was restricted and, at any rate, quite different from that of men. But surely the many tribes differed greatly in this regard. In some California tribes and among the Navajo, women played important ceremonial roles. In Plains cultures, they were restricted to private events, whereas musical performances in public or for addressing the supernatural were men's activity. In modern Native American culture, women have played increasingly prominent roles. For one thing, they have often held onto older traditions better than men. Judith Vander found that Shoshone women knew and could sing old songs, including those of the Ghost Dance, better than men. My male informants among the Blackfoot sometimes turned to their wives for jogging their musical memories.

The matter of gender sometimes played a special rule in musical life. In some Plains cultures, Berdaches—men who dressed as women and did women's work and might be homosexual—were sometimes extolled as great singers. And among the Blackfoot, women identified as "manly-hearted," often daughters of influential men, associated themselves culturally with men, could be hetero-sexually promiscuous, and carried out the male roles in ceremonies, singing men's songs in men's singing styles.

As observed at North American Indian Days in Montana, women have increasingly become active as members of drums, or powwow singing groups. In the powwow tradition of 1960, a drum was usually based on the men of an extended family—father, sons, nephews, sons-in-law—along with some close friends. Occasionally a woman of the family might sit in. Gradually, however, the participation of women increased, to the extent that many drums have several female members, and a number of drums traveling the powwow circuit consist entirely of women. Some drums consisting largely of men have female leaders.

Popular Music Of particular interest is Native American music's entry into the mainstream of American popular music. There is a genre known simply as "Indian rock music," which combines the use of some traditional tunes, the percussive sound of Native American songs, and texts derived from or referring to Native American culture. Among the famous exponents of this music in the 1960s and 1970s was the jazz-rock musician Jim Pepper, a Native American musician performing with a multiracial ensemble. His popular "Newly-Wed Song" uses material from the two forty-nine songs that we previously heard. As early as the mid-1960s, rock groups devoting themselves more explicitly to protest, such as XIT, came to the fore, along with Native American singers, such as Buffy Sainte-Marie and Peter LaFarge, who performed Western-style popular music with words about Native American issues.

Photo of Tony Bellamy.
Source: Gary Null/© March 25, 2011 NBCUniversal/Getty Images

In the 1990s, the Navajo flutist Carlos Nakai developed a variety of styles based on, or referring to, Native American culture, composing for traditional, popular, and classical music contexts, performing solo and with Western instruments. The ensemble Ulali, led by a female singer, performs music syncretizing Western and Native style, singing Plains-like tunes but in vocal harmony and backed by chords on synthesizers and guitar. Flutes, which played a modest role in many Native cultural traditions, have increased in importance, to the extent that flute music accounts for perhaps half of the Native music recordings produced for the mass market. This shift in emphasis probably results from the importance of instruments in Euro-American culture.

These recent developments in musical sound and in ideas about music as well as contexts for performance show that Native American music is very much alive. Native American peoples use it, and dance, more than anything else to show to each other and to other Americans that they are a distinct ethnic group. To them, music functions both as a way of maintaining their cultural integrity and as a form of mediating between themselves and other culture groups. In this sense it continues a tradition, for in earlier times, too, its function had been that of mediation, but between humans and the forces of the supernatural.

 **EXPLORE**

Native American Rock

In historic times, Native American tribes were probably concerned about their natural environment, as is evident in the attention to wildlife as natural phenomena in their traditional ceremonies. No doubt, however, they sometimes also violated the environment, taking occasion, for example, to slaughter more buffalo than needed for survival. In the second half of the twentieth century, they became increasingly involved in preservation and protection, as their areas of residence were affected by large-scale industry, mining, fishing, and agriculture. Much of the modern popular music produced by Native American musicians speaks to environmental issues, and Euro-Americans have increasingly interpreted Native American culture as symbolic of environmental and spiritual concerns and made it part of the "New Age" cultural movement. Native American musicians have sometimes accepted these attitudes, seeing the New Age movement as an ideological ally as well as a market for Native art and music. Thus, for example, one can find numerous CDs of Native American flute music labeled as appropriate for meditation.

Much of the Native American popular music does not differ in its musical style and sound from mainstream rock, blues, and pop, but its words deal with social, economic, and political issues faced by American Indians. Traditional-sounding music such as the powwow repertory, but also including other nonceremonial genres, continues to be hugely popular in Native American communities as indicated by the thriving CD and prerecorded cassette market. Recent surveys uncovered twenty-three different tapes and CDs of Blackfoot music in a shop frequented by Blackfoot customers in Montana and thirty-three CDs of older traditional, modernized, New Age, and popular Native American music in a large bookstore in a Midwestern college town.

REVIEW CHAPTER RESOURCES

SUMMARY

Our explorations conclude with a brief review of the main sounds of and ideas about music in Native American life. Native American songs tend to be very short, and are generally sung in large groups for specific rituals. Individual skill is not valued as highly as group participation in performance. The voice, moreover, is the primary instrument. Drums, rattle, scrapers, and flutes are the most widespread percussion and wind instruments. Native American singing style usually features a tense, pulsating voice, though this does vary a bit among the seven "music areas" that we have identified as having common musical cultures. The Yuman music area, for instance, is known for a more relaxed vocal quality than is the Plains musical area.

In traditional Native American culture, music serves as a mediator between humans and the supernatural world. In recent memory, music has continued to serve a mediating function in this way (i.e., Peyote Songs), but has also been used to mediate representations of Native American culture to non-Native American listeners and to their fellow Native Americans. Since the coming of white people, new forms—such as the Ghost Dance and Peyote Song—have developed, and intertribal musical styles have become prevalent. Today,

KEY TERMS

Ghost dance
Grand entry
Hako
Incomplete repetition
Intertribal
Music area
Peyote music
Plains indians
Potlatch
Powwow
Terraced melody
Vocable
Yeibechai

Western pop influences—including rock and hip hop—have led to a new type of intertribal popular music. The vitality of Native American popular music continues to suggest creative ways of addressing Native American concerns about the environment and related to presenting Native American history to new audiences.

BIBLIOGRAPHY

North America as a Whole Tara Browner, Ed., *Music of the First Nations: Tradition and Innovation in Native North American Music* (Urbana, IL: University of Illinois Press, 2009); Tara Browner, *Heartbeat of a People: Music and Dance of the Northern Pow-wow* (Urbana, IL: University of Illinois Press, 2002); Bryan Burton, *Moving Within the Circle: Contemporary Native American Music and Dance* (Danbury, CT: World Music Press, 1993); Beverley Diamond, "Native American Contemporary Music: The Women" in *The World of Music* Vol. 52, No. 1/3, the world of music: Readings in Ethnomusicology (2010), pp. 387–414; Marcia Herndon, *Native American Music* (Hatboro, PA: Norwood, 1980); Richard Keeling, Ed., *Women in North American Indian Music: Six Essays* (Bloomington, IN: Society for Ethnomusicology, 1989); Richard Keeling, "Animal Impersonation Songs as an Ancient Musical System in North America, Northeast Asia, and Arctic Europe" in *Ethnomusicology* Vol. 56, No. 2 (Spring/Summer 2012), pp. 234–265; Luke Eric Lassiter, Clyde Ellis, and Ralph Kotay, *The Jesus Road: Kiowas, Christianity, and Indian Hymns* (Lincoln, NE: University of Nebraska Press, 2002); Victoria Lindsay Levine, *Writing American Indian Music: Historic Transcriptions, Notations, and Arrangements* (Middleton, WI: A-R Editions for the American Musicological Society, 2002); Bruno Nettl, *North American Indian Musical Styles* (Philadelphia, PA: American Folklore Society, 1952); Michael Pisani, *Imagining Native America in Music* (New Haven, CT: Yale Univeristy Press, 2005); Helen H. Roberts, *Musical Areas in Aboriginal North America* (New Haven, CT: Yale University Press, 1936); John William Troutman, *Indian Blues: American Indians and the Politics of Music, 1879–1934* (Norman, OK: University of Oklahoma Press, 2009.)

Plains Cultures Frances Densmore, *Teton Sioux Music* (Washington, DC: Bureau of American Ethnology, 1918); James Howard and Victoria Levine, *Choctaw Music and Dance* (Norman, OK: University of Oklahoma Press, 1990); Luke E. Lassiter, *The Power of Kiowa Song* (Tucson, AZ: University of Arizona Press, 1998); Alan P. Merriam, *Ethnomusicology of the Flathead Indians* (Chicago, IL: Aldine, 1967); Bruno Nettl, *Blackfoot Musical Thought: Comparative Perspectives* (Kent, OH: Kent State University Press, 1989); William K. Powers, *War Dance: Plains Indian Musical Performance* (Tucson, AZ: University of Arizona Press, 1990); Christopher A. Scales, *Recording Culture: Powwow Music and the Aboriginal Recording Industry on the Northern Plains* (Durham, NC: Duke University Press, 2012); Robert Witmer, *The Musical Life of the Blood Indians* (Ottawa: National Museum of Man, 1982).

Other North Native American Peoples Rani-Henrik Andersson, *The Lakota Ghost Dance of 1890* (Lincoln, NE: University of Nebraska P, 2008); Beverley Cavanagh, *Music of the Netsilik Eskimo: A Study of Stability and Change* (Ottawa: National Museum of Man, 1982); Charlotte Frisbie, ed., *Southwestern Native American Ritual Drama* (Tucson, AZ: University of Arizona Press, 1980); Chris Goertzen, "Powwows and Identity on the Piedmont and Coastal Plains of North Carolina" in *Ethnomusicology* Vol. 45, No. 1 (Winter, 2001), pp. 58–88; Anna Hoefnagels and Beverley Diamond, Eds., *Aboriginal Music in Contemporary Canada: Echoes and Exchanges* (Montreal: McGill-Queens University Press, 2012); Kristina Jacobsen, "Rita(hhh): Placemaking and Country Music on the Navajo Nation" in *Ethnomusicology* Vol. 53, No. 3 (Fall 2009), pp. 449–477; Thomas Johnston, *Eskimo Music by Region: A Comparative Circumpolar Study* (Ottawa: National Museum of Man, 1976); Richard Keeling, *Cry for Luck: Sacred Song and Speech Among Yurok, Hupa, and Karok Indians of Northwestern California* (Berkeley, CA: University of California Press, 1992); David P. McAllester, *Peyote Music* (New York: Viking Fund Publications in Anthropology, 1949); David P. McAllester, *Enemy Way Music* (Cambridge, MA: Peabody Museum of American Archeology and Ethnology, 1954); Frank Mitchell, *Navajo Blessingway Singer*, Ed. Charlotte J. Frisbie and David P. McAllester (Tucson, AZ: University of Arizona Press, 1978); Ruth Murray Underhill, *Singing for Power: The Magic of the Papago Indians of Southern Arizona* (Berkeley, CA: University of California Press, 1938); Judith Vander, *Songprints* (Urbana, IL: University of Illinois Press, 1988); Judith Vander, *Shoshone Ghost Dance Religion: Poetry, Songs, and Great Basin Context* (Urbana, IL: University of Illinois Press, 1997).

Instruments Paula Conlon, "The Native American Flute: Convergence and Collaboration as Exemplified by R. Carlos Nakai" in *The World of Music* Vol. 52, No. 1/3, (2010), pp. 118–131; K.G. Izikowitz, *Musical and Other Sound Instruments of the South American Indians* (Götesborg, Sweden: Kungl, Vetenskap-och Vitterhets-Samhälles and lingar, 1935); Thomas Vennum, Jr., *The Ojibwa Dance Drum* (Washington, DC: Smithsonian Institution Press, 1982); Beverley Cavanagh Diamond and others, *Visions of Sound* (Chicago, IL: University of Chicago Press, 1995).

DISCOGRAPHY

Anthologies *A Cry from the Earth: Music of the North American Indians* (Folkways FC 7777; 1979); *An Anthology of North American Indian and Eskimo Music* (Ethnic Folkways FE 4541; 1973).

Blackfoot *An Historical Album of Blackfoot Indian Music* (Ethnic Folkways FE 4001; 1979); *Blackfeet* (Indian IR 220; ca. 1980); *Blackfeet Pow-Wow Songs* (Canyon C-6119; 1974).

Other North American Peoples *American Indians of the Southwest* (Ethnic Folkways P 420; 1951); *Music of the Sioux and Navajo* (Ethnic Folkways P 401; 1949); *Kiowa Peyote Ritual Songs* (American Indian Soundchief Kiowa-590; ca. 1970); *The Great Plains* (Canyon ARP 6052; 1966); *Indian Music of the Canadian Plains* (Ethnic Folkways FE 4464; 1966); *Papago Dance Songs* (Canyon 6098; 1973); *Popular Dance Music of the Indians of Southern Arizona* (Canyon C-6085; 1972); *Inuit Games and Songs* (UNESCO Collection Musical Sources, Philips 6586 036; 1978); *Indian Songs of Today* (Library of Congress AFS L36; ca. 1960); *Omaha Indian Music* (American Folklife Center, Library of Congress AFC L71; 1984); *Inuit Games and Songs* (Auvidis Unesco AD 090); *Native American Traditions: Music of New Mexico* (Smithsonian/Folkways SF 40408); *Creation's Journey: Native American Music* (Smithsonian/Folkways SF 40410); *Heartbeat: Voices of First Nations Women* (Smithsonian/Folkways SF 40415); *Dancing Buffalo: Cornel Peewardy and the Alliance West Singers;* Dances and Flute Songs from the Southern Plains (Music of the World CDT-130); *Talking Spirits: Native American Music from the Hopi, Zuni, and San Juan Pueblos* (Music of the World CDT-126).

Recent Developments *Spirit Horses: The Music of James Demars* [*Concerto for Native American Flute and Chamber Orchestra*] (Canyon CR 7014); *Solo Flights: Various Native American Artists* (Soar 1245-CD); *Ulali: Mahk Jchi* (Thrush Records CD 0605287581); *Walela: Unbearable Love* (Triloka 7930185209–2); *Northern Wind: Jingle Dress Songs* (Arbor Records AR-11282).

MUSIC OF ETHNIC NORTH AMERICA

Byron Dueck

MUSIC, ETHNICITY, AND POLITICS IN PUBLIC PERFORMANCE

On a cold October day in 2002, the city of Winnipeg in the western Canadian province of Manitoba welcomed Queen Elizabeth II. She was touring the country as the nominal head of state—Canada is, unlike the United States, a constitutional monarchy—to commemorate the fiftieth year of her reign. Two public concerts were organized for the occasion, the first in the afternoon at a park in the city center, the second in the evening on the grounds of the provincial legislative buildings.

At the first event, the Queen and Prince Philip strolled through the grounds of the Forks Historic Site at the juncture of the two rivers that meet in the center of the city. The afternoon was devoted to performances by young amateur

CHAPTER

13

musicians and celebrated the ethnic diversity of the province. When immigrants began to pour into Manitoba from around the world in the late nineteenth century, they often came in large groups and settled in geographic blocs, inspiring early twentieth-century commentators to remark on a patchwork ethnic "mosaic" in the western provinces. Fittingly, then, the visitors were met on their walk by performers who represented some of these historical communities, including a Ukrainian dance troupe and Mennonite and Icelandic youth choirs.

Upon reaching the shore of the Red River, the royal guests were seated for a short program of performances. A choir of students from the northern port town of Churchill sang the national anthem in French, English, Cree, and Inuktitut

Queen Elizabeth II greets members of a Canadian Indian dance troupe during welcoming ceremonies in Winnipeg. *Source:* ADRIAN WYLD/AFP/Newscom

(the country's official languages and two Indigenous ones). A group of young French Canadian women presented an exhibition of folk dancing in the distinctive Franco-Manitoban style, the dancers doing an animated "jig" step while moving through intricate ensemble patterns. A high-school dance group performed "Cabaret" from the musical of the same name, and there were speeches from a number of politicians. The program culminated in a performance of *Spirit of the Rivers*, a work for choir, narrator, dancers, and prerecorded musical accompaniment.

The event organizers had clearly put a great deal of thought into how this concluding performance might represent the cultural diversity of the province. *Spirit of the Rivers* had lyrics in English and French, but also in Cree. The music was in a contemporary Western choral idiom, but the prerecorded accompanying track incorporated a number of prominent elements that suggested Indigenous music: rattle, drum, and a series of high-pitched cries of the kind sometimes heard in the powwow singing of the northern plains (see Chapter 12). As the piece moved into an untexted instrumental coda, dancers from various traditions joined in: a group of young ballet dancers occupied the center of the stage, while dancers representing the province's Scottish, Irish, Portuguese, Ukrainian, and Afro-Caribbean communities performed behind them.

This performance synchronized through music and dance the various social groups that are often held to comprise Canada as a nation. The languages sung corresponded to the three populations that have been most active in negotiating their sovereignty relative to one another throughout the country's history: anglophones, francophones, and Indigenous Canadians. Meanwhile, diverse dance styles represented other immigrant ethnic groups. In short, the event brought together members of the communities whose interrelationships and integration have long been the subject of national political discussions. (Political philosopher Will Kymlicka, for instance, describes the historical development of Canada as involving "the federation of three distinct national groups (English, French, and Aboriginals)" supplemented by a fourth, "polyethnic" population of immigrants [1995: 12–13]). Dance and song made the national mosaic visible and national polyphony audible.

And yet a second welcoming concert, held at the provincial legislative grounds later that day, occasioned a decidedly less consonant display of national coexistence. In the period leading up to the Queen's visit, spokespeople from a number of First Nations groups had voiced concerns about the federal government's failure to live up to the obligations outlined in the treaties signed with Indigenous communities in what is now the province of Manitoba. The living conditions in these communities, which were generally much poorer than anywhere else in the province, were a particularly sharp grievance, as was recently proposed legislation understood to threaten Indigenous sovereignty. First Nations leaders asked to meet with the Queen during her visit, but their request was refused. Following this, a number of them announced that, having been denied a voice in the planning of the welcoming ceremonies, they would organize their own greeting. And thus it was that on the day of the Queen's arrival, a group of protesters, including a number of prominent Manitoban Indigenous leaders, marched to the legislative grounds, where the second concert was to take place. They made their way down Salter Street, a north-south artery that travels through the North End and Central neighborhoods, where a considerable portion of the city's Indigenous population lives, to the provincial legislative grounds, the symbolic center of the city and province. The procession was headed by a drum group whose members sang songs in the Northern Plains style (see Chapter 12).

Upon arriving at the legislative grounds, where thousands of people were gathering to enjoy the concert and the following fireworks, the protesters, still led by the drum group, moved toward the roadway where the Queen's vehicle was to arrive. Meanwhile the event was getting underway. In contrast to the afternoon program, it gave pride of place to professional adult performers, including dancers from the Royal Winnipeg Ballet and new-age harpist and singer Loreena McKennitt. The drum group sang throughout, right in the middle of the rest of the audience. This didn't sit well with some of the people trying to listen to the "official" performance, and they began angrily shouting at the protesters. I began to worry that something unpleasant might occur. Members of the police came to speak to the drum group, urging them to move back, but they nonetheless continued to sing. Toward the end of the concert, the Queen arrived, and the protesters momentarily pressed closer to the road to greet her with another song. Having welcomed her as promised, they moved back and away from the stage. As fireworks lit up the sky and the orchestra played Handel's *Music for the Royal Fireworks*, they grouped one last time near a war memorial north of the legislative grounds to sing a few more songs.

UNITY, DIVERSITY, AND DIFFERENCE IN NORTH AMERICAN MUSIC

As this account suggests, music is an important part of North American social and political life, and an essential element at moments of celebration and solemnity. But what is particularly North American in this account? Certainly one distinguishing factor is the nature of the cultural diversity on display. In Canada and the United States, Indigenous residents comprise a statistical minority, whereas the great majority of the inhabitants are immigrants and descendents of immigrants, or descendents of slaves who were forcibly taken from their lands of origin. This ethnically diverse population is, moreover, continually being supplemented by new arrivals. Accordingly, much of the music and dance that people regard as their own has origins in other lands, or emerged because preexisting practices were creatively fused and exchanged by the new inhabitants of North America.

As the chapters in this book show, there are other ethnically diverse cultural areas, and there are many countries with significant immigrant populations. But North American social relations and musical life reflect a particularly long-standing series of encounters between original Indigenous inhabitants, long-resident immigrant populations, and newer arrivals. Musical dynamics have for centuries involved negotiations between newcomers and older communities, and the expression of multiple, potentially conflicting, identities and affiliations. Thus, some ninety years before the royal visit described previously, in the same city, the annual industrial exposition held a "Foreign Night" to welcome members of various recently established immigrant communities. Over the course of the evening, a band played patriotic songs from France, Germany, Russia, Italy, and Iceland to an audience of appreciative foreign-born Winnipeggers. At the conclusion of the event, probably as a way of suggesting where the deepest loyalties of this cosmopolitan audience ought to lie, a picture of the reigning monarch, George V, was created in fire (*Manitoba Free Press*, July 15, 1911, pp. 1, 14). Moreover, such events are clearly not unique to Canada: festivals of ethnic diversity are also widely celebrated across the United States, including the St. Paul Festival of Nations in Minnesota and the Albany Festival of Nations in New York.

As these accounts suggest, musical performances of ethnicity play an important role in North American expressions of political ideals. On days of national celebration, North Americans often affirm concepts of national unity in diversity. Bright costumes, sounds, and dances are brought together, and the eyes and ears of the public witness a variegated multicultural nation emerge as the sum of ethnic difference. Yet, as the opening vignette suggests, performances of ethnic music and dance may also reveal political divisions and tensions, or advance alternative social and political visions. The 2002 welcoming ceremonies for Elizabeth II affirmed, from one perspective, a unified ideal, but they also evidenced the misgivings of some groups. The two clashing welcomes— one claiming to represent the province, the other its First Nations inhabitants —demonstrated in a dramatic way the limits of the government's ability to represent its constituent populations, musically and otherwise. They also suggested that the relationship between ethnicity, nationality, and various other forms of affiliation is rarely simple or straightforward.

THEMES IN NORTH AMERICAN MUSIC

This chapter examines music in North America, paying special attention to how it helps to organize and enrich social life. We will look at a variety of musical genres on this excursion, including children's singing games, ballads, fiddling, dance music, gospel singing, blues, and jazz. Several broad themes will accompany us as well. We have already seen how music asserts ethnic differences, and how musical performances make political relationships between groups audible and visible. We will also explore how music shapes experiences of passing time and of changing social states and relationships; investigate how ethnic groups maintain distinct and particular musical traditions even as they borrow musical elements from other communities and groups; and consider musical phenomena that seem, by contrast, to be shared across many boundaries, whether of community, ethnic group, or region. We will then spend some time examining the special contribution of African American music to North America. Finally, we bring our excursions to a close by considering how music is conceptualized.

Three broader questions underlie these investigations. The first concerns difference and similarity. Many North American ethnic, religious, regional, and community groups have their own unique musical styles and practices. At the same time, certain widespread cultural elements play a significant role in shaping North American musical life, even across social boundaries. These include Christianity, the legacy of slavery, economic structures such as labor specialization and capitalism, and widespread musical forms such as the two-part fiddle tune and common-practice harmony. One challenge for this chapter (and for ethnomusicology more generally) involves accounting for these widely distributed aspects of North American musical life, while also recognizing the ways they are complicated and challenged by ethnic, religious, and regional particularities and local practice.

A second broad question has to do with the differences between professional and nonspecializing musicians, and between everyday musical activity and more extraordinary moments of performance. Consider the performances by the schoolchildren at the afternoon welcoming ceremony previously described. To prepare for such events, "ordinary" children have to spend long hours practicing on their own and rehearsing with colleagues in classrooms, community halls, church basements, and other spaces of assembly. Calendars have to be coordinated and money spent on travel and costumes. In short, ethnic performance is a special, passing moment made possible by a much longer engagement with ethnic community. And thus ethnicity is not experienced solely in moments such as the one just considered. It is also lived in everyday interactions that prioritize certain groups of people, specific ways of interacting, and particular musical activities.

A third broad question involves the concept of performance, broadly conceived: what do musical acts accomplish? Here again, it is useful to refer back to the opening vignette. Ritual festivity in this case presented national unity from a certain perspective—but from another it made apparent deep differences of opinion about the government's right to represent certain constituencies. Ethnic music and dance were not simply "symbolic" expressions of unity or diversity here. They actively made these abstractions concrete—or, from another perspective, failed to do so. The performance of *Spirit of the Rivers* did not only represent unity: it integrated participants in collective activity. Conversely, the singing protest at the evening concert did not simply symbolize Indigenous difference, but rather actively produced it. In launching a welcome that competed with the one on the main stage, the protesters brought their difference into being as a social and musical fact—a difference that would not otherwise have been audible within the unity being showcased.

SOUNDLY ORGANIZED TIME

The winter holiday season in North America is distinguished from other, more ordinary times of the year by music above all else. On tinny-sounding outdoor speakers, on the radio, and especially in stores and shopping malls, pop songs celebrate snow, reunions with loved ones, the giving of gifts, and a certain jolly old elf. Many of these songs were composed in the 1930s and 1940s and resemble other Tin Pan Alley tunes from that era: they have catchy, singable melodies and make frequent use of the 32-bar **AABA** form ("Santa Claus Is Coming to Town" and "Rudolph the Red-Nosed Reindeer," for example). Alternating with the pop songs are Christmas carols and hymns: pieces that make explicit reference to the birth of Jesus and its theological implications. These are, predictably, especially prevalent at the church services and devotional events that lead up to Christmas and on the day itself. Also parts of the annually transformed soundscape are pieces from the world of art music: here an excerpt from Handel's *Messiah*, there a piece from Tchaikovsky's *The Nutcracker*. Yet the seeming ubiquity of Christmas music masks a North American musical life that is anything but unified. Those who observe Christmas do so through widely varying repertories: songs, melodies, lyrics, and performance styles differ from community to community and ethnic group to ethnic group. Not all Christians even observe holidays at the same time: Old Calendar Orthodox Christians, for instance, celebrate Christmas in early January. And, of course, as the success of Adam Sandler's "The Chanukah Song" suggests, there are many who do not observe Christmas, whose year is structured around quite different celebrations and solemnities, and who perhaps feel a sense of distance from these annual musical transformations.

Music shapes the experience of passing time, and does so at a number of different levels. For instance, people have an innate ability to follow regular patterns of pulsation (see Clayton, Sager, and Will 2004). This universal ability is expressed through a wide range of culturally specific rhythmic and metrical practices: for instance, the interlocking patterns of sub-Saharan African music (see Chapter 8) or the complex structures of Indian tal (see Chapter 2). But "slower" levels of temporality are likewise shaped by musical experience, and human societies around the world have imbued the daily, monthly, and yearly cycles with various culturally specific musical associations.

Similar ways of organizing time are evident in North America. But, as might be expected on a continent of such ethnic and regional diversity, social groups establish commonalities and differences in part through distinctive ways of structuring the calendar. Ethnicity and identity come into being through the temporal and musical division of life, in both its everyday aspects and its more memorable and festive ones. Let's explore a few of these.

Liturgical Cycles

The cultural organization of time is perhaps most evident in religious liturgies, where music and various forms of heightened speech (for instance, chant and sacred readings) establish and consecrate daily, weekly, and annual cycles. Sacred time is organized on a weekly basis in a number of traditions, of course: Christian churches privilege Sunday as a day of worship, Jewish congregations meet on the Sabbath (from sunset on Friday to sunset on Saturday), and Muslim congregational prayer occurs on Fridays. In all three religious traditions, these meetings incorporate the reading, recitation, or singing of special and sacred texts. Not all of these practices are considered to be "music" by practitioners (see Chapter 3); in most cases, however, the texts are declaimed using some form of heightened speech (an intoned or cantillated vocal delivery in some cases, and song in others).

Sacred liturgies also articulate daily cycles. Some Christian traditions observe the **Office** (based on the canonical hours), a set of daily worship services in which certain prayers, readings, and chants are performed at fixed times: matins in the morning and vespers in the evening, for instance. The Islamic call to prayer, heard five times a day, is another example. At a more mundane level, the largest and loudest musical instruments in many cities are the bells in church steeples. Their hourly or even quarter-hourly pealing might be heard to do the ongoing work of sacralizing passing time, albeit in a manner that has become so familiar it often goes almost unnoticed. Occasional controversies over the public broadcast of the Islamic call to prayer tend to ignore that the pealing of church bells is an even more prevalent example of religious expression being publically broadcast.

Turning to longer cycles of temporality, liturgy also shapes the organization of the year. For instance, the Christian year begins with Advent (the four Sundays preceding Christmas) and progresses through the celebration of the Nativity to Epiphany. After a period of "ordinary time" comes the second major period of special observance, beginning with Lent, reaching a peak during Easter celebrations, and moving through to Pentecost. These events are associated with particular kinds of music; many hymnals, for instance, contain sections devoted to Advent, Christmas, and Easter. And as the opening of this section suggests, some of these songs—Christmas carols, most notably—are heard well outside the confines of liturgical practice.

In Jewish and Islamic practice, too, congregations and communities mark the passing of the year through ritual, moving through sequences of holy days and associated observances. In Judaism, the most important events are the High Holy Days: Rosh Hashanah (the New Year Festival) and Yom Kippur (the Day of Atonement), which arrive in autumn. The central holiday in Islam is the month of Ramadan, which occurs in the ninth month of the lunar year (accordingly, several days earlier every solar year). In both Jewish and Islamic practice, these events are observed in part through special assemblies and the recitation of special texts.

OFFICE
Organized to correspond to the canonical hours, the Office (also called the Divine Hours) is a set of daily worship services in which certain prayers, readings, and chants are performed at fixed times. The services include matins, vespers, and compline, among others, and the practice is generally associated with Catholic, Orthodox Christian, and Anglican/Episcopal traditions, though other traditions include these services in their worship as well.

Rabbi Moshe Wilansky of Chabad of Maine blows the shofar before the start of a Rosh Hashanah service at the Italian Heritage Center in Portland. *Source:* Portland Press Herald/Getty Images

Although musical articulations of time are most extensively connected to liturgical practice, there are also more secular manifestations. Some are connected to the standardized work week that holds for many North Americans (although this work week, too, has its origins in the religious calendar). For example, special radio programs of talk and music accompany morning and evening commutes. On Friday and Saturday nights some radio stations play nightclub-like dance mixes, acknowledging the arrival of the weekend and its pleasures. It could be suggested that music helps to mark the distinctions between productive but onerous work and pleasurable but prodigal leisure. Again, as in the case of sacred music, sounds do not simply reflect the social division of time but rather actively help to shape it: North Americans' work and leisure are experienced through the sounds and silences associated with them.

Music is coordinated with temporal cycles and religious structures in societies around the world, although rarely in the same ways. North American society is distinctive in part because of the great variety of ways of organizing temporality. Yet this diversity should not obscure certain larger trends. For instance, the prevalence, indeed the near ubiquity, of Christmas carols and church bells in public spaces attest to the significance of Christianity in shaping North American soundscapes and musical temporality.

Music and Age Categories

If the daily, weekly, and yearly rounds are organized by music, so too is the life cycle. Certain genres of music are associated with social categories, including age and gender. Of these, children's music is perhaps the most readily distinguished. In North America, there are significant bodies of repertory that are closely associated with children—especially, but not only, girls—of elementary school age.

The performances of "Miss Sue from Alabama" present fragments of everyday life for children in the New York of the 1970s and perhaps today, too: mama, father, brother, and a new baby; the somewhat obscure world of adult life, where fathers drink in the alley and mothers have babies; locations both familiar (the elevator and its floors) and imagined (Alabama). There are hints of simmering sibling antagonism: just what is being sent down the elevator in this song, for instance? Present too are many of the elements Kyra Gaunt (2006) identifies in her book on African American girls' games: quotations from popular culture alongside other orally circulating elements, and above all a playful, musical physicality. What is also highlighted in this pair of examples is the diversity and particularity of children's musical games. Edet describes finding ten different versions of another song, "Here We Go Willoughby," in an eight-block radius. As this suggests, children's games differ from playground to

LISTENING
GUIDE

"MISS SUE FROM ALABAMA"

 LISTEN

TRACK 13.1 Recorded by Edna Smith Edet in New York City

THESE GAME SONGS were recorded in New York, probably in the 1970s, where they were sung by what sounds like a chorus composed largely of girls. In performances of the songs, according to the notes of the recordist, Edna Smith Edet, the children move in a circle and perform actions that are coordinated with the words. In the first version of "Miss Sue from Alabama," they move their hands to the words "chicka boom," move their feet on "tic, tac, toe," and "waddle and shake shoulders on 'boom tick a wally wally.'" In the second version, which emerges from the first, they mime "curl," "toy," "wrap," and "down," stopping all motion on "stop." The circle game ends with the children tickling each other.

[0:00] Miss Sue from Alabama (1)

Miss Sue (clap clap), Miss Sue (clap clap),
Miss Sue from Alabama;
Now let's have a party,
Chicka boom, chicka boom,
Chicka boom boom boom.

[0:13] Now let's have a tic tac toe,
A tic, a tac, a tic tac toe.

[0:19] Now Mama's in the kitchen
Peeling white potatoes,
Father in the alley
Drinking white ladle [?White Label?],
Brother in the [playpen],
Waiting for the clock to go,
Boom tick tock, boom tick a wally wally

[0:51] Miss Sue from Alabama (2)

Miss Sue, Miss Sue,
Miss Sue from Alabama,

[0:57] [Now let's,] My mother had a baby
And father's going crazy.
But if it's a girl,
I give it a curl
And if it's a boy,
I give it a toy,
Wrap it up in toilet paper
Send it down the elevator

[1:19] First floor, stop, ticking over,
Second floor, stop, think it over,
Third floor, you better watch out,
'Cause S T O P spells stop.

playground and community to community, reflecting locality, but also the creative work of young innovators and improvisers.

Other forms of musical activity tend to be associated with certain social categories as well, although perhaps not quite so exclusively. Young people, and especially young men, invest immense amounts of energy learning to perform genres such as rock, metal, and hip-hop. Youthful pop singers and boy bands are marketed aggressively to adolescent girls. And it is a North American commonplace that paired adults often take up couple dancing in later life—for instance, learning ballroom dancing or Chicago stepping—while younger singles are more likely to dance apart, to genres such as rock and roll and electronic dance music. But these generalities are complicated by ethnic, regional, and class variations, which give particularity to musical and choreographic experiences of age and gender. For some young North Americans, youthful musical experiences probably do involve dancing in highly individuated styles suited to electronic dance music, and adulthood and committed partnership are embodied in the dance lessons they take to prepare themselves for wedding receptions and similar occasions. But for many others, couple dances may be the very form in which youthful good times are experienced: in dancing the country two-step or *pasito duranguense* (see below), for instance.

Music and Rites of Passage   Music is not only connected to particular stages of life, but also and especially to ritual undertakings that mark and effect movements from one stage or state of social life to another. Through these rites of passage, communities imbue the life cycle with meaning in a way similar to how they organize the passing of time through liturgy. Birth rites—for instance circumcisions and baptisms—commemorate the moments when new persons join communities, whereas funerary rites—wakes, funerals, viewings, and memorial services—mark departures. Other rites of passage accompany and affirm transformations from childhood to adolescence and adolescence to adulthood, or various stages of educational achievement; for instance, bar and bat mitzvahs, *quinceñeras*, confirmations, and various graduations. Still others perform marriages. Music plays an important role at many such events.

Take, for instance, wedding ceremonies. In the late 1980s and early 1990s I occasionally accompanied weddings at a Mennonite church in a small western Canadian town. Observant Mennonites are Christians who tend to practice adult baptism, nonresistance (for many this means refusing to do military service), and, in many cases, a wariness of ideas and practices deemed to be too worldly. The rejection of worldliness has had musical implications: in some Mennonite churches instruments have been disallowed. The church where I played was relatively liberal in this respect, however, and, in addition to the piano, there were amplified guitars and even a drum set. Indeed, weddings made extensive use of instrumental music. At the opening of a service, the pianist typically performed pleasant music—nothing too showy or harmonically unusual—as wedding guests moved to their seats. Once everybody was in place, the bridal party processed in, not uncommonly to an arrangement of Pachelbel's Canon in D. The length of the processional was often worked out the night before the wedding so that there would be exactly enough music to get the parents, bridesmaids, groomsmen, and groom down the aisle to the front of the church. There was no telling, however, whether nerves or mistakes would change the speed of the procession on the actual day of the wedding, so whoever was playing had to be prepared to cut things short. The entrance of the bride required special music, of course, and this was typically picked with care and in consultation with her in advance. During the service itself, the congregation sometimes sang a hymn, and there was typically a song on the themes of love and marriage, performed by a friend or relative of the bride or groom. After the pronouncement of marriage, the pianist played a recessional as the couple went back down the aisle. This last, obviously, had to sound grand and joyful, and it was usually showier than the music played at other points during the service.

Music served a number of purposes at the ceremony. First, it demonstrated the taste of the bridal couple and their families and reinforced the grandness and consequentiality of the event. The quality of the music was important for some of the same reasons that the quality of the food and the clothing of the bridal party were concerns. This said, the music was by no means the most important element of the service. It tended to occupy a moderate register, without drawing too much attention to itself, and it had to be timed correctly to accompany the movements of the ritual participants into the sanctuary and out of it. In fact, there were only two moments when the music was the primary focus of attention: during the congregational hymn and the solo song. At both of these moments, the texts sung expressed important beliefs shared by the bridal party and the assembled witnesses: concerning, for instance, the love between God and humanity, or the loving relationship between a married couple.

All in all, these ceremonies progressed like many North American Christian weddings, and stood in a reasonably close relationship to the continental mainstream. In other ways they were quite distinct. For instance, the ceremonies were typically followed by a reception, but rarely by a dance. The community and the church were conservative in a number of respects, and many disapproved of drinking and dancing. In other nearby communities and congregations, these were important parts of the wedding reception, and hosts hired a DJ or even a full band to perform at the function. Indeed, there existed a widespread tradition in the region of the pre-wedding social: engaged couples raised money for their nuptials by holding a dance at a community hall. But the congregation I played for eschewed such activities, or at least the majority of its members (those who wanted them as part of their wedding typically held the reception in a neighboring town). By excluding drinking and dance from weddings, the church actively distinguished itself from surrounding communities and from the worldly North American mainstream. Nevertheless, to characterize these differences in behavior simply as boundary maintenance (that is, a way of separating one's own community from others) does not do them justice: they were also a creative way to address a theological imperative to moral behavior. Thus, although church services incorporated a piano, amplified instruments, and worship songs that drew upon pop precedents, they avoided certain equally common North American musical behaviors deemed morally problematic. Evident here too is an inventive, selective engagement with the world beyond the community.

The place of music in this wedding ceremony certainly cannot be generalized to all of North America—it is rooted in a specific place and time. Neighboring communities celebrated weddings in different ways, depending on their own cultural and religious particularities. Neither is ritual practice historically stable. When I worked as a pianist in the 1980s and 1990s, weddings only occurred between men and women: today of course it is possible for same-sex couples to be wed in Canada and the United States, opening up possibilities for creative elaborations of ritual and musical practice. A quick perusal of wedding videos on the Internet suggests both continuity and change. Music continues to play processional and recessional roles in many ceremonies, both traditional and new: a lesbian couple walks down the aisle to Pachelbel's Canon in one video; in another, a chorus sings "San Francisco" as a postlude at a wedding between two men in that city in 2008 (the year a ban on same-sex marriages was overthrown in California). So it is that specificities of history and place intersect with widely distributed musical practices in shaping North American ritual life.

To sum up, North American ethnicity is performed and experienced through musical practices that coincide with, and effect transitions between, temporal divisions and life stages. Christian and English-speaking traditions enjoy particular prominence, but are in no way universal. The preceding accounts demonstrate that ethnicity is lived not only at moments of solemnity and festivity, but also during the everyday stretches these punctuate. Moreover, it is performed into being through the ongoing musical organization of life and passing time.

MUSICAL PARTICULARITY AND HISTORICAL CONTINUITY

Social groups value those practices that distinguish them from one another. Perhaps particularly important for many ethnic communities are the practices that connect them to their original homelands. Yet in many cases these traditions are quite different from what arrived with the original immigrants. Subsequent generations have modified them in ways that acknowledge a new, North American, context. Moreover, musicians, instruments, genres, and practices have in the intervening generations moved among groups. Hence many communities have a complicated relationship to their valued musical traditions, which may have come to them well after their arrival in North America. All of this suggests two key characteristics of North American musical life identified by Philip V. Bohlman (2008): its simultaneous adaptability and particularity. On the one hand, musical practices and technologies move between communities, regions, and ethnic groups. On the other hand, community members feel a strong sense of ownership of, and connection to, these practices, including some that have been recently adopted. Some of the complexities of these musical movements and senses of ownership are explored in the following case studies.

EXPLORE

Anglo American Ballad

Anglo-American Ballads   Clarence Ashley first recorded "The House Carpenter" for Columbia Records in 1930 (Smith [1952]: 3), and then again after he was "rediscovered" during the 1960s. The song is an example of American music from Appalachia (the highlands that extend from Pennsylvania to Alabama). It is a ballad: that is to say, a song that tells a story. Straightforward musical structures reinforce the centrality of the narrative element in this performance. The song has a basic strophic form, all verses being set to the

Banjo player, guitarist and singer Clarence Ashley on stage at the Newport Folk Festival in Rhode Island. *Source:* The Estate of David Gahr/Getty Images

same repeated melody. Supporting this structure, the banjo accompaniment ticks along in the background, rarely drawing attention to itself.

"The House Carpenter" seems to have originated in England and been brought to North America by immigrants from Great Britain, Northern Ireland, or both, sometime between the late seventeenth and early nineteenth century. It proliferated in the North American context, and regionally differentiated versions of the song emerged in Newfoundland, New England, the Midwest, the West, and especially Appalachia (Burrison 1967: 282, Gardner-Medwin 1971: 426). In fact, this particular ballad seems to have flourished much more widely in North America than on its island of origin (Burrison 1967).

So, immigrants brought "The House Carpenter" with them to North America from their original homeland and preserved it in their new one. Yet Ashley's recording suggests transformation as well as perpetuation. For instance, the ship carpenter in the British version of the song has become a house carpenter in the American one. This reflects a new performance context: ship carpenters were rarer in Appalachia than in Britain, whereas house carpenters were well known in the highlands, where the wood construction of houses was quite common (Gardner-Medwin, 1971: 421).

But the instrumentation of the recording reveals something even more telling about the new American musical context. Clarence Ashley accompanies himself on the banjo, which has its roots in an instrument of African origin, brought to the Americas by slaves (Epstein 1975). Banjo-type instruments are documented amongst Caribbean blacks in the [late] seventeenth century and African Americans by the middle of the eighteenth (ibid.). They were initially played

**LISTENING
GUIDE**

"THE HOUSE CARPENTER"

 **LISTEN**

TRACK 13.2 **Clarence Ashley, vocals and banjo**

The House Carpenter

1. *"Well met, well met," said an old true love,*
   "Well met, well met," said he.
   "I'm just returning from the salt, salt sea
   And it's all for the love of thee."

2. *"Come in, come in my old true love,*
   And have a seat with me.
   It's been three fourths of a long, long year
   Since together we have been."

3. *"Well I can't come in or I can't sit down,*

   For I haven't but a moment's time.
   *They say you are married to a house
   carpenter*
   And your heart will never be mine."

4. *"[Now I saw] I could have married a king's
      daughter dear.*
   I'm sure she'd have married me.
   But I've forsaken her crowns of gold

   And it's all for the love of thee."

5. *"Now will you forsaken your house
      carpenter*
   And go along with me?
   I'll take you where the grass grows green

   On the banks of the deep blue sea."

6. *She picked up her little babe,*

   And kisses gave it three,
   *And said, "Stay right here, my darling little
      babe*
   And keep your papa company."

7. *Well, they hadn't been on ship but about
      two weeks,*
   I'm sure it was not three,
   And his true love began to weep and mourn
   And he [???] most bitterly

8. *Says, "Are you weeping for my silver or my
      gold,"*
   Says, "Are you weeping for my [store]
   Are you weeping for that house carpenter
   Whose face you never see any more?"

9. *"No, it's I'm not a-weeping for your silver
      or your gold,*
   Or neither for your [store].
   I am weeping for my darling little babe

   Whose face I'll never see any more."

10. *Well, they hadn't been on ship but about
      three weeks,*
   I'm sure it was not four,
   *And they sprung a leak in the bottom of the
      ship*
   And it sunk for to rise no more.

This song is a version of a ballad for which there is printed evidence dating back to the seventeenth century. It seems particularly close to a variant first published in London around 1785, entitled "The Distressed Ship Carpenter" (Burrison 1967: 271–272). Compare the first two verses of the following ballad with the first and fourth of the previous.

continued

The Distressed Ship Carpenter

1. *Well met, well met, my own true Love*
    Long time I have been seeking thee,
    I am lately come from the salt, salt Sea,
    And all for the Sake, Love, of thee.

2. *I might have had a King's Daughter,*
    And fain she would have married me,
    But I've forsaken all her Crowns of Gold,
    And all for the Sake, Love, of thee.

3. *If you might have had a King's Daughter,*
    I think you much to blame,
    I would not for Five Hundred Pounds,
    That my Husband should hear the same.

4. *For my Husband is a Carpenter,*
    And a young Ship Carpenter is he,
    And by him I have a little Son,
    Or else, Love, I'd go along with thee.

by black musicians but eventually adopted by whites, first it seems in the course of local music making, and later in the context of minstrelsy (see below for a description of this musical style).

Ashley's banjo points to a social and musical context unique to the United States, where black slaves and free white men historically played similar music on similar instruments. In fact, as work by Alan Jabbour and others suggests (Jabbour 2001, Epstein 2003, Wells 2003), much of the instrumental music that today is widely associated in the popular imagination with white musicians was also historically played by blacks, as is evidenced by the fact that many American fiddle tunes employ complex rhythmic syncopations that suggest the influence of African musical traditions (see Chapter 8).

Tecnobanda and *Duranguense*: Other Migrating Musical Styles

Similar developments have occurred in the more recent past. For instance, the 1990s and 2000s saw a surge in the popularity of a number of musical styles on Spanish-language radio stations in the United States—including **tecnobanda** and **música duranguense** and the related **quebradita** and *pasito duranguense* dance crazes (see Hutchinson 2007, Simonett 2001). In these genres, singers perform in close vocal harmony, in alternation with melodic fills by brass, reed, and electronic keyboard instruments, and dramatic bursts of sound from the kit drum and tambora (a combined bass drum and cymbal, sometimes called the tamborón). Much of the music makes use of dance rhythms—including the polka, waltz, and cumbia—that are common enough in North America, but quite different from those that are prominent in mainstream dance music oriented to young people. Especially in earlier recordings, singers and the instrumentalists accompanying them sometimes strayed from the center of the pitch, performing on what some listeners would consider the "sharp" (high) or "flat" (low) side

EXPLORE
Tecnobanda

EXPLORE
Durangnense

TECNOBANDA
A popular dance music derived from blending the instruments and repetory of traditional banda ensembles (brass bands) with electronic instruments.

MÚSICA DURANGUENSE
A popular dance music that developed in Chicago. A variant of technoband, the musical style is derived from blending banda with electronic instruments. It is notable for its emphasis on percussion lines and for the generally faster tempos at which the repertory is performed. The accompanying

dance is characterized by western attire and a typical dance step, called pasito, derived from the traditional dancing in Durango, Mexico. Duranguense is popular in both Mexico and the United States.

QUEBRADITA

A dance craze, accompanied by technobanda ensembles and privileging cumbia dances, which became especially popular in Los Angeles, northern Mexico, and throughout the Southwest. Characterizes by western attire, hat tricks, and flips.

of the notes. Given that some of this music came to prominence at a moment when producers of English-language popular music were enthusiastically embracing electronic methods of pitch correction to ensure vocal and instrumental parts were "in tune" with each other, the more discrepant songs stood out dramatically on the radio dial and in urban public spaces. Thus, through language, instrumentation, dance rhythms, and tuning, the music established distance from the anglophone popular musics that otherwise dominated the soundscapes of American cities. In so doing, it also contributed to the elaboration of a certain kind of Mexican-American musical ethnicity (without constituting it in full, of course).

Many elements of tecnobanda and duranguense can be traced to rural Mexican musical traditions of longer standing. The genres emerged as updated and electrified versions of traditional village banda (band) music from the northwestern Mexican state of Sinaloa, as Helena Simonett (2001) and Sydney Hutchinson (2007) explain. The Sinaloan banda traditionally incorporated melodic wind and brass instruments, a tuba to play the bass line, and the tamborón and snare drum as percussion instruments. (The mariachi ensembles discussed in Chapter 10 represent another example of the importance of brass instruments in Mexican music cultures.) To this, the newer genres added instruments like the electric guitar and electronic keyboards.

A closer look at banda and its descendents, however, reveals that its history is not simply that of a rural Mexican genre carried northward, including to American cities by Mexican immigrants. Rather, a long history of border crossing and musical borrowing is evident. Musicians have long moved back and forth between the northern Mexican states and Texas, establishing deep musical connections between Spanish-speaking communities on both sides of the border (Peña 1985). Moreover, the polka and waltz rhythms that are common in genres descended from traditional banda point to an important German influence in that region. Both polka and waltz circulated internationally in the nineteenth century, but their popularity in northern Mexico was probably also due to the presence of German immigrants in Texas and in the city of Monterrey in the state of Neuvo Leon. These immigrants brought dances and instruments—particularly the accordion—with them when they settled in these areas, making a significant impact upon the music culture of the border area (Hutchinson 2007: 27).

This cross-border borrowing and migration is just as complicated in the case of two dance crazes growing out of the banda tradition—quebradita and pasito duranguense—and the music associated with them. Duranguense, most dramatically, emerged in Chicago, led musically by the ensemble Grupo Montéz de Durango (see the discography for a short list of recordings and performers in the various tecnobanda genres). The style incorporates some elements that can be found in music and dance from Durango and evidences the influence of previous Mexican popular styles. In other ways it is innovative, however; for instance, women musicians contribute on a previously unprecedented scale. Crucially, duranguense was not "brought along" by migrants from Mexico but rather emerged in the United States. And from the beginning it addressed an audience on both sides of the border.

As in the case of "The House Carpenter," the model of immigrants preserving old traditions in a new country does not seem adequate. Immigrant communities borrow instruments and stylistic elements from one another, they adapt musical practices to suit new social circumstances, and the resulting transformations sometimes double back to impact musical practices "back home."

Not all practices undergo dramatic developments and transformations; nor do all musicians appropriate elements from neighboring music cultures upon arrival in North America. In some instances old repertories continue to be practiced, often in similar circumstances to those in which they originated, and within communities that have retained strict boundaries. But even in these situations, musical activity and discourse frequently reflects the new North American context. For example, the Hutterites, a Protestant group whose members live communally, abide by strict guidelines concerning comportment and dress, speak a relatively rare Central European language, and maintain a conservative musical tradition. Hutterite music tends to be **monophonic** and unaccompanied, eschewing instruments and especially secular subjects (Wulz 2002). Yet even these musically conservative communities occasionally borrow sacred songs from other communities, import new melodies, and engage in discussions about introducing certain new practices. Thus the everyday production of ethnicity involves, at some level, an acknowledgment of neighboring communities and broader mainstreams. Sometimes this means borrowing genres, stylistic elements, and technologies from neighbors, and sometimes it involves the explicit rejection of their musical practices.

MONOPHONY
One melody line is played by all musicians, with no harmonic accompaniment.

PARTICULAR AND GENERAL MUSICAL PRACTICES

The "mosaic" metaphor introduced at the beginning of the chapter is one of the ways that North Americans characterize the cultural diversity of their countries. Another metaphor, perhaps more closely associated with the United States, is the "melting pot"—the idea of a national culture that emerges as various contributing traditions blend together. These characterizations are familiar and comfortable but not entirely accurate: musically speaking, evidence of both "melting" and "sustained" difference can be found in North American music. There is on the one hand a tendency toward distinctiveness: ethnic groups, regions, and communities actively differentiate themselves through musical means. On the other hand, there is a tendency toward musical borrowing, seemingly even in the most conservative music cultures. Communities appropriate musical sounds and technologies from one another, and these sometimes change hands altogether. As we've seen, music that is frequently associated with white Appalachian musicians is in fact a hybrid music, making use not only of

String band playing at a Saturday night dance with a kitty for contributions, Tulare migrant camp, California. *Source:* © Everett Collection Historical / Alamy Stock Photo

British songs and genres but also of traditional African-American instruments. Meanwhile tecnobanda and duranguense are often associated with a northern Mexican identity, but they reflect the musical influence of German musicians, and their popularity was as much an American as a Mexican phenomenon. Thus the paradox: musical materials circulate, but the resulting hybrid practices are nevertheless held to belong closely to particular communities, regions, and populations (see Bohlman 2008).

A similar tension emerges when we explore the relationship between stylistic particularities and generalized practices in North American fiddle traditions, where numerous regional styles are distinguishable from broader national or international ones. In fiddling from Cape Breton in the Canadian maritime province of Nova Scotia, fiddlers are typically accompanied by pianists, who play in a unique syncopated style. The **strathspey**, a dance tune of Scottish origin in duple time, is particularly prominent, as are patterns of melodic embellishment that are borrowed from bagpipe traditions. By contrast, in Quebec (but also in many Canadian Indigenous communities) fiddlers perform rhythmic "clogging" patterns with their feet as they play. And the fiddle style of the "upper South" in the United States is characterized by a distinctive syncopated bowing style that reflects the influence of African American musicians (Jabbour 2001).

Thus, a great deal of regional and ethnic musical diversity can be catalogued based on musical particularities. But it is just as important to acknowledge that certain musical structures are widely distributed, and even normative, in North American musical practice. Close study of Dwight Lamb's performance of

STRATHSPEY
A dance tune, associated with Scotland, in 4/4 meter. Charaterized rhythmically by dot-cut, or Scotch "snaps" (a short note followed by a dotted note).

**LISTENING
GUIDE**

"ROCKY ROAD TO JORDAN"

TRACK 13.3 **Dwight Lamb, fiddle; Lynn Holsclaw, guitar**

I▌**F YOU LISTEN CLOSELY**, you should be able to hear that the tune has two sections that alternate throughout the piece. The first, labeled **A**, begins in a lower range and lasts until about [0:17] into the track. At that point, the second part, labeled **B**, begins, marked by a shift into a higher register. Further close listening will reveal that the melodic material in both **A** and **B** is repeated; so, for instance, [0:09–0:17] is a repetition of [0:00–0:09]. For this reason, the tune is said to be in **AABB** form. This structure is carefully synchronized with the underlying pulse. If you count along with the music, which ticks along at about 120 beats per minute, you should be able to hear that there are exactly 16 beats in each of the four sections of the tune, for a total of 64 in each iteration. In 2/4 meter (two beats per measure, or bar) these 64 beats translate to 32 measures or bars. This 32-bar **AABB** dance form and other closely related ones are used throughout North America. To be sure, these forms are broken or elaborated by fiddlers, and in certain fiddling traditions they are treated much more freely than in others, but they are nevertheless very widely practiced.

TIME	SECTION
0:00	**A** Section.
0:09	**A** Section repeated.
0:17	**B** Section.
0:25	**B** Section repeated.
0:33	**A** Section.
0:41	**A** Section repeated.
0:49	**B** Section.
0:57	**B** Section repeated.
1:05	**A** Section.
1:13	**A** Section repeated.
1:21	**B** Section.
1:29	**B** Section repeated.
1:37	**A** Section.

Close attention to the guitar part reveals another element of musical structure, equally important but somewhat more abstract: harmony. Each section of the tune moves through harmonic progressions, most evident in chord changes in the guitar part that, by and large, track what goes on in the fiddle melody. It might be difficult to hear these progressions if your ears are not attuned to them, but if you listen closely you should notice that there are three different harmonies in play in total. North American music theorists—and many musicians—call these harmonies the tonic, subdominant, and dominant,

continued

or alternatively, chords I, IV, and V. Each of these comprises three simultaneously sounding pitches drawn from the seven-note diatonic scale, and each is named for the lowest of those three pitches. In the diagram that follows, chord I is associated with D, the first note in the D major scale, chord IV with G, the fourth note, and chord V with A, the fifth.

Harmonic structure in the guitar part to "Rocky Road to Jordan"

	Bar 1	Bar 2	Bar 3	Bar 4	Bar 5	Bar 6	Bar 7	Bar 8
A section	I	I	V	V	I	IV	V	I
B section	I	I	V	V	I	IV	V	I

Harmonies in the key of D major

I	II	III	IV	V	VI	VII	I

Dmajor   Eminor   F#minor   Gmajor   Amajor   Bminor   C#diminished   Dmajor

Harmony can be a complex business, and many North American music scholars devote entire careers to unlocking its secrets and structures. A few key points can be suggested here. First, the guitar playing in this piece stands in dialogue with the most widespread ways of organizing harmony: the common practice system, which is built upon a fundamental opposition between tonic and dominant, chords I and V. In common practice music, the fundamental motion is from I to V and back to I again. Two elaborations of this fundamental motion are evident in Section **A** of "Rocky Road to Jordan," one in each four-bar half. In the first four bars, the harmony moves from I to V (I–I–V–V), where it is interrupted. The second four bars introduce the tonic again and, this time, articulate a complete version of the fundamental pattern, moving from I to V to I via IV (I–IV–V–I). The completion of the I–V–I pattern creates a sense of musical closure, especially because it coincides with the end of a rhythmic and formal grouping.

"Rocky Road to Jordan" exemplifies two such generalized musical structures: the **AABB** dance form, found widely in fiddle music, and a standard harmonic pattern that uses the tonic, dominant, and subdominant chords.

Lamb is an American fiddler and accordionist of partial Danish descent. His musical repertory was shaped by both family connections and engagement with mass media: his maternal grandfather was an accordionist and his father was a fiddler, but he also learned tunes by listening to musicians who performed on the radio, particularly a fiddler named Uncle Bob Walters, who later in life became a personal friend (Lamb 1999). Lamb's repertoire reflects a diverse array of fiddling and dancing practices—the fiddlers in his circle played Danish,

German, Scottish, American, and Canadian fiddle tunes. And yet, his varied repertory makes frequent use of the formal and harmonic patterns just mentioned.

The formal structures and harmonic patterns in fiddle tunes typically reinforce one another. Experienced musicians are aware of this correspondence at some level (in many cases probably unconsciously) and gauge their activity so that everything more or less matches up. A general feel for these forms and patterns helps fiddlers to learn new tunes and remember old ones, and it allows accompanists to play along with tunes they don't recall particularly well or have not heard before. As long as a tune follows the standard form and stands in dialogue with common harmonic practice, fiddlers and accompanists can, so to speak, slot melodic and harmonic patterns into appropriate places within the structure. The match may not always be exact—as in this performance, where there is sometimes a little tension between the guitar chords and the fiddle melody—but such patterns make everyday music making possible. Indeed, the common practice system and its associated harmonic patterns inform a very wide range of North American folk and popular music practices, including not only fiddling, gospel song, country music, and some forms of the blues and jazz, but also duranguense and other Mexican-American genres.

That said, there are many other options for harmonization—if none so widespread and well established as common-practice ones. Some tunes, genres, and performers draw upon a wider harmonic palette, incorporating a broader range of chords than those used in "Rocky Road to Jordan." In other cases, the dominant-tonic relationship is not as central as it is in common-practice harmony. In still other instances, tunes are based on scales or modes that are not easily harmonized using I, IV, and V. For instance, on the same album from which the preceding example was drawn, Dwight Lamb plays a tune in the Dorian mode (a seven-note mode distinct from both major and minor); it is harmonized by two chords, I and VII rather than I and V.

Though slightly less widespread, these alternative harmonic structures are themselves musical commonplaces, known to, and practiced by, musicians across North America. And as in the former case, when they are employed it is relatively easy to pick up how a given tune should be accompanied, particularly when a standard 32-bar form is in play. My broader point is this: although there is considerable regional diversity in North American fiddling, and although there are no North American universals, there do seem to be musical practices—including the harmonic and formal structures just discussed—that extend across regions and unite many musical traditions across the continent. Ethnic and regional differences—but also individual creativity—become apparent when musicians stray from, or elaborate, these commonalities.

THE AFRICAN AMERICAN CONTRIBUTION TO NORTH AMERICAN MUSIC

One of the most characteristic aspects of North American music—and particularly music of the United States—is the important contribution of African

American music and musicians. This is not to say that black music has not also made a significant contribution in other parts of the world (as Chapters 10 and 11 illustrate). It is rather to say that African Americans, despite being demographically in the minority in the United States, and subject for centuries to slavery and, later, to legalized forms of discrimination, have played a central role in shaping the country's traditional, popular, and art musics. During the long twentieth century of America's global influence in matters economic, political, and musical, moreover, African American music has exerted an unprecedented influence upon the rest of the world. Many of the genres that emerged in the United States and went on to have a global impact during this period came into existence thanks to originating or otherwise significant contributions by African Americans, including ragtime, blues, jazz, rhythm and blues, rock and roll, soul, funk, disco, hip-hop, and electronic dance music. Other American musical genres would be unimaginable in their present forms without the influence of African American music and musicians: these include country music and bluegrass, the Broadway musical, and American art music, whether in its more tonal manifestations or in its avant-garde expressions.

Culturally speaking, at least two factors seem to be responsible for the prominence of African American contributions to the music of the United States and to musical practices in many parts of the world. First, music has been an important means of creating and expressing collectivity for African Americans themselves. Second, African American music has been a central element of American musical life more generally, and as such has continually been incorporated into the musical traditions of European-Americans and others. African American music has been an object of fascination for other North American music cultures—and in at times problematical fashion, as during the era of minstrelsy (further discussion follows). It is probably for both of these reasons that music has been a consistent site of African American cultural innovation and creativity.

Expressing Collective Experience and Resistance

Millions of Africans were forcibly taken across the Atlantic Ocean to the Americas during the centuries in which the slave trade was legal. With them they brought a number of musical practices and technologies that survived despite the crushing circumstances of slavery. Dena Epstein (1975) has suggested that louder African wind and percussion instruments were regarded with suspicion by slave owners, and that for this reason quieter instruments such as the banjo (and the fiddle) became particularly important amongst African Americans. But it is in the realm of musical structures rather than instruments that key African retentions are most evident. Many of the characteristics of sub-Saharan African music (identified in Chapter 8) are present in African American music, including cyclical forms, interlocking parts, dense timbres, and musical divisions into core and elaboration parts. So it is that even as African American musics

EXPLORE

The Blues and Tin Pan Alley

make use of a wide variety of structures of European origin, they have transformed these to bring them into line with an African American aesthetic. These have, in turn, been incorporated in North American music more generally.

Early accounts suggest that music played an important role in the collective expression of the experiences of slave life. Epstein's research points to an array of musical practices, including work songs, sacred music, and music for socializing and dancing on days of rest. Music expressed sorrow, it protested the conditions of slavery, and it expressed hopes for a better life. Early accounts make it clear, too, that music was useful as a means of resistance, both overt and covert. Drumming, singing, and dancing accompanied an uprising that occurred in Stono, South Carolina in 1739 (Epstein 2003), in which slaves fought for freedom from their oppressors. And song often enabled the expression of sentiments and the passing of information that would have been dangerous to convey in speech (Maultsby 2011).

African American music was not strictly separate from other forms of American music, however, but stood in complex relationships of exchange. Black fiddlers were particularly common in early American life, for instance, and they appear to have accompanied the dances of both blacks and whites using Anglo-Celtic tunes and genres (see Wells 2003). Whites borrowed music and dance they understood to come from black practice; thus a description of Virginia life published in 1776 remarked, "Toward the close of an evening, when the company are pretty well tired with country-dances, it is usual to dance jigs; a practice originally borrowed . . . from the Negroes" (Epstein 2003: 121). Moreover, the complex syncopation frequently found in American fiddle music seems to have been an African American innovation that was appropriated by whites and then spread across the continent to become the characteristic sound of American fiddling.

In fact, African American music became an object of considerable fascination for white Americans. Or perhaps it would be more accurate to say that the music became the object of ambivalent fascination, for there existed simultaneously a love for African American music and a refusal to respect the people who made it. This was most evident in the phenomenon of minstrelsy, which emerged around the middle of the nineteenth century. In minstrel shows, white actors and musicians blackened their faces with cork and played parts as stereotypical African Americans. These minstrels played instruments commonly used by blacks and made music that drew upon African American performance practices, but their representations of blackness consisted of grotesque caricatures. Minstrelsy was immensely successful as a popular culture movement, and continued in various forms well into the twentieth century. Its prevalence suggests that, however negative and stereotypical white representations of blacks were—however much whites asserted a distance between themselves and blacks—black music was becoming a central element of white expressive culture.

EXPLORE

African American Spirituals

African American Music: From Emancipation to Today

In the decades following Emancipation (1865), black music continued to offer possibilities for collective expression and action even as it held an enduring fascination for non-blacks. New technologies—beginning with newspapers and other print media, then recording and radio, and finally the Internet—helped spread local musical traditions to new audiences. Many forms of black music became more prominent and more widely dispersed as a result. A few examples will illustrate this point.

Sacred Music   Listen to "Precious Lord, Take My Hand" as performed by the singers of the First Independent Holy Church of God—Unity—Prayer from Marion, Alabama. Frederic Ramsey, who recorded the song in 1954, described the church as a tiny congregation ("more than eight persons") that met every Wednesday evening in the front room of the cabin of church elder Effie Hall (Ramsey 1962). Both the music and lyrics of the song are striking. The singing is propelled by the insistent rhythmic accompaniment of a bass drum, tambourine, and guitar, the latter played almost like a percussion instrument in its own right (and in a manner that does not always correspond to the harmonies implied by the vocal line). In dramatic contrast, the lyrics project absolute despondency ("I am tired, I am weak, I am worn") and plead for divine help.

As the lyrics of "Precious Lord, Take My Hand" suggest, African American religious observance and sacred song often focused on life's difficulties (see Maultsby 2010). These tended to be considerable in an era when blacks faced not only the same concerns faced by many other Americans—poverty, illness, crime, and the uncertainties of love (though in greater proportion)—but also the ongoing consequences of slavery and the crushing effects of legalized racism. In these circumstances, gospel song offered opportunities for collective reflection upon shared circumstances, for mutual affirmation, encouragement, and support, and for expressions of solidarity. This in part helps to explain the quick dissemination of Dorsey's song, which had reached even tiny congregations like the one in Marion, Alabama some two decades after it was first published.

The emerging gospel music movement preserved many valued elements of African American musical and religious practice. For instance, Dorsey's gospel songs were notated in a style that left room for improvisation and free elaboration, in keeping with African American performance practice (Maultsby 2010). Perhaps not surprisingly, the melody of the performance you have just heard differs from the published version in a manner that suggests local elaboration. Songs like the foregoing circulated through print and, later, by means of radio and recordings. In this way, they connected local communities and congregations to a broader, continental group of African American musical practitioners. Put another way, the dissemination of musical publications, and their performance from week to week in local congregations, helped to build a black American musical public, distinguished from the Euro-American public

"PRECIOUS LORD, TAKE MY HAND"  **LISTEN**

TRACK 13.4 **Elder Effie Hall and congregation of First Independent Holy Church of God— Unity—Prayer. With Annie L. Fitts, Elma Sawyer, Jennie Jackson, and Brother Williams. Recorded Marion, Alabama, 15 April 1954**

SLAVES AND FREE BLACKS seem to have begun to adopt Christianity widely in the nineteenth century (Epstein 1963) and, as they did so, they adapted it in ways that suited African American sociability and aesthetics. For instance, in the realm of worship, African American congregations tended not to practice the more staid forms of observance characteristic in many other Christian traditions, rather incorporating elements such as rhythmic movement and spontaneous spoken and sung expression (Burnim 2001). Worship became a way of expressing and affirming the shared African heritage of participants, shaped by the experience of slavery and the encounter with Christianity. African Americans adopted Christianity, but in doing so they transformed it into something that was their own.

The early decades of the twentieth century saw many African Americans move from rural southern contexts to urban northern ones. Coinciding with this Great Migration to the cities of the north was the emergence, in the 1930s, of a dynamic form of gospel music that fused black gospel hymns, elements of secular popular music, and a spontaneous, unconstrained performance style (Burnim 2001). Thomas A. Dorsey, a former blues and jazz musician who moved from Atlanta to Chicago during World War I (Oliver 2011), was a key figure in this development. It was he who composed the song, following the death of his first wife in 1932.

TIME	SECTION
0:00–0:06	Introduction
0:07–0:28	**Chorus**: Notice the prominent voice of the female leader and also the percussion that is added to the accompaniment as the singing begins.
0:29–0:49	**Verse 1**: See if you can hear the way that the guitar serves more percussive than harmonic functions here. There are a few moments when the chord implied by the melody is not performed on the guitar, for example at [0:37–0:39] and again at [0:46–0:47]. But the strumming pattern remains consistent and insistent throughout, driving the singers through the verse.
0:49–1:09	**Chorus**: Now that you're hearing the chorus again, listen carefully to how the whole performance hangs together, with percussion and guitar driving the singers through each section of the song.
1:10–1:29	**Verse 2**: Now turn your attention to the subtle differences you can hear in each singer's approach to the melody. Some singers are adding harmony, others are embellishing the melody in their own way. You should get the distinct impression of a spontaneous and partially improvised rendition of a song well known by all the participants.
1:30–2:10	**Chorus**: Repeated twice here for emphasis as the song comes to an end.
2:10–2:23	**Conclusion**: Listen for the informal way that the guitarist brings the song to an end here.

Blind Lemon Jefferson.
Source: GAB Archive/
Redferns/Getty Images

EXPLORE

Blues

not only by the history of slavery and experiences of racism, but also by the collective development and elaboration of shared musical practices. This is not to suggest any sort of strict insularity, however. In fact, Dorsey's "Precious Lord, Take My Hand" became one of the most widely known gospel songs of the twentieth century, thanks in part to recordings by Mahalia Jackson and Elvis Presley, made just a few years after the one you have heard.

Secular Music   Listen to 'Matchbox Blues' by the Texas blues musician Blind Lemon Jefferson. This is an example of rural blues, a style that appears to have come into being in the southern United States in the early twentieth century. Paul Oliver (2011) suggests that the blues drew upon the solo vocal style of post-Emancipation work songs called field hollers and musical elements of black ballads, and that the earliest blues probably circulated in the repertories of traveling "songsters."

Jefferson's lyrics suggest areas of similarity and contrast with sacred music. On the one hand, the blues, like gospel music, were a genre that allowed singers and listeners to reflect on unhappy circumstances. On the other hand, the blues were more amenable than gospel music to discussions of earthly love, sexuality, money, and the various ways they intersect—in terms both euphemistic ("If she flag my train, papa Lemon's going to let her ride") and direct ("Seems like my heart going break"). It can be added that while this example paints a picture of strained relationships between the sexes from a man's point of view, these relationships were explored from quite distinct perspectives by women blues singers.

Although there are notable differences between the subject matter treated in sacred and secular songs, it is important not to draw too strict an opposition between them. In fact, the same musicians were often active in both areas: as we saw, Thomas Dorsey was a blues singer before he became a composer of gospel music, and Blind Lemon Jefferson sang and recorded sacred songs alongside blues numbers. Moreover, both repertoires played an important part in the work of building a black musical public, circulating through print, broadcasts, and recordings, and connecting local, particularized practices to a broader imagined community.

Importantly, none of these genres has had a solely black listenership, or remained an entirely black practice. Non-black audiences have also been captivated by these musical styles, and non-black musicians have performed them and contributed to their histories. These genres appealed to a broad audience for a variety of reasons: the frank discussions of love and money in blues lyrics, for instance, addressed subjects that were of concern to many North American

LISTENING GUIDE

"MATCHBOX BLUES"   **LISTEN**

TRACK 13.5   **Blind Lemon Jefferson**
Recorded: Chicago, c. Apr. 1927

FOLLOWING A BRIEF instrumental introduction, you should be able to hear that the song moves through a repeating lyrical and harmonic pattern seven times. Each of these verses comprises two rhyming lines, the first sung twice and the second only once. The same harmonic progression supports each verse, Jefferson elaborating it in creative ways from iteration to iteration. The tonic chord, I, accompanies the first statement of the first line. In the second statement of that line, the harmony moves to the subdominant, chord IV, for a time, and then back to the tonic. The final line moves to the dominant, chord V, and then back to the tonic. Using the fourth verse (1:27–1:48), in which the harmonic progression is more audible than in some others, as an example, the structure of the song's verses can be sketched as follows:

I can't count the times I stole away and cried;
Tonic (I)
Can't count the time I stole away and cried;
Subdominant (IV)   Tonic (I)
Sugar the blues ain't on me, but things ain't going on right.
Dominant (V)   Tonic (I)

This formula is well established and indeed might be thought of as the basic pattern elaborated in many other blues songs. It is important to note, however, that Jefferson frequently breaks away from it in other performances (see Evans 2011), as do many other blues performers.

This recording was made using the acoustic equipment of the day, and existing copies tend to be well-worn; therefore it is difficult to transcribe the lyrics with complete certainty. This transcription attempts to capture what is actually sung, but there is a chance that some words are inaccurate, or that you may hear something differently!

I sat there wondering: will a matchbox hold my clothes?
I sat there wondering: will a matchbox hold my clothes?
I ain't got so many matches, but I got so far to go.
I said, "Fair brown, who may your manager be?
Oh, mama, who may your manager be?
We've asked so many questions; can't you make arrangements for me?"
I got a girl across town: she crochet all the time;
I got a girl across town: she crochets all the time;
Mama if you don't quit crocheting, you going lose your mind.
I can't count the times I stole away and cried;
Can't count the time I stole away and cried;
Sugar the blues ain't on me, but things ain't going on right.

continued

If you want your lover, you better pin him to your side;
I say, if you want your baby, pin her to your side;
If she flag my train, papa Lemon's going to let her ride.
Ain't seen my good gal in three long weeks today;
Ain't seen my good gal in three long weeks today;
Lord it's been so long, seems like my heart going break.
Excuse me mama for knocking on your door;
Well, excuse me mama for knocking on your door;
If my mind don't change, I'll never knock here no more.

whites as well. In some ways their appeal probably continued the dynamic of ambivalent fascination and imitation evident in minstrelsy (an enthusiasm for musical styles that, while enjoyed, could nevertheless be dismissed as "someone else's"). But the immense social transformations that accompanied Emancipation, Reconstruction, and the Civil Rights Movement insistently pointed white North Americans toward a more respectful engagement with African Americans and their musics (an incomplete transformation that continues into the present moment).

Changes in the social status of black musicians are especially evident in the history of jazz, and even more particularly those musicians who became active during the 1940s, 1950s, and 1960s—the period immediately leading up to the civil rights reforms in the United States. Perhaps the most iconic musicians in this respect are those associated with the bebop movement. Bebop, emerging in the 1940s, was a demanding style that required great musical facility and flexibility. Musicians improvised at extremely fast tempos, negotiating intricate musical structures at speed. They elaborated preexisting musical and harmonic forms—including the basic blues pattern just introduced—by means of complex harmonic progressions. Consequently, although jazz musicians of previous eras earned renown as artists, it was bebop that definitively won jazz recognition as an art music. Indeed, as George Lewis (1996) has argued, its complexities seem to have spurred developments in other western art music traditions, including a new emphasis on **indeterminacy** and improvisation. As a complex, cutting-edge practice in which black musicians played a particularly prominent role, and which emerged at a moment when blacks were still regularly denied the same rights as white Americans, bebop made a powerful argument for equality.

Although bebop innovators were by and large African American, their audience extended well beyond that community. Moreover, the language of bebop was widely adopted by non-black musicians. The style is now a central component of the training of young jazz musicians around the world (McGee 2011) and an important part of the musical language of many performers. Here again the migration of musical practices between social groups and across social boundaries is evident. Jazz—speaking broadly here, and not simply about bebop—incorporates fundamental African retentions, including collective

INDETERMINANCY
A term used to describe a compositional technique, increasingly common in Western art music composed after World War Two, in which elements of the composition are left to chance or the preference of the performer.

improvisation, and integrates elements of older African American traditions, most notably the blues. At the same time, it has seen important contributions from non-black and non-American musicians, and been a site for collaborations between jazz performers of many backgrounds. Further, its influence is extensive: it is evident in the swung rhythms of classic country music and the improvisatory elements of postwar avant-garde performance. So it is at once a fundamentally African American practice and one that has shaped music making across North America and the globe. In this sense it epitomizes the centrality of African American music to the United States. It also underscores the paradoxical way in which North American music is deeply felt to belong to particular groups even as it is regularly taken up by others.

NORTH AMERICAN MUSICAL CONCEPTS

Dizzy Gillespie plays his trumpet during a jam session. *Source:* Allan Grant/Getty Images

One embarrassing but useful activity I sometimes undertake in the first world music class of a semester asks students to compile a list of the songs they can sing. The responses often reveal a division of the class into two groups. The smaller group comprises singers—amateurs, semiprofessionals, and music students—who claim to know some songs, whereas the larger group consists of students who claim to know few or none. "I know a bit, but not all the words," is a common response. It soon becomes apparent that many students believe they are being asked whether they know any "real" songs—pop tunes, jazz standards, art songs—and whether they know them in full. Only when asked if they know the national anthem or "Twinkle, Twinkle, Little Star" is it evident that the larger group of students possess a sung repertory after all: children's clapping games, simple lullabies, sacred music, "Ninety-nine Bottles of Beer on the Wall."

Responses to that exercise suggest a number of things about how music is frequently conceptualized in North America. First, it tends to be understood as something done by professional or specialist artists. Second, it is typically imagined to be something that one encounters in, and performs for, the public sphere. Music learned from intimates—schoolmates, schoolteachers, parents, fellow congregants—is less likely to spring to mind than music that is made available in a somewhat more formalized way, as printed sheet music, an mp3, or a concert performance. Third, music tends to be understood as "music for music's sake" rather than music that is associated with the daily and weekly lives and everyday activities of the people who make it. To some degree, this chapter has sought to balance out these default understandings of music by examining several examples of music performed by non-professionals in everyday settings that is being performed not simply for its own sake, but also to accomplish something, or help accomplish it. To this end, in addition to music played by professional musicians, we have discussed congregational worship, dance music, children's music, and music of welcome and protest.

There are a number of reasons why North Americans tend to conceptualize music in the ways listed above (keep in mind I am suggesting that this is a particularly common way to think of music, not the only one!). Prevailing social and economic conditions have a great deal to do with it. First, North American societies are highly specialized economically, and this professionalization extends to the musical world. Music is thus widely perceived to be the purview of artists who devote the majority of their efforts to it. Second, North American societies are capitalist, and consequently the work of musicians is often understood as a commodity—goods or services available to the public by the unit or the hour. It follows that music is often conceived as something you hear at a concert, or purchase from iTunes, or watch between ads on YouTube. It is perhaps also easy to understand how lullabies and children's games—which circulate in the alternative economies of the home and playground—sometimes come to mind a little later.

So, North Americans often understand music as a commodity produced by specializing artists. Interestingly, the two elements in play—commodification and specialization—do not always mesh smoothly. For they are associated with two different, and sometimes opposing, ways of valuing. From an economic perspective, it is financial success that is esteemed, whereas from a specialist or professional perspective, it is artistic excellence that is measured. Producers of commodities are expected to make music with a wide appeal, whereas artists are expected to make music that evidences talent and craft and pursues excellence. These ends are not always the same.

Indeed, art and commerce often stand in a tense relationship. Fans of popular music will be familiar with certain forms the conflict between them takes: when a metal, country, or indie rock band starts to court a mainstream audience, concerns are often voiced that the music will lose its authenticity and artistic vitality. Critics worry that, in seeking to fill concert halls, symphony orchestras are relying too much upon familiar works and shirking the artistic imperative to program challenging new ones. Lovers of old-time music express concern that fiddlers are abandoning local styles and taking up more virtuosic national ones in order to win contests and cultivate professional careers (for a discussion of how local styles are defended see Goertzen 1996). Commercially successful music is often alleged to be artistically compromised, and it is sometimes argued that it is pushed on relatively helpless audiences by companies with no interest in art, craft, or tradition. Looking at the conflict from the other side, it is sometimes alleged that art music is too subtle (or even too deliberately abstruse) to be of any value to a wide audience. Its failure as a commodity is deemed to be a symptom of a deeper inability to communicate, and therefore both predictable and deserved. Such quarrels, again, exemplify the tensions that arise in a society where both artistic and commercial success are valued.

However unresolved these arguments, North American behavior suggests that one set of values has precedence over the other. Year upon year, North Americans pour vast amounts of effort into developing and refining musical skills—playing virtuosic guitar solos, improvising in contemporary jazz styles, writing thoughtful lyrics, entering "battle of the bands" contests, and interpreting challenging classical compositions. They do so in full knowledge that their efforts may see little or no financial reward.

Nevertheless, music lovers still get into heated discussions about, for instance, whether avant-garde music should be subsidized, or whether a beloved artist has sold out. But to devote too much space to the tensions between art and commerce—a generative paradox of valuing that isn't going to disappear any time soon—is potentially to ignore two other important issues. The first is that music extends beyond the worlds of art and commerce. It is also a democratic, participatory, and everyday phenomenon. A culinary analogy might be helpful here. The existence of fast-food chains and Zagat-rated restaurants does not change the fact that people still cook at home (and that they garden, fish, and hunt). As this chapter has illustrated, music continues to play a role in the home, the playground, and the community. It acknowledges the passing of the year, assists in rites of passage, coordinates playground games, puts babies to sleep, and teaches the alphabet. And it continues to be implicated in moments of solidarity, helping families, communities, and larger groups to express and experience their bonds to one another. The second concern is North American diversity. Concepts of art and commerce stand in complex and contradictory relationships, not only to one another, but also to ethnic, regional, and community musical priorities. They need to be understood, not as universal North American structures, but rather as two particularly powerful ways of valuing among many. Our task, then, is to consider how the dominant ways of valuing music in North America are challenged and qualified by various ethnic and local ways of assessment.

SUMMARY

As we have seen, music helps to give meaning to the passing of time, assisting in the cultural work that vests the daily, weekly, and yearly cycles with significance, and in the rituals that effect transitions between stages of the life cycle. Just as it helps to do the work of shaping temporality, it plays a part in other kinds of organization and differentiation. It coordinates and integrates the efforts of persons and groups (whether under the banner of a nation or some other form of affiliation) and it distinguishes communities, ethnic groups, regions, and nations from one another. Clearly, some kinds of differentiation are unhappier than others, and they are imposed from without by powerful forces, as the legacies of colonialism, slavery, and minstrelsy illustrate. On the other hand, many North American ethnic groups actively pursue cultural and musical paths that distinguish them. Musical differentiation can come from without or within.

**REVIEW
CHAPTER
RESOURCES**

KEY TERMS

32-bar song form
Anglo-american ballad
Bebop
Indeterminancy
Liturgical cycle
Minstrelsy
Monophony
Música duranguense
Office
Quebradita
Ritual
Strathspey
Tecnobanda
Rural blues

In the process of considering differentiation, some interesting complications became evident. First, many North American groups have borrowed musical technologies and stylistic elements from neighbors, as the use of the banjo by Appalachian whites and the presence of German dance rhythms in Mexican-American popular music demonstrate. Nevertheless, these musics are closely associated with their practitioners, by insiders and outsiders alike. Second, despite extensive local and regional variation, widely generalized musical practices can be identified: for instance common-practice harmony, or the **AABB** dance form. Third, certain musical particularities seem particularly subject to cross-cultural appropriation, as the extraordinarily broad circulation of African-American musical practices shows.

Finally, many of our examples have suggested a close connection between music, ethnicity, performance, and the everyday. The performance of ethnic music does not simply symbolize difference, but rather actively produces it. Singing improvised gospel music on a Sunday morning, playing the fiddle at a local dance, or turning the radio to the station that plays duranguense at work are generative acts that help bring ethnicity into being. And this North American diversity is not simply produced and reproduced during heightened moments of solemnity and celebration, as in, for instance, the welcoming ceremonies described at the opening of this chapter. It also involves day-to-day activity, and the ongoing practices of musicians both ordinary and extraordinary.

BIBLIOGRAPHY

Works Cited and Consulted Philip V. Bohlman, "Ethnic North America," Bruno Nettl et al., *Excursions in World Music*, 5th ed. (Upper Saddle River, NJ: Pearson Prentice Hall, 2008); Horace Clarence Boyer, "Black Gospel Music," Harry Eskew et al., "Gospel music," *Grove Music Online, Oxford Music Online* (accessed February 17, 2011); Mellonee V. Burnim, "Religious Music," pp. 624–636, "African American Musics," Ellen Koskoff, *The United States and Canada, The Garland Encyclopedia of World Music*, Vol. 3 (New York: Garland Publishing Company, 2001); John Burrison, "'James Harris' Britain Since Child," *The Journal of American Folklore* 80 (1967): 271–284; Martin Clayton, Rebecca Sager, and Udo Will, "In Time with the Music: The Concept of Entrainment and its Significance for Ethnomusicology," *ESEM Counterpoint* 1 (2007): 3–75; Edna Smith Edet, *Songs for Children from New York City*, Folkways 07858, liner notes (1978); Dena J. Epstein, "Slave Music in the United States before 1860: A Survey of Sources (Part 1)," *Notes* 20.2 (1963): 195–212; Dena J. Epstein, "The Folk Banjo: A Documentary History," *Ethnomusicology* 19.3 (1975): 347–371; Dena J. Epstein, *Sinful Tunes and Spirituals: Black Folk Music to the Civil War* (Urbana, IL: University of Illinois Press, 2003); David Evans, "Musical Innovation in the Blues of Blind Lemon Jefferson," *Black Music Research Journal* 20.1 (2000): 83–116; Alisoun Gardner-Medwin, "The Ancestry of 'The House-Carpenter': A Study of the Family History of the American Forms of Child 243," *The Journal of American Folklore* 84 (1971): 414–427; Kyra Gaunt, *The Games Black Girls Play: Learning the Ropes from Double-Dutch to Hip-Hop* (New York: New York University Press, 2006); John Murray Gibbon, *Canadian Mosaic: The Making of a Northern Nation* (Toronto: McClelland and Stewart, Limited, 1938); Chris Goertzen, "Balancing Local and National Approaches at American Fiddle Contests," *American Music* 14.3 (1996): 352–381; Alan Govenar, "Blind Lemon Jefferson: The Myth and the Man," *Black Music Research Journal* 20.1 (2000): 7–21; Sydney Hutchinson, *From Quebradita to Duranguense: Dance in Mexican American Youth Culture* (Tucson, AZ: The University of Arizona Press, 2007); Alan Jabbour, "Fiddle Tunes of the Old Frontier," lecture delivered as the Joseph Schick Lecture at Indiana State University, December 6, 2001, accessed online www.alanjabbour.com/Fiddle_Tunes_of_the_Old_Frontier_Schick.pdf (February 17, 2011); Will Kymlicka, *Multicultural Citizenship: A Liberal Theory of Minority Rights* (Oxford: Clarendon Press, 1995); Dwight Lamb, liner notes to *Dwight Lamb: Joseph Won a Coated Fiddle and Other Fiddle and Accordion Tunes from the Great Plains*, Rounder CD 0429 (1999); George E. Lewis, "Improvised Music after 1950: Afrological and Eurological Perspectives," *Black Music Research Journal* 16.1 (1996): 91–122; Portia K. Maultsby, "African American," Richard Crawford et al., "United States of America," *Grove Music Online, Oxford Music Online* (accessed February 17, 2011); Kristin McGee, "'New York Comes to Groningen': Jazz Star Circuits in the Netherlands," Jason Toynbee and Byron Dueck, Eds., *Migrating Music* (London: Routledge, 2011); Paul Oliver, "Blues," *Grove Music Online, Oxford Music Online* (accessed February 17, 2011); Peña, Manuel, *The Texas-Mexican Conjunto: History of a Working-Class Music* Austin, TX:

University of Texas Press, 1985; Frederic Ramsey, Jr., *Music from the South*, Vol. 9, *Songs and Worship*, Folkways FW02658, liner notes (1962); Helena Simonett, *Banda: Mexican Musical Life Across Borders* (Hanover, CT: Wesleyan University Press, 2001); Harry Smith, *Anthology of American Folk Music*, Smithsonian Folkways Recordings SFW 40090, liner notes (1952); Eileen Southern, *The Music of Black Americans: A History*, 3rd ed. (New York: W.W. Norton, 1983); Thomas Turino, *Music as Social Life: The Politics of Participation* (Chicago, IL: University of Chicago Press, 2008); Paul F. Wells, "Fiddling as an Avenue of Black-White Musical Interchange," *Black Music Research Journal* 23.1/2 (2003): 135–147; Helmut Wulz, "Musical Life among the Canadian Hutterites," Philip V. Bohlman and Otto Holzapfel, Eds., *Land Without Nightingales: Music in the Making of German-America* (Madison, WI: University of Wisconsin, 2002).

General Works on North American Music Marius Barbeau and Edward Sapir, *Folk Songs of French Canada* (New Haven, CT: Yale University Press, 1925); Richard Crawford, *America's Musical Life: A History* (New York: W.W. Norton, 2005); Richard Crawford and Larry Hamberlin, *AN Introduction to America's Music* 2nd ed. (New York: W.W. Norton, 2013); Beverley Diamond and Robert Witmer, Eds., *Canadian Music: Issues of Hegemony and Identity* (Toronto: Canadian Scholars' Press, 1994); Charles Hamm, *Yesterdays: Popular Song in America* (New York: W. W. Norton and Company, 1979); Charles Hamm, *Music in the New World* (New York, W. W. Norton, 1983); Ellen Koskoff, *The United States and Canada, The Garland Encyclopedia of World Music*, Vol. 3 (New York: Garland Publishing Company, 2001); Helmut Kallmann, Gilles Potvin, and Kenneth Winters, Eds., *Encyclopedia of Music in Canada*, 2nd ed. (Toronto: University of Toronto Press, 1992); a more recent online edition is available at <www.thecanadianencyclopedia.com/index.cfm?PgNm=EMCSubjects&Params=U2>; Conrad Laforte, *Le Catalogue de la chanson folklorique française*, 6 volumes (Quebec City: Les Presses de l'Université Laval, 1977–87); Kip Lornell and Anne K. Rasmussen, Eds., *Musics of Multicultural America* (London: Schirmer Books, 1997); Timothy J. McGee, *The Music of Canada*, 2nd ed. (New York, W. W. Norton and Company, 1985). Gillian Mitchell, *The North American Folk Music Revival: Nation and Identity in the United States and Canada, 1945–1980* (Aldershot and Burlington: Ashgate, 2007); Judith Tick, Ed., *Music in the USA: A Documentary Companion* (Oxford: Oxford University Press, 2008).

African American Music Leroi Jones/Amiri Baraka, *Black Music*, reissue (Brooklyn: Akashic Books, 2010); Paul Berliner, *Thinking in Jazz: The Infinite Art of Improvisation* (Chicago, IL: The University of Chicago Press, 1994); Samuel A. Floyd, *The Power of Black Music: Interpreting Its History from Africa to the United States* (Oxford: Oxford University Press, 1995); Ted Gioia, *The History of Jazz* (Oxford: Oxford University Press, 1997); Glenn Hinson, *Fire in My Bones: Transcendence and the Holy Spirit in African American Gospel* (Philadelphia, PA: University of Pennsylvania Press, 1999); Charles Keil, *Urban Blues*, 2nd ed. (Chicago, IL: The University of Chicago Press, 1991); Ingrid Monson, *Saying Something: Jazz Improvisation and Interaction* (Chicago, IL: University of Chicago Press, 1996); Guthrie P. Ramsey, *Race Music: Black Cultures from Bebop to Hip-Hop* (Berkeley and Los Angeles: University of California Press, 2004); Ronald Radano, *Lying Up a Nation: Race and Black Music* (Chicago, IL:

University of Chicago Press, 2003); Eileen Southern, *The Music of Black Americans: A History* (New York: W.W. Norton, 1997).

Asian Music in North America Adelaida Reyes, *Songs of the Caged, Songs of the Free: Music and the Vietnamese Refugee Experience* (Philadelphia, PA: Temple University Press, 1999); Nitasha Tamar Sharma, *Hip Hop Desis: South Asian Americans, Blackness, and a Global Race Consciousness* (Durham, NC: Duke University Press, 2010); Oliver Wang, *Legions of Book: Filipino American Mobile DJ Crews in the San Francisco Bay Area* (Durham, NC: Duke University Press, 2015); Deborah Anne Wong, *Speak it Louder: Asian Americans Making Music* (New York: Routledge, 2004); Su Zheng, *Claiming Diaspora: Music, Transnationalism, and Cultural Politics in Asian/Chinese America* (Oxford: Oxford University Press, 2001).

Latino and Hispanic Music Vernon Boggs, *Salsiology: Afro-Cuban Music and the Evolution of Salsa in New York City* (New York: Greenwood Press, 1992); Cathy Ragland: *Música Norteña: Mexican Migrants Creating a Nation between Nations* (Philadelphia, PA: Temple University Press, 2009); John Storm Roberts, *The Latin Tinge: The Impact of Latin American Music on the United States*, 2nd ed. (Oxford: Oxford University Press, 1999); Daniel Sheehy, *Mariachi Music in America: Experiencing Music, Expressing Culture* (Oxford: Oxford University Press, 2005).

Music of European Ethnic Groups in North America Bertrand Bronson, *The Singing Tradition of Child's Popular Ballads* (Princeton, NJ: Princeton University Press, 1976); Philip V. Bohlman and Doris J. Dyen, "Becoming Ethnic in Southwestern Pennsylvania," paper given at the annual meeting of the American Folklore Society in October 1985, Cincinnati; Philip V. Bohlman and Otto Holzapfel, Eds., *Land Without Nightingales: Music in the Making of German-America* (Madison, WI: University of Wisconsin, 2002); Aili Kolehmainen Johnson, "Finnish Labor Songs from Northern Michigan," *Michigan History* 31.3 (1947): 331–343; Doreen Klassen, *Singing Mennonite: Low German Songs Among the Mennonites* (Winnipeg: The University of Manitoba Press, 1989); Robert B. Klymasz, "'Sounds You Never Before Heard': Ukrainian Country Music in Canada," *Ethnomusicology* 16.3 (1972): 372–380; Alan Lomax, *The Folk Songs of North America in the English Language* (Garden City, NY: Doubleday, 1960); Barbara Lorenzkowski, *Sounds of Ethnicity: Listening to German North America 1850–1914* (Winnipeg: University of Manitoba Press, 2010); Miller, Rebecca S., "Irish Traditional and Popular Music in New York City: Identity and Social Change, 1930–1975," Ronald H. Bayor and Timothy J. Meagher, Eds., *The New York Irish* (Baltimore, MD: The Johns Hopkins University Press); Colin Quigley, "Catching Rhymes: Generative Musical Processes in the Compositions of a French Newfoundland Fiddler," *Ethnomusicology* 37.2 (1993): 155–200; Paula Savaglio, "Polka Bands and Choral Groups: The Musical Self-Representation of Polish Americans in Detroit," *Ethnomusicology* 40.1 (1996): 35–47; Mark Slobin, *Tenement Songs: The Popular Music of the Jewish Immigrants* (Urbana, IL: University of Illinois Press, 1982).

Music and Multiculturalism Elizabeth Barkley, *Crossroads: The Multicultural Roots of America's Popular Music* (London: Routledge, 2006); Charles Hiroshi Garrett, *Struggling to Define a Nation: American Music and the Twentieth* Century (Oakland, CA: University of California Press, 2008); Pauline Greenhill, "Backyard World/ Canadian Culture: Looking at Festival Agendas," *Canadian University Music Review* 19.2 (1999): 37–46; Josh Kun, *Audiotopia: Music, Race, and America* (Berkley and Los Angeles: University of California Press, 2005); Marina Peterson, *Sound, Space, and the City: Civic Performance in Downtown Los Angeles* (Philadelphia, PA: University of Pennsylvania Press, 2010); Robert Cantwell, *Ethnomimesis: Folklife and the Representation of Culture* (Chapel Hill, NC: University of North Carolina Press, 1993).

Sacred Music in North America Philip V. Bohlman, Edith Blumhofer, and Maria Chow, Eds., *Music in American Religious Experience* (New York: Oxford University Press, 2006); Kay K. Shelemay, "Music in the American Synagogue: A Case Study from Houston," Jack Wertheimer, Ed., *The American Synagogue: A Sanctuary Transformed* (Cambridge: Cambridge University Press, 1986); Jeffrey Summit, *How Shall We Sing? Music and Identity in Contemporary Jewish Worship* (Oxford: Oxford University Press: 2000); Jeff Todd Titon, *Powerhouse for God: Speech, Chant, and Song in an Appalachian Baptist Church* (Austin, TX: University of Texas Press, 1988).

Monographs Focusing on Specific Genres Robert R. Faulkner and Howard S. Becker, *"Do You Know . . . ?" The Jazz Repertoire in Action* (Chicago, IL: The University of Chicago Press, 2009); Murray Forman and Mark Anthony Neal, *That's the Joint: The Hip-Hop Studies Reader* 2nd ed. (London: Routledge, 2011); Aaron A., Fox, *Real Country: Music and Language in Working-Class Culture* (Durham, NC: Duke University Press, 2004); Gage Averill, *Four Parts, No Waiting: A Social History of American Barbershop Harmony* (New York: Oxford University Press, 2003); Karl Hagrstom Miller, *Segregating Sounds: Inventing Folk and Pop Music in the Age of Jim Crow* (Durham, NC: Duke University Press, 2010); Gillian Mitchell, *The North American Folk Music Revival: Nation and Identity in the United States and Canada, 1945–1980* (Aldershot, UK: Ashgate, 2007); Matt Sakakeeny, *Roll With it Brass Bands in the Streets of New Orleans* (Durham, NC: Duke University Press, 2013); Roger Wood, *Texas Zydeco* (Austin, TX: University of Texas Press, 2006).

DISCOGRAPHY

Song An immense array of North American ethnic music is available on disc and via streaming or purchased download. Given this abundance, some general orientation is followed here by a short list of recordings, in sections corresponding to the genres introduced in the preceding chapter.

The Library of Congress offers a collection of mp3s of traditional music and spoken word on their website http://memory.loc.gov/ diglib/ihas/html/afccards/afccards-home.html. The library's Archive of Folk Culture has released many compilations of American folk music over the years; see www.loc.gov/folklife/folkcat.html. Several of these have been rereleased by Rounder Records (as described in the sections that follow) on CD; others remain available from the Archive of Folk Culture on audio cassette.

Smithsonian Folkways offers recordings of folk music from around the world; its North American collections include field recordings of a scholarly nature, popular music, and albums for children. A good place to start for American music is Harry Smith's *Anthology of American Folk Music* (SFW 40090) originally released in 1952 and now available on compact disc with an extensive set of liner notes. For a compilation of Canadian music, see *Classic Canadian Songs from Smithsonian Folkways* (SFW40539). Rounder Records also offers a significant selection of folk music, especially old-time music, although it is more commercially oriented than Folkways. New World Records offers some recordings of folk and ethnic music. So far as early popular music is concerned, JSP Records issues remastered compilations of early blues, country, jazz, and popular song recordings.

Smaller independent labels continue to produce recordings of music oriented primarily to ethnic communities. One such is Sunshine Records, a Canadian company that publishes recordings of fiddle music, gospel song, Ukrainian music, and polka.

Children's Music For a list of recordings of children's folksongs housed in the Archive of Folk Culture at the American Folklife Center, see the following online resource: www.loc.gov/folklife/ guides/Children.html.

Anglo-American Ballads *Anglo-American Ballads*, Vols. 1 and 2, recorded in various parts of U.S. by Alan Lomax and others in 1934–41 (Vol. 1) and 1937–42 (Vol. 2), Rounder CD 1511 and Rounder CD 1516 [originally released by Archive of Folk Song as AFS L 1 and AFS L 7]. *Ballads and Songs of the Blue Ridge Mountains: Persistence and Change*, Folkways FW 03831.

Fiddle Music *American Fiddle Tunes*, Rounder CD 1518 [a wide-ranging collection of American fiddle music, edited and with extensive liner notes by Alan Jabbour, originally released by the Archive of Folk Song as AFS L 62]; *Ashley MacIsaac: fine(r) thank you very much (a traditional album)*, Ancient Music 79602 2002–2 [Cape Breton fiddle music]; *Old Time Fiddle Tunes Played by Jean Carignan*, Folkways FW03531, 1960 [Quebec fiddle music].

Duranguense and Tecnobanda *Banda Maguey: La Estrella de los Bailes*, Fonovisa [tecnobanda]; *Los Creadorez del Pasito Duranguense: Recio, Recio Mis Creadorez*, Disa Records [duranguense]; *Grupo Montéz de Durango: De Durango a Chicago*, Disa Records [duranguense].

Gospel Music *The Clark Sisters: The Definitive Gospel Collection*, Word Entertainment; *Mahalia Jackson: The Apollo Sessions 1946–1951*, Pair; *Precious Lord: Recordings of the Great Gospel Songs of Thomas A. Dorsey*, Columbia.

Blues *Negro Blues and Hollers*, recorded in Arkansas, Mississippi and Tennessee by Alan Lomax, Lewis Jones, and John W. Work, Rounder 1501 [originally released by the Archive of Folk Song as AFS L 59]; *Rural Blues: A Study of the Vocal and Instrumental Resources*, Folkways FWRF202.

GLOSSARY

Abhinaya: (South Asia). Gestural interpretation of text in dance.

Aerophone: Scientific term for all types of wind instruments, including trumpets, flutes, and the organ.

Afoxe: (Latin America). A secular manifestation of candomblé, connected to carnival and performed on the streets.

Ageng: (Indonesia). Large, as in gong ageng (Jv.).

Ageuta: (Japan). A type of song in higher vocal range used in Noh plays.

Agogó: (Africa) (Latin America). Double bell of West African origin, also used in Brazil.

Agrarian bureaucracy: (Korea). A term used to describe the social structure of pre-20th century Korea and China, denoting a complex hierarchy of farming classes, administrative classes, elites, and various outcastes.

Aguê: (Latin America). A gourd rattle of West African origin containing cowries, pebbles, or dry seeds and with a net covering to which additional noise makers are fixed.

Aḥwash: (Middle East and North Africa). Communal festival dance music in Berber villages of Morocco.

Akadinda: (Africa). Large twenty-two-key xylophone of the Ganda.

Akan: (Africa). A major ethnic group in Ghana.

Akía: (Latin America). An individually owned and sung song of the Suyá Indians of Brazil.

Alap(anam): (South Asia). Raga improvisation in free rhythm.

Animism: (Korea). A religion that holds that material things are possessed of spirits.

Angklung: (Indonesia). A kind of pitched bamboo rattle.

Anupallavi: (South Asia). Second section of kriti or other Carnatic song form.

Apache fiddle: (North American Indian). Bowed instrument with one string, probably made in imitation of the Western violin, used in the culture of the Navajo and Apache peoples.

Arab-Andalusian music: (Middle East and North Africa). Refers to a number of related art music traditions of North Africa that trace their origins to the Islamic courts of medieval Spain.

Arabesk: (Middle East and North Africa). A popular music form of twentieth-century Turkey that drew heavily on Arab aesthetics.

Aragoto: (Japan). Rough-style acting in the kabuki theater.

Aria: (Europe). A self-contained, often highly virtuosic piece for solo voice, most commonly used in opera, that affords the character a moment of reflection on a particular sentiment, issue, or dilemma taking place within the plot.

Arja: (Indonesia). A type of Balinese opera.

Asymmetrical phrases: Phrases not equal in length.

Atabaques: (Latin America). Drums of West African origin, used in Brazilian candomblé music.

Atouta: (Japan). The last song in the jiuta cycle.

Atsimevu: (Africa). Large Ewe (Ghana) lead drum.

Atumpan: (Africa). Paired drums central to the Akan people of Ghana.

Axatse: (Africa). Ewe shaker with beads on a net on the outside the gourd.

Aymara: (Latin America). Indigenous Andean language, second-largest indigenous ethnic group in the Andean region.

Bağlama: (Middle East and North Africa). A fretted, long-necked Turkish lute.

Bajo sexto: (Latin America). A twelve-string guitar used in Mexican norteño music.

Balo: (Africa). A Mande xylophone.

Balungan: (Indonesia). Skeletal melody in Javanese music.

Ban: (China). Generic term for Chinese clappers.

Banda Sinaloense: (Latin America). Brass bands developed in the Mexican State of Sinaloa and playing a wide range of traditional Mexican repertory.

Bandoneon: (Latin America). A type of concertina commonly associated with tango music and particularly popular in Argentina and Uruguay.

Bandura: (Europe). Ukrainian plucked lute of different sizes and ranges, often played in ensembles.

Bansuri: (South Asia). Hindustani flute.

Bantu: (Africa). A major group of African languages.

Baqqashot: (Middle East and North Africa). Hebrew songs sung during night vigils of Sephardic Jews.

Barong: (Indonesia). (1) A mythical lion-like creature in Balinese sacred dramas; (2) a trance dance ritual adopted for performances for tourists.

Barung: (Indonesia). Specifying the middle range of some types of Javanese gamelan instruments.

Bauls: (South Asia). A community of itinerant musicians in West Bengal and Bangladesh who preach tolerance and oneness through music and dance.

Baya: (South Asia). Small, bass kettle drum of tabla pair.

Becar: (Europe). Instrumentalist and musical specialist in southeastern Europe, often distinguished by great mobility.

Bedhaya: (Indonesia). Sacred court dance of Java.

Bendīr: (Middle East and North Africa). Handheld circular frame drum, often with snares.

Berava: (South Asia). The caste of Sinhala Buddhist drummers, dancers, and ritualists in Sri Lanka who perform all-night rituals to protect and heal communities.

Bhajan: (South Asia). Hindu devotional song.

Bhangra: (South Asia). Pop music of the South Asian diaspora combining aspects of hip-hop, trance, and remix techniques with a traditional folk dance music from the state of Punjab.

Bharata Natyam: (South Asia). Major dance style of South India.

Bin: (South Asia). Hindustani plucked lute associated with dhrupad style.

Bira: (Africa). A Shona religious ceremony involving spirit possession.

Birimintingo: (Africa). An instrumental interlude or "break" during which a Mande jali departs from the basic ostinato.

Biwa: (Japan). A type of lute.

Bol: (South Asia). Rhythmic syllable in Hindustani music.

Bomba: (Caribbean). An Afro-Puerto Rican music and dance complex.

Bonang: (Indonesia). Multioctave bronze instrument responsible for elaboration in Javanese gamelan.

Bonsan: (Japan). Japanese Buddhist chants in Sanskrit.

Boogaloo: (Latin America). A musical genre envisioned as a crossover between Latin and North American popular musics and actively pursued during the 1960s.

Brahmin (Brahman): (South Asia). The highest varna, or caste, in Indian society.

Broadside ballad: (North America). A printed version of a folk song, usually combining a well-known melody with a topical text; printed on large sheets and sold inexpensively.

Bubaran: (Indonesia). A small-scale Javanese gendhing having sixteen beats.

Buddhism: Religion of compassion and salvation based on the teaching of the Indian prince Siddharta ("the Buddha," 563–483 BCE). Influential in Chinese, Japanese, and Korean societies.

Bugaku: (Japan). Japanese court dance with instrumental accompaniment.

Buka: (Indonesia). Introduction to a Javanese gendhing.

Bunraku: (Japan). The main form of puppet theater in Japan.

Cadence: A pause or ending in music.

Cai Yuanpei (1868–1948): (China). Chancellor of Peking University (Beida) from 1916 to 1926. Important supporter of the May Fourth Movement.

Caja: (Latin America). A large, indigenous snare drum used to accompany pinkillu ensembles.

Cajun: (North America). French-speaking culture of Louisiana, with historical links to French-speaking Canada.

Call-and-response: The alternation or interlocking of leader and chorus musical parts or of a vocal and instrumental part.

Canboulay: (Caribbean). Processions that commemorated the harvesting of burnt cane fields before emancipation.

Candombe: (Latin America). An Afro-Uruguayan music and dance complex.

Candomblé: (Latin America). An Afro-Brazilian religion heavily involving West African religious beliefs and musical practices.

Canonization: (Korea). The selection from a broad range of musical practices of a core of sanctioned pieces.

Canto pop: (China). Popular song genre sung in the Cantonese dialect produced in Hong Kong since the 1970s.

Caranam: (South Asia). Last of three sections in Carnatic kriti or other song form.

Carnatic: (South Asia). In music, referring to South Indian music style.

Cariso: (Caribbean). Traditional French creole song. Early form of calypso, often employing insulting or satirical lyrics.

Cavaquinho: (Latin America). A small, four string instrument belonging to the guitar family and used in Brazilian choro music.

Celempung: (Indonesia). The plucked zither of Javanese gamelans.

Çeng: (Middle East and North Africa). Classical Turkish harp.

Champeta: (Latin America). An Afro-Colombian popular music associated particularly with the címarron (maroon) village of Palenque de San Basilio and centered in the city of Cartagena.

Changga: (Korea). A turn of the 20th century genre with origins in Western folk songs and Christian hymns, modally similar to the music of central and southeastern Korea.

Chen Gexin: (China). Composer of popular songs active in Shanghai between the 1930s and 1940s.

Chicha: (Latin America). A popular music mixing Andean musics like wayno with the sounds of cumbia and rock music.

Chobo: (Japan). The Gidayu (musico-narrative) duo on the kabuki stage.

Chord: A group of at least three tones sounded simultaneously in combination.

Chordophone: Scientific term for all types of string instruments, including violins, guitars, and pianos.

Choro: (Latin America). An instrumental Brazilian form of popular music.

Chou: (China). Generic name for a clown role in Chinese theater.

Chowtal: (Caribbean). A form of folk music associated with phagwa (holi) in Trinidad and having roots in Indian (Bhojpuri) folk music.

Church modes: (Europe). Seven-note scales, thought by many to characterize more recent styles of folk music.

Chutney-soca: (Caribbean). Popular music style of Trinidad that combines elements of two earlier styles, soca and chutney.

Cinquillo: (Caribbean). A rhythmic cell common throughout the Caribbean, containing five separate articulations and organized into a long-short-long-short-long pattern.

Colonialism: The administrative, economic, and political control of a territory (colony) by a colonial power (such as the British Empire). This condition is maintained through exploiting unequal power relationships and by force, benefiting the colonial power and its center (the métropole) to a much greater degree than the colony itself in the process.

Colotomic (Japan). Marking or delineating major phrases in a musical composition. Used to describe percussion instruments that have this function.

Colotomic structure: (Indonesia). The marking of fixed beats within the metric structure of a musical piece by particular instruments; in gamelan music these include gong, kenong, kempul, and ketuk.

Colotomy: (Indonesia). The structure of a Javanese gendhing determined by the total number of beats it contains and which of those beats are sounded on particular instruments.

Compadrito: (Latin America). A stereotypical character in the early history of tango. A male of modest means who makes do, both within and outside of the law, managing life with flair.

Comparsa: (Latin America). The name given to the entire group of candombe revelers, including dancers, masqueraders, and drummers.

Compás: (Latin America). Within Mexican traditional musics a rhythmic gesture, spread across two equal halves, that shifts the accent patterns to create syncopation.

Concertina: (North America). The button-box accordion favored in polka bands of the Midwest.

Confucianism: System of ethics based on the teachings of Kongfuzi (Confucius, 551–479 BCE). Confucianism formed the dominant ethic of Chinese social units from the imperial government to the peasant family. It is also influential in Korean and Japanese societies.

Conjunto norteños: (Latin America). Popular dance bands originally associated with northern Mexico and southern Texas, featuring three-row button accordion, bajo sexto (12-string guitar), bass, and drums.

Conventillos: (Latin America). Tenements around Buenos Aires.

Copla: (Latin America) (Caribbean). An Iberian-derived verse form with four octosyllabic lines per stanza.

Corrido: (Latin America). Mexican ballads usually on historical or topical themes using the copla text form.

Counter-Reformation: (Europe). A period of Catholic revival (mid-16th to mid-17th centuries), energized in response to the Protestant Reformation.

Criollo: (Latin America). In some regions criollo refers to American-born Spaniards, or largely European-derived ethnicity in Latin America, "white."

Cultural Revolution: (China). Complex social and political upheaval that began as a struggle between Mao Zedong and other top Communist Party leaders for domination of the Party and went on to affect all China with its calls for "continuing revolution" and "class struggle." Dates for the movement are usually given as 1966 to 1976.

Cumbia: (Latin America). A Colombian traditional music combining Amerindian, African, and European musical ideas and instruments. It has, since the middle of the twentieth century also become an internationally important popular music.

Currulao: (Latin America). Afro-Colombian, Afro-Ecuadorian dance context in the Pacific Coast region in which marimba is featured.

Dabke: (Middle East and North Africa). Popular folk dance of the eastern Arab region.

Da-daiko: (Japan). The largest of gagaku drums.

Dahina: (South Asia). Treble drum of tabla pair, having a tunable head.

Dalang: (Indonesia). Master puppeteer of the Javanese shadow-puppet play.

Dalits: (South Asia). The politically correct name for the formally "untouchable" community called the Paraiyars, who traditionally performed the parai frame drum at funerals in South India and Sri Lanka.

Daluo: (China). Big Chinese gong.

Dan: (China). Generic name for a female role in Chinese theater.

Dan: (Japan). A musical section in Japanese music of various forms.

Dangdut: (Indonesia). Popular Indonesian musical style that combines Western rock and Indian film music influences.

Danmono: (Japan). Sectional form.

Danpigu: (China). A single-headed drum used in Chinese theater.

Darbūka: (Middle East and North Africa). A goblet-shaped drum.

Dastgah: (Middle East and North Africa). Melodic mode in Persia/Iran.

Datangu: (China). A big Chinese barrel drum.

Debayashi: (Japan). The on-stage musicians of the kabuki theater.

Décima: (Caribbean). An Iberian-derived, octosyllabic verse form with ten octosyllabic lines per stanza. The rhyming scheme is **ABBAACCDDC**.

Degatari: (Japan). On-stage musicians in Kabuki theater. This group is divided functionally into two separate ensembles, called the chobo (storytellers) and debayashi (ensemble specializing in performing nagauta, or "long song").

Demung: (Indonesia). The low-range saron.

Devadasi: (South Asia). A Carnatic dancing girl whose art was dedicated to temple deities.

Dhalang: (Indonesia). Puppeteer of wayang kulit.

Dhikr: (Middle East and North Africa). A Sufi devotional practice involving the chanting of names of God.

Dhrupad: (South Asia). A severe classical song and instrumental form of Hindustani music.

Diaspora: (Caribbean). A term describing the movement of a group of people (generally sharing ethnic or national history) into forced exile. This exile in a place other than the group's ancestral homeland generally also precludes the possibility of return. The Jewish and African diasporas are two paradigmatic examples.

Diatonic: Refers to the European, seven-note (do-re-mi) scale.

Didgeridoo: Long trumpet, made of a hollowed eucalyptus branch, used in Australian aboriginal cultures as a drone accompanying singing, and more recently, a general symbol of Australian musical identity.

Disike (Disco): (China). A recent Chinese popular song style.

Dizi: (China). A Chinese transverse bamboo flute with six finger holes.

Dondon: (Africa). Ewe hourglass-shaped "talking drum."

Donkilo: (Africa). The basic sung melody of Mande jali songs.

Drut: (South Asia). Fast.

Dùndún: (Africa). Hourglass-shaped "talking drum" of the Yoruba of Nigeria.

Duranguense: (North America). A popular dance music that developed in Chicago. A variant of tecnobanda, the musical style is derived from blending banda with electronic instruments.

It is notable for its emphasis on percussion lines and for the generally faster tempos at which the repertory is performed. The accompanying dance is characterized by western attire and a typical dance step, called pasito, derived from the traditional dancing in Durango, Mexico. Duranguense is popular in both Mexico and the United States.

Eduppu: (South Asia). The beginning of a phrase in Carnatic music used as a cadence for improvisations.

Elima: (Africa). A Pygmy puberty ceremony for which women are the primary singers.

Ennanga: (Africa). Ganda bow-harp.

Entenga: (Africa). Royal Ganda tuned drum ensemble.

Erhu: (China). A two-stringed Chinese spike fiddle with hollow wooden cylindrical sound box.

Erhuang: (China). Basic aria-rhythmic patterns used in the Peking Opera.

Eurovision Song Contest: (Europe). The largest popular-song contest in the world, established in 1956 by the European Broadcasting Union and pitting national entries against each other in an annual spectacle judged by telephone voting from the entering nations.

Fangman jiahua: (China). Literally, "making slow and adding flowers." A technique through which the tempo is slowed to achieve temporal space between the notes of the melody. This space is then ornamented with additional notes.

Fasıl: (Middle East and North Africa). Multi-sectional organizational scheme for a performance of Turkish art music, featuring melodic modal unity and rhythmic modal diversity.

Fei Shi: (China). The pseudonym of an early twentieth-century Chinese reformer.

Filmigit: (South Asia). Popular songs composed for Indian films.

Flat: Pitch lowered by a half tone.

Forró: (Latin America). A Northeast-Brazilian traditional music that has, since the middle years of the twentieth century also found expression as popular music.

Fret: A device of metal or string that divides the fingerboard of plucked instruments and against which the player presses the playing strings to get different tones.

Fuga: (Latin America). A term used throughout Peru to indicate an animated concluding section to a dance piece.

Fujian nanqu: (China). A genre of song suite with instrumental accompaniment popular in Fujian province in southern China and in Taiwan as well.

Fushi: (Japan). A term for melody in general.

Gagaku: (Japan). Japanese court orchestral music.

Gaita: (Latin America). A duct flute, played in gendered pairs. The female gaita hembra has six holes and the male gaita macho is made with two holes. The gaita is an integral part of the traditional Colombian cumbia ensemble.

Gaku-so: (Japan). The gagaku zither.

Gambang: (Indonesia). A xylophone instrument in the Javanese gamelan; an archaic instrument, g. gangsa, is related to the saron.

Gambuh: (Indonesia). An archaic type of Balinese court opera and its accompanying orchestra.

Gambus: (Indonesia). A type of Islamic song having Arabic influence; the name of the plucked lute used to accompany this song.

Gamelan: (Indonesia). An ensemble of instruments such as those found in the central Javanese courts.

Gamelan Arja: (Indonesia). A type of Balinese opera.

Gamelan Gambuh: (Indonesia). An archaic type of Balinese court opera and its accompanying orchestra.

Gamelan Gong Gede: (Indonesia). Older Balinese court music, used for court and temple rituals, similar in sound and style to the Javanese gamelan.

Gamelan Gong Kebyar: (Indonesia). A modern type of Balinese music and the dance it accompanies, which is noted for its virtuosic and unpredictable playing style.

Gamelan Semar Pegulingan: (Indonesia). Large, Balinese court orchestra that plays instrumental versions of gamelan gambuh melodies.

Gankogui: (Africa). Ewe double bell.

Gaşba: (Middle East and North Africa). An end-blown flute of North Africa, associated with early Algerian raï.

Gatra: (Indonesia). A four-beat phrase in Javanese music.

Gat-tora: (South Asia). The section of Hindustani instrumental performance, accompanied by tabla, in which a short composed melody, the gat, is alternated with improvisational passages, tora.

Gaucho: (Latin America). Residents of the South American pampas and particularly important to the national imaginations of Argentina, Uruguay, and Chile. A term roughly equivalent to the North American cowboy.

Gboba: (Africa). Large Ewe (Ghana) lead drum.

Gede: (Indonesia). Large, as in gamelan gong gede.

Gender: (Indonesia). An instrument having thin bronze slab keys individually suspended over tube resonators.

Gender Wayang: (Indonesia). Four-piece ensemble of genders that typically accompanies the Balinese shadow play.

Gendhing: (Indonesia). A piece of Javanese music for gamelan.

Gerongan: (Indonesia). A male chorus that sings with Javanese gamelan.

Gesangbuch: (North America). Meaning "songbook," a printed collection of Amish religious songs, many entering from outside the community.

Gesellschaft für Musikfreunde: (Europe). "Society for the Friends of Music"; institutional home to concert halls, archives, and artistic monuments that recognize the past history of Austrian music.

Geza: (Japan). The off-stage music of the kabuki theater.

Gharana: (South Asia). A school of professional musicians who originally traced their heritage to a family tradition but which now includes non-biological descendants as well.

Ghazal: (South Asia). A form of poetry associated with Perso-Arabic Muslim culture enthusiastically taken up by Urdu speakers in North India and Pakistan, where it is often sung.

Ghost Dance: (North American Indian). Native American (principally Plains) religious movement of protest against U.S. government excesses of the 1880s.

Gidayubushi: (Japan). A major Japanese musical narrative style accompanied by the Shamisen created by Takemoto Gidayu.

Gisaeng: (Korea). A class of female professionals, many of whom were professional entertainers who were foundational in the history of Korean traditional music.

Gong: (Indonesia). Gong.

Gongan: (Indonesia). A phrase concluded with a stroke on gong ageng or siyem.

Gu: (China). Generic name for Chinese drum.

Guacharaca: (Latin America). A wooden scraper played with a fork consisting of many wire prongs mounted into a wooden handle. Part of the traditional Colombian vallenato ensemble.

Guangdong yinyue: (China). A genre of Chinese instrumental ensemble music originating in Guangdong province, which became popular not only in other parts of China but also Chinese ethnic enclaves in the West known as "China Town."

Guellal: (Middle East and North Africa). Goblet-shaped drum of Algeria, associated with early Algerian raï.

Gugak: (Korea). "National music," a neologism generally used to describe music officially sanctioned as Korean traditional music.

Guiro: (Caribbean). A rattle made out of a vegetable gourd.

Guitarrón: (Latin America). In Mexico, a large acoustic bass guitar with a convex back.

Gumbrī: (Middle East and North Africa). Three-stringed lute used in Tunisian stambeli.

Guru: (South Asia). A Hindu teacher.

Guru-Shishya parampara: (South Asia). Teacher-student tradition. A system of musical learning in India where a student undertakes a long, arduous apprenticeship with a teacher.

Gūshe: (Middle East and North Africa). Melodic phrases that constitute the main musical pieces of the Persian dastgah.

Gusle: (Europe). Bowed lap fiddle, played throughout southeastern Europe, especially to accompany narrative epic repertories.

Gwangdae: (Korea). Professional male entertainers omnipresent in the musical landscape of 19th-century Korea.

Habanera: (Latin America). Another name for the condradanza, a slow duple meter Cuban dance popular in the nineteenth century. It refers specifically to the rhythm prominent in the contradanza.

Ḥaḍra: (Middle East and North Africa). The musical ritual ceremony of Sufis in North Africa.

Haji: (Indonesia). A male Muslim who has made a pilgrimage to Mecca.

Hako: (North American Indian). A complex ceremony of the Pawnee, carried out for the general welfare of the tribe and the world, requiring four days of singing, dancing, and ritual.

Halam: (Africa). A West African banjo-like lute with a neck, gourd sound box, and skin stretched over the face of the sound box.

Han: (Korea). A complex emotional cluster often translated as "resentful sorrow." Thought by many to be essentially Korean, and by many others to be the product of modern, post-colonial efforts to create a "Korean" essence.

Hanamichi: (Japan). A ramp used in the Kabuki theater that connects the back of the theater to the stage.

Hardanger fiddle/Hardingfele: (Europe and North America). Elaborate Norwegian folk fiddle, with elaborate woodwork and extra resonating strings.

Harmonium: (South Asia). Portable reed organ, with a single keyboard and a handoperated bellows; of European origin, but used widely in the sacred and semiclassical musics of Pakistan and North India.

Hayashi: (Japan). Generic name for ensembles of flute and drums.

Heterophony: Two or more performers play the same melody, but with small differences in timing or ornamentation.

Heuriger: (Europe). Austrian wine garden, which is often a site for traditional music.

Hexatonic: A scale of six tones.

Hichiriki: (Japan). A double-reed gagaku instrument.

Highlife: (Africa). A form of urban-popular dance-band music of Ghana; also played in Nigeria and elsewhere in West Africa.

Hindustan (South Asia). Region of North India, with a distinct musical tradition —Hindustani.

Hindustani: (South Asia). In music, referring to North Indian musical style.

Hispaniola: The name of the large Caribbean island shared by the modern nation-states of Haiti and the Dominican Republic.

Hocket: (Latin America). Interlocking pitches between two or more sound sources to create a single melody or part.

Hogaku: (Japan). Native Japanese music.

Hogoromo: (Japan). A noh play.

Hosho: (Africa). Large gourd shakers, used in Zimbabwe to accompany mbira music.

Hua San Liu: (China). A Chinese instrumental piece belonging to the Jiangnan sizhu repertory.

Hui: (China). Position markers on the qin.

Hummel: (Europe). Dulcimer played widely throughout Sweden and associated historically with Swedish folk styles.

Iberian: Referring to Iberian Peninsula, Spain, and Portugal.

Idiophone: Scientific term for all instruments whose bodies vibrate as the principal method of sound-production, including rattles and many other percussion instruments.

Ikagura (Japan). Japanese court religious (Shinto) music.

Improvisation: Performance that is spontaneous rather than predetermined.

Incomplete repetition: (Native America) (North American Indian). A song structure common in intertribal and Plains style and consisting of two sections. The first section includes a short melodic phrase, called a "push up" or "lead," followed by a repetition of that melody by another singer. This repetition is called the "second." The second section, called the "chorus" generally consists of two or more phrases and is, itself, repeated.

Indeterminacy: (North America). A term used to describe a compositional technique, increasingly common in Western art music composed after World War II, in which elements of the composition are left to chance or the preference of the performer.

Interlocking: The practice of fitting one's pitches and beats into the spaces of other parts, or alternating the pitches or phrases of one part with those of others to create the whole; hocket.

Intertribal: (North American Indian). Songs or dances based on the Plains styles with which traditions of various other tribes are combined, developed for performances at modern powwows.

Interval: The distance between two pitches.

Jaipongan: (Indonesia). Popular Indonesian music that is derived from the native folk entertainment of Sunda (West Java).

Jali. pl. jalolu: (Africa). The term for a hereditary professional musician in Mande society, who serves as an oral historian and singer/performer.

Jaliscan Harp: (Latin America). A wooden, 36-string, diatonically tuned harp using nylon strings. Was once the primary bass instrument in Mariachi ensembles but has been replaced by the more flexible guitarrón.

Jangdan: (Korea). Rhythmic patterns that underlay Korean traditional music.

Jenglong: (Indonesia). An archaic Javanese instrument.

Jeong-ak: (Korea). "Proper music," a broad category which encompasses the music of the traditional upper classes.

Jhala: (South Asia). The concluding section of instrumental improvisation following jor in Hindustani music during which the performer makes lively and fast rhythmic patterns on the drone strings of an instrument.

Jiangnan sizhu: (China). A type of Chinese chamber instrumental ensemble made up of strings ("silk") and winds ("bamboo") popular in the areas around Shanghai.

Jianzipu (Abbreviated characters tablature): (China). Tablature for the Chinese seven-stringed zither, the qin; it is made up of clusters of abbreviated Chinese characters.

Jing: (China). Generic name for a painted-face role in Chinese theater.

Jingge: (Energy Song): (China). A recent Chinese popular song style.

Jinghu: (China). The leading melodic instrument in the Peking Opera theater. It is a two-stringed bamboo spike fiddle with a very high and piercing range and timbre.

Jingju: (China). Chinese term for Peking Opera. It means "theater of the capital."

Jit, also jiti: (China). Informal Shona village dance, song, and drumming. Also a genre played by electric guitar bands in Zimbabwe.

Jiuta: (Japan). A major koto genre that combines techniques of both kumiuta and danmoto. Sometimes also called tegotomono.

Jo-ha-kyu: (Japan). A basic aesthetic concept in Japanese music. Jo denotes "introduction"; ha denotes "development"; kyu denotes the final section of a composition.

Jor: (South Asia). The section of Hindustani instrumental performance that follows alap and introduces a pulse.

Jùjú: (Africa). A form of Nigerian popular music associated with the Yoruba that combines electric instruments with indigenous drums and percussion.

Junkanoo: (Caribbean). A Bahamian festival, celebrated on Boxing Day (December 26) and New Year's Day and including music, costume arts, and dance.

Kabaka: (Africa). King of Buganda.

Kabuki: (Japan). The main form of Japanese popular musical theater.

Kaganu: (Africa). Small ewe (Ghana) accompanying drum.

Kagura: (Japan). A generic term for Shinto music.

Kagura-bue: (Japan). A flute used in Shinto music and court music.

Kakegoe: (Japan). Vocal drum calls used in noh theater.

Kakko: (Japan). A small horizontal drum used in court music.

Kamanja: (Middle East and North Africa). Middle Eastern fiddle (*kemençe* in Turkish).

Kang Youwei (1858–1927): (China). Confucian scholar, influential in late Qing reform movements.

Kansan: (Japan). Japanese Buddhist chant in Chinese.

Karawitan: (Indonesia). Learned music in the Javanese tradition.

Kebyar: (Indonesia). A modern type of Balinese music and the dance it accompanies.

Kecak: (Indonesia). A type of dance drama accompanied by a large male chorus that chants rhythmically, usually performed for tourists.

Kempul: (Indonesia). A type of small suspended gong in the Javanese gamelan having a colotomic function.

Kena (quena): (Latin America). An indigenous Andean end-notched flute of pre-Columbian origin with six top finger holes and one back hole.

Kendang: (Indonesia). Javanese double-headed drum.

Kenong: (Indonesia). A relatively large horizontal gong in the Javanese gamelan having a colotomic function.

Kenongan: (Indonesia). A colotomic phrase in Javanese music marked by a kenong stroke.

Ketawang: (Indonesia). A type of Javanese gendhing having thirty-two beats.

Ketuk: (Indonesia). A small, horizontal gong in Javanese music having a colotomic function.

Ketuk tilu: (Indonesia). A small, Sundanese ensemble consisting of rebab, gong, three ketuk, and drums. This ensemble accompanies a female dancer/singer.

Key: The pitch at which the major or minor scale begins.

Khyal: (South Asia). The major vocal style of Hindustani music.

Kidi: (Africa). Middle-sized ewe accompanying drum.

Klasik: (South Asia). The classical music of Afghanistan, founded by Hindustani musicians from hereditary Muslim families who moved from North India to Kabul in the nineteenth century.

Klezmer music: (Europe). Jewish instrumental music, performed in social events and rites of passage in Eastern Europe prior to the Holocaust and revived in Europe and North America at the end of the twentieth century.

Klezmer musicians: (Europe). Jewish instrumental ensembles that performed, often professionally, for both Jewish and non-Jewish social functions.

Koma-bue: (Japan). A flute used in court music.

Komagaku: (Japan). Japanese court music of Korean origin.

Kontingo: (Africa). A five-stringed plucked lute played by Mande jalolu with a skin head stretched over a gourd sound box.

Kora: (Africa). A twenty-one-string bridge harp played by Mande jalolu.

Kotekan: (Indonesia). Often virtuosic and rapid interlocking rhythms important within gamelan kebyar performances and consisting of two parts (a lower part and a higher part) played on two separate instruments. Generally, multiple pairs of instruments are simultaneously involved in performing kotekan.

Koto: (Japan). A thirteen-stringed zither with movable bridges. It is Japan's main zither.

Kotoba: (Japan). A heightened speech style used in the noh theater.

Ko-tsuzumi: (Japan). A small hourglass-shaped drum.

Krakowiak: (Europe and North America). Duple-meter folk dance, associated with the region near Cracow.

Kraton: (Indonesia). Javanese royal court.

Kriti: (South Asia). The major song type of Carnatic music, divided into three parts: pallavi, anupallavi, and caranam.

Kroncong: (Indonesia). A type of popular Indonesian music originating from Portuguese derived sources.

Küdüm: (Middle East and North Africa). A small pair of Turkish kettledrums.

Kumbengo: (Africa). The basic instrumental ostinato, which serves as the foundation for Mande jali performance.

Kumiuta: (Japan). A suite of songs accompanied either by the koto or the shamisen, or by both.

Kunqu: (China). Classical Chinese musical drama.

Kuse: (Japan). The dance section of the first act of a noh play.

Kushaura: (Africa). "To lead the piece"; the first part, or lead part played by one Shona mbira player.

Kutsinhira: (Africa). "To accompany"; the second accompanying part played by a second Shona mbira player.

Kyogen: (Japan). Literally, "mad words"; it is a comic play inserted between noh plays.

Kyogenkata: (Japan). The clapper player in the kabuki theater.

Ladino: (Europe). The pre-Italian Latinate dialects of the southern Alps in Italy and Switzerland. Ladino is also the Romance vernacular language historically spoken by Sephardic Jews.

Lamellaphone: A general class of musical instruments that have tuned metal or reed tongues set on a bridge mounted to a soundboard or box; it is played by striking the keys. The mbira is but one example of this instrument type. Other lamellaphones used in Zimbabwe include the karimba, njari, and matepe.

Laras: (Indonesia). Javanese tuning system; there are two primary types (1) slendro (with a five-note scale) and (2) pelog (with a seven-note scale).

Lay(a): (South Asia). Tempo.

Li Jinhui (1891–1967): (China). Modern Chinese composer and innovator of the first modern Chinese popular song genre, the liuxing gequ of Shanghai.

Li Shutong (1880–1942): (China). Poet, educator, and pioneer of the modern Chinese School Song. He later became a Buddhist monk.

Liang Qizhou (1873–1929): (China). Student of Kang Youwei and also an influential reformer. He used his writings to raise support for the reform movement.

Liminality: (Korea). The quality of being on the threshold between states of being, characterized by loosening of social structure and the possibility of transformations such as healing and initiation.

Liu Jinguang: (China). Famous composer of Shanghai liuxing gequ and younger brother of Li Jinhui.

Liuxing gequ: (China). Popular song produced in Shanghai since the late 1920s that is a hybrid of various Western and Chinese musical genres. Its lyrics are sung in the Chinese national tongue, the so-called Mandarin.

Living tones: (Korea). Experimentalist Kim Jin-I's term for describing how pitches in Korean music are not fixed, but alive—moving up and down, undergoing dynamic and timbral transformations.

Llamada: (Latin America). The name given to the drum ensembles featured in Uruguayan candombe.

Lunfardo: (Latin America). A particular approach to language (slang) that developed in the tenements of late nineteenth- and early twentieth century Buenos Aires. Associated with early tango.

Lute: A stringed instrument with a sound box and a distinct fingerboard, the strings stretching over both.

Ma'lūf: (Middle East and North Africa). The Arab-Andalusian art music of Tunisia.

Maeuta: (Japan). The first song in a jiuta cycle.

Major: Referring to the quality of a scale having its pitches arranged as follows: tone, tone, semitone, tone, tone, tone, semitone.

Makam: (Middle East and North Africa). Melodic mode in Turkey.

Malambo: (Latin America). A form of Argentine improvised male dance competition important to the early development of tango.

Maqām: (Middle East and North Africa). Melodic mode in the eastern Arab world.

Mao Zedong (1893–1976): (China). An early member of the Chinese Communist Party who rose to party leadership in the 1930s. Led the Party on the Long March and then to establish the People's Republic of China in 1949. Until his death in 1976, he was the paramount political leader and theorist of Chinese communism.

Mariachi: (Latin America). Ensemble type originally from Jalisco, Mexico, consisting of two or more violins, vihuela, guitarrón, two trumpets, and various guitars.

Marimba: (Latin American). Wooden keyed xylophone, originally from Africa, widely popular in Latin America.

Marímbula: (Caribbean). A large box lamellaphone used as a bass instrument in a variety of Caribbean ensembles.

Mawwāl: (Middle East and North Africa). Solo vocal improvisation in the Arab world, usually involving the singing of a piece of poetry.

May Fourth Movement: (China). Term used to describe student demonstration that took place in Tiananmen Square on May 4, 1919, in protest against unfair terms of the Treaty of Versailles. Also refers to the period of iconoclastic intellectual ferment that followed the protest.

Mazurka: (Europe). Polish and Polish American folk dance, often stylized in art-music compositions.

Mbaq'anga: (Africa). A South African urban-popular music featuring electric instruments and horns, with the bass often particularly prominent.

Mbira: (Africa). A twenty-two-key Shona lamellaphone, originally associated with the Zezuru Shona of central Zimbabwe.

Mbube: (Africa). "Lion," one name for Zulu migrant choral music.

Melismatic-syllabic: (Europe). Performing a single syllable of text by singing multiple notes or pitches is called a melisma (melismatic). Syllabic singing, by contrast, matches one syllable to a single note or pitch.

Melodic modes (e.g., maqām): (Middle East and North Africa). Named musical scales that have conventions for how the pitches are used; in performance and may be associated with particular moods or extramusical associations.

Membranophones: Scientific term for all instruments using a stretched membrane for sound production, that is, all true drums.

Mentalité: A collective way of thinking, expressed in the cultural activities of a group or community.

Merengue: (Caribbean). Popular dance music of the Dominican Republic.

Mestizo: (Latin America). A relative term referring to people and a social identity involving the blending of European and Amerindian beliefs and cultural practices. Although in the past used as a racial category, it now more accurately denotes the variable incorporation of Iberian (Spanish and Portuguese) and indigenous cultural heritages.

Metallophone: An instrument classification term for idiophonic instruments made of metal.

Meter: A measure of musical time that organizes beats into larger units also called *measures* or *bars*.

Métropole: From Metropolis, or "mother city." Also used for any colonizing "mother country."

Mevlevi: (Middle East and North Africa). Turkish Sufi order in which a whirling dance and the preservation of Ottoman classical music play important roles.

Mikagura: (Japan). Japanese court religious (Shinto) music.

Milonga: (Latin America). A style of song popular in the more rural areas of the Rio de la Plata region and influential during the early development of tango.

Minnesinger: (Europe). Medieval singer, who often accompanied himself on the lute and was one of the first musical professionals.

Minor: Referring to the quality of a scale having its pitches arranged as follows: tone, semitone, tone, tone, semitone, (tone, tone) or (tone and a half, semitone).

Minyo: (Korea). "Folk song," a term invented in Japan as a literal translation of the German volkslied, and adopted into Korean musicological discourse in the late 19th and early 20th centuries.

Mode: Generic term for a concept indicating tendencies or rules for composing melody. Examples of modes include Indian ragas, Persian dastgahs, and Arabic maqams.

Molimo: (Africa). A Pygmy ceremony for the forest; a straight valveless trumpet used in the ceremony.

Monophonic: Referring to music comprising a single melody; without chords or other melodic or harmonic parts.

Monophony: One melody line is played by all musicians, with no harmonic accompaniment.

Montuno: (Caribbean) (Latin America). A term designating both the improvisatory call-and-response section of a Cuban rumba or son performance (and, later on, the same section within salsa performances) and the technique of arpeggiating chords on the piano.

Mridangam: (South Asia). Double-headed, barrel-shaped drum of Carnatic music.

Mu'adhdhin (Turk. Muezzin): (Middle East and North Africa). The person responsible for intoning the call to prayer (*adhān*; Turk. *Azan*) five times per day in Islamic communities.

Mukhra: (South Asia). Initial phrase of a khyal or gat used as a cadence for improvisational passages in Hindustani music.

Música Duranguense: (North America). A popular dance music that developed in Chicago. A variant of tecnobanda, the musical style is derived from blending banda with electronic instruments. It is notable for it's emphasis on percussion lines and for the generally faster tempos at which the repertory is performed. The accompanying dance is characterized by western attire and a typical dance step, called pasito, derived from the traditional dancing in Durango, Mexico. Duranguense is popular in both Mexico and the United States.

Musica humana, musica mundana, and musica instrumentalis: (Europe). Medieval distinction of different domains of music-making: humanly made music, music of the spheres, and music played by instruments.

Musica mizraḥit: (Middle East and North Africa). A late twentieth-century popular music genre of Israel, associated with working-class immigrants from Middle Eastern countries.

Mūsīqā: (Middle East and North Africa). Music, but refers mainly to secular and instrumental musical traditions and the object of study for Middle Eastern music theorists (Persian: *Mūsīqī*).

Musical bow: (Africa). A bent stick with a single string that is struck with another stick or plucked; a gourd resonator is attached to the bow or, on a second type, the mouth cavity serves as resonator.

Music area: (North American Indian). A group of Native American tribes who share similar musical styles, roughly corresponding to the cultural areas (but not by language).

Muyu (Wooden fish): (China). A carved, hollow, wooden Chinese instrument struck with a pair of wooden sticks.

Nagauta: (Japan). A lyric genre of shamisen music.

Naoba: (China). A small pair of Chinese cymbals.

Naqqarāt: (Middle East and North Africa). Small kettledrums in North Africa.

Nāqūs: (Middle East and North Africa). General term for metallic idiophones in the Middle East and North Africa; in Moroccan Berber music they may be played on found metal objects.

Narodnik Movement: (Europe). A Russian agrarian socialist movement of the late nineteenth century.

Natural: A pitch that is neither raised (sharped) nor lowered (flatted).

Natyasastra: (South Asia). An early Indian treatise on the performing arts attributed to Bharata and concerned with music, dance, and theater and drama.

Nautch: (South Asia). An English colonial name for various kinds of Indian dance, derived from a word in Indian languages for "dance."

Nāy: (Middle East and North Africa). End-blown flute used throughout the Middle East and North Africa.

Netori: (Japan). Introductory section of gagaku music.

Niraval: (South Asia). A type of improvisation in Carnatic music that retains the text and its rhythmic articulation but alters the pitches of the melody.

Ngelik (Indonesia). A section in ketawang pieces that contrasts with the surrounding material (ompak) and is usually longer than one gongan. It is also usually where the gerongan sings the melody of the ketawang composition.

Noh: (Japan). Japanese classical drama that originally developed in the early fourteenth century.

Nohkan: (Japan). The flute used in noh.

Noraebang: (Korea). Korean karaoke, private rooms where people gather to sing songs to the accompaniment of a song machine.

Nortec: (Latin America). A popular music centered in Tijuana that combines sonic markers of Mexican traditional ensembles (including bandas sinaloenses and norteño groups) with electronica (especially techno).

Notation: Graphic representation of music.

Nyamalo: (Africa). Craft specialists in Mande societies, a category including professional musicians.

Obeah: (Caribbean). Bahamian folk belief and practice derived from African religious models and concerned with controlling and deploying powers in service of both good (i.e., healing) and evil (i.e., vengeance).

Oberek: (North America). Polish and Polish American folk dance in triple meter.

Office (Divine Hours): (North America). Organized to correspond to the canonical hours, the Office (also called the Divine Hours) is a set of daily worship services in which certain prayers, readings, and chants are performed at fixed times. The services include matins, vespers, and compline, among others, and the practice is generally associated with Catholic, Orthodox Christian, and Anglican/Episcopal traditions, though other traditions include these services in their worship as well.

Oito baixos: (Latin America). An eight-bass accordion used in Brazilian forró ensembles.

Old Style and New Style: (Europe). The major stylistic categories of Hungarian folk music.

Ompak: (Indonesia) Refers to the opening, usually repeated gongan in ketawang pieces.

Organology: The study of musical instruments.

Orisha: (Caribbean): A spirit understood as one of the manifestations of God within Yoruba and Yoruba-derived religious practice.

Orixa: (Latin America). A spirit or deity in the Yoruba religion of Nigeria.

Orquesta: (Latin America). Orchestra.

Orquesta tipica: (Latin America). A mixed ensemble of European instruments and indigenous Andean flutes.

Ostinato: (Africa) (Caribbean). A repeated or cyclical melody or rhythmic pattern.

O-tsuzumi: (Japan). A large hourglass-shaped drum.

Palenquero: (Latin America). A creole language, developed in Colombia, and mixing Spanish with Bantú.

Pallavi: (South Asia). The opening section of a Carnatic song form.

Pandeiro: (Latin America). A frame drum used in a variety of Brazilian musical genres.

Panerus: (Indonesia). The types of saron or bonang having the highest ranges.

Pansori: (Korea). Solo epic story-singing with barrel drum (buk) accompaniment.

Parallel harmony: Refers to two or more melodic lines moving in parallel motion, or consistently remaining the same harmonic interval apart, for example, parallel thirds, a common trait in Latin American music.

Parlando rubato: (Europe). Identified by Béla Bartók and characterized by a speechlike style that stresses the words while incorporating a great deal of give-and-take in the rhythmic structure. It is associated most closely with "old style" Hungarian folk song.

Pathet: (Indonesia). A particular way of using a scale or laras in Javanese music.

Peking: (Indonesia). The saron with the highest range.

Peking Opera (Jingju Theater): (China). The main type of Chinese popular musical theater that first emerged in the Chinese capital Beijing (Peking) in the later eighteenth century.

Pelog: (Indonesia). The heptatonic tuning system of Javanese music.

Pentatonic: Having five pitches.

Pentatonicism: Melodic structure based on scales with five pitches, often revealing an historically early stage of folk-music style.

Pesindhen: (Indonesia). Javanese female vocal soloist.

Peşrev: (Middle East and North Africa). Instrumental prelude in Turkish art music.

Peyote music: (North American Indian). Songs, in a characteristic style, accompanying a ceremony surrounding use of peyote, a drug derived from a cactus. The peyote religion is a major component of twentieth-century Native American culture of the Plains and Southwest.

Pífano: (Latin America). A small flute, similar to a piccolo, often used in traditional Brazilian forró ensembles.

Pinkillu (Aymara, pinkullu, Quechua): (Latin America). Andean vertical duct flute usually made of cane, but also of wood in some regions.

Pipa: (China). A pear-shaped, four-stringed plucked lute with a short bent neck and many frets.

Pitu: (Latin America). Andean cane side-blown flute.

Piyyut: (Middle East and North Africa). Jewish liturgical poem, often sung.

Plena: (Caribbean) (Latin America). A Puerto Rican folk song style associated with political and social protest and accompanied by frame drums and scrapers.

Polka: (Europe and North America). Dance in duple meter, originally Czech but disseminated throughout European and North American regions and ethnic groups.

Polyphonic: (Europe) (Native America). Generic term referring to all music in which one hears more than one pitch at a time, for example, songs accompanied by guitar, choral music, orchestral music, or two people singing a round together. Refers more specific-ally to music which incorporates two or more simultaneous melodic lines or parts.

Pongzhong: (China). A pair of small Chinese handbells.

Portamento: A slide or sweep between two pitches.

Potlatch: (North American Indian). A ceremony once common among the peoples of the North Pacific Coast, held to exhibit personal wealth and family status, and often commemorating important events in the life of the host (i.e., marriage, death, birth of a child, etc.). Potlatch ceremonies usually included a feast and the giving of gifts.

Powwow: (North American Indian). Tribal or intertribal gathering in twentieth-century Native American culture; a principal venue for performance of traditional and modernized music and dance.

Pungmul: (Korea). Farmers' percussion and dance bands ubiquitous throughout traditional Korea, and adopted by post-colonial protest movements.

Punta rock: (Caribbean). Popular music style developed by the Garifuna, featuring call-and-response vocals and a rich percussion accompaniment derived from traditional punta music.

Pusaka: (Indonesia). Javanese royal heirloom.

Qānūn: (Middle East and North Africa). Plucked zither (spelled *kanun* in Turkey).

Qafla: (Middle East and North Africa). Melodic cadence that marks the end of a section in Arab music.

Qaşīda: (Middle East and North Africa). A vocal piece based on classical Arabic poetic form of the same name.

Qawwali: (South Asia). A genre of Sufi Muslim music popular throughout North India and Pakistan, which uses harmonium and tabla, and involves the singing of Persian poetry (particularly the poetic form called ghazal).

Qin: (China). A Chinese seven-stringed zither. It is the most revered instrument and was patronized by members of the educated class.

Qinqin: (China). A two- or three-stringed plucked lute with a long, fretted neck.

Qirā': (Middle East and North Africa). Recitation of the Qur'an.

Qiuge (Jail Songs): (China). Popular Chinese songs of the 1980s and 1990s. Their lyrics deal with convicts' lives in labor reform camps.

Qur'an: (Middle East and North Africa). The holy book of Islam, considered the word of God.

Quadrille: (Caribbean). A dance, originating in Europe and adapted to Caribbean contexts. It was historically performed by couples arranged in a square formation and following a series of set dance figures.

Québecois: (North America). French-speaking residents of the Canadian province of Québec.

Quebradita: (North America). A dance craze, accompanied by tecnobanda ensembles and privileging cumbia dances, which became especially popular in Los Angeles, northern Mexico, and throughout the Southwest. Characterized by western attire, hat tricks, and flips.

Quechua: (Latin America). The most widespread indigenous Andean language; the state language of the Inca, largest indigenous ethnic group in the Andes.

Radif: (Middle East and North Africa). In Persian classical music, the body of music, consisting of 250–300 short pieces, memorized by students and then used as the basis of point of departure for improvised performance.

Rag(a)(m): (South Asia). A scale and its associated musical characteristics such as the number of pitches it contains, its manner of ascending and descending, its predominant pitch, and so forth.

Ragam/Alapanam: (South Asia). An improvisation performed before the kriti, that demonstrates the musician's abilities to interpret the ragam (or mode) in which the kriti is written.

Ragam-tanam-pallavi: A form of Carnatic music that favors improvisation.

Raï: (Middle East and North Africa). A late twentieth-century popular music form of Algeria, Morocco, and the North African diaspora in France.

Rake 'n' Scrape: (Caribbean). A traditional Bahamian music, usually played on accordion, saw, and goatskin drum.

Ranchera: (Latin America). A Mexican song genre with rural and working-class associations.

Rasa: (South Asia). The affect or emotional state associated with a raga or other artistic expression.

Rebab: (Indonesia). A type of Javanese bowed lute.

Rebāb: (Middle East and North Africa). Upright fiddle of one or two strings.

Recitative: (Europe). A style of barely sung recitation in which the action or plot is carried forward. Often used in operas, oratorios, and cantatas, it imitates the rhythm and cadence of speech and is generally sparsely accompanied.

Rhythmic modes (e.g., īqāʿ): (Middle East and North Africa). Named rhythmic patterns played in repeated cycles; they have conventions for how they are played and may be associated with particular moods or extramusical associations.

Rig-Veda: (South Asia). A collection of poems that tell the stories of the Indian gods. There are three other Vedic texts, called the Yajur-Veda, Sama-Veda, and Atharva-Veda.

Riqq: (Middle East and North Africa). Middle Eastern tambourine.

Ritsu: (Japan). A basic Japanese scale.

Roma (Europe). Transnational communities of people pejoratively referred to as Gypsies; active participants in Europe throughout history and across the continent.

Rough beauty: (Korea). Percussionist and improviser Kim Dong-Won's term for the stylized roughness—raspy timbres, irregular instrument construction, and so on—intentional gestures toward nature and materiality that pervade much of Korean traditional music.

Rumba: (Caribbean). Cuban dance form that developed at the end of the nineteenth century. The typical Rumba ensemble consists of a lead vocalist, a chorus, clave, palitos, and congas.

Rways: (Middle East and North Africa). Traditionally itinerant musicians of the Berber communities of Morocco.

Ryo: (Japan). A basic Japanese scale.

Ryuteki: (Japan). A flute used for Togaku music in the gagaku repertory.

Saami: (Europe). Circumpolar peoples, living in northern Norway, Sweden, Finland, and Russia, whose musical practices in Europe mix indigenous and modern sounds.

Sageuta: (Japan). A type of song in lower vocal range used in Noh plays.

Saibari: (Japan). Shinto songs meant to entertain the gods.

Sam(am): (South Asia). The first beat in a tala.

Samāʾ: (Middle East and North Africa). The act of listening, associated particularly with Sufism.

Salsa: (Latin America). A style of popular Latin dance music.

Samba: (Latin America). The most important Brazilian musical genre often associated with Carnival in Rio but performed in other rural and urban contexts.

Samulnori: (Korea). A new genre of percussion music for stage performance derived from the farmers' band traditions and the traditions of *namsadang* travelling entertainers.

Samurai: (Japan). Warrior.

Sanghyang: (Indonesia). A heavenly spirit who may possess certain performers in Javanese and Balinese trance dances.

Sangita: (South Asia). Music and associated performing arts.

Sangitaratnakara: (South Asia). This thirteenth century treatise on music, the last to be referenced by both Hindustani and Carnatic musical traditions, marks the beginnings of a distinction in style between the Northern and Southern classical traditions.

Sanjo: (Korea). Originally suites of improvisations for solo instrument with hourglass drum (janggo) accompaniment based on rhythmic patterns of generally accelerating tempo; now generally notated and played rote.

Sankyoku: (Japan). Jiuta music played by a trio.

San-no-tsuzumi: (Japan). An hourglass-shaped drum used in court music.

Santur: (South Asia). A Kashmiri hammered dulcimer now used in Hindustani music.

Sanxian: (China). A three-stringed plucked lute with a long, fretless neck and an oval-shaped sound box.

Saqras: (Latin America). Dance drama group of Paucartambo, Peru, representing devils.

Sarod: (South Asia). A fretless, plucked string instrument of Hindustani music originally coming from Afghanistan.

Saron: (Indonesia). A type of Indonesian instrument having thick bronze slab keys lying over a trough resonator.

Sataro: (Africa). A speechlike vocal style performed by Mande jalolu.

Satokagura: (Japan). Folk Shinto music.

Saz: (Europe). Lutelike instrument used widely in Turkish art music and spread throughout the regions of southeastern Europe, into which the Ottoman Empire extended.

Scale: A set of pitches arranged in ascending or descending order.

Schrammelmusik: (Europe). "Schram-mel-Music": urban folklike music of Vienna, named after a family of musicians.

Sertaõ: (Latin America). A region within Northeastern Brazil.

Sesquialtera: (Latin America). The combination/juxtaposition of duple and triple rhythmic patterns, both simultaneously in different instrumental parts, or sequentially in the same part, hemiola.

Session: A traditional gathering of musicians at an Irish pub to play together in an intimate jam session.

Shagird: (South Asia). Pupil of Muslim master.

Shakubyoshi: (Japan). Clappers used in court singing.

Shakuhachi: (Japan). An end-blown flute.

Shamanism: (Korea). Typically a form of animism in which ritual specialists channel and manage complex pantheons of spirits and their place in the material world.

Shamisen: (Japan). A three-stringed plucked chordophone.

Sharp: A pitch raised by a half tone.

Shenai: (South Asia). A Hindustani double-reed instrument.

Sheng: (China). A Chinese free-reed mouth organ; also generic name for a male actor in Chinese theater.

Shen Xingong (1870–1947): (China). Educator and pioneer of modern Chinese School Song.

Shinnai-bushi: (Japan). A musical narrative form accompanied by the shamisen, found in Shinnai Tsuruga.

Shinto: (Japan). Native religion of Japan literally meaning "the way of the gods."

Shishya: (South Asia). Pupil of a Hindu master.

Shite: (Japan). Principal actor in noh.

Sho: (Japan). A mouth organ.

Shoko: (Japan). A suspended bronze drum used in gagaku.

Shomyo: (Japan). Japanese Buddhist chanting.

Shqāshiq: (Middle East and North Africa). Metal clappers used in Tunisian stambeli.

Siku: (Latin America). Andean instrument consisting of different lengths of reed or cane tubes, lashed together, each tuned to a specific note. The performer blows across the top of a cane to make it sound. The siku is a double-row panpipe, divided between two players, the pitch row alternating between the two rows.

Simsimiyya: (Middle East and North Africa). Five-stringed lyre, used primarily in Egypt and Yemen.

Sinawi: (Korea). A genre of simultaneous improvisation modeled after the music of shamanist ritual, particularly of Southwestern Korea.

Sinminyo: (Korea). "New folk song," an early 20th-century genre that combined quasi-traditional Korean melodies with Western instrumentation and harmonies.

Sinti (Europe). One of the largest communities of Roma, with a particularly strong presence in Central Europe.

Sitar: (South Asia). Primary plucked string instrument of Hindustani music.

Siyem: (Indonesia). The smaller of the two large gongs in the Javanese gamelan.

Slendro: (Indonesia). The pentatonic tuning system of Javanese music.

Sogo: (Africa). Middle-size ewe (Ghana) accompanying drum.

Sokyoku: (Japan). Popular koto-and-vocal music of the Edo period in Japan.

Son: (Latin America). A strophic song usually on romantic themes and in many regions characterized by sesquialtera rhythm.

Songs for the Masses: (China). Chinese communist political songs.

Soundscape. A combination of "sound" and "landscape" to indicate how sounds are experienced within a particular area.

Speech Islands: (Europe). *Sprachinseln*, or the German-speaking cultural islands in Eastern Europe, given nationalist significance by Germany prior to World War II.

Sruti: (South Asia). The twenty-two subdivisions of the octave within Indian classical music theory.

Ssikkim gut: (Korea). A ritual dedicated to assisting a recently deceased spirit in moving on to its next life.

Staatsoper: (Europe). National, or "State," Opera of Austria, serving the Habsburg court during the Austro-Hungarian Empire, until World War I.

Stambeli: (Middle East and North Africa). A healing trance music developed by people of sub-Saharan heritage in Tunisia.

Steel band: (Caribbean). A band composed of oil drums that have been "tuned" to play a range of pitches.

Strathspey: (North America). A dance tune, associated with Scotland, in 4/4 meter. Characterized rhythmically by dot-cut, or Scotch "snaps" (a short note followed by a dotted note).

String quartet The ensemble of European chamber music that idealizes the social and musical equality of the modern era—two violins, viola, and violoncello.

Strophic form: Song form in which the verses change but the music used to accompany each verse remains the same.

Sufism: (Middle East and North Africa) (South Asia). Form of Islamic worship involving communal ritual ceremonies featuring participatory practices such as singing, chanting, music, and dance.

Sula: (Africa). Social category in Mande societies, referring to "ordinary people" in contrast to craft specialists.

Suling: (Indonesia). Indonesian vertical flute.

Suona: (China). A Chinese conical double-reed oboe.

Suyá: (Latin America). Amazonian Indian group of Brazil.

Suzu: (Japan). A small bell tree used in some Shinto dances.

Svarakalpana: (South Asia). Improvised singing of pitches using their names in Carnatic music.

Syncopation: Accenting rhythms where they would not normally be accented.

Syncretism: (Latin America). A term, used within religious studies, to describe processes of mixture between religious traditions.

Ṣabā: (Middle East and North Africa). Melodic mode in North Africa.

Tabla: (South Asia). A pair of drums used in Hindustani music.

Taiko: (Japan). A generic term for drum; also a drum struck by a pair of sticks used in the noh theater.

Takht: (Middle East and North Africa). Small traditional ensemble in the Arab world, typically including the 'ūd, nāy, kamanja, and riqq.

Tajwīd: (Middle East and North Africa). Style of reciting the Qur'an based on principles of maqām.

Tal(a)(m): (South Asia). Meter.

Tamboo bamboo band: (Caribbean). Bamboo percussion band that accompanied cariso songs during the late nineteenth and early twentieth centuries.

Tambora: (Latin America). The bass drum in a traditional cumbia ensemble. Also identifies the bass drum in banda sinaloense.

Tambor alegre: (Latin America). The improvisational drum within a traditional cumbia ensemble.

Tambor llamador: (Latin America). The "calling" drum within a traditional cumbia ensemble, it plays a very steady rhythm, helping the other instruments to orient themselves around that beat.

Tambura: (South Asia). A stringed drone instrument.

Tamburitza (Tamburitza orchestra): (Europe). String ensemble of southeastern Europe and in the diasporas of ethnic and national groups from the Balkans, with distribution of voices from low to high.

Taan: (South Asia). A rapid and florid kind of improvised melodic passage in Hindustani music.

Tanam: (South Asia). The improvised instrumental or vocal performance that follows Carnatic alapanam and that introduces a pulse.

Tango: (Latin America). A form of popular dance music developed primarily in Buenos Aires and the greater Río de la Plata region.

Tango-canción: (Latin America). A form of tango music designed to be listened to instead of danced.

Tanjidor: (Indonesia). Musical ensemble from the outskirts of Jakarta that blends European-derived band instruments with local instruments.

Taqsīm: (Middle East and North Africa). Solo instrumental improvisation.

Ṭār: (Middle East and North Africa). North African tambourine.

Ṭarab: (Middle East and North Africa). Heightened state of emotion or musical enchantment associated with listening to traditional Arab music.

Ṭarīqa: (Middle East and North Africa). A Sufi order (lit. "path" or "way").

Tarka: (Latin America). An Andean wooden duct flute.

Tarola: (Latin America). The snare drum in the banda sinaloense ensemble.

Tavil: (South Asia). A double-headed barrel drum played with a stick and thimble-covered fingers to accompany nagasvaram.

Tecnobanda: (North America). A Popular dance music derived from blending the instruments and repertory of traditional banda ensembles (brass bands) with electronic instruments.

Tegoto: (Japan). Instrumental interludes in koto music.

Tegotomono: (Japan). A generic term for instrumental koto music; it is also used as another term for jiuta.

Tempo giusto: (Europe). Identified by Béla Bartók and characterized by a dancelike style that stresses strict adherence to meter. It is associated most closely with "new style" Hungarian folk song.

Terraced melody: (North American Indian). A melody structured so that it begins in a high register and "steps" or "cascades" down to a low concluding pitch.

Teuroteu: (Korea). Korean pop balladry which originated in colonial-era Japanese popular music, but changed to express the struggles of colonial and post-colonial Korean life.

The Trinity: (South Asia). Three foundational composers of Carnatic music: Tyagaraja (1767–1847), Muthuswami Dikshitar (1775–1835), and Syama Sastri (1762–1827).

Thumri: (South Asia). A lyrical type of Hindustani song and a style of instrumental performance modeled on it.

Tihai: (South Asia). A formulaic cadential pattern, normally repeated three times with calculated rests between each statement so that the performance ends on sam.

Togaku: (Japan). Court music of Chinese and Indian origin in the gagaku repertory.

Tongsu yinyue (Light Popular Music): (China). Chinese popular music of the 1980s and 1990s.

Torimono: (Japan). Shinto songs in praise of the gods.

Traditionalization: (Korea). The transformation of modern music to make it resemble older musical forms.

Traditionesque: (Korea). Describes cultural practices that reference tradition but maintain a flexible relationship to the past and its forms.

Trajes de charro: (Latin America). Fancy western Mexican "cowboy" costume worn by mariachis.

Triadic harmony: A European style of harmony with three pitches sounding simultaneously, each a third apart.

Trikala: (South Asia). A type of Carnatic improvisation in which the durational values of the notes in a phrase or piece are systematically augmented or diminished.

Tritone: The interval, or distance between two pitches, whose dissonant character caused it to be associated with the devil.

Tsuri-daiko: (Japan). Suspended drum used in gagaku.

Tsuyogin: (Japan). A strong-style noh music.

Twenty-one Demands: (Japan). Issued by Japan in 1915, in which Japan demanded various economic and political concessions from the Chinese government touching off popular Chinese protests.

'Ūd: (Middle East and North Africa). Plucked lute of the Middle East, usually with four to six pairs of strings.

Urumi Melam: (South Asia). A drum ensemble in Malaysia and Singapore that plays fast, brash music to accompany Hindu devotees undergoing penance in Hindu festivals.

Ustad: (South Asia). A Muslim teacher.

Usul: (Middle East and North Africa). Rhythmic mode in Turkish music.

Vallenato: (Latin America). A traditional music of Colombia that has also found expression as popular music since the middle of the twentieth century.

Varna: (South Asia). Division of society in Indian culture, sometimes translated as "caste."

Vedas: (South Asia). The holy scriptures of Hinduism, traditionally recited by Brahmins and passed down by them orally.

Vedic chant: (South Asia). Intoned verses for ancient religious ceremonies performed by Brahman priests.

Venu: (South Asia). Carnatic flute.

Vichitra vina: (South Asia). A Hindustani plucked string instrument whose strings are stopped with a ball of glass; *see* Gottuvadyam.

Vihuela: (Latin America). In Mexico, a small five-string guitar variant with a convex back, used for percussive strumming.

Vilambit: (South Asia). Slow.

Villancicos: (Latin America). A form of polyphonic song, either secular or sacred, important to the development of Latin American art music from the late fifteenth to the eighteenth century.

Vina: (South Asia). Primary plucked string instrument of Carnatic music.

Violão: (Latin America). Tenor guitar used in early Brazilian choro ensembles.

Vocables: (North America). Nonsemantic syllables that are sung; "nonsense syllables."

Volkslied: (Europe). German term for "folk song," coined by the philosopher Johann Gottfried Herder at the end of the eighteenth century.

Volkstümlich: (Europe). "Folklike" music of Central Europe, in which traditional folk and modern popular musics are often mixed.

Wagon: (Japan). A six-stringed zither.

Waki: (Japan). The supporting actor in noh.

Wankara: (Latin America). Sometimes called bombos, these large, double-headed drums are used to accompany siku ensembles.

Wasan: (Japan). Buddhist hymns in Japanese.

Waşla: (Middle East and North Africa). Multi-sectional organizational scheme for a performance of eastern Arab music, featuring melodic modal unity and rhythmic modal diversity.

Wayang kulit: (Indonesia). Indonesian shadow play accompanied with gamelan music.

Wayno, or huayno: (Latin America). The most widespread Andean mestizo song-dance genre in Peru, also performed by some indigenous musicians. The song texts are strophic, and the tunes comprise short sections in forms such as **AABB**. Waynos are in duple meter with a rhythmic feel varying between an eighthand-two-sixteenth-note figure and an eighth-note triplet.

Wenchang: (China). The instrumental ensemble in Peking Opera made up of melody instruments.

Wenzipu (Prose Tablature): (China). Archaic Chinese tablature for the qin written in prose.

Westernization: (Korea). The variously voluntary and involuntary processes by which so-called non-Western cultures and societies adopt their versions of the qualities of "The West."

Wuchang: (China) (Japan). The instrumental ensemble in Peking Opera made up of percussion.

Xiao Youmei (1884–1940): (China). Chinese composer, music educator, and reformer. He established the first modern Chinese music department at Peking University in 1920, and in 1927 he established the first modern Chinese music conservatory in Shanghai, the Shanghai Conservatory of Music, which is still in existence today. Xiao served as its director until his death in 1940.

Xiao: (China). A Chinese end-blown flute with six finger holes.

Xiaoluo: (China). Small Chinese gong.

Xiaotangu: (China). A small Chinese barrel drum.

Xibei feng (Northwestern Wind): (China). Popular Chinese song genre of the 1980s and 1990s. It combines a disco beat with Chinese folk music, and its lyrics are deliberately artless and simple.

Xipi: (China). Basic melody-rhythmic patterns used for arias in the Peking Opera.

Xylophone: An instrument with keys made from wooden slabs.

Yangqin: (China). A Chinese dulcimer struck with a pair of bamboo sticks.

Yayue: (China). Literally meaning "elegant music," it was Chinese court music of imperial China.

Yeibechai: (North American Indian). A major curing ceremony, lasting nine days, of the Navajo; also known as "Night Chant."

Yoiking: Traditional vocal repertory of the Saami people of circumpolar Europe, reflective of the Saami interaction with the nature of the Arctic, for example, reindeer herding.

Yokyoku: (Japan). Choral singing in noh.

Youlan (Orchids in a Secluded Valley): (China). The earliest extant qin piece; it was notated in "prose tablature" in a manuscript dating from sixth century CE.

Yowagin: (Japan). Soft-style noh music.

Yuan Shikai (1859–1916): (China). Leader of the powerful North China army who was instrumental in arranging the abdication of the Qing emperor in 1912. Because of Yuan's strength, Sun Yat-sen, the founder of the Chinese republic in 1912, offered Yuan the presidency of the new republic. Yuan abused the office and proclaimed himself emperor in 1915, but he died six months later.

Yueqin: (China). A four-stringed Chinese plucked lute with a round sound box.

Yunluo: (China). A Chinese suspended gong set.

Zabumba: (Latin America). The drum used in traditional Brazilian forró ensembles.

Zeng Zhimin (1879–1929): (China). Modern Chinese music educator and a pioneer in writing modern School Song.

Zhao Yuanren (Y. R. Chao) (1892–1982): (China). Influential modern Chinese composer of songs, choral works, and piano compositions, Zhao was also an internationally known linguist. He received his education first from Cornell University and then from Harvard University; he later joined the faculty of the University of California at Berkeley.

Zither: An instrument with strings that stretch along the whole length of the sound board.

Zouk: (Caribbean). Popular music style of the French Antilles, popularized in the 1980s by the band Kassav'.

Zydeco: (North America). African American popular music from Louisiana, also including Caribbean and Cajun elements.

INDEX